LEARNING LEGAL RULES

A Students' Guide to Legal Method and Reasoning

Tenth Edition

James Holland LLB, PhD, Barrister (Middle Temple)

Emeritus Professor of Employment Law
University of the West of England, Bristol

Julian Webb BA, LLM, LLD, FRSA

Professor of Law
University of Melbourne, Australia

Foreword to the First Edition by the Rt Hon Lord Templeman MBE

OXFORD
UNIVERSITY PRESS

OXFORD
UNIVERSITY PRESS

Great Clarendon Street, Oxford, OX2 6DP,
United Kingdom

Oxford University Press is a department of the University of Oxford.
It furthers the University's objective of excellence in research, scholarship,
and education by publishing worldwide. Oxford is a registered trade mark of
Oxford University Press in the UK and in certain other countries

© J.A. Holland and J.S. Webb 2019

The moral rights of the authors have been asserted

Seventh edition 2010
Eighth edition 2013
Ninth edition 2016

Impression: 1

Public sector information reproduced under Open Government Licence v2.0
(www.nationalarchives.gov.uk/doc/open-government-licence/open-government-licence.htm)

Published in the United States of America by Oxford University Press
198 Madison Avenue, New York, NY 10016, United States of America

British Library Cataloguing in Publication Data
Data available

Library of Congress Control Number: 2019940594

ISBN 978-0-19-879990-0

Printed in Great Britain by
Bell & Bain Ltd., Glasgow

Links to third party websites are provided by Oxford in good faith and
for information only. Oxford disclaims any responsibility for the materials
contained in any third party website referenced in this work.

This book is dedicated to the memories of our respective parents
Julie and Jim Holland, and Lucy and Sidney Webb.

Contents

Foreword to the First Edition

The Rt Hon. Lord Templeman MBE,
Lord of Appeal in Ordinary

This book answers all the questions which a student of the law ought to ask and propounds answers to questions which every lawyer and every judge should ask himself from time to time.

The lawyer is a manipulator of words; this is an assertion and not a criticism. Language is the means of disclosing facts, expressing ideas, and applying principles. The ultimate solution of any legal problem is to be found in the application of basic principles to ascertained facts. The difficulties which obstruct the ultimate solution lie in the selection of appropriate principles and the rejection of irrelevant facts. The practice of the law is an art and not a science because the applicability of principle and the analysis of complicated facts depend on the language employed. The judge resembles a conductor of a nineteenth-century symphony. The conductor and the judge must establish the main themes, eliminate discordant sounds, and present a harmonious whole. Modern litigation, like a twentieth-century symphony, suffers from the obscurity of themes and the tyranny of discordant sounds. In this book the authors set out to teach the art of conducting the law.

For the student the first task is to become well acquainted with the instruments of English law and Community law, namely, primary legislation, delegated legislation, judicial authorities, and textbooks. The first four chapters introduce all these sources of the law. The fifth chapter deals with the interplay of law, fact, and language. The authors illustrate the fact that the flexibility of words affords a danger to logic as well as an effective aid to explanation. Rhetoric and jargon may disguise principle and obscure uncomfortable fact. The sixth and seventh chapters are invaluable guides to the dissection and application of precedents—those themes which enable the lawyer and the judge to determine the presence or absence of compatible variations. The ninth and eleventh chapters manfully grapple with the different problems of construing English and Community legislation. The differences are substantial: Articles 30 and 35 of the Treaty of Rome, prohibiting quantitative restrictions on imports and exports, enabled the European Court of Justice to establish a free trade regime which could only have been established by about four English statutes containing 500 sections and 15 Schedules and hundreds of statutory instruments. The interplay of UK law and Community law is explored, not always in agreement with the House of Lords.

The book is aimed at law students but is valuable to the citizen who knows no law, the lawyer who has forgotten some law, and the judge who fears that a just result may be buried under torrents of oral and written words. The book should enable all its readers to guard against asking a silly question and thus provoking a silly answer. The language of the book is clear and the style interesting and thought-provoking.

The authors make a new contribution to legal literature and, at the same time, illuminate and recognise old controversies.

Templeman
House of Lords

Preface to the Tenth Edition

In writing the preface to our first edition, nearly thirty years ago, we said our primary aim was to provide a practical, user-friendly, and critical introduction to legal method and reasoning; to demystify the subject. That is still very much our intention today.

Why you should read this book

If you are studying law it is extremely easy to get focused on the substantive aspects of the subject—the concepts, rules, and principles that go to make up contract, tort, crime, etc. There is a risk that, in the process, we lose sight of the glue that holds all these things together:

(i) that the substantive law is constructed within the context of a set of institutions that make up the legal system; and

(ii) that these institutions themselves make and develop the law within the framework of a further set of values, rules, and principles that determine the legitimate limits of law-making, interpretation, and application.

This book is intended to help you develop both the knowledge and reasoning skills that will support your understanding of this context, and thus also support and enhance your performance in your substantive law subjects. Legal method does not exist in isolation. In reality, it is a key part of your toolkit for making sense of how law works. The most common problem a law student faces is not *'What are the rules?'* but rather *'How do I make use of the rules?'* This requires that you develop the abilities that are the core focus of this book:

- to *find* and *'make sense'* of the primary and secondary sources of law (see **Chapters 1–3**);
- to *interpret* and *apply* authorities; and by the term 'authorities' we mean primarily the legislation and reported cases that can be found in a law library (see **Chapters 6–11**);
- to *construct* arguments both about the facts of a case, and as to how and why a particular authority should or should not be applied in a given situation (see chiefly **Chapters 5–7, and 9**);
- to *write* clearly and in an appropriate (legal) style, making reference to authority as necessary, and *citing* sources in the proper academic form (see **Chapter 4**).

In supporting you to develop these skills, and to acquire the requisite knowledge, we have tried to stress not just what the rules and principles are, but to understand why they are as they are, and what consequences they have. We remember our own frustrations as undergraduates trying to make sense of legal method (though when we were students explicit courses on legal method were the exception rather than the norm, which made the job even harder). When we started to write *Learning Legal Rules,* we therefore set out to try to answer the sorts of questions we had as students. We hope you will find that useful.

Although the most common comment we hear about *Learning Legal Rules* is that it is clear and user-friendly, we sometimes hear the complaint that we make legal method more complicated than it needs to be. We don't think that is true. The reality is that any topic can be addressed at a number of levels. A lot of general 'English legal system' books deal, in a single chapter, with topics that take us two or three chapters to address. Equally, there are even more specialist texts that take a whole book to cover a topic that we cover in a couple of chapters. In other words, we have tried to steer a middle course, between the very detailed knowledge required by the specialist (i.e. the advocate arguing technical points of precedent and interpretation in the higher courts) and the oversimplification of some more generalist student texts. We don't believe understanding is achieved by oversimplification. The reality is that legal method and reasoning can be quite complex, and we want you to achieve an adequately complex understanding of how they work. In the same way that you would not expect your doctor to 'give up' on the difficult bits, lawyers have to face up to the complexities of legal argument and acquire the skill and knowledge to deal with them.

How to use this book

Learning Legal Rules can be used either to support a course of study in legal method or as a self-teaching guide to the subject. We are aware that many people study law by independent or distance-learning methods, and have tried to anticipate their needs, in addition to those of students on traditional full- or part-time courses. We would, however, say that the course of study laid down in this book cannot be wholly followed without access to, at least, a basic library containing some primary sources (law reports and statutes) and a good internet connexion!

We have also sought to organise the contents in a sequence that supports you to build your knowledge sequentially from **Chapters 1–11**. On the whole it makes sense, therefore, (with the possible exception of **Chapter 5**, which is more optional material) not to read the later chapters until you have worked through the earlier material.

In order to make the text easier to follow, we have avoided the use of footnotes. All case references appear in the text. References to books and articles in the text are cited using what is called the Harvard reference system, rather than the OSCOLA method often used in Law Schools. The Harvard referencing system gives the name of the author followed by date of publication and (if appropriate) the page number, thus, 'Smith (1986: 123)'. The full citation of references is listed at the end of each chapter. Some of those references are marked with an asterisk (*). This indicates a text which we consider particularly suitable for further reading; though you should (where possible) be guided by your teachers with regard to what additional reading is required for your course.

This book is also supported by a set of online resources (which can be accessed at www.oup.com/uk/holland-webb10e). These resources are regularly updated, and contain a variety of resources for both students and lecturers, including: a test bank of multiple-choice questions and answers with feedback; updates on recent cases and legislation; ideas for seminars and lecturers; and additional web links.

As part of our step-by-step approach to the mechanics of legal reasoning, we have included a range of practical exercises which are designed to enable you to gain experience in, as well as knowledge of, the area. Learning by experience really is the key to understanding legal method. If you are following a formal course in legal method and/ or legal system, do make the most of the opportunities to learn by experience that seminars or tutorials provide. Whether or not you are following such a course, the paper and online exercises that go with this book will provide you with an opportunity to deepen your understanding of the topics discussed.

Changes from the Ninth Edition

As ever, we are grateful to those users (lecturers and students from around the world) who have given us feedback on the strengths and weaknesses of the ninth edition. In the light of this feedback we have made a number of changes. Indeed, legal method itself has changed substantially since we wrote the first edition and continues to evolve. In 1991 it was not even a recognised law subject in many law schools; now it is a given. We have sought to reflect these changes as to how legal skills, and particularly legal method, have been viewed in each new edition. This edition sees the most extensive changes to the text since we introduced the chapter on the Human Rights Act in the early 2000s. **Chapter 1** has been further revised from the ninth edition to offer a slightly shorter and more focused Introduction,while **Chapter 2** has been revised primarily to include additional material on OSCOLA. Although the aim of this book is to examine legal method, not wider legal skills such as mooting etc., we have added further guidance in **Chapter 4** on the presentation of written work. **Chapter 5** is, essentially, a new chapter, replacing the former Chapters 5 and 12 with an extended treatment of legal reasoning, drawing on leading works in legal theory, which seeks to blend practical description with conceptual explanation and critique. We do not expect that this chapter will be for everyone, but we hope that it will address concerns expressed by some teachers, that the former chapters tried to do too much, and over-simplified the theoretical aspects of legal reasoning. For more advanced students, we trust it will enable a deeper understanding of the subject, as well as offering a substantial taster of the kinds of issues and approaches involved in the study of legal theory or jurisprudence. **Chapter 10** has been substantially re-written to clarify and, in some respects simplify, its description of the Act's substantive provisions and operation, which had, over the past few editions, become rather more detailed than necessary for a text primarily on legal methods, and **Chapter 11** on European Legal Method has had a major re-write, with much excision of material, to account for Brexit. **Chapter 12** has been removed and replaced with the new **Chapter 5**. All chapters have been updated and we are grateful to the many helpful comments we have received on the text generally. We have sought to state the law as it stood at 1 October 2018.

In writing this tenth edition we have sought to preserve the strengths of previous editions. It is still our firm belief, as we noted in 1991, that the study of law is challenging but also immensely rewarding and enjoyable; we hope that you will find it so.

James Holland
Julian Webb
December 2018

Acknowledgements

This book has been shaped and influenced by the contributions and support of many friends and colleagues over the years. Our particular, and continuing, thanks are due to Emeritus Professor Adrian Chandler, Carol Crowdy, and Julie Hamley at the University of the West of England, Bristol, Dr Rachel Fenton at Exeter University, and Professor Lisa Webley at Birmingham Law School. At Warwick University, Dr James Harrison and Helen Riley were instrumental in developing the MELS course, which in turn had an influence on previous editions. We would also like to acknowledge Jo Kendal's research assistance at UWE in previous editions, and Emily Hoyland, our editor at Oxford University Press, not least for her enthusiasm, professionalism, and perseverance in attempting to keep us to deadlines. And we could not forget the assistance of those university and college teachers and students from countries around the world who have shared their experiences of using *Learning Legal Rules* with us over various editions: thank you too. In particular, as first appeared in the ninth edition, we are grateful to Maureen Maksymiw at Nottingham Trent University for her fascinating comments on the different advertisements that appeared in the case of *Carlill* v *Carbolic Smoke Ball Company* (covered in **Chapter 7**).

We have an enduring debt to two key people. The first is Alistair MacQueen (1944–2008). Alistair was one of the founders of Blackstone Press (the original publishers of this work) and the man who really was responsible for *Learning Legal Rules* seeing the light of day. Our second debt is owed to the Rt Hon. Lord Templeman MBE, former Lord of Appeal in Ordinary, for agreeing to write the Foreword to this book, and for the continuing interest he showed in the text throughout its entire history from that point until his death in the summer of 2014, aged 94. We believe Sydney was the first sitting Law Lord to write such a piece for an undergraduate text and he insisted on reading and sometimes debating every word in the book before he would lend his name to it. As per his reputation in practice, described below, we did not get off lightly. His obituaries demonstrated how loved and admired he was across the legal world. The Daily Telegraph put it this way: 'Off the bench, Sydney Templeman was a genial character entirely lacking in pomposity; on it, however, he could be distinctly fierce. . . . His peremptoriness resulted in his being affectionately known as "Syd Vicious" by some of the barristers who appeared before him.'

Sydney believed fervently in every student having the chance to fulfil his or her own potential and, to this effect, he established and funded scholarships for UK and overseas students as well as prestigious prizes in a number of Law Schools in the UK. At UWE, Bristol he also frequently judged moots and gave talks to students on life as a judge and on how legal method related to real-world legal argument. He is sadly missed both in academia and practice, especially by the authors of this book.

The authors and publishers also wish to thank the following for permission to reprint copyright material: RELX (UK) Limited, trading as LexisNexis for extracts from the All England Law Reports; the Incorporated Council of Law Reporting for England and Wales for permission to reproduce *DPP* v *Bull* [1994]; Thomson Reuters (Professional) UK for permission to reproduce extracts from *Pierrel SpA and others* v *Ministero della Sanità* [1995] from the Common Market Law Reports along with screenshots from westlaw.co.uk; and Reed Elsevier (UK) Limited, trading as LexisNexis, for screenshots of their online services.

Table of Cases

1

Understanding the Law

1.1 Introduction

Law is everywhere. It governs our work, the products we buy and sell, our relationships, and even helps shape the physical environment in which we live. This first chapter sets out to introduce some fundamentals that will underpin your understanding of law and 'legal method'—that is, those core principles and techniques that underpin the process of legal reasoning. We do this by, first, introducing you to the idea of 'law' and some of the major functions of law, and then by looking at the main sources of law that you will become familiar with as you work through this book: primarily *legislation* as well as other less 'formal' categories of legal rules, and *case law* as it is developed by the courts. We will also look at the institutions responsible for making and shaping those laws—chiefly Parliament and the courts—and consider the impact of Europe on English (and UK) law. So, let's start at the very beginning.

1.2 What is law?

At first glance this seems a very simple, if not a rather strange, question to ask. After all, as the poet W.H. Auden said, 'The law is The Law' and we tend to know it when we see it. But it is also a question that philosophers and legal theorists have expended many pages in trying to answer. Why do you think that is? And what answers do you think they might have come up with?

Some of the philosophers' answers, reduced to their most basic form, are:

- law is a system of rules laid down by a body or person with the power and authority to make law;
- law is what legislators, judges, and lawyers 'do';
- law is a tool of oppression used by the ruling class to advance its own interests; and
- law is a system of rules grounded on fundamental principles of morality.

Each of these characterisations has the capacity to tell us something useful about the nature of 'law' and how it operates—at least within Western legal systems; whether each (or any of them) offers 'the truth' about law is a different question, and not one that we intend to dwell on here. We think 'what is law' is a useful question for at least three reasons.

First, at its simplest, understanding law presupposes the ability to find and read the law. This in turn assumes that we know how to identify it in the first place, which leads us back, in a sense, to that fundamental question: 'What is law?'

Secondly, even asking the question obliges us to think about how we conceptualise complex phenomena like 'law'. Being able to conceptualise something and describe it in language is a crucial step on the path to understanding that thing and the ideas and beliefs which shape and are shaped by it.

Our third reason for asking the question also flows from this: namely, that understanding in turn helps us to determine how we should make sensible or reasoned choices about what constitutes law in any given situation. This too can be a complex issue for legal theory, but it is also of real significance, for example, in assessing the perennial problem of whether and how we can determine if a law is 'good' or 'bad'; and if it is bad, what we can (or should) do about it. We will touch on some basic issues of conceptualisation in **Chapters 3** and **5**, entitled 'Reading the Law' and 'Understanding Legal Reasoning', respectively. But for the moment we will focus on something a little more concrete.

1.3 A sample legal problem

A friend who is a shopkeeper has recently received a consignment of camping and other knives, including a small number of flick knives. She is concerned that the police may take action if she were to display and sell these flick knives to the public, and asks you for advice. In considering this problem, we are going to ask you two questions:

1. Why might the sale of flick knives be a matter for law in the first place?

2. How can you find out if she would be breaking the law?

These look like very different kinds of question. Asking *why* something might be a matter for law requires us to think about the role and purposes of law—what it *ought* to do. It might also imply that there are some things law should not do, or activities it ought not interfere with. We will look at this question first, under the heading the 'functions of law'. Our second question seems much more mechanical: how do we find the law? But that in turn assumes certain knowledge and skills: sufficient knowledge to identify, first, the different kinds of rules that are recognised as 'law' in the relevant legal system; secondly, the appropriate search skills to find the rules and principles you need; and, thirdly, enough understanding of what the rules actually mean (and how they are likely to be applied) to advise. As we shall see over the course of this book, finding and understanding the law is not quite as straightforward as it sounds, but a good starting point is to be aware of the range of rules that are developed by the important institutional sources we have already mentioned. We will come back to this in sections **1.6**, **1.7**, and **1.10**.

1.4 The functions of law

Thinking functionally about law is an important part of studying because it helps us to focus beyond what law *is*, to what law *does* and *why* it may be an appropriate tool of social policy. Learning law is not just a rote exercise; it is not just about learning the rules (despite the title of this book!). In learning law, we need also to pay attention to the bigger picture of what law in general is *for*. This is one of the things that can make understanding the law both exciting and important. Moreover, it is not just a social policy question, it can take us into some quite deeply philosophical territory—if you take a module in legal theory or philosophy of law, you will certainly look at some of those larger issues, though these philosophical questions can be raised in virtually any substantive subject too.

For our present purposes it is enough to note that a functional perspective emphasises the extent to which law performs a range of 'coercive', 'protective', and 'facilitative' roles. The coercive function of law is the one with which we are most familiar, where law acts as a power over our conduct, notably in criminal law matters, though the coercive force of law can also be much more subtle than fining someone or throwing them in prison! The flip side of such coercion is that law also serves to protect and defend the rights and interests of legal persons, and to stabilise social conduct and expectations (e.g. by blocking conflict, or diverting it into an acceptable—i.e. institutionalised—form). Law—and lawyers—also perform an important enabling (facilitating) role in society. Law in this latter sense makes a whole range of interpersonal, business, and even interstate transactions possible: from getting married, to selling a house, buying products for a business, liquidating a company, through to constructing a bilateral or multilateral trade agreement between states.

Linked to this is the rather obvious point that specific laws also tend to be made for a particular *purpose*. Such purposes may well be significant considerations in interpreting and applying the law. To that extent the functional question, 'What is *this* law for?', can be of real practical importance. This is a theme to which we will return at a number of points in this book.

1.4.1 Maintenance of public order and safety

The law is often regarded as a critical part of the 'glue' that holds the fabric of society together, and protects us from the risks of social disorder and anarchy. The criminal law, in particular, is important in this respect, since it defines those behaviours which are regarded as sufficiently antisocial or potentially damaging to the public good to be outlawed and punishable by the state. At the same time, there is a real risk that the state itself can use the law to legitimate its rule and to suppress dissent by force. This abuse of law can be seen in many repressive regimes, and it is therefore considered important that political and legal authority in the state are kept reasonably separate and subject to a range of checks and balances, for example, by ensuring that lawyers, the police, and courts are independent of executive government.

1.4.2 The protection of individual rights and liberties

An important function of law in liberal democratic societies is that it should curb the capacity of the state and other powerful social actors to infringe the rights and liberties of individual citizens. This is often encapsulated in notions like the 'rule of law', which requires that no person or organisation be above the law, and 'freedom under the law', which implies that individual autonomy can only be constrained by a legitimate exercise of law. The protection of fundamental rights and liberties such as the right to a fair trial, the freedom of speech, and of lawful protest are important in constraining potential abuses of state power. Increasingly, in the context of the international and national human rights movements, the language of (negative) civil liberties and freedoms is being superseded by a language of positive, enforceable, rights such as the right not to be discriminated against because of one's sex, race, age, sexual orientation, or disability.

This dimension of the law presents the courts with many of their most complex and politically and/or morally challenging problems. One such example is the case of the conjoined twins, referred to pseudonymously in proceedings as 'Jodie' and 'Mary': see *In re A (Children) (Conjoined Twins: Surgical Separation)* [2000] EWCA Civ 254; [2001] Fam 147. Shortly after their birth, it became clear that both babies would die within a matter of months if not separated. If they were separated it was equally certain that Mary would die during or very shortly following the procedure, while Jodie had a very strong chance of survival and, subsequently, of a reasonable quality of life. While doctors were willing to undertake the surgery, the parents felt, on religious grounds, unable to consent to an operation that would actively take the life of one of their children. The medical team also needed to know that they would not be prosecuted for murder if the operation went ahead.

The case was without legal precedent, and raised fundamental questions of human rights, family law, and criminal law that all had to be considered by the court. In a unanimous judgment the Court of Appeal allowed the operation to go ahead, but the complexities of the issues were such that the three judges came to that conclusion by quite different routes.

1.4.3 The organisation and control of the political sphere

Although we often think of law and politics as necessarily distinct systems, the reality is more complex, as law performs an important part in preserving the political structure and processes, and politics plays an increasing role in shaping the law, not least through the extensive annual legislative programme of Parliament.

In many countries the relationship between law and state is defined primarily by a written constitution. The United Kingdom, by contrast, is distinctive in retaining an unwritten constitution, but this does not mean that there is no constitutional law, nor that the courts lack any authority over the political and legislative process. Moreover, major legislative reforms such as the European Communities Act 1972, the Human Rights Act 1998, the various devolution Acts, and the Constitutional Reform Act 2005 all point to ways in which our constitutional arrangements are becoming increasingly embedded in written—statute—law. We will touch on a number of these developments in the course of this chapter, and later in the book.

1.4.4 The regulation of economic activity

Within the dominant ethos of market capitalism, law plays an important function in facilitating and encouraging national and international trade in goods and services. It does this by creating legal frameworks and conditions for facilitating trade, and by establishing principles of risk allocation and dispute resolution for when things go wrong. At the same time, the law also plays a role in restricting the activities of economic entities, and protecting citizens, states, and the environment itself—for example, from unsafe labour practices, abuses by an entity of a dominant market position, and other forms of unfair exploitation. Achieving a balance between these aims is often extremely difficult, and, as the recent banking crisis has shown, regulatory failure can have massive economic and social impact.

1.4.5 The regulation of human relationships

The law serves to legitimate and control various aspects of personal relationships. This includes laws on marriage and civil partnership; setting principles governing the distribution of family property on relationship dissolution or death; regulating parent–child relationships, and those situations where the state and the courts may take measures to protect the welfare of a child, even against the rights of the parent. The law may also play some part in regulating our most intimate relationships, by setting limits to what constitutes lawful sexual activity, and regulating both abortion and assisted reproduction.

1.4.6 The preservation of a moral order

Closely related to the law's role in regulating both public order and human relationships is another idea: that the law plays an important role in the reproduction and enforcement of certain moral principles and values. Both laws and moral principles share a characteristic that legal philosophers describe as 'normativity'—that is, they describe behavioural 'norms', or statements of what we *ought* to do. However, laws become distinct from purely moral norms by virtue of acquiring a particular material form (as statute or case law) developed within and legitimated by the institutional framework of a 'legal system'. This does not mean that laws have no moral content, or that law necessarily lacks moral functions and values. There are, of course, many specific areas of law which try to reflect a current moral consensus within society—for example, laws protecting freedom of religion, and others which attempt to control certain 'immoral' behaviours, such as the public display of pornography or racist 'hate speech'. Beyond these sorts of specifics, however, some would also argue that the law itself is grounded upon certain core moral values—a commitment, for example, to ideals of order, justice, and individual freedom (Stein and Shand, 1974). We consider some of the implications of the (contested) interplay between law and moral norms in relation to models of legal reasoning in **Chapter 5**. The rise of 'human rights' (**Chapter 10**) similarly can be regarded as a predominantly moral discourse that has sought to embed notions of human dignity and fundamental rights within national legal systems.

1.4.7 The regulation of international relations

International relations are governed primarily by a form of law called public international law. This creates rules, for example, for the recognition of states as legal entities, the setting of their territorial boundaries, and the conduct of diplomacy between them. Wars and armed conflict are also governed by international legal rules; principles of international humanitarian law exist to protect those caught up in conflict, and, increasingly, those accused of war crimes and other crimes against humanity are liable to be judged before international tribunals according to standards set by international criminal law. At the interstate level, international trade is also increasingly regulated, chiefly by the World Trade Organization in Geneva, but also by regional trade systems such as the European Union (which is the most closely harmonised, and most like a regional legal system of all the trading blocs), the US–Mexico–Canada Agreement

(USMCA), and the Association of South East Asian Nations (ASEAN) Free Trade Area. These bodies exist as negotiating *fora*, and offer systems of dispute resolution for trade disputes between states within their jurisdiction.

1.4.8 Why thinking functionally matters

A good academic, and often a good practising lawyer too, needs to be able to think critically about the law—about what it can, and also what it *ought* to do. Examining its social, political, economic, or moral role and consequences opens up a whole range of arguments and issues that we might not consider if our thinking stopped at just a technical analysis of the rules themselves. As we shall see later, particularly in **Chapters 9, 10**, and **11**, thinking about law in this kind of 'purposive' way is also something judges do when they are making a decision, or interpreting legislation. But for now, we return to the question of what law is, by looking at how it differs from other forms of regulation and what we can call 'social rules'.

1.5 Regulation: legal rules and social rules

One of the words that kept cropping up in section **1.4** was 'regulation'. Law is commonly used to regulate aspects of individual and institutional behaviour; indeed, legislation in particular is sometimes seen as a paradigm form of regulation. But law is not the only means of regulating.

The term regulation can be seen as encompassing 'all forms of social control, whether intentional or not, and whether imposed by the state or other social institutions' (Morgan and Yeung, 2007: 3–4). If we think about it, law does not operate in isolation from other forms of regulation. Any society is governed by a mass of other rules which are not laws in the formal sense, but merely private rules or more general social conventions—perceptions of 'proper' behaviour. These are also a means of regulating social conduct, but the focus on regulation reminds us that societies have a choice about what and how they regulate. Thus, while most of us would accept that anyone stealing the possessions of another, or possibly someone selling flick knives, should be liable to a penalty under the criminal law, we might be surprised to see someone in court for eating peas off their knife! Regulating table manners is not really so important to our society as to require the force of law.

Thinking about law as one of a number of possible ways of regulating helps us understand what is distinctive about law, and the way it relates to other social rules, thus:

(i)   Laws tend to perform the important regulatory functions that often could not be performed (at all or as well) by other kinds of rule.

(ii) Law may be particularly important because of its formal character and the specialist sanctions or remedies that are not available to other forms of regulation.

(iii) The choice of formal or less formal mechanisms employed may well reflect different priorities, or different social values, regarding the behaviour in question.

(iv) The use of law and legal sanction is also symbolic: it sends out a powerful message about what society *does* value.

Decisions about regulatory tools and approaches may also reflect judgements about the effectiveness of different forms of regulation. In some contexts, regulation may be much more effective if it makes little or no use of law. Economic policy may thus be used to regulate market behaviour; or design principles may be applied in such a way as to regulate the ways in which buildings or roads, etc. are used. Consider, for example, how traffic-calming measures, or putting pedestrians and car users into a shared space, may control drivers' speed more effectively than (just) a speed limit. Governments and regulators are becoming more aware of how different kinds of rules, together with a variety of other regulatory tools, can be used purposefully, recognising that, in some settings, it may be sufficient to guide or steer conduct, rather than deploy the full force of traditional legal regulation.

Generally, laws are identifiable by the fact that they take a form which distinguishes them from other social rules and conventions. Their form tells us that they are derived from an 'institutional' source that is socially recognised (and some would say accepted) as having the power to create law. Only rules so created can be said to be *legally binding* upon the individual, or even upon the state itself. Thus, our first step in finding the law governing the sale of flick knives would be to discover whether any of the legal institutions have had anything to say on the matter. In sections **1.6–1.10** we turn our attention more specifically to the forms and sources of English law.

In English law there are currently four main institutional sources which we shall consider: Parliament, the courts, the European Union, and the European Convention on Human Rights (ECHR). By taking them as our starting point, we are defining legal material by concentrating on the 'law-makers'. This is a rather narrow basis, but it does emphasise the importance of what are often called the 'primary' sources, and distinguishes them from 'secondary' or literary sources of law that provide only a commentary on or analysis of the rules (see **Chapter 2**).

1.6 Parliament and legislation

Parliament is significant for three reasons. First, it is the originator of what is probably the single most important modern source of law—that is, **statute law**. Secondly, through its legislative powers, Parliament is able to give law-making powers to other bodies, such as local councils, government departments, and other agencies. This results in a form of law that is called **subordinate** or **delegated legislation**. Thirdly, Parliament's delegatory powers are being widely used to create less formalised regulatory systems which operate within a framework of formal rules created by statute.

1.6.1 The importance of legislation

It is critical that you understand what legislation is and how it operates. Legislation matters because statutes are constitutionally the highest form of law in the UK legal systems, and, practically speaking, because most new laws over the past 100 or so years have had their basis in legislation. Against this background you should not be surprised to find quite a lot of legislation governing the display and sale of flick knives, for example.

The growth in legislation has been a key feature of the modern English legal system. It reflects the extent to which social life has become more complex, and government has extended its control over our activities, both in the areas of business and commerce and in the social sphere, where many important fields, such as employment, child care, and social security law, owe their modern existence almost exclusively to statute.

This has meant that over the past fifty to sixty years the amount of legislation in force has grown significantly. This reflects two processes: first, a tendency of law to accumulate, because 'old' laws are not necessarily removed at the same rate that new ones are created, and, secondly, a higher level of legislative activity by Parliament than in the past. If we look at the nature of that legislative activity, however, it is not simply that we are seeing more Acts of Parliament every year. In fact, the number of Acts being passed per parliamentary session actually peaked in the 1970s (see Miers, 1986; cf. Cracknell and Clements, 2012). So, what is happening to make the statute book continue to expand?

(i)   The amount of statute law judged by the number of *pages* of legislation passed has still tended to grow decade on decade. Miers (1989) has thus shown that the volume of primary legislation rose steadily from an average of 745 pages per session in the 1950s to 1,525 pages in the 1980s. By the end of the 2000s, that average had increased to 3,224 (our figure, based on data in Cracknell and Clements, 2012).

(ii)   This has also been accompanied by a growth in the amount and length of secondary legislation. We return to this in section **1.6.3**.

So, what this tells us is not that there is simply more legislation, but that the way in which legislation is being designed and used is changing. Acts are becoming longer and perhaps therefore more complex, and, at the same time, more and more law-making is being channelled through delegated legislation.

1.6.2 Statute law

A statute is a document which contains laws made by Parliament. Statutes are also referred to as *Acts of Parliament*. You will learn more about their design in **Chapter 3**.

Statutes are now found in virtually all fields of law and govern all sorts of activities. Many statutes affect our lives without us even knowing about them. For instance, how is the date of Easter calculated? For the answer to that one has to turn to a strange Act of 1750—the Calendar (New Style) Act. This Act determined many calendar calculations, including leap years and Easter. The strangest provision, however, came with the calendar itself. In 1750 Britain used the old Julian calendar. Many other countries had switched to the more accurate Gregorian calendar. There was a difference of eleven days between these calendars. When it was the end of September here, it was October elsewhere. A change had to be made. The question was: how? The Act provided the answer by stating that 2 September 1752 was to be followed by 14 September 1752. Eleven days were thus simply deemed not to exist! This clearly illustrates the power and authority that legislation has. Unfortunately, in this case, it also led to riots in the streets; not least because some people were not getting birthdays in September 1752, and everyone was suddenly eleven days older!

Statutes are created directly by Parliament, following procedures laid down in both the House of Commons and the House of Lords. A statute becomes law only after it has been introduced into Parliament as a 'Bill', been approved by both Houses of Parliament, and has satisfied the formality of obtaining the Royal Assent. Once an Act has been passed it is unimpeachable, so far as English law is concerned. As Lord Campbell put it in *Edinburgh & Dalkeith Railway* v *Wauchope* (1842) 8 Cl & F 710: 'no Court of Justice can inquire into the mode in which it was introduced into Parliament, nor into what was done previous to its introduction, or what passed in Parliament during its progress'.

Lord Campbell's statement still rings broadly true today. There is no single UK court with the power equivalent to, say, the American Supreme Court to declare domestic legislation unconstitutional and therefore invalid. This absence of constitutional review reflects a principle called *parliamentary sovereignty*, or sometimes 'supremacy'. This is the idea that Parliament is the primary law-maker, and that an Act of Parliament is the supreme form of English law. The supremacy of Parliament is important for legal method, both because it creates a division between law-making and judicial functions in the state and because it raises questions about the proper boundaries between rule-making and the subject matter of this book—rule interpretation and application. According to the conventional view, the role of judges is to interpret the law, not to make it; however, as we shall see over the course of this book, the reality is rather more complicated than this simple idea suggests.

This is because the boundary line is being tested in the context of the UK's adoption of laws that voluntarily set limits on what Parliament can do. These are primarily the small category of so-called 'constitutional statutes', including the Act of Union 1707, the European Communities Act 1972 (currently under threat of repeal), the Human Rights Act 1998, and the Scottish and Welsh Devolution Acts. These Acts involve important self-constraints on Parliamentary sovereignty to legislate, for example, inconsistently with European Law, or international human rights norms, or to legislate over matters within the exclusive authority of the devolved governments. Cases which raise questions under these Acts therefore have the potential to challenge boundaries between the courts' established powers merely to 'apply' the law, or legitimately to challenge Parliament's competence to legislate in certain ways inconsistent with its obligations, and its capacity to challenge the very validity of legislation. For judicial discussion of where some of these boundaries lie, see, for example, *Ahmed* v *HM Treasury* [2010] 2 AC 534; *R (Jackson and Others)* v *Attorney-General* [2005] UKHL 56; *H* v *Lord Advocate* [2012] UKSC 24.

It is at least of note that in two of these cases—*Jackson* and *H*—the possibility of a judicially constrained sovereignty is openly considered by members of the highest court in the United Kingdom. This in itself signals a perceptible shift in judicial thinking about the relationship between the courts and Parliament in the twenty-first century.

1.6.3 Delegated legislation

Acts of Parliament are not only a major source of law in their own right; they also provide a legitimate means whereby Parliament can pass on, or delegate, its law-making powers to another body or person. Parliament's power of delegation has in fact been widely used for many years, but because its exercise is much less visible than the act of legislating, it is easy to lose sight of the importance of delegated legislation. The volume of secondary legislation is in fact considerable: 11,888 UK statutory instruments were made in 2009 alone (Cracknell and Clements, 2012). Statutory instruments are not just quantitatively important. It is worth remembering that, in practice, the operation of whole areas of law, such as social security and immigration, is dependent upon a network of regulations, which will be of greater day-to-day significance than much of the statute law. As most of this book focuses on primary legislation and case law, we will look at delegated legislation in some detail here.

Delegated legislation takes primarily one of two forms, called *secondary* or *tertiary legislation*. Be aware, however, that terminology in this area is not entirely consistent. You may also come across the concept *quasi-legislation*, which seems to cover a broad spectrum of rules (what we will here refer to as tertiary legislation and 'soft law') that are not directly enforceable by the courts.

The most important secondary legislation is published as a **statutory instrument (SI)** (individual instruments may also be called *Regulations*). The term SI derives from the Statutory Instruments Act 1946, s. 1, which provides:

> (1) Where by this Act or any Act passed after the commencement of this Act power to make, confirm or approve orders, rules, regulations or other subordinate legislation is conferred on His Majesty in Council or on any Minister of the Crown then, if the power is expressed—
>
> (a) in the case of a power conferred on His Majesty, to be exercisable by Order in Council;
> (b) in the case of a power conferred on a Minister of the Crown, to be exercisable by statutory instrument,
>
> any document by which that power is exercised shall be known as a 'statutory instrument'....

Most secondary legislation is published in the form of an ordinary SI. However, there are a number of specialised forms of secondary legislation of which it is useful to be aware. These are:

- Orders in Council, which are orders issued under statutory authority by the Crown on the advice of the Privy Council. They can be used for a wide variety of functions, but tend to be used for administrative and governance matters for which SIs are not deemed appropriate. For example, the transfer of specific ministerial powers from the UK government to ministers of the devolved governments in Wales and Scotland was completed by Orders in Council.

- Legislative Reform Orders (LROs), which were created by the Legislative and Regulatory Reform Act 2006 and enable ministers, subject to certain safeguards, to amend primary legislation by SI. The intention is that LROs are used to reduce regulatory burdens without having to resort to amending legislation.

- Remedial Orders: where a UK court or the European Court of Human Rights has found a specific UK statutory provision to be incompatible with a Convention right, a minister may, where this is possible, amend or repeal the offending provision by remedial order.

The Statutory Instruments Act 1946 also lays down a number of clear rules about the form or style that SIs must adopt, and SIs, in theory at least, are subject to parliamentary oversight. In practice, however, many are not actually 'laid before Parliament'—a technical term, meaning that copies are given to Parliament to scrutinise—as the level of scrutiny depends on the enabling legislation.

Delegation always requires the express authority of an Act of Parliament, which, in respect of any delegated legislation created under its authority, will be referred to as the *parent or enabling Act*. The parent Act will not only give authority to the process of delegation, but also will set the parameters of the delegated power.

Where a public body attempts to act outside the authority of the powers delegated to it by Parliament, or fails to follow proper or prescribed procedures in the exercise of its power, then the courts may intervene and declare such actions unlawful because they are *ultra vires*, meaning 'beyond the powers'.

Statutes can also delegate law-making authority to a wide range of government ministers, public agencies, and even private organisations or corporations. The rules made by such bodies are now commonly referred to as 'tertiary legislation'. The word 'tertiary' is somewhat confusing, because it seems to suggest that this type of law is at a level below secondary legislation. It isn't. It is still a direct delegation from Parliament, and so at the same 'level' as secondary legislation, but the style of the regulation is different, and there is no expectation of parliamentary scrutiny. These two points represent the key distinctions between statutory instruments and tertiary legislation, though in practice, as we have noted, the *actual* level of scrutiny of SIs and tertiary legislation may often not be very different.

A good example of tertiary legislation is Code of Practice 'C' governing the detention and questioning of persons held at a police station. Codes of Practice governing the conduct of police are made by the Home Office under powers contained in the Police and Criminal Evidence Act 1984 (PACE). Code of Practice 'C' is not directly enforceable in the courts, by virtue of PACE, s. 67. This means that breaches of the Code are not themselves breaches of law; however, the Act does allow them to be used by a court to justify excluding any item of evidence that has been improperly obtained by the police (see, e.g., *R v Samuel* [1988] QB 615; [1988] 2 All ER 135).

The term *tertiary legislation* is also used in the context of European Union Law, where it has a very specific but different meaning from that used here—see further section **1.10**.

1.6.4 'Soft law'

Legislation may also enable other bodies to issue a variety of 'soft law'. This term is used to describe a range of measures that are less formal than tertiary legislation and often non-binding in their effect. Such measures tend to be administrative in character, providing guidance to officials or sometimes advice and information to citizens. Despite its relatively informal character, soft law is recognised as an important source of rights and duties, and such policy statements may be sufficiently clear or 'hard-edged' to be justiciable in the sense that they are open to interpretation by the courts, even if not enforceable as 'hard law'. As Lord Steyn put it in *Re McFarland* [2005] UKHL 17; [2004] 1 WLR 1289 at [24]:

> …in respect of the many kinds of 'soft laws' with which we are now familiar, one must bear in mind that citizens are led to believe that the carefully drafted and considered statements truly represent government policy which will be observed in decision-making unless there is good reason to depart from it. It is an integral part of the working of a mature process of public administration. Such policy statements are an important source of individual rights and corresponding duties. In a fair and effective public law system such policy statements must be interpreted objectively in accordance with the language employed by the Minister. The citizen is entitled to rely on the language of the statement, seen as always in its proper context. The very reason for making the statement is to give guidance to the public.

> The decision-maker, here a Minister, may depart from the policy but until he has done so, the citizen is entitled to ask in a court of law whether he fairly comes within the language of the publicly announced policy…. This is not to say that policy statements must be construed like primary or subordinate legislation. It seems sensible that a broader and wholly untechnical approach should prevail. But what is involved is still an interpretative process conducted by a court which must necessarily be approached objectively and without speculation about what a particular minister may have had in mind.

The distinction between soft law and more formal regulation is not always straightforward. Neither the stated intention of the rule-maker nor the name of the measure will be determinative. Codes of practice, circulars, guidance, etc., may be either tertiary legislation or soft law. Their legal nature and effect can only be determined by examining the material in question within its whole context (including the legal powers under which it was made), to assess whether or not it has the character of a rule or is just information, advice, or guidance as to how the requirements of a rule might be met: *R (on the application of Alvi)* v *Secretary of State for the Home Department* [2012] UKSC 33.

In summary, then, we have seen how both statute and, with it, delegated legislation have expanded over the past thirty to forty years. This creates a challenge for those seeking to know and use the law: there is quite simply a lot more of it, and it is more widely distributed across a range of legal instruments. Consequently, in advising our friend about her business, we need to look not just for statute law, but whether Parliament has delegated relevant authority to make regulations about flick knives, and then exercised that power to make regulations, and/or authorised any other bodies (such as local councils) to issue guidelines or other controls.

Practically, the ability to delegate carries great advantages to the government, and sometimes to the legal system, for example in times of emergency, or whenever we need to be able to change the law quickly and easily. Soft law and informal rules similarly are adaptable and can provide a flexible way of providing authoritative advice and guidance to citizens and officials. They can be instrumental in guiding officials in the use of their discretion, and can actually impose significant restraints upon it. The risk of soft law, however, lies in the extent to which public power is thus being exercised from within less public places: (semi-)autonomous government agencies and the private sector, and according to rules found in guides and manuals rather than statute books and published regulations. These are not necessarily beyond the reach of the supervisory powers of Parliament and the courts, but the scope for judicial oversight and intervention tends, by definition, to be less.

1.7 The courts

Although legislation is extremely important, it cannot operate in isolation. Legislation requires implementation. On a day-to-day basis that is the function of a wide variety of officials, whose job is either itself to carry out Parliament's commands or else to make sure that other organisations or private individuals are doing so. In this process, questions may be raised about the effect of a particular piece of legislation. Often these will involve technical questions of *interpretation*. Officials are constantly engaged in interpreting both primary and secondary legislation, but sometimes we require a more authoritative statement of what the law means. That authoritative process of interpretation is usually undertaken by the courts.

The courts, moreover, are not only important as interpreters of legislation, but they are also the second major source of English law in their own right, through the development of the **common law**, a term which we first need to define.

1.7.1 The meaning of 'common law'

This term is used in two ways:

(i) **to distinguish common law from statute:** 'common law' is used to describe all those rules of law that have evolved through court cases (as opposed to those which have emerged from Parliament) over the past 800 years. Despite the growth of statute, English law is still generally understood in common law terms. By this we mean that the way in which we think about law, and categorise laws, is still heavily influenced by the old common law *forms of action* which determine what types of problem we now call 'contract', 'tort', etc.

(ii) **to distinguish common law from other legal systems:** comparative lawyers have long used the term 'legal families' to group together legal systems which share certain common features. More recently, the term 'legal tradition' has become more popular as a way of thinking comparatively about different legal systems and cultures (see, e.g., Glenn, 2010).

Tradition in this setting emphasises both the influence of (legal) history—the continuing presence of the past in shaping the law—and the complex, dynamic nature of legal culture. The philosopher Alasdair MacIntyre (1988) summarises this idea of a 'living tradition' as 'an historically extended, socially embodied argument, and an argument precisely about the goods that constitute that tradition'. In other words, 'tradition' becomes a way of understanding and explaining the norms and values that make up a particular conception of the legal world, and the ways in which that legal world embraces both continuity and change. Tradition as an idea of both historical continuity and a reinterpreting of the past through the present (and *vice versa*) is quite fundamental to our understanding of law, where the past constitutes a continuing source of reference, authority, and value-conformity.

In the Western world, there are two dominant 'traditions' which we call civil and common law, though there are a number of legal systems, such as the Scottish, which reflect elements of both traditions. The term 'common law' is thus used as a means of defining all those legal systems in the world whose laws are derived from the English system. We use the term 'English' rather than 'British' with good cause. For reasons of history, not only Scotland, but also Northern Ireland, and even the Isle of Man and Channel Islands, have evolved as separate legal systems from England and Wales (the Channel Islands, for instance, are part of Great Britain but not part of the United Kingdom or the European Union). Although much of the legislation passed by the Westminster Parliament now governs the whole of the United Kingdom, there remain substantial differences in law and the legal processes that apply in the different jurisdictions that make up the British Isles; indeed, with devolution of powers to Scotland and Wales, the differences are increasing.

The common law world remains extensive; it includes the federal laws of the United States, and most existing or former members of the British Commonwealth, such as Australia, Canada, India, New Zealand, and Singapore, though in many such systems the English influence may coexist with elements of local customary law or even with other legal traditions, such as Islamic law or Hindu law (see, e.g., Glenn, 2010). This does not mean that these countries have all developed uniform responses to particular legal problems. To survive transplanting, the common law has had to respond to the different needs and conditions of each jurisdiction. This has often meant departing from the established (English) rules. Such variation is generally seen not so much as a dilution of the common law, but rather as a sign of its capacity to adapt (see, e.g., *per* Lord Diplock in *Cassell* v *Broome* [1972] AC 1027 at 1127; [1972] 1 All ER 801 at 871; *per* Lord Lloyd in the New Zealand case of *Invercargill City Council* v *Hamlin* [1996] 1 All ER 756, at 764–5). Courts, legislators, and lawyers in the common law world still share a more or less common approach to legal reasoning, and, as Lord Lloyd put it in *Invercargill*, a willingness to learn from each other. For example, it is not that uncommon, particularly in areas where the law is uncertain, for judges to refer to decisions from several common law jurisdictions, thereby enabling them to analyse a range of potential solutions to the problem.

1.7.2 The contrast with 'civil law'

The term *civil law* describes those systems which have developed out of the Romano-Germanic legal tradition of continental Europe. It is the civil law tradition which dominates within the present European Union. Only two Member States—the Republic of Ireland and the United Kingdom, subject to the caveat regarding Scotland—belong to the common law world as such. (One other Member State, Cyprus, shares some of the common law tradition, but is best seen as a mixed system, rather like Scotland.) As large sections of this book are concerned with comparative issues between English and 'European' law, we will come back to the differences between the common law and civil law traditions at various points, but for now we return to the other meaning of common law as a source of judge-made English law.

1.7.3 The court structure

To understand how the common law works, we need to understand the English court structure and its role in making *precedent*. We begin with two basic distinctions: one is the difference between *trial* and *appellate* courts; the other is between *civil* and *criminal* courts.

The function of trial courts, such as the county court, is to hear cases 'at first instance': that is, to make a ruling on the issues of fact and law (this is a distinction that we shall discuss in detail in **Chapters 3** and **5**) that arise in the case. This distinguishes them from appellate courts, whose function it is to reconsider the application of legal principles to a case that has already been heard by a lower court. Some appeal courts also have jurisdiction to reconsider disputed issues of fact—i.e. disputes about the events leading to the legal action. Thus, any one case may well be heard by more than one court before the issues are finally resolved. Rights of appeal can be a complex subject in their own right, governed by a whole set of procedural rules; the detail of these falls outside the scope of this book, and we shall only outline the general principles that apply.

Trial and appellate functions are often combined within one court; the system is not simple enough for us to say that court X is solely a trial court, while court Y is purely appellate.

Civil and criminal law are significantly different in their aims, and employ different legal procedures. This latter point is particularly true of rules of evidence, for example. 'Evidence' describes the legal rules which control what facts may be proved, and the manner of their proving, before the courts. If you were to study the law of evidence, you would soon be struck by the greater evidential restrictions governing criminal as opposed to civil cases.

Criminal law describes those wrongs—*offences*—which are sufficiently important for society, usually through the intervention of the state, to outlaw as crimes, and to impose special penalties on the wrongdoer (such as a fine or term of imprisonment). If you haven't studied law before, this is probably what you most immediately think of when you think about 'law', whereas, in reality, the criminal law is a relatively small part of the totality of English law.

The term *civil law* (as opposed to 'civil (romano-germanic) law' as considered in section **1.7.2**) is also used to describe all those areas of law which are not criminal. Areas that govern the relationship between legal persons—i.e. individuals and corporations—such as contract, employment, or tort (itself an umbrella term used to describe a whole variety of specific wrongs, not 'offences', which is a term reserved for criminal matters) and areas such as negligence, libel, and trespass are all classed as civil law. In civil law matters the injured party will, if they succeed, be entitled to a 'remedy'. This will most commonly be in the form of financial compensation for the harm suffered, and where that compensation is awarded by the court it is called 'damages'.

By and large there is a fairly clear distinction between those courts having civil law and those having criminal law responsibilities (what lawyers call *jurisdiction*). **Figures 1.1** and **1.2** provide a basic guide to the structure of the English civil and criminal court systems.

With the exception of the lay magistracy, and some specialist tribunals, the English judiciary is overwhelmingly drawn from legal practice. Unlike many civil law countries, where there is an established career judiciary which functions, usually as a branch of the civil service, judicial appointments in England and Wales are made generally on the basis of private practice experience, with most judges commencing their judicial careers after around ten or more years as practitioners. This means that English judges tend to have a substantial body of legal experience already behind them, but, on the downside, it means that the lack of diversity apparent in the more senior levels of the legal profession tend to be amplified in appointments to the judiciary. Thus, in 2017, 93 per cent of court judges identified as white, and 70 per cent as male (as compared with a European average of 49 per cent male). Around two-thirds of all judicial appointments are still made from the Bar, which represents some 10 per cent of the practising profession. (All statistics cited are drawn from the *Judicial Diversity Statistics* 2017 published at www.judiciary.uk.)

The Supreme Court of the United Kingdom

The Supreme Court is at the top of the hierarchy of English courts. It is the final court of appeal in civil and criminal matters in England, Wales, and Northern Ireland, and for civil appeals from Scotland. The Court was created by the Constitutional Reform Act 2005 to replace the Appellate Committee of the House of Lords. It commenced work

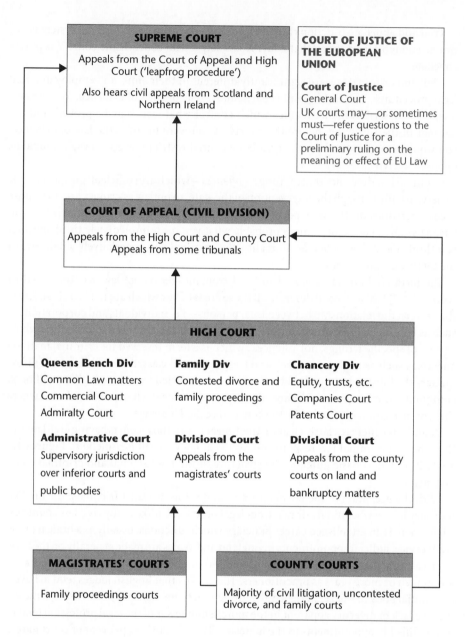

Figure 1.1 The civil courts of England and Wales, and the CJEU

on 1 October 2009. The Court comprises twelve judges in total, called Justices of the Supreme Court (JSC). Only eleven Justices were appointed by the time it commenced sitting. Ten of these were already sitting as judges in the House of Lords, including the first President of the Supreme Court, Lord Phillips of Worth Matravers.

The current President of the Court is Lady Brenda Hale (Baroness Hale of Richmond), who took up the role in September 2017. Lord Reed took over from Lady Hale as Deputy President of the Court on her appointment. Lady Hale is the first woman to lead the UK's highest court, having also been the first woman to be appointed to its predecessor,

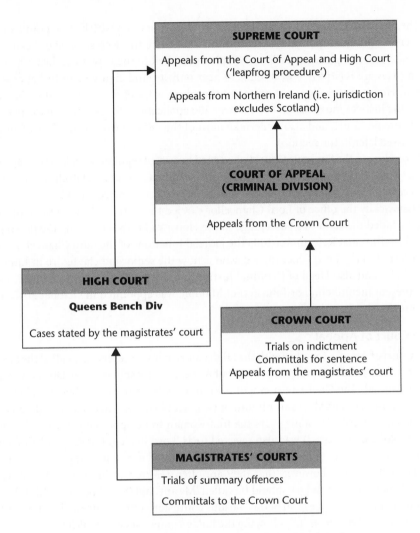

Figure 1.2 The criminal courts of England and Wales

the House of Lords, in 2007. She was joined in 2018 by two further female Justices: Lady Arden and Lady Black. In an historic moment for the Court, the case of *Re D*, in October 2018, became the first case to be heard by a panel on which women Justices were the majority.

The majority of appeals to the Supreme Court come from the Court of Appeal in England and Wales. Although it may also hear appeals direct from the High Court by a special procedure (called 'leapfrog'), such cases are rare.

Cases in the Supreme Court are normally heard by five judges, or, exceptionally, by as many as seven or nine judges if the case is felt to raise issues of special importance or difficulty. *HM Treasury* v *A and Others*, the very first case to be heard before the Supreme Court on 5 October 2009, was one of three joined appeals listed to be heard by a bench of seven Justices. For earlier examples, see *Pepper* v *Hart* [1992] 3 WLR 1032; [1993] 1 All ER 42 and *R* v *Bow Street Metropolitan Magistrate, ex parte Pinochet Ugarte (No. 3)* [1999] 2 All ER 97.

The Supreme Court only hears appeals in respect of cases which raise points of law of 'general public importance'—that means that there must be some significant area of doubt regarding the operation of a rule of law before the Court will hear the case. Such cases are relatively few; it tends to hear only around eighty or so full appeals in a year. However, this does not represent the whole work of the Court and its Justices, since the Justices must also sit to hear over 200 applications for permission to appeal to the Supreme Court, and also undertake most of the judicial work of the Privy Council (discussed later in the section).

Procedure in the Supreme Court is governed by a set of regulations called the Supreme Court Rules 2009, and by 'Practice Directions' set down by the Court itself. These can all be accessed from the Supreme Court website (at www.supremecourt.uk).

Historically the office of Lord Chancellor carried the status of head of the judiciary, and included the right to sit as a judge in the House of Lords. Following the passing of the Constitutional Reform Act 2005 the judicial functions of the Lord Chancellor were transferred to the Lord Chief Justice, who is now the senior judicial figure in England and Wales and also Head of Criminal Justice (but does not sit in the Supreme Court). The present incumbent, Lord Burnett of Maldon, was appointed in October 2017, having previously sat in the Court of Appeal.

The Court of Appeal

The Court of Appeal, together with the High Court, constitute what are called the Senior Courts of England and Wales. The Court of Appeal itself is split into two Divisions, Civil and Criminal. The Civil Division will hear appeals from the High Court and county courts. Cases are heard by a minimum of two, but normally three, judges called Lords Justices of Appeal. For some years the first woman to be appointed (Dame Elizabeth Butler-Sloss, now retired) was also referred to as 'Lord Justice', but she (and all female judges subsequently appointed to the Court) are referred to now as 'Lady Justice'. Female judges will tell you, however, that they are often referred to in all manner of ways. Thus, female District Judges should be called 'Ma'am', but 'Sir', 'Your Worshipfulness', 'Madam', and even 'Lovey', all betray various confusions or prejudices. The title Lord or Lady Justice is written as 'LJ' following the judge's name—hence 'Smith LJ'.

The Court's Civil Division is headed by a senior judge known as the Master of the Rolls, who is also Head of Civil Justice in England and Wales. He (as yet there has never been a female Master of the Rolls) is referred to by whatever title is appropriate with the suffix 'MR'. The present incumbent is Sir Terence Etherton MR, who was also, in 2008, the first openly gay man to be appointed to the Court of Appeal.

The Criminal Division will hear criminal appeals against either conviction or sentence from the Crown Court. Criminal cases will normally be heard by at least two or three judges drawn from among the Lord Chief Justice, the Lords Justices of Appeal, and the Judges of the High Court.

Sir Rabinder Singh (appointed July 2017) is the only Court of Appeal judge with black or Asian ethnic origins. In 2017, nine (24 per cent) of the thirty-eight Lords Justices of Appeal, were women. This compares with eight (21 per cent) in 2015.

The High Court

This is the most complex of the courts to understand. The best way to grasp how it operates is to consider the trial functions of the various elements.

You can see in **Figure 1.1** that the Court is subdivided into three divisions, each of which has a separate jurisdiction to hear cases at first instance (i.e. trials). These divisions are the **Queen's Bench**, which deals with the main areas of common law, such as contract and tort, and some criminal and public law matters; **Family**, which deals with matrimonial cases and the wardship and adoption of children; and the **Chancery Division**, which deals chiefly with certain property, corporate, and tax matters. That seems simple enough, but now it begins to get more complicated. The English courts have long been important in the development and adjudication of both 'local' and international commercial disputes, not least because of Britain's (and particularly London's) historical importance as a centre of international trade and commerce. Because commercial law itself and the demands of court users have become increasingly complex and specialised, there has been a growing need for specialisation within the two divisions, which have significant commercial law jurisdictions: Queen's Bench and Chancery. As a consequence, a number of specialist, commercial, trial courts have been created *within* each of those divisions, with judges being assigned specifically to those courts. The oldest of these is the Admiralty Court, which existed originally as a separate common law court in its own right, but was, in the late nineteenth century, amalgamated into a rather curious hybrid, the Probate, Divorce, and Admiralty (PDA) Division. The functions of the old PDA division were dispersed across all three divisions when the present system was created. The other specialist courts are of relatively recent creation. Their location and jurisdictional responsibilities are represented in **Table 1.1**.

Table 1.1 Specialist courts of the High Court

Chancery Division	Queen's Bench Division
Bankruptcy and Companies Court	**Admiralty Court**
Personal actions for bankruptcy. Compulsory liquidation of companies and other matters arising under Insolvency and Companies Acts.	Deals principally with the legal consequences of collisions at sea, salvage, and damage to cargoes.
Patents Court	**Commercial Court**
Deals with a range of intellectual property matters, not just patents. Hears appeals from decisions of the Comptroller General of Patents, Designs and Trade Marks.	Wide jurisdiction over banking, international credit, and international trade matters, including shipping contracts that are not within the Admiralty Court's jurisdiction. Judges of the Commercial Court also have jurisdiction to arbitrate commercial disputes.
Intellectual Property Enterprise Court (IPEC)	**Technology and Construction Court**
Replaces the Patents County Court in dealing with intellectual property matters (copyright, patent, and trade mark infringements and breach of confidence) where damages recoverable are below £500,000. Higher-value claims continue to go to the specialist Patents Court.	Specialist jurisdiction over building and engineering disputes, and computer litigation. Cases may be heard in London or at a number of regional court centres.

Each division has its judicial 'head', normally appointed from among the Lords Justices of Appeal. The head of the Chancery Division is now called the Chancellor of the High Court. The present incumbent is Sir Geoffrey Vos. The Family Division is led by a President, currently Sir Andrew McFarlane. The head of the Queen's Bench Division was, historically, the Lord Chief Justice; however, the Constitutional Reform Act relieved him of that role by creating a new post of President, currently occupied by Sir Brian Leveson.

In addition to these first instance jurisdictions, each division has appellate functions performed by a 'Divisional Court'. A Divisional Court will normally be presided over by two or three judges. The Divisional Courts of the Chancery and Family Divisions have jurisdiction over certain appeals from the county and magistrates' courts. The main function of the Divisional Court of the Queen's Bench Division has been to exercise what is called the 'supervisory jurisdiction' of the High Court; that is, the power to oversee the quality and legality of decision-making in inferior courts and tribunals. It also (occasionally) hears criminal appeals '*by way of case stated*' on points of law from the magistrates' courts and Crown Court. Following recommendations in the Bowman Review of the judicial review process, the Divisional Court of the Queen's Bench Division was renamed the 'Administrative Court' in October 2000.

At first instance cases are heard usually by a single puisne (pronounced 'puny') judge, referred to as 'Mr Justice . . .' and written as, for example, 'Brown J.' (plural—'JJ.'). As of July 2015, there were only three High Court judges who declared themselves to be from a black or minority ethnic background (representing 3 per cent of the total (and down from 4.5 per cent in 2012)). Twenty-one judges (20 per cent) out of the total of 106 sitting in the High Court were women. They have conventionally been called 'Mrs Justice', regardless of marital status; however, Dame Alison Russell on her appointment in 2014 became the first British High Court judge to be permitted to adopt the style 'Ms Justice'.

The county court

Whereas the High Court can trace its ancestry back to Norman times, the county courts are essentially nineteenth-century creations. Two types of judges sit in the county courts: Circuit Judges (the more senior) and District Judges. Work is divided among these judges on a set of procedural rules which are outside the ambit of this book. An appeal from the decision of a District Judge (the right to appeal is based on limited grounds) will go to a Circuit Judge. An appeal from the decision of a Circuit Judge goes to the Court of Appeal.

The High Court and the county court deal with the same sort of legal issues. The difference is that the High Court deals generally with the more legally complex and/or higher monetary value claims. Major changes to the procedure of the High Court and the county courts were introduced on 26 April 1999, following recommendations in Access to Justice (1996)—often referred to as the 'Woolf Report', after its author, the then Master of the Rolls, Lord Woolf. While much of the detailed application of these rules goes beyond the scope of this book, we will briefly consider some of the consequences in section **1.8**.

The Crown Court

This court deals almost exclusively with criminal trials and appeals. Most of its case load involves the trial at first instance of the more serious criminal offences, such as homicides, serious physical and sexual assaults, and property offences involving loss or damage of a 'high value'. It is in this context that the Crown Court remains the only court in the English system in which a judge regularly sits with a jury. The function of the judge is to advise the jury on the law; the jury, however, remains the sole tribunal of fact, and it is for the jury alone to decide whether an accused is guilty or innocent as charged. The Crown Court has an appellate function whereby it also hears appeals (without a jury) from the magistrates' courts on issues of fact or law.

The magistrates' courts

Magistrates' courts are purely courts of first instance. The bulk of their case load involves the trial of less serious criminal offences (in fact over 90 per cent of all criminal cases are tried by magistrates), though the courts also have a civil jurisdiction over some licensing, tax arrears, and matrimonial matters. The magistrates' court is unique in that the great majority of cases are heard before Justices of the Peace—lay persons with little formalised legal training, though they are advised on the legal issues by a legally qualified Justices' Clerk. Legally qualified magistrates may sit alone to hear cases: they were formerly called stipendiaries but now have the title of District Judge (Criminal).

Administrative tribunals and other courts

In addition to the formal courts, there is a plethora of administrative tribunals, many of which have been created only since the Second World War (though some, like the Commissioners of the Inland Revenue, are far older). They control a vast range of activities from the issuing of passenger licences to airlines, through employment disputes, to adjudicating on parking fines or the award of social security entitlement. The tribunal system has been significantly restructured and rationalised by the Tribunals, Courts and Enforcement Act 2007, bringing many individual tribunals within the structure of a standardised 'First-Tier Tribunal' with rights of appeal to an 'Upper Tribunal', which has taken over the appellate jurisdiction of the Administrative Court in respect of a large number of tribunals. One very important set of tribunals still sits outside this structure. These are the Employment Tribunals (until 1998 known as 'Industrial Tribunals'). Appeals from these tribunals go to a specialist appeal forum known as the Employment Appeal Tribunal, and from there any appeal goes to the Court of Appeal.

In England and Wales there are a number of other local or special courts in existence, which are rather too specialised to merit discussion here. However, you should be aware of three other courts which, formally speaking, are not a regular part of the English court system, but are still of considerable importance to it. These courts are the Court of Justice of the European Union, the European Court of Human Rights, and the Privy Council.

The **Court of Justice of the European Union (CJEU)** is the final authority on points of interpretation of European Union law. The Court actually comprises three courts: the Court of Justice, the 'General Court', and the EU Civil Service Tribunal. For our purposes the Court of Justice has been the most important court in the CJEU structure. It exercises a range of judicial oversight powers over EU institutions and legislation, and courts in the EU Member States can refer points of European law to it for clarification and ruling (see further section **1.10** and **Figure 1.1**), though note that the CJEU's importance in relation to the UK is likely to be greatly diminished in the context of Brexit.

The **European Court of Human Rights** is the international court created by, and with power to adjudicate cases involving the application of, the European Convention on Human Rights. It is a wholly separate institution from the CJEU, and the two should not be confused. Again, we discuss the nature and role of this court more fully later, this time in **Chapter 10**.

The **Judicial Committee of the Privy Council** (normally abbreviated to just 'Privy Council') acts as the final court of appeal for a number of UK dependent territories and independent Commonwealth states, though its jurisdiction has been steadily eroded by continuing UK and international reforms. Today it tends to hear anywhere between thirty and fifty cases a year, mostly from the Commonwealth Caribbean and the Channel Islands. It has a number of rather esoteric functions in the English legal system, relating to matters such as Admiralty cases and appeals from the disciplinary decisions of the General Medical Council. Its jurisdiction was extended in 1998 to include adjudicating on the 'legislative competence' of the devolved governments of Scotland, Wales, and Northern Ireland, though these powers have now been transferred to the UK Supreme Court.

Cases before the Privy Council are normally heard by the Justices of the Supreme Court. Senior judges from other Commonwealth states are entitled to sit, but that right is not always exercised. Given the status of the judges, Privy Council decisions may carry some considerable weight within the English legal system (see the discussion in **Chapter 6**), as well as being binding in the jurisdictions for which it remains the final court of appeal.

1.7.4 Precedent and the common law

The common law has not, as a system of rules, evolved from the totality of case law. It would be physically impossible to maintain records of and develop principles from every decision of every court that has ever heard a case. Rather, the origins of the common law can be traced back to the practice which developed in medieval England, whereby records of arguments used in the Royal courts were kept and circulated, at first unofficially, among the judges, student advocates, and practitioners. This practice gradually hardened into an officially sanctioned system of *precedent*, whereby important cases were recorded and subsequently used as authority for specific rules of law. As a reflection of that original practice, precedent is still created only by the superior courts—the High Court, the Court of Appeal, and the Supreme Court. Some of the major tribunals have separately created their own internal systems of precedent, and where rights of appeal to the courts exist, they will also be bound to follow the precedents set by those courts. Precedent is, in theory, binding on all inferior courts (and tribunals). These include, chiefly, the Crown Court, magistrates' courts, and county courts; the details of our system of precedent will be discussed at much greater length in **Chapters 6** and 7.

So, in advising our friend we would almost certainly have to take some account of case law, either because the legal rules concerned are actually a creation of the common law, or because the courts have considered the operation and effect of some relevant statutory provision. In advising her, we would not only have to know what cases (if any) existed, but also, by reference to the doctrine of precedent, assess what impact those cases might have on any future proceedings against her, which leads us onto our next point: what might those proceedings involve?

1.8 The importance of procedural law

When someone goes to court, there are two kinds of law that need to be taken into account in managing their case. The first is what we call the **substantive law**, that is, the specific rules which tell us what the law of contract or crime says about selling flick knives (to continue with our example). The second is the **procedural law**, which lays down the process by which a case is brought before the court, and how it is tried. Thus, the procedural law will prescribe the process by which a claim is made or criminal action commenced, and the pre-trial steps required (under judicial supervision) to bring it to trial. Procedural and evidential rules also set some parameters on the conduct of trials and on what evidence may be admitted.

The procedural law tends to operate differently in civil disputes and criminal prosecutions. Generally procedural and evidential rules tend to be rather more restrictive in criminal cases, not least because an individual's liberty is often at stake.

The details of procedural law are not widely taught in English law schools before the stage of professional training, but a basic knowledge of how cases come to court, and the systemic assumptions underpinning that process, is useful in understanding how and why cases get to court (and sometimes into the law reports) in the way they do. Moreover, because the continuing development of the common law system depends to a significant extent on cases getting into the superior courts, the processes by which cases get before those courts are important for legal method, because they will also help determine the future shape of the common law, and the pace of change.

1.8.1 The adversarial process

One thing procedurally that virtually all common law civil and criminal courts (it is much less true of tribunals) have in common is the assumption of what is commonly called an *adversarial process*. This was described by Justice (1974: 18) as:

> a fight, a pitting of strengths and wits against each other, a display of aggression mitigated only by the ritual of a complex set of rules and conventions.

This notion of 'trial by battle' is deeply embedded, both historically and psychologically, within the common law tradition. It has created a system in which, traditionally, it is the parties themselves who make the running in any case. It is they, not the judge, who select the facts and the legal issues upon which a case is to be fought. This is reflected in both the role of the judge and the ethical obligations borne by the advocates.

Traditionally, the role of the judge is thus, in theory, restricted to passive umpire, overseeing proceedings and ensuring that the trial is pursued according to the rules of the legal game. Judicial neutrality is, of course, a fundamental principle. Judges are expected to remove themselves (or risk being removed) from hearing cases in which they have a personal interest, or where, viewed objectively, they have acted in a manner that demonstrates actual or apprehended bias or prejudice. Of course, this does not mean that the judge is a silent bystander; he is quite at liberty to interject, for example, to direct a witness to answer questions, to test the quality of the legal arguments being put forward, to seek clarification of some point of fact or law, or to prevent an improper line of questioning. And judges can legitimately be quite robust or forthright in their language without that of itself leading to a finding of bias.

Unlike the judge, the advocate's role in common law systems is, it follows, essentially partisan. Their job is to represent their client, though this too is subject to certain ethical limitations: most notably, the lawyer's partisanship is qualified and balanced by duties to the court and, to a lesser extent, third parties and the profession at large. Professional codes of conduct in the UK thus make it a disciplinary matter actively to mislead the court or other parties to the proceedings, though the boundaries of such obligations may themselves be a matter of some debate (see generally Herring, 2017: ch. 4).

Even so, it is sometimes said that the system is of limited efficacy. The promise of adversarialism is a pragmatic commitment to procedural fairness, which may in practice be significantly undermined by resources and other inequalities between parties. Defenders of the system nonetheless argue that the law is doing the best it can. In *Air Canada v Secretary of State for Trade (No. 2)* [1983] 1 All ER 910, Lord Wilberforce put it in these terms (at 919):

> In a contest purely between one litigant and another, such as the present, the task of the court is to do … justice between the parties … There is no higher or additional duty to ascertain some independent truth. It often happens, from the imperfection of evidence, or the withholding of it, sometimes by the party in whose favour it would tell if presented, that an adjudication has to be made which is not and is known not to be, the whole truth of the matter; yet if the decision has been in accordance with the available evidence, and with the law, justice will have been fairly done.

This traditional adversarial approach differs somewhat from the *inquisitorial* procedure in the majority of civil law systems, though those differences are often overstated. The inquisitorial process is typified by a far more pro-active judicial role than we would expect to find in a true adversarial system.

There is not an assumption in civilian systems that the court's function is to vindicate the winner, to establish that one party has a legal right. Rather there is a more open and free-ranging search for 'truth'. This difference in perception affects the substantive procedures used. Because there is no perceived battle between two sides, there is less requirement to control inquisitorial proceedings by restrictive procedural and evidential rules. Whether it is more effective at finding the truth is debatable. While it is common to draw quite a stark contrast between these two types of process, in reality that is rather artificial. There have always been legal institutions in common law countries (including England) which adopt a form of inquisitorial process. Equally, there are civilian legal systems (such as Italy) where adversarial procedure is more in evidence. Moreover, trends towards greater judicial control and 'case management' of proceedings in England and Wales also potentially narrow the gap (see, e.g., Partington, 2018: ch 8).

1.8.2 Legal method and the limits of the trial

Most infringements of the law never get before a court, either because they are never identified as such, or never pursued, or resolved by less formal means. Moreover, contrary to common belief that societies are becoming more litigious, long-term studies of trends in both England and the United States indicate that there is actually proportionately *less* civil litigation than fifty or sixty years ago (Kritzer, 2004; Genn, 2009), Procedural changes in England and Wales since the late 1990s have, in the words of one leading commentator, converted the trial and rendering of judgment in the civil courts into a 'solution of last resort' (Roberts, 2009: 458). This has been achieved, for example, by front-loading the costs of going to trial, reframing the objective of pre-trial proceedings as being to promote settlement, and actively diverting cases to mediation.

In criminal matters, the trial has not been de-centred from the legal process to anything like the same degree, but it should be borne in mind that the great majority— around 98 per cent—of criminal cases are dealt with at the lowest level of the system, by magistrates' courts, and most proceed no further. Moreover, many matters in the criminal justice system are resolved by the decision to plead guilty, or by 'plea bargains': agreements (or a kind of 'settlement') between prosecution and defence that also result in a guilty plea, and thus obviate the need for a full trial (see, e.g., Sanders *et al.*, 2010).

Trials are thus only the tip of a (potential) disputes iceberg; and appeal cases, which shape the rules discussed in this book, are in turn only a fraction of a fraction of that total activity. Why is this rather self-evident fact important for legal method?

First, the growth in a settlement culture, whilst in many respects a good thing, does involve a substitution of private for public forms of dispute resolution. Negotiated and mediated settlements are usually confidential to the parties and, by definition, there is no adjudication of a claim. Some commentators have raised concerns about the wider implications of this shift from public to private ordering. In the United States, for example, Professor Owen Fiss (1984) has argued that more private resolution of disputes reduces the power of law to articulate public values, to bring, in Fiss's words, 'a recalcitrant reality closer to our chosen ideals'. It might even be argued that too great a reliance on private and alternative forms of dispute settlement potentially reduces the opportunity for courts to establish points of principle through the public deciding of cases and the development of precedent.

Secondly, if we think about the cases that get to the higher courts, we cannot avoid seeing case-law development as other than a relatively *ad hoc* and possibly even inefficient process (though that latter assertion is difficult to confirm empirically). The evolution of legal rules through court decisions depends on a number of variables, not least:

- the 'right' legal claims arising. Common law development can be seen as a bit of a lottery. The way the law evolves depends on the factual matrices and 'strength' of the cases coming to court. However, we have no idea when or whether the 'right' cases will emerge from the primordial soup of human (mis)conduct. Unless the issue is serious enough to justify legislation, the (lower) courts may consequently be stuck with 'bad' law for a considerable period, until either the right case comes along, or Parliament considers it important enough to legislate change.

- the resources of the parties. Even if we do have a potential case with the appropriate facts, that case will only become a precedent if the parties have the power, resources, and willingness to pursue the issues through the appellate courts.

- the prevailing 'judicial practice'. As we shall see (in **Chapters 5** and **6**), precedent is not simply a matter of courts blindly following a set of concrete rules or principles. Rather, it is best understood as a 'judicial practice' (see, e.g., Geary *et al.*, 2013: ch. 6); that is, an activity that is shaped by the interplay of rules and principles in the context of a particular judicial culture. Though judicial cultures tend to be relatively stable, they will vary not just over time but possibly between courts in the hierarchy, and even between cases, as regards, for example, the extent of judicial activism or creativity that is permissible and appropriate.

Thirdly, it also reminds us that, while the rules and principles explained in this book are incredibly important for understanding how the higher reaches of 'the law' work, and how the law itself evolves according to its own logic, this is only part of the story. Much of the legal process operates at 'street level', below the radar of the higher courts. You do need to be aware that the law in books and the law in action can be surprisingly different creatures, and that you will be seeing only a part of the picture from a doctrinal analysis of law.

Before we close this chapter, there are two areas of European law which have had a significant impact on the English legal system and legal method, which we need also to consider.

1.9 English law and the European Convention on Human Rights

The European Convention on Human Rights (ECHR) is an international treaty which was created in the aftermath of the Second World War. It has been signed by most European governments, including the United Kingdom, as a statement of their commitment to the protection of certain fundamental human rights, such as freedom from torture and slavery, freedom of religion, freedom of expression, and the right to a fair trial. The ECHR is not one of the EU treaties and is not part of EU law; consequently, the UK's legal relationship with the ECHR is not affected by Brexit. Nor is the ECHR controlled by EU institutions. The political governing body with oversight of the Convention is an organisation called the Council of Europe. Although there is a separate EU Charter of Fundamental Rights (based on the ECHR), this was introduced only because the EU institutions were not bound by the ECHR (see Opinion 2/94 of the Court of Justice: *Accession by the Community to the European Convention for the Protection of Human Rights and Fundamental Freedoms* [1996] ECR I–1759) and does not significantly change the relationship of EU Member States to the ECHR itself.

Whether or not individuals can enforce their rights under the ECHR within their own legal systems depends on the rules and structures of each legal system. Many, though not all, Western European legal systems are framed so that treaty obligations entered into by their governments are automatically incorporated into domestic (i.e. national) law. In that situation, a citizen could pursue a Convention right through the domestic courts. The legal position in Britain is different. Here, international legal rights can be directly enforced only where the treaty has been expressly incorporated into law. This normally requires an Act of Parliament. Although the courts and Parliament sometimes made reference to the ECHR in defining the scope of rights and duties under English law, there had been, prior to 1998, no express incorporation. Consequently, British citizens seeking redress under the ECHR had to rely exclusively on an international institution called the European Court of Human Rights at Strasbourg. There have been a significant number of such cases on a variety of issues, including the freedom of the press; the rights of transsexuals to have public documents such as passports and birth certificates changed to record their 'reassigned' rather than 'genetic' sex; the detention and trial of 'political' prisoners in Northern Ireland; and the use of corporal punishment in schools. Indeed, the British government had a relatively poor track record before the Court, having been found in violation of the ECHR in a total of fifty cases (see Greer, 1999: 5); this has been one of the key reasons why the political pressure for incorporation of the ECHR into English law steadily increased, though for many years neither Labour nor Conservative governments had supported the move to incorporation as part of government policy.

That changed in 1996 when the Labour Party published an influential policy paper called *Bringing Rights Home*, proposing measures for the incorporation of the ECHR. This policy came to be reflected in Labour's 1997 election manifesto and its first legislative programme after that election. Consequently, after a sometimes rather bumpy ride through Parliament, the Human Rights Bill received the Royal Assent in November 1998. In addition, the original legislation devolving powers to the new Scottish and Welsh assemblies also contained provisions requiring those bodies to legislate consistently with the rights contained in the ECHR. The Human Rights Act 1998 (HRA) came into force in England on 2 October 2000. We shall explore the role of the Act in greater detail in **Chapter 10**.

Politically and legally the passing of the HRA has been a landmark moment in English law, fundamentally reshaping legal discourse and the legal accountability of the state to maintain human rights standards. Anyone following media debates about human rights will be aware that the HRA generates strong opinions both for and against. This is not new. Lord McCluskey, in his 2000 Reith lecture, for example, warned that 'we are going to have to struggle to avoid being buried in new claims of right' (*Guardian*, 8 May 2000). In fact, the feared deluge of claims has not really materialised, with debates focusing far more on the kinds of claims being allowed than the volume. Nevertheless, as we shall see further in **Chapter 10**, there have been growing calls for reform of the HRA, with members of both the last coalition and present Conservative government pushing for the Act's replacement by a 'British Bill of Rights' more independent of the ECHR. When, or indeed whether, such legislation will be introduced is, at the time of writing, uncertain. For us, as lawyers, the HRA has created a whole new set of concepts and rights which must be understood and developed through practice in courts and tribunals. As we will see, the Act has had a notable impact on that part of legal culture we call 'legal method'. At the same time, there are things that the HRA will not do, partly because of the internal limits and restrictions built into the Act (see further **Chapter 10**), and partly because there is much that the ECHR itself does not do. Human rights remain a developing area of law, and many of our conceptions of fundamental rights have evolved and changed since the Convention was drafted nearly fifty years ago. There are newer forms of human rights, some of which are not yet fully recognised or understood, and about which the ECHR is largely silent (see Rainey *et al.*, 2014: 7; Macklem, 2015). These include:

- the group rights of minority peoples;
- economic rights (so our seller of flick knives could not use the HRA to argue that laws restricting trade in particular goods are an unwarranted restriction of her right to engage in a particular business) and cultural rights; and
- so-called 'third-generation' rights, which include the recognition of individual and community rights over the environment.

Nevertheless, as we shall see in **Chapter 10**, just as the influence of EU law has gradually overtaken this book (as we predicted it would in the first edition), so too issues of human rights have taken on an increasingly pervasive role in shaping British law.

1.10 English law and the European Union

The European Union is a political and legal organisation of twenty-seven Member States (not including the UK, on the assumption that some form of Brexit will happen). It was founded as the European Economic Community (EEC) by the original six members (France, Germany, Italy, and the Benelux countries—Belgium, the Netherlands, and Luxembourg), and given international legal status by the Treaty of Rome in 1957. The European Union grew out of the EEC, and was formally established by the Treaty of Maastricht on 1 November 1993.

Following the passing of the European Communities Act 1972—an Act of the Westminster Parliament—the United Kingdom became a member of the European Community/Union on 1 January 1973. The European Communities Act made the EU treaties and legislation emanating from the EU institutions enforceable as part of UK law. Under s. 2 of the Act, UK courts were required to interpret domestic law consistently with our European law obligations. UK courts were also empowered to refer questions on the interpretation of European Law to the EU's court, the Court of Justice of the European Union (CJEU). This did not (as it has sometimes been represented), make the CJEU a court of final appeal (since questions remitted to the CJEU were always remitted to the English courts to make a decision on the actual facts of the case), but it did mean that the CJEU operated as the final, authoritative *interpreter* of EU law in the UK legal systems.

As a consequence of EU membership, there has been a gradual but substantial mingling of European and English concepts within the legal system for the past forty-five years.

However, in the wake of the 2016 Brexit referendum, Britain's membership of the EU potentially comes to an end in March 2019, following the repeal of the European Communities Act by the European Union (Withdrawal) Act 2018. Extraordinarily, however, at the time of writing this edition, it is still unclear, whether, let alone on what terms the UK will leave.

Membership of the EU was never designed on the assumption that members might one day want to leave the club. It is an extremely complicated process, not just in negotiating the terms of withdrawal, but because so many of the UK's obligations under international trade law are subsumed within its EU membership, and these relationships, and the UK's future relationship with the EU itself, require substantial (re)negotiation. Moreover, while the Withdrawal Act, may signal our departure from the European Union, it does not mark the end of EU law's influence. Unless the UK crashes out in a so-called 'no-deal Brexit' there is also likely to be a transition period in which EU law will continue to apply.

Even after any transition period has ended, the Withdrawal Act maintains EU law influence in two ways. First, it automatically converts existing EU-derived law into English law. Though much of this will likely require amendment, or may face repeal, to accommodate the new relationship between the United Kingdom and the European Union, this will not happen overnight. Secondly, the 2018 Act also establishes, for the sake of legal certainty and continuity, that UK courts below the Supreme Court will continue to be bound by the jurisprudence of the CJEU in respect of law and decisions in force pre-Brexit. The extent of divergence will thus depend significantly on the approach taken by the Supreme Court In short, EU law will not be quickly or easily consigned to the history books.

For these reasons we continue to discuss EU law, though in rather less detail than before, both in specific contexts throughout the book, and more substantially in **Chapter 11**.

CONCLUSION

In this chapter we have explored the functions of law, the variety of forms that law takes, and have glimpsed some of the ways in which English law has been shaped by external influences. In solving any legal problem, including the one set at the beginning of this chapter, we need to be aware of these many dimensions of English law. Any advice we give must take into account the kind of issue with which we are dealing. Is it a question of criminal or civil law? Have we considered all relevant Acts (if any), and checked on the existence of any subordinate legislation? What about case law? Are there any human rights implications? Have the courts said anything about the matter, either in interpreting a relevant statute or in applying rules of common law? It is only by appreciating this context that we can, ultimately, find the relevant law to solve our problem. In practice, of course, you quickly overcome the need to run through the kind of checklist we have just presented. Your knowledge and understanding of substantive areas of law will help to make the job of researching legal issues much simpler. Even so, no one can retain sufficient detailed knowledge to make legal research redundant. **Chapter 2** is intended to help you develop the basic research skills necessary to find the law on any basic legal problem.

CHAPTER REFERENCES

CRACKNELL, R. and CLEMENTS, R. (2012), 'Acts and Statutory Instruments: The Volume of Legislation 1950–2012', Standard Note SN/SG/2911, House of Commons Library (available at www.parliament.uk/briefing-papers/SN02911).

EWING, K.D. (1999), 'The Human Rights Act and Parliamentary Democracy', 62 *Modern Law Review*, 79.

FISS, O. (1984), 'Against Settlement', 93 *Yale Law Journal*, 1073.

GEARY, A., MORRISON, W., and JAGO, R. (2013), *The Politics of the Common Law: Perspectives, Rights, Processes, Institutions* (2nd edn, Abingdon: Routledge).

GENN, H. (2009), *Judging Civil Justice* (Cambridge: Cambridge University Press).

GLENN, H.P. (2010), *Legal Traditions of the World* (4th edn, Oxford: Oxford University Press).

HERRING, J. (2017), *Legal Ethics* (2nd edn, Oxford: Oxford University Press).

JUSTICE (1974), *Going to Law: A Critique of English Civil Procedure* (London: Stevens).

KRITZER, H.M. (2004), 'Disappearing Trials? A Comparative Perspective', 1 *Journal of Empirical Legal Studies*, 735.

MACINTYRE, A. (1988), *Whose Justice? Which Rationality?* (Notre Dame, IN: University of Notre Dame Press).

MACKLEM, P. (2015), 'Human Rights in International Law: Three Generations or One?', 3 *London Review of International Law*, 61.

MIERS, D. (1986), 'Legislation, Linguistic Adequacy and Public Policy', 7(2) *Statute Law Review*, 90.

MIERS, D. (1989), 'Legislation and the Legislative Process: A Case for Reform?', 10(1) *Statute Law Review*, 26.

MORGAN, B. and YEUNG, K. (2007), *An Introduction to Law and Regulation: Text and Materials* (Cambridge: Cambridge University Press).

PARTINGTON, M. (2018), *An Introduction to the English Legal System 2018–19* (Oxford: Oxford University Press).

RAINEY, B., WICKS, E., and OVEY, C. (2014), *Jacobs, White and Ovey: The European Convention on Human Rights* (6th edn, Oxford: Oxford University Press).

ROBERTS, S. (2009), '"Listing Concentrates the Mind": The English Civil Court as an Arena for Structured Negotiation', 29 *Oxford Journal of Legal Studies*, 457.

SANDERS, A., YOUNG, R., and BURTON, M. (2010), *Criminal Justice* (4th edn, Oxford: Oxford University Press).

STEIN, P. and SHAND, J. (1974), *Legal Values in Western Society* (Edinburgh: Edinburgh University Press).

 ONLINE RESOURCES

Test your knowledge by trying the self-test questions that accompany **Chapters 1–6**. Visit: www.oup.com/uk/holland-webb10e

2

Finding the Law

Let's begin by considering again the problem of the shopkeeper, which we introduced in **Chapter 1**. We now know that the answer to her question is likely to lie somewhere in either existing legislation, or in case law, or perhaps in a combination of the two. We also know that there is a vast amount of that primary material to be searched.

How do we go about finding the law on a particular issue? That is a question of developing the appropriate research skills to do the job. Research skills matter, particularly for new lawyers, not just at university or college, but when working in a wide range of trainee and paralegal roles. Indeed, it is no exaggeration to say that research skills are a key element of both academic and professional learning. For example, for those of you who do go into practice, you will have an ethical obligation to represent your clients competently and with appropriate skill and diligence. Competence expressly includes the ability to do effective research, or as the Solicitors Regulation Authority's *Competence Statement* puts it, to use '*appropriate* methods and resources to undertake research' (our emphasis). The point is not an insignificant one. A recent and substantial review of legal education and training, commissioned by the main legal services regulators, reported concerns that:

- Trainee lawyers appear generally to be unfamiliar with paper-based resources by comparison with digital resources
- Trainees depend too much on one-hit searching and thus do not check their findings thoroughly and contextually
- Trainees use Google extensively, and their searches tend to be shallow and brief
- Trainees also appear to lack the skills to organise their research.

(LETR Report, 2013: 45)

An aim of this and the following chapters is therefore to set you on the right path, and help you avoid at least some of those problems.

When we were writing the first edition of this book back in 1990, 'research skills' pretty much meant the ability to use a physical law library. Even in the wake of developing commercial platforms (Lexis, the precursor to LexisNexis, for example, was launched in 1973) and despite the growth in specialist legal informatics during the 1980s and early 90s (Bing, 2010), we could still quite confidently proclaim that 'law is above all else a library-based subject'. In a sense that is still true, but today the 'library' and the associated research skills involved in finding and using legal information have moved substantially from physical to virtual space.

This process of digitisation has not simply been about converting print media into an electronic form. Consequently, the skills, tools, and processes we are talking about in this and **Chapter 3** need to be thought of not simply as discrete 'legal research skills', but as part of a broader package of (particularly digital) information *literacy*. By 'information literacy' we mean the set of capabilities necessary for learning and working in an information-rich, digital society—see further section **2.2**. Though, as the LETR Report reminds us, we cannot ignore paper entirely (yet).

This chapter thus starts out by outlining how not just access to information, but information itself, and legal information in particular, is changing and why that matters. It then explores the skills and capabilities you need to develop to function effectively in this environment, before discussing the specific kinds of sources you need to be familiar with, and some of the research tools you will use in legal settings.

2.1 Law and legal information in a digital society

Let's begin with what may seem like a bit of a digression, though it serves to put what follows in context. The massive growth of computer processing power over the past thirty years has been at the heart of the information revolution. It is this that has enabled us to digitise and move large amounts of information (text, sound, images, or any combination thereof) around the globe.

The public launch of the World Wide Web in 1992 opened up the potential for individuals and small businesses to use communication technologies which a few years previously had been the preserve of governments and large corporations, and, only a few years before that, had simply not existed. In 1994, there were fewer than 3,000 websites (LaFrance, 2015); twenty-one years later the figure is over 943 million. E-commerce has become big business and robotics and artificial intelligence (AI) are out of the lab and changing (often quite imperceptibly) the way we live and work.

2.1.1 The implications for law

Even a relatively traditional field like law is not immune from this transformation. New information technologies are changing the subject matter of law itself. Digital media have created new challenges, for example for intellectual property law, for data security and protection, and for the criminal law, in responding to a wide range of electronic crime (from online theft and fraud, through control of extreme internet porn, to policing the online activities of terrorist groups). Financial regulatory systems globally are having to come to terms with digital currencies such as bitcoin, but also moving significantly to use technology itself as a mode of regulation—the so-called 'fintech' revolution. The military applications of robotics, for example in constructing semi-autonomous and autonomous weapon systems have profound implications for the laws of war, and so on. Scientific and technological innovations are thus creating many of the most interesting and cutting-edge challenges for today's lawyers and legal systems (Brownsword, 2015).

Technology is also changing the way lawyers work, and even the kinds of job that exist in the legal services market (Susskind, 2017). Large-scale litigation has been simplified by the ability to digitise and organise vast swathes of documents and share them through electronic disclosure protocols; the use of visual and audio evidence in the courts is increasingly widespread; private systems of online dispute resolution are expanding. Firms are investing in legal technology to standardise and automate more of their routine transactional work. New hybrid roles are emerging that combine legal and other technical know-how in, for example, knowledge and process engineering, project management, or legal risk management: it is not just about being a solicitor, barrister, or paralegal.

In sum, technology is having a profound impact on the substantive law, the practice of law, and also, more subtly, on how we think conceptually about the subject (see, e.g., Parker, 2011; Sherwin, 2011). As Marshall McLuhan didn't quite say, the medium really does change the message. This has important implications for how we think about legal information and legal research.

2.1.2 Information in the digital society

Let's start with the obvious: digitisation has led to an information explosion of unimaginable proportions. As Professor Richard Susskind (2017: 11) observes, quoting Google's Eric Schmidt, we now create in every two days as much information as existed 'from the dawn of civilization up to 2003'.

Of course, not all of that is legal material, or even material about law; but a lot is, and the amount is growing all the time. In part this reflects the underlying trend for primary legal information (cases, statutes, regulations, and other sources of law) to expand, and never contract. Payne (1983) put it more graphically:

> The Ten Commandments consist of 120 words, the Magna Carta 63 Clauses and the American Declaration of Independence 500 words. The Common Market regulations concerning duck eggs run to no fewer than 120,000 words!

But it also reflects (and has facilitated) an explosion of information *about* law. Information put out by courts and advice agencies, publications from law firms, research and policy documents prepared by government, regulatory bodies, and interest groups; academic articles, working papers, and conference proceedings; media reports; and all sorts of self-publishing through blogs and other social media. All of these might, to a greater or lesser degree, be considered research resources.

The sheer amount of information, however, is only one part of the story. Two other crucial things have happened that make digitisation significant for our present purposes.

First, digitisation has, to an extent, democratised access to and control over information and, in the process, changed the nature of information itself. This is particularly true of web-based information, which is fundamentally non-hierarchical and (in quality terms) loosely controlled. As Tim Berners-Lee, the inventor of the World Wide Web acknowledges, this facet is fundamental to the design principles and architecture of the web:

> the Web is about anything being connected with anything. It is a vision that provides us with new freedoms, and allows us to grow faster than we could when we were fettered by hierarchical classification systems into which we bound ourselves.
>
> (Berners-Lee, 2000: 1)

In some respects, this makes the web an amazing resource, and in other ways it makes it incredibly unhelpful, particularly for academic and professional work where the quality and authenticity of research resources matter. In sum the main problems are:

- There is no all-seeing editor. To put it crudely, anyone with basic resources can publish on the web and basic web architecture does not help us distinguish an idiot from an Einstein. This does not mean that self-published content is intrinsically poor (there are some extremely good legal blogs—or 'blawgs'—for example), but you do need to develop robust criteria for evaluating them.

- Document history and provenance can be difficult to ascertain. The web is not intrinsically interested in authorship, or whether a document is an original or a copy, real or fake, draft or final version.

- As scale increases, depth of research declines. If you have only ten 'hits' it is pretty easy to search all of them. It is a different matter if your search returns 164,000 items. Remember that search algorithms tend to use a wide range of indices in ranking pages: popularity and 'freshness' of the source, relevance to the search, and (technical) page-quality indicators tend to be significant. These may provide only a weak proxy for the intrinsic quality of the page content.

Secondly, digitisation has also radically blurred the distinction between users and producers of information. This has been a particular function of the kinds of Web 2.0 technologies we associate with social media. It creates a couple of significant challenges in academic and professional contexts:

(i) It has changed our relationship to the ownership and authorship of information. Digital information often occurs as a public resource, something we can share freely and readily on Facebook or Instagram. This is, however, a bit of a myth. Outside the digital commons, where authors actively reduce or give up their ownership rights, all information belongs to someone. In the academic and professional worlds acknowledging ownership ('attribution') is important, and the failure to do so has consequences. At university or college such behaviour may be considered 'plagiarism', a kind of cheating that might lead to you failing a module, or even your whole degree (we revisit this in **Chapter 4**). At work it may be embarrassing (a number of law firms, for example, have had to apologise and remove material after lifting content from other firms' websites!) or have disciplinary consequences.

(ii) It has changed the nature of authorship in all sorts of ways. For example, it increases the capacity and, perhaps, the tendency to respond instantaneously to events. This can be great for currency, sometimes less good for quality. Web technologies also facilitate collaborative authoring, with Wikipedia a well-known example. Collaboration fundamentally blurs the line between users and producers, and can be a highly creative and valuable process, but it can also pose risks for other users. The quality of the content depends fundamentally on the skills, knowledge, and interest of the community editing that content. As we see with Wikipedia itself, public content may be provisional, and even disputed; quality and accuracy can be very variable between topics and even within single pages, and consequently academic advice is generally against relying on Wikipedia as an authoritative source. In sum, you need to look carefully at who is authoring anything, in what context, and with what quality controls in place.

So, in the light of all this, what sort of skills should you be aiming to develop?

2.2 Developing your information and research skills

Developing your own information literacy and research skills involves a mix of domain (i.e. legal) knowledge, plus functional IT, research, and communication skills. Visually we can represent it as shown in **Figure 2.1**. We will say a little about each element here.

2.2.1 Five core capabilities

Domain knowledge is an obvious requirement, and it is not just about 'knowing' some law, it is about developing ways of constructing (or deconstructing) legal problems. To be an effective researcher, you need to develop some sense of how lawyers think about legal issues (i.e. the terminology and concepts they use, how legal information is structured and classified, what might be more standard or creative solutions, etc.). This does mean that, to start with, legal research can be really slow and frustrating as you try to find your way around the material. Persevere—it becomes easier with experience.

Understanding your relationship to the problem may also help define the kind and level of research you need to undertake. What is your standpoint? (Learner, legal adviser, friend ...) What is your task, and your objective? Are you reading to fill in

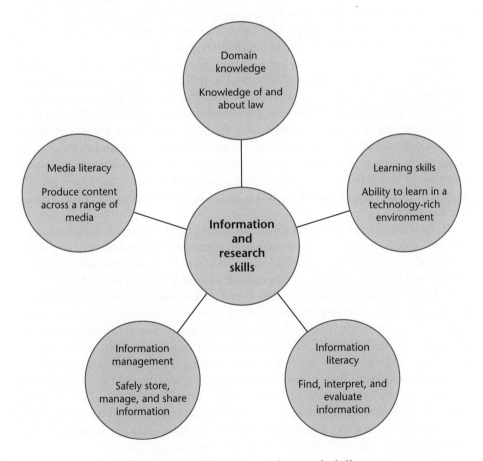

Figure 2.1 Information and research skills

the background of a subject, to enhance your own understanding, or to provide a detailed study of some issue or point of law? Are you producing a letter of advice or an academic essay? Each of these locations and activities may require rather different research strategies (we develop this further in **Chapter 3**), and may influence your choice of sources.

Learning skills: information literacy builds on a good platform of general learning skills. Part of being at university involves learning how to learn in ways that prepare you for the next stages of your career. In particular, it requires developing greater independence as a learner, i.e.:

- actively and critically engaging with material;
- taking responsibility for finding things out rather than waiting to be taught;
- reflecting on your own learning and how you might close any gaps you identify.

The approach we take in this book is particularly geared to helping you develop those skills. That is why we ask questions and include self-tests. It is why we do not pretend that everything is really simple, and include material that is designed to stretch you as a learner.

Information literacy is the primary business of this chapter and **Chapter 3**. It involves finding, reading, and understanding the law. You should also be aware that finding the law increasingly requires a reasonable level of ICT literacy: a basic knowledge of computers, and some understanding of how digital information is stored and retrieved. This will help you construct more effective information searches.

Information management: once you have your information you need to consider how to organise it and store it safely and securely. Dumping everything into a single default documents folder becomes a recipe for overwhelm. Think about how you want to organise your file space, whether it is a hard drive or cloud-based application. Develop good habits in naming files, so you can easily identify the contents. Think about version control: include version numbers or dates in filenames so you can readily see which is the most recent version of a file. Keep secure backups of documents separate from your main PC or laptop hard drive, and back up regularly. These days, as excuses go, 'The computer ate my essay' is generally going to garner about as much sympathy as 'The dog ate my essay'!

Media literacy is, at a minimum about communicating the outcomes of your research. It is still something that plays little real part in legal education, and much of it falls outside the scope of this book. By media literacy we mean the capability to select and use a range of media in ways that are appropriate for your audience and your activity.

At law school many of your assessments and related tasks will involve written communication skills. Most of them may take the form of conventional essays and exams (and we focus on these in **Chapter 4**). Some law schools have opened up their assessment to include multiple forms of writing (professional communications, reflective journals, blogs, etc.), and to allow multimedia use—making videos, dramatic performances, blogs, apps, and so on. These opportunities are really useful. Writing for or speaking in different formats will sharpen your communication and presentation skills, provided you really focus on understanding how these different formats, and different audiences, influence the way in which you communicate. Look out for extra-curricular courses or student societies that will give you access to these sorts of experience.

The remainder of this chapter is about getting you on the path to finding and researching the law.

2.2.2 Getting started: the sources

Lawyers have essentially two types of library and information sources: what we call **literary** and **primary** sources. These may be further subdivided. Accordingly, we have split the following discussion into four constituent parts, covering:

(i)   literary sources;

(ii) case law;

(iii) legislation; and

(iv) EU law.

2.3 Literary sources

The term 'literary sources' is used to describe books *about* law, as opposed to those books *of* law, which contain 'official' copies of legislation or case reports. It thus includes student textbooks, books for practitioners, and articles from professional and academic journals and newspapers. We might also include new media—blogs and commentary on websites—in this category.

We start with literary sources because the simplest way to begin researching a problem is often to find a book about it. This is also going to seem more familiar to you at the start of your law career than going to the cases and statutes themselves (though that is important, as we shall see). Literary sources are sometimes also referred to as *secondary* sources, to distinguish them from those books of law, which are *primary* sources. Be careful that you don't confuse the term 'secondary', meaning literary, with other uses of the term, particularly in relation to secondary legislation.

2.3.1 Books and journals

In terms simply of quantity, textbooks are the main literary source of law. We conventionally make a distinction between academic and practitioner texts. That distinction is slightly arbitrary, as many books may be as useful to the practitioner as to the academic lawyer, but, to generalise, academic texts tend to be less concerned with matters of procedure, and to offer a more critical perspective on the law than practitioner texts. Many academic texts now take a specifically *contextual approach* to law; that is, an approach that attempts to place law in a social, political, or economic perspective, rather than just concentrating on what we call *black-letter* law—i.e. the rules themselves. Accordingly, the answers you find may well reflect the function of the text and the perspective of the author on the subject.

Law journals also take a wide variety of forms. Some, such as the *Law Society Gazette*, are primarily practitioner journals, which will contain articles of interest to legal practitioners on matters of substantive law or practice management; they will also normally maintain an element of updating, with short case notes and information about recent or planned legislation. Many of the more 'heavyweight' journals, such as the *Law Quarterly Review*, appeal to both practitioner and academic audiences. Of these, the majority have some kind of specialist focus—hence we have titles like the *Journal of Business Law, Industrial Law Journal, Legal Ethics*, and *Journal of Social Welfare and Family Law*. Others, such as the *Modern Law Review, Oxford Journal of Legal Studies*, and *Journal of Law and Society*, have a broad coverage of subject matter, but a primarily academic outlook. Most of the main journals have adopted a similar format, with each containing a number of leading articles and book reviews. Some may include shorter articles on recent cases or new legislation.

2.3.2 Finding literary sources

As a starting point in your studies you will almost certainly be given guidance on what texts are required for the course, though for most purposes you will be expected to read more widely than just the required or recommended text. So, sooner rather than later, you will be required to look for other sources (both textbooks and journal articles) from which to work. There are a number of ways of going about this.

- *Check your reading or study guide.* Most lecturers include additional readings and references in their course materials. These will often include alternative and 'key' sources.

- *Start with your textbook.* This is one strategy, but not necessarily the best one. Textbooks will tend to focus on the primary and most important secondary literature, and so are certainly helpful. But they may also be quite selective, particularly in referencing other textbooks ('the competition'!), and they inevitably get out of date, so will not necessarily include the latest works.

- *Access the library catalogue.* All university libraries have an online catalogue of their collection. This will enable you to search by keywords (usually title and/or subject based) and by author, and will link you to available online content from your library. This is a good starting point, but still a fairly limited technique for in-depth searching, as catalogues contain relatively general search terms, so it is unlikely you would find, for example, any references to the law on flick knives this way! Catalogues also do not reference specific journal articles.

Most university libraries have access to extensive digital book collections, as well as a print collection. If you are not used to using digital books, they are worth exploring. Digital platforms increasingly have the capacity to change *how* we interact with information. For example, the more sophisticated e-book readers are more than just reading platforms. They enable us to interact with the text in a multiplicity of ways: bookmarking, adding marginalia and 'sticky notes' (as you might with hardcopy), but also cutting and pasting and linking to other online resources in ways that were never possible with paper sources.

Journal articles and notes can be a very useful resource for a number of purposes, including:

- researching recent developments, which may not have made it into your textbooks;
- identifying different opinions about the purpose and/or effects of a particular legal principle; and
- finding empirical research about the way the law works in the 'real world'.

Searching for journal articles now is best done through electronic resources, of which there are a number, including Westlaw, LexisLibrary, and Lawtel (discussed in section **2.7**), though none of these has a complete set of even the most commonly cited academic journals. For example, none of these databases carries the *Cambridge Law Journal* or *Legal Studies*. There are, however, various other databases to which many law libraries subscribe, including:

- **HeinOnline:** this is a US-based database containing a very extensive full-text library of journal articles, mostly from North America, but including some UK and Australasian academic journals as well. It also holds copies of English case reports from 1212–1865. Because all its content is converted into pdf format, it is not as up to date as Ingenta or the publishers' own sites.

- **Commercial online resources:** all the major publishing groups provide full-text online access to their journals, and often a range of online books as well. You will only have full-text access to those journals and e-books for which your library has a subscription. Non-subscription items can be purchased for a fee. The major databases include Oxford Journals, Ingentaconnect, Taylor & Francis Online, and Wiley Online Library. None of these are purely law-specific, and all are limited in the sense that they only carry their own publications, so you cannot use them to search 'across the board'.

- **JSTOR:** this is a large and multi-disciplinary not-for-profit archive project. It does not carry the most recently published issues of journals (usually those for the last three to five years), but users can link from the JSTOR archive to the publisher's site or sometimes to another online source. Its law collection overlaps with and is much smaller than Hein, but it includes archive copies of the *Modern Law Review, Cambridge Law Journal, Harvard Law Review, Legal Studies, Oxford Journal of Legal Studies*, and *Yale Law Journal* and may be useful, especially if you do not have access to HeinOnline.

In addition to these specific sites, you can use a number of published indexes to search for journal articles by subject or other keywords. These do not necessarily give you direct access to the full text of the article, but can be a useful way of building up a bibliography for further research. There are three that may be of value to you:

- **The Legal Journals Index:** this, the most useful, commenced publishing in 1986, and contains full details of all the legal journals published in the United Kingdom, and so provides an extremely important research resource. It is published online as part of the Westlaw database and can be searched by 'free text' or by subject keyword.

- **Index to Legal Periodicals and Index to Foreign Legal Periodicals:** these are both US publications and are available in paper and electronic forms. The former is an index to all US journals, plus a selection from Britain, the Republic of Ireland, and the Commonwealth from 1981 to date. In the electronic version, details of articles in UK, Irish, North American, and Australasian legal journals for 1908–1981 are held in a separate database called 'Index to Legal Periodicals Retrospective'. The Index to Foreign Legal Periodicals indexes articles on international and comparative law, and on the municipal law of all countries which do not appear in the Index to Legal Periodicals.

2.3.3 Citations

When textbooks and articles make reference to other journal publications, they will do so using relatively standardised modes of referencing or 'citation'. The ability to understand and use systems of citation is critical both to finding and referencing legal materials. We introduce the topic here, and further discuss the importance of referencing in the context of your own writing in **Chapter 4**.

In law there is no internationally, or even nationally, agreed system of citation, though there have been various attempts to standardise within jurisdictions; thus, US law journals mostly adopt the infamous (for its complexity) 'Blue Book' citation system; Australian journals mostly adopt the *Australian Guide to Legal Citation* (AGLC); and in the United Kingdom a number of journals have adopted the *Oxford University Standard for Citation of Legal Authorities* or OSCOLA (more about this later in this section). A comparison of these highlights the problem of multiple citation systems, which is their lack of uniformity. Differences are often fairly small, but still significant.

In general, references may be *in-line*, that is, they are incorporated in the text itself, using the author–date systems of citation, such as the Harvard system, or, more commonly, references appear in footnotes or endnotes.

In-line, author–date systems, such as Harvard, are less commonly used in law. They do not use footnotes for referencing purposes, but refer to sources in the text by author and year of publication, thus: 'Tadros (2008)'. The full reference is then reserved to the bibliography, for example, Tadros, V. (2008) 'Crimes and Security', *Modern Law Review*, 71(6), 940–70. Note that the Harvard citation includes not just the volume but also the issue or part number—here (6), which is often excluded from conventional law citations.

If you are using a footnote and endnote system of citation, this means that your in-text citation will simply be a small superscript number which then links to a full text description of your source within a footnote (or endnote). Footnote styles tend to adopt structures similar to those shown in **Figures 2.2** and **2.3**.

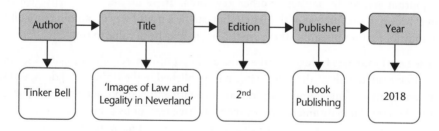

Figure 2.2 Construction of a book citation

OSCOLA is a footnote system of citation that has been widely adopted by UK law schools, and is favoured by a number of journals and publishers. If your school has adopted OSCOLA you should familiarise yourself with the system before you start researching and writing. Like all such citation systems, it is quite complex and requires an eye for detail. The full standard (4th edition, 2012) and a quick guide can be downloaded at www.law.ox.ac.uk/research-subject-groups/publications/oscola.

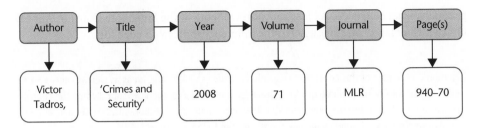

Figure 2.3 Construction of a journal citation

We provide a short introduction to OSCOLA here; essentially there are three basic points to note.

First, it has precise criteria for the referencing of different types of source material—cases, statutes, books, journal articles, government reports, webpages, and so on. The point of this is to ensure that referencing is both complete and consistent, so that the reader can easily identify the type of source material and locate it online or in a physical library. These formats should be followed exactly. You should rely on the official guide for the format of each of type of source; some are hard to guess, and you will almost certainly get it wrong!

Secondly, many of the OSCOLA citations use established abbreviations to denote the source. This is particularly so for law reports—see our discussion of these in section **2.4.1**—but also for journal names (MLR for *Modern Law Review,* PL for *Public Law,* etc.), and official paper series such as parliamentary debates, Law Commission reports, and so on. Until you get familiar with the most common abbreviations, this can make finding legal sources a bit of a trial. Again, you should use The Guide to help, as this provides a substantial list of abbreviations in part 4.2. A comprehensive list of the longer established citations are also listed in Raistrick (1981).

Thirdly, although OSCOLA itself only recommends the use of lists of cases and legislation cited and a separate bibliography in longer works, many law schools require reference lists at the end of *any* piece of submitted work, in addition to footnotes. Expectations may vary, so please check your own institution's requirements. A common practice, however, is to require a case list first, identifying all cases cited, with full names and citations. This should then be followed by a list or table of legislation cited in the work, with the bibliography of secondary sources (books, etc.) following that.

We include a checklist with our online resources which highlights the absolute basics that you should aim to get right when using OSCOLA.

Do be precise in your use of references. This is not just a matter of pedantry; it is a way of ensuring that we are all 'speaking the same language' and that references can be easily traced. We will come back to the importance of citation in **Chapter 4**.

A guide to legal abbreviations has been written by Donald Raistrick (2008); and a list of the main abbreviations in use is also contained in the online resources accompanying this book.

2.3.4 How authoritative are literary sources?

Literary sources do not really contain 'the law'; they contain the author's interpretation of it, and often normative commentary regarding how it might be different. This is not, generally, what courts do. As Justice Andrew Phang of the Singapore Court of Appeal (and a former law professor), asserts, the difference indicates a need for:

> caution on the part of this Court. Unlike academic articles which float ideas as well as concepts of every stripe with no immediate or direct practical consequences, the law laid down by the courts constitutes the law of the land which carries with it immediate and direct practical consequences and implications on those bound by the law and the parties before the court.
>
> *Bom v Bak* [2018] SGCA 83 at [165]

This view is reflected generally in the way the common law courts have made (limited) use of literary, and particularly academic sources. Indeed, at one time, it was the practice that no living author could be cited in court—a rather arbitrary rule, which seemed to suggest that death gives an author authority that he or she may never have had when alive! This restriction has largely fallen into disuse, and some well-established texts are now quite widely cited.

Although academic journal articles and books are increasingly being cited, it is not so much as authoritative texts in and of themselves, but more as an influence on the court's thinking and reasoning. Thus, in *R v A* [2001] UKHL 25; [2001] 2 AC 45, their Lordships referred to a number of academic analyses of the procedural rules governing the bringing of evidence of a complainant's previous sexual experiences in the trial of various sex offences. Judges may also refer to their own, or their colleagues' extra-judicial writing, even if only sometimes, to point to its lack of relevance to the issues—see, for example, *R (Westminster City Council) v National Asylum Support Service* [2002] UKHL 38 at [5], per Lord Steyn, though, judges do also seem on the whole to exercise that same cautious in differentiating between their extra-judicial thoughts and their work in deciding cases (see e.g., Sumption, 2016: 213).

2.3.5 Legal encyclopaedias

Encyclopaedias are usually designed to provide a reasonably complete statement of the law in a relatively concise form. They come in a variety of shapes and sizes. Many of them are subject-specific—so, for example, there are encyclopaedias on consumer protection, social welfare law, employment law, and so on. Most of these are large, loose-leaf volumes designed mainly for legal practitioners. Other significant multi-volume sets for practitioners include the *Encyclopedia of Forms and Precedents* and *Halsbury's Statutes.*

One of the most valuable starting points, particularly if you are researching a topic about which you have little or no existing knowledge, is the legal encyclopaedia called *Halsbury's Laws of England.* This is available in hard-copy format and online as part of the LexisLibrary service (discussed in section **2.7**). The online search facility makes using the electronic version very simple. Searching is not so straightforward with the paper version.

As this is an important source, and one which in practice you may well have to consult in paper form, we have included a brief guide to searching in *Halsbury's* among our online resources, available at www.oup.com/uk/holland-webb10e.

2.4 Cases

The operation of our system of precedent is dependent upon us being able to find out what the courts have said about any given question. This means that we must have a record of the courts' decisions. These records are referred to as 'law reports'.

Whenever possible you are recommended to look at actual reports of cases rather than just to accept the interpretation given in textbooks. This section is intended to give you some guidance to the English system of law reporting, and then to help you to find and update specific cases.

2.4.1 Law reporting

The tradition of law reporting is very ancient in the English legal system, though many of these early reports are now regarded as highly unreliable. In essence, the law reports can be divided into two historical phases, pre- and post-1865.

Before 1865, there were two main sources of case reports:

- **Year books:** established about 1285, these continued in existence until 1535. They were probably derived from the notes of cases taken by student advocates. Consequently, they are not consistently reliable: would you want to rely on your notes as law reports? They are often difficult to read and make relatively little sense to anyone except a legal historian.

- **Private reports:** sometimes called 'nominate reports' because each series is named after the lawyer who compiled them. Hundreds of reports appeared in this era. The same case could be reported by a range of reporters, and in such cases, it is not unusual for the contents, even the decision, to vary as between reports! The significance of these reports, however, lay in the evolution of more precise methods of recording judgments; for example in about 1765 Burrow's Reports introduced the idea of a 'Headnote' (a summary of the facts, decision, and reasoning—a device which is used in every report today). Some were good, for example Coke's Reports [1600–58]; others were not so, for example Espinasse's Reports [1793–1807], of whom it was said: he was deaf; he heard only half of what went on in court, and reported the other half. These reports are now collected together in The English Reports. Cases from the nominate reports are still cited, though increasingly rarely. Some of the most important have also been reprinted in a series called the All England Law Reports Reprint (cited as All ER Rep), which contains a selection of cases from between 1558 and 1935, and the most important ones have been digitised and appear on LexisNexis or Westlaw.

Even after 1865, there remains no single 'official' (in the sense of state-sponsored) source of law reports in the English legal system. This is yet another respect in which our system differs from much of continental Europe. For example, in France there are separate criminal and civil series of the *Bulletin des arrêts de la Cour de Cassation* (the final court of appeal in most civil matters) dating back to 1798, while in Germany there are about twelve current sets of official law reports; these tend to be published separately by reference to the particular court in which the cases were heard. Thus, for example, the Federal Supreme Court (*Bundesgerichtshof*) and Federal Constitutional Court (*Bundesverfassungsgericht*) reports constitute separate series.

In England, in 1865, a body called the Incorporated Council of Law Reporting (ICLR) introduced what is now recognised as the 'official' source of law reports. The Council is still responsible for these today, though there are a number of other organisations which publish various law reports, as well as a body of case law that is never published. We shall consider each of these in turn.

The Law Reports and alternatives

The so-called 'Law Reports' consist of Queen's Bench Reports (abbreviated to QB), Chancery (Ch), Family (Fam), the Industrial Cases Reports (ICR) and Appeal Cases (AC). This broadly reflects the division of work between the superior courts, as Queen's Bench, Chancery, and Family Reports will contain reports of both High Court and Court of Appeal decisions. The ICR, as the name implies, covers employment law in the Employment Appeal Tribunal and above. Appeal Cases contain chiefly Supreme Court, House of Lords, and Privy Council cases. The Council also publishes the Weekly Law Reports (WLR), which are published ahead of the main series and are relied upon by many practitioners.

There are other reputable reports not published by the Council. The All England Law Reports (All ER), published by Butterworths, is a prime example. These are probably the most widely used alternative. Indeed, many smaller law libraries in the United Kingdom and abroad rely purely on the All England Law Reports, which are also available electronically through LexisLibrary, discussed in section **2.7**. The Incorporated Council of Law Reporting also publishes the Law Reports in an online version, (though behind a paywall) and free electronic case summaries. Originally called the Daily Law Reports, these are now published on the ICLR website (see section **2.7.2**) as the Weekly Law Reports (Daily)—WLR (D). Both the Weekly Law Reports and the All England Reports are published in weekly paper parts as well as annual bound volumes. Electronic versions of all the law reports are available from a range of other sources, discussed in section **2.7**.

The Law Reports are generally preferred to other reports in the case of any conflict, and, in terms of court practice, represent the authoritative version of a judgment, which must be used where available—see the *Practice Direction (Citation of Authorities)* (2012) issued by the Lord Chief Justice and published on the judiciary website (at www. judiciary.uk/publications/practice-direction-citation-of-authorities-2012). This preference is because judgments in the Law Reports are revised either by the judges themselves or with their cooperation.

This should ensure that they are a more reliable source of what was said. However, the opportunity for correction enables a judge sometimes to introduce changes to the text which may reflect what he meant to say, rather than what he actually said. This is perhaps a rather more controversial practice, though in some cases it has enabled judges to amend or clarify their reasoning in the light of criticisms directed at the unreported transcript—see, for example, Lord Denning's judgment in *Ghani v Jones* [1970] 1 QB 693, and Jackson (1970: 3).

Conflicts between the various law report versions of a case are comparatively rare, but not wholly unknown. For an example you might like to look at the reports of *Davies v Swan Motor Co. (Swansea) Ltd* [1949] 2 KB 291, at 319; [1949] 1 All ER 620, at 629, where there is a small but confusing discrepancy in the reporting of the judgment of Evershed LJ. See if you can spot it!

Specialist reports

There are many and varied specialist reports such as the Criminal Appeal Reports, Reports of Patents Cases, and Industrial Cases Reports. These are of considerable assistance to subject specialists. A list of the majority of such reports can be found in Raistrick (2008).

Unreported cases

Cases in the inferior courts are not routinely reported. Cases in the higher courts and tribunals may be reported because those are formally 'courts of record', i.e. courts which are required to maintain a full transcript of proceedings. Historically, limited resources meant that not all cases could be reported, and decisions had to be made by the editors as to which cases would appear in the printed volumes. Sometimes they got it wrong. This happened in 1973, for example, with the case of *Mesher* v *Mesher*, which introduced a new kind of 'property adjustment order' for use in divorce cases. Initially the case had been picked up only by *The Times* (a point that seems to have been forgotten, as the case was widely cited as unreported). Even so, the Mesher Order (as it was called) became very popular with the divorce courts, with the result that the case was belatedly reported in the All England Law Reports in 1980 (see *Mesher* v *Mesher and Hall (Note)* [1980] 1 All ER 126). Practically speaking, the higher up the structure one goes, the more likely it is that a case will be reported. All decisions of the Supreme Court and the Privy Council are thus reported as a matter of course. However, reporting today is rather less critical as digitisation has significantly reduced the proportion of unreported cases.

As a matter of general principle, the citing of unreported cases is discouraged. The 2012 Practice Direction states at para. 10:

> Where a judgment has not been reported, reference may be made to the official transcript if that is available, not the handed-down text of the judgment, as this may have been subject to late revision after the text was handed down. Official transcripts may be obtained from, for instance, BAILLI (www.bailii.org). An unreported case should not usually be cited unless it contains a relevant statement of legal principle not found in reported authority.

Clearly, there is some merit to the core of this argument, to the effect that lawyers should only cite cases that actually lay down or explain a principle of law.

2.4.2 How to cite a case

Cases are cited by their name and their 'neutral citation' and/or location in the law reports. Taken together, these provide a means of identification as unique as a fingerprint. The name of any case in English law is normally based upon the parties involved—hence some of the case names we have already seen, such as *Mesher* v *Mesher* or *R* v *Shivpuri*. The case reference is more properly called its **citation**. For the paper volumes of the law reports the most common form of citation of any case will be made up of the following elements:

YEAR	VOLUME (if any)	REPORT	PAGE
[1989]	2	QB	123

This tells us that the case is to be found in volume 2 of the Queen's Bench Law Reports for 1989, beginning at page 123. There is one significant variation on that, which affects the style of citing dates and volume numbers. Some series of law reports in the twentieth century, and a few modern sets, have consecutively numbered volumes, year by year—for example the case of *Bowker* v *Rose*, which is reported only in (1978) 122 Sol Jo 147. Theoretically, the date there is not significant—we could find that case merely by knowing that it is in volume 122 of the *Solicitor's Journal*. For that reason, where the set of reports is consecutively numbered, the date is cited in round brackets. If the date is in square brackets, it is vital to the finding of that case, because the volume number will only refer to volumes *within that particular year*.

With the growing use of online sources, the courts needed a system of citation that could cope with the fact that cases were being published online from transcripts more quickly than they could appear in the traditional law reports. The system devised adopts what is termed a 'neutral' form of citation, and came into operation in 2001.

Every case before a court of record is given a neutral citation that takes a similar form to conventional citations, thus:

[YEAR]   Court   Ref No

The identifiers for each court, which form the core of the neutral citation, are as follows:

- UKSC for the UK Supreme Court;
- UKHL for the House of Lords;
- UKPC for the Privy Council;
- EWCA for the Court of Appeal (followed by 'Civ' or 'Crim', respectively for the Civil and Criminal Divisions); and
- EWHC for the High Court (followed by the abbreviation for the Division of the High Court, or 'Admin' for the Administrative Court).

Though these are the most important for our purposes, they are not the only citations. The system has also been adopted by the courts in Scotland and Northern Ireland, and for a number of specialist courts and tribunals not included here. The result is that we now have a uniform, UK-wide system of neutral citations for all electronically reported case law.

To see how the system works, let's say we have a case of *Smith* v *Jones*, which is the tenth case in 2014 to be decided by the Court of Appeal (Civil Division). It will thus appear as: *Smith* v *Jones* [2014] EWCA Civ 10. The official number (here, 10) will now always have to be cited on at least one occasion whenever a reference is made to *Smith* v *Jones* in later cases. The judgment itself will also be organised by paragraph (not page) numbers. These will appear identically in both the electronic and printed forms of the report. The paragraph numbers do not start and stop with each judge's judgment, but run throughout the case report sequentially, thereby both facilitating searching in electronic form, and enabling comparison of electronic and paper versions. If reference is to be made to, say, paragraph 59, in our fictitious case, the citation becomes: *Smith* v *Jones* [2014] EWCA Civ 10 at [59]. Multiple paragraph references will take the form of: *Smith* v *Jones* [2014] EWCA Civ 10 at [1], [7], and [30]–[42].

Once the judgment has been reported in the printed reports the neutral citation will appear in front of the law reports citation described earlier in this section: thus, *Smith v Jones* [2014] EWCA Civ 10 at [42]; [2014] QB 113 at [42]; [2014] 1 All ER 88 at [42]. The Law Reports produced by the Incorporated Council of Law Reporting are, as we noted earlier, still judicially preferred in the High Court and Court of Appeal, and should be cited where available. This was confirmed in the 2012 Practice Direction, discussed in section **2.4.1**.

The style of citing cases is, as with journal citations, rigidly adhered to. You may find the system rather complex and confusing at first, but it will soon become familiar. We have already indicated the main reports, with their abbreviations. If you need help, fuller lists of specialist, and of US and Commonwealth, reports with their abbreviations can be found in Raistrick (2008).

2.5 Legislation

Legislation, you will recall, can be divided chiefly into Acts of Parliament and statutory instruments. The publication of each of these is a separate activity, so separate search techniques are required.

2.5.1 Acts of Parliament: the sources

Before we begin, one important thing you need to know about an Act is the way in which it is cited. Like cases, Acts of Parliament have a unique signature. This is not based solely upon their name (or **short title**, to use the technical term), however. Many different Acts share a common name—for example, there are presently five statutes in force bearing the title 'Criminal Justice Act'. This means that the year in which the Act became law will be crucial in identifying it. Additionally, every Act passed has a 'chapter number' which may also be used in its identification. In practice, it is quite possible to find legislation by reference to the year and chapter number alone. The citation of an Act as '1988 c. 33', for example, could refer only to the Criminal Justice Act 1988.

Until comparatively modern times, Acts were not formally given short titles (though such titles were quite widely used on an informal basis) so that all legislation was identified by chapter number and **regnal year** (that is, a number assigned to the year in which it was passed, counting it from the first year of that monarch's reign). Hence, the famous Poor Law Amendment Act passed in 1834 was properly cited as '4 & 5 Will. IV c. 76'. This indicates that it was the 76th statute passed in the Parliamentary session which overlapped the fourth and fifth years of William IV's reign.

The tradition of citing regnal years gradually declined after the Second World War, and the system was formally dropped in 1963. Since there are numerous older Acts of Parliament still in force, the old system of citation cannot be wholly disregarded. However, do remember that when writing about any statutes it is conventional now to refer to them, wherever possible, by their short title and date only.

Acts of Parliament are published in a variety of paper series and online. The initial responsibility for publication lies with the Stationery Office which, as the government printer, is required to publish individual copies of all statutes as they are passed. These are ultimately brought together in the annual bound editions of the *Public General Acts and Measures*. All statutes passed since 1988 are also published online through the National Archives (at www.legislation.gov.uk). The site contains either the full text of the Acts as originally passed or revised versions which incorporate later amendments. The majority of legislation is held in revised format, but revisions are by no means entirely up to date, so it is important that you check for warnings where there are revisions pending. As these versions may be less current than LexisLibrary and Westlaw (which contain fully annotated versions of legislation), and the site has relatively limited search functionality by comparison with those others, you should, if you have access to Lexis or Westlaw, use one of those in preference.

In addition to the government printer's versions, there are a number of other paper series which are worth knowing about. The most widely available of these are the *Law Reports: Statutes, Halsbury's Statutes*, and *Current Law Statutes Annotated*.

Law Reports: Statutes

This rather incongruously named collection is also published by the Incorporated Council of Law Reporting—hence the title. The contents are not annotated or revised, and so they do not provide anything different from the Stationery Office copies.

Halsbury's Statutes of England

This provides a partner series to *Halsbury's Laws*, containing an annotated version of all legislation presently in force, organised by subject. It is therefore the main resource for discovering whether legislation exists on any topic.

Current Law Statutes Annotated

All Acts are published in a loose-leaf format soon after coming into force. Of these, those which the editors judge to be sufficiently important are annotated by someone who is a specialist in that area of law. The annotations are not part of the Act, and do not, of course, have any legal effect, though they can be very useful in explaining the background, scope, and operation of the Act. During the course of each year, bound volumes of the *Current Law Statutes Annotated* are published; they are printed in order, according to the chapter numbers of the Acts.

2.5.2 Tracing the legislative history of an Act

Since the House of Lords' decision in *Pepper* v *Hart* [1993] 1 All ER 42, the courts have also been entitled to refer to the Official Reports of proceedings in Parliament (Hansard) as an aid to construction in cases where the language of the Act is unclear (we discuss the parameters of this principle further in **Chapter 9**). This means that lawyers today also need to be familiar with the research techniques necessary to make sense of the legislative history of an Act. The potential scale of this change is indicated by the fact that *Pepper* v *Hart* affects not only Acts passed since 1993, but *all* Acts in force.

Every Parliamentary Bill has to go through both the Commons and the Lords before receiving the royal assent and becoming law. In this process, the Bill will normally be introduced by its promoter at the so-called second-reading stage, where you may find some general statements about purpose or legislative intent; it will also be debated before both Houses, sometimes briefly, sometimes in some detail. It will also be analysed clause by clause in standing committee—this is often the most useful part of the process for our purposes, as in *Pepper* v *Hart* itself. You need to check all of these stages. The following research strategy should work in most cases (see Tunkel, 1993: 18 for further information and alternative approaches).

For established legislation, the best starting point is an annotated version of the Act, though none of these are guaranteed to make the job entirely simple, as much depends on the quality of annotation, which is sometimes variable. Westlaw includes specifically what it refers to as '*Pepper* v *Hart* Notes' amongst its annotatations. LexisLibrary uses *Halsbury's Statutes* annotations, which may also contain references to legislative history. Amongst paper sources, it follows that *Halsbury's Statutes* may be useful, although the *Current Law Statutes* version of the Act will give you all the Hansard references to debates in both Commons and Lords. It will also generally (though not always, especially with older Acts) refer to the discussion in standing committee. Once you have identified the relevant debates, etc. these can be followed up through Hansard. This is published online at the UK Parliament website (see **Table 2.2**), with separate pages for the House of Commons and House of Lords. The online version includes debates in the Commons and in the House of Lords from 1804 to the present day. If you are using the paper volumes, these are bound in separate volumes for the Commons and the Lords, by parliamentary session rather than calendar year. The main Hansard Commons series does not include reports of standing committees. These are published as a separate series.

2.5.3 Statutory instruments

Statutory instruments (SIs) are also published by the Stationery Office, separately, in the annual bound volumes of *Statutory Instruments* (entitled, until 1948, *Statutory Rules and Orders*), and in electronic form on the www.legislation.gov.uk website (from 1987), as well as on LexisLibrary and Westlaw.

The main alternative (paper) source for SIs is *Halsbury's Statutory Instruments*, a multiple-volume set organised by subject, with a Current Service containing instruments passed since the publication of the bound volumes. *Halsbury's* contains information on all instruments in force, though not necessarily in a full-text form.

Note that SIs also have their own mode of reference, which is made up of their title, the year in which they were passed, and the instrument number. So, for example, we have the UK Borders Act 2007 (Code of Practice on Children) Order 2008, SI 2008/3158.

2.5.4 Legislation of the Scottish Parliament and Welsh Assembly

Under the devolution Acts, the Scottish Parliament and Welsh Assembly each have the power to create legislation in their own right. The Scottish Parliament can create primary and secondary legislation. The primary legislation is known as 'Acts of the Scottish Parliament' (the Scotland Act 1998, s. 28(1)). These are published independently of the laws passed by the Westminster Parliament, and are available electronically as well as in paper form. They generally fall outside the scope of this book, since Acts of the Scottish Parliament extend only to the law of Scotland, not to England and Wales.

Under the original devolution Act, the Welsh Assembly could only make secondary legislation. However, Part 3 of the Government of Wales Act 2006 extended the powers of the National Assembly for Wales (as it is now properly called) and gave it the power to pass primary legislation on matters within its legislative competence. Within Wales this has the same authority as an Act of the UK Parliament. Between 2006 and 2011 these legislative acts were called 'Assembly Measures'. Following a referendum on 3 March 2011, the National Assembly for Wales was granted further primary law-making powers. The twenty areas in which the Assembly now has competence are listed in Schedule 7 to the Government of Wales Act 2006. Primary legislation passed by the Assembly under these extended powers are known as Assembly Acts.

Assembly legislation in force is printed with authoritative versions in both Welsh and English. Together with all Welsh statutory instruments, they are published electronically on the Welsh government website and on the www.legislation.gov.uk website—see www.legislation.gov.uk/browse/wales. Assembly Bills, with information on their progress, can be accessed online from the Welsh government website: https://gov.wales/assembly-bills.

2.6 EU law

Because the EU has separate law-making institutions from the United Kingdom, it is hardly surprising that much EU law is found in locations distinct from those we have so far discussed.

However, elements of EU law can often be found in the kind of sources we have already considered. Both *Halsbury's Laws* and *Halsbury's Statutes* have volumes specifically on European Union law, for example.

In addition to occasional articles in the journals already considered, there are quite a number of journals which specialise in EC law matters. These include the *European Law Review, Common Market Law Review*, and *Legal Issues of European Integration*. Articles on the Community may also be found in the main journals of International Law, such as the *International and Comparative Law Quarterly*. These all appear in the *Legal Journals Index*.

The various English law reports can also include cases concerned with EU law—where the English courts are considering the application of EU law either *ab initio*, or in response to a preliminary ruling of the Court of Justice of the European Union (CJEU). Furthermore, it is becoming more common to find decisions of the Court of Justice (particularly, though not exclusively, those involving the United Kingdom) reported in the usual English law reports.

Despite this, there are a number of specific sources of EU law with which you ought to be familiar.

2.6.1 European Court Reports

The European Court Reports (cited as ECR) are the official reports published by the European Court of Justice (ECJ). The Reports are available in all the Community languages, including English, but the demands of producing multiple translations of every case do mean that there are substantial delays between the Court handing down its decision and that case being reported. In the early 1990s, the time lag was such that even the first reports—in French—were taking over a year to appear in the ECR. Since 1994, steps have been taken to reduce delays by excluding the Report of the Hearing from the published version, and also by excluding most staff cases heard by the General Court from publication in the ECR.

Following the creation of the Court of First Instance (CFI, now the General Court) in 1989, the ECR has been divided into two parts: ECR I, which reports decisions of the Court of Justice, and ECR II, which contains decisions of the General Court.

2.6.2 Common Market Law Reports (CMLR)

The CMLR are an 'unofficial' series published weekly in English by the European Law Centre. They cover cases before the CJEU, and before national courts within the EU. Although unofficial, the relative speed of publication makes them largely preferable to the ECR.

Both series are indexed by subject and case name or number. The case number is an important feature of ECJ decisions. The proper mode of citation is to give the case *number* first, followed by its name, and then the citation of any report. Thus, for example, one of the leading cases on the impact of EU membership on national sovereignty is properly cited as Case 6/64 *Costa* v *Ente Nazionale per l'Energia Elettrica (ENEL)* [1964] ECR 585. The case number, it can be seen, contains two elements: the actual number at which the case was listed (here, no. 6) and the year in which the application or reference was made (64—indicating 1964). Since the creation of the CFI, a further element has been introduced into the citation of cases. Now all case numbers have the prefix 'C–' or 'T–'. This indicates that the case was listed, respectively, either before the ECJ or the CFI/General Court.

Note also that the year contained in the case number will not be the same year that judgment was given, or that the case was reported. For example, the reference for a preliminary ruling in *R* v *Secretary of State, ex parte Factortame Ltd* was made in 1989. The case therefore received the number C–213/89. Judgment by the Court, however, was not handed down until June 1990. In fact, several years may elapse between the reference and the case being heard. You should also be aware that some English textbooks do not adopt the full European mode of citation, and either disregard the case number or place it after the names of the parties.

2.6.3 Online access to EU cases

EU cases can also be retrieved electronically from the Court of Justice's 'Curia' website (at http://curia.europa.eu and from Lexis or Westlaw. The Curia site can be accessed in all of the official languages, and contains full-text versions of judgments from both the Court of Justice and General Court from 17 June 1997 (though formally speaking until 2011, only the paper reports of cases in the General Court constituted the official version of judgments). Earlier case law can also be accessed from the Eur-Lex site (discussed in section **2.6.4**). From its homepage the Curia website enables you to browse recent decisions and search for specific cases by official case number, or by the names of parties. It does allow keyword searching, but this is not obvious—you have to click the advanced search icon on the homepage, and it will take you to a separate search page to do that.

Commercial systems like LexisLibrary and Westlaw offer more powerful search tools. In Westlaw, for example, you can search for both UK and EU cases together by keyword within the general UK database.

2.6.4 The *Official Journal*

The *Official Journal* (OJ) is the primary organ of legal information within the EU. It is published almost daily and thus provides an extremely current source of legal information. Mastering the OJ is one of the major challenges of researching EU law, though it is much simpler to search online than via the paper version. The *Journal* is made up of several sections, of which the most important are referred to as the *L, C, and CE Series*. The *L Series* contains a record of all Community legislation, whereas the *C Series* covers a wide range of information generally falling under the heading of 'Communications'. The *CE Series* commenced publication in January 2008. It contains the preparatory acts in the legislative process and is only available electronically in the EUR-Lex database. The full text of the OJ *L* and *C Series* is freely available on the EUR-Lex website (at http://eur-lex.europa.eu/en/index.htm). Their current coverage is explained in **Table 2.1**.

Table 2.1 Sections of the *Official Journal*

L Series	Section I	Legislation whose publication is obligatory under the EC or Euratom Treaties—i.e. regulations, directives, and decisions of the Parliament and Council addressed to all Member States.
	Section II	Legislation whose publication is not mandatory under the EC or Euratom Treaties—chiefly Commission or Council decisions and recommendations.
	Section III	Legislative acts (e.g. decisions, common positions, and declarations) adopted under the EU Treaty.
C Series	Section I	Resolutions, recommendations, and opinions of the EU institutions.
	Section II	Information from EU institutions and bodies.
	Section III	Preparatory acts—i.e. proposals for legislation, including the draft text and explanatory memoranda—now published separately under the tab 'preparatory acts' on the EUR-Lex homepage].
	Section IV	Formal notices from the EU institutions and other bodies, and notices from Member States.
	Section V	Announcements from the Institutions (e.g. on changes to administrative procedures, announcements on competition policy; commencement of proceedings, orders, and summaries of judgments before the ECJ and CFI; staff vacancies, etc.).

Journal references to legislation are usually cited by year, series, issue number, and page. For example, the 1985 Product Liability Directive is found at [1985] OJ L210/29—meaning L Series, issue number 210, of 7 August 1985 at page 29 (note that the date of the citation is to the OJ reference, not the date that the Act was passed). Cases reported in the C Series of the Journal are usually cited in the same form, thus[1990] OJ C146/9 refers to Case C–70/88 *European Parliament* v *Council of the European Community*. The OJ is quite a useful source of basic information on Court decisions, as the summaries usually appear substantially in advance of any full reports.

2.6.5 Citing EU legislation

The system for citing EU legislation looks different from what we are familiar with in the UK, though the underlying principle is similar. Each piece of legislation has its own identifiers, based on the year it became law and its own unique 'act number' (rather like the chapter number of a UK Act or the reference number of an SI). So, for example, the important Equal Treatment Directive of 1976 (on sex discrimination) is cited as 'Directive 76/207' (i.e. number 207 of 1976). The same format applies to decisions and recommendations. That numerical sequence, however, is reversed in respect of regulations, hence we speak of 'Regulation 1408/71', not 71/1408.

Full references will also indicate the institutional source of the legislation. Thus, for example, directives, decisions, and recommendations under the authority of the EC Treaty use, depending on their age, for example the suffix 'EC' or 'EEC'—thus Directive 76/207/EEC, but Directive 2009/36/EC. Regulations, strictly speaking are cited in the form 'Commission Regulation (EC) No. 312/2009' or 'Council Regulation (EC) . . .'.

2.6.6 Other legislative sources

The texts of the Treaties and of all international agreements entered into by the EU are available on the EUR-Lex site. This also contains a searchable directory of all EU legislation currently in force. Lawtel, LexisLibrary, and Westlaw also carry full-text EU legislation, and there are also specialist subscription services, such as Justis CELEX, which are built around the official EU multilingual CELEX database.

2.7 Online resources

Computerised and online legal information retrieval systems have developed substantially since the 1970s and are a key part of the legal research toolkit. The advantages of such systems are fairly obvious. They have the potential to store, with relative ease, large quantities of information in electronic form, which can be searched thoroughly and accessed far more quickly than by traditional means.

The amount of computer-based legal information has grown exponentially since the early 1980s. The earliest systems to develop were those which required dedicated online searching, i.e. using a special terminal to connect, via the public telephone network, to a commercial database in another location. Today, these kinds of subscription service have been integrated into PC-based internet technologies, and supplemented by a growing number of public information services that are freely available across the web.

2.7.1 Commercial systems

The main online legal information systems available in the UK are LexisLibrary, Westlaw, and Lawtel; the same or similar services exist in many other common law jurisdictions. Their core coverage of primary legal materials is quite similar, but they vary in the range of other resources on offer. If you are studying law at university your library will almost certainly offer you dedicated training in the systems to which you have access, so we have only included brief guides in this chapter.

LexisLibrary

The LexisNexis database, marketed in the UK as **LexisLibrary** (see **Figure 2.4**), offers full-text legal information retrieval to a range of sources, including:

- over 600,000 UK law reports;
- UK statutes in force, consolidated, giving access to over 86,000 Acts;
- over 290 practitioner texts (predominantly Butterworths/LexisNexis titles), and a range of 126 full-text journals, including titles from Oxford and Cambridge University Presses, Hart/Bloomsbury, and DeGruyter;
- *Halsbury's Laws of England.*

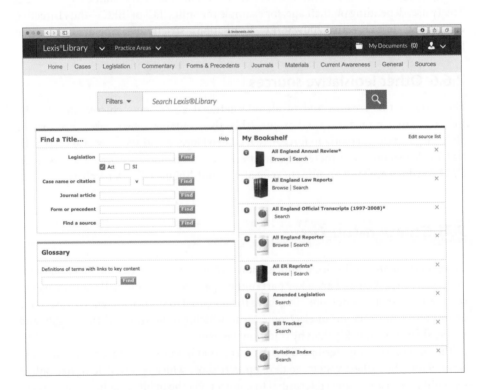

Figure 2.4 LexisLibrary homepage
Reproduced by permission of RELX (UK) Limited, trading as LexisNexis.

The extent of one's access is determined by the range of services to which a user has subscribed. The user interface can be customised and it provides a good platform for searching multiple kinds of content. The basic search techniques draw substantially on Boolean search methodology, which we discuss in section **2.7.3**.

Westlaw

Westlaw, like LexisLibrary, was originally a US-based service and also provides access to an extensive full-text retrieval system (see **Figure 2.5**). Features of the Westlaw UK system include:

- over 400,000 UK law reports in full text;
- UK statutes in force, consolidated, plus full coverage of devolved legislation;
- access to Sweet & Maxwell's Common Law Library and a selection of practitioner texts;
- full-text access to 110 journals—from Sweet & Maxwell, Oxford and Cambridge University Presses, Bloomsbury Professional, and Emerald;
- access to journal abstracts via the Legal Journals Index and Financial Journals Index; and
- national, regional, and international news and business updates.

Figure 2.5 Westlaw homepage
Reproduced with permission of Thompson Reuters (Professional) UK Limited.

Both LexisLibrary and Westlaw also have very extensive US, Commonwealth, and international case libraries, and EU resources. Both allow 'natural language' as well as keyword searching (discussed in section **2.7.3**).

Lawtel

Lawtel has a more limited database and relies more on summaries, with the result that some aspects of the system are far more geared to updating and preliminary, rather than in-depth research. The main data available include:

- links to the original (i.e. not consolidated) text of statutes passed since 1987, and section-by-section information on the commencement, amendment, and repeal of statutes from 1984;
- summaries of cases (60,000+), both unreported and from the main generalist and some specialist law reports (from 1980 on), with links to full-text transcripts for the High Court, Court of Appeal, and Privy Council from 1990, and for the House of Lords/UK Supreme Court from 1980;
- full text of all parliamentary Bills from 1997/98;
- publication details of all Command Papers from 1997/98 with links to full-text versions where available; details of government Green and White Papers from 1992/93; and
- summaries of articles published in a range of key practitioner journals.

2.7.2 Free online legal information

The massive improvements in both communications and database technology over the past decade have unleashed the potential for storing and sharing large quantities of legal information across the web. The global Legal Information Institutes (LII) network, which started in the United States, Australia, and the Netherlands in the 1990s in particular has become a central pillar of what is known as the Free Access to Law Movement and the WorldLII collaborative portal now provides access to over 800 databases from forty countries. In fact, the quality and quantity of free legal information is improving very rapidly, to the extent that, as long ago as 2008, the American Bar Association's *Legal Technology Survey Report* found that, for the first time slightly more lawyers in the United States were making use of free legal information retrieval than subscription services. This does not yet mean that we can obtain from public sites everything that is available commercially, nor does it mean that searchability is necessarily as easy or sophisticated, but public access has nonetheless improved considerably in terms of quality and quantity. We will look at what is available, first, in terms of primary sources, and then secondary sources.

Primary sources

Table 2.2 provides details of some key free legal information providers, particularly useful for UK law students. The basic reliability of information from these sites is as good as the commercial sites, though it will lack the add-ons that you pay for—essentially annotation, updating, and the slicker interface and search functionality.

Table 2.2 Useful 'free' websites for legal research

Legislation:	www.legislation.gov.uk	Full text of all public Acts of the UK Parliament from 1988. Acts of the Scottish Parliament (1999–) and Northern Ireland Assembly (2000–), and Welsh Assembly Acts (2011–) and Measures (2007–11). UK SIs from 1987; Northern Irish statutory orders (1991–), Scottish and Welsh SIs (1999–).
	www.bailii.org	The British and Irish Legal Information Institute's full text database of UK statutes (1988–), Northern Irish statutes (1945–), Irish statutes (Republic) (1922–), Acts of the Scottish Parliament and Welsh Assembly Measures. Also, a range of English, Scottish, Irish, and Welsh SIs.
	https://services.parliament.uk/bills	Full text of Bills presented before Parliament in the current session, and Bills from previous sessions since 2001–02.
Case law:	www.bailii.org	Full text of decisions of the Supreme Court (2009–), HL, PC, CA (all complete from 1996–) and the High Court (from various start dates). Also, decisions of the Scottish Court of Session (1998–) and High Court (1998–), and of the Northern Ireland Court of Appeal (1998–). ECJ decisions since 1954; all CFI/GC decisions. A range of reported tribunal decisions. Content is being added regularly to earlier years.
	www.supremecourt.uk	Full text of Supreme Court decisions (from October 2009).
	https://publications.parliament.uk/pa/ld/ldjudgmt.htm	Full text versions of all House of Lords judgments from 14 November 1996 to 30 July 2009.
	www.iclr.co.uk	Incorporated Council of Law Reporting site, containing its 'WLR Daily' feature. This service, updated daily Monday–Friday provides summaries of important new decisions of the ECJ, HL, CA, and High Court prior to their appearing in the published Law Reports series.
	www.curia.europa.eu	Court of Justice of the European Communities: contains documentation relating to the ECJ, all cases decided by the ECJ and CFI since June 1997, and a weekly list of recent proceedings (opinions and judgments).

Table 2.2 Continued

	www.echr.coe.int	European Court of Human Rights: searchable full-text database of cases. Also has full text of the Rules of the Court and the ECHR and its Protocols.
UK Parliament:	www.parliament.uk	Gateway to House of Lords and House of Commons websites, with information on their functions and activities, and access to the Information Offices of both Houses. Can also be used to access parliamentary publications.
	https://hansard.parliament.uk	Full text of the House of Lords Hansard (debates, oral and written questions) from May 1804. Full text of House of Commons Hansard (debates, oral and written questions); complete from the start of session in April 1804.
Other useful sources:	www.worldlii.org	1,829 databases of legal information from 123 countries and territories, including the UK and Ireland (based on the BAILII databases), the United States, Canada, Hong Kong, South Africa, Australasia, and the South Pacific. Also provides access to over 20,000 journal articles, chiefly from Australasia.
	www.gov.uk	Gateway to a vast range of sites created by UK central government departments (including the Ministry of Justice and the Home Office), government agencies, and local authorities. Of variable utility.
	www.justice.gov.uk	UK government's Ministry of Justice site: contains useful information on law reform, the administration of justice, court rules, and Ministry-supported research publications.
	http://europa.eu	Gateway to the multilingual EU website. Contains information, statistics, and extensive documentation on the EU, its legislation, and institutions, including the courts.
	www.judiciary.uk	Judiciary of England and Wales site. Includes statistics, judicial biographies, practice directions, and guidance.

 An extended version of this table is available with the online resources accompanying this book. Visit www.oup.com/uk/holland-webb10e.

Secondary sources

It is also becoming easier to access some secondary sources online, though coverage is far more patchy and *ad hoc*, and you need to take steps to verify the quality of what you have found.

Useful websites worth considering, include:

- **Social Science Research Network (SSRN)** at http://ssrn.com: the SSRN is a large multi-disciplinary searchable database containing abstracts of around 635,000 scholarly working papers and forthcoming papers and an Electronic Paper Collection currently containing over 523,000 downloadable full-text documents in Adobe Acrobat pdf format. A Legal Scholarship Network Research Paper series forms a significant part of this database, with the Network primarily made up of contributing law schools. There is a predominance of US material, but a significant number of leading law schools from the United Kingdom and other jurisdictions are using SSRN to profile their research. It includes both externally published work and institutional 'working papers'.

- **WorldLII** (see **Table 2.2**): includes a limited range of journals in full text. The material is predominantly from Australia and New Zealand, and includes virtually all of the university-based law reviews in those jurisdictions, plus a small amount of material from Europe and Asia-Pacific.

- **ResearchGate and Academia**: these are used by growing numbers of academics to publicise and self-publish their work. There is no editorial or institutional quality control, though a high proportion of the papers uploaded are drafts or final versions of published work. It is most easily searched by author name or keyword, though publications may also show up via more refined Google searches.

- **Institutional repositories and research centres**: for more specialist work, where you are concentrating on a specific research topic, or want to follow up the work of a particular individual or research centre, it is worth checking their university webpages, as some full-text publications may be accessible there.

None of these strategies will give you the range or depth of material you would find via commercial databases, largely because of the copyright restrictions imposed by some journal publishers. There is also no specialist search engine that is particularly effective at distinguishing academic publications from other material, though Google Scholar can be helpful in identifying published research, for which free access copies are also available. If you are not familiar with Google Scholar, you can access it by typing 'scholar' in the Google search box. For easy access you can also install a Scholar 'button' from the settings page into your browser.

There is thus much more public access to legal information than there used to be, and it is increasingly stable: most of these sites and URLs have not changed since the last edition of this book in 2015, and many have now been in existence for fifteen to twenty years, which is an eternity in IT terms. We are thus already at a point where public knowledgeability of law is determined far more by access to computer resources than to conventional library materials.

2.7.3 Search techniques

Most online systems (commercial and public) have little in the way of organising or indexing, other than into broadly thematic but large-scale libraries of data. So, what most systems use is a technique of searching by matching keywords or phrases entered by the user to the text contained in the database.

In technical terms this involves a system of what is called 'Boolean searching' (Leith, 1991). This engages fairly simple word-matching techniques, so that, for example, if you search for cases containing the word 'knife', that is precisely what you will get—all cases in which the word 'knife' appears, regardless of its legal significance. You will likely be familiar with this problem already from your experience of using generic search engines like Google or Bing. This is probably the greatest practical limitation of such systems, as it means they are not very effective if you are trying to research concepts, particularly concepts which are difficult to define.

An example of such is 'good faith', which is an important concept relating to contract law. However, it is extremely difficult to define, is not always identified by name, and arises in a range of legal contexts, as well as being a term that may be used colloquially. As a result, it is almost impossible to construct an effective Boolean search related to that concept.

Against this, these systems do have the advantage of being *interactive*. It is not necessary to get one's search terms exactly right first time; it is quite possible to modify a search request in response to the information that one has received from the system already. In developing search terms, it is important to note that various systems use particular words to enable you to structure your request with some degree of precision. These special words are normally referred to as *connectors* or *logical operators*. This means that those particular terms will not actually be searched for, but will tell the system how your search terms relate to each other. The main connectors can be described diagrammatically, as shown in **Figure 2.6**.

As you can see, there are essentially three ways in which search terms can be connected; we have identified them by the most commonly used connectors, AND, OR, and NOT (the precise terms used and variety of connectors will vary from system to system):

- AND will search documents for terms A and B, and will retrieve those only where both terms are discovered (here represented by the shaded area in the two circles). LexisLibrary and Westlaw also have a rather more sophisticated proximity connector which enables you to specify the maximum number of words you want separating your search terms, for example 'cat w/3 dog' in LexisLibrary will retrieve only those documents where 'cat' occurs within three or fewer words either side of 'dog'; similarly 'cat/s dog' in Westlaw will find documents where cat and dog are in the same sentence (whereas AND will retrieve any documents where both your research terms occur, regardless of proximity).

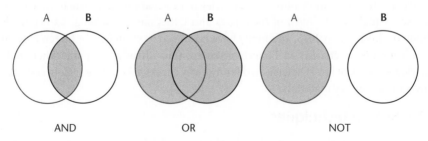

Figure 2.6   Logical operators

- OR will retrieve all documents containing *either or both* search terms A and B.
- NOT enables you to search for term A, but *excludes* documents which also contain word B.

The technicality of Boolean searching undoubtedly limits the research utility of electronic systems, and may well be one reason why it is estimated that Boolean searching alone may retrieve as little as 25 per cent of the relevant information from a system (Poynder, 1994). A number of search engines such as Google and information retrieval systems, including LexisLibrary and Westlaw, have developed a facility for *natural language searching*, which enables you to enter search terms in 'natural language', or 'free text' as it is sometimes called—in other words, 'plain English', if you prefer. The process of keyword selection and pattern matching is then completed by the software. Natural language searching is not necessarily superior to Boolean. Most natural language systems simply convert into Boolean by selecting those words that appear to be searchable. The selection mechanism can be relatively crude, so a natural language search can actually throw up more irrelevant material than a well-constructed Boolean search.

2.7.4 Verifying electronic sources

If you are drawing on material from sites other than credible commercial or public legal information services, you need to think carefully about whether that material is likely to be accurate and from a credible source, and therefore something you should rely on. You need to be able to evaluate whether you have something written by the idiot or by Einstein, or someone somewhere between the two. There is no absolutely foolproof test of quality, but the following checks are common sense, and will help in most cases:

- Who is the author? If the paper doesn't have a name, that may be a warning in itself, though it is not determinative as some publications are 'staff papers' written under the name of the employing institution. Equally, even if a paper has a person's name and their institutional (e.g. university) affiliation, how do you know whether they are a student or a professor? If there is a name, search against it: what do they do? Where are they employed? What else have they published?

- Who is the publisher? Has the paper been published by a reputable publisher or institution? Or is it self-published? If so, it may be risky to rely on it without further contextual information about the author and the paper's provenance. For example, is it a pre-publication draft? If so, can you find anything to indicate that the published version exists? Can you get the final published version?

- What else can you find out from the paper itself? Read it, don't just cherry-pick the bit you like! Does it make sense? Is it well written? Does it reference other work or relevant legal sources that you might expect to see?

- What can you learn from its context? What other kinds of material are on the same website? Are there links to other sites? If there is an 'About us' section, what does it tell you about the organisation?

- Has it been referred to by anyone else? Put the title into Google Scholar and see if it comes up with any citations. Don't worry too much if the number is relatively small; most academic work gets read chiefly by closest collaborators, immediate family, your worst enemy, and the occasional pet hamster. (Except, of course, where the pet hamster is a co-author: see A.K. Geim and H.A.M.S. ter Tisha, 'Detection of Earth's Rotation with a Diamagnetically Levitating Gyroscope' (2001), *Physica* B 294–5, 736–9. You can get away with things like that when you are a Nobel prize winner.)

 ## CONCLUSION

In this chapter we have introduced you to some of the challenges of research in a digital age; to the core dimensions of information literacy, and to the main resources and techniques required to undertake both conventional paper and electronic legal research. Research skills are critical. They are emphasised both in the Quality Assurance Agency's 'Benchmark' statement of skills required of the law degree and in the requirements of the Solicitors Regulation Authority and Bar Standards Board at the professional stage of training, and there are concerns about students' performance in this area. But you will not get proficient in these skills just by reading this book. We have provided you with a start, and some reference resources to dip into if you get stuck; that is all. As with all skills, mastery lies in action, not reading! Get familiar with your library, use the training available, and get comfortable with the technology—the days are now long gone when any lawyer—academic or practising—can afford to be a technophobe. Finally, before moving on to **Chapter 3**, you will find a couple of exercises based upon some of the material in this chapter, and intended to help you to test your research skills.

EXERCISE 1 Flick knives for sale

If you were wondering whether you would ever find the answer to the problem we have used to develop the themes of this book, now is *your* chance to find out. See if you can find answers to the following questions. If you can, you will have the basic material to advise our fictitious friend.

QUESTIONS

(a) Using the paper or online version of *Halsbury's Laws*, find the volume number and paragraph containing information on criminal liability for the display and sale of flick knives.

(b) Using any appropriate research strategy, what is the current *statutory* provision governing that liability?

(c) Can you find any *cases* on the interpretation of that provision?

(d) Using your research, what is your advice?

ANSWERS

(a) In this case a simple online search for 'flick knives' or 'flick knife' will give you three options: 'hire of chattells'; 'carrying offensive weapons in a public place', and (bingo!) 'manufacture and sale, etc., of arms and offensive weapons'. The same result can be achieved using the paper index. Both refer you to vol. 11(1),

continued

EXERCISE 1 *continued*

para. 705 (2006 reissue). Be aware that a simple search like this doesn't always produce results, or, more likely, it will produce too many results, most of which are not relevant. In that situation you need to refine your search (and that sometimes means doing some initial research to discover more, or more effective keywords that you could use).

(b) Volume 11 of *Halsbury's* refers you to the Restriction of Offensive Weapons Act 1959 s. 1(1), as amended. The latest amendment noted in that volume refers to the Criminal Justice Act 1988. On the electronic version, you can click on the section and it will take you to the source statute within LexisLibrary. If you scroll that page to the heading 'Amendment', it shows that the section has not been further amended since 1988. Searching online for related commentary will also quickly disclose that a separate offence exists of selling knives to persons under eighteen under s. 141A of the Criminal Justice Act 1988, but that knives expressly covered by s. 1 of the 1959 Act are excluded from that provision (meaning that sale to a person under 18 would be charged under the 1959 Act, s. 1, not s. 141A of the 1988 Act).

(c) Volume 11(1) para. 705 mentions no cases; that is misleading, they do exist! Interestingly, if you search from s. 1 for related cases online, it only comes up with one case, *British Car Auctions* v *Wright* (1972), which cites *Fisher* v *Bell*, but is not otherwise on point. This just goes to show that the online systems are not foolproof. However, if you go to s. 1 again and click on related commentary, it will lead you to *Blackstone's Criminal Practice*, and this cites a number of cases: *Lawrence* (1971) 57 Cr App R 64; *Allamby* [1974] 1 WLR 1494; *Gibson* v *Wales* [1983] 1 WLR 393; and *Simpson* [1983] 1 WLR 1494.

(d) Your advice should take into account that, though initially it was not an offence to offer a flick knife for sale (*Fisher* v *Bell*), the Act has been amended. As a result, it is now an offence not only to sell, but also to have on display or in one's possession, a flick knife for sale.

EXERCISE 2 Researching the web

Using web-based legal resources, where would you find the following?

Q **QUESTIONS**

(a) The latest reported decision on circumstances in which a court may make a declaration of incompatibility under section 4, Human Rights Act 1998.

(b) The text of the Criminal Procedure Rules 2015.

(c) Statistics on the number of ethnic minority judges in England and Wales.

(d) Information on the progress of Bills in the current session of Parliament.

(e) The names of the Advocates General of the European Court of Justice.

(f) The decision of the House of Lords in *Pepper* v *Hart* [1993].

continued

EXERCISE 2 *continued*

(g) Citations of *Pepper* v *Hart* in UK cases decided after 1 January 2003.

(h) References to the case 202/89 *European Commission* v *United Kingdom* in later decisions of the ECJ.

(i) An authoritative version of Article 62 of the Treaty of Rome.

(j) An authoritative version of Article 3 of the European Convention on Human Rights.

For obvious reasons we have not given the answers here—you will find them with our online resources at www.oup.com/uk/holland-webb10e.

CHAPTER REFERENCES

BERNERS-LEE, T. (2000), *Weaving the Web* (New York: HarperCollins).

BING, J. (2010), 'Let There Be LITE: A Brief History of Legal Information Retrieval', 1(1) *European Journal of Law & Technology*. Available at http://ejlt.org/article/view/15.

BROWNSWORD, R. (2015) 'In the Year 2061: From Law to Technological Management', 7 *Law, Innovation and Technology*, 1.

JACKSON, R. (1970), 'Police Search—Law Reports—Law Reform by Precedent', *Cambridge Law Journal* 1.

LAFRANCE, A. (2015), 'Raiders of the Lost Web', *The Atlantic*, 14 October 2015. Available at www.theatlantic.com/technology/archive/2015/10/raiders-of-the-lost-web/409210.

LEITH, P. (1991), *The Computerised Lawyer* (London: Springer-Verlag).

LETR REPORT (2013), *Setting Standards: The Future of Legal Services Education and Training Regulation in England and Wales* (Coventry: Legal Education and Training Review). Available at http://letr.org.uk/the-report/index.html.

PARKER, J. (2011), 'The Soundscape of Justice', 20 *Griffith Law Review*, 962.

PAYNE, R. (1983), 'Lawtel: A Prestel-based Legal Retrieval Service', in *The Progress in Legal Information Systems in Europe* (Strasbourg: Council of Europe).

POYNDER, R. (1994), 'Beyond Boolean', *Information World Review*, July/August, 14.

RAISTRICK, D. (2008), *Index to Legal Citations and Abbreviations* (3rd edn, London: Sweet & Maxwell).

SHERWIN, R.K. (2011), *Visualizing Law in the Age of the Digital Baroque: Arabesques and Entanglements* (New York: Routledge).

SUMPTION J. (2016), 'A Response', in N. Barber, R. Elkins, and P. Yowell (eds), *Lord Sumption and the Limits of the Law* (Oxford: Hart Publishing).

*SUSSKIND, R. (2017), *Tomorrow's Lawyers: An Introduction to Your Future* (2nd edn, Oxford: Oxford University Press).

TUNKEL, V. (1993), 'Legal Research after *Pepper* v *Hart*', 90 *Law Society's Gazette*, 12 May 1993, 17.

 ## ONLINE RESOURCES

Test your knowledge by trying the self-test questions that accompany **Chapters 1–6**.
Visit: www.oup.com/uk/holland-webb10e

3

Reading the Law

In this chapter we focus on another important dimension of legal information literacy: the ability to read critically and with understanding. This is a fundamental precursor to the third major arm of literacy (discussed in **Chapter 4**), the ability to produce academic and, ultimately, professional communications appropriate to your audience.

Much of this book is concerned with principles of interpretation—both of legislation and of cases. At its heart, any process of interpretation is one of reading. Reading is an activity that can be carried on at different levels. If you have ever studied literature, you will be familiar with the idea of reading as a search for layers of meaning. For example, one does not find in Dickens's *Hard Times* just the story of the characters involved, but also a powerful critique of mid-Victorian social values, and a particular attack on the doctrine of utilitarianism which dominated that age.

Legal texts can similarly be seen as displaying layers of meaning. These layers broadly correspond to the three questions that we might ask about a legal text, what we call the *What, How & Why* of law, that is:

(i)   *What* kind of law is it?

(ii)   *How* does it affect existing law?

(iii) *Why* was it made?

At the first level (*what*), the form of the document itself tells us something about it. If, for example, it takes the form of an Act of Parliament, we know that it takes precedence over case law.

At another level (*how*) we must work out what it is actually about; this is a matter of constructing meaning from the text. Again, the way in which legal documents are put together can sometimes help us in this task, but can also hinder (see further **Chapter 8**).

At a third level, legal texts contain a deeper meaning, which may help us to answer the question *why* the law has developed in such a way. Legislation has a history which may reflect particular economic, political, or social values. Court decisions may also reflect a variety of underlying influences, for example: the values which the legal system has traditionally served; the prejudices of a particular judge; or the perceived internal logic of the case-law system. Asking *why* may involve an element of historical analysis (e.g. to see how a law has developed over the years—though note that, traditionally, reading the law has been treated as a largely ahistorical process), or a consideration of governmental or judicial policy making. This will help us to understand the reasoning behind the court's decision in a case, or why an Act with those particular provisions was passed at that particular time.

In this chapter, we shall consider primarily the questions *what* and *why*. In looking at the structure of legal rules, we may occasionally trespass on the territory of *how*, though that will generally be left to later chapters. In so doing, we have broken this chapter down into three sections: reading legislation; reading cases; and reading literary sources.

3.1 Reading legislation

In this section we will look at two kinds of legislation in depth: UK Acts of Parliament and EU regulations and directives.

3.1.1 Acts of Parliament

Once a bill has received the royal assent it becomes an Act of Parliament. An Act (note that the word 'Act' when used in this sense is always capitalised) is a public document and must be published by The Stationery Office; it will also, as we have seen, be published in a variety of other sources. A copy of such an Act is reproduced in **Figure 3.1**.

3.1.2 The elements of an Act of Parliament

Any modern Act of Parliament will take the following form (each number here corresponds to that on **Figure 3.1**):

(1) short title;

(2) citation;

(3) long title;

(4) date of royal assent;

(5) sections; and

(6) marginal note.

In addition to these, copies of the statutes may also contain:

(i)   enacting formula;

(ii)   textual amendments and annotations;

(iii) date of commencement; and

(iv) schedules and tables.

We shall now consider each of these in the order in which they appear in the Act. The numbers or letters in bold text after each heading refer to the illustration.

Long and short titles (3) and (1)

Modern Acts will have both a **long** and **short title**:

- the long title describes the general scope of the Act; and
- the short title is for convenience of citation.

Early Acts were enacted without a short title, and therefore tended formally to be known by their long titles. Thus, the famous Bill of Rights 1689 was originally known as *An Act Declaring the Rights and Liberties of the Subject and Settling the Succession of*

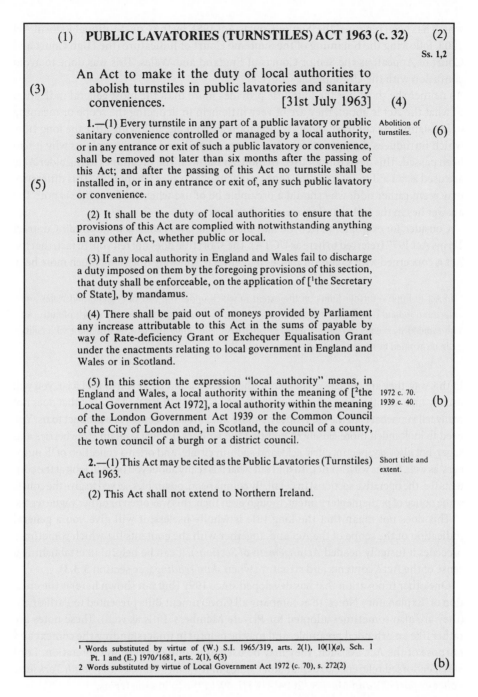

(1)   **PUBLIC LAVATORIES (TURNSTILES) ACT 1963 (c. 32)**   (2)

Ss. 1,2

(3)   An Act to make it the duty of local authorities to abolish turnstiles in public lavatories and sanitary conveniences.   [31st July 1963]   (4)

1.—(1) Every turnstile in any part of a public lavatory or public sanitary convenience controlled or managed by a local authority, or in any entrance or exit of such a public lavatory or convenience, shall be removed not later than six months after the passing of this Act; and after the passing of this Act no turnstile shall be (5)   installed in, or in any entrance or exit of, any such public lavatory or convenience.

Abolition of turnstiles.   (6)

(2) It shall be the duty of local authorities to ensure that the provisions of this Act are complied with notwithstanding anything in any other Act, whether public or local.

(3) If any local authority in England and Wales fail to discharge a duty imposed on them by the foregoing provisions of this section, that duty shall be enforceable, on the application of [¹the Secretary of State], by mandamus.

(4) There shall be paid out of moneys provided by Parliament any increase attributable to this Act in the sums of payable by way of Rate-deficiency Grant or Exchequer Equalisation Grant under the enactments relating to local government in England and Wales or in Scotland.

(5) In this section the expression "local authority" means, in England and Wales, a local authority within the meaning of [²the Local Government Act 1972], a local authority within the meaning of the London Government Act 1939 or the Common Council of the City of London and, in Scotland, the council of a county, the town council of a burgh or a district council.

1972 c. 70.
1939 c. 40.   (b)

2.—(1) This Act may be cited as the Public Lavatories (Turnstiles) Act 1963.

Short title and extent.

(2) This Act shall not extend to Northern Ireland.

---

¹ Words substituted by virtue of (W.) S.I. 1965/319, arts. 2(1), 10(1)(a), Sch. 1 Pt. 1 and (E.) 1970/1681, arts. 2(1), 6(3)
2 Words substituted by virtue of Local Government Act 1972 (c. 70), s. 272(2)   (b)

Figure 3.1 A Public General Act from *Statutes in Force*

the Crown. It only formally acquired the short title of the Bill of Rights by virtue of a later enactment—the Short Titles Act 1896—which created short titles for a number of important earlier statutes. Very occasionally the short title of an Act may be changed by later legislation. This has happened more recently with the Supreme Court Act 1981, which has been renamed the 'Senior Courts Act 1981' by the Constitutional Reform Act 2005, following the renaming of the Supreme Court of Judicature (the High Court and Court of Appeal) as the Senior Courts of England and Wales. This was done to avoid confusion with the UK Supreme Court.

As neither the short nor the long title provides more than the most general indication of what the Act is about, they are of very little help in deducing the scope or meaning of legislation. By contrast, older Acts contain a *Preamble*, following after the long title, which introduces the legislation, often in some detail, and usually explains why it had been passed. This device is not used in modern statutes. The Preambles to the older Acts are used as an aid to interpreting those particular Acts (see **Chapter 9**). This difference may seem rather odd; why should a preamble be of use when the long title is not? The answer lies in the fact that they serve diverse functions.

Consider, for example, an Act you may meet in the law of contract: the Unfair Contract Terms Act 1977 (referred to here as UCTA). The short title does not tell you, in fact, that the Act is concerned with exclusion clauses in contracts. The long title is not much more help.

> An Act to impose further limits on the extent to which under the Law of England and Wales and Northern Ireland civil liability for breach of contract, or for negligence or other breach of duty, can be avoided by means of contract terms or otherwise, and under the Law of Scotland civil liability can be avoided by means of contract terms.

In this way, they are perhaps analogous to the label on a jam jar. If you look at a jar, you will usually find the title in large letters on the front—STRAWBERRY JAM—but that does not really tell you what is in the jar. It does no more than broadly identify the product to us. You need to look much more closely to find that the jar does not just contain strawberries and sugar, but also, say, pectin, citric acid, and sodium citrate, and often a collection of 'E numbers' as well. So it is with an Act. To find out what it is really about you need to look at the contents (i.e. the operative sections) in detail. By comparison, preambles served to give the courts some notice of parliamentary intent, though even then, this was often in rather vague terms.

This does not mean that the long title is wholly useless; it will give you a general indication of the scope of the Act and, together with the contents list which sometimes precedes it (usually headed *Arrangement of Sections*), it can be helpful in establishing a sense of the Act's contents and structure when *skim reading* (see section **3.3.3**).

One other innovation that has developed since 1999 (but not shown here) is the creation of 'Explanatory Notes' to accompany all Government Bills presented to Parliament (they are also sometimes adopted for Private Members' Bills as well). These notes are rather like an extended preamble, and may be helpful in understanding the context and purpose of the Act. As such, they may be used as a limited aid to interpretation. Lord Steyn endorsed reference to explanatory notes in *R* v *Chief Constable of South Yorkshire Police ex parte LS and Marper* [2004] UKHL 39, in the following terms:

> Explanatory Notes are not endorsed by Parliament. On the other hand, in so far as they cast light on the setting of a statute, and the mischief at which it is aimed, they are admissible in aid of construction of the statute. After all, they may potentially contain much more immediate and valuable material than other aids regularly used by the courts, such as Law Commission Reports, Government Committee reports, Green Papers, and so forth.

The fact that they are not endorsed by (or capable of amendment by) Parliament sets a significant limit on their utility. As Lord Steyn also observed, this time in *Westminster City Council* v *National Asylum Resource Service* [2002] UKHL 38 at [6]:

> If exceptionally there is found in Explanatory Notes a clear assurance by the executive to Parliament about the meaning of a clause, or the circumstances in which a power will or will not be used, that assurance may in principle be admitted against the executive in proceedings in which the executive places a contrary contention before a court. This reflects the actual decision in *Pepper v Hart* [1993] AC 593. What is impermissible is to treat the wishes and desires of the Government about the scope of the statutory language as reflecting the will of Parliament. The aims of the Government in respect of the meaning of clauses as revealed in Explanatory Notes cannot be attributed to Parliament.

Citation (2)

Statutes obviously have their short title and the year of their creation cited, but, as we explained in **Chapter 2**, they also have what is known as a **chapter number**. If a statute was the fiftieth to be passed in 1977, then it will have that number. This is a means of reference only and is therefore neither very helpful nor very exciting.

Royal assent (4)

No statute is law until assented to (i.e. formally agreed to) by the Monarch. The date of assent is given in the statute—in UCTA it is 26 October 1977. Frequently this is the date on which the Act becomes law. However, the Act may state that all or part of it will come into effect at a later date (in UCTA's case this was 1 February 1978) or at a date to be appointed by the appropriate minister. Different parts of the Act can thus come into effect at different times. Obviously, this may have important practical consequences for the advice that lawyers give. Inevitably it can make life very complicated, where you need to know which rules have already come into force, which have an agreed date for their introduction, and which do not.

Enacting formula (a)

Although not always reproduced in *Statutes in Force* (they are missing from our example), these are introductory words which appear in every Act stating that both Houses of Parliament and the Monarch have passed the Act. The form of words used is identical in every case, and is of long historical standing. They are of little practical legal significance, though the publication of the Act with these words is taken as conclusive evidence that the Act has been passed and is good law. Because of their different legislative competence Acts of the Scottish Parliament and Welsh Assembly Acts and Measures have differently worded enacting formulae, but the underlying principle is the same: it creates the presumption that the legislation is properly made.

The enacting formula normally follows directly after the long title. In online versions of the statutes (at www.legislation.gov.uk) these are now jointly referred to as 'Introductory Text'.

Sections (5)

All Acts are divided into sections—these are usually cited in an abbreviated form as s. 1 or s. 2, or (in the plural) ss 2 and 3. Sometimes it may be possible to perceive a logical development of concepts as the sections progress, but this is not always the case, so you may, in resolving a single problem, find yourself starting at s. 1, which is qualified by something in s. 3, which contains terms defined in s. 45 and repeals part of an earlier enactment listed in sch. 4! We provide further discussion and specific examples of how statutes are organised in **Chapter 8**.

Each section will often be divided into **subsections**—cited as s. 1(1) or s. 1(4). After subsections we can have **paragraphs**—cited as s. 1(1)(a) or s. 1(2)(g); and even **sub-paragraphs**, as in s. 1(1)(a)(i). Section 3 of UCTA has such a division. If you have ever tried to draft the rules of a committee or a game, you will appreciate that this device can be used to split up ideas or clarify particular points. Thus, each separate section of an Act may deal with a separate issue (though these sections may often remain closely related), and each subsection (etc.) within a section may express a different aspect of that issue. For example, if you have a definition section, it may be that the phrase to be defined has more than one statutory meaning, in which case you could use a different subsection for each meaning.

Often, you will also find that groups of sections dealing with the same point have *headings* and that very large groupings are divided into *parts*. These titles are of little value as an interpretative aid; they are essentially a form of indexing. At best they will indicate some general thematic coherence among the sections under that heading.

Marginal notes (6)

Most Acts display marginal notes as a kind of quick reference mechanism to help you find the section you want.

Amendments and annotations (b)

In *Statutes in Force*, and the revised statutes on www.legislation.gov.uk, it is normal for any amendments to an Act made subsequent to its passing to be incorporated into the text. As in the illustrated Act, the amendments are shown within square brackets in *Statutes in Force*, and by a different text colour on www.legislation.gov.uk. These amendments are cited as being part of the Act, and have the full force of law. Any foot-notes or commentary annotated to an Act (as, e.g., in *Current Law Statutes Annotated*) do not form part of the Act and, of course, have no direct legal effect.

Date of commencement (c)

Acts will normally have a specific commencement section near to the end of the statute. It may either state that the Act, or parts of the Act, will come into force on a specific date or dates, or that it comes into force on a date to be fixed by the relevant government minister. On the latter occasions the normal form of words runs more or less as follows:

> this Act shall come into force on such day as the Secretary of State may by order appoint; and differ-ent days may be so appointed for different provisions or different purposes of the same provision...

This gives the minister *carte blanche* in deciding what comes into force and when.

Schedules (d)

Schedules (the term may be abbreviated to 'sched.' or 'sch.') can be found at the end of most Acts of Parliament. Schedules are parts of an Act that provide more detail regard-ing sections or groups of sections. Sometimes they give examples of how to calculate things contained in the Act, such as pensions, tax assessments, and so on; sometimes they simply expand upon phrases; sometimes they define phrases; or sometimes they contain detailed amendments of earlier legislation. As such, they may be quite detailed, perhaps even exceeding the length of the rest of the Act. Each provision within a schedule is called a **paragraph**, and there may also be **sub-paragraphs**. So, a provision is properly cited in the form 'sch. 1, para. 3(a)'.

A schedule, normally the last, tells you which earlier Acts the present statute repeals. This is important because, generally speaking, once an Act is passed it remains in force until repealed by another Act. This is why vestiges of the Witchcraft Acts were still in force as late as 1951 and why other such anachronisms remain 'on the Statute book'. By an odd quirk it also meant that, in English law, the United States did not gain its independence until 1963!

Note, here, that though lawyers sometimes talk of Acts being 'obsolete', there is no formal basis upon which an Act could be disapplied by the courts simply because it has become old or out of date. At most it can be argued that a statute should not apply to a novel situation, because that situation was not within the original legislative intent; this reflects what is sometimes called *the principle of contemporary exposition*: see *Aerated Bread Co. Ltd v Gregg* (1873) LR 8 QB 355. In this case Blackburn J. refused to apply provisions of the Bread Act 1836 regarding 'fancy bread' to the plaintiff's product, because at the time the Act was passed, the term had a very specific meaning, which could not be applied to the disputed product some thirty-six years later.

Some obsolete legislation is periodically repealed by the passing of Statute Law Revision Acts or Legislative Reform Orders, which are purely administrative measures intended to tidy up the statute book.

3.1.3 European legislation

As we noted in **Chapter 1**, European legislation comprises a combination of treaty articles, regulations, directives, and decisions. In style these follow a broadly similar pattern. In terms of EU legislative acts (note: not capitalised), this structure reflects the Rules of Procedure for drafting laid down by the European Council—see Council Decision 2006/683/EC, Euratom (OJ L 285, 16 October 2006, p. 47)—which require the following components:

(i)   title of the legislative act;

(ii) enacting formula;

(iii) reference to the 'legal basis' of the legislation;

(iv) a statement of reasons;

(v)   the 'enacting terms'; and

(vi) signatures.

EU legislative acts may vary from two or three pages to very lengthy, technical, documents. We have not produced an actual facsimile here; however, we will discuss the main points, and particularly the points of difference from UK legislation, that it may help you to be aware of:

(i)   **Title**: the title of each legislative act states its legal form (regulation, directive, decision), its unique identifier, date of adoption, and a narrative description of its subject matter, akin to what we, in the English context, would think of as the long title, thus:

> DIRECTIVES
>
> **DIRECTIVE 2009/12/EC OF THE EUROPEAN PARLIAMENT AND OF THE COUNCIL**
>
> **of 11 March 2009**
>
> **on airport charges**

There is no formal equivalent in EU legislation to the UK concept of a 'short title'. Note also that the formal date of adoption will commonly be different from the date the legislative act as a whole, or the dates at which different specific provisions, come into force. The latter will be spelled out as part of the enacting terms:

(ii) **Enacting formula**: this takes a very different form from UK legislation. It has two simple parts, bracketed around elements (c) and (d) below: it starts by identifying the law-maker, and then uses the words, 'has adopted' to indicate the process of enactment. So, for example:

> THE COUNCIL OF THE EUROPEAN UNION . . .
> HAS ADOPTED THIS REGULATION

(iii) **Legal basis**: all EU legislation must have a basis in one of the founding treaties. Without such a basis it would not be valid law. Consequently, it is necessary to identify the relevant treaty under which each legislative act is made, thus:

> Having regard to the Treaty establishing the European Community, and in particular Articles 60 and 301 thereof

The legal basis will also often make reference to other legislative acts and opinions that provide the legal context within which this legislative act will sit:

(iv) **Statement of reasons**: this is akin to the preamble in a UK Act, or what we call the recitals of a treaty. It helps to provide a context for interpretation by explaining how and why the act has come about, and in particular explains the legislative background or history of the legislation. This may include references to earlier proposals and consultation documents. These are called *travaux préparatoires* ('working papers' or 'preparatory texts'), which may help identify why the legislation was introduced, and thence how it should be applied. This explicit mapping out of the background makes that legislative history transparent to anyone reading the legislation, and therefore easier to research. It is introduced by the word 'Whereas'.

(v) **Enacting terms**: i.e. the substantive, operative, provisions of the act. These are conventionally organised as 'Articles' (broadly equivalent to our 'sections') and in larger and more complex pieces of legislation, these are grouped into thematically organised parts variously called 'chapters', 'titles', or (confusingly for us) 'sections'. At the detailed level, the actual style of drafting is rather different from what we are used to in the United Kingdom. Articles are written in more 'everyday' language (so far as possible), and in a more narrative style—generally with less subdivision into subsections and paragraphs than in English legislation. This reflects the strong influence of civil law drafting traditions on EU practice (see **Chapter 8**).

(vi) **Signatures**: every piece of legislation is signed by an authorised signatory of the relevant law-making institution or institutions, for example the President of the Commission or Council, or the relevant commissioner responsible for that part of the Commission's legislative programme.

The complexity of the EU legislative process is quite considerable (see Robinson, 2008). Although each legislative act is drafted and revised in only one authoritative language— usually English or French—it must normally be translated into all of the official languages of the EU. Strict guidelines therefore exist on the layout and formatting of legislation, and on language usage in the official languages. Nevertheless, there have been longstanding concerns about the quality (Robinson, 2008: 182–6) and quantity of legislation. An extensive simplification and codification process began in 2005.This reduced the EU 'statute book' by some 5,000 pages in the first four years. Moreover, data suggest that the volume of new legislation being passed has also slowed since the early 2000s. Even so, it has been estimated that (using data to 2012) the EU still approves a lot of legislation: on average 80 directives, 1,200 regulations, and 700 decisions per year (Toshkov, n.d.).

3.2 Reading cases

In this section we will look first at the form of English reports and then of EU cases.

3.2.1 English law reports

Like statutes, modern English law reports tend to follow a standard format, similar to the illustration (see **Figure 3.2**) from *Finnegan* v *Clowney Youth Training Programme Ltd* [1990] 2 All ER 546. Running down the pages, you will find:

(1) the name of the case;

(2) the court in which it was heard;

(3) the names of the judge(s) presiding;

(4) the hearing date(s);

(5) the headnote;

(6) notes of cross-references to *Halsbury's*;

(7) a list of cases referred to;

(8) details of the appeal;

(9) the names of counsel appearing in the case;

(10) the judgment(s) (not shown);

(11) letters in the margin.

Some of these are quite self-explanatory, so we will be selective in the points we discuss.

546   All England Law Reports   [1990] 2 All ER

Finnegan v Clowney Youth Training Programme Ltd

(1)

a

HOUSE OF LORDS (2)

LORD BRIDGE OF HARWICH, LORD GRIFFITHS, LORD ACKNER, LORD OLIVER OF AYLMERTON AND
LORD LOWRY

(3)

2 APRIL, 17 MAY 1990   (4)

b

*Northern Ireland – Employment – Discrimination against a woman – Provision in relation to
retirement – Female employees required to retire at 60 whereas men retiring at 65 – Northern
Ireland and English legislation identical – English legislation passed before adoption of EEC
equal treatment directive whereas Northern Ireland legislation passed subsequent to directive
– Whether Northern Ireland provision passed to implement directive – Whether Northern Ireland* *c*
*provision to be construed differently from English provision – Whether unlawful discrimination
for women to be required to retire earlier than men – Whether necessary to refer question
to European Court – Sex Discrimination (Northern Ireland) Order 1976, art 8(2)(4) – Council
Directive (EEC) 76/207, art 5(1).*

European Economic Community – National legislation – Construction – Construction of legislation *d*
*relating to death or retirement – Determination of case not dependent on question of Community
law – Whether court should make reference to European Court.*

In February 1986 the employee, who was employed by the employer as a supervisor, was
told that she would be required to retire on 1 April 1986 following her sixtieth birthday
on 22 March. Her request to be allowed to continue working beyond her sixtieth
birthday was refused and her employment was duly terminated on 1 April. The employee *e*

(5)   made a complaint to an industrial tribunal alleging that she had been unlawfully discriminated
against by the employer on the grounds of sex, contrary to art 8(2)ᵃ of the Sex Discrimination
(Northern Ireland) Order 1976, in that she had been forced to retire at the age of 60 whereas
male employees retired at 65. The employer relied on art 8(4)ᵇ of the 1976 order, which *f*
provided that art 8(2) did not apply to provisions relating to death or retirement. The tribunal
upheld the complaint and awarded the employee compensation, on the ground that art 8(2)
and (4) had to be construed consistently with art 5(1)ᶜ of Council Directive (EEC) 76/207
(the equal treatment directive), which prohibited discrimination in working conditions,
including conditions governing dismissal, on grounds of sex. The employer appealed to the *g*
Court of Appeal in Northern Ireland, which allowed the appeal on the ground, inter alia,
that art 8(2) of the 1976 order was to be given the same meaning as identical legislation
in England which had been construed as permitting discrimination in retirement ages. The
employee appealed to the House of Lords, contending, inter alia, that the English legislation
was distinguishable since it had been passed before the equal treatment directive was adopted
whereas the 1976 order had not been made until after the adoption of the directive, so that *h*
the order had to be construed in the light of the directive. The employee also requested (11)
the court to seek a preliminary ruling from the Court of Justice of the European Communities
under art 177 of the EEC Treaty on the question which arose on the appeal.

Held — (1) Since art 8(4) of the 1976 order was in identical terms and in an identical
context to the English legislation it must have been intended to have identical effect and
should not be presumed to have been made for the purpose of implementing the equal

---

a   Article 8(2), so far as material, provides: 'It is unlawful for a person, in the case of a woman employed by him at
an establishment in Northern Ireland, to discriminate against her . . . (*b*) by dismissing her, or subjecting her to any
other detriment.'

b   Article 8(4) provides: 'Paragraphs . . . (2) do not apply to provision in relation to death or retirement.'

c   Article 5(1) is set out at p 548 *h*, post

Figure 3.2 An English law report

HL   **Finnegan v Clowney Youth Training Ltd**   **547**

a treatment directive, notwithstanding that the order was made subsequently to that directive. It followed that although the employee's compulsory retirement at the age of 60 was a contravention of art 8(2) of the 1976 order, since it discriminated against her on the grounds of sex, it was a provision in relation to death or retirement which fell within the exception permitted by art 8(4) and therefore did not constitute unlawful discrimination. The employee's dismissal therefore did not contravene art 8(2). The appeal would accordingly be dismissed

b (see pp 551 *a b d* to *f h* to p 552 *b*, post); *Duke v GEC Reliance Ltd* [1988] 1 All ER 626 applied; *Marshall v Southampton and South West Hampshire Area Health Authority (Teaching)* Case 152/84 [1986] 2 All ER 584 considered.

(2) Since it was for the United Kingdom courts to interpret the 1976 order and since the equal treatment directive did not have direct effect between citizens the determination of the appeal did not depend on any question of Community law. Accordingly, a reference

c to the European Court under art 177 was not necessary (see p 551 *h* to p 552 *b*, post).

Notes
For discrimination against employees, see 16 Halsbury's Laws (4th edn) paras 771·2, 771·5, and for cases on the subject, see 20 Digest (Reissue) 588-593, *4495-4515*.

For Community provisions on equal treatment of employees, see 52 Halsbury's Laws (4th

d edn) paras 21·13, 21·17.   (6)

For references to the Court of Justice of the European Communities for a preliminary ruling, see 51 ibid paras 3·79-3·81.

For the EEC Treaty, art 177, see 50 Halsbury's Statutes (4th edn) 325.

Article 8 of the Sex Discrimination (Northern Ireland) Order 1976 corresponds to s 6 of the Sex Discrimination Act 1975. For s 6 of the 1975 Act, see 6 ibid 702.

e

Cases referred to in opinions
Burton v British Railways Board Case 19/81 [1982] 3 All ER 537, [1982] QB 1080, [1982] 3 WLR 387, [1982] ECR 555, CJEC.

Duke v GEC Reliance Ltd [1988] 1 All ER 626, [1988] AC 618, [1988] 2 WLR 359, HL.

f Litster v Forth Dry Dock and Engineering Co Ltd [1989] 1 All ER 1134, [1990] AC 546, [1989] 2 WLR 634, HL.   (7)

Marshall v Southampton and South West Hampshire Area Health Authority (Teaching) Case 152/84 [1986] 2 All ER 584, [1986] QB 401, [1986] 2 WLR 780, [1986] ECR 723, CJEC.

Note [1966] 3 All ER 77, [1966] 1 WLR 1234, HL.

g Pickstone v Freemans plc [1988] 2 All ER 803, [1989] AC 66, [1989] 2 WLR 634, HL.

von Colson and Kamann v Land Nordrhein-Westfalen Case 14/83 [1984] ECR 1891.

Appeal
Frances Finnegan (the employee) appealed with leave of the Court of Appeal in Northern Ireland against the decision of that court (Hutton LCJ and Mac Dermott LJ) on 28 November

h 1988 allowing the appeal of the respondent, Clowney Youth Training Programme Ltd (the employer), by way of case stated by an industrial tribunal (J E Maguire chairman) sitting at Belfast on 23 November 1987 in respect of its decision that the employer had unlawfully discriminated against the employee on grounds of sex, contrary to the provisions of art 8 of the Sex Discrimination (Northern Ireland) Order 1976, SI 1976/1042, in compulsorily (8)

j retiring the employee at 60 when comparable male employees were allowed to work until the age of 65. The facts are set out in the opinion of Lord Bridge.

Patrick Coghlin QC and *Seamus Treacy* (both of the Northern Ireland Bar) for the employee. (9)
Patrick Markey QC and *Brian Kennedy* (both of the Northern Ireland Bar) for the employer.

Their Lordships took time for consideration.

Figure 3.2 Continued

The name of the case (1)

It was said in **Chapter 2** that English case names follow the names of the parties involved. In this respect, common law case citations tend to differ from the forms adopted in many civilian systems, which often adopt a more anonymous, administrative title, based usually on the court, and a case number or date, though this is not always so. The French, for example, use both styles. Cases before the *Cour de Cassation* are cited by giving an abbreviated version of the division concerned (*civile, criminelle, sociale, commerciale*), the date of the decision, and its location in the relevant case reports. Conversely, decisions of the *Conseil d'Etat* are cited by case name.

By comparison, the more consistent English system sounds simple, but, as is so often the case, that impression is misleading; there is a wide array of forms that the case name can take. However, these forms can tell us quite a lot about the nature of the case.

In *civil* cases the normal mode of citation is the name of the person bringing the case or appeal (**claimant**, formerly *plaintiff*, or **appellant**) first followed by the name of the **defendant** (or **respondent** in an appeal): thus, '*Smith* v *Jones*'. The 'v' means *versus*, that is 'against' (reflecting the adversarial nature of the process); it is usually spoken as 'and', hence 'Smith and Jones'—spoken citations can thus sound confusing if there are more than two parties, as you will have a multiplicity of 'ands', one of which is a 'v'! If Jones were to lose his case and appeal, the form of citation should switch to '*Jones* v *Smith*'. For an apparently unfathomable reason this does not always happen. Four other forms of civil citations crop up with some regularity.

First, in shipping cases (a number of which come up in contract and commercial law), it is a convention to abbreviate the case name to that of the ship involved, so, for example, the case of *Compania Financiera Soleada SA, Netherlands Antilles Ships Management Corp. and Dammers and van der Heide's Shipping and Trading Co.* v *Hamoor Tanker Corp. Inc.* (1981) is mercifully known as *The Borag*. That abbreviation will be sufficient to find the case in most books or citators.

Secondly, cases may appear in the form '*Re Smith*' (where '*Re*' roughly means 'concerning'). This form arises in some property cases, particularly those relating to trusts or the estates of deceased persons. It is also used in cases where the court is considering its wardship jurisdiction (where the court effectively takes ultimate control over the affairs of a child). In the latter cases the name of the child will not normally be disclosed, and the case citation will appear as '*Re M*', for example. They are usually indexed under the name referred to, not under '*Re*'. (There are also other situations where the court will grant the parties anonymity to protect their privacy, so that parties are identified only by an initial letter, in the form of '*A* v *B*'.)

Thirdly, you may come across cases cited as '*In B*' or '*In E*'. These cases arise in the law relating to wills and estates. '*In B*' stands for '*In Bonis*' (in the goods of). '*In E*' stands for '*In the Estate of*'. The distinction arose because, prior to the 1897 Land Transfer Act, personal representatives could only deal with a deceased's goods, not their land. The citations reflect this. The equivalent cases nowadays use the form '*Re*', so it is increasingly unlikely that you will come across this form of citation.

Finally, another form appears where the Administrative Court has exercised its public law jurisdiction judicially to review the administration or an inferior court. These cases were for a long time cited in the form '*R* v *Bloggs, ex parte Smith*', though with the move to anglicise English legal terminology the form of citation has changed, thus: *R (on the application of Smith)* v *Bloggs*. This is the only context when the Crown ('*R*') is commonly cited in civil proceedings. It reflects the fact that technically the action has been taken by the Crown, on the application of some other party, under what are, historically, the *prerogative* powers of the Crown. The term *ex parte* properly denotes someone who is outside the proceedings. In this situation it seems rather peculiar, though strictly correct, as it identifies the person who made the application for judicial review. *Criminal* cases are normally cited as '*R* v *Smith*'. The '*R*' stands for *Rex* or *Regina* (Latin for king and queen), denoting the state's role as **prosecutor**; the accused is normally cited as the **defendant**. The oral form of the citation is 'the Crown against Smith', although it is usually abbreviated to just *Smith*.

Once again, there is a variety of alternative forms. Some criminal prosecutions can be commenced only with the approval of one of the government's law officers—the Attorney General (A-G) or the Director of Public Prosecutions (DPP). In such cases that official's title will appear instead of the Crown as prosecutor. Some cases, notably those which commenced in the magistrates' courts before the Crown Prosecution Service was set up in 1985, bore the name of the (police) prosecutor (see, e.g., *Albert* v *Lavin* [1982] AC 546; [1981] 3 All ER 878). This principle still applies in those very rare cases where a member of the public brings a private prosecution.

The court and presiding judge(s) (2) and (3)

These are perhaps of greater significance than you might at first think. Given that our system of precedent depends upon a ranking of courts, we need to know whereabouts in the 'batting order' this particular case is placed. Furthermore, in cases before the Supreme Court (or House of Lords before that), Court of Appeal, and a Divisional Court of the High Court, it is normal to have more than one judge presiding. Sometimes the number, and even the status, of the judges presiding will influence the weight of that decision. It is notable that the use of larger panels of seven or even nine judges to hear important or especially difficult cases in the Supreme Court and Privy Council has increased since the Presidency of Lord Phillips.

The headnote (5)

This does three things. First, it provides a brief statement of the **material facts** of the case. By facts we are talking about the description of events leading up to the case (see further **Chapters 5** and **7**); the term *material* denotes those facts which the judge considered important in deciding the case (we discuss the concept of materiality in detail in **Chapter 7**). Secondly, it will normally indicate the legal issues (usually called the **questions of law**) to be considered by the court. Thirdly, the headnote contains a summary of the court's decision on the issues of fact and law (as appropriate), including details of any *dissenting* judgment (where one or more judges disagree with the majority view).

It will also frequently give some indication of the effect of this decision on existing case law. This is indicated by the use of the following terms in conjunction with the citation of the relevant case:

Affirmed: this indicates that the court has agreed with the decision of a lower court in respect of the *same* case.

Applied: this means that a court has regarded itself as bound by an earlier decision, and has therefore employed the same reasoning in the instant case. The alternative would have been to distinguish the earlier case (see the relevant heading later in this section).

Approved: this is used where a higher court states that another case before a lower court was correctly decided.

Considered: this seems to be something of a residual category. If the court has discussed a reported case (particularly one decided by a court of equal status) but not reached any dramatic conclusion about its application, then it will probably appear as 'considered'.

Distinguished: an earlier case will be distinguished where a court has no power (or no wish) to overrule it, but does not want to apply it either. The court will therefore find some ground for saying it is different, and should not be followed. Distinguishing is an important category as it provides one of the main mechanisms by which the common law refines the scope of legal principles. Distinguishing may be restrictive or non-restrictive. Where it is restrictive, the act of distinguishing will materially affect the scope of the earlier authority; where it is non-restrictive, the court is simply saying that there is a material difference, but not one that will affect the ambit of the rule for the future. For example, in *Rickards* v *Lothian* [1913] AC 263, Rickards was the landlord and manager of property occupied by Lothian and other tenants. Lothian ran a bookselling business on the second floor. One night, water overflowing from a tap left running on the fourth floor ran down into Lothian's premises, causing considerable damage to his stock. It was established that the accident was not caused by Rickard's negligence. Lothian consequently sought to bring an action under the tort of *Rylands* v *Fletcher* (1868) LR 3 HL 330 which, regardless of fault, makes the occupier of land liable for damage caused to another by the 'escape' from his property of anything likely to do harm, provided that the use of the land was 'non-natural'. Hence in *Rylands* v *Fletcher* itself, the claim was founded on the 'escape' of water from a reservoir constructed on the defendant's land—this construction being declared a non-natural use of the land. By contrast, in *Rickards* v *Lothian*, although there was an escape of water, the Privy Council held that the provision of a bathroom with running water was not a non-natural use of the defendant's property. Consequently, this case could be distinguished from *Rylands* v *Fletcher* on its material facts, precisely because there was no non-natural user in the later case. This was, therefore, a non-restrictive distinction.

Now, suppose the facts had been slightly different. Assume that instead of an escape of water, the damage in *Rickards* had been caused maliciously by a trespasser who set fire to the property. This would clearly be a non-natural use, but the court might, arguably, still not allow Lothian to recover, because the case could again be distinguished from *Rylands* v *Fletcher*. In *Rylands*, the non-natural use was authorised by the owner; in our new version of *Rickards*, it was not. If the court was so to hold, this would be an example of restrictive distinguishing. We would now say that liability under the principle in *Rylands* v *Fletcher* was restricted to those cases where the use was authorised by the owner or occupier of the land.

Overruled: this is used to show where a court has rejected and invalidated an earlier decision of a court of lower (or sometimes equal) status to itself. The power to overrule is thus limited by a court's position in the hierarchy. Sometimes, as an alternative to overruling, you will see the comment '**Not followed**'. This is used where the decision in question is persuasive authority, for example, from another jurisdiction. 'Not followed' does not affect the status of the precedent within its own jurisdiction, but it will certainly cast doubt on the value of that decision within the jurisdiction that has declined to follow it.

Reversed: this is the opposite of affirmed. It means that the higher court has decided that the lower court in the *same* case came to the wrong decision.

Although the headnote is intended as a summary of the whole case, it is not authority for anything within the case. It is simply a *résumé* provided by the publishers of the report. Though they are usually fairly reliable, mistakes are sometimes made. For example, in *O'Grady* v *Saper* [1940] 3 All ER 527, which concerned an appeal from an action originally brought against an employer in respect of unpaid wages during the employee's absence for sickness, the headnote reads:

> *Held*, the facts proved showed by implication that there was no agreement that the respondent should be paid wages while absent through illness and he was not entitled to recover.

This significantly distorts the contractual point which was made in that case. What the Court actually said was that the respondent (the employee) could not recover because there was an implied contractual term that he was *not* to be paid wages during any sick leave. So be careful in relying upon the headnote of a case—it certainly should not be used as a substitute for reading the judgments.

List of cases (7)

Most law reports will contain two separate lists. The first is a list of cases cited by the judge(s) in the judgment. That list is useful if you are trying to discover how the courts have subsequently used a particular decision. In other words, it provides a list of possible precedents used in that case. The second list (if there is one) will refer to additional cases cited in argument by counsel. Since the judge has not cited them, they are obviously of much less significance, but they can sometimes be worth considering if you are undertaking detailed research into the rationale of a decision, as they may show up points that the judge has apparently ignored or rejected, but without referring to the case in the written judgment.

Details of the appeal (8)

Here, the report gives a short history of the case, stating the parties, the previous hearing(s) of the case, and usually the legal findings which form the basis of the appeal.

There are a number of basic points regarding appeal terminology that we can deal with here. In most cases, the case will refer simply to an 'appeal', which may be an appeal on a point of law, or fact, or both, depending upon the jurisdiction of the court. However, there are three particular procedures that you may confront quite frequently, which require a little more explanation:

(i) **Appeal by way of case stated**: this most commonly arises in appeals from the magistrates' court to the High Court, either where the applicant believes the magistrates have made an error of law (e.g. misinterpreted a statute) or acted outside their jurisdiction. The magistrates state a case by submitting to the High Court a statement of facts found by the justices, together with the question(s) of law or jurisdiction on which guidance is sought. The High Court may then come to its own decision on the issue, or refer the case back to the magistrates for reconsideration in the light of the High Court's opinion. Further rights of appeal exist on a case stated. These lie directly to the Supreme Court in criminal cases. A good example of the whole appeal process is provided by the case of *Albert* v *Lavin*, already mentioned. The law report includes the form of words used by the magistrates to state a case concerning police powers of arrest for a breach of the peace. In civil cases the appeal is normally to the Court of Appeal. In *Finnegan* v *Clowney Youth Training Programme Ltd* the appeal shows that a case was stated by an industrial tribunal to the Court of Appeal in Northern Ireland. This particular procedure is unique to the Northern Irish system; though there are a number of contexts in which an English civil case can be stated for the High Court, these tend to be rare.

(ii) **Interim application**: in civil proceedings an interim application (formerly called an interlocutory application) is an application to the court for some kind of temporary order that will take effect until the case comes to a full trial at a later date. Such applications most commonly arise as requests for an *injunction* (an order requiring the other party to do, or stop doing, something). They are thus meant to preserve the *status quo* until the trial. Interim applications will normally be heard by a single judge in the High Court, with a right of appeal to the Court of Appeal.

(iii) **'Leapfrog appeal'**: under the Administration of Justice Act 1969 Part II, a civil case could exceptionally move from the High Court direct to the Supreme Court, provided all the parties consented and both the Supreme Court and the High Court agreed. The circumstances in which such appeals could be made were extremely narrow; the case must have involved a point of law of general public importance relating to the interpretation of primary or secondary legislation; and the High Court had to be bound on that point of law by a precedent of the Court of Appeal or Supreme Court.

Consequently, the procedure seemed to be used in only a relatively few cases (see discussion in Drewry, 1973); however, attempts to revive it have been made as a result of amendments in the Criminal Justice and Courts Act 2015, ss 63–66, which came into force in August 2016.

These provisions have somewhat relaxed the conditions for a leapfrog appeal from the High Court, by removing the consent requirement and permitting cases to leapfrog where they raise issues of 'national importance', or where the result is of 'particular significance', or where the benefits of not delaying consideration by the Supreme Court outweigh the benefits of consideration by the Court of Appeal. Appeals will, however, still have to be on a point of law of general public importance. The 2015 Act also introduced equivalent leapfrog appeals from a number of High Court-equivalent tribunals to the Supreme Court, namely the Upper Tribunal (s. 64), the Employment Appeals Tribunal (s. 65), and the Special Immigration Appeals Commission (s. 66). It is still too early to say much about how these new, and rather subjective grounds are being interpreted, or their impact on the caseload of the Supreme Court.

The names of counsel (9)

Historically, the only lawyers entitled to appear before the High Court and above were barristers. Changes to the rules in the Courts and Legal Services Act 1990, s. 27 extended rights of audience to solicitors who have undergone additional advocacy training.

In the majority of cases before the higher courts, each side will be represented by two barristers, a leader and a junior counsel. Until late 1977, this was a formal requirement where the leader was a 'QC' (Queen's Counsel). Now a QC may appear alone, though she or he can decline to do so.

The judgments (10)

The judgments are the most important part of any case, and as we shall see in **Chapters 6** and **7**, they are crucial to the operation of the English doctrine of precedent. It is normally the practice that, where there is more than one judge sitting, each is entitled to deliver his own opinion on the case. The first judgment given tends to be that of the senior judge presiding. However, do not assume that because it is first it is therefore the 'main' or 'leading' judgment. Indeed, where there are multiple judgments, it can be dangerous to assume that any one has precedence over the others—though sometimes you can get an intuitive sense that one judgment is the most significant, perhaps because the other judges refer to it extensively, or because it seems to be the most comprehensive or to provide the best analysis. The judges following may then either give a full judgment of their own, either supporting or dissenting from the decision of one or more of the other speakers, or give a brief *concurring* judgment, which may be no more than 'I agree'. The chief exception to this practice is the Privy Council, where a unanimous or majority opinion is presented by one judge alone, and only dissenting voices from that have a separate right to be heard. It is notable, however, that, following a steady decline since the early 1990s, the number of single judgments issued by the Supreme Court has increased, to a point where, by 2013, single judgments constituted 55 per cent of decisions (Paterson, 2015).

So far as the formalities of judgments are concerned, there appear to be none of any real significance, though there are many points of style, particularly in respect of forms of address. Titles are always given—a matter of style which is normally followed in academic writing, though the judges are also strong on ritual courtesy. A fellow judge is seldom anything less than 'learned', even where the discussion of his judgment strongly suggests that the speaker considers him to have the reasoning powers of a codfish.

The style of judgments tends to be quite individual. Some judges adopt a clear narrative pattern; Lord Denning was a prime—in his later decisions one might say an extreme—example of this style, whereby the facts and the law are woven into a continuous 'story' (note also the discussion of *Miller* v *Jackson* in **Chapter 5**). Others have a far more formal style, which can produce some very dense prose indeed. A more recent innovation, which has been widely adopted, is to break up the text with headings and sub-headings, which can much improve the clarity of the argument. Levity is unusual but not unknown. Court of Appeal judge Sir Alan Ward became something of a legend in this regard. His opening lines in one particular unreported case have rapidly passed into legal folklore: 'This case involves a number of—and here I must not fall into Dr Spooner's error—warring bankers' (Regan, 2014).

Sadly, Sir Alan retired in 2014 (an event, we hasten to add, not in any way linked to the judgment above), leaving the Court of Appeal a slightly more predictable place.

One final feature of English cases, which differentiates our process from that of most other countries, has been the high proportion of *ex tempore*, or 'off-the-cuff', judgments. It has been common practice in the High Court, though less common in the Court of Appeal, for judgment to be given either immediately after the conclusion of argument, or following a brief adjournment. There are certainly anecdotal indications that the practice is much less common as more and more of the relatively straightforward cases are dealt with by county courts, or diverted to alternative dispute resolution, meaning that it tends to be the more complex cases that come to trial. Where the judge is not prepared to give his or her decision *ex tempore*, judgment is said to be **reserved** for presentation at a later date. The House of Lords always reserved its decisions, and the Supreme Court follows this practice. In the lower courts it is for the judges to decide.

Where a judgment in the law reports has been reserved, that is usually indicated (at a point just preceding the judgment(s)), by the abbreviation '*Cur. adv. vult*'. This is short for *Curia advisari vult*, meaning 'The court wishes to be advised'. Judgments in the House of Lords were preceded, as here, by the more mundane: 'Their Lordships took time for consideration'. These editorial devices do not, of course, appear in the official transcript, though reservation can be inferred from any difference between the hearing and judgment dates.

Letters in the margin (11)

These are a useful addendum to the page number, which may be cited in the form 'p. 123a'. (Note also that, conventionally, the 'p.' denoting the page can be dropped when citing pages of the law reports.) Taken together, they can be used to locate more accurately a piece of text which is being referred to in court, in the headnote to a law report, or in an essay, and so on. As we noted in **Chapter 2**, with the rising use of online sources, it is now the normal practice that paragraphs are numbered continuously throughout the published version of the judgments. This reduces the significance of the pagination and marginal lettering when citing cases.

3.2.2 European reports

As we also noted in **Chapter 2**, decisions of the Court of Justice of the European Union (CJEU) are reported in two main series of English language reports the *European Court Reports* (ECR) and the *Common Market Law Reports* (CMLR). There are slight but mostly insignificant differences in the way in which these two sets of reports are laid out. For our purposes, therefore, it is sufficient to focus on just one version—the CMLR. To do this we have chosen Case C–83/92 *Pierrel SpA v Ministero della Sanità* [1995] 1 CMLR 53, a decision on a point of conflict between Italian law and Community law governing the marketing of pharmaceuticals (see **Figure 3.3**); the issues in the case are not significant for our purposes, the structure of the report is. Rather than take you through each element of the report, we have highlighted only the significant differences from an English law report:

(1) the boxes;

(2) the court and chamber;

(3) the personnel;

(4) date of judgment;

(5) the headnote;

(6) advocates appearing;

(7) Advocate General's Opinion (not shown); and

(8) the judgment.

(1)   (1)

ECJ*   EEC   1993
                                                                        ‾
PIERREL SpA AND OTHERS *v.* MINISTERO DELLA SANITÀ   *Pierrel SpA*
              (Case C–83/92)   v.
                                                              Ministero
                                                              della Sanità
BEFORE THE COURT OF JUSTICE OF THE EUROPEAN COMMUNITIES   (2)   ‾
                  (5th CHAMBER)   European
                                                               Court of
                                                               Justice
(*Presiding*, Moitinho de Almeida PC; Joliet and Rodríguez (3)
                    Iglesias JJ.)
        Herr Carl Otto Lenz, *Advocate General.*

                                      7 December 1993 (4)

Reference from Italy by the Consiglio di Stato under **Article 177**
                          EEC.

Provisions considered:
  Dir. 65/65
  Dir. 75/319
  Dir. 83/570
  Dir. 92/27

    Regulation of trade. Pharmaceuticals. Article 21 of the (5)
    Pharmaceuticals Specialties Directive 65/65 means that the
    suspension or revocation of a marketing authorisation for a
    proprietary medicinal product may be decided only on the
    grounds laid down in that directive or other relevant provi-
    sions of Community law. [23]
        CLIN-MIDY SA *v.* BELGIAN STATE (301/82): [1984] E.C.R.
        251, [1985] 1 C.M.L.R. 443, *confirmed.*
    Regulation of trade. Pharmaceuticals. National rules,
    according to which marketing authorisations for proprietary
    medicinal products which are not used within a specified
    period are to lapse, breach the Pharmaceuticals Specialties
    Directive 65/65, as amended. [30]

  * This box indicates the court or, for national systems, the class of court which
delivered this judgment. The box on the right indicates the country or jurisdiction
to which the court belongs.

The Court *interpreted* the Pharmaceuticals Specialties Directive 65/65, as amended and
supplemented by Directives 75/319, 83/570 and 92/27, *in the context of* Italian legislation
which provided that authorisations to market proprietary medicines lapsed if they were
not used within 18 months *to the effect that* the grounds laid down by the directives for the
revocation or suspension of such authorisations (which did not include failure to use them
within a specified period) were exhaustive, *that* the lapse of an authorisation was analogous
to a revocation since they both resulted in termination, and so *that* the Italian legislation
breached the directive, it being irrelevant that it had been amended after the national
court's **Article 177** reference.

Figure 3.3 A decision of the ECJ

Professor Luigi Ferrari Bravo, Head of the Department of Contentious Diplomatic Affairs at the Ministry of Foreign Affairs, assisted by *Oscar Fiumara* and *Francesco Guicciardi*, Avvocati dello Stato, for the Italian Government.

Luis Ines Fernandes, Director of the Legal Department of the Directorate-General for the European Communities at the Ministry for Foreign Affairs, *Maria Luisa Duarte*, Legal Adviser at the Directorate-General for the European Communities, and *Cláudio Monteiro*, Legal Adviser at the Directorate-General for Medicinal Products, for the Portuguese Government as *amicus curiae*.

Antonio Aresu, of the Legal Service of the E.C. Commission, and *Virginia Melgar*, a national official seconded to the Legal Service, for the Commission as *amicus curiae*.

The following case was referred to in the judgment:

1. CLIN-MIDY SA v. BELGIAN STATE (301/82), 26 January 1984: [1984] E.C.R. 251, [1985] 1 C.M.L.R. 443.

The following further cases were referred to by the Advocate General:

2. GUNA SRL v. E.C. COUNCIL (C–437/92), not yet decided.
3. ANGELOPHARM GmbH v. FREIE UND HANSESTADT HAMBURG (C–212/91), 25 January 1994: [1994] 1 E.C.R. 171, [1994] 3 C.M.L.R. 573.
4. MARLEASING SA v. LA COMERCIAL INTERNACIONAL DE ALIMENTACIÓN SA (C–106/89), 13 November 1990: [1990] 1 E.C.R. 4135, [1992] 3 C.M.L.R. 305.

The following additional cases were referred to in argument:

5. ALGERA v. COMMON ASSEMBLY (7/56 & 3–7/57), 12 July 1957: [1957–58] E.C.R. 39.
6. RE THE MARKETING OF MEDICINES: E.C. COMMISSION v. ITALY (C–145/82), 15 March 1983: [1983] E.C.R. 711, [1984] 1 C.M.L.R. 148.

TABLE OF PROCEEDINGS	PAGE
Opinion of Lenz A.G., 15 July 1993	58
Judgment of the European Court of Justice, 7 December 1993	64
Language of the proceedings: Italian	

Figure 3.3 Continued

The boxes (1)

This is a particular feature of the CMLR. The CMLR include cases from courts of national as well as international jurisdiction, and the publishers therefore needed to develop a system which would make it clear to readers in any country what the status of a decision was. This is the system they devised. The box on the left indicates the class of court as follows (variations reflect the structure in place at the time the case was reported):

   ECJ—the Court of Justice of the EC

   CFI—the Court of First Instance of the EC

   EFTA—the Court of the European Free Trade Association.

For courts of national jurisdiction, the CMLR identify decisions according to the level of the court in the national hierarchy. Level I thus, indicates a court of first instance, or trial court; Level II covers all intermediate courts (like the English Court of Appeal); and Level III indicates a final court of appeal (e.g. the Supreme Court). The use of this system enables us roughly to gauge and compare the relative significance of decisions of national courts on points of EU law.

The box on the right of the page indicates the court's jurisdiction, e.g. 'EEC' for courts with jurisdiction across the Communities, or 'UK–England' for English courts, etc.

The court and chamber (2)

The formal title of the court is given together with, where appropriate, the chamber in which it is heard. This is not a reference to the English practice of hearing some (mostly interim) applications in private in the judge's office (called 'chambers'); rather it refers to the procedural process of assigning the case to a particular group of judges. Each of the EU courts is divided into chambers, with each chamber having its own President, elected by the judges. In most of their cases the Court of Justice and General Court sit as a regular chamber of three or five judges, or as a Grand Chamber of fifteen judges, or, very exceptionally as a 'plenary' (full) court. The Court itself determines whether to hear proceedings in plenary session or as a chamber, and, if the latter, whether comprising a panel of three, five, or fifteen judges (the last being referred to as a 'Grand Chamber'). In the Court of Justice this decision is taken by the Court at the close of the written proceedings, and after the Advocate General has been heard. It is based simply on an assessment of the importance or difficulty of the issues raised. Member States and any Community institutions involved in the proceedings can require the trial to be conducted before the full Court. The General Court, also with a total of twenty-eight judges, operates in a very similar fashion, though it has only very rarely exercised its power to sit as a plenary court.

The personnel (3)

There are a number of key personnel within the CJEU. In addition to the judges, there are the eleven Advocates General and the Registrar of the CJEU. We will consider each of these roles in turn.

There are twenty-eight judges at present: one from each Member State. Under the terms of the Treaties, the judges are appointed for a renewable term of six years on the basis either of substantial professional expertise and seniority (the first option), or on the basis of academic scholarship (the second option). The alternative nature of these qualifications is particularly significant in the British or Irish context where, unlike most continental jurisdictions, academics *per se* are not eligible for domestic judicial appointment. To date, however, the United Kingdom has not nominated a judge who would not satisfy the first option, though two of the judges have also held chairs at British universities. David Edward, for example, was both a Scottish QC and Salveson Professor of European Institutions at Edinburgh University before his appointment, first to the CFI, and then, in 1992, to the ECJ. If Brexit proceeds, the United Kingdom will most likely lose its seat on the Court, and its current Advocate General, Eleanor Sharpston.

Each chamber of the Court has a President elected, by its members, annually in the case of chamber of three judges, or for a three-year term where there are five judges in the chamber (in practice, this means that each judge serves as President in rotation). The Court of Justice also has an overall President and Vice-President who are elected for a (renewable) three-year term. The President of the Court presides at plenary hearings and has ultimate responsibility for the judicial administration of the court. Other than the presidents, all judges rank equally, though seating positions in court are determined by 'seniority in office'—in effect, length of service as a judge.

Each case has assigned to it a *Judge-Rapporteur*. This is a judge nominated by the President of one of the smaller chambers to undertake the preparatory inquiry phase once an application has been lodged with the court. The *Judge-Rapporteur*'s role is akin to that of the investigating magistrate in civilian court procedure, i.e. to undertake an inquiry and produce a report on the case for the Court to consider (see the CJEU website for a brief outline of its procedures: http://curia.europa.eu/jcms/jcms/Jo2_7024). This report is used by the Court to determine procedure for the hearing of the matter—for example what witnesses (if any) may be called, whether the case is heard by the chamber to which it was assigned, or by a chamber of five judges or plenary court. The *Judge-Rapporteur* is also normally present at oral hearings, and is entitled to put questions to the advocates.

The *Advocates General* are perhaps the most distinctive element of the proceedings, having no equivalent in common law procedure. Advocates General are very much a part of the court, and subject broadly to the same conditions of appointment, tenure, salary, etc. as the judges (indeed, over the years, a number of Advocates General have become judges, and *vice versa*). In a sense, then, in true civilian style both Advocates General and judges are part of the same Community *magistrature*. In much the same way, in France we see a functional distinction between judges of the *siège* (i.e. those who sit in judgment 'on the bench') and judges of the *parquet* (the 'floorboards') who take responsibility for the prosecution of cases, but this does not alter the fact that both are part of the career judiciary. The analogy is not exact, of course, as the Court of Justice has no direct equivalent of the *parquet*, and it has been suggested that their role more clearly reflects the court's early links (both procedural and personal) with the French *Conseil d'Etat* (see further Vranken, 1996: 40–8).

The idea of an Advocate General is a familiar one in continental legal systems. The Advocate General is an 'adviser' to the court, performing a task which might be likened to 'sifting' through the law on behalf of the Court in each case. In practice this has meant that the Advocate General has tended to play an important part in the proceedings. He receives all the details of the case from the parties, investigates the law relating to the issues raised, and delivers his opinion on the case to the Court as to what decision it should reach. He sits with the judges on the Bench (opposite the Registrar) but plays no part in their deliberations. He delivers his opinion after the case has been heard by the court, and often at a later hearing. This can be highly influential on the reasoning of the court. We discuss the nature and role of the Advocate General's opinion in more detail later in this section.

The procedure governing cases before the General Court is slightly different. There is no general requirement of an Advocate General to prepare the case, and no formal or permanently established body of Advocates General for the General Court. When the Court sits in plenary session, a judge of the General Court will normally be appointed to act as Advocate General. In addition, under the Court's rules of procedure, an Advocate General may be appointed to assist the Court where the case is to be heard before a chamber, and the legal difficulty or factual complexity of the case so requires. In practice, however, this power is seldom used (see Biavati, 2011: 79). Where appointed, an

Advocate General has the same functions before the General Court as before the Court of Justice.

Note that since 1982 there has been no hyphen in the spelling of Advocate General. The plural of an Advocate General is Advocates General. This distinction is not a popular question on game shows.

Last, there is the *Registrar*, who is in charge of the court Registry (i.e. its administrative arm) and deals with the procedure and administration of the court. His role is perceived as something more important than the title would imply under our system—he even sits with the judges in court, but takes no part in the decision. There are also two Assistant Registrars who take day-to-day responsibility for the administrative and judicial sides of the Registry's work, respectively.

Date of judgment (4)

Again, this is self-explanatory; note, however, that, unlike the English law reports, no separate hearing dates are given. Note too that the CJEU always reserves its judgments.

The headnote (5)

The form of a headnote differs substantially from that used in English law reports. Opening with a reference to the procedure whereby the case reached the Court (here, an Art. 177—now Art. 267—Reference) and citations of the relevant Community legislation, it then identifies the subject matter of the case, together with references to key paragraphs in the judgment (in square brackets) and refers to any authority cited in the judgment—but *not* authorities referred to by the Advocate General.

The advocates (6)

Parties before the CJEU must normally be represented by a lawyer. In addition, in reference proceedings, legal representatives from other Member States having an interest in the ruling may submit observations to the Court in both the written and oral proceedings. The Commission also always submits observations in reference proceedings. In the *Pierrel* case, you can see that observations were received from the Commission and from the Portuguese government.

Advocate General's opinion (not shown)

The Advocate General's opinion is often an important part of the case, and one that has no direct counterpart in the English legal system. In his opinion the Advocate General will normally go through the facts, the law, and various authorities (including case law and academic commentary), and usually in far more detail than does the judgment of the court. Practically speaking, therefore, it makes a lot of sense to read the opinion before the judgment, as that will (especially if the opinion is followed by the court) give you significant insights into the development and rationale of the law.

The Advocate General's opinion is not part of the court's judgment and is in no sense 'binding' either on the Court to which it is presented or on any other later court. It may, however, be referred to and used as a kind of persuasive authority in later cases before the CJEU. Thus, for example, in T–3/90 *Prodifarma* v *Commission* [1991] ECR II-11154, the Advocate General's opinion in a previous Court of Justice decision was taken up by the Court of First Instance. It is also quite common practice for Advocates General to cite each other's opinions. The division between the Advocate General's

opinion and the judgment has become rather more blurred by the more modern practice of the judges in some cases simply adopting the opinion in its entirety by 'direct
reference'. For an example of the practice, see Case C–284/91 *Suiker Export* v *Belgium*
[1992] ECR I-5473.

Whatever the procedure, estimates (albeit now rather dated) suggest that the Advocate
General's opinion is followed in something like 70–85 per cent of cases (Vranken, 1996:
61). Note, however, that there are also some indications of a gradual reduction in the
importance of the opinion. The increased maturity of the Court of Justice's jurisprudence, and the development of a settled body of relevant precedents has somewhat
diminished the need for an opinion in all cases. Consequently, after the Treaty of Nice,
it was decided that the need for a mandatory Advocate General's opinion would be
removed in respect of those cases that raise no novel questions of law (see Art. 20(5) of
the CJEU Statute).

The judgment (not shown)

There are two particular points to note about the style of judgments of the Court of
Justice and the General Court.

First, all decisions are *collegial*. A decision is reported as a decision of the court, without the individual (or idiosyncratic!) voices we often associate with English judgments.
Collegiality also means that, following the civilian tradition, there is no provision for
dissenting judgments. Decisions will follow the majority reasoning if unanimity cannot
be achieved, but, unlike the common law approach, no record of the minority view is
retained to trouble posterity. That said, the European courts work very hard to achieve
unanimity, and this sometimes means that decisions reflect a 'lowest common denomi-
nator of conflicting opinions' (Edward, 2004: 124). Though collegiality may thus set
limits on the development of EU law, or the CJEU's creativity, that is not necessarily a
'bad thing', and it can also be argued that collegiality might be the only way in which a
court such as the CJEU could work:

> The principle of collegiality is an incentive to judicial modesty, as it is intended to be, and it is well
> adapted to the needs of a court that has to work in the multilingual, multinational and multicultural
> environment of the European Union. The individual Judges cannot be criticised for disloyalty to the
> interests of their own country nor, correspondingly, can the member states find an excuse for not
> accepting the Court's judgment on the ground that 'their' Judge did not vote for it.
>
> (Edward, 2004: 124)

Secondly, it follows that the form and style of the decision are also rather different from
those found in English law reports. To start with, the judgment is presented in the form
of numbered paragraphs, a practice which has only relatively recently been adopted by
English courts. These provide a reference point when citing the decision. Note also that
the actual ruling of the Court always appears at the end of the judgment. It is often quite
short, and is identified by the opening phrase 'On those grounds…' from the French
'*pour ces motifs*'. There are some other relatively minor stylistic differences between
reports which can reflect the age of the case (the principles governing the format for
judgments were relaxed in 1978) or small variations in 'house-style' between the ECR
and CMLR. They are not significant for our purposes. Now to a more substantial issue.

The contents of the judgment also appear distinctive to lawyers of the common law tradition. But this is not just a matter of style—it reflects the different legal cultures involved, and particularly assumptions about the judicial function. Unlike the rather more rhetorical approach of many English judges, the language used by the CJEU tends to be more measured, if not downright flat. This is sometimes said to reflect the compromise nature of many decisions and is a consequence of the collegiality principle. If a camel is a horse designed by committee, European judgments can sometimes be the judicial equivalent of the camel. Judgments are also relatively short. This is not least because they commonly lack the detailed factual and legal analysis which is the feature of many English judgments and of the Advocate General's opinion. Relatively few cases may be cited in support of the decision (though references to case law have become much more common) and older judgments rarely made any direct reference to the opinions of Advocates General—not even the opinion given in that case (though as we have seen, that too is changing).

This is not to say that EC decisions suffer from a lack of rigour or rationalisation: they are presented in a very logical, developmental form in which point follows point in a seemingly inexorable sequence. This form of presentation can sometimes make European decisions easier to read and understand than their English counterparts, but it does mean that points of uncertainty or argument get rather lost in what is packaged as a rational, deductive process (we explore some of the reasons behind this approach in **Chapter 5**). It can also mean that the Court is often reluctant to explore the implications or boundaries of the law beyond the issues directly raised by the case at hand. This contrasts with English practice, where judges will frequently speculate on the scope or implications of a particular ruling. Lawyers asking the question '*What if . . .*' of the CJEU will seldom find guidance in the judgment. Arguably this has meant that the Court has actually generated a lack of legal certainty through an unwillingness to provide fuller reasoning of its decisions in cases like *Francovich* (see, e.g., Bebr, 1992) and *Faccini Dori* (see our discussion of these cases in **Chapter 11**).

3.2.3 A beginning, not an end

Thus far we have provided you with a basic road map to the structure of the law reports. The detail may seem rather dull, at worst, a bit overwhelming to start with. You will get used to it, provided you practise the skills of going back to these original sources, and not just relying on summaries in textbooks. Textbooks are useful (otherwise we wouldn't have written one), but there are times when you need to understand the nuances and the detail that you get from the original source material. Reading and observing how the judges actually structure their arguments can also help you learn how to compose and organise legal argument.

So far all we have given you is some basic tools to help you find your way around a case:

- to identify its position in the hierarchy of decision-making;
- to find the structural features that the editors of law reports have introduced to help you to identify the issues, locate the case in the existing law, and understand the principles that the court has adopted or developed in its reasoning; and
- to understand some of the technical terminology used, and its significance.

These tools by themselves will not be enough to enable you to make full sense of a law report. You do need to understand something about the substantive law in the area discussed by your case (that's where textbooks and articles really do play a part), and you also need to understand the principles and practices of legal reasoning, which we will come back to in the later chapters of this book. But you also need to develop a further set of reading and analytical skills that will support you in dealing with materials of the length and technical complexity that you will encounter in law. That is what we will turn to in section **3.3**, and though we focus on using these skills in the context of books and articles, the basic principles can help you with complex primary sources too.

3.3 Reading books and articles

How do you read a book or article?

This may seem like a silly question, but it is not. Educational research has shown that many of us are very inefficient in the way we approach academic reading. Given the time pressures you will face as a student, it is vital that you develop an efficient technique. One that is worth trying is commonly called **SQ3R** (see, e.g., Williams, 1989: 4–5). It describes a sequence of five steps you should follow when looking at books and articles: Survey, Question, Read, Recall, and Review.

3.3.1 Survey

Start by getting a 'feel' for the publication and its potential usefulness. You can do this by looking at the elements outlined in the following subsections.

The title

Yes, we are starting with the obvious, but mind that it is not so obvious that you overlook it! The title may tell you a lot about the author's aims. Consider, for example, what you might be able to tell about the contents from the following (real) book titles:

> *The Law of Contract*
>
> *A Casebook on Contract*
>
> *Nutshells—Contract Law*
>
> *The Rise and Fall of Freedom of Contract*
>
> *Contract Law—Questions and Answers*
>
> *Understanding Contract Law*
>
> *Sourcebook on Obligations and Legal Remedies*

Similarly, phrases in titles or subtitles like 'a student's guide', 'a critical approach', or 'handbook' can also help indicate the level of difficulty or type of approach being taken.

The 'blurb', editorial, or abstract

Books almost invariably have a brief summary of their aims or arguments on the back cover or inside the jacket (if hardback). This is often written—or at least revised—by the author and should provide a reasonable indication of what the book is about, though do not forget that it is also written with the aim of selling the book! Similarly, some, though by no means all, journals either contain an editorial summarising the contents of the particular issue or require authors to provide a brief summary or 'abstract' of their article which gives a guide to the contents. This may provide a useful framework around which you can organise your own notes from your reading.

The date of publication

In a book this is given on either the face or obverse of the title page. In a constantly changing field such as law, recency of publication is important. Most law books will become progressively more out of date as time goes on. Always check the date of publication and be prepared to update accordingly. If the book is more than three or four years old, it is often worth checking a publisher's catalogue to see if there is a later edition or finding a more up-to-date alternative. With journal articles, the problem is more acute. These are not generally updated by revised versions and it can be difficult to check for accuracy other than by returning to primary sources. The older the article, the more careful you may have to be. Having said that, there is no general rule that can tell us when a piece of legal writing is past its 'sell by' date.

Contents page

A quick check of the contents page can also give a useful overview, not just of the bare contents of a book, but of how the material is structured and used. It is a curious reflection on academic cultures that many North American law journals will publish much longer articles than their British or European counterparts. In the United States particularly, articles of 25,000 words or more are not uncommon. It is perhaps unsurprising therefore that in the US journals major articles will normally have their own table of contents.

Preface

A lot of readers will skip the preface or introduction and just focus on the main text of a book. This is often a bad idea. Most prefaces, etc. are written by authors expressly as a way of explaining the thinking behind their books.

3.3.2 Question

Worthwhile reading requires more than staring at the page and trying to soak up the contents like a sponge. You *must* ask yourself questions both before and during your reading. Consider first your objectives in reading the text: what is it you want from this book or article?

- Are you looking for an overview of a topic?
- Are you trying to answer a specific question or legal problem?
- Are you looking for a critical perspective on the law or the context in which it has evolved?

  Use these to focus and cross-check your reading.

3.3.3 Read

Think about how you have been using this book. Have you read everything we have written? Has your reading been all at the same speed, or to the same depth? In fact, it is highly unlikely that you have read every word, and even if you have, you will have varied the depth and pace of your reading. You are almost certainly using a range of reading techniques already, according to the purpose for which you have been reading at the time. It is worth thinking about how you might harness those techniques to make yourself a more efficient and productive reader. In practice we suggest there are three stages to effective reading:

(i)   *Skim* the text for an overview. This can often be best achieved by taking the text a paragraph at a time. When skim reading it is often sufficient to read just the opening sentence or two of each paragraph. Let us explain why. Most well-constructed paragraphs can be split into three elements (this idea is useful in developing your writing skills too): an opening sentence or two, incorporating the 'topic sentence'; an explanatory or discursive middle element; and a closing sentence, which commonly serves to develop the topic sentence as well as to complete the paragraph. The topic sentence is crucial; it provides the main idea of the paragraph and all other sentences develop it and are dependent on it to some degree. Consider the following paragraph as an example (we have given each sentence a number, in brackets, for reasons which will become apparent in a moment):

> Lord Woolf has proposed fundamental and radical changes to the way litigation should be conducted. [1] His diagnosis is that civil justice is in crisis because (among other things) it takes too long, costs too much money and, even when people win, they are unhappy with the process. [2] Although this analysis is far from new, I agree with it. [3] I also agree with Lord Woolf that radical change is needed, not cosmetic surgery. [4] However, reforming the civil justice system for the better 'ain't easy'. [5] This is why, despite some sixty reports in England on aspects of civil procedure since 1851, there has been no lasting solution to the twin problems of cost and delay. [6] The same is true of North America. [7] Our predecessors were neither foolish dullards nor acting in bad faith; reform is simply very difficult. [8] The challenge is not simply to propose change: it is to propose reforms which significantly improve the current position. [9]
>
> (Watson, 1996: 63)

Here, the topic sentence is the first sentence: it tells us that the subject of the paragraph is Lord Woolf's proposals for the reform of civil justice. The later sentences relate back to the topic sentence (TS), albeit at different levels, to expand on or explain the theme it introduces. By identifying the TS, we can quickly spot the focus of that paragraph and thus decide whether to ignore it or return to it for a further reading and analysis. In longer paragraphs it can sometimes be helpful to skim the last sentence or two as well, to help us see where the argument is going.

(ii)   It follows, then, that the second stage is to *identify* those elements of the text which need to be read in detail. Do not make notes at this stage, other than to identify the bits to which you will return. You need to concentrate on understanding the text at the level of an overview first. Only once you have done this are you really ready for the next stage.

(iii) *Read in detail*. This is never the first stage in effective reading. Indeed, you will often find that there is material you will never have to read in detail because by surveying the text and skim reading you can establish that *it is of absolutely no use to you whatsoever*. If you start by reading in detail, you risk wasting time on something that is of little or no practical help, whatever its intrinsic worth may be!

Reading in detail will usually involve two distinct processes:

(a) reading for understanding; and

(b) reading critically.

Again, we will take each of these ideas in turn.

You can really know something only if you understand it. Reading for understanding is therefore a central part of the learning process. Often you will find understanding does not come easily. The ideas represented in a piece of writing may be complex; sometimes they may not be clearly expressed. It may be necessary for you to work hard at unpicking the meaning. Here again, it is often helpful to work through the text a paragraph at a time. If you can make sense of the structure and order of the writer's ideas at this level, you will have a better chance of grasping their meaning. There are better ways of doing this than staring at the page and waiting for inspiration.

Think back to what we said about paragraph organisation in the section on skim reading. You will recall that we said that all sentences in a paragraph relate back to the topic sentence (TS), but at different levels. So, there will be sentences which are directly subordinate to the topic sentence (Level 2 sentences), but also other sentences which illustrate or modify the Level 2 sentences and so are subordinate to them (Level 3 sentences) and, in more complex paragraphs, so on. Maughan and Maughan (2015) have shown how we might use a tree diagram more effectively to identify this relationship and thereby to extract the meaning from a paragraph (see **Figure 3.4**).

We suggest that this technique can help us to untangle long and complex paragraphs. We can, however, start with a straightforward example, using the extract from Garry Watson's paper quoted earlier in the section. If we apply their approach here, we get a structure that looks like this (the numbers in brackets correspond to the sentence numbers in the text).

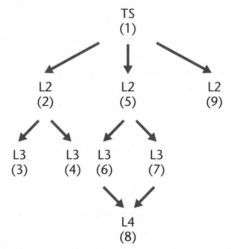

Figure 3.4. Topic and subordinate sentences

Thus Sentence 1, the TS, introduces the main theme:

Lord Woolf has proposed radical reforms.

This is developed by Sentence 2 (L2):

Woolf says reform is necessary because of delays, etc.

which is then modified by Sentences 3 and 4 (L3):

I agree with Lord Woolf.

Sentence 5 (L2) returns to the topic sentence to qualify it:

But reforming civil justice is not easy.

The statement in Sentence 5 is then justified by Sentences 6 and 7 (L3):

Just look at the impact of previous attempts in the UK and N. America

and Sentence 8 (L4) then emphasises the point by saying, in effect:

and it was not for want of trying.

Lastly, Sentence 9 returns to the TS with a final modification that is crucial to the later development of the argument:

Proposing radical reform is one thing: making a difference is another.

It is quite possible that you would analyse this, or any paragraph, slightly differently from us. That is because it is ultimately your interpretation of what the writer is saying, and which sentence is subordinate to which may well be debatable. That relationship is not really important for our purposes. What is important is that you can see a logical structure to the paragraph which establishes, develops, and ultimately modifies or transforms a basic theme. Once you can see that development, it becomes much easier to understand what the writer is trying to achieve. We do not suggest that you need to work through everything as systematically as this, but you would probably find this technique helpful with any material you are struggling to understand. Note also that in our analysis we have used paraphrases of Watson's text, rather than verbatim quotations. This too is deliberate—the process of translating another person's words into your own is also an important step on the path to understanding.

If your purpose is critical, in that, for example, you are attempting to analyse or challenge the ideas presented by a particular author, your reading must be directed to that purpose. In that case you must consider how the author has developed his argument. Has he:

(i)   made any unsupported or unrecognised assumptions?

(ii)   reached conclusions unsupported by his argument?

(iii) ignored counter-arguments that exist?

Often, a comparison of different texts can help you sort out the range of arguments and counter-arguments which exist. Do not fall into the trap of being dependent upon a single book or article when constructing any kind of critical analysis. Literary sources may also be of assistance if you are attempting some critical analysis of a case or statutory provision.

Finally, always remember, when reading, what your purpose is. If you are unsure, stop, think, and read again.

3.3.4 Recall

In the recall phase you are really trying to test yourself on what the text was about. It is at this point that you should begin to make notes.

Note-taking is an integral part of effective, detailed reading. Simply photocopying text and going through it with a highlighter is a poor substitute for the kind of mental processing of information that takes place when making notes on your source material. Whether making handwritten notes is more effective than using a laptop or tablet may be moot. Research into the cognitive processing of lectures tends to suggest that typing and handwriting lecture notes result in appreciably different learning outcomes. Experiments show that those who write out notes by hand tend to have a stronger conceptual understanding and are more successful in applying and integrating the material than laptop users. Though the latter are able to take more verbatim notes, they may, consequently, process the material less, leading to lower retention of the information (see, e.g., May, 2014).

Do *not* take verbatim notes as you read. Read first, then make your notes. Obviously longer pieces of text need to be broken down into manageable chunks for this technique to work—no one can make meaningful notes on a whole book at one, two, or even three sittings! But why not make notes as you read? We advise against this for three reasons. First, it is difficult to assess just how critical any part of the text is before you have completed the whole; you are therefore more likely to misrepresent your source this way. Secondly, delaying note-taking encourages you to think about what you have read. Thirdly, it reduces the likelihood of one kind of *plagiarism*, that is, of quoting someone else's work without attribution. This is an academic cardinal sin, and can be a ground for failure under the academic regulations of every law degree we have come across. However, it can be very easy to confuse quoted or paraphrased material from your own notes if you are not careful about maintaining that distinction. If you must take down verbatim extracts, make sure it is clear to you what is quoted material and what is not. Williams (1989: 30) also suggests the following guidelines for good note-taking practice:

(i) **Record your source**: make sure that you keep a note of the full reference for your source material. You will need this for any works you cite in your bibliography, and you may need to locate it again. Note the author(s), the title, publisher, or journal name, year, and page reference(s). If it is a library book, it can save time later if you note the library (shelving) classification too. If you are doing an extended piece of project work, where you are likely to have a large number of references, it may be helpful to note each reference on individual index cards which can be stored as a permanent record. Alternatively, there are a number of cheap 'shareware' computer programs which can enable you to produce an electronic index of references that can be downloaded to a document file for word processing, or you may use specialist bibliographic software like *Zotero* (see www.zotero.org)—which is a free, web-based research database tool—or commercial equivalents such as *Endnote*, to which you may have access via your university network.

(ii) **Show the main ideas clearly**: what are the key points/arguments to come out of the text? Identify them! Show also how the main ideas are linked and what supporting points are used for each.

(iii) **Be brief**: do not take copious notes unless you have to. It may be better to take brief notes at first, and come back to the source later if more detail proves necessary.

(iv) **Be selective**: avoid lengthy illustrations, asides, etc. If an example helps you to understand a point, outline it briefly. Make a note of the page reference of any examples you are uncertain about using.

(v) **Leave notes well spaced on the page**: this enables you to fill in with more detail later on (if necessary).

3.3.5 Review

Williams (1989: 5) also suggests that the review process has two elements. One is retrospective, the other prospective. First, you can quickly review the first four stages of **SQ3R** to check your progress:

- *Survey* the whole text to remind yourself of the structure.
- *Question*—what was your purpose? What were the specific questions to which you wanted answers?
- *Read* the text by skimming only. Are there any points you have missed?
- *Recall*—check your notes. Are there any gaps? Have you found answers to your questions?

From here you need, finally, to think about what you will do with your notes. It may be that they will serve a one-off purpose, contributing to an essay, say. Even so, it is worth putting them aside for a day or two, to see if they still make sense or whether they need further revision or correction. However, it is more likely that they will form part of your knowledge bank for the future (for end-of-year examinations perhaps), in which case you will need to consider what future strategies of review and refinement you intend to adopt as part of your preparation for that event.

EXERCISE 3 SQ3R squared

Ask yourself the question, 'How can the SQ3R method improve my study skills?' Now, using SQ3R, work through the relevant sections of this chapter, and see what answer you come up with.

Of course, we are not going to give you an answer to this one—that is for you to decide! Having said that, the technique is tried and trusted, and most people should get something of value from it. You should consider trying out SQ3R on an assignment. Do not be put off just because it may take you longer than your conventional research and reading methods. The time invested should pay off in the long run, both in terms of greater conceptual understanding as you progress through your course and in terms of better (and, hopefully, easier) preparation for examinations.

✦ CONCLUSION

In this chapter we have provided you with a set of concepts and tools to enable you better to understand both primary and secondary legal sources. There is perhaps a danger at this stage of having replaced the myth that the law can be found in one book with another, more sophisticated version, which says that law is simply about constructing a solution from a variety of written sources. Provided your research is adequate, and you understand how to go about reading what you have found, you will come up with the answer. To an extent there is some truth in that, but the reality is rather more uncertain.

In practice, the process of reading the law does not operate in a vacuum; it is not an arid activity, but one that is applied in real legal disputes. Going to law is not simply a case of lawyers dusting down the appropriate statutes and cases, and reading them (though that will inevitably be part of it); it is, at its heart, a process of reconstructing disputed events ('the facts') and proposing a legal solution to them. We touch on this again, briefly, in **Chapter 5**, but before we get there, we turn our attention from the process of reading to writing.

EXERCISE 4 Attempting the impossible

Before attempting this exercise, you are advised to read and make notes on:

(a) The case of *R v Shivpuri* [1986] 2 All ER 334—an important case in both criminal law and legal method. You are advised to use the All England report, as the answers make specific reference to that version.

(b) The introductory parts and s. 1 of the Criminal Attempts Act 1981.

Make sure that you understand the basic context of the dispute—i.e. what the case was about; why it was before the particular court hearing the case; what that court decided; and why. Once you have done so, you should be ready to test your comprehension against the following questions.

Q QUESTIONS

1. Starting with the Criminal Attempts Act, let us check your basic information:

(a) What is its full citation?

(b) When did it receive the royal assent?

(c) What is the subject of Part I of the Act?

2. Is the short title (Answer YES or NO to each of the points):

(a) an accurate statement of what the Act is about?

(b) capable of assisting our interpretation of the Act?

continued

EXERCISE 4 *continued*

3. Answer TRUE or FALSE to each of the points:
Section 1 of the Act:

(a) makes it a statutory offence to attempt to commit an indictable offence;

(b) seeks to exclude from criminal attempts any significant steps towards a crime where the offence is in fact impossible to complete;

(c) includes within the definition of an attempt any acts of an accused which he believes would involve the commission of a crime, but which, if completed, would not, in reality, be criminal.

4. Turning to *R* v *Shivpuri*:

(a) Which court's decision appears in the report cited?

(b) In which court(s) had the case appeared previously?

5. Which of the statements that follow contain(s) a material (i.e. important) fact (there may be more than one)?

(a) The accused believed he was carrying heroin or cannabis.

(b) The substance in the suitcase was not a prohibited drug.

(c) The full offence of 'dealing' could not be committed.

6. Which of the statements that follow reflect(s) the legal issue(s) at the root of the appeal? Again, there may be more than one right answer:

(a) A merely 'preparatory' action constitutes an attempt in English law.

(b) It is possible to be convicted of attempting to commit an offence where the facts make its actual commission impossible.

(c) The requirement that the accused acted 'knowingly' means that the prosecution must prove that the accused knew it was a particular controlled drug.

7. Do the judges all agree on the outcome of the case (YES or NO)?

8. Was that outcome:

(a) that the appeal was upheld on the question of attempting the impossible?

(b) that the appeal was dismissed because the judge had wrongly advised (*misdirected*) the jury?

(c) that the appeal was dismissed on the question of attempting the impossible?

(d) that the appeal was dismissed on both issues (i.e. attempting the impossible and on the misdirection of the jury)?

9. What was *Shivpuri*'s impact on the standing of the earlier decision in *Anderton* v *Ryan*? Did it:

(a) overrule it?

(b) apply it?

(c) distinguish it?

continued

EXERCISE 4 *continued*

 ANSWERS

1. (a) It is cited as the Criminal Attempts Act 1981, c. (i.e. chapter) 47.

   (b) It received the royal assent on 27 July 1981 (the date given just below the long title).

   (c) Simply 'Attempts, etc'! This is to distinguish it from the repeal of the so-called 'sus' laws created under the Vagrancy Act 1824, which form the subject of Part II (see the 'Arrangement of Sections' and long title).

2. (a) is correct; it is a brief but accurate description.

   (b) No is the correct answer here: if you got this wrong, think back to the 'Strawberry Jam' analogy used earlier in this chapter.

3. (a) **TRUE**: this is the combined effect of subsections (1) and (4)—the latter restricts liability only to indictable (i.e. serious) criminal offences.

   (b) **FALSE**: this statement actually reverses the effect of subsection (2), which deals with cases of 'factual impossibility'—e.g. the situation where A attempts to poison B with a substance which is, in fact, harmless.

   (c) **TRUE**: this is the most difficult to work out. Subsection (3) is concerned with the intention of the accused. So long as the accused intends to commit the offence, it does not matter that, because of some mistake on his part about the law, what he does is not a crime. A widely cited example is the situation where A has sexual intercourse with B, believing her to be under the legal age of consent. Technically, A has committed the offence of attempting unlawful sexual intercourse, even though B is not in fact 'under age'.

4. (a) The House of Lords.

   (b) The Crown Court and Court of Appeal—see 335i.

5. This comes close to being a trick question! All three of (a), (b), and (c) would have been material questions of fact. That this is the case with (a) and (b) should be reasonably evident. The accused's belief and the nature of the substance are both material to the question of attempting the impossible; they are both matters which are proved by evidence. Item (c) is rather more difficult. The definition of an offence is a matter of law; but that is not the point here. Here, the issue is one of proving that the accused could not commit the offence. That, we suggest, is a matter of fact.

6. (b) and (c) are both correct. Statement (b) is probably the more obvious answer, but the issue identified by (c) also arises, e.g. at 339b *per* Lord Bridge. (a) is incorrect; though this point has arisen in a number of cases, it was not critical here—see e.g. Lord Bridge, at 342g.

7. Yes is the right answer, though they do not necessarily arrive at the same outcome for the same reasons. If you got this one wrong it is probably because you have confused the result of the appeal with the reasoning used by the judges to come to their decision (see further the answer to Question 9). They should always be kept separate in your mind.

continued

EXERCISE 4 *continued*

8. (d) is the correct answer. The misdirection point is less obviously a ground of the appeal, but it is raised by the defence and discussed by the House of Lords. They held that though there had been a technical misdirection, it had caused no miscarriage of justice, and so could be disregarded under their Lordships' statutory powers—see Lord Bridge, at approximately 341d–h.

9. The correct answer is (a). The decision of the House was unanimous in this respect; though Lords Hailsham and MacKay state that they would have been content to distinguish *Anderton* v *Ryan* (see 337b and 345h), they do not actually dissent from the judgment given by Lord Bridge.

CHAPTER REFERENCES

Bebr, G. (1992), 'Case Law', 29 *Common Market Law Review*, 577.

Biavati, P. (2011), *European Civil Procedure* (Alphen aan den Rijn, The Netherlands: Wolters Kluwer).

Drewry, G. (1973), 'Leapfrogging—and a Lord Justice's Eye View of the Final Appeal', 89 *Law Quarterly Review*, 260.

Edward, D. (2004), 'Luxembourg in Retrospect: A New Europe in Prospect', 16 *European Business Journal*, 120.

Maughan, C. and Maughan, M. (2017), 'Legal Writing', in J. Webb et al., *Lawyers' Skills* (21st edn, Oxford: Oxford University Press).

May, C. (2014), 'A Learning Secret: Don't Take Notes with a Laptop', *Scientific American*, 3 June 2014. Available at www.scientificamerican.com/article/a-learning-secret-don-t-take-notes-with-a-laptop.

Paterson, A. (2015), '*Final Judgment* Revisited', 21(1) *European Journal of Current Legal Issues*. Available at http://webjcli.org/article/view/418/531.

Regan, D. (2014), 'Ward of Court', *New Law Journal*, 19 September 2014. Available at www.newlawjournal.co.uk/nlj/content/ward-court.

Robinson, W. (2008), 'Drafting of EU Acts: A View from the European Commission', in C. Stefanou and H. Xanthaki (eds), *Legislative Drafting: A Modern Approach* (Aldershot: Ashgate).

Toshkov, D. (n.d.), '55 years of EU Legislation', online presentation. Available at www.dimiter.eu/Eurlex.html.

Vranken, M. (1996), 'Role of the Advocate General in the Law-making Process of the European Community', 25 *Anglo-American Law Review*, 39.

Watson, G. (1996), 'From an Adversarial to a Managed System of Litigation: A Comparative Critique of Lord Woolf's Interim Report', in R. Smith (ed.), *Achieving Civil Justice* (London: Legal Action Group), 63.

*Williams, K. (1989), *Study Skills* (Basingstoke: Macmillan).

ONLINE RESOURCES

Test your knowledge by trying the self-test questions that accompany **Chapters 1–6**. Visit: www.oup.com/uk/holland-webb10e

4

From Reading to Writing

The processes of reading and note-taking will often be the precursor to a specific writing task—an essay or examination script. In this chapter we will consider briefly the techniques involved in basic academic legal writing, an aspect of one of the key skills required by employers, namely, written communication. There are many good, specialist, books on the market which cover general academic skills such as oral communication, mooting, team work, etc. (we have listed some at the end of the chapter), but here we want to introduce you to some of the basic requirements for producing what is still the most common form of assessment: written pieces of work.

4.1 Writing legal essays

Writing legal essays is essentially about three things:

- conveying information;
- constructing an *argument* based on the information you have acquired;
- applying the information and the arguments to the essay title or the problem posed.

4.1.1 Conveying information

Any essay you are asked to write will require you to tell the reader what you know about the subject under discussion. This requires more than the mere description of cases or statutes, or a summary of a textbook. *Description* is not the same as *explanation*. Lecturers, examiners, or judges want to see your analysis and an explanation of your argument. As with poor TV sports commentators, simply telling the viewer/reader what they can already see is not much use.

In conveying that information there are three cardinal rules, set out as follows.

Cardinal rule 1: be accurate

Try to be as precise as possible in the information you put down. Vagueness is a sure sign of a lack of understanding or insufficient thought. If it is not possible to give an accurate statement of the principles involved (perhaps because the law is in a muddle), then say that there is no single answer and *clearly distinguish any alternatives that seem to exist.*

Precision involves accuracy and clarity of meaning. 'Accuracy' speaks for itself: make sure your source material is up to date and that you present the material or any summary of it correctly. Clarity depends upon the *style* of presentation that you use. By this we mean your choice of words, construction of sentences, and use of grammar. Style is important because a good style enhances the exposition of your arguments, which can be only as good as your ability to express them. Do not ignore the fact that language has its own rhythm, and this can often guide you to sentences or phrases which do or do not work. Some people find that reading work aloud helps in this, because if a phrase sounds wrong it probably is wrong. Some people test out their work on friends who know nothing about the subject to see if the essay is clear enough.

An example of a very good writing style (even when the decisions are questionable) can be found in most of Lord Denning's judgments. He tended to favour a mixture of short and long sentences (with the balance in favour of short sentences). This creates a pattern that most people find attractive to read. Here is one of Lord Denning's more famous openings (from the case of *Hinz* v *Berry* [1970] 2 QB 40):

> It happened on 19 April 1964. It was bluebell time in Kent. Mr and Mrs Hinz, the plaintiff, had been married some ten years, and they had four children, all aged nine and under. The youngest was one. The plaintiff was a remarkable woman. In addition to her own four, she was foster mother to four other children. To add to it, she was two months pregnant with her fifth child.

This was a case about negligence in a car accident and claims for nervous shock. You might not know this from the opening paragraph. So, forget about the content: look at the patterns created and how they draw you into the narrative. It is a homely style, but one which engages you. We are not suggesting you copy the homeliness of the style: merely that you see the pattern of sentences and how they easily convey meaning. Here is another example (from a case called *Thornton* v *Shoe Lane Parking* [1971] 2 QB 163). The passage centres on the point at which a contract is formed when driving up to an automated ticket machine. Lord Denning starts by referring to existing authorities that dealt in general terms with terms appearing on tickets. Again, look at the use of short and long sentences:

> These cases were based on the theory that the customer, on being handed the ticket, could refuse it and decline to enter into a contract on those terms. He could ask for his money back. That theory was, of course, a fiction. No customer in a thousand ever read the conditions. If he had stopped to do so, he would have missed the train or the boat. None of those cases has any application to a ticket which is issued by an automatic machine. The customer pays his money and gets a ticket. He cannot refuse it. He cannot get his money back. He may protest to the machine, even swear at it; but it will remain unmoved. He is committed beyond recall. He was committed at the very moment when he put his money into the machine. The contract was concluded at that time. It can be translated into offer and acceptance in this way. The offer is made when the proprietor of the machine holds it out as being ready to receive the money. The acceptance takes place when the customer puts his money into the slot.

A similar style can be found in the judgments of Laddie J. (e.g. here in a case called *Series 5 Software Ltd* v *Clarke* [1996] 1 All ER 853). Note how the learned judge mixes short and longer sentences, as needed, to explain the points:

> The basic outline of the dispute between the parties is as follows. The plaintiff is a company which is engaged in the development, production and sale of computer software for use in the printing and publishing industry. It commenced trading in June, 1992. Its main product is a software system called 'QC 2000' which enables print shops to quote, manage and schedule their production. It claims that it employed Mr Jenkinson, the fifth defendant, in February, 1995 as a technician, Mr Clarke, the first defendant, in June, 1995 as a sales manager and Mr Wheeler, the fourth defendant, as a computer programmer. The employment did not last long. By letters of August 25, 1995 all the defendants resigned. The three defendants say that this was because they had all been treated very shabbily. Their salaries were paid with cheques which were not honoured or they simply were not paid at all. There is little dispute as to this…

An example of how to refer to case law in a simple manner can be found in Dillon LJ's judgment in *Interfoto Picture Library Ltd* v *Stiletto Visual Programmes Ltd* [1989] QB 433, at 438:

> Counsel for the plaintiffs submits that *Thornton* v *Shoe Lane Parking Ltd* [1971] 2 Q.B. 613 was a case of an exemption clause and that what their Lordships said must be read as limited to exemption clauses and in particular exemption clauses which would deprive the party on whom they are imposed of statutory rights. But what their Lordships said was said by way of interpretation and application of the general statement of the law by Mellish LJ in *Parker* v *South Eastern Railway Co.*, 2 C.P.D. 416, 423–424 and the logic of it is applicable to any particularly onerous clause in a printed set of conditions of the one contracting party which would not be generally known to the other party. Condition 2 of these plaintiffs' conditions is in my judgment a very onerous clause.

This has two long sentences and one short sentence, but clearly lays out a pattern, a structure that is easy to follow. His Lordship sets up the proposition (put by counsel), disagrees with this by reference to his interpretation of the authorities, and then sets about applying that analysis to the facts. Note also that in **Exercise 11** in **Chapter 7** we give some examples of how cases can be cited in essays.

It is equally important to avoid jargon or words you do not understand. Do not be like the famous Mrs Malaprop in Sheridan's play 'The Rivals', with her 'nice derangement [arrangement] of epitaphs' and her 'very pineapple [pinnacle] of politeness'. If in doubt, use a dictionary or a thesaurus to bring in alternative vocabulary.

Cardinal rule 2: be relevant

Do not introduce something you know or suspect to be irrelevant into an answer. There is a great temptation to throw every possible bit of information you have at the question, and hope that some of it is right (what many lecturers call a 'shotgun' approach). This does not look impressive, as it again suggests a lack of forethought. Keeping to what is relevant is not magic; it is simply a question of familiarity with and understanding of your material. If you have taken the time to analyse the question, and thought out what is expected of you, there should be no need to adopt such an approach.

Cardinal rule 3: be concise

In our experience, lecturers do not award marks on the basis of the number of pages filled. It is obviously impossible for us to state what the 'average' acceptable length of an essay is, as criteria vary from course to course and year to year. You should always be guided by your tutors as to what is required. If you are given an indication of the appropriate length or there is a word limit, then any significant shortfall normally indicates that something is missing and any excess may incur penalties.

Brevity is not, ultimately, just about the number of words you use; it is about how you use them. Again, it is a matter of clarity. As seen under 'Cardinal rule 1: be accurate', you can use short sentences but you can also add interest and explain related ideas by using some longer sentences. Remember, though, that a sentence should always make sense, and that each separate issue you discuss deserves its own paragraph. For example, a common misuse of sentences seems to be the 'hanging sentence' such as this:

- *'Whereas the claimant has a good case. Therefore he should be advised to bring a claim.'* The first 'sentence' does not make sense: it goes nowhere and is technically not a sentence at all.

Here is another example:

- *'As counsel failed in her professional capacity to secure the company's costs. Then surely she should pay the costs herself as she was engaged as a competent and qualified person.'* You might just be able to run these together (with some amendments) to make one sentence, but, as they stand, neither 'sentence' does its job.

A sentence is a complete idea, capable of standing on its own. Forgive us for also making the basic point that a sentence begins with a capital letter and ends with a full stop. In addition, it must contain a main clause that usually has a subject, verb, and object, though it may contain much more. In our first example the student probably meant to write something like: *'The claimant appears to have a good case and should be advised to bring a claim.'*

Sentences full of long words do not impress unless they convey a meaning not otherwise possible. Lawyers, perhaps more than any other profession, have a reputation for pomposity. It is a reputation that is not wholly undeserved.

4.1.2 Language

Formal legal writing is still perceived to be very different from everyday English. Indeed, there are those who suspect that its connexions with the English language are little more than coincidental. This is because, at its worst, it not only uses technical terms outside the general language, but also uses forms of language and phrasing that are archaic and often redundant—documents full of jargon interspersed with the occasional 'whatsoever', 'wheresoever', 'heretofore', and 'hereafter'. In a brilliant parody, James D. Gordon III (1991: 1689) offers a classic example of such 'legalese'; a lawyer's translation of the phrase, 'I give you this orange':

> Know all men by these presents that I hereby give, grant, bargain, sell, release, convey, transfer, and quitclaim all my right, title, interest, benefit and use whatever in, of, and concerning this chattel, otherwise known as an orange, or citrus orantium, together with all the appurtenances thereto of

skin, pulp, pip, rind, seeds and juice, to have and to hold the said orange together with its skin, pulp, pip, rind, seeds and juice for his own use and behoof, to himself and his heirs in fee simple forever, free from all liens, encumbrances, easements, limitations, restraints or conditions whatsoever, and all prior deeds, transfers or other documents whatsoever, now or anywhere made to the contrary notwithstanding, with full power to bite, cut, suck or otherwise eat the said orange or to give away the same, with or without its skin, pulp, pip, rind, seeds or juice.

Fortunately, this kind of 'supernatural incantation' (to borrow Gordon's phrase) is becoming far less common in legal practice, where there is a growing tendency to simplify documents and to move towards a system of 'plain English' drafting (see Watson-Brown, 2009). Although mastery of technical legal language is a requisite for both the study and practice of law, jargon used for its own sake has no place in the law school. Do not let your choice of words turn your work into a parody of legal language.

However, there is no escaping the fact that legal language is littered with Latin and Norman-French words: *ratio decidendi, stare decisis, autrefois acquit, puisne* judges, to name but a few. Many of these have, quite rightly, been abandoned—at least when talking to clients. However, that is a recent development and the law reports are full of such terms, so when you read a report from, say, 1950 you will encounter these and it is best to have a working knowledge of what they mean. Oddly enough, the one Latin term most lawyers come across very early in their studies (*mens rea*) does not mean what most textbooks say it means ('guilty mind') but just means 'mind thing' and the Romans never used this as a legal term anyway.

Legal jargon can also arise in unexpected quarters. A question once asked of one of the authors by an employment tribunal judge in Truro in an unfair dismissal case ('Are you asking me to read that *eiusdem generis* with the rest of the section so as to incorporate a notion of *mens rea?*') would not have been well received with a response of: 'I have no idea what you are talking about.' The case later went to the Court of Appeal on this very point: the question of whether one should use the criminal law concept of *mens rea* in employment misconduct cases.

All this need not be as terrifying as it first appears: we use Norman-French and Latin words every day. In a legal setting the following are all of Norman-French derivation yet they are used widely: accused, defendant, perjury, judgment, jury, arson, and dungeon. In a non-legal setting, we have words such as bacon, pork, and beef (which, when out in the fields and not on the table, retain their Saxon names of pig and cow). Latin phrases such as *caveat emptor, ad nauseam, per se,* and *et cetera* are used frequently in ordinary conversation. English developed from a whole range of languages—chiefly, Latin, Ancient Greek, Norman-French, the Germanic and Scandinavian languages, and later Hindi and Urdu—adopting and adapting them when necessary. This is one of its great strengths.

4.1.3 Constructing an argument

Essay writing is about constructing an *argument* based on the information you have acquired. Essay questions inevitably ask you to structure your material in one way or another. The clue usually lies in the first or last words of the question: 'Consider critically'; 'Discuss'; 'Evaluate', and so on. The greatest failing of all is to miss the significance of those words and simply 'write all you know' about a topic without bringing any critical faculty into play. 'Discuss' is the most general of these: anything else tends to narrow the field of enquiry.

The key thing to remember about argument in academic writing is that there are certain conventional rules about what constitutes a 'good argument'. If you have had little or no previous experience of this type of writing, it is something you will certainly need to think about and practise. There are many useful publications on study skills, and we have listed some of them at the end of this chapter. We can briefly summarise the techniques here.

Authority

When lawyers use the word 'authority' we are referring to *legal* authority, i.e. cases and legislation together with academic sources, such as textbooks and journals. A good legal argument requires authority: it is insufficient to rely on your own value judgements or 'common sense'. **Any arguments you advance must be supported by authority from primary source (cases, legislation) or at least secondary sources (legal academic literature). Primary sources take precedence over secondary sources**.

Your own value judgements do not constitute evidence of how things work. To be blunt: your opinion does not matter unless it is backed by legal authority. Value judgements also personalise the debate, so that your arguments will lack a sense of objectivity. You may bring an element of value judgement into play in a conclusion, for example, where you have to choose between two established alternative arguments, but even then, you should indicate why one argument is to be preferred. Your preference should be supportable on rational grounds, not just on the basis that 'I think it is the better answer' or 'this is fairer'. Common sense is of no more worth than one person's value judgement. New bulletins are replete with interviews following court cases where one hears: 'A great example of British justice' from the winners, and 'A mockery of British justice' from the losers. These are obviously (often heartfelt) subjective views.

An argument is not necessarily true because the proponent believes most other people would support it. For instance, it is 'common knowledge' that before Christopher Columbus discovered America everyone thought the world was flat. First, he did not discover America (even from a European perspective) and secondly, at the time of his journey in 1492 very few people thought the world was flat—and had not thought so since the time of the Ancient Greeks. He was trying to sail around the world to find a quicker route to Japan/India; that is how he raised the money for the voyage, so a flat world would have been a problem. Nevertheless, possibly under the influence of the lyric 'They all laughed at Christopher Columbus when he said the world was round' (in the song 'They all laughed' by Ira and George Gershwin), there is the commonly held belief that our ancestors were a little on the stupid side. So much for generally held beliefs.

Having a plan

A good argument is built up carefully. In developing that argument, it is important to have a plan of where you are going and, to persuade most people, arguments need to be developed gradually. A good essay comprises three elements:

- introduction;
- discussion; and
- conclusion.

Your introduction should explain what you are setting out to do. Your discussion should display the relevant information, derived from the appropriate sources, and show clearly on what side of the argument each piece falls. The conclusion should sum up the main points you have made and make clear your conclusions regarding the question asked. Keep these separate functions clearly in mind. Do not fall into the trap of presenting a lengthy ramble through the detail of the law, followed by a final paragraph containing a number of disparate critical remarks. That does not constitute an argument.

We return to this theme in **Exercise 11** in **Chapter 7**. There we have set out how an essay may be written using the structure described earlier and how you would cite relevant authorities. As the 'essay' concerns points discussed in **Chapters 6** and **7** we have left this fuller account until you have read those chapters.

Use of visual aids

You may find it helpful when planning an answer to reduce your plan to a diagrammatic form. Space precludes us from exploring the options in any depth, but you should be aware that there are a number of techniques you can use, including flowcharts and 'decision trees', which help you to construct a logical framework for ideas or processes, and 'mind maps' (see Buzan, 2002), which provide, it is said, a less formally structured way into a problem, and therefore a less restrictive and more powerful way of identifying the issues and making connexions between ideas. For examples of how each of these can be used to support legal problem solving, see Maughan and Webb (2005: ch. 10). **Figure 4.1** is a simple flowchart which could be used to examine the question of offer and acceptance in the law of contract.

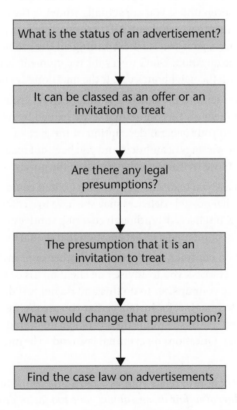

Figure 4.1 Law of contract: offer and acceptance

A final word of warning: good planning and good writing technique can never wholly disguise a lack of content. It can, however, enable you to use your knowledge to its best effect. Failure to abide by the basic rules can be met with the kind of indignity once meted out to an attorney by the United States Supreme Court. The Court returned a brief with the instruction that a whole new set of papers be filed in a form that was 'logically arranged... concise and free from burdensome, irrelevant and immaterial matter...' (*Gilchrist* v *Interborough Rapid Transit Co.* (1929) 279 US 159). Back in the United Kingdom, in 2008, one judge referred to a prosecutor who kept saying 'grievious bodily harm' instead of 'grievous bodily harm' as 'an illiterate idiot'. We hope that none of your work receives a similar response.

4.1.4 Applying the information

We will explore this more fully in section **4.2** as regards the key topic of 'problem questions' but the idea of 'application' also relates to writing what may be termed 'pure essays' (the ones that have a quote or statement followed by 'Discuss' or something similar). The basic rule with these essays is to try to relate your answer throughout the text to the statement posed (i.e. do not write everything you know about a topic and then have a conclusion which starts, 'So, as can be seen, the statement is true...'). Here are some preliminary matters you need to note which concern all legal problems and essay questions set at academic stage:

- There is always a potential problem of proving the facts (a question of evidence). With such questions, however, unless you are actually studying the law of evidence, this is not something you need to worry about. All these questions are posed on the basis that the facts can be proven, so if you start examining all the problems of proof you will not be answering the question. Don't worry for the moment as to how we know that 'Patrick wanted to kill the neighbour's cat'. If the question says he did, then he did.

- Pure essay questions tend to present you with an extract from a book or judgment and ask you to comment on this. More marks are gained by relating your answer to the quotation than to your general description of the area of law in question. If the question is about the writings of author X and you have not read her words and do not relate your essay to those writings you have missed the point.

- The question might ask you to discuss X's possible guilt. It could ask something different, for example, 'What possible defences may she have to a charge of murder?' or 'For what crimes might X be charged?' Although covering similar ground, these questions raise slightly different points and it is that question that should be answered specifically.

- In problems based on contract, negligence, and other civil matters it is quite common for the examiner to ask you to advise one client on his or her potential liability. If this is so, structure your answer to do this and do not just describe the legal position generally. Try to imagine, for instance, that you are giving advice to a real client sitting in front of you. He or she wants their problem answered, not a general lecture on the law of trespass. Questions on criminal law tend to be more straightforward: is X guilty or not?

Here is an example of how to relate your essay to a title which reads: '*Most employers now believe that the law of unfair dismissal has gone too far in providing all employees with statutory rights which restrict the managerial prerogative of employers. Discuss.*' The statement asks for comment on a specific issue, not for a rambling exposition of the law on unfair dismissal. The comment is deliberately provocative and reflects how many employers mistakenly perceive the law on unfair dismissal to be biased in the employees' favour (the irony being that most employees think it is balanced in the employers' favour). So, one comment (early on) could be:

Before we discuss the merits of the claims made in the essay title we should note that the statement contains a common fallacy: it is based on the premise that *all* employees have the right to claim unfair dismissal. This is not true: in most cases only those employed for two years or more gain this right.

Another example might be:

When the statement in issue refers to 'managerial prerogative' it begs the question: what is 'managerial prerogative'? If it means that employers should have the right to dismiss without reason or justification, then it is certainly the case that the law restricts their freedom.

4.2 Answering legal problems

In studying law many of you will encounter what law teachers call 'problem questions' for the first time. Most students find these the best part of studying law because, to a limited extent, you are trying to apply the law to the facts as if in real life. Indeed, as we noted in section **4.1.4**, a good way to approach these questions is to imagine a real client asking you for advice (and then to imagine how, if you were the client, that advice addresses your concerns). The basic techniques of introduction and discussion which we have already considered apply to problems as much as essays, but you must be aware of the fact that you are dealing with a different kind of question.

The essence of any problem question is that it requires you to analyse some fictitious situation and consider questions of legal liability that it creates. As with arguments in court, your best friend is a sound structure. Take the reader/judge on a clearly defined path, perhaps laying out the pattern you wish to follow from the start, as in 'There are three aspects to the case here: A, B, and C. All must be proven before liability can be imposed. Should the claimant fail on any one ground it is submitted that that will be enough for the case to be dismissed. I will deal with these in turn.' (In court you have to insert a lot of 'May it please your Honour' and other displays of good manners—or obsequious comments depending on your viewpoint.) Essays should generally be framed in the 'third person' as in 'It is submitted that . . .'.

The precise scope of your answer will depend on what you are asked to do. The facts will normally be followed by some such request as 'Discuss'; 'Advise Ann'; or 'Advise Ken of his liability to Lee'. Do not ignore this: questions of standpoint and objective are as important to the student as the practitioner; so, in dealing with problems always remember who you are advising and what you are trying to do. For example, it may be that the problem concerning Ken and Lee also involves a third party, Mary. But if you have not been asked about Mary's rights or liabilities, it would be a serious error to discuss them. If 'Discuss' is used, then you have a freer rein.

Problem questions are usually constructed on a number of levels. Chiefly, this enables teachers to differentiate more clearly between the various qualities of answer. Most will therefore have one or two major issues, plus a number of less obvious legal points, or 'twists' to the facts which, for example, could distinguish the events from an earlier case which you might cite as a precedent. Particularly in examinations, it can be difficult to sort out the factual material and assess its legal implications in the time available. There is no instant solution to this. The answer lies in having a good working knowledge of the relevant law (this helps you to identify those facts which will have legal significance) and in adopting a systematic approach to the question.

By 'systematic' we mean that you must learn to use the question to help construct an answer. Let us explain. Most problems involve a sequence of events, so that x happens, followed by y, then z. Often x, y, and z have separate legal consequences, so by following the facts as laid down you can explore the consequences of each event, as it 'happens'. This should help ensure that you do not miss elements of the question completely. However, you may also need to rearrange the discussion.

For instance, imagine you are studying the law of wills (often called the law of succession) and the question states that, 'Ms Lee was an elderly lady who rewrote her will on her deathbed to leave everything to her solicitor. Her previous will left all her estate to two of her children (Ann and Bob) in equal measure but omitted any reference to her third child, Christopher. Ann and Bob wish to challenge the latest will and Christopher wishes to challenge both wills. Discuss.' Probably the best way to deal with this is to concentrate on the final will first and test its validity (it may not be valid because the solicitor exercised undue influence or even fraud, or perhaps it was not witnessed properly). Why start there? Because if that will stands, then, as it is the final expression of Ms Lee's wishes, no further discussion would be necessary in reality. However, the examiner would expect you to cover all eventualities and to analyse the position where that 'final' will is invalid, because the question states that Christopher wishes to challenge both wills. (If the question simply told you he had been excluded, this would be an example of an 'unspoken' question in the problem and would still require your attention.) You would introduce this with a sentence which begins: 'Assuming, however, that the final will is invalid . . .' and then go on to discuss the possibilities. So, if the final will is invalid we need to examine whether the law allows the first will to be revived in these circumstances and, if it can be revived, whether it can validly exclude Christopher.

You would need to examine how he might challenge the will. You then need to explain the consequences of that first will being either valid or invalid. Here, you have worked chronologically, but in reverse.

Above all else, developing a good problem-solving technique takes practice; do not miss out because of a lack of it. On most law courses that practice is offered in seminars, tutorials, or workshops which 'test out' different answers to legal problems.

One key weakness identified by lecturers all over the world seems to be that of 'applying' the law to the facts, so here is an exercise in that as regards the use of case law (you will find similar exercises on answering legal questions on precedent at **Exercise 11** in **Chapter 7** and concerning the interpretation of statutes at **Exercise 17** in **Chapter 9**). **As we have not fully discussed the operation and importance of statutes or case law, we will take some shortcuts here, but you may find it useful to return to this exercise when you have read Chapters 6 and 7**. Our example here concerns the law on age discrimination.

EXERCISE 5 An age of discrimination

Outline of the law: Employers can no longer dismiss an employee 'for retirement' at age 65 or any other age unless they can demonstrate why this is not 'unfair' (as statutorily defined) and why this would not be age discrimination.

 QUESTION

Keith is 57 and is employed by a company which specialises in removing asbestos from old buildings. He is told by his employer that he will be forced to retire in six months' time when he reaches 58 as this is the company's 'normal retirement age'. He does not wish to retire and so challenges this as amounting to discrimination and unfair dismissal. He points out that his colleague, Xena, who works in the finance department is the same age as Keith and she is not being 'retired'. The company claims that because of the strenuous nature of the work it has a general policy of retiring workers in Keith's job at 58 for health reasons. Discuss Keith's claims for discrimination and unfair dismissal.

 ANSWER

First you need to marshal your information (as noted earlier). This will mean acquiring information on: (a) the relevant legislation (if there is any); and (b) case law on 'retirement'. You find that the legislation is mainly contained in the Equality Act 2010 and follows the outline described above but that there is quite a lot of UK and EU case law on the meaning of 'retirement'. You must now read that case law in depth. One thing you notice from the case law is that an employer can force someone to retire at a particular age—called an 'employer-justified retirement age' (EJRA)—but it must not be discriminatory and the justification must clearly apply to the particular employee affected. The next paragraph shows how you might apply that information (we have not used real case names or section numbers).

> The Equality Act 2010 prevents employers dismissing employees on the grounds of 'retirement' (see section x) but allows for a company to have an EJRA (see section y). However, the case of *A v B* set out the conditions for establishing an EJRA. One key aspect of that case was that the EJRA must not be discriminatory itself—there must be a legitimate aim, as set out in section z—and that it had to be clear that the EJRA applied directly to the affected employee (here, Keith). The case of *C v D* also emphasised that this must be clear from the contract: that something did not constitute an EJRA just because that was what normally happened—there must be a contractual requirement to retire at that age.

(Comment: this is good at establishing the basic ground on which to build the application. It is not the application itself because we have not related our findings to the question yet; we have not solved Keith's problem—now we need to do that.)

continued

EXERCISE 5 *continued*

Here is how you could apply your research:

> In our problem, Keith is 58 at the point of 'retirement'. Any dismissal for retirement reasons will be unfair unless there is an effective 'employer-justified retirement age' (EJRA) at the company which could apply to him (see Case *A* v *B*). The company's general policy might be an EJRA if it can clearly be shown to apply to Keith, but the case of *C* v *D* requires an additional step: there must be a clear contractual term to this effect, and the case of *E* v *F*, a German case in the Court of Justice of the European Union, tells us that there must also be some 'social policy' ground for the retirement age (an aspect of 'legitimate aim'). The evidence we have from Keith (which may be disputed) is that the contract does not allow for this. If Keith is correct (*note here that if the question does not tell you about a key point, the examiner expects you take account of both possibilities*), there can be no EJRA and the dismissal is unfair. (*This applies your finding on the facts to the law you have discovered so that you can reach a conclusion as to consequence.*) Only if (a) the 'company policy' can be interpreted as a contractual term which applies directly to Keith; (b) the 'company policy' is a proportionate means of achieving a legitimate aim; and (c) there was no way of achieving this in a less discriminatory manner will the company have an effective EJRA to enforce against him. We know that *C* v *D* established that 'company policies' will generally not be regarded as binding contractual terms, so (*here we see an application of that case to the facts*) it seems unlikely that the policy will bind Keith. Further, even if they have a policy which is deemed a term of the contract but they do not enforce it against, say, female secretaries, then this will mean the EJRA is discriminatory and not effective. The company may, however, overcome the claim of discrimination if they can show justification (here, related to the so-called health reasons—which should fall within the reasoning of the Court of Justice in *E* v *F*). (*These last points show a lawyer's caution in accepting that we may possibly lose the argument on whether a policy is a contractual term, but we have a reserve argument on discrimination. The evidence in Keith's favour is given in the question—the reference to Xena. On the whole, examiners do not put in facts without a reason, so this should always be a clue for you. This is an example of a 'hidden fact' or 'twist' inasmuch as the question does not ask you about discrimination explicitly but hints at it through the reference to Xena. This is not unfair: very often you have to extract this sort of thing from real clients in practice as they do not know the significance of the facts themselves.*)

Note that what we have not done here is to make general statements about how older people should be treated, nor have we tried to say whether we think such treatment 'fair' or 'unfair' except in the statutory sense. We have taken the key points in the question and *applied* those to the statute and case law. *In other words, we have tested the facts as given against the law we researched in the same way as if responding to a real client.* It is vital, when dealing with problem questions, to actually address the problem raised. However banal or obvious this seems, the major reason that law students do badly when answering problem questions (other than lack of knowledge) is their failure to attempt to solve the client's problem.

4.3 How to present your answer

There are a number of models and strategies available. Though some law teachers take the view that these can be too formulaic, we think they are a useful tool in developing competence and confidence in answering problem questions. One of the most widely used is '**IRAC**'. This requires you to break your answer down into four elements:

- Introduce the **Issues**: show that you have correctly identified that the problem raises the issues (say) of the *mens rea* in homicide and defences to murder, or of what steps can constitute consideration in contract.

- Discuss the **Rules**: this enables you to show that you know the law. Don't use it as an opportunity just to write everything you know about murder, or negligence. Keep it focused to the issues, but don't stray into the detailed analysis of fact at this stage. Imagine, for instance, that the problem posed is this: '*Tired of being kept awake at night by the howling of the local fox population, Alex takes his shotgun, goes into the garden, and fires at some foxes. He kills two but with the third shot he misses a fox as it passes by a house, the shot goes through an open window into the house, and kills Bob. Alex is charged with murder. Discuss.*'

The question clearly relates to the problem area of the lines to be drawn between murder (with intent or recklessness) and manslaughter. For these purposes we will concentrate on intent and recklessness. Your research reveals that *Blackstone's Criminal Practice 2018* [at A2.6] says that recklessness is 'essentially concerned with unjustified risk-taking' and that 'the precise meaning of the term "recklessness" has been the subject of great controversy . . .'. The text then shows that there are many ways intention and recklessness can overlap. Now, if all you do is to copy and paste section A2.6 there is little to reward. You need to explore the cases and the classifications given by Blackstone's, but keeping in mind A's case, not just a general description:

- **Apply** the rules to the facts in this scenario. Make sure here that you state the legal implications of all the material facts, and identify any issues of doubt. Cross-refer to authorities (statute, precedent, or maybe even academic authority) wherever possible—most of these you will have already discussed in the Rules part of your answer. What does your research tell you about Alex's case? When he fired at the fox (as it passed a house) what category of intent or recklessness (if any) did he fit into according to any legal authorities you have explored?

- **Conclude** by summarising your analysis. This is an opportunity to make clear that you have appreciated your instructions. If the question says, 'Advise Diana', then phrase your conclusion as legal advice to Diana—make it clear (so far as the information given to you allows) whether, on these facts, you think Diana is liable. If you cannot come to a definite conclusion, clearly state why and identify what information you would need to complete your advice.

4.4 Planning your answer

Whatever you are writing, take note of two fundamental principles. First, there is one vital ingredient in any writing—will power. Unfortunately, essays do not write themselves, and most universities enforce strict deadlines. The hardest part of any piece of writing is actually to sit down at your desk and begin. It is much easier to go and make the tenth cup of coffee that evening, or decide that cleaning the fridge *now* is imperative. Such delaying tactics can reflect a whole variety of difficulties—from a lack of confidence to total boredom with the subject matter, though normal human inertia is probably the most common cause. We cannot pretend to have a magic cure, but offer the following advice:

- Find a period in which you can work reasonably undisturbed. Time to think and plan is normally vital to producing good written work, particularly as careful planning can remove much of the apprehension that surrounds the writing process.

- The hardest parts to write are often the introduction and/or the conclusion, so leave these until last. Draft the various points of your argument first and then come back to the finishing touches. Probably the worst thing you can do is to try to finalise your opening sentence before anything else has been written.

- Pace yourself. Many of us justify leaving things to the last minute on the basis that we 'work better under pressure'. That is nearly always a myth. Perhaps some of us *only* work under pressure; but it is rarely the best that we can do. Instead it is usually hurried and full of half-developed ideas that sound fine at 2.00 a.m., but are much less convincing in the cold light of day.

The second piece of general advice is: never miss an opportunity to check your work before submitting it. Many minor errors can be found this way. We all make these mistakes. They can be humorous at times (e.g. one student who meant to write, 'The jury is the last bastion of freedom left in the English legal system', but wrote, 'The jury is the last bastard of freedom…') or the shop sign in Exeter which read 'Buy your wedding gown get a Bridesmaid half price', but frequent occurrences demonstrate carelessness. Re-reading also gives you an opportunity to review your own writing critically, and make sure that it makes sense. A student who begins an essay on the cost of litigation with the sentence 'Litigation is expensive, particularly if the defendant contests the case' will probably be given the benefit of the doubt; but repeat that sort of error too often in one piece of work and the marker will inevitably question your understanding of the subject.

4.4.1 Spelling and punctuation

Do these things matter? The short answer is yes—lawyers deal with words and the presentation of information. Universities are more tolerant of mistakes than practitioners, especially if there is a question of dyslexia. Clients, on the whole, are not tolerant of anything which does not serve their purpose. A badly written essay will annoy but probably will not be penalised (certainly under examination conditions); a badly written letter or claim will annoy judges and clients alike.

This is not a text on spelling, grammar, syntax, etc. However, we would advise that you do all you can to avoid or correct mistakes and to try to be observant. If you see that in some cases a word is spelt, say, as 'principle' but in others it appears as 'principal', or you see 'discrete' and 'discreet', or 'prescribe' and 'proscribe', or 'uninterested' and 'disinterested', or 'substantive' and 'substantial', or even 'prostrate' and 'prostate' and do not know the differences, do not dodge the issue: find out why they are different. Arm yourself with a good dictionary, a good legal dictionary, and any other help you can find—and do not always trust your computer's spellchecker to save the day.

Common mistakes which appear in essays (and online material in particular) to be guarded against are:

- **writing 'you' when the author means *your* (meaning belong to you) or *you're* (abbreviation for you are)**: an example is, 'This was not you argument' or 'This was not you're argument'. Related to this is not understanding the difference between 'there' (as in a place or direction, for instance), 'their' (meaning belonging to them), and 'they're' (meaning 'they are').

- **the so-called grocer's apostrophe** (because the mistake is seen so often in such shops): putting an apostrophe and the letter *s* at the end of a word to signify the plural form, as with potato's, car's, dog's and so on. The obverse of this comes with putting an *s* where an *'s* is required: it was his sisters cat, the landlords house. To make a word plural in English you generally just add an *s*; where you see *'s* at the end of a word it is usually a way to indicate the 'possessive', i.e. something belonging to the subject—the court's decision, the judge's robe, etc. For words ending in *s*, such as plural possessives, there is some debate on how to write this, but perhaps the safest route is to go for just adding an apostrophe, as in the *dogs'* dinners when talking about a lot of dogs eating or *Chris'* pen (here, some will argue this should be '*Chris's* pen'). The *'s* can also appear as a contraction of 'is', as in 'Where's the book?' or 'Who's outside?'

- **confusing 'its' and 'it's'**: given what has just been noted above, it would be logical to assume that 'it's' is the possessive, but it is not. 'It's' is a contraction of 'It is' (as in, 'It's an open and shut case'); but 'its' is the possessive (as in, 'its judgment', 'its history').

- **the missing apostrophe**: here words have been joined together as an abbreviation, but appear as one new word: 'wasnt' for 'wasn't', 'couldnt' for 'couldn't'.

- **'could of', 'should of', 'would of'**: because most English speakers say 'would've' or even 'woulda' instead of 'would have' it is often assumed that the abbreviation relates to 'of' instead of 'have'. In any case, in written English it would be better to write 'would have', etc.

- **a mute point**: this should be a 'moot' point (meaning a debatable one, not a silent one).

- **using 'literally' for emphasis without knowing that if something 'literally' happens, then it actually occurs**: to say, 'I was literally blown away' would need to involve a hurricane or a blast. Try to avoid overuse of 'basically' as well.

- **confusing 'affect' and 'effect'**: this can be a difficult one but, briefly, 'an effect' describes a consequence (a noun, but can also be a verb as in 'it effected a change') and one 'affects' (influences) an outcome (a verb) or is 'affected' (emotionally moved) by a book.

- **finally, 'to' and 'too'**: the latter means 'also'.

There are many other examples, and there is also some disagreement on the use of particular terms and phrases: many readers are upset by phrases which split the infinitive ('to boldly go' for instance), some object to using the word 'due' when it should be 'owing to'. Sentences which end with a preposition are often frowned upon (as with this sentence). All we are advocating here is caution.

By way of consolation, even experienced lawyers can make some interesting mistakes (and we recognise we may have been guilty of such errors in this text too). Here is a Practice Direction from 1965: 'The Lord Chancellor and the Lords of Appeal in

Ordinary have agreed that from the beginning of next term Queen's Counsel appearing before the Appellate Committee of the House of Lords will only wear full-bottomed wigs when their Lordships are sitting in the Chamber either for the hearing of appeals or for delivering judgments.' The idea of barristers appearing *only* in full-bottomed wigs needs no further comment.

An extreme example of how punctuation can turn apparent nonsense into sense is the sentence: '*Where James had had had Julian had had had had had had had my approval*'. This can be made to make sense with the careful placement of punctuation. Imagine James had written an essay which included the sentence, 'The lawyer had permission from the court but had failed to make use of it' but Julian had more accurately written, 'The lawyer had had permission from the court but had failed to make use of it'. The teacher prefers Julian's use of the pluperfect tense in his sentence ('had had') and comments on the essays thus: "*Where James had had "had", Julian had had "had had";* "*had had" had my approval*'. This conundrum has been around for some time: see for example, *A New Miscellany-at-Law* by R.E. Megarry (2005: 203). In the real legal world, it has not been unknown for the fate of millions of pounds to rest on the placing of a comma in a sentence.

4.5 Referencing your work

4.5.1 The significance of referencing

Referencing is an important skill, particularly if you are undertaking coursework or completing a project. Referencing matters for two main reasons:

- Without showing that you have legal authority to make a point all you are doing is giving your opinion and, as we noted in section **4.1.3**, that does not carry any weight.

- Referencing is really a matter of integrity. It demonstrates that you have credited someone else's thoughts or words. In practical terms it also means that you cannot be accused of plagiarism. Many students think that by showing where they obtained an idea, they will lose marks for lack of originality. The opposite is true: all tutors welcome originality but will also give credit for sound research and clear authority. **So, citing your sources is a sign of strength, not weakness**. Effective referencing should: (a) be clear and accurate enough for your reader to identify precisely the sources you have used and your care and accuracy in using them; (b) enable you to show accurately the breadth and depth of your research, and hence to obtain the credit you deserve for that effort. The originality can come into play when you bring all your sources together and then come up with a good argument.

4.5.2 How should you reference your work?

There are a number of approaches, and you may find that your law school (or even a particular tutor) has a preferred style. As noted in **Chapter 2** at section **2.3.3**, the most widely used system in law schools is one known as OSCOLA (Oxford Standard for Citation of Legal Authorities). It is also the standard form of presentation in legal texts. The OSCOLA system makes use of footnotes. In this text you will have noticed that we do not have footnotes. We use a different system: a modified form of the Harvard Referencing system (detailed below). The reason for this is historical: the original publishers of this text (Blackstone Press) preferred text which did not include footnotes as they believed it flowed more easily.

Your law library will most likely provide instruction on how to use the OSCOLA method, if that is employed where you study. Both the quick reference guide and the full standard Guide (4th edn, 2012) can be downloaded at www.law.ox.ac.uk/research-subject-groups/publications/oscola. The explanations are clear and detailed.

In **Chapter 2**, at section **2.3.3**, we provided a short introduction to OSCOLA and noted that there are three basic points to note. First, OSCOLA has precise criteria for the referencing of different types of source material—cases, statutes, books, journal articles, government reports, webpages, and so on. These formats should be followed exactly. You should rely on the official guide for the format of each of type of source; some are hard to guess. Secondly, many of the OSCOLA citations use established abbreviations to denote the source. This is particularly so for law reports (see our discussion of these in section **2.4.1**), but also for journal names (MLR for *Modern Law Review*, PL for *Public Law*, etc.), and official paper series such as parliamentary debates, Law Commission reports, and so on. The Guide provides a substantial list of abbreviation in part 4.2. A comprehensive list of the longer established citations are also listed in Raistrick (2013).

Thirdly, longer works (such as dissertations) using OSCOLA should provide reference lists. For books (such as textbooks) lists of primary sources will appear at the beginning of the text, while references to secondary sources will normally appear at the end; for undergraduate work reference lists of primary sources (should this be required) will usually appear at the end, alongside a bibliography of secondary sources such as books and articles used. This is obviously useful in research terms, as it may save trawling through footnotes. The traditional sequence of materials is as follows: a case list should come first, identifying all cases cited, with full names and citations; this should be followed by a list or table of legislation cited in the work, with the bibliography following that (and in bibliographies, unlike footnotes, OSCOLA requires that the author's name precedes his or her initials—see p. 11 of the full Guide). All secondary sources should appear in alphabetical sequence, by the first author's family name (or equivalent). Further details can be found in sections 1.6 and 1.7 of the full OSCOLA Guide.

In legal essays you are expected to reference your work as noted above, using footnotes unless told otherwise by your tutors. The following examples should be considered.

Footnotes

Footnotes appear at the bottom of the page on which the reference is referred to. All good word-processing packages have automatic footnote facilities which make the creation of notes relatively easy. If you are using footnotes, you should provide a full reference to your sources:

- When citing **books**, identify author(s), title, edition, publisher, and year of publication, thus: James Holland and Julian Webb, Learning Legal Rules (10th edn, Oxford University Press 2019). Refer to the OSCOLA Guide for specific conventions to employ when citing, for example, edited collections.

- **Articles** should cite the author(s), title, year, journal name, and first page of article. If there is a volume number, this is given after the year. The title of the journal may either be cited in full or, if there is one, by using a recognised abbreviation (see the list of citations provided), thus: Julian Webb, 'Being a Lawyer/Being a Human Being' (2002) Legal Ethics 130 or Julian Webb, 'Being a Lawyer/Being a Human Being' (2002) LE 130.

- When citing **cases**, OSCOLA demands that you should 'give the party names, followed by the neutral citation, followed by the Law Reports citation (e.g. AC, Ch, QB)'. The neutral citation contains the year, court, and number. The law report citation contains the year, volume, report abbreviation, and first page. Thus, the OSCOLA Guide provides the following example of a full citation, including both neutral citation and law report: *Corr v IBC Vehicles Ltd* [2008] UKHL 13, [2008] 1 AC 884. Where a case with a neutral citation has not been reported, give only the neutral citation. For example: *R v Simpson* [2003] EWCA Crim 1499. Of course, if the case dates from before the creation of the 'neutral citation' in 2001 it will only have a law report reference. In this case, give the Law Reports citation followed by the court in brackets. If a case is not reported in the Law Reports, cite the All ER or the WLR, or failing that a specialist report. Thus, for example: *Actavis UK Ltd v Merck & Co Inc* [2008] EWCA Civ 444, [2009] 1 All ER 196. If you wish to cite a particular paragraph, the old citations may require you to put a page number and the letter of that paragraph, such as at *A v B* [1984] AC 111 at 111F. With the introduction of the 'neutral citation' there are no 'pages' so one needs to cite paragraph numbers in order to make what OSCOLA calls a 'pinpoint' reference. These can be identified as a number in square brackets, as in *B v C* [2015] EWCA 13 [46]. If you wish to cite a particular judge, then the method is to provide the relevant name after the citation (here the reference is to Lord Justice Laws): *Arscott v The Coal Authority* [2004] EWCA Civ 892, [2005] Env LR 6 [27] (Laws LJ).

It is acceptable for the footnote to just give the year and citation for that reference where the case name appears in the text. Thus, a text may run: 'The principle of negligence was first developed in Donoghue v Stevenson'. In this example, you would have a footnote number beside the name, as in Donoghue v Stevenson[1] and in the text of the footnotes you would have the citation (as in 1. [1932] AC 562 or 1. *Donoghue* v *Stevenson* [1932] AC 562).

- **Statutes**: the OSCOLA method cites the name and then the section (Human Rights Act 1998, s 4), though more commonly one has the section and then the name (s.1 Human Rights Act 1998). Be aware: wherever you are quoting or paraphrasing a particular passage of a book, case, article, or statute, you must reference it. Your reference should include the specific page or paragraph number of the resource to which you refer. Otherwise, that passage either lacks authority or may be seen as plagiarism.

Harvard referencing

For the reasons noted earlier in the section, we use a modified form of Harvard referencing in *Learning Legal Rules*. This form of referencing is much less used in legal scholarship than it is in the social sciences, but you may come across this style in interdisciplinary or socio-legal materials and courses, so it is helpful to be aware of how it works. The system works like this:

- Works are cited in the text by author and year only (with page references if appropriate), thus: 'a number of writers (e.g. Flood, 1996; Martiny, 1999) argue that the international law firms are extremely sensitive to "choice-of-law" problems that may arise when conflicts occur in their clients transnational business transactions'; or you could say 'Flood (1996: 170) argues that...' (where 170 is the relevant page number).

- The references in the text are then cross-referable to your bibliography where they should appear thus: Flood, J. (1996) 'Megalawyering in the Global Order: The Cultural, Social and Economic Transformation of Global Legal Practice', *International Journal of the Legal Profession*, 3: 169. (Note: here '3' is the volume number and '169' is the first page; note also that standard journal abbreviations are not used with the Harvard method.)

- The format for citing books is similar, thus: Downes, D. and Rock, P. (2003) *Understanding Deviance*, 4th edition (Oxford: Oxford University Press).

- Cases and statutes must be cited in the text when you are using Harvard. It is acceptable to use the standard system of case citation, however.

- Current UK Law Report and journal citations were dealt with in **Chapter 3**.

4.6 How are law essays marked?

We have already seen that any answer to a legal question must contain authorities (generally cases or legislation but also the published views of other academics and practitioners). Marks are always given for the use of authorities, as long as they show something relevant. However, a list of cases alone is not enough—there must be some comment/application.

4.6.1 Marking standards

There is an ongoing debate across education about how to define exactly what constitutes a first-class mark or a bare pass. Each university (and subject area) adopts similar guidelines, but there are variations. **You need to check with your own university's regulations to see how each category is defined. If that guidance differs from the general points given here, then the former wins.**

Taking direction from various 'quality assurance' bodies over the years and our experience in different universities, our basic guidance would be that students gaining a **first-class** mark (70%+) will produce an answer which builds upon a full, extremely accurate, and well-structured exposition of the subject area. The answer may contain sophisticated criticism or originality but there must be a clear and rigorous analysis of source materials and authorities, and a sustained, detailed consideration of alternative arguments. First-class answers are not perfect answers but they are ones that are exceptionally good for undergraduate level. Excellence in one or more of these areas should be in addition to the qualities expected of an upper second-class answer.

An **upper second-class** answer (60–69%) will be a critical and perceptive piece of work with an extensive and authoritative deployment of source materials. There will be a sustained development of the theme or analysis of the problem and conclusions will be reached by confident manipulation and synthesis of materials and authorities. One is looking for a mature and developed style of writing with a precise attention to detail and physical presentation. This class of answer covers a wide band of students. Some will be only marginally better than a lower second-class answer; some will only just fall short of a first-class mark. The work should be well ordered, with major and minor issues spotted, and legal argument accurately and comprehensively addressed. An accurate conclusion must summarise the work undertaken.

A **lower second-class** answer (50–59%) will be an accurate and ordered exposition of the subject area with proper use of source materials, both primary and secondary, containing a logical development of the theme with conclusions which show a clear understanding of the topic. Consistent and correct use of authorities and sound physical presentation should be present. An acceptable level of competence is required. A lower second-class answer may be an answer which is good in parts but there is insufficient attention to detail, or one which displays only average analytical ability.

For a **third-class** answer (40–49%) one would expect an adequate exposition of the subject area, with either insufficient or partially inaccurate use of authorities. This answer is likely to contain an ill-defined structure, with poor or no development of the theme, containing little or no criticism. The answer will not always be lucid and there will be inattention to detail. A third-class answer is one that demonstrates some knowledge or understanding but may be weak in a number of areas.

A **fail** clearly does not even make it to the bottom of the third-class category. Apart from lack of knowledge, many students fail because they fall foul of some of the points made in section **4.6.2**.

4.6.2 Common errors

Here we list some of the things to be avoided in a piece of written work. This should be read in conjunction with all we have already noted:

- **Poor structure:** by this we mean answers which jump all over the place, dealing with one point and moving onto another, only to return to the first later. Structure is very important in legal argument, so think about this carefully (use headings, etc. if this will help).

- **Questions you do not want the reader to ask when they have read a sentence, paragraph, etc. which you have written:**

  So, what is the point or conclusion you are making?

  Why did you say that?

  On what legal authority is that argument based?

  What else is there (e.g. case law or statutes)?

- **'Wolf in sheep's clothing' phrases:** these are phrases you might use which look like your friend—but they are not:

  Therefore...

  Thus...

It follows…

As can be seen…

Surely…

It is obvious that…

This seems unfair…

Clearly…

Why are these phrases dangerous?

In themselves they are not, but usually there is little or no substance to justify them and they often demonstrate a personal view, rather than a legal argument. For instance, say you read the following passage:

> The law of negligence demands that there must be a direct link between the accident and the injury or damage suffered. We have seen that Adam and Berni were involved in an accident in which Berni says Adam failed to slow down approaching the junction and that Berni has suffered a broken leg from the collision. Therefore (or 'Thus', or 'Clearly', or 'Surely', etc.) Adam is liable to compensate Berni for all her injury.

There is a superficial air of logic about this, until you analyse it. What does the 'therefore' relate to? The first sentence is a general proposition (generally correct as it turns out). But after that all we really know is that Adam and Berni had a collision. We do not know whose fault it is (presumably this is being disputed). And even assuming Adam was negligent (and there are a number of other factors to consider before making that judgement), we do not know if Berni contributed to the accident in some way, so that Adam would not be liable to pay for *all* her injuries.

Here is another example:

> We know from the facts that Maud shot Simon at close range and that he died of his wounds. Surely she is therefore guilty of murder.

The one word 'Surely' betrays such a lack of knowledge in terms of both dealing with evidence and the law on homicide that this sentence is quite frightening. Even a non-lawyer would be able to see that Maud may not have meant to fire the gun or she may have fired it in self-defence. Once you have studied criminal law, you will also see that there may be other technical reasons why she is not liable for murder. So, the use of the word 'surely' is very dangerous: it pretends that there cannot possibly be any other answer and, in doing so, reveals an inability to think (never mind to think like a lawyer).

Essay openings to be avoided

- 'X is clearly liable'—**Really? So why was the question asked? Do not start with a conclusion.**
- Saying everything about the area of law when most is irrelevant—**The classic 'shotgun' approach. This fails to answer the question posed. Merely describing the law (however accurately) does not bring with it many marks.**

- Saying nothing; simply listing cases with some joining text. **The 'I've learned all this so I must pass' approach. As this shows no analysis or application (but may show a good memory), it will fail or be a borderline pass at best.** Here is an example of this bad practice: 'The law on nuisance was summed up in Case A and will apply here. Thus, the landowner may be liable to others (see cases B, C, and D along the same lines).'

Incorrect use of cases

- 'X will be liable for his offer: see *Carlill* v *Carbolic Smoke Ball Company*.' **So, exactly why should we see *Carlill*? Does it cover X's case as well? This cannot be given credit as there is no reasoning present. Cases are authorities, to be used to demonstrate an argument, not pieces of jewellery to be worn ostentatiously.**
- 'The case of *Carlill* will apply here.' **But I'm not going to tell you how. This is a key point in our description of applying the law: merely noting or listing something is not application. What is needed instead is something like: 'In *Carlill* the specific terms set out in the advertisement (mainly the promise that money had been deposited at the local bank) turned an invitation to treat into an offer. The specific terms in our case are similar in that the company has offered a "guarantee" for all its work...'**
- '*Carlill* clearly established that advertisements can amount to offers.' **Well, it did in part, but this does not explain the reasoning why an advertisement may sometimes constitute an offer (and there are cases which demonstrate when an advertisement will not amount to an offer too, so this is an incomplete summary).**
- 'As *Donoghue* v *Stevenson* does not apply on these facts, there can be no negligence.' **This tells us nothing: the dodge phrase is 'on these facts' and this really amounts to telling the reader to do the analysis themselves.**

All these points are simple examples. They are real: we have come across them in many essays across many universities. You need to avoid them because they will damage all your good work. Instead, we would advise you to follow the simple approaches we have advocated.

4.6.3 Plagiarism

One of the most damning accusations in academic circles, classed as a form of cheating by many, is that the essay plagiarises the work of someone else. Plagiarism is defined in subtly different ways and your own university may have specific guidance on it. Essentially, the definition is a simple one: if you pass off someone else's work or someone else's idea as your own, then you have committed plagiarism. It is a form of literary theft and is taken very seriously in universities.

The music industry is littered with examples of plagiarism, most often unconscious plagiarism but nevertheless ones that cost the plagiarising author a share of royalties. John Lennon, George Harrison, Oasis, Vanilla Ice, Coldplay, amongst many others, have fallen foul of plagiarism and, as we write, Led Zeppelin's Jimmy Page and Roger Plant are in dispute with the estate of Randy Wolfe (again) over the chord sequence and opening melody to 'Stairway to Heaven'.

With music the difference between being 'influenced' by another artist and copying can be difficult to define, and chord patterns, for instance, do not have unlimited variations. The position is different where you can cite the source in an essay. Here, plagiarism can be avoided very easily and the plea of 'unconscious plagiarism', or 'I didn't mean it' is not so persuasive.

By way of contrast, in the art world 'plagiarism' basically means forging and many works of art exist which never saw the paintbrush of Rembrandt, Monet, Van Gogh, for example, but make claims to have done so. And this is at the heart of what we are discussing here: a work presented as being painted by J.M.W. Turner which is not actually by Turner is a fraud and an essay by you which you never really wrote is also a fraud, though admittedly not many forgers 'accidentally' create a Rembrandt whereas some students do, to be fair, 'accidentally' plagiarise.

Nor should you think that plagiarism is limited to 'borrowing' the work or ideas of established authors. Relying on or even copying the work of fellow students is also plagiarism, as we shall note below.

Examples of plagiarism

- You come across an idea that you wish to use, though you are not going to use a direct quote. Let us say that the idea you have discovered is that in order to understand contract law properly you need to place it in its historical context—originally concerning a set of laws about market dealings which underwent severe reform in the late nineteenth century in favour of consumers. You obtained this idea from two old textbooks. By all means present the idea, **but give credit**, for example by saying, 'the eminent jurists Alex Down and Henry Burek both suggested that the real origins and explanations of modern contract law lie in analysing nineteenth-century reforms. They note that before judges such as Bowen LJ shaped the law of contract the idea of "consumer" rights barely existed in legal terms.' That is all it takes.

- If Down or Burek actually said these words, then the words themselves need to be credited, for example, 'As Down said "The real origins and explanations of modern contract law. . ."' and then give the page, etc. using the systems we described in section **4.5**. This is not difficult and does avoid having a note (or worse) in your essay pointing out the plagiarism.

As one of the authors to this text wrote on a student essay once: 'I agree with this statement—but I would, as I wrote it and you haven't bothered to credit that fact.' One error of this kind is annoying; many errors may lead to a plagiarism hearing and penalties being imposed.

The same applies to quoting a judge in a case. Indeed, forget plagiarism for the moment: if you are in court and you claim to be citing a judge in a case, you will have to have very specific references available, otherwise you will feel the wrath of the court. Again, this is straightforward—credit the judge, put the extract in quotation marks and show where it is from, for example, '. . . As Foster J. said in *Morning Star Co-Operative Society Ltd* v *Express Newspapers Ltd* [1979] FSR 113, at 117 when answering the question whether the title "Morning Star" might lead someone to buy that paper thinking it was the "Daily Star"': "'if one puts the two papers side by side I for myself would find that the two papers are so different in every way that only a moron in a hurry would be misled".'

Avoiding plagiarism

It makes no sense to rely on the 'moron in a hurry' defence. However, there are tactics you can use to avoid being accused of plagiarism:

- Keep a note of any quotation or idea you have come across and, when you write your essay, give credit to the originator of that thought. You will not lose marks; you will most likely gain marks. As we have already seen, the use of authorities in law is a key aspect of both legal academia and practice, so citing those authorities accurately is not going to do you down. If you cannot find the quote again because you did not reference it properly, then leave it out. Further, giving credit can be achieved in different ways. One obvious method is to put quotation marks around the section you are using and then give the name of the author and the source (universities use different styles for this, as noted in section **4.5**, so check on what is expected from you). Another method is to paraphrase an author but say something along the lines of: 'As Dickens says, we should regard this as the Law of Torts not the Law of Tort because there has never been a coherent development of this area (see *The Strange Case of Christmas Past* (2015) SPQR, 13).' Again, you will need an accurate reference. It is not enough just to add a book or article title to your bibliography—the reference needs to be more specific and more closely tied to the text.

- It should also be noted here that merely stringing together quotes from authors or accurately citing their ideas without any original input or comment provided by you is bad academic practice and unlikely to win awards. You may have avoided a charge of plagiarism but you have not created anything along the way.

- As seen in the examples above regarding contract law, plagiarism is not just about transcribing another person's words. Even if you paraphrase someone else's work (however expertly) you need to credit them with the original thought.

- Make use of the guidance provided by your university; not just as regards the rules (whether 10 per cent 'duplication' counts as plagiarism or not, for instance) but also the advice given online or in handbooks.

- Make use of online checkers. There is a long list of such programs and your university may well suggest some to use.

- Do not read fellow-students' work, even 'for inspiration' and, if you work together with a colleague, then make sure the final product is yours and does not contain structures and approaches you may both have found or discussed.

- Do not lend out your work. One risk in doing this is that the other student copies your work and you both end up facing a charge of collusion. It is no defence to say your work was stolen when you facilitated this.

- Do not buy material from websites, etc. This has become big business in recent years. Presenting someone else's work as your own is outright cheating.

- Do not use material you have written before and used in another essay (this applies particularly if you are unfortunate enough to be resitting a subject). Copying from yourself—however strange it appears—counts as self-plagiarism. Our best example here combines these last two points: one student was resitting a subject and was found to have apparently copied from an essay traced to an online 'help' site (i.e. an essay-writing service). This came to light when another student in that year presented the same essay.

Further investigation showed that the first student had actually written the essay and sold it to the site the year before. The first student had passed his coursework in his 'fail' year—it was the examination that was his downfall. Both students were penalised. The lecturer also had to explain why he had set the same essay two years running!

- Remember that to be found guilty of plagiarism you do not have to have intended to steal another's work. The authors have sat on many panels dealing with cheating and plagiarism charges. As with our famous songwriters, in many cases the actions were unintentional and born of bad research practice. You may just escape punishment if your error is a minor breach (sometimes referred to as bad academic practice) but tolerances are low and all the stories about time pressure, last-minute illnesses, being ignorant as to the meaning of plagiarism, or the dog dying have all been tried before. It does not matter if your plea is genuine in these circumstances; you face a jaundiced audience.

 ## CONCLUSION

As we said at the start of this chapter, this is a very brief guide on 'writing' styles. The books mentioned in the References section are much more detailed and their sole purpose is to help students in the art of studying (rather than the art of 'thinking like a lawyer', which is our purpose). In one form or another, every text makes the same basic points we have made:

- Your aim is to convey information. **Chapters 1–3** of this text demonstrate how to find that information and understand it.
- You need to construct an *argument* based on the information you have acquired. **Chapters 5–11** in this text demonstrate how to do this using the skills that all lawyers have at their fingertips.
- You must *apply* that information and the arguments to the essay title or the problem posed.

Legal authority is everything. Your opinion has no weight unless you can tie it in to some established case, statute, or legal text. This does not mean you cannot be original, but you must show how you derive your argument, your originality, from legal sources. The exceptional students will be able to take these sources and develop them into something special, but legal thinking is most often centred on a 'building blocks' technique of applying and distinguishing authorities (on which we have more to say in the next few chapters). To ensure that you do this convincingly you need to do the following:

- Structure your answer carefully. The easier you make the task of reading, the more you carry the reader with you. Plan your essay and decide whether you need to adopt a chronological approach or one which addresses each legal point or each person's case separately. Use summaries, headings, sub-headings; in fact, use any device which makes your answer clear. Practising lawyers do this in court with what are termed 'skeleton arguments' and many judges now do this in their judgments (this was not always the case). Follow their example. It is quite common now, for instance, for judges to split their judgment into sections, headed, 'Facts', 'Arguments', 'Discussion', 'Legal authorities', 'Conclusions', etc.

- Cite your authorities, both because this lends weight to your argument and also because it avoids any problems of plagiarism. The pupil master to one of the authors (some time in the past) once advised on legal ethics: 'if you are an honest person and the act you are considering feels wrong in any way, then it is wrong'. The same applies to literary theft: if the ideas are not your own or the words are not your own, then you have stolen them unless you acknowledge the source.

 CHAPTER REFERENCES

BRYSON, B. (2002), *Troublesome Words* (3rd edn, London: Penguin).

*BUZAN, T. (2002), *How to Mind Map: The Ultimate Thinking Tool That Will Change Your Life* (London: Thorsons).

FINCH, E. and FAFINSKI, S. (2017), *Legal Skills* (6th edn, Oxford: Oxford University Press).

FOSTER S. (2016), *How to Write Better Law Essays: Tools and Techniques for Success in Exams and Assignments* (4th edn, London: Pearson).

*GORDON, J.D. (1991), 'How Not to Succeed in Law School', 100 *Yale Law Journal*, 1689.

GOWERS, SIR ERNEST (2015), *Plain Words* (Originally *The Complete Plain Words* (1948), now revised and updated by Gowers, R.) (London: Penguin).

GREETHAM, B. (2008), *How to Write Better Essays (Palgrave Study Skills)* (2nd edn, Basingstoke: Palgrave MacMillan).

HIGGINS, E. and TATHAM, L. (2010), *Successful Legal Writing* (2nd edn, London: Sweet & Maxwell).

LEVIN, P. (2009), *Write Great Essays!* (2nd edn, Maidenhead: Open University Press).

MCVEA, H. and CUMPER, P. (2006), *Exam Skills for Law Students* (2nd edn, Oxford: Oxford University Press).

*MAUGHAN, C. and WEBB, J. (2005), *Lawyering Skills and the Legal Process* (2nd edn, Oxford: Oxford University Press).

*MEGARRY, R.E. (2005), '*A New Miscellany-at-Law*' (Oxford: Hart Publishing).

RAISTRICK, D. (2013), *Index to Legal Citations and Abbreviations* (4th edn, London: Sweet & Maxwell).

STRONG, S. (2018), *How to Write Better Law Essays & Exams* (5th edn, Oxford: Oxford University Press).

TRASK, R.L. (2002), *Mind the Gaffe: The Penguin Guide to Common Errors in English* (London: Penguin).

TRUSS, L. (2009), *Eats, Shoots and Leaves* (London: Fourth Estate Limited).

WARBURTON, N. (2007), *The Basics of Essay Writing* (London: Routledge).

*WATSON-BROWN, A. (2009), 'Defining "Plain English" as an Aid to Legal Drafting', 30 *Statute Law Review*, 85.

WEBLEY, L. (2016), *Legal Writing* (4th edn, Abingdon: Routledge).

 ONLINE RESOURCES

Test your knowledge by trying the self-test questions that accompany **Chapters 1–6**. Visit: www.oup.com/uk/holland-webb10e

5

Understanding Legal Reasoning

5.1 Introduction

In **Chapters 5–9** following we will take you through the 'mechanics'—the principles and techniques—of legal reasoning as applied by the courts in their decision-making. This chapter, however, focuses on legal reasoning more conceptually. The aim here is to help you develop a deeper understanding of what is involved in legal reasoning within the process of adjudication. Legal reasoning in this specific sense is a distinctive interpretative practice conducted in accordance with the norms of a very specific community: lawyers and judges.

Legal reasoning is both a highly theorised topic and a practical, *purposeful* activity: it focuses on how legal arguments both seek to persuade and provide **justification** for specific decisions. Some of its practical virtue lies in the idea that it also possesses **predictive value**; that is, if we understand the forms of argument that are not just permissible, but perhaps preferred by judges, we can better advise clients about the likely legal consequences of their behaviour, and the merits of their case. (Though as we shall see, theorists are divided on the predictive value of the rules and principles, with some arguing that they are too general to provide any real practical constraint on judicial decision-making.)

To help you understand legal reasoning we present it in this chapter, first as a theoretical construction about which there is much debate, and then as a specific process. Our task is thus, in part, a descriptive one; however, the discussion also cannot simply remain at the level of description, since legal reasoning also has a large **normative** dimension: as we shall see, there are multiple theories about how legal reasoning *ought* to work. Consequently, we will be stepping into the philosophical territory occupied by legal theory (or 'jurisprudence'). Conceptually, that makes this possibly one of the more challenging chapters of the book. We therefore suggest there are two ways you can approach this material, depending on whether you prefer to start with the big picture or the detail. It can thus be either read first, as a theoretical, 'big picture', prelude to the mechanics of legal reasoning discussed in the later chapters, or you can come back to it when you feel you have a better understanding of the practical techniques and principles.

To get us started, consider the following scenario, from the Scottish case of *MacLennan v MacLennan* [1958] ScotCS CSOH_5; 1958 SC 105:

> Mr & Mrs MacLennan were married in Scotland in 1952. The marriage, however was not a success and they separated in 1954, without getting divorced. Following the separation, Mrs MacLennan migrated to America, and in June 1955, some 14 months after separating from her husband, gave birth to a daughter in Brooklyn, New York. Mr MacLennan, having done the maths, quite reasonably assumed the child could not be his. He commenced divorce proceedings in Edinburgh, alleging adultery. His

wife, however, raised as a defence that the child had been conceived through assisted reproduction, specifically, artificial insemination by donor (AID) as it was then called, albeit without her husband's consent. The question before the court was therefore whether AID in these circumstances could, and should, constitute adultery.

So, *how* should the court in *MacLennan* decide? Must it simply find and follow an existing legal rule? What if there are no directly applicable existing rules? Can it make up the law as it sees fit? Even if there is applicable law, if the court thinks the applicable law is wrong, can it ignore or change it? Can it refuse to decide?

5.2 A starting point: are judges presumptively rule followers?

We have already highlighted in **Chapter 1** that the very concept of law and 'legal tradition' involves some sense of an obligation to follow the rules. This obligation applies not just to citizens, but to the courts as well—that is inherent in our notion of a society that operates according to the rule of law. Classically, this idea is reflected in the seemingly rather banal claim that courts interpret the law, not make it. In reality, of course, that distinction can be, at best, a fine one, and at worst, downright misleading: the courts' obligation to follow and apply the law is complicated by the fact that they are also able to say with some authority what that law *is* in the first place! We will come back to this tension later, but for now we will focus on this interpretative task. What does it mean when we say that the job of the courts is to interpret and apply the law? We will frame this inquiry initially around the juxtaposition of two broad and influential schools of thought about legal reasoning: legal formalism and legal realism.

5.2.1 Legal formalism

The formalist account of legal reasoning has been a significant approach within the common law tradition since at least the nineteenth century. Formalism generally can be associated with what we would call a 'judicial style' that favours restraint over activism (see section **5.7**). It is associated with both a relatively strict approach to precedent and respect for what is termed 'settled (i.e. well-established) law and a 'plain-meaning' theory of statutory interpretation. By the latter we mean the idea that statutes should be interpreted so that the words and phrases used are given their ordinary meaning. Plain-meaning approaches are also associated with the limited and cautious use of legislative history and related policy arguments, especially where those would result in an interpretation that differs from the ordinary meaning of the statutory language.

Legal formalism is grounded on three claims about how legal reasoning works (MacCormick 1994; Leiter, 2010):

(i) Law is defined as a system of known, general, rules that can be applied to specific fact situations;

(ii) In any given fact situation, the process of asserting a legal conclusion is one of rational justification. Such justification involves giving reasons for the decision that are determinate, i.e. they settle the question, and if the judge has chosen correctly from what Leiter (2010: 111) calls 'the class of legitimate legal reasons available', no other outcome would be proper;

(iii) Such legal reasons, moreover, are autonomous and independent of other (normative) reasons; they are therefore a sufficient justification for adjudication, without reference to normative standards drawn from morality or the political sphere.

This seems to put the focus of legal reasoning squarely on the practice of rule following. But does that mean adjudication is just some narrow, technical process? If so, shouldn't we just replace judges with computers that could be programmed to apply the rules mechanistically, and probably more consistently than human beings? Well, not necessarily. The better formalist accounts recognise that what is often described as 'rule following' should be understood as a complex and sophisticated process. The judge in *MacLennan*, for example, isn't just picking the right rule and mechanistically applying it, but engaging in a process of rule identification, interpretation, and differentiation, which the formalists say is itself *rule-governed* in quite sophisticated ways. Moreover, formalism is not the only game in town.

5.2.2 Legal realism

On the other side of our dividing line are what we will call the realists. We use this term to encapsulate a set of positions that are deeply sceptical of the formalist account as a description of what judges really do. At the heart of this group is a loose 'school' of jurisprudence called American legal realism —represented in this chapter in the work of scholars such as Karl Llewellyn and Jerome Frank. This was an influential movement in legal theory during the first half of the twentieth century and still has adherents today in various forms of post-realist, Critical, and new realist scholarship.

The central claim of realism stands in direct contrast to that advanced by legal formalism: namely realism argues that adjudication is *indeterminate*; that is, it is unable through formal legal reasoning to predict the one right answer to questions of law arising in appellate cases (Leitner, 2010: 113). At the heart of this 'indeterminacy thesis' is a position described by realists as *rule scepticism*. There are two key insights of rule scepticism relevant to us here. First, it reminds us that rules are not results: 'if there is a core idea in Legal Realism it is that for most purposes . . . talk of rules is not enough. . . . [B]are statements of legal rules are generally not self-enacting, self-interpreting, self-applying, self-invoking, self-enforcing or self-legitimating' (Twining, 2009: 300). Rules require interpretation, application, and enforcement, and that requires people, institutions, and (more) rules to undertake these tasks, and brings an inevitable level of complexity to them. Secondly, it suggests that rules actually impose little real constraint on the judges. In the language of regulation, we might say that the realists believe rules are much less effective as choice-reduction tools than we conventionally think. Why is this? Rumble (1968) provides a number of reasons that are central to the classic rule-sceptic's thesis:

- Ambiguity in legal language means cases and statutes are open to different interpretations that cannot be resolved by the rules alone;

- The scope of a given precedent is uncertain: how do you decide whether or when to interpret it broadly, or narrowly? On what basis do you determine whether an existing precedent was meant to be extended to cover a new fact situation, or not?

- No two cases are ever entirely identical; there is always scope for distinguishing (differentiating the cases on their material facts);
- The sheer volume of case law means that you can generally find authority to support almost any view.

So, if judges are not substantially constrained by rules, nor necessarily as deferential to them as they think they are (or tell us they are), what is going on? According to the realists, two things; first legal decision-making in their view is much more about consequences than rules. Rather than start with the rules and work forwards to an outcome, judges tend to reason backwards from what appears to be the right result (on the particular facts) to the rules. Secondly, they suggest law is not as distinct from politics and policy considerations as the formalist account indicates. Indeed, realists of various stripes have been keen to uncover the ways in which formalism arguably hides the extent to which legal decisions are policy decisions, shaped by considerations from outside the legal system.

In presenting these two broad schools of legal theory, our job is not to convince you one is right and the other is wrong. Both have their distinctive insights, which together tell us some important things about how legal reasoning works (or ought to work). Moreover, these two positions are not the only options open to theory. In this chapter we will also draw on the work of theorists like Hart and Dworkin, who take intermediate positions that, to an extent, share, draw on, or respond to formalist or realist viewpoints.

One point that may have struck you is the extent to which legal formalism corresponds with what judges at least appear to be doing when judging. Decisions are presented as the outcome of a careful analysis of the facts and the applicable law, comparing the features of this case to the relevant terms of the statute or the appropriate precedents, often without reference to extraneous moral or social norms. The judgment in *MacLennan*, for example, can be read in just such formalist terms. While noting the moral uncertainties around the issue of donor insemination, the presiding judge was clear that the only issue that fell to be decided 'by the objective standard of legal principles as these have been developed' was the 'narrow issue of whether this form of insemination constitutes adultery in the eyes of the law'. In reading the formalist account, you may also have sensed its apparent similarity to the IRAC model of problem analysis that we discussed in section **4.3**. IRAC, you will recall, involves four steps: identifying the issues in the case; identifying the applicable legal rule(s); applying those rules to the facts; and coming to an appropriate conclusion. At the core of this chapter we explore the process of legal reasoning following (more or less) the IRAC stages, but before we do, there is one more point we need to make about the context of legal reasoning.

5.3 The context of legal reasoning: easy vs hard cases

Legal method has an understandable, to some extent necessary, but also somewhat pathological preoccupation with 'hard cases', which are often seen as the grist to legal reasoning's mill. Broadly, a hard case is one in which rule indeterminacy or conflict means that the judge cannot rely primarily or exclusively on the rule itself as a justification for the decision.

The existence of hard cases also implies, of course, that there are such things as 'easy cases', where the answer *can* be found by a straightforward application of rules. This assertion, though seemingly obvious, is not without its own problems, and at the very least, we should recognise two things. First, we don't actually know much about the functioning and location of such cases in the real world; as Leiter (2010) acknowledges, the question about where and how often the formalist model of decision in 'easy' cases applies, as compared with competing models of decision in difficult cases, remains unanswered. Secondly, it is tempting to assume that there is a bright-line distinction between 'easy' and 'hard' cases, whereas the reality is more complex. Cases more likely reflect a continuum between reliance on the formal rules (easy) and reliance on non-rule-based reasons (hard) (Green, 2003). As Jackson (1988:145) argues, the distinction between hard and easy cases in fact turns on three distinct but conceptually related questions: 'What makes a case appear "hard" or "easy"?'; 'What strategies should we adopt to resolve hard (or easy) cases?'; and 'What strategies should we adopt to justify those decisions?'

5.3.1 What makes for a hard case?

Frederick Schauer (1985: 415–23) offers a neat summation of the possible causes and characteristics of hard cases. He posits that a case may be hard for any one or more of four reasons:

(i) the case turns on a rule the meaning of which is linguistically vague or ambiguous, so that the answer to a legal question cannot be determined by a 'straightforward reading' of the rule (this Schauer describes as the 'prototypical' hard case);

(ii) the rule may appear linguistically 'easy', but when applied to the facts of a given case, the outcome is contrary to the purpose of the rule;

(iii) there are two (or more) applicable rules, which dictate different outcomes. As Schauer observes 'In the calculus of rules, too many rules are no better than none at all'; and

(iv) the rule in question may be linguistically straightforward, and applied consistently with its purpose, but the outcome of the case is 'hard' because it is morally, socially, or politically undesirable.

Hard cases may be hard by virtue of uncertainties arising in the application of either statute or common law, or some combination of both. We can, of course, see this in the *MacLennan* case. Divorce in Scotland (as in England) was a creature of statute. The statute made adultery a ground for divorce, but did not define the term; definition was thus left to the courts, so that the boundaries of adultery became fixed by precedent, not the statute itself. Notwithstanding some differences of opinion, the weight of case law and academic opinion over the centuries appeared to narrow the essence of adultery down to the act of sexual intercourse with a partner other than one's spouse. So, had Mrs MacLennan conceived in the more usual way, there would have been no question that her conduct was adultery as the law defined it. But AID introduced a factual variation/complexity to the law. The ultimate question before the court was therefore a novel one: could AID constitute adultery, even though there was, as the court expressed it, no 'carnal union'?

Thus, *MacLennan* could be regarded as a hard case on at least two of Schauer's grounds: the facts highlighted the opacity of adultery as a legal concept, and even if the court did adjudge that precedent had established a sufficiently clear meaning of the term, an outcome that excluded Mrs MacLennan's conduct from the definition may well have attracted moral and political opprobrium at the time. As Lord Wheatley observed in the case, Mrs MacLennan's conduct could be interpreted as 'a grave and heinous breach of the contract of marriage'.

5.3.2 Why hard cases matter: interpretation and justification

Hard cases, we suggest, matter both practically and conceptually. The case of *MacLennan* neatly shows that hard cases raise questions of real importance to the parties and, often, society at large. Divorce in the 1950s was fault-based and laden with a great deal of moral baggage. This was particularly true of cases involving adultery. The adulterous party to the marriage was described as the 'guilty party' in proceedings, and a finding of adultery, particularly against a woman, had serious economic and familial consequences. If the claim against her was upheld, it would be unlikely that Mrs MacLennan would be granted financial support from her ex-husband (and she would probably have been denied custody of any children of the marriage, had there been any). Moreover, in societal terms, the practice of donor insemination in the 1950s was recognised as a legal minefield and treated with a degree of moral suspicion. It raised questions regarding not just adultery, but the status of children so conceived, as well as fears about the consequences of the levels of secrecy surrounding the practice. Consequently, arguments were still being advanced into the 1960s that AID should be made entirely illegal, on the basis that it was contrary to good public policy (see Allan, 2017:15–20). But these individual and societal factors, though important, do not tell us why hard cases matter *for legal reasoning*.

Practically speaking, hard cases are also valuable to us as teachers and students (and sometimes practitioners) of law. The reasoning skills involved in arguing and resolving hard cases are self-evidently important to developing an understanding of how law works, and, as students you will likely find that the problem questions you are asked to resolve in seminars and assessments have an element of hard case about them. They are also useful to us because they often oblige judges to be more explicit about what they are doing in a way that simpler and more routine cases do not. The problem with routine legal reasoning is that it tends to sit quietly in the background, just doing its job. Hard cases, by contrast, can offer a laboratory in which we can both observe the process of legal reasoning and develop a better understanding of the principles and assumptions that are at play. This is one of the reasons we stress the importance of actually reading cases, not just textbook summaries.

At the same time, judges are sometimes not explicit in acknowledging that X v Y is a hard case, and may present their decision as if it involves a straightforward application of the rules, even though a fair degree of creativity and fancy footwork may have gone into the reasoning process. This reflects the realist insight that there may be a marked difference between the grounds on which judges actually decide cases and those reasons that they use as formal justification. This in turn brings us closer to the core question of why hard cases are conceptually important for legal reasoning.

Conceptually, hard cases matter because they oblige us to consider what the courts do—or in more normative mode, ought to do—when the rules start to run out. These are questions over which legal theorists disagree, sometimes quite profoundly.

First, a critical preliminary point; part of what makes hard cases interesting is that they seem to change both the role of the judge and the function of rules in legal reasoning. In easy cases, the rule itself does the explanatory work of the law. It is applied by the judge to resolve the case and serves as (formal) justification for the decision. In hard cases, however, the rule itself lacks that explanatory force. The rule instead becomes the thing to be explained by the judge (Jackson, 1988: 146). This raises an important question: if in easy cases rules sit in the justificatory foreground of the legal system, what, if anything, sits in the background doing the explanatory work for the rules in hard cases? We will outline three leading accounts that offer alternative answers.

First, Hart (2012), a critic of both formalist and realist accounts, argues that, in essence, there is nothing within the legal system sitting behind those rules which are socially designated to be authoritative (as 'law'). However, this does not mean that rules are ultimately determinative of every dispute. Rules are imperfect tools, even if they work for the majority of cases. In the context of what Hart calls the 'open texture' of language, and the almost infinite possibilities of factual variation, a point will come 'where their application is in question' (Hart, 2012: 127–8). The answer in hard cases, is that the judge must use discretion to adapt and extend pre-existing rules to new fact situations. Such discretion is 'strong' in that it is subject to few express limits, but it is never complete or absolute. The duty to give reasons by way of justification provides a formal constraint on discretion, though for Hart that constraint is not 'legal' but 'extra-legal', drawing on ordinary standards and arguments regarding justice, morality, or public policy. Hart's position thus seeks to reject the determinism and purely formal legal rationality of the formalists, whilst seeking to show that the indeterminacy claimed by the realists was ordinarily resolvable by reference to norms other than the legal rules.

Hart's view of the importance of strong judicial discretion came to be opposed by another of the twentieth century's leading theorists, Ronald Dworkin, who was also Hart's successor as Professor of Jurisprudence at Oxford. Dworkin does not wholly reject the idea that judges have discretion, but he sees it as only a very weak discretion that is fundamentally constrained by the operation of interpretative principles and practices. These principles constitute a part of the law, and provide (in Dworkin's view) a sufficient resource for finding the right answer to any hard case (see Dworkin 1977 and 1986). This rejection of discretion in favour of principle reflects Dworkin's (normative) position that strong discretion is in opposition to the rule of law, since it implicitly places rule by intuition above rule by rules and principles. Dworkin's fear is that strong discretion undermines both the predictability of legal decision-making and the accountability of judges.

Dworkin's view of discretion also reflects two larger disagreements with Hart (and some legal formalists). First, Dworkin rejects a clear distinction between the law-finding and law-creating functions often ascribed to judges, arguing, in effect, that what judges 'do' is interpretation all the way down. Secondly, insofar as law for Dworkin is not merely a matter of applying and adapting past decisions according to socially authorised norms, it is a *moral* practice that seeks to achieve 'integrity' (see Dworkin, 1986: ch. 7). This requires some explanation. Dworkin does not use the term as a synonym for truthfulness or honesty (as it is often used), but in its alternative sense of a thing that is whole or complete. 'Integrity' in this sense is a core value of legal reasoning. It describes the (idealised) function of the judge to find an interpretation which (a) 'fits', i.e. is consistent with, the existing law; and also (b) morally *justifies* the decision.

Justification thus also takes on a special meaning in Dworkin's work (see particularly 1977: ch 4); it is not just the obligation to give reasons, but an obligation to find the best reason(s) for a decision. In hard cases the test of 'fit' by itself is often not enough—competing or conflicting rules may preclude the judge from finding a single right answer (and while Hart's discretion may give an answer, there is no guarantee it is the best). Consequently, the judge needs to dig deeper, and ask, first, 'What *normative theory* best justifies the existing law in this area?' Dworkin describes such justificatory arguments as arguments of 'principle'. Put at its simplest, principles are different from rules; they are derived from and reflect the interpretative traditions of the legal community, and represent an appeal to moral ideas about fairness and rights. Unlike rules, they guide but do not necessarily determine a legal outcome.

While Dworkin was by no means the first legal theorist to talk about principles (indeed, the idea that common law rules are reflections of broader principles that are in turn grounded in moral reasoning is one of considerable antiquity—see Simpson (1981)), he was the first to associate their use so centrally with the resolution of hard cases. However, as Waldron (2008) also observes, Dworkin's constructionist view of law as integrity remains vulnerable to attacks from those theorists who would argue that such a univocal view of the interpretative legal community flies in the face of claims that legal reasoning is suffused with principles that are fundamentally contradictory or otherwise in opposition.

Just such a radical attack on legal interpretation has been mounted against traditional legal thought by our third theory, termed critical legal studies (CLS). During the 1980s and early 1990s CLS scholars sought, initially at least, to fuse radical philosophical thought and political activism into a movement for legal reform. Conceptually, the essence of the CLS critique can be reduced to two arguments, commonly characterised as the 'indeterminacy thesis' and the 'ideology thesis'. The indeterminacy thesis we have already met. CLS builds directly on the realist claim that the convoluted forms of legal reasoning act as a screen for judicial discretion (Hutchinson and Monahan, 1984). David Kairys (1998: 4) puts it thus:

> The problem is not that courts deviate from legal reasoning. There is no legal methodology or process for reaching particular, correct results. . . .
>
> The lack of required, legally correct rules, methodologies, or results is in part a function of the limits of language and interpretation, which are subjective and value laden. More importantly indeterminacy stems from the reality that the law usually embraces and legitimizes many or all of the conflicting values and interests involved in controversial issues and a wide and conflicting array of 'logical' or 'reasoned' arguments and strategies of argumentation, without providing any legally required hierarchy of values or arguments or any required method for determining which is most important in a particular context. Judges then make choices, and those choices are most fundamentally value based, or political.

As will be apparent, however, CLS goes further than many of the realists in arguing for a radical or fundamental indeterminacy; in so doing critics of the Critics, like Dworkin, have argued that CLS somewhat arbitrarily conflates (resolvable) competition between principles with a more fundamental contradiction of principles (Solum, 1987).

The ideology thesis also makes a relatively straightforward argument that the apparent formalism and objectivism of conventional legal reasoning of itself disguises the ideological content of law and its lack of neutrality. To quote Kairys again (1998: 14–15):

> Decisions are predicated upon a complex mixture of social, political, institutional, experiential, and personal factors; however, they are expressed and justified, and largely perceived by judges themselves, in terms of 'facts' that have been objectively determined and 'law' that has been objectively and rationally 'found' and 'applied'. … The results are not, however, random; [judges] particular backgrounds and experience—in which law schools and the practice of law play a significant role—result in a patterning and some consistency in the ways they categorize, approach, and resolve conflicts. This is the great source of the law's power: it enforces, reflects, constitutes, and legitimizes dominant social and power relations without a need for or the appearance of control from outside. …

CLS scholars, moreover, would not necessarily see a material difference between 'easy' and 'hard' cases, or certainly not in those terms. Ease or predictability are no more neutral or objective qualities of a case than its 'hardness': 'a relative societal consensus or a lack of controversy regarding particular values, issues, or results can create a false sense of determinacy' (Kairys, 1998: 4). At the same time, hard cases are functionally useful to Critical scholarship because it is often in such cases that (in their view) the formalist façade cracks to expose the partisan and political choices that favour certain principles over other available counter-principles (Unger, 1987).

So, what lessons, as a minimum, might we draw from this excursion into the jurisprudential jungle?

EXERCISE 6 Synthesising and distinguishing ideas

Review and make notes on the summary you have just read. Can you identify three key points of similarity (i.e. where all three, or at least two out of the three theories seem to agree), and three points of substantial difference regarding legal reasoning in hard cases?

 ANSWERS

Key similarities and differences are often closely interrelated, so we can see that often 'high-level' or abstract similarities break down into meaningful differences at the level of detail. Here are some examples:

- There is broad acceptance that rules (narrowly understood) are not determinative in hard cases, though different theories take different views on what does the interpretative work when the rules run out—is it other standards (Dworkin's principles) or something broader and less definable (Hart's discretion, or public policy, where the judge went to school, etc.)?

- All three theories reflect a recognition of the importance of what we have called the 'background' of legal reasoning as distinct from the (formalist) foregrounding of legal rules, though, again, the background may be defined in substantially different ways.

continued

EXERCISE 6 *continued*

- Legal reasoning is ultimately a matter of *justification;* valid justification, especially in hard cases, goes beyond the response 'because the law says so'—there must be some reference to *reasons,* whether or not one sees them as based on formal or substantive grounds, or social and political values (Hart) or embedded in the legal community (Dworkin). Note that here CLS becomes the little nagging voice in your head that says, 'Whatever, it's really all about legitimating bare political power.'

- It follows that legal reasoning seems in hard cases to be at least partly, if not substantially values-based, but again there are disagreements at the level of detail as to whose values and how they are represented. Hart and Dworkin seem to assume that the work of judges is to interpret and apply some notion of 'community' values, though they disagree as to whether judges draw those values from outside the legal system or from what another theorist (Lon Fuller, 1958) would call an 'internal morality' of law. By contrast, the Crits, at best, view legal decisions primarily as reflecting the values of those in power, or, at worst, treat values-talk itself as a device used to disguise the exercise of economic and political power.

- One other difference worth noting is the extent to which the realists and the Crits would treat the very notion of a hard case as something of an artificial construct. This is obviously not reflected in the other schools of thought that we have examined.

You may have noted also that there has been little substantive discussion so far, outside of Dworkin's work and its emphasis on fit and coherence, regarding what some of the core 'principles' underpinning legal reasoning might be. The answer to this question matters for the reason we have already touched on: that formally at least, such principles appear to have some justificatory role in legal reasoning, perhaps because they act as what Bell (1986) refers to as 'general values' and 'steadying factors' in shaping the boundaries of acceptable legal argument. A number of other theorists have touched on this topic, including writers from the positivist and formalist traditions who would not in other ways seem to be allies of Dworkin. Candidate principles thus include:

- *Coherence*—MacCormick (1984, 1994), for example, stresses the importance of both 'normative' and 'narrative' coherence as qualities of legal reasoning, the latter being central to the justification of legal decisions on fact (1984: 245–9; 1994: ch. 7), and the former to decision-making on questions of law. Both MacCormick and Raz (1994) see normative coherence as a desirable quality of reasoning insofar as it means legal decisions satisfy or reflect a more general unity of principle—i.e. the decision points to, and is justified by coherence with already established law.

- *Consistency*—according to MacCormick (1994) consistency means that legal rules should so far as possible exist with an absence of mutual contradiction (again, be aware that consistency in this relatively narrow sense is different from overlap or competition between rules; legal rules might share a normative space, but that does not of itself make them contradictory: problems of inconsistency would only arise where, e.g., case 1 defines certain conduct as lawful and case 2 defines substantively the same kind or class of conduct as unlawful).

continued

EXERCISE 6 *continued*

- *Generality*—or what MacCormick calls 'universalisability'—reflects the idea that legal rules should be of general application and also, like consistency, requires the law to treat like cases alike. The risk with hard cases is that they encourage too much particularism—a bending and fitting of the rules to the demands of a specific case in a way that may distort the underlying legal principle. Moreover, as even Dworkin acknowledged, principles themselves are not always mutually exclusive, and may exist in tension with, if not contradiction to, each other—for example, the (formal) commitment to achieve consistency of interpretation will commonly push up against the (substantive) expectation of 'fairness'—that outcomes properly reflect the merits of the case.

- *Certainty*—the double requirement that decisions be made according to legal rules, and its pre-requisite, that legal norms are identifiable as such (Radbruch, 1950). This is perhaps the most fundamental principle of all. It operates as a 'general principle' in European Law and in England can be seen as underpinning a number of the principles of statutory drafting and construction, including the presumption against laws having retrospective effect. It also provides a key rationale for the doctrine of binding precedent itself. Another strong example of the principle of certainty in action is the concept in US Constitutional Law that a statute may be void for vagueness, making it unenforceable. There is no equivalent judicial power in English Law.

- Again, the realists and the Crits would evince a fair degree of scepticism that such principles have substantive meaning or act as a real constraint on decision-making, rather than operating as mere post-hoc justifications. You may nonetheless find it interesting, and even helpful in terms of understanding the formal legal reasoning in cases, to look at where and how arguments of 'fit', coherence, consistency, certainty, and generality are used by judges to frame their decisions. For a specific example, see the House of Lords decision in *Sweet v Parsley* [1969] 1 All ER 347 at 359 (per Lord Wilberforce), which MacCormick (1984) cites as an example of the use of coherence reasoning.

5.4 Hard cases and the problem of 'underdetermination'

The distinction between hard and easy cases may also tell us something useful about the problem of 'indeterminacy' in legal reasoning. Just how important is it, and how does it show up as a problem? Obviously, we can't say quantitatively how important it is without empirical data, but we can at least make some intuitive assessment, as follows.

If, on the one hand, we accept that there are such things as easy cases, then the strong indeterminacy thesis looks to be in some trouble. It is one thing to say that law does not (or does not significantly) constrain the set of legally correct outcomes in some cases; it is quite another to say that law does not constrain adjudication in most, or even all situations. On the other hand, the existence of hard cases seems to support a view that limited or moderate indeterminacy is a problem for legal reasoning, though we should be careful not to assume, without more that all hard cases are based on *rule* indeterminacy in some form. Some, as Kairys observed, may be more conceptual, reflecting underlying indeterminacy or contradiction of values.

What is the cause of the problem? Given the difficulties with the indeterminacy thesis, let's start with a little redefinition that may be a more helpful—and a more moderate— way of putting the problem in the first place. What we might be better saying is that hard cases demonstrate that rules are at least *underdetermined*; that is, that in certain cases the primary rules by themselves cannot get us to 'the' or perhaps even 'a' right answer by themselves. Underdetermination therefore matters, both because it is a (qualitatively) significant problem for legal reasoning and because it also offers an explanation for the development of the rules and principles of legal reasoning themselves, i.e. as a mechanism to try to resolve such uncertainties.

If we accept this premise, then, before we move on to look at the process and stages of legal reasoning more specifically, it will be helpful if we say a little more specifically about the *causes* of underdetermination, since those provide a further context for understanding how legal reasoning works and why it matters.

Underdetermination arises for multiple reasons; rather than try to be exhaustive here, we highlight two overarching forms of underdetermination and offer some examples.

First, and most importantly, underdetermination is, as Hart argued, often a consequence of language. Lawyers commonly face three problems in respect of the meaning of words.

(i)   *Semantic vagueness or ambiguity*: where the meaning of words or phrases is vague or ambiguous this will create linguistic uncertainty about the legal effect of the text. As a general principle, we can assume that the meaning of words is often clarified by its context, and there is a legal presumption that ordinary words should be given their ordinary commonsense meaning (see *Brutus* v *Cozens* [1973] AC 854), but this is not always as simple as it sounds. For one thing, it assumes that words have a central meaning that would be widely accepted as their most ordinary meaning, and that such meaning is language- rather than context-determined (Schauer, 2008: 1111). This is not necessarily self-evident. Whilst we would likely agree with the Court of Appeal that attempting to call a jet-ski a ship is patently absurd (see *R* v *Goodwin* [2005] EWCA Crim 3184), what if we are asked where to draw the line on what constitutes a 'vessel' (we look at a real case where this question arose later in the chapter). That term would under normal circumstances surely include a ship, but would it also include a jet ski? What if, like the QE2, the ship is permanently moored up in Dubai as a floating hotel? What about an oil platform—is that a vessel? This kind of inquiry directs us to a further phenomenon that Hart (2012) referred to as the 'open texture' of legal rules. To talk of terms as 'open textured' is to recognise that every word, every sentence, has the *potential for vagueness* when confronted by the unplanned or unexpected (see Schauer, 2008: 1126–7). However, Schauer also argues that the unexpected situation does not mean that our language fails us, but rather that our *law* does; we are not caught out by the open texture of language so much as the open texture of law. Schauer thus essentially sides with Hart in arguing that in the great majority of cases, there is a 'core' meaning that will provide an answer without us having to focus on the wider context or purpose of the rule. His analysis also usefully reminds us that not all legal uncertainty points back to rule indeterminacy. As we have observed, sometimes legal uncertainty arises in hard cases because the *consequences* of applying the (linguistically) plain meaning are deemed undesirable. This is a problem familiar to law, but it is not a problem of indeterminacy or even underdetermination.

(ii) *Generality:* legal standards are frequently expressed at a high level of generality using terms like 'fair', 'reasonable', or 'foreseeable'. The use of such terms may leave the meaning of the rule significantly underdetermined precisely because it requires the judge or other decision-maker to make a context-specific determination about some behaviour. The indeterminacy of such words may be reduced by partial definition and similar devices, but this is not always easy, or necessarily desirable. This highlights another point about underdetermination: sometimes it is a positive policy choice because the legislature wants to leave the decision-maker with some discretion, or does not want to risk unduly narrowing the rule by overdetermining it. Do not just assume that underdetermination is a 'bad thing', or in error.

There is also sometimes the obverse problem where the level of specificity in a rule may actually over-determine its meaning or scope. This may be a problem, for example, in rapidly changing areas of law, where there may be difficulties of 'pacing' legal change to the changing environment, or a desire to try and legislate for as yet unknown technological advances. The underlying problem is thus one of legal redundancy and doubt about whether new innovations are captured by existing laws. To paraphrase Windeyer J in the Australian case of *Mount Isa Mines Ltd v Pusey* (1970) 125 CLR 383, the risk is that law marches with technology, 'but in the rear and limping a little'. *MacLennan* itself is an example, where the court had to determine whether the relatively new technology of donor insemination could constitute adultery, not least because that appeared the most plausible of specific grounds then available.

(iii) *Syntactic ambiguity:* words are, of course, the constituent parts of more complex linguistic structures, such as phrases and sentences, and in reality these can create separate problems from those which arise in the interpretation of a single word. A common problem of syntactic ambiguity in statutory construction is the extent to which the use of qualifying phrases and dependent clauses within a sentence or paragraph creates a problem of ambiguity or other indeterminacy. Bryan Niblett (1980: 10–11) exemplifies this problem by reference to what computer programmers call the 'dangling else' ambiguity. Thus:

if (condition 1) then if (condition 2) then
(statement 1) else (statement 2).

If we consider this expression, it does not take long to work out how the ambiguity arises. If conditions 1 and 2 are satisfied, there is no problem, since statement 1 obviously applies; but what if neither condition is satisfied, or only condition 1? When does statement 2 come into play? The ambiguity is there because we do not know from this expression to which *then* the *else* is an alternative. The ambiguity thus does not depend upon the words used but upon the way the expression is structured. It follows therefore that the problem cannot be resolved by language alone—it will require an element of contextual reasoning, or reliance, perhaps, on a principle of statutory interpretation to solve the problem—see, for example, *Hobson* v *Gledhill* [1978] 1 WLR 215; [1978] 1 All ER 945, where the meaning of s. 1 of the Guard Dogs Act 1975 had to be untangled.

Secondly, underdetermination can be a consequence of the structure and complexity of legal rules themselves. This uncertainty may also have a linguistic quality. Somewhat paradoxically, the very search for precision in legislative rule construction may reduce intelligibility and legal certainty, especially in complex regulatory schemes (Braithwaite, 2002). Such 'structural' underdeterminations may also arise in common law matters as well, where it is built in to the whole system of precedent. We can see this in two instances that are fundamental to the system.

(i)   When a new legal principle emerges from case law, its scope will be neither settled nor entirely predictable. It takes an accumulation of cases to work out the parameters of the rule. This in itself, of course, also makes the rule harder to define. It doesn't have a single authoritative version that we can start from, unlike the sections of a statute; it has to be pieced together and construed from multiple sources.

(ii) Precedent works partly through analogy—a system of pattern matching based on material similarities and differences in the factual matrix of the cases. A precedent may thus be *distinguished* where its facts are adjudged to be too different from the facts at issue in the case to be decided. To permit every difference in fact to be a basis for distinguishing would, however, render the system of precedent useless— we would have a system of cases all determined according to their unique facts. Logically, there has to be a boundary line, but at the same time, there are certainly no general rules that tell a lawyer or a judge when a difference in material facts warrants distinguishing. It is a matter for argument and persuasion—see further section **7.8.1**).

We will continue to draw on the problematic nature of hard cases and the theoretical insights that have been generated about interpretation and underdetermination at various points in the remaining discussion, which turns now to the basic stages of the reasoning process, via the IRAC model.

5.5 Identifying the issues: facts in the context of law

In discussing hard cases we have focused on the process and values of legal interpretation, but interpretation of a rule must, first, be distinguished from the task of fact-finding under a rule. Fact-finding is, of course, a core function of courts and the first step in the IRAC model. No legal system interprets law in the abstract, so in any dispute the first question is always, *what actually happened here?* 'What happened' questions are called *questions of fact*. The interpretation of a rule, by contrast, is what is commonly called a *question of law*. As the latter term implies, we are asking the basic question, 'What is the applicable legal rule here?'

This distinction between questions of law and fact has important practical and institutional consequences. Questions of law are exclusively for the judge to decide (normally after argument from counsel). By contrast, questions of fact are to be determined by the 'tribunal of fact'. Generally, this is also the judge; it is frequently her job to determine both questions of fact and of law. The chief exception to that is in serious criminal cases, where the trier of fact is the jury, so in such cases the functional distinction between findings of fact and law is reflected in a formal separation of roles. However, even where the judge performs both roles, findings of fact and law are, and must be kept, conceptually distinct. This is because the grounds for challenging any finding of fact tend to be much more restrictive than the grounds for questioning findings of law. Moreover, decisions on questions of fact do not normally create precedents, whereas decisions on questions of law do.

We can illustrate the basic difference between questions of fact and law with reference to the *MacLennan* case, thus:

Questions of fact—i.e. what did Mrs MacLennan (allegedly) do:

(i)   Did she separate from her husband?

(ii) Did she get pregnant by donor insemination?

(iii) Did her husband consent to the AID?

(iv) Did she give birth to a child 14 months after the separation?

Note that these are all things that can demonstrably be proved by *evidence* to have happened (or not). That doesn't necessarily mean they are easily proven—given the secrecy around donor insemination, Mrs MacLennan might actually have found it quite difficult to bring evidence that conception was by AID, but ease or difficulty of proof does not change the fact that these are questions of fact. In contrast, what do you think was the question of law in *MacLennan?*

If you said, 'What is adultery?' (or words to that effect), you'd have actually missed a step. The initial question of law is much more generic. It should be something like 'What are the legal consequences of donor insemination on a marriage where the husband does not consent?' 'Adultery' is incorrect because that is actually the answer to another question: what Endicott (1998) calls the question of *application*. As the IRAC model illustrates, we can't answer that question until we have determined what the applicable law is. We therefore come back to that in section **5.5**. For now, we focus on the role of facts in cases

Fact-finding is a primary function of trial courts, yet remarkably little attention has been paid to the process of reasoning about facts in either jurisprudence or legal method (see Twining, 2005). In this section we focus, therefore, not so much on 'high theory', but on the basic legal functions that are performed, and on some of the conceptual and empirical arguments about the nature of legal fact-finding.

The preparatory work of evidence-gathering and presentation in the common law tradition falls primarily on the parties' lawyers, not the court. The adversary system requires that separate explanations of the case are constructed by the parties to the dispute, and, as part of this, certain facts are, of course, likely to be contested by them. An important preliminary task for the parties and their representatives is therefore to clarify those facts that are actually in dispute, and marshal the evidence that each side intends to bring to court. This process happens in both civil and criminal cases, albeit in rather different ways, the details of which are outside our present concerns.

The task of initial fact-finding is the province of trial courts, which make decisions based on a direct and often detailed hearing of the evidence. Whilst, in the English tradition, appellate courts have broad powers to rehear cases, they are often cautious in the extent to which they will re-open the factual issues. Legal systems do not want the issues in a case to be capable of endless re-litigation. This obviously would increase the costs of litigation, and tie up more court time—itself a relatively scarce resource. Re-opening questions of fact normally requires at least some element of presenting evidence, possibly even a new trial, and this is more expensive than just rehearing a case 'on the papers'. It could also be open to abuse, enabling those with the deepest pockets to turn litigation into a game of 'double or quits'. It also potentially offends against the principle of finality. Finality recognises the importance of providing the certainty of an endpoint to litigation. It is reflected in a number of substantive procedural rules which prohibit the re-opening of matters already litigated, except where the failure to do so would constitute a real injustice to one of the parties, for example, where evidence emerges that an earlier judgment was obtained by fraud,: see *Joint Stock Company 'Aeroflot Russian Airline' v Barakovsky* [2014] EWCA Civ 20 (per Arden LJ); *Henderson* v *Henderson* (1843) 3 Hare 100. The other side of this reluctance to re-open factual issues is that the appellate courts are also relatively cautious in their approach to the findings of fact made by the trial judge. Contrary to what is sometimes said, this is not in deference to the trial judge's view, but is a basic recognition that trial courts have an advantage in seeing and hearing the witnesses, and thereby making direct assessments of the weight and credibility of evidence.

This also does not mean that the facts 'as found' are now irrelevant to the appeal. Even where the appeal is on a question of law only, the judges are responding, as the realists claim, 'primarily to the stimulus of the facts' (Leiter, 1997: 269). This stimulus can be important in at least two ways.

First, an appeal cannot be used to run a purely hypothetical argument, hence the given facts set some boundaries for legal analysis. Although parties can raise legal arguments on appeal that were not raised before the trial court, the scope of those arguments are still confined, at least to some extent, by the so-called material facts. A fact is material if it is one that would affect the outcome of the case. What is material is thus not self-evident, it can only be assessed in terms of the legal issues, i.e. by what the law requires to be proved. This highlights the intrinsic synergy that exists between law and fact, which is fundamental to the process of legal reasoning, and particularly to our understanding of how the common law develops through precedent (see **Chapter 7**, where we offer some more practical examples).

Secondly, the material facts do not just set boundaries; they are often the motor that drives the appeal (just as they frame questions of law before the trial court). It is thus the very uncertainty created by a new set of facts that raises the question 'What rule of law applies here?' We can see this self-evidently in *MacLennan*. If Mrs MacLennan had conceived her daughter in the more usual fashion, there would have been no new legal issue. It was already well-established law that where a married person had sex with someone other than their spouse, this constituted adultery. The novel question in *MacLennan* thus depended entirely on the new fact of donor insemination.

This procedural and evidential framework strives to achieve a degree of formal objectivity around cases in court. By that we mean that the rules enable cases to be prepared and heard before an impartial judge in ways that are relatively uniform and—procedurally—predictable. However, as Bennett and Feldman (1981: 33) observe,

> Referring to justice processes as objective does not imply that they hold any special purchase on revealed truth or infallibility. ... [T]he ways in which stories represent the incidents in legal disputes produce often radical transformations of 'reality' that are hard to reconcile with commonsense understandings about objectivity.

This is in part because the underlying 'reality', it is argued, is that the 'facts' are essentially constructed within the courtroom, and are as much a matter of rhetoric and persuasion as they are of knowledge and 'truth' (Bennett & Feldman, 1981; Hutchinson and Monahan, 1984; Jackson, 1988). Consequently, it may be said that outcomes often depend in the end on which side can tell the best story. In talking about stories, we don't mean that people simply make stuff up (though sometimes clients and witnesses most certainly do); the point is both subtler, and more fundamental than that. 'Fact-finding' according to this account is something of a misnomer. Courts do not simply 'find' facts that already exist; the court process itself creates what counts as fact for its purposes, or, as Susan Haack puts it, 'legal truths are [only] made true by legal decisions' (Haack, 2008: 1008).

This sense of the constructed nature of facts extends into legal reasoning. The question 'What facts are material?' is also somewhat contingent. The answer to it depends on how the parties (and the court) read both the law and the facts. To take the example of one of the most famous cases in the legal lexicon, *Donoghue v Stevenson* [1934] AC 562, what are the material facts? Are they that a decomposed snail was found in an opaque ginger beer bottle? Or are they more generally that there was a hidden defect in a product sold to a consumer? The difference could be significant: hypothetically, the court might decide there is something so heinous about a production process that fails to remove snails from ginger beer bottles that there should be a tort of strict liability to cover such situations, whereas lesser defects might only attract liability if it can be shown that the manufacturer was negligent. The realists and their followers point out that the resolution of such interpretations of fact is not, or at least not to any useful degree, rule-governed. Cases will commonly display differences of fact that might or might not be material; and there is no 'rule' about the level of fact-specificity or generality at which issues should be argued; we thus have no cast-iron way of predicting how these questions of fact interpretation will affect the legal outcome of the case (see, e.g., Stone, 1950).

This kind of uncertainty has led some realists to adopt a position of not just rule-scepticism but fact-scepticism. Jerome Frank (1970: 162) thus argued that '[i]n a profound sense the unique circumstances of almost any case make it an "unprovided case" where no well-established rule authoritatively compels a given result'. Moreover, he continued, the very formalities of legal reasoning conceal the extent of this contingency because 'the judge so states the facts that they appear to call for the application of a settled rule' (Frank, 1970). Many theorists, not just legal formalists, baulk at Frank's claims of *radical* fact as well as rule indeterminacy—but that does not exclude the possibility of a more moderate position: namely that the finding (or defining) of facts is an active and important part of the reasoning process; that judges, at least in more difficult cases, have some discretion in defining what facts are material and why, and to that extent the implicit objectivity of the language of 'fact-finding' and 'questions of fact' may disguise situations where the judge is in reality retrofitting the facts and the law to a desired or 'right' outcome.

5.6 Identifying, applying, and interpreting the applicable rules: law in the context of the facts

Legal theory and legal method tend to treat the application of law to fact as the core element of legal reasoning, but what does it actually mean to say judges apply the law?

In this section we will relatively briefly distinguish between three related parts of the process. These are:

- identifying the applicable law;
- interpreting the applicable law;
- applying the applicable law.

These three stages are at the heart of formal legal reasoning. Before we look at each in turn, we need to explain how they fit together as both a logical and conceptual process.

5.6.1 Logic and legal reasoning

Many textbook discussions of legal reasoning start with the basic forms of logical—deductive and inductive—reasoning. These are the main kinds of reasoning process that we routinely employ in making decisions in life as well as law. In *Zen and the Art of Motorcycle Maintenance*, Robert M. Pirsig thus uses the example of locating a fault in a motor cycle to illustrate each of these modes:

> Inductive inferences start with observations of the machine and arrive at general conclusions. For example, if the cycle goes over a bump and the engine misfires, and then goes over another bump and the engine misfires . . . and then goes over a long smooth stretch of road and there is no misfiring, and then goes over a fourth bump and the engine misfires again, one can logically conclude that the misfiring is caused by the bumps. That is induction: reasoning from particular experiences to general truths.
>
> Deductive inferences do the reverse. They start with general knowledge and predict a specific observation. For example, if from reading the hierarchy of facts about the machine, the mechanic knows the horn of the cycle is powered exclusively by electricity from the battery, then he can logically infer that if the battery is dead the horn will not work. That is deduction.
>
> (1974: 107)

Deductive reasoning is exemplified in the form of the 'syllogism'. This is a formal (logical) device which demonstrates the move from a general rule to particular application. It is constructed out of two limbs, a major and minor premise, each of which is verifiably true, thus:

(Major premise—general principle):	All men are mortal.
(Minor premise—particular case):	Socrates is a man.
(Conclusion):	Therefore, Socrates is mortal.

The power of deductive reasoning is that, provided the major and minor premise are both correct, the conclusion has to be correct: there is only one answer. Note that 'correctness' here is a formal quality; we can say the answer is correct because it follows from the proper logical structure of the syllogism. In both Pirsig's example and the syllogism above, the statements all have a quality of empirical or factual 'truth' about them. This gives the syllogism its justificatory weight (its 'truthiness' if you like!), but this is not necessarily the same as saying that the answer is substantively 'good'. This distinction is somewhat blurred when we move into legal analysis. In legal reasoning, the quality of both the major premise and the conclusion changes: they are both normative rather than purely factual statements, so the syllogism becomes a prediction of what *ought* to happen if the rule is 'properly' interpreted and applied.

In legal reasoning, the rule constitutes the major premise, the material facts, the minor premise. Note that the syllogism can only be constructed once the hard work of interpretation and fact analysis have been done. Interpretation itself is not a deductive process. We can see this clearly in the act of reasoning from precedent. Edward Levi (1949: 2) described this as a 'three step process':

- *Step one* is where a judge sees a relevant factual similarity between an earlier case, or cases, and the present one.
- In *step two*, the judge identifies the rule of law on which the previous case(s) rested.
- Finally (*step three*), he or she applies that rule to the present case.

In theory, the common law reasoning process is almost stubbornly inductive. In its simplest terms it can be represented thus:

> In case *x*, factors A, B, and C existed. Judgment was given for the claimant.
> In case *y*, factors A, B, and C existed. Judgment was given for the claimant.
> In case *z*, factors A, B, and C exist. Judgment should, therefore, be given for
>   the claimant.

In reality, however, given the scope and scale of modern case law, the task of reasoning by analogy from the mass of precedents is too great, so that the reality becomes that the court interprets a rule, usually from a selection of relevant leading cases, which is then applied deductively to the facts. Thus, we can say, as a reasonable generalisation that in both statutory and case-based reasoning, the outcome of the case is the product of deduction.

Although you won't generally find judges using syllogisms in their opinions, this basic structure of 'Rule + fact = conclusion' appears to be fundamental to legal reasoning because it is treated as a *necessary* component of justification (MacCormick, 1994).

5.6.2 Identifying applicable law

In practical terms, given the fact that litigation is party-led, the judges actually play a secondary role to the lawyers in identifying applicable law. Just as the parties' lawyers are responsible for determining the factual grounds of a claim, they also take the lead in determining the legal grounds (cause of action/charge, defence, grounds of appeal) that will form the basis of the case. As law students, this task is fairly straightforward: if you are studying Contract, and are given a problem question to solve as part of that subject, it is a pretty safe bet that the question will be about contract law. By contrast, in theory at least, practising lawyers are confronted with an entire 'lawscape' to choose from, though increased levels of specialisation, and the routine nature of many legal problems, both help simplify the task in reality. So, how do they decide? We can best describe this as a mix of finding the proper rules and eliminating inapplicable law. This involves:

- starting from the known facts of the case;
- using keywords and key concepts to identify:

- jurisdiction—i.e. the question of which legal system's rules apply;

- subject matter—whether the facts disclose an action (e.g.) in contract or tort, and then what specific kind of action (usually shaped by the remedy being sought);

- relevant sources—remember, actual rules of law are found in cases, statutes, and secondary legislation, not in books about the law—see the discussions of 'finding the law' and 'reading the law' in **Chapters 2** and **3**;

- testing whether selected rules are applicable by further research and attempted application;

- checking validity and 'weight': are the rules in force? Have they been amended since the version you have used? Have any precedent cases been distinguished or over-ruled? Are there any doubts about their formal validity or applicability: for example is delegated legislation *ultra vires*, or is a precedent readily distinguishable?

This practical perspective, however, does not tell us much about what identifying applicable law involves at a deeper level. Conceptually speaking, we can think of this first stage as a search for what MacCormick (1994) calls relevancy or what Dworkin (1977) describes as fit. As the name suggests, relevancy asks, what is the relevant legal rule? Relevancy is a question of both factual and legal construction.

It is factual because every rule is ultimately reducible to its factual conditions or 'predicates'. For example, the offence of theft is defined as the taking of another's property with the intention permanently to deprive that other of it—see s. 1, Theft Act 1968. So, we can say that if Joh takes Kat's bicycle with the intention of keeping it, then Joh will have committed theft. The facts of the case satisfy the factual predicates of the rule.

The task of finding the relevant law is obviously critical, and not just mechanical. In more legally uncertain and complex matters, the lawyer or judge does not just 'find' an obviously 'right' rule, there needs to be some identification and assessment of the parameters and scope of the rule that make it the appropriate reference point. Dworkin's idea of fit makes a similar point, that the task is to see which rule or rules apply by *analogy*—that is, by reference to their fit with the facts of the case, but also in terms of *coherence* with the larger legal landscape. Relevancy and fit can also be conceptually important in the task of carving out exceptions. Don't forget that legal interpretation can be as much about explaining why a rule *should not apply* to a case.

However, abstract terms like 'fit' and 'relevancy' don't get us very far without some interrogation of what they mean in the practice of interpretation. The fundamental problem of any kind of analogical reasoning is determining our criteria of fit: on what basis do we say the analogies are sufficiently the same or sufficiently different? 'Relevancy' or 'fit' have to be understood as having some content. By itself this is a pretty big question in philosophy in general, not just legal theory (see Bartha, 2016, for an overview). What we can say here is that in law, like life, the approach seems largely intuitive. Drawing on Bartha (2016), we suggest that legal analogies are thus more likely to be deemed 'good' if (e.g.):

- there are more similarities between the two cases (conversely. the more differences, the weaker the analogy);

- the similarities in the earlier case have 'weight', for example they are likely to make a difference to the conclusion in the present case;

- differences from the earlier case lack weight or are superficial;
- the relevant similarities and differences were treated as highly relevant to the conclusion in the precedent;
- there are multiple analogies supporting the same conclusion.

You should also be aware too that in some instances the search for relevance or fit may identify a gap in the rules. Obviously, that makes both the advocate's and the judge's task harder. It shifts the balance of analysis further away from rule-finding and more on to the task of rule interpretation, into the realm of looking for analogies that may be useful often at a high level of general principle.

5.6.3 Interpreting applicable law

You will already be getting a sense that the distinction between finding, interpreting, and applying law to particular facts is not entirely clear cut. Finding the rule requires some interpretation in the context of the facts, albeit in the broad sense of scoping potentially applicable laws, and the distinction between interpretation and application is also often blurry. If a judge says, 'This is a case of negligence', she is saying something that is both an interpretation of the rule ('negligence is . . .'), even though it may say little about the nature and boundaries of negligence in general, and particularistic about the law that applies to this case. This insight has implications for how we understand the acts of rule interpretation and application.

We suggest it makes sense to think of interpretation expansively as a two-step process of general and particular interpretation, which blends into the final stage of application. In (relatively) simple terms, the interpretation of the law must logically come before its application to the detailed facts of the case. Application of a rule to the facts is better seen as a particular instance and end-point of (general) interpretation. To use a classic example, the rule 'No vehicles in the park' seems reasonably clear in most instances. If one of us decides to drive a car into the park, there is little doubt we would be breaking the rule. But does the rule prohibit skateboarding? Would it prevent you bringing in a toy radio-controlled car? Would it prohibit an ambulance from entering the park to tend to someone who has collapsed whilst jogging?

Each of these examples illustrate the extent to which even a seemingly straightforward rule requires interpretation (which is why this particular example has spawned an enormous secondary literature: see, e.g., Fuller 1958; Hart, 1958; Schauer, 2008). Of course, a lot of such apparent conflicts can in fact be readily resolved by common-sense reasoning, but that will still have formal and substantive consequences in a rule-based domain like law.

The crucial initial question is thus where do we start our process of interpretation—with the rule in general or with the rule as it applies to the facts of our particular case? The answer matters because our starting point might well give us different outcomes. Thus, if we start with the rule 'No vehicles in the park', we might be struck by the absolute nature of the prohibition and the absence of any exceptions. On that basis, a judge might well say that, since the rule admits of no exceptions, an ambulance is clearly a vehicle and by entering the park it breaches the rule. This might seem *consequentially* on the facts like a bad answer, but the defence offered by numerous theorists, including sophisticated formalists like Schauer, is that such approaches put the responsibility on getting the law 'right', where it properly belongs, with the democratically elected legislature, rather than the judges.

The point is that there might be a *policy argument* for creating an exception and admitting ambulances to the park, but it is important that this is considered as such and not hidden behind the façade of interpreting the language of the rule. Policy arguments, moreover, often come at the cost of creating more, not less uncertainty. If the judge creates an implied exception to the rule, permitting access by ambulances, this presents us with a raft of new problems. What is the extent of the implied exception? Does it cover just ambulances or other emergency vehicles? Must the emergency be within the confines of the park, or would the exception also protect an ambulance driving through the park to reach an emergency on the other side of town? Might there be other circumstances that should be deemed exceptional? If Wendy is pregnant and unexpectedly goes into labour, can Harry take a shortcut through the park because it is the fastest route from their home to the hospital? And so on.

Scenarios like this are commonly used in formalist accounts to highlight the risks and uncertainties of too much judicial interpretation and creativity. Rules are intended to be of general application, and if judges get too focused on the particulars, they risk distorting the law in unpredictable and possibly undesirable ways. This is what sits behind a saying you may have heard, that 'hard cases make bad law'. It is why, at least as a starting point, it makes sense to look to the language and scope of the existing rule in the abstract. We can at least then say whether the instant case fits within the terms of the provision or highlights an uncertainty or a gap in the law.

Of course, this is easier where we have reasonably well-defined legislative rules rather than badly drafted legislation or a broad common law 'rule' to interpret. Because common law rules rarely emerge fully formed from a single case, or may be complicated by a lack of clarity over the reasons for a given decision (see, e.g., our discussion of multiple *rationes* in section **7.8.2**), this process of 'abstract interpretation' is not straightforward and may give the judge a relatively high degree of freedom of interpretation.

In the second phase of interpretation, we start to get more detailed, in the sense that we need to identify the *specific* interpretative questions raised by the facts of the case. This is not strictly rule application, because we still have not clearly defined the *scope* of the rule to be applied, but in reality, it tends to merge imperceptibly into the process of application.

5.6.4 Applying the law

In formal logical terms, as we have seen, rule application is primarily deductive—the application of a defined rule to the facts. This statement works as a straightforward description of what happens when applying a clear rule to known facts, but in hard cases the process tends to be more complex, because the rule indeterminacy highlighted by the facts often force the judges into a greater use of inferential or analogical reasoning, or into the realm of policy arguments, which involve a different style of reasoning again. To get a sense of this in practice we will look at each of the two forms of 'rule-based' reasoning (statute and common law) and policy reasoning separately.

First, inferential reasoning is widely used as part of the process of textual interpretation of statutes. This is most obviously seen in the function of special rules and maxims of statutory interpretation (see **Chapter 9**) such as the literal and golden rules, and maxims like *eiusdem generis* (meaning 'of the same kind'). These rules and principles facilitate the textual analysis of statutes because they tell the lawyer or judge what they may be permitted to infer from the statutory language, without having to go behind the text to look for some further meaning. Thus, the literal rule provides that, if the language of an Act is plain and unambiguous, then we are entitled to—indeed should— infer from that that Parliament intended the plain meaning to have effect. Although these inferential rules and principles are important, and widely used (which is why we spend a whole chapter discussing them!), they are often not conclusive and suffer from their own indeterminacy problems. This is because:

(i)   they are often framed in general terms and so capable of both broad application, and competition. Indeed, in a well-known law review article, Karl Llewellyn (1950) argued that, for pretty much any case where one 'canon' or principle of interpretation could be said to apply, another could be found to contradict it;

(ii) they are as much in need of interpretation as the rules to which they are applied. So, for example, we might be able to construe alternative 'kinds' or classes in applying *eiusdem generis*, and there is no legal formula for identifying the 'right' class.

Secondly, statutory interpretation will also often involve a significant element of inductive reasoning or analogy, notably where:

- the meaning of words used may be derived from analogous statutory provisions (so that some legal argument or justification needs to be made for the appropriateness of the analogy—for example of a justificatory principle; see our discussion of whether statutes are *in pari materia* in section **9.4.7**);

- there are doubts about the scope of a statutory rule, which have to be resolved on the basis of arguments about statutory meaning derived from case law. These cases will usually need to be interpreted in their own right before they can be applied (inductively) to the facts in issue. Again, this process may be affected by underdetermination because there are competing analogies, or because the scope or meaning of the analogy is itself in doubt.

A well-known US case, *Stewart v Dutra Construction Company* (2005) 543 US 481; 2005 US LEXIS 1397 illustrates the latter point. In this case Mr Stewart was seriously injured while working on the 'Super Scoop', the largest dredger in the world, which was employed in digging out Boston Harbour to build a new tunnel. The case turned on whether or not the Super Scoop was a 'vessel'; if the answer was 'yes', then Stewart was a seaman and his claim fell to be determined under the Jones Act, which would have had significant advantages for him as a plaintiff. Alternatively, Stewart's claim would be resolved under a statutory workers' compensation scheme, the Longshore Harbor Workers' Compensation Act (LHWCA), which would have been a worse outcome for Stewart, but better for his employer.

   According to s. 3 of the US Code of 1873, which defined 'vessel' for both the Jones Act and the LHCWA, a vessel is a watercraft 'used, or capable of being used, as a means of transportation on water'. What made this a hard case was that, while the dredger had other characteristics consistent with the common understanding of a 'vessel', it had little or no capacity for self-propulsion, and had to be towed around the harbour. This led the District Court to determine that the dredger's primary purpose was dredging, not transportation, so that Stewart's claim for Jones Act status would fail.

On Stewart's appeal to the US Supreme Court, Dutra argued, from a range of analogous cases, that the Supreme Court had implicitly limited the s. 3 definition by denying vessel status to watercraft that were not practically capable of transporting people or cargo from place to place. The Court, however, rejected this submission. Dutra was misinterpreting the analogy to be drawn from these cases; a watercraft need not be used primarily for transportation to qualify as a vessel. The *ability* to be used for transportation is enough. Rather, the Court found that the critical distinction was between watercraft or platforms that are permanently attached to the shore or the ocean floor for extended periods of time and those that are only temporarily immobile. The Super Scoop was capable of movement, even if not under its own power, and was routinely moved and used as a means of transporting workers. Consequently, it was capable of being a vessel.

Thirdly, we turn our attention to the process of rule application in case-based or 'common law' reasoning. Case-based reasoning is materially different from statutory interpretation, and this is largely because the basic material—the precedent—is a significantly different kind of rule. This is reflected in a number of fundamental challenges that make the most difficult part of case-based reasoning *getting to the point of applying the law.* As we have observed, we have to have a 'rule' before we can apply it, and, given the nature of case-based material, neither 'finding' the analogous cases nor interpreting a rule from them is necessarily straightforward. But, once we get to the point of application, what are judges actually doing? Ultimately, once the rule is settled, case-based reasoning involves the same deductive process as the application of statutory rules. As with any form of deductive reasoning in law, the flexibility that judges have at this stage to characterise facts (the minor premise) in more than one way means that the deductive process may be less determinative than it looks. This is another way in which the process gives the judge a degree of freedom to apply the rule or distinguish the precedent.

We can see this process of rule interpretation and application taking shape through Lord Wheatley's judgment in *MacLennan*. His lordship concluded that the court needed to consider one crucial question of law: whether adultery could be constituted by reference to the end result— pregnancy by another outside of the marriage—or whether the essence of adultery at law lay in the act of sexual intercourse as such. A detailed review of authorities led him to the view that adultery *as a matter of law* was narrowly defined as 'consensual sexual intercourse between a married person and a person of the opposite sex during the subsistence of the marriage'. Logically, in his lordship's view, donor insemination was not analogous to having sex with someone:

> Just as artificial insemination extracts procreation entirely from the nexus of human relationships in or outside of marriage, so does the extraction of the nexus of human relationship from the act of procreation remove artificial insemination from the classification of sexual intercourse ...

Consequently, Mrs MacLennan's actions were not capable of being adultery under the law. Moreover, expressed in such terms, the outcome seems both obvious and sensible, and that, of course, is commonly the intention.

Finally, we consider the role of and reasoning involved in policy-based arguments. One way in which courts deal with both problems of underdetermination in deductive and inductive reasoning and hard cases where there is an undesirable 'right answer' is through the use of policy arguments. Policy arguments conventionally work in conjunction with formal reasoning, but they are not of the same logical form. Whilst analogical and deductive forms of reasoning start from a rule (some right, duty, or entitlement) which must be applied, policy arguments focus on the consequences of an interpretation.

Underlying policy-based reasoning is an assumption that laws are policy instruments that have a purpose. Policies themselves are not general rules that can be applied deductively; rather they are the 'ends' to which the rules are a means. This substantially changes the reasoning process. Instead of starting with the rule, the judge must identify the policy objective underlying the rule, and then assess whether or how, on the facts of this case, the rule(s) should be interpreted and applied to produce the outcome required by the policy considerations. What constitute policy considerations tends to be fairly open ended—considerations of cost, desirable or undesirable consequences for a stakeholder or for 'society', changes in social norms and values, and big concepts like fairness, certainty, or justice may all come into play.

Policy arguments are thus fundamentally different from arguments based purely on primary sources of law. While policies, like rules, can be stated at different levels of generality, policy arguments are perhaps more prone to arguments about weight and the balancing of competing objectives. Such exercises of course involve an assessment not of meaning but of merit. Policy argumentation also draws on a wider range of sources and considerations than those found in the formal sources of law, including 'social facts'—a general knowledge of the world often based on judicial common sense and intuition, judgements about the relationship of means to ends, and value-judgements about the relative weight of policy considerations; sometimes it may even include empirical data.

In practice we see policy arguments coming into cases primarily in one of two ways:

(i)   the judge comes to a provisional view of the effect of the rule interpreted and applied in the normal way, but then explains why that outcome is undesirable in policy terms, and uses policy reasoning to identify an alternative outcome; or

(ii) the judge, sometimes adopting what we would call a 'grand style of legal argumentation (see section **5.7**) goes straight for the policy argument.

The former is common in statutory interpretation, where a judge first rejects an outcome based on plain meaning in favour of a more purposive interpretation. The latter is possibly less common overall. For examples, see the judgments of Lord Scarman and Lord Diplock in *Royal College of Nursing* v *DHSS* [1981] AC 800.

We also cannot rule out the extent to which policy arguments may sometimes operate silently in the background. For example, a possibly interesting feature of the 'No vehicles in the park' debate has been Hart's expressed uncertainty whether a bicycle is a vehicle. A common dictionary definition of 'vehicle' is 'a thing used to transport people or goods on land'. Applied literally, a bicycle therefore would be a vehicle, It would seem unlikely Hart would have made such a category mistake, so clearly something else is going on. Either he has implicitly a narrower definition in mind, so that vehicles are things powered other than directly by human beings (which is at least arguable), or, somewhere in Hart's thinking is an objective of ensuring that parks are quiet places that can be enjoyed free of 'traffic' of any kind. In other words, as Fuller suggests, there may be situations where the idea of purpose might unconsciously infect our definition. Of course, where a policy consideration is introduced silently into a rule in this way, it does not visibly change the form of reasoning into one of policy argumentation.

Finally, we step away from the formalities of different stages and forms of reasoning to look again at a question implicit in the realist critique: if it isn't all about the rules, what else could be going on?

5.7 Does 'judicial style' matter?

The relationship between form and (proper) function is a close one. A simple example makes the point for us: if a piece of writing begins with the phrase 'Once upon a time' we expect (other things being equal) that what follows will be a fairy story. If a judge were to begin her judgment with the phrase 'Once upon a time', this would (without more) seem not just odd, but transgressive. It does not fit with the formalities we expect, and by virtue of that fact alone, we might question its legitimacy as a judgment. The principles and practices that prescribe the structure of judgments (discussed in **Chapter 3**) themselves play a part in vesting the text with the formal authority and legitimacy of the law, but, more important is to understand that the ways in which judges actually use rules, principles, and language are not the same, and not without effect. We will refer to these elements as constructing a 'style' of judicial reasoning, which will be deployed to construct and justify a legal argument. Let's start this discussion by looking at two decisions on the law of negligence.

In negligence, it is necessary for the plaintiff to show that the injuries suffered are 'reasonably foreseeable' if the claim is to succeed. In *Bradford* v *Robinson Rentals Ltd* [1967] 1 All ER 267, the High Court had to deal with an unusual claim. The plaintiff's action was in respect of frostbite suffered as a result of driving his employer's unheated van during an exceptionally harsh winter. The plaintiff succeeded in his claim; the employer was negligent in allowing the plaintiff out in such a vehicle and the plaintiff's injuries were a reasonably foreseeable consequence of that action, despite the fact that the precise kind of injury suffered was extremely uncommon in England.

In *Tremain* v *Pike* [1969] 3 All ER 1303, however, a seemingly similar claim failed. The plaintiff, a farm worker, contracted a rare disease called Weil's disease, which is caused by the sufferer being infected by an organism found in rats' urine. He claimed that his employer had been negligent by allowing the the farm to become infested with rats. The Court did not deny that such behaviour was negligent, but it refused the plaintiff's claim on the basis that the type of injury was not foreseeable. What was foreseeable was a more obvious kind of 'rat injury' such as a bite. In effect, the Court held that you cannot foresee a rare disease.

Is the latter decision inconsistent with the former? If the approach in *Bradford* had been followed in *Tremain*, there would certainly be grounds for suggesting that contracting Weil's disease is no less foreseeable than contracting frostbite. As the Court in *Tremain* was not bound by *Bradford*, the judge had greater freedom of justification in applying the reasonable foresight test than he might otherwise have done. What makes the comparison relevant to us is that, while both judges applied the same test, their approaches to the test were different. In the second case, the judge took a very restrictive view, requiring that the precise type of injury should be reasonably foreseeable. In *Bradford*, the judicial view was more relaxed. It was foreseeable that some kind of injury would follow from being thus exposed to the extreme cold, and that was taken to be sufficient. It was not necessary that the precise nature of the injury should be foreseen. This difference cannot readily be explained on formal grounds, which raises the intuition that maybe it has something to with the way the judge conceives of the interpretative role.

This is not a new or particularly radical insight. Sixty years ago, Karl Llewellyn distinguished between 'grand' and 'formal' styles of reasoning. We look at this formulation again in **Chapter 9**, but, briefly, we can say that Llewellyn (1960) describes the grand style as broader, based on an appeal to reason, common sense, and policy considerations, with a more flexible approach to the use of precedent, whereas the formal style is, as you would expect, much more formalist: rules of law decide the cases and precedents are interpreted more strictly; policy is for the legislature, and not the courts. Llewellyn described these styles as dominant features of different periods of judging, not as descriptors of individual judges' decision-making. However, we suggest that style can also be thought of in more individualised terms; thus, we might say that the judge's decision in *Bradford* was more in the formal style, while the judgment in *Tremain* was more in the grand style.

Empirical studies of the judiciary (albeit substantially from the United States) offer some support for this view, suggesting that individual judges can differ quite markedly in their approaches —see, for example, Cross and Lindquist (2009); Yung (2013). Judges will vary in their attitudes to legal change, along a spectrum from conservative, incremental, or even resistant approaches, to more pragmatic and creative 'judicial activist' stances. Some judges will strongly value consensus-building and collegiality on the bench, whereas others are less averse to a diversity of opinion, and even conflict. Such differences in attitude may well have real, though often hidden impact on the outcome of cases, reflected, for example, in their effects on variables such as 'social leadership' of the court (Paterson, 2013) and the ability to persuade other judges to one's point of view, as well as more obviously, perhaps, in the different rates of dissenting opinions that we see across judges of the same court (see, e.g., Groves and Smyth (2004); Graham (2018)). Moreover, as continuing debate about the nature and proper extent of activism shows (including debate within the judiciary itself, cf. Sumption, 2011; Sedley, 2012), such limits as exist are relatively informal, and likely only a limited constraint on style.

Whilst we think style is a useful construct for understanding what judges do, it must also be used with some degree of care. There are dangers in (a) treating style as too much a fixed quality; (b) in over-emphasising the individual nature of style; and (c) in understating the ways in which style may *constrain* both the form and substance of judicial decision-making. We now take each of these points in turn.

First, while judges may portray some fairly consistent preferences, we are doubtful whether any judge necessarily has a clearly 'fixed' style. Indeed, common law reasoning itself would seem to militate against such fixity. As we have seen, it has a strongly contextual and pragmatic quality that often favours responsiveness to factual nuance over deeper conceptual consistency. The relative freedom of justification involved in the selection of interpretative principles can also serve as readily to permit a judge to adopt a diversity of styles as to craft a single style.

Secondly, while we have suggested judicial style varies between individuals, we should also not underestimate the extent to which it is shaped by organisational cultures and practices. Particularly at the higher appellate level, the impact of different legal styles is also likely to be evened out by a mix of organisational and cultural norms. The fact that judges in the appellate courts sit *en banc* of itself may serve to limit the effect of individual differences. The increased use of 'backroom' meetings to discuss cases and the sharing of draft opinions, for example, can also operate in part to build collegiality and consensual decision-making, and reduce individual differences (cf. Paterson, 2013).

Thirdly, we should be careful not to read into the notion of judicial style an assumption that it is a strong feature of legal indeterminacy. Judicial style only makes sense inside a wider context of an accepted framework and understanding of legal decision-making (this is part of what Dworkin (1977) means when he talks of judges as an interpretative community, though his account goes perhaps too far in treating that community as univocal). Rather, as Llewellyn's analysis shows, what is 'acceptable' in a given period both creates *and* constrains the space for interpretation and sets some limits to freedom of justification. Judicial style in this context thus needs to be understood (at least) as much as a conservative and unifying force as it is a symbol of a potential diversity of attitudes and values. Moreover, it might be argued that the realists underestimated the degree of institutional and cultural respect within the judiciary for the more formalistic norms of judging, and the perceived integrity of the legal reasoning process (see Duxbury, 2008; Paterson, 2013), which means that those whose style tends to sit outside the norm risk undermining their own legitimacy within the court. This may apply as much to the form and language of a judgment, as to its content. Where a judgement breaches these stylistic norms, this too may undermine its legitimacy. Consider as an example the judgment of Lord Denning in *Miller* v *Jackson* [1977] QB 966; [1977] 3 All ER 338.

EXERCISE 7 It's just not cricket!

Consider the following passage taken from Lord Denning's judgment at [1977] 3 All ER 338, 340–1:

> In summer time village cricket is the delight of everyone. Nearly every village has its own cricket field where the young men play and the old men watch. In the village of Lintz in County Durham they have their own ground, where they have played these last 70 years … The village team play there on Saturdays and Sundays. They belong to a league, competing with the neighbouring villages. On other evenings after work they practise while the light lasts. Yet now after these 70 years a judge of the High Court has ordered that they must not play there any more. He has issued an injunction to stop them. He has done it at the instance of a newcomer who is no lover of cricket. This newcomer built, or has had built for him, a house on the edge of the cricket ground which four years ago was a field where cattle grazed. The animals did not mind the cricket. But now this adjoining field has been turned into a housing estate. The newcomer bought one of the houses on the edge of the cricket ground. No doubt the open space was a selling point. Now he complains that, when a batsman hits a six, the ball has been known to land in his garden or on or near his house. His wife has got so upset about it that they always go out at weekends. They do not go into the garden when cricket is being played. They say that this is intolerable … And the judge, much against his will, has felt that he must order the cricket to be stopped; with the consequences, I suppose, that the Lintz Cricket Club will disappear. The cricket ground will be turned to some other use. I expect for more houses or a factory. The young men will turn to other things instead of cricket. The whole village will be much the poorer. And all this because of a newcomer who has just bought a house there next to the cricket ground.

continued

EXERCISE 7 *continued*

Q QUESTIONS

From this statement can you:

(i) predict Lord Denning's decision on the law: did he find in favour of the cricket club, or of the Millers?

(ii) distinguish fact from supposition within that case?

A ANSWERS

The answer to (a) will probably come as little surprise. Lord Denning found in favour of the cricket club. He held that there was no actionable nuisance by the club, and discharged the injunction. His Lordship was not, in the end, wholly successful in carrying the rest of the Court of Appeal with him. The other two judges found that there was an actionable nuisance; however, only one of them felt that it was such that an injunction (a discretionary remedy) should be granted, so that Lord Denning was in a majority in favour of dismissing the injunction granted by the High Court.

Is it not rather odd that we can guess the final decision from what is supposed to be a statement of facts? Yes, it is. Lord Denning's comments illustrate, as Twining (1990) notes, the way in which facts can be formulated so as to advance a particular argument, albeit that, here, Lord Denning's formulation is far more explicitly biased than one would normally expect from a judge.

In respect of (b), the construction of a narrative built upon both fact and supposition and a strongly disapproving style of language is another aspect of Lord Denning's attempt to carry us along to his conclusion. Consider, for example, how he creates a picture of socially undesirable consequences that might flow from the continued injunction: the replacement of the cricket ground with houses or a factory; the fear that young men will turn 'to other things' which, though remaining unspoken (or perhaps *because they are unspoken*), are clearly undesirable. This is all supposition.

The overall effect of the judgment's style is thus unsettling. The narrative does not even pretend objectivity, and subtly substitutes rhetorical effects for logical argument. As Jackson (1988) argues, through its choice of language and a range of rhetorical techniques, it builds an image of a rural community bound together by its love of cricket, and an idyllic way of life threatened by an outsider who is no part of that world. The effect is to create a narrative framework 'laden with disapproval' (1988: 96). The effect is powerful, but also not judicial.

 CONCLUSION

In this chapter we have sought to present a reasonably sophisticated overview of the legal reasoning process, and to introduce you, through the context of legal reasoning, to some central works in Anglo-American legal theory.

By way of conclusion, we suggest seven major points that can be drawn from this chapter.

First, a common mistake made by students in the early stages of studying law is to assume that legal reasoning is all about 'the rules'. The idea that every legal question can be resolved by reference to some existing rule is a pervasive one, that often appears to be supported by judicial practice and sometimes in the work of textbook writers operating within the doctrinal and formalist traditions. This view, however, risks treating rules as over-determinative and understates the extent to which (i) legal reasoning involves other processes, such as the exercise of discretion or the use of principles and policy considerations; and (ii) legal reasoning may be, in a wide sense of the term, applied politics, and 'style'.

Secondly, facts and fact-finding matter. Facts drive not just the reasoning process in individual cases (as the formalist and realist accounts indicate), but particularly through the operation of precedent, over time, they come to shape the substantive law itself. This also points to the extent to which the situational problems raised by cases act as a primary driver of legal change. The *MacLennan* case itself illustrates this, as an example of where the court has had to respond to the legal uncertainties created by unregulated donor insemination.

Thirdly, while facts are important, they also have their own indeterminacy problems and care should be taken, in practice and in theory, to recognise the possible contingency of facts 'constructed' for and in the courtroom.

Fourthly, there is reasonable agreement that law often suffers from an underdetermination problem, but less agreement about its extent. The causes of underdetermination are most commonly linguistic, but also embedded in the forms and structures of legal norms (e.g. the difficulty we may encounter in formulating a specific common law rule).

Fifthly, the primary *tasks* for legal reasoning are to find, interpret, and apply the law to a given set of facts. Finding the law is both conceptual (the search for relevance), and practical (getting the right sources). Interpretation is a complex phenomenon that tends to pervade and dominate the legal reasoning process in hard cases. It involves constructing both a general and particular reading of the relevant legal rule(s) before applying them to the case. It primarily uses standard forms of logical reasoning, but is assisted in that process by a broad range of rules and principles of legal interpretation (discussed in later chapters), though these too will suffer from problems of underdetermination/indeterminacy. Rule application, finally, is essentially a deductive process, except where policy grounds may intervene and change the reasoning process into a consideration of policy consequences.

Sixthly, the primary *function* of legal reasoning is to *justify legal decisions*. Justification is the requirement to give 'good' reasons, which generally in the legal sphere means reasons that are authoritative and constructed in accordance with the interpretative practices of the courts. In hard cases in particular, authoritative arguments may reflect moral or other non-legal standards, though there is commonly disagreement amongst theorists about whether such standards are sourced from within or outside the law.

Finally, lawyers and judges can be expected to deploy only certain kinds of argument by way of justification for a legal outcome; these may be:

- substantive (rule-based) arguments asserting formal legal rights and obligations;
- inferential arguments based on rules or principles of legal interpretation that can be used to clarify the scope and application of the primary legal rules;

- principle-based arguments which can be used to evaluate and justify the choice of primary rule (e.g. arguments of fit, consistency, coherence, and certainty);

- consequentialist arguments regarding appropriate policy considerations, which may or may not override the outcomes of more conventional rule-based reasoning.

You will also have seen as this chapter has developed that there is considerable scope for reasonable disagreement about the way legal reasoning works, and that this extends to both descriptive and normative accounts of legal reasoning within legal theory. If you like having a single right answer to everything, you will likely have found this difficult and frustrating. Our advice is stick with it; the capacity to deal with uncertainty and complexity is a fundamental quality of being a law graduate. It can be difficult to be effectively critical and evaluative about the law if you are not comfortable with the idea that the whole enterprise, in an oddly paradoxical way, has uncertainty at the heart of what it does.

 CHAPTER REFERENCES

ALLAN, S. (2017), *Donor Conception and the Search for Information: From Secrecy and Anonymity to Openness* (Abingdon: Routledge).

BARTHA, P. (2016), 'Analogy and Analogical Reasoning', in E. Zalta (ed.), *The Stanford Encyclopedia of Philosophy* (Winter 2016 Edition), https://plato.stanford.edu/archives/win2016/entries/reasoning-analogy.

BELL, J. (1986), 'The Acceptability of Legal Arguments' in N. MacCormick and P. Birks (eds), *The Legal Mind: Essays for Tony Honoré* (Oxford: Clarendon Press).

BENNETT, L. and FELDMAN, M. (1981), *Reconstructing Reality in the Courtroom : Justice and Judgment in American Culture* (Brunswick, NJ: Rutgers University Press).

BRAITHWAITE, J. (2002), 'Rules and Principles: A Theory of Legal Certainty', 27 *Australian Journal of Legal Philosophy*, 47.

CROSS, F. and LINDQUIST, S. (2009), 'Judging the Judges', 58 *Duke Law Journal,* 1383.

DUXBURY, N. (2008), *The Nature and Authority of Precedent* (Cambridge: Cambridge University Press).

DWORKIN, R. (1977), *Taking Rights Seriously* (Cambridge, MA: Harvard University Press).

DWORKIN, R. (1986), *Law's Empire* (London: Fontana).

ENDICOTT, T. (1998), 'Questions of Law', 114 *Law Quarterly Review,* 292.

FRANK, J. (1970), *Law and the Modern Mind* (Gloucester, Mass: Peter Smith).

FULLER, L. (1958), 'Positivism and Fidelity to Law—A Reply to Professor Hart', 71 *Harvard Law Review,* 630.

GRAHAM, L. (2018), 'Lady Justices and Dissent on the Court of Appeal of England and Wales', *UK. Constitutional Law Blog* (15 November 2018), https://ukconstitutionallaw.org/2018/11/15/lewis-graham-lady-justices-and-dissent-on-the-court-of-appeal-of-england-and-wales.

GREEN, L. (2003), 'Legal Positivism', in E. Zalta (ed.), *Stanford Encyclopedia of Philosophy* (Spring 2018), https://plato.stanford.edu/archives/spr2018/entries/legal-positivism.

GROVES, M. and SMYTH, R. (2004), 'A Century of Judicial Style: Changing Patterns in Judgment Writing on the High Court 1903–2001', 32 *Federal Law Review,* 255.

HAACK, S. (2008), 'Of Truth, in Science and Law', 73 *Brooklyn Law Review,* 985.

HART, H. (1958), 'Positivism and the Separation of Law and Morals', 71 *Harvard Law Review,* 593:

HART, H. (2012), *The Concept of Law,* (3rd edn, Oxford: Clarendon Press).

HUTCHINSON, A. and MONAHAN, P. (1984), 'Law, Politics and the Critical Legal Scholars: The Unfolding Drama of American Legal Thought', 36 *Stanford Law Review,* 199.

JACKSON, B. (1988), *Law, Fact and Narrative Coherence* (Liverpool: Deborah Charles).

KAIRYS, D. (1998), 'Introduction', in D. Kairys (ed.), *The Politics of Law: A Progressive Critique* (3rd edn, New York: Basic Books).

LEITER, B. (1997), 'Rethinking Legal Realism: Toward a Naturalized Jurisprudence', 76 *Texas Law Review,* 267.

LEITER, B. (2010), 'Legal Formalism and Legal Realism: What is the Issue?', 16 *Legal Theory,* 111.

LEVI, E. (1949), *An Introduction to Legal Reasoning* (Chicago, Ill: University of Chicago Press).

LLEWELLYN, K. (1950), 'Remarks on the Theory of Appellate Decisions and the Rules or Canons about How Statutes are to be Construed', 3 *Vanderbilt Law Review,* 395.

LLEWELLYN, K. (1960) *The Common Law Tradition* (Boston, Mass: Little Brown).

MACCORMICK, N. (1984), 'Coherence in Legal Justification', in A. Peczenik, L. Lindale, and B. Van Roermund (eds), *Theory of Legal Science* (Dordrecht: Reidel).

MACCORMICK, N. (1994), *Legal Reasoning and Legal Theory* (2nd edn, Oxford: Clarendon Press).

NIBLETT, B. (1980), 'Computer Science and Law: An Introductory Discussion', in B. Niblett (ed.), *Computer Science and Law: An Advanced Course* (Cambridge: Cambridge University Press).

PATERSON, A. (2013), *Final Judgment: The Last Law Lords and the Supreme Court* (Oxford: Hart).

PIRSIG, R. (1974), *Zen and the Art of Motorcycle Maintenance* (London: Bodley Head).

RADBRUCH, G, (1950), 'Legal Philosophy', in E. Lask, G. Radbruch, and J. Dabin (eds), *The Legal Philosophies of Lask, Radbruch and Dabin,* (trans. K. Wilk) (Cambridge, Mass: Harvard University Press).

RAZ, J. (1994), 'The Relevance of Coherence', in J. Raz (ed.), *Ethics in the Public Domain* (Oxford: Clarendon Press).

RUMBLE, W. (1968), *American Legal Realism: Skepticism, Reform and the Judicial Process* (Ithaca, NY: Cornell University Press).

SCHAUER, F. (1985), 'Easy Cases', 58 *Southern California Law Review,* 399.

SCHAUER, F. (2008), 'A Critical Guide to Vehicles in the Park', 83 *New York University Law Review,* 1109.

SCHAUER, F. (2009), *Thinking Like a Lawyer: A New Introduction to Legal Reasoning* (Cambridge, Mass: Harvard University Press).

SEDLEY, S. (2012), 'Judicial Politics', 34(4) *London Review of Books,* 15, www.lrb.co.uk/v34/n04/stephen-sedley/judicial-politics.

SIMPSON, B. (1981), 'The Rise and Fall of the Legal Treatise: Legal Principles and the Forms of Legal Literature', 48 *University of Chicago Law Review,* 632.

SMILLIE, J. (1996), 'Formalism, Fairness and Efficiency: Civil Adjudication in New Zealand', [1996] *New Zealand Law Review,* 254.

SOLUM, L. (1987), 'On the Indeterminacy Crisis: Critiquing Critical Dogma', 54 *University of Chicago Law Review,* 462.

STONE, J. (1959), 'The Ratio of the Ratio Decidendi', 22 *Modern Law Review,* 597.

SUMPTION, J. (2011), 'Judicial and Political Decision-Making: The Uncertain Boundary', 16 *Judicial Review,* 301.

TWINING, W. (1990), *Rethinking Evidence: Exploratory Essays* (Oxford: Basil Blackwell).

TWINING, W. (2005), 'Taking Facts Seriously—Again', 55 *Journal of Legal Education,* 360.

TWINING, W. (2009), *General Jurisprudence: Understanding Law from a Global Perspective* (Cambridge: Cambridge University Press).

UNGER, R. (1983), *The Critical Legal Studies Movement* (Cambridge, Mass: Harvard University Press).

WALDRON, J. (2008), 'Did Dworkin Ever Answer the Crits?', in S. Hershovitz (ed.), *Exploring Law's Empire: The Jurisprudence of Ronald Dworkin* (Oxford: Oxford University Press).

YUNG, C. (2013), 'A Typology of Judging Styles', 107 *Northwestern University Law Review*, 1757.

 ONLINE RESOURCES

Test your knowledge by trying the self-test questions that accompany **Chapters 1–6**.
Visit: www.oup.com/uk/holland-webb10e

6

The Doctrine of Judicial Precedent

6.1 Introduction

In this chapter we begin to examine how we use case law to solve legal problems. In the study and practice of law we seek to analyse legal principles; and the 'principles' in English law are derived from pure case law or from case law dealing with statutes.

6.1.1 What is case law?

So, what exactly do we mean by 'case law'? In earlier chapters we discussed the idea of cases and we examined procedure and law reporting. In this and **Chapter 7** we discuss case law in much greater depth. Although this is not a book on the English legal system, we will begin with an explanation of some basic points on what 'cases' are and how they come about.

Criminal law cases, of course, come about because the police make an arrest and charge the accused, the legal arguments of the case being taken up by the Crown Prosecution Service (CPS). Indeed, the CPS may well have been involved at the 'charging' stage, advising on the strength of the evidence, etc. The CPS then brings the prosecution on behalf of the Crown. The charge must be clearly defined. Lay people often talk of a person being 'charged with theft' (or rape, or murder, etc.), but the CPS has to frame the charge according to strict rules and with reference to established and recognised common law or statutory crimes. This will lead to what is termed the 'indictment', which will first set out the charge (e.g. 'Arson contrary to section 1(2) and (3) of the Criminal Damage Act 1971'). There will then appear the 'Particulars of the offence'—the basic facts—such as 'Claude Nero on October 3rd 2015 did without lawful excuse damage by fire a caravan, having a value of £17,000, belonging to Vyacheslav Molotov intending to damage such vehicle by fire and intending by such damage to endanger the life of Vyacheslav Molotov'). These will be given to the jury at the start of the trial.

Before the matter comes to trial (in front of magistrates for lesser offences or, in the Crown Court, before a judge and jury) there will be other preliminary matters to deal with and perhaps even detailed legal arguments about admissibility of evidence. Many of these cases are reported in the local and national press, but they are only really interesting to a lawyer if and when they go on appeal, for it is at that point that the key legal arguments start to bite.

Civil cases are obviously different. Here, the usual position is that one individual or company is suing another for some form of compensation arising from a loss. But suing for what? A litigant cannot just 'sue' someone: they have to sue them for some identifiable legal reason. They must have what is called a 'cause of action'. This means that the set of facts must show something which the law recognises as giving rise to potential liability. If you are injured in a car accident, for instance, you do not just 'sue' the other driver, you must sue for and show 'negligence'; if someone does not do what they promised to do you may have a claim (a cause of action) for breach of contract. If someone floods your land, you may have claims in negligence, breach of contract, or nuisance (to name but a few).

The point of this is that when you fill out your claim form you must identify what it is you are suing for—otherwise neither the court nor the defendant can respond. Indeed, the importance of establishing the cause of action lies even earlier than this: if you write to a potential defendant in advance of bringing a claim (which you have to do in many instances under what are known as 'Protocols') you must spell out why you think they are liable. You must also specify the damages (or compensation) you are seeking. Be careful here: the cause of action identifies what legal right you are claiming has been breached, the damages you are seeking is your **remedy** for that breach. Unless you establish your cause of action and meet all the requirements to be found there, you cannot receive any damages.

So, from the moment a client walks into the office and starts to tell her story, a lawyer has to be thinking:

(i)   What legal principles are involved (what is the cause of action here)?

(ii) What is the relevant law regarding these principles (where can the up-to-date authorities be found)?

(iii) What evidence will we need to prove or defend the case? and

(iv) Which court do I have to apply to?

In fact, this is a very similar thought process to that in a criminal law case—just substitute the word 'charge' for 'cause of action'.

Concentrating on civil cases: let us assume all attempts to settle the case fail. As with the criminal justice system there are procedures to go through before trial (these form part of what is generally called the 'case management' system). These will include things such as disclosing and exchanging relevant documents, obtaining experts' reports, and agreeing how long the case will take. These are often dealt with before a judge in what is referred to as a 'Directions hearing'. Here, the parties agree or are told what 'directions' the judge is giving on the management of the case. Assume these have happened but the case is going to trial—perhaps in a county court (in Bristol, London, Leeds, etc.—wherever is appropriate). The case is for a relatively small amount and is heard by a District Judge.

As we have noted previously, our system is an 'adversarial' one: when it comes to trial, each side presents and argues their case according to rules of evidence and procedure, but before the trial each party must know what the other party's evidence will be. The idea that one side can 'surprise' the other with new evidence on the day of the trial is not part of our system. Further, during the trial judges may intervene and ask pertinent questions (especially if one side is not represented by a lawyer) but they are anxious to avoid 'stepping into the arena': it is not a judge's job to argue the case for either litigant.

The judge sees all the documents, sees any witnesses being examined and cross-examined, hears arguments on the law, and makes a decision. One party loses (there is no system of 'drawing'). In most cases they will have to pay some form of damages and possibly the costs of litigation for both sides (e.g. any court fees or lawyers' costs). And, as an aside, at no time in an English court does a judge ever use a gavel, no matter what contrary image TV and films portray.

The losing party wishes to appeal. In nearly all instances they can only do so on points of law. They will need permission from a court to do so (it is not an automatic right) and they must lodge the appeal within a prescribed time. Let us assume they get permission, but lose again. The same mechanism operates. Now let us say they have arrived in the Court of Appeal. This is the stage where most decisions will be reported in the law reports (it can happen lower down in the hierarchy but, aside from specialist courts such as the Employment Appeal Tribunal, this is not common). All the arguments are about the legal principles involved. The facts are taken as proved by that stage. The same is true of criminal cases: the lower courts deal with both law and fact, but by the time a case reaches the Court of Appeal (Criminal Division) the issues tend to be purely legal ones.

So now, when we talk later in the chapter about precedents, *ratio decidendi*, and other matters, we are usually talking about cases heard in the Court of Appeal or the Supreme Court. What we are concerned with is not who won or lost but the legal principles that can be extracted from the case. As a law student, this is the setting you are most concerned with (if you become a practitioner you will, of course, have had to deal with questions of fact, evidence, and procedure, as well as the law, in the lower courts).

This is a very sketchy view of case law procedure, but it serves our purpose. We now know that:

- there must be a cause of action (or a charge/indictment in criminal cases) such as negligence, breach of contract on the civil side, and arson, theft, etc. on the criminal side;
- that analysing this involves matching the facts to legal principles; you could not, for instance, claim for negligence if the person you are suing does not have a duty of care to your client because this concept of 'duty of care' is central to the principles of negligence (i.e. the cause of action);
- that the facts must be proved in court (balance of probabilities in civil actions, beyond all reasonable doubt in criminal cases);
- that it is generally arguments about the legal principles that form the basis of appeals; and
- that it is the legal analysis in these appeals which forms the basis of 'law reports' and therefore precedents.

'Case law' is the term we use to describe the collection of all the legal principles emanating from all the reported cases on a given topic. The case law on the law of negligence, for example, consists of thousands of individual cases, all building one on another, year after year, exploring different aspects of the law and seeing whether the principles of law apply or do not apply (or need changing) to different sets of facts. Each case 'tests out' the relevant principle in the light of new facts.

Indeed, it is often said to be a strength of English law that it is built upon the concrete examples of case law rather than hypothetical models. This contrasts with the European approach, which does depend upon 'models' (called 'Codes'). As regards the common law fixation with a case-by-case development of the law, it is worth noting the observations of Lord MacMillan that, unlike the civil law lawyer, the Englishman:

> has found that life is unconformable to any fixed theory and that principles always fail because they never seem to fit the case in hand, and so prefers to leave theory and principle alone.
>
> (1937: 81)

We shall explore the significance of this statement over **Chapters 7** and **8**. One difficulty with this case-by-case development is that it does leave us with a slight 'Goldilocks problem' in that when there are very few cases on a topic we cannot be sure how far the precedent will be applied or changed and when there are hundreds of cases we have trouble sorting through all the detailed applications to get to the general principle—rarely are things 'just right'.

6.1.2 What is precedent?

The doctrine of judicial precedent is concerned with the importance of case law in our system. It is about achieving consistency. It is really the lawyer's term for legal experience. We all tend to repeat things we have done before if they proved successful: law is essentially no different. Nor should it be if we want some degree of certainty in our law. If one case has decided a point of law, then it is logical that that solution will be looked at in the future. Even small children recognise the need for consistency and certainty in how they are dealt with and how they deal with others. The US judge, Oliver Wendell Holmes Jr, once said that: 'The life of the Law has not been logic; it has been experience.' Miles Kington put it rather more cynically in *Punch*: judicial precedent means: 'A trick which has been tried before, successfully'.

But if judicial precedent is simply legal jargon for experience, why does it deserve our attention? Why can we say that, during your training in law and afterwards, you will have to possess a clear understanding of the intricacies of judicial precedent? The answer lies in the fact that the term 'experience' only begins to describe the situation.

First, even when a layperson uses the term 'precedent' there is an implication that what was done before should be done again—that a starting point in trying to solve a problem is to see what examples exist where this (or similar) problems have been tackled before. The example—the precedent—is at least a good guide and probably will be followed. This achieves consistency, if nothing else. As was said by the Court of Appeal in *Howard de Walden Estates Ltd* v *Aggio and others; Earl Cadogan and Cadogan Estates Ltd* v *26 Cadogan Square Ltd* [2007] EWCA Civ 499; [2007] All ER (D) 408 (May): 'This principle serves the interests of legal certainty. The need of litigants and their advisers to know where they stand is not served if a lower court is free to create a conflict of authority by declining to follow the relevant decision of a higher court.'

The corollary is that people making decisions are often afraid to do something in case 'it creates a precedent'. As MacCormick stated:

> To understand case-law … is to understand how it is that *particular* decisions by particular judges concerning particular parties to particular cases can be used in the construction of *general* rules applying to the actions and transactions of persons at large.
>
> (1987: 155)

In other words, combining the remarks of Lord MacMillan and MacCormick, the principles of English law are derived from observing the development of a line of particular cases on a particular topic. This is a key factor in English law. Because English lawyers are so avidly fixed on case law, principles do not develop unless claimants bring cases. Academics and practitioners may speculate on the development of legal principles, but it takes real-life cases to settle them. And the judges in each case, to a greater or lesser extent, draw upon the principles established in those earlier cases in reaching their decision. It should be noted, however, that there are also weaknesses in this system, and we will return to these later.

As we have already noted on the development of case law in negligence, this is a piecemeal, case-by-case progression. In 1950 the head of the judiciary in Scotland, Lord Cooper, put it this way: 'The civilian [i.e. lawyers using the Civil Law system] naturally reasons from principles to instances, the common lawyer from instances to principles' (Cooper: 1950). Lord Wright had already put it even more graphically in 1938 when he described how the common law judges 'proceed from case to case, like the ancient Mediterranean mariners, hugging the coast from point to point, and avoiding the dangers of the open sea . . .'. Lawyers like security. Richard Buxton (2009: 60) also notes that: 'The purpose of any case is to decide the issue between the parties, and not to reform the law.' There are many intriguing academic aspects in the study of law, but this quote emphasises that the purpose of law is to solve problems and disputes.

Slavish adherence to precedent has also been described whimsically as one which 'follows the trail of the calf'. The metaphor goes: many hundreds of years ago a calf wandered home and cut a path through the wood. The calf wandered all over the place but the trail it made was clear. Other animals followed this indirect path because it was easier to do so. Eventually there was a road, but one which did not necessarily go in a straight line. However, everyone subsequently followed that route. There are a number of sources for this idea, for example a 1905 poem by Sam Walter Foss called the 'Calf-Path'. It was quoted by Professor Max Radin (a nineteenth-century US jurist) in 'The Trail of the Calf' (1946: 137, 150), but the author goes on to show that the adherence to precedent is not as passive as this analogy leads us to believe: the path is not always followed slavishly but is in fact subject to modifications by its followers. Nevertheless, it is a fun way to visualise the somewhat meandering development of case law.

As an example of this more active and thoughtful case-by-case development of precedent imagine a case in, say, 1930, which decided that any person selling parrots was under an implied contractual duty to ensure that the parrot could talk. A layperson reading about this case might think it interesting, especially if he has just bought an unwanted dumb parrot. A lawyer, however, immediately starts to think of the ramifications of the case: what is its wider significance? How does it stand with other cases? What level of court made the decision? Thus, to the lawyer, the case presents further questions:

(a) Would this principle still apply if the pet shop owner clearly told the customer that the parrot could not talk?

(b) Does the same principle apply to similar birds such as budgerigars?

(c) Should the principle apply to any bird (e.g. that they twitter pleasantly even if they are not 'talkers')?

(d) Wider still, is there a general principle to be found in the case that might mean that a similar duty (say as to standards of health) might apply to the sale of all animals?

Thus, as MacCormick indicates, the particular case concerning parrots may consequently be seen as giving birth to a more general principle on the duties owed by pet shop owners to their customers, for example that they owed a duty always to deal in good faith. It is not beyond speculation that the same principle might one day then be applied to sellers of other types of goods such as televisions (not even in common use in 1930) or cars. Eventually a textbook writer will sum up the case law in one general statement on the duties owed by vendors of goods. Looking back at the history of the cases, we might find that the principle concerning one case about a mute parrot is now applied to all cases on defective merchandise.

The case of *Whittall* v *Kirby* [1947] KB 194 serves as a good, simple example to illustrate the development, from one case to another, of a legal principle, and we shall return to this throughout **Chapters 7** and **8** to demonstrate different aspects of judicial precedent.

In 1946 Henry Kirby was convicted of driving his lorry while intoxicated. This meant he would lose his licence unless, under the Road Traffic Act 1930, there was a 'special reason' not to disqualify him. The magistrates decided that, as he had no previous convictions, drove the lorry for a living, and had been given a substantial fine, these constituted special reasons not to disqualify him. On appeal by way of case stated (a special provision dealing with legal points alone) it was held that none of these reasons was a 'special reason': to be a 'special reason', that reason (it was said) had to be special to the facts of the offence, not to the offender. Being a lorry driver was only something special to the offender and so not enough to avoid disqualification. Something else would be needed to avoid disqualification. At this point, in 1947, however, would we know whether the same principle applied to, say, a taxi driver or to a commercial traveller? We only have one concrete example: a lorry driver. At its most obvious level the case can only concern lorry drivers. However, it is at this point that the specific words used by the judge in his judgment provide some guidance for later judges. Here, Lord Goddard stated: 'That a man is a professional driver cannot, as it seems to me, by any possibility be called a special reason.' This rather indicates that the case will be authority on the wider class of professional drivers, not just lorry drivers. But in 1947 lawyers did not know what this might mean; it would take further cases to establish this. Therefore, we will return to this example later to demonstrate the workings of case law and how this decision 'panned out' in future cases.

One interesting development as regards creating a form of 'restatement' of the law came in *R* v *Hunter* [2015] EWCA Crim 631; [2015] 2 Cr App R 9, where the Court of Appeal effectively issued a diktat, stating [103]: 'We have deliberately conducted a very thorough review of the case law so that it will be unnecessary in future for other courts to do the same. Reliance on this judgment, [and two other named cases] should suffice.'

In our legal system the idea of 'doing the same thing when faced with the same set of facts' was formalised as far back as the twelfth century, when judges would return to Westminster from their journeys around the country and compare their decisions. It is a form of standardising so that everyone in similar circumstances is treated the same. Where our Common Law system differs from others can be seen in section **6.2**: the idea of **binding** precedent, which arose much later.

6.2 The idea of binding precedent (*stare decisis*)

We now need to add one further ingredient. It is this: an important and distinctive element of English law is that the reasoning and decisions found in preceding cases are not simply considered with respect or as a good guide, but can be **binding** on later courts. This is known as the principle of *stare rationibus decidendis*; usually referred to as *stare decisis*. It translates simply as 'Let the decision stand.' *Stare rationibus decidendis* is the more accurate statement because, as we shall see, it is the reasoning (*rationibus*) that is the vital binding element in judicial precedent. However, nobody actually refers to it this way.

What *stare decisis* means in practice is that when a court makes a decision in a case, then any courts which are of equal or lower status to that court must follow that previous decision if the case before them is similar to that earlier case. Thus, as Lord Neuberger explained in *Willers* v *Joyce (No. 2)* [2016] UKSC 44; [2016] 3 WLR 534 para [5]:

> The doctrine is, of course, seen in its simplest and most familiar form when applied to the hierarchy of courts. On issues of law, (i) Circuit Judges are bound by decisions of High Court Judges, the Court of Appeal and the Supreme Court, (ii) High Court Judges are bound by decisions of the Court of Appeal and the Supreme Court, and (iii) the Court of Appeal is bound by decisions of the Supreme Court. (The rule that a Circuit Judge is bound by a decision of a High Court Judge is most clear from a 'Note' included at the end of the judgment in *Howard De Walden Estates Ltd* v *Aggio* [2008] Ch 26).

At para **[6]**, his Lordship continued, 'The position is rather more nuanced when it comes to courts of co-ordinate jurisdiction.'

We shall return to consider that last sentence in due course. What is made clear here, though, is that, once one court has decided a matter other inferior courts are bound to follow that decision, whether they agree with it or not.

You must be careful: the 'decision' of a case can mean a number of different things. At its simplest, the 'decision' is that X won and Y lost. Thus, X and Y are (subject to any appeal) bound by that decision; this is referred to as *res judicata* (a matter which has been adjudicated upon). But when we use the word 'decision' in the context of legal analysis we are referring to something much wider. We are referring to the *whole* reasoning process that went into deciding that X won—we are referring to *why* X won and we shall explore how we set about this later. For instance, in *Whittall* v *Kirby* (see section **6.1.2**) the decision was not merely that a lorry driver convicted of being drunk in charge could be disqualified, but that he was disqualified *because* the idea of a 'special reason' under the statute had to be special to the offence and not the offender. In analysing cases you are looking for the 'because', not just the result.

So, you must be aware right at the start that legal reasoning is not simply a process of matching one case against another; it is not merely a question of drawing direct analogies. Finding analogous cases is a good starting point, but there will always be differences in the facts of the two cases, if nothing else. Equally, the status and therefore the importance of the decision depends upon which court made it. We shall look at the court structure and which court is bound to follow the decision of another court in section **6.4**.

Before that, however, we need to be clear on what we mean by 'similarities' and 'differences' between cases. It is very easy to fall into the trap of comparing cases on their facts without, as we noted above, looking at the *reasoning* used in reaching that decision. For instance, just because the facts of two cases are apparently similar does not mean they should be decided in the same way. You would not, for instance, say that if a tabby cat called Henry miaows like a banshee, then every other tabby cat called Henry will do so too.

We can translate this into something more realistic and legally orientated.

EXERCISE 8 Zebras on the North Circular

Let us say that in *case (1)* a man driving a Ford Mondeo runs over an old lady who was lawfully using a zebra crossing. The man is held to be liable in negligence.
Let us say that in *case (2)* a woman driving a BMW runs over an old man who was crossing the road.

 QUESTIONS

Should she be found liable, too, or do you need to ask some further questions? If there are other questions, what might they be?
We do not present a formalised answer to this, because we wish to explore the ramifications of the issues it raises, but you may check your ideas against the comments which follow in the text.

We have seen in earlier exercises that a proper assessment and analysis of factual detail is essential to the application of rules. You might wish to know, for instance, what were the weather conditions in each case, whether either of the drivers was speeding, whether the old man was crossing the road at a safe point.

All these matters will come out in the evidence given by the parties. The judge will decide, on the strength of the evidence, which version of the 'truth' he or she believes. The judge will then apply the law (i.e. the existing judicial precedents) to the facts of this case to decide whether, on the facts as found, the defendant is liable to pay damages to the claimant. The more similar the facts of this new case are to existing precedents, the easier it is for the judge to decide that the law which is found in those precedents applies to the new case; the more the new facts differ from existing precedents (or raise completely novel points), the more difficult it will be to find a match. As you have seen in **Chapter 5** there are various reasoning techniques a judge may employ (reasoning by induction, deduction, analogy, or even through policy considerations), but the basic idea is that he or she has to choose whether the new case should be decided in the same way as the older cases. This leads us to ask: what similarities or differences in the facts might be significant here. Are the cases, for instance:

(i)   sufficiently similar that the decision of *case (1)* should be applied in *case (2)*; or

(ii)   sufficiently different that the decision of *case (1)* should not be applied (never mind be considered binding) in *case (2)*; or

(iii) different in, at first sight, minor, but in reality, significant ways so that *case (1)* is likely to be applied to *case (2)*; or

(iv) are the facts different, but the principle underlying the decisions in the cases similar?

Point (iv) is the most difficult one. Here you need to be sure of the **principle** that was established in the first case: does the reasoning—the '*why?*'—in the first case apply to the second, even though the facts differ? In some instances, this may even involve using one case in, say, shipping law, to answer a question about the liability of a fairground company to a local authority in the law of contract (as was the point in a real case dealt with by one of the authors). The factual settings are miles apart but the contractual principle involved might be common ground. In this particular example, for instance, involving such widely different facts, the legal *principle* in question was whether a contract could exist when there were three parties involved and, if so, between which parties (the fairground, the local council, and a booking agent on the one hand and, in the nineteenth century shipping law case, a yacht club and two race contestants).

In **Chapter 7** we shall explore in more depth how we assess the '*why?*' in a case. For the moment, though, we shall concentrate more on how precedent operates throughout the hierarchy of the courts. To do this, we return to our injured pedestrians. Imagine that when you read the report of *case (1)*— the Ford Mondeo hitting the lady on a zebra crossing—you found that the case went all the way to the Supreme Court, which pronounced that whenever a driver injures a pedestrian, irrespective of how careless the pedestrian was, the driver is to be held to be at fault. This would mean that, whatever the differences in fact between *case (1)* and *case (2)* (which in our example involved a woman driving a BMW running over an old man who was crossing the road), it looks as if the driver in *case (2)* will be liable because the **general** principle established in *case (1)* would apply. The principle enunciated by the Supreme Court would be so wide as to make all car drivers 'strictly liable' for an accident; negligence would be irrelevant.

On the other hand, perhaps the principle found in the Supreme Court's decision in *case (1)* was simply that drivers will always be held to blame if pedestrians are injured while using a zebra crossing. If that is the principle established in *case (1)*, then the presence or absence of a zebra crossing is of utmost importance and it is arguable that the decision in *case (1)* should not apply to the facts of *case (2)* as *case (2)* did not involve a zebra crossing.

6.3 Establishing the principle in a case

As can be seen from this discussion, the doctrine of judicial precedent is not simply a mechanical process of matching similarities and differences as in some weird game of 'Snap'. It is not merely a science of comparisons for it embodies the art of interpretation; the art of propounding the **principle** to be derived from each case. It also involves the lifeblood of a lawyer: argument. We will deal with this aspect of precedent in depth in **Chapter 7**. However, by way of introduction we can look at one case from the nineteenth century (the one which appears in the box below: *Household Fire Insurance* v *Grant*) and see how it was treated as a precedent when cases, which at first sight seemed quite similar to it, came before later courts.

Household Fire Insurance Co. v Grant (1879) 4 Ex D 216

Grant made an application in writing to the company for shares. A deposit was paid, the remainder to be paid within 12 months. The company allotted shares to Grant and posted the allotment to him. The letter never arrived. The company later went into liquidation and the liquidator sought the balance of Grant's application, which was still outstanding. Grant maintained he had no contract with the company because his offer had not been accepted. No contract would mean no liability to pay. The company/liquidator maintained that the offer had been accepted when the letter of acceptance had been posted, even though it never arrived.

In case you have not studied contract law yet (or are not going to), we should explain that a contract is formed when there is an offer which is accepted, without the addition of new terms, by the other party. A person making an offer is termed the *offeror* (in the earlier example that would be Grant); the person receiving the offer is the *offeree* (Household Fire Insurance). The general rule is that acceptance has to be communicated by the offeree. There is no contract simply because, in his or her own mind, the offeree is willing to accept. However, a major problem arises when the parties are not face to face. If they communicate by post, for instance, when does the acceptance take place? Should it be when the letter of acceptance is posted by the offeree, or only when it arrives with the offeror?

Prior to the case of *Household Fire Insurance* v *Grant* there existed a number of authorities on what is now termed the 'postal rules' of acceptance in contract. These stretched back to *Adams* v *Lindsell* (1818) 1 B & A 681, but the key case under scrutiny was to be the House of Lords case of *Dunlop* v *Higgins* (1848) 1 HLC 381; 9 ER 805. In this case Dunlop wrote to Higgins offering to sell some iron, reply to be by return of post. The offer was accepted by Higgins in a letter but bad weather delayed the post. In the meantime, there had been an increase in the price of iron. It was in Dunlop's interest to argue that no contract had been concluded with Higgins because then Dunlop would still own the iron and be able to sell it to other customers at the new (higher) price. So, Dunlop informed Higgins that the reply had not been made by return of post and so was invalid. The House of Lords decided otherwise: a contract existed when the letter of acceptance was posted.

What was the reasoning behind that decision? In *Household Fire Insurance* v *Grant* all three judges in the Court of Appeal analysed whether *Dunlop* v *Higgins* applied to the case before them. Lord Justice Thesiger said that the decision in *Dunlop* v *Higgins* rested 'upon a principle which embraces and governs the present case'. He believed that to say that the acceptance takes place when the letter is posted and arrives late (as with *Dunlop* v *Higgins*) but not if it never arrives (as with *Household Fire*) would be illogical. The principle was, therefore, that once the letter of acceptance was posted both parties were bound. Of course, evidence would be needed to show that the letter of acceptance was posted, but that point of evidence was irrelevant to the legal principle.

However, when the next judge, Bagallay LJ, examined *Dunlop* v *Higgins* he concluded (at 227–8):

I think that the principle established by that case is limited in its application to cases in which by reason of general usage, or of the relations between the parties ... or of the terms in which the offer is made, the acceptance of such offer by a letter through the post is expressly or impliedly authorised.

Thus the principle in *Dunlop* v *Higgins* was seen by Bagallay LJ as being more limited than Thesiger LJ's approach—it would not apply in all cases where the post was used, only to cases where it was general practice or specifically agreed that the acceptance would be by post. On the facts Bagallay LJ decided that the present case still fell within the rule because the offer had stated that reply should be by return of post.

Lord Justice Bramwell dissented. He thought there was *no contract* because the letter never arrived. He argued that *Dunlop* v *Higgins* had been completely misinterpreted: at best it was authority for the rule that acceptance takes place on posting only where the letter arrives (albeit late and within a reasonable time).

So, the same authority was used by two Lords Justices to find for the company but they had quite different interpretations of what the precedent case of *Dunlop* v *Higgins* really decided. Bramwell LJ, of course, read the same case, decided it stood for something very different, and held against the company—showing at least that simply knowing about the existence of a case is not enough; you must be able to argue its relevance or irrelevance to the case in hand. This means that you must read cases in depth. Such advice has always been unpalatable, but if you choose not to, then you run the risk of being caught out by your opponent in a legal argument. To adapt slightly a quote from Mark Twain: the person who does not read cases has no advantage over the person who cannot read them.

In this chapter we shall concentrate on the position where the facts are sufficiently similar that the cases are 'alike'. How will the doctrine of *stare decisis* affect our analysis? In answering this question, it becomes important that we should look at the mechanical side of precedent. The courts stand in a defined hierarchy: which courts are **bound** to follow the decisions of which other courts? This is not usually perceived as the most exciting part of legal studies, but understanding the workings of *stare decisis* depends upon having a sound grasp of the court structure. In turn, an efficient system of precedent depends upon dependable law reporting. You should familiarise yourself with the court structure and know how to use a law library. You will find these matters explained in **Chapters 2–4**, detailed in any text on the English legal system, and nearly every law course now also includes extensive instruction on how to use a law library (both hard copy and legal databases).

6.4 The mechanics of *stare decisis*

The system of precedent itself involves a fair degree of detail, but the basic principle to keep in mind is that the precedents created by superior courts bind lower courts and, generally, courts of equal status. We considered the basic court structure in **Chapter 1** (at **1.7.3** and **Figures 1.1** and **1.2**). You are advised to refer to **Figures 1.1** and **1.2** to see the relationship of the courts discussed hereafter. It is also interesting to note that this idea of **binding** precedent was not always present in our law and, in reality, was only clearly established as late as 1898. Prior to that, as Lundmark notes (2003:161), 'case decisions in their totality were [seen] as a reflection of the law' rather than individual precedents.

One other idea you need to bear in mind is that not all precedents are binding. For if some precedents are binding, there must be others which are not. These we call **persuasive** precedents. **Persuasive** precedents arise out of a number of contexts:

(i) Decisions of lower courts such as the County Court and tribunals, which cannot bind. They may be persuasive.

(ii) Decisions of the High Court at first instance (i.e. the trial stage), which are persuasive authority for later cases in the High Court (but are binding on lower courts such as county courts).

(iii) Decisions of the Judicial Committee of the Privy Council.

(iv) Decisions of the Scottish and Northern Irish courts.

(v) Decisions of other courts within the common law world: see, for example, the use of the Australian case of *Sutherland Shire Council* v *Heyman* (1985) 60 ALR 1 in *Murphy* v *Brentwood DC* (1990), detailed in section **6.4.1**.

6.4.1 The Supreme Court (formerly the House of Lords)

The decisions of the Supreme Court/House of Lords bind all lower courts. For some 100 years the Law Lords also considered themselves bound by their previous decisions (though, oddly, the Judicial Committee of the Privy Council, consisting of the same people but hearing the final appeals of the British Empire, strictly speaking did not). This changed with the *Practice Statement (Judicial Precedent)* [1966] 1 WLR 1234, where the House of Lords said that though the doctrine of being bound had many commendable points, 'too rigid adherence to precedent may lead to injustice in a particular case and also unduly restrict the proper development of the law'. The Supreme Court has not re-issued the Practice Statement but, in *Austin* v *Southwark London Borough Council* [2010] UKSC 28, [2010] 3 WLR 144, at para 25, Lord Hope DP (with whom all other members of the Court agreed) stated that this 'has as much effect in [the Supreme Court] as it did before [in the House of Lords]'. This view has been incorporated into Practice Direction 4 of the Supreme Court, which details how to make an application to the Supreme Court.

The Lords decided that they could depart from their own previous decisions, but would do so only in rare circumstances (there is a technical distinction between the lesser idea of *departing from* a decision and the more damning one *overruling* it, but the terms are used interchangeably even by the House of Lords itself). Remember that the Supreme Court/House of Lords is the highest court in the land. Its pronouncements (only about 100 a year) need to be seen to create an air of certainty in business dealings, in criminal law, in land law, and so on. Changing its mind may do 'justice' to a particular case, but at the cost of certainty. The level of reluctance can be seen in Lord Hoffmann's words in *Horton* v *Sadler* [2006] UKHL 27; [2007] 1 AC 307 (at [40]):

> But the fact that the House as now constituted would have decided *Walkley* differently is not a sufficient reason for departing from a decision which has stood for nearly 30 years and which the House has followed on two subsequent occasions. If the House in its judicial capacity has erred, it is usually better to leave it to Parliament to change the law prospectively than for the House to undo its mistake with retrospective effect.

Again, the reluctance to disturb legal positions which have been adopted widely by practitioners on the basis of previous House of Lords/Supreme Court decisions can be seen in the words of Lord Hope in *Austin* v *Mayor and Burgesses of the London Borough of Southwark* [2010] UKSC 28 at [31]: 'There are very good reasons for accepting that the law as declared in Thompson [1987] 1 WLR 1425, however unsatisfactory it can now be seen to be, should not be disturbed.' This view is often repeated, as in *Haile* v *London Borough of Waltham Forest* [2015] UKSC 34 at [73], where Lord Reed JSC said: 'First, we should be very slow before departing from an earlier decision of this court or the House of Lords.' The same logic appears in another common law jurisdiction, that of the Irish Supreme Court (see *Desmond* v *Moriarty* [2018] IESC 34), which talks about 'compelling reasons' being required to overturn earlier Irish Supreme Court decisions. However, despite this, the Law Lords (and now the Justices of the Supreme Court) have changed their minds. As Lord Hoffmann continued in *Horton* v *Sadler* (discussed earlier in this section): '[T]he situation which has been created by *Walkley* falls squarely within Lord Reid's description in *R* v *National Insurance Commissioner, ex parte Hudson* [1972] AC 944, 966 of a case in which it would be right for the House to depart from a previous decision.' There, Lord Reid had said: 'It is notorious that where an existing decision is disapproved but cannot be overruled courts tend to distinguish it on inadequate grounds. . . . On balance it seems to me that overruling such a decision will promote and not impair the certainty of the law.'

The same was seen in *A* v *Hoare* [2008] UKHL 6; [2008] 1 AC 844, where their Lordships chose to overturn one of their decisions which was barely fifteen years old (*Stubbings* v *Webb* [1993] AC 498). The reason for this was that *Stubbings* was found to have placed too much weight on authorities external to the statute in question and so was simply wrongly decided (we cover which authorities can be used in **Chapter 9**). In general terms, it would seem to need a fundamental change in circumstances or evidence that adherence to a previous decision will result in unforeseen serious injustice to generate such departures.

A further example comes where decisions of the Court of Justice of the European Union (CJEU) or the European Court of Human Rights contradict earlier House of Lords' or Supreme Court decisions (see **Chapter 11** as regards the role of the CJEU after Brexit). The primacy of these courts in their respective jurisdictions means that the Supreme Court must consider departing from its own precedents.

So, though it is rare for the Supreme Court to depart from previous decisions, it is certainly not unknown. To adopt the Irish Supreme Court's terminology: compelling reasons have been found. We list below some examples of this occurrence, but these cases do not reveal one unifying principle. Some concern older decisions having run their course when placed in modern society, some concern removing House of Lords' decisions which later courts have been trying to avoid following by making very fine distinctions, some just seem to concern a general sense of 'fairness' (see also the now ageing but still excellent analysis of this topic in Harris (2002)).

British Railways Board v *Herrington* [1972] AC 877; [1972] 1 All ER 749

Public policy and developments in the law: the Lords faced a number of nineteenth-century and early twentieth-century decisions wherein they had held that there was only a limited duty of care in negligence owed to children who trespassed onto property. This duty was that the occupier should not act recklessly with regard to children whom he knew to be there; and public policy dictated that there was no duty at all to keep out such children or to make the premises safe for them. Since then changes in perceptions of public policy and the development of the law of negligence had altered the approach to the whole topic of responsibility for negligent actions. Thus, their Lordships felt able to ignore the earlier decisions and impose on British Railways a duty of care in keeping railway line fences repaired.

Miliangos v *George Frank (Textiles) Ltd* [1976] AC 443; [1975] 3 All ER 801

Changes in how trade was conducted: the House of Lords had previously decided that all awards of damages in an English court had to be made in sterling. In this case, however, because of changes in international trade and the status of sterling they felt the time had come not to adhere to their previous decisions.

R v *Shivpuri* [1987] AC 1; [1986] 2 All ER 334

Getting it wrong analytically: the case concerned the law as to criminal attempts. A decision of the House of Lords one year earlier (*Anderton* v *Ryan* [1985] AC 560; [1985] 2 All ER 355) had received great criticism. In *R* v *Shivpuri* the House of Lords changed its mind on whether it was possible to attempt to do the impossible. This is a rare example of the House of Lords overturning its own decisions simply because it felt that the earlier decision was wrong. Usually the Lords look for wider policy considerations (cf. our earlier discussion in section **6.2**).

Murphy v *Brentwood District Council* [1990] 3 WLR 414; [1990] 2 All ER 908

Faulty analysis and academic criticism: their Lordships were again prepared to overturn one of their previous decisions (*Anns* v *Merton London Borough Council* [1978] AC 728; [1977] 2 All ER 492) and there were various reasons given by their Lordships for why they were prepared to do this. Lord Mackay, the (then) Lord Chancellor, felt that the earlier case was taken as a preliminary issue of law so that the facts had not been considered in detail (i.e. the point had not been argued fully, so the authority was weak). The case may have worked in theory but did not relate to real facts. On the other hand, Lord Keith looked at *Sutherland Shire Council* v *Heyman* (1985) 60 ALR 1, an Australian case which had rejected *Anns*, and some US cases which had analysed the older cases on which *Anns* itself was based and proved these earlier authorities to be faulty. Thus, said Lord Keith, departure from *Anns* could be justified on the ground that the case was 'unsatisfactory'. Lord Oliver also noted academic criticism of the decision in *Anns*.

Arthur J.S. Hall & Co. (a firm) v *Simons* [2002] 1 AC 615

Public policy: the House of Lords, by majority, departed from their own decision of *Rondel* v *Worsley* [1969] 1 AC 191 and removed the immunity from being sued previously enjoyed by advocates (for alleged negligence in the conduct of civil proceedings). This was done on the basis that the public policy reasons for the immunity being granted no longer stood up to scrutiny in today's society.

R v *Jogee (Ameen Hassan)* [2016] UKSC 8; [2017] A.C. 387

Misinterpretation of earlier authorities: the case concerned the concept of 'joint enterprise liability' in criminal law. This is a doctrine under which a person who assists or encourages another (the principal) to commit a crime is guilty of the same offence as the principal: there is no need to establish which elements of the offence were committed by which person. So, all those engaged in a bank robbery, from the person funding the operation to the 'lookout' (the accessories) are guilty of the same offence as the masked robber. But what happens when the principal goes beyond what is expected and kills someone? That was the problem before the court. A Privy Council case (*Chan Wing-Siu v The Queen* [1985] AC 168) had established that where the plan is to commit one crime but another is committed, all parties carry the responsibility for the second crime if it could have been foreseen that the principal might have acted in the way he did, even if this was not the accessory's intention. This had been followed by the House of Lords in two later cases. At para [**79**] of *Jogee*, the Supreme Court ruled that: 'In plain terms, our analysis leads us to the conclusion that the introduction of the principle was based on an incomplete, and in some respects erroneous, reading of the previous case law, coupled with generalised and questionable policy arguments.'

The Justices also noted that s. 44 of the Serious Crime Act 2007 did not use this idea of 'foreseeability' as a test for whether there had been encouragement or assistance in the commissioning of the intended offence, so it seemed inappropriate to apply that test to an unintended consequence. Thus, the foreseeability test should be converted into one which asked 'whether the accessory intended to encourage or assist Defendant 1 to commit the crime, acting with whatever mental element the offence requires of Defendant 1. . . . If the crime requires a particular intent, Defendant 2 must intend (it may be conditionally) to assist Defendant 1 to act with such intent' [para 90].

Knauer v *Ministry of Justice* [2016] UKSC 9; [2016] 4 All ER 897

Outdated methodologies: this was a technically complicated case on how one calculates damages being claimed by a widow under the Fatal Accidents Act 1976 for the death of her husband (here, down to mesothelioma arising from exposure to asbestos). In ordinary 'personal injury' cases (e.g. a road traffic accident) the approach is to calculate losses up to the date of trial and award a lump sum in respect of those. This is a very easy calculation. Any future losses from date of trial are then calculated on what is termed the 'multiplier/multiplicand' approach. The 'multiplier' is the life expectancy of the victim and the 'muliplicand' is the annual figure for loss sustained. One then uses tables (such as one called the Ogden Tables) to multiply all these figures, allowing for discounts for early receipt of monies, etc., to get to a final award (so 20 years at £20,000 a year gives losses of £400,000 before deductions). It is a relatively scientific method. In fatal accident cases, however, such as here, the appropriate method had been mapped out by two earlier House of Lords' cases as being: take the multiplier as at the date of death and then deduct from it the time which elapsed between death and trial. As Lord Neuberger PSC commented, although the Supreme Court 'should be very circumspect before accepting an invitation to invoke the 1966 Practice Statement', nevertheless these differences in calculation methods resulted in unfairness to the claimant and mixed up a calculation based on properly considered actuarial principles with an arbitrary arithmetical deduction. Further, when the earlier House of Lords' cases (in 1979 and 1983) had been decided there were no Ogden Tables and the Law Commission had since recommended that the earlier House of Lords' decisions should not be followed. All these reasons justified the use of the 1966 Statement.

Patel v *Mirza* [2016] UKSC 42; [2017] AC 467

Public policy and review of the underlying purpose of the doctrine: in *Holman* v *Johnson* (1775) 1 Cowp 341 at 343 Lord Mansfield stated that, 'No court will lend its aid to a man who founds his cause of action upon an immoral or an illegal act.' Thus was born the doctrine of 'illegality' and the cases since that time have based their analysis on whether the person claiming was relying on their illegal act as the basis of their claim: if so, their claim failed. In *Patel* v *Mirza* [2016] UKSC 42; [2017] AC 467 (a case concerning 'insider dealing') the Supreme Court reviewed the cases, such as the House of Lords' decision in *Tinsley* v *Milligan* [1993] 3 All ER 65; [1994] 1 AC 340, and decided that the concept of 'reliance' was outdated and too simplistic. Instead, claims should not be barred just because they were based on illegality: there was a discretion involved centred on the nature of the circumstances themselves.

As we have commented, there is no obvious pattern to be found and nor can there be in reality. In the end the House of Lords/Supreme Court has had to—and will continue to have to—try to balance questions of certainty, flexibility, legal, commercial, and social developments and the influence of European and international law. These concepts are often in direct conflict. It is hardly surprising, therefore, that no model emerges as to when the Supreme Court will change direction. And, amidst all this, it should not be forgotten that the Supreme Court will often *not* change its mind, as with *R* v *Kansal (Yash Pal) (No. 2)* [2001] UKHL 62; [2002] 2 AC 69 (again with dissenting voices), where the House criticised their own previous decision in *R* v *Lambert (Steven)* [2001] UKHL 37—on the application of the Human Rights Act 1998 to matters arising before that Act came into force—but did not overrule *Lambert*.

The problem is no different when considering criminal law cases as opposed to civil matters: the function of the Supreme Court is to lay down clear and just principles in both areas. There is, however, another problem which lies hidden in all this: it travels under the name of 'prospective overruling' and we shall examine that in section **6.4.2**.

It is worth noting here, though, by way of an aside, that some time ago, in *Food Corp. of India* v *Antclizo Shipping Co.* [1988] 1 WLR 603; [1988] 2 All ER 513, Lord Goff (on behalf of the court) stated that their Lordships would not depart from a previous House of Lords' decision unless:

(i)   it felt free to depart from both the reasoning and decision of the earlier case; and

(ii) such a review would affect the resolution of the actual case before them and not be of mere academic interest.

This decision, however, has not had the impact first anticipated and has not been referred to on many occasions. But the *Antclizo* case does allow us to say one further thing, to which we shall return. That is, when a case first appears, stating a principle of law, one can never really be sure of the impact the case will have. At the instant it appears, when there are no other cases which have attempted to apply it, one can only speculate as to its impact.

This is the difficulty that faces practitioners every time a new case appears—what is the legal principle of the case and how far-reaching will it be? We noted with *Whittall* v *Kirby* (in section **6.1.2**), for instance, that in 1947 we did not know for sure whether the reasoning as to what constituted a 'special reason' applied to all professional drivers or just to lorry drivers.

6.4.2 Retrospective and prospective overruling

As we have already seen, courts make findings on disputed questions of fact, identify and apply the relevant law to the facts agreed by the parties or found by the court, and award appropriate remedies. But when a court is faced with a decision on what the law means (whether on 'pure' case law or the interpretation of statutes) it might depart from or overrule a previous decision. When it does this the court can adopt one of three different approaches:

(i) *Approach 1*: say that the law is [x] and, if that differs from what everyone thought the law was, then hard luck—it was always [x] but we did not know it until now. Here, any decision which changes the law from what it was previously thought to be operates *retrospectively* as well as *prospectively*. It is retrospective in that the parties to the case are caught by the ruling and so are all those who have, say, created leases or contracts on the basis of what was thought to be the law. Despite their best endeavours, it now turns out they were wrong. You can imagine that this can produce very unfortunate results. *Approach 1* is also prospective in that this is the 'new law' so all future cases will be decided this way. In the case of *In Re Spectrum Plus Ltd (In Liquidation)* [2005] UKHL 41; [2005] 3 WLR 58 Lord Nicholls explained the position this way:

[7] The ruling will have a retrospective effect so far as the parties to the particular dispute are concerned … Further, because of the doctrine of precedent the same would be true of everyone else whose case thereafter came before a court. Their rights and obligations would be decided according to the law as enunciated by [the court] in that case even though the relevant events occurred before that decision was given.

[8] People generally conduct their affairs on the basis of what they understand the law to be. This 'retrospective' effect of a change in the law of this nature can have disruptive and seemingly unfair consequences.

The *retrospective* effect of precedents has been made abundantly clear in the House of Lords case of *Kleinwort Ltd* v *Lincoln City Council* [1999] AC 349; [1998] 4 All ER 513.

In this case, the House of Lords overruled long-established Court of Appeal authorities and abolished the rule that money paid under a mistake of law could not be recovered. Their Lordships were agreed that the idea of retrospective effect means that once the law has been changed it applies not only to the case in hand but to all subsequent cases coming before the courts, even though the events in question occurred *before* the previous authority was overruled. What they were not in agreement over was how this applied to the actual case on whether a mistake of law arose *at the time of the contract* when the law was later changed; on this they were divided 3:2 in favour of saying there was a mistake of law:

(ii) *Approach 2*: say that the law is [x] but, because everyone has organised their affairs until now on the basis that the law was [y], the new view of the law only affects events occurring *after* the decision. So, using our previous examples, only contracts or leases formed *after* the date of the judgment would be affected by the 'new' law, [x]. Contracts and leases, etc. formed *before* the judgment would continue to fall under the 'old' law, [y]. This is the 'purest' form of *prospective* overruling. It was popular in the US courts for a while. Most statutes work on this basis. The law is said to 'change' only from that decision in the case onwards. Prospective overruling (sometimes described as 'non-retroactive overruling') is therefore a judicial tool fashioned to mitigate the adverse consequences of making major changes in the law. This is what Lord Nicholls had to say:

[9] In its simplest form prospective overruling … has the effect that the court ruling has an exclusively prospective effect. The ruling applies only to transactions or happenings occurring after the date of the court decision. All transactions entered into, or events occurring, before that date continue to be governed by the law as it was conceived to be before the court gave its ruling.

(iii) *Approach 3 (mixtures)*: it is possible to come up with other variations on this theme. For instance, the decision might be held to be prospective as regards everyone not involved in the case but retrospective in its effect as between the parties to the case in which the ruling is given. Or the ruling may be prospective as regards everyone not involved in the case but retrospective as between the parties in the case in which the ruling was given *and also* as between the parties in any other cases already pending before the courts on the same issue.

What does this mean in practice? Imagine that you have just completed some complicated contractual negotiations, basing your law on a case from 1990. One morning you read that the Supreme Court has 'changed' the law of contract: it is no longer what you (and everyone else) thought it was. Under this new interpretation the deal you have just concluded is worthless. Now, you know that this means if you are negotiating a contract *today* you must take into account the 'new law'. But does the ruling affect the contract you concluded last week? If the Supreme Court ruling is *retrospective*, then the answer is 'yes'. If it is only *prospective*, then your contract is safe (it will be interpreted under the 'old' law) but any new contracts with new clients would have to be drafted with the recent decision in mind. The idea of prospective overruling therefore looks attractive but it hides a real problem: we could have different laws applying to the same types of contract—the only differences being when they were dated.

You may have guessed from the earlier quotes that the House of Lords' decision in *In Re Spectrum Plus* reviewed the law regarding retrospective and prospective overruling—and Lord Nicholl's crystal-clear speech is worth reading for its explanation of case law. In the end, Lord Nicholls showed some enthusiasm for allowing prospective overruling (but only in exceptional circumstances) and Lords Hope and Walker agreed with Lord Nicholls; Lords Steyn, Scott, and Brown accepted that one should never say never about such matters, but were not in favour of using prospective overruling—Lords Steyn and Scott expressly stating that they would not allow prospective overruling in relation to statutory interpretation, only 'pure' case law.

On this basis, retrospective overruling is still the norm—so, in our contract example, you would be advised to try to negotiate new terms.

6.4.3 The Court of Appeal

The importance of this court, both because of its place in the hierarchy and because of its heavy workload, means that you need to be aware of how it deals with precedent. Most of the important cases you will deal with in your studies were reached by this court or its nineteenth-century predecessors such as the Court of Exchequer Chamber.

There are two important questions concerning the Court of Appeal and the notion of *stare decisis*. They are: (i) to what extent is the Court of Appeal bound to follow the decisions of the House of Lords/Supreme Court; and (ii) to what extent is it bound to follow its own decisions?

To what extent is the Court of Appeal bound to follow decisions of the House of Lords/Supreme Court?

Strictly speaking, the answer is always. But there have been campaigns in the Court of Appeal to overcome the principle. The principal crusader was Lord Denning MR. His retirement in 1982 signalled a halt to the conflict, but the analyses still apply.

The *per incuriam* campaign

In his major attack Lord Denning advocated that if a House of Lords' decision had been made *per incuriam* it need not be followed. A *per incuriam* decision is one where a court failed to take into account all the relevant and vital statutes or case authorities and that this had a major effect on the decision. The analogy might be made with the writing of a scientific paper. Let us say a famous scientist produces a theory, and that a few years later it is discovered that his research was faulty: he had not read two of the leading papers. Would you say there are grounds for arguing that the theory should be open to scrutiny, or even doubt?

The *per incuriam* rule is a well-established technical rule; but you must be careful here. Saying that a decision was made *per incuriam* does not simply mean that the earlier court got things wrong. It only means that there was a significant oversight. As we shall see later in this section, not only must there have been a failure to take account of relevant authorities, that fault must also have been such a major defect that it seriously affected the reasoning in the case and would have affected the outcome. So, with the example of the scientist, if it is now discovered that if he had researched thoroughly and read the two leading papers this would still have had no effect on his theory, the fault is a technical one of methodology and does not affect the conclusions drawn.

Lord Denning MR tried this form of reasoning in *Broome v Cassell* [1971] 2 QB 354; [1971] 2 All ER 187, convincing the other members of the Court of Appeal that an earlier House of Lords' decision (*Rookes v Barnard* [1964] AC 1129; [1964] 1 All ER 367) was a decision made *per incuriam* because it had failed to consider even earlier House of Lords' authorities. However, when *Broome v Cassell* went to the House of Lords, the Law Lords rebuked Lord Denning for adopting such a rule because they believed he had plainly looked for an excuse not to adhere to *stare decisis*. Lord Hailsham, the (then) Lord Chancellor, said: 'In the hierarchical system of courts which exists in this country, it is necessary for each lower tier, including the Court of Appeal, to accept loyally the decisions of the higher tiers': [1972] AC 1027, at 1054.

The 'lapsed rule' campaign

Let us say that the House of Lords reached a decision some years ago based upon a particular rule or set of facts, for example that damages in English courts can be given only in sterling because of the stability of the currency and established forms of procedure. Now let us say that the reason for the rule has disappeared: the forms have changed and sterling has lost its stability. Should the precedent created by the House of Lords be followed even though the whole basis of this precedent has disappeared?

This was the question considered by the Court of Appeal, led by Lord Denning, in *Schorsch Meier GmbH v Hennin* [1975] QB 416; [1975] 1 All ER 152. Like so many things in law, a Latin maxim describes the rule Lord Denning wished to use: *cessante ratione legis, cessat ipsa lex* (with the reason for the rule ceasing, the law itself no longer exists).

On this occasion the Court of Appeal was split. Lord Denning and Foster J agreed that a 1961 decision of the House of Lords (*Re United Railways of Havana and Regla Warehouses Ltd* [1961] AC 1007; [1960] 2 All ER 332) had run its course. In fact, the rule that damages should be awarded only in sterling seems to have existed for over 300 years. Lord Justice Lawton, however, did not recognise that the Court of Appeal had such power and found himself bound to follow the House of Lords.

This case did not go on appeal to the House of Lords. However, as seen in **6.4.1** above, the House of Lords soon had opportunity to comment on this issue in a case named *Miliangos* v *George Frank (Textiles) Ltd* [1977] QB 489; [1976] 3 All ER 599; and once again disapproved Lord Denning's attempts to vary the notion of *stare decisis*. With a touch of irony, though, their Lordships did overrule their own previous decisions on the same grounds proposed by Lord Denning, i.e. the 'lapsed rule' idea.

The same question was raised in *WB (a protected party through her litigation friend the Official Solicitor)* v *W District Council (Equality & Human Rights Commission intervening)* [2018] EWCA Civ 928. This case concerned a person who was homeless and who suffered from mental illness, making an application for housing under the Housing Act 1996. In 1993, the House of Lords had held that a homeless person with mental disabilities, who could not understand the choices she had to make when offered accommodation, could not be treated as a person in priority need for the purposes of the Housing Act 1985. It was argued, amongst other points, that the attitude to disabled people had changed since that decision, so it should be ignored. On that point of precedent Arden LJ in the Court of Appeal stated at [**51**]:

> In the present case we are faced with a decision of the House of Lords on precisely the same point. The statutory language has not changed. Indeed it has been re-enacted by Parliament following the decision of the House of Lords. It is perfectly true that attitudes toward disabled people have changed radically since then, and those changes may be enough to persuade the Supreme Court to depart from the previous decision of the House of Lords as it is entitled to do under the *Practice Statement (Judicial Precedent)* [1966] 1 WLR 1234. However, that is not enough to enable this court to refuse to follow an otherwise binding decision of the House of Lords unless it can be said that subsequent statutes have impliedly changed the rule laid down by the House.

Thus, it is for the Supreme Court to change its mind, not for the Court of Appeal to decide the issue for it. On the positive side, this helps to create certainty. Equally, such strict adherence to *stare decisis* may increase costs (because of the need for further appeals), as well as appearing to invite the veneration of rules whatever the logic or perceived justice. This is an age-old problem in law: balancing the need for certainty with the desire for the law to be flexible.

To what extent is the Court of Appeal bound by its own previous decisions?

This is the key area as regards questions of *stare decisis*. The basic rule is that it is bound. This was decided in *Young* v *Bristol Aeroplane Co. Ltd* [1944] KB 718, though three exceptions were given by Lord Greene MR on behalf of the court. This is the case you will see cited time and again on this topic. The exceptions to *stare decisis* given in this case are considered in the subsections below.

The first exception: the Court of Appeal can choose between its own conflicting decisions

Such conflict should not arise in an ideal world, but it does, and Lord Greene MR did not explore *which* of the conflicting decisions should be followed. Academic and judicial debate over the years tended to indicate that a later Court of Appeal faced with this problem would probably be free to decide which authority it should follow, with the result that the one not chosen is overruled (for a full debate, see Cross (1991: 144)). If a general rule has emerged, it has been that the latest case would probably be followed in preference to the earlier decision.

The situation can occur for a number of reasons; the most usual ones are:

- because the Court of Appeal does not hear one case at a time (there may be two or three hearings going on at the same time in different courtrooms in the Strand, before different members of the court). Further, each case may be heard on a number of days spread over a period of months. These cases may involve similar legal principles and the various courts may reach different conclusions which later appear contradictory. When the Court of Appeal decided *Young* there were only six Lords Justices. Now there are up to twelve courts sitting at any time with over forty members of the Court (plus others who are entitled to sit), which means there is a greater possibility of conflicting judgments;

- it is also possible that some earlier cases may not have been reported;

- equally, one court may look at the previous decisions and consider them distinguishable for one reason or another, while another may think they are not distinguishable and should be followed (which highlights the point we have made before on this being a matter of interpretation rather than pure science).

It was this last reason that gave rise to the problem in *Starmark Enterprises Ltd* v *CPL Distribution Ltd* [2001] EWCA Civ 1252; [2002] 4 All ER 264. The case concerned a rent review clause in a lease of property. Two earlier Court of Appeal decisions (which we shall simply call decisions 1 and 2) had followed on from, considered, and applied an even earlier decision of the House of Lords. Unfortunately, the two Court of Appeal cases appeared to be in conflict. In *Starmark* the landlord argued that decision 2 (the latest) was unsupportable and decision 1 should be preferred; alternatively, that decision 2 was distinguishable on the facts from the present case. It should therefore be ignored and, again, decision 1 should be followed. The tenant argued that there was no conflict between decisions 1 and 2 and decision 2 was entirely consistent with the original House of Lords' approach; equally, the facts in the present case and decision 2 were indistinguishable and so decision 2 plainly had to be followed.

Lord Justice Kay decided that decisions 1 and 2 *did* conflict and that he preferred the views expressed in decision 1 (which was also the minority judgment in decision 2) and was bound to follow the reasoning in decision 1. Lady Justice Arden held that decisions 1 and 2 involved the same principle and could not be reconciled; it was not possible to distinguish them. But Her Ladyship agreed with Kay LJ and held that decision 2 was faulty and should not be followed. The final judge, Peter Gibson LJ, stated at [97]:

> Where the ratio of an earlier decision of this court is directly applicable to the circumstances of a case before this court but that decision has been wrongly distinguished in a later decision of this court, in principle it must be open to this court to apply the ratio of the earlier decision and to decline to follow the later decision. In my judgment the majority of this court in [decision 2] wrongly distinguished [decision 1]. The ratio decidendi in [decision 1] ... should in my judgment have been applied in [decision 2] and is decisive of this case.

Thus, in *Starmark*, the latest authority was not followed. Lord Justice Kay's remark (at [3]) perhaps sums up the frustration of encountering conflicting decisions, when he said: 'It is unfortunate that over 15 years after ... [cases 1 and 2] ... were decided, the legal effect of a common provision in a rent review clause is still unknown. This is the common law at its least impressive.' The Court followed the same approach in *Patel* v *Secretary of State for the Home Office* [2012] EWCA Civ 741 and decided to go with the decision it preferred when faced with what it termed 'irreconcilable differences' between two of its own previous judgments.

It is also worth noting that Lord Denning led another attack on what he clearly perceived to be the fetter of *stare decisis* in the case of *Davis* v *Johnson* [1979] AC 264; [1978] 1 All ER 1132 (HL); [1978] 2 WLR 182; [1978] 1 All ER 841 (CA). This was not an instance of cleverly adopting rules to excuse departure from precedents. Here, Lord Denning sought to apply the 1966 Practice Statement to the Court of Appeal as well as the House of Lords. The argument was that, if the Court of Appeal could simply depart from previous decisions when justice demanded (as the House of Lords can now do), this would save wasting time and costs of further appeals to the House of Lords. Once again, however, the attempt failed (not least because Lord Denning had conveniently forgotten that procedures already existed whereby a case could be allowed to 'bypass' the Court of Appeal for this very reason: see section **6.6**).

The second exception: if its own previous decision has been overruled expressly or impliedly by the Supreme Court/House of Lords, it need not be followed

Thus, if the order of cases ran:

- Court of Appeal's decision (1954);
- Supreme Court decision (disapproving the Court of Appeal's reasoning—see, for example, *Ivey* v *Genting Casinos (UK) Ltd trading as Crockfords* [2017] UKSC 67; [2018] 2 All ER 406, which overruled the well-established Court of Appeal decision in *R* v *Ghosh* [1982] QB 1053, on the meaning of dishonesty);
- your case in the Court of Appeal (today);

then the Court of Appeal in your case *must* follow the Supreme Court and not the first Court of Appeal decision.

But this does not answer the question which path should be chosen where the order of cases is:

- House of Lords' decision (1980);
- Court of Appeal's decision (2008)—which, for some reason, is contrary to the earlier House of Lords' decision;
- your case in the Court of Appeal (today).

Now the Court of Appeal is caught between two rules: one saying it is bound to follow its own previous decisions, the other that it is bound to follow the House of Lords.

This situation arose in *Miliangos* v *George Frank (Textiles) Ltd*. Only a year after the Court of Appeal (in the *Schorsch Meier* case) had ignored earlier House of Lords' authority and decided to award judgment in a currency other than sterling, the same issue came before the Court of Appeal again. Should it follow its decision in *Schorsch Meier* or follow the decision of the House of Lords which had been bypassed in *Schorsch Meier*? You may wish to speculate as to which answer, which strand of *stare decisis*, you think should be the most appropriate.

The Court of Appeal in *Miliangos* chose to follow its own previous decision and not the House of Lords. When the case went before the House of Lords their Lordships agreed that judgment could be given in a currency other than sterling, thereby overruling their own previous decision; but took the opportunity to criticise Lord Denning's approach in the *Schorsch Meier* case for ignoring the doctrine of *stare decisis*. However, to add to the confusion, whereas Lord Simon in the House of Lords agreed that the Court of Appeal in *Miliangos* should have followed its own precedent created in *Schorsch Meier*, Lord Cross felt that the Court of Appeal in *Miliangos* should have ignored its own precedent in *Schorsch Meier* because that decision was in conflict with the earlier House of Lords' decision. So, the short answer is: nobody really knows.

6.5 A combination of exceptions

The latest examination of these first two exceptions arose in *Henderson (a protected party, by her Litigation Friend the Official Solicitor)* v *Dorset Healthcare University NHS Foundation Trust* [2018] EWCA Civ 1841. Henderson had been convicted of manslaughter for the killing of her mother. It was manslaughter because of Ms Henderson's diminished responsibility at the time of the incident (a psychotic episode). She sued her care home for negligence in their care of her when she was under a restriction order. The Trust opposed the claim for damages on the grounds of public policy and that it was based on illegality. Since the eighteenth century the principle has existed that one cannot benefit from one's own illegal act. Did this prevent Henderson claiming?

There were two barriers to Henderson's claim: (i) an earlier Court of Appeal case (*Clunis* v *Camden and Islington Health Authority* [1998] 3 All ER 180) had rejected a similar claim on the grounds of public policy; and (ii) a 2009 House of Lords' case (*Gray* v *Thames Trains* [2009] 4 All ER 81) held that recovery is barred for loss suffered in consequence of one's own criminal act—here another killing when suffering post-traumatic shock after being involved in a train accident. On a strict application of precedent, the Court of Appeal should have determined that Henderson could not succeed because her claim was based on an illegality (the killing of her mother).

However, there existed another Supreme Court case, *Patel* v *Mirza* [2016] UKSC 42, [2017] AC 467 (noted in **6.4.1**) which dealt with the concept of illegality and which had held that claims should not be barred just because the claimant had relied on some illegal act as part of the claim. One difficulty was that the *Patel* v *Mirza* case was on an entirely different area, namely the recovery of money in contract, and the principle of illegality was being triggered not by a killing but by insider trading.

So, the argument in *Henderson* was that the second exception to the concept of binding authority set out in *Young* v *BAC* would be triggered if the Court of Appeal decision in *Clunis* had effectively been set aside (indirectly overruled) by the later Supreme Court ruling in *Patel* v *Mirza*. Further, the second obstacle of the binding precedent of the House of Lords' authority of *Gray* v *Thames Trains* would not be binding if *Patel* v *Mirza* had also effectively (though obviously not expressly) utilised the 1966 Practice Statement to overrule it.

The argument was: the earlier Court of Appeal and House of Lords' authorities cannot stand with the subsequent and different decision of the Supreme Court in *Patel* v *Mirza,* even though that case was on an entirely different area of law. The concept of illegality was common to all the cases. Just because *Henderson's* claim was based on an illegality (the manslaughter of her mother) did not in itself preclude her from suing the Trust. This argument failed. The Court of Appeal was not prepared to allow *Patel* v *Mirza* to be used to impliedly overrule the earlier cases. At para [87], the court stated:

> [I]n view of the actual contractual and unjust enrichment issue in *Patel*, considerable caution must be taken, in the context of the rules of binding precedent, in determining whether there are any other cases in other areas of the law which the Supreme Court in *Patel* held by necessary implication to be overruled or such that they should no longer be followed.

It needs stronger stuff for the exceptions in *Young* v *BAC* to kick into action. As a side point, it is interesting to note that Lord Greene's statement in *Young* v *BAC* (that the Court of Appeal is bound by its own decisions) actually conflicts with some earlier Court of Appeal decisions which stated that the Court of Appeal was *not* bound by its own previous decisions. The sort of panic that this can send a student into should be avoided; Lord Greene's words reflected the history of the Court of Appeal since its creation and are generally taken as gospel today.

The third exception: the Court is not bound by its own decisions found to have been made *per incuriam*

We noted the *per incuriam* rule earlier. For some reason this rule appeals to students and it tends to be used on many occasions (usually incorrectly). It is worth repeating, therefore, that it does not simply mean that the Court made a mistake. The fact that the case being examined had weaknesses in argument, or in the judgment, does not make the decision *per incuriam*. Thus, in *Morelle* v *Wakeling* [1955] 2 QB 379; [1955] 1 All ER 708, Lord Evershed MR limited the use of the *per incuriam* rule to cases where:

- there was ignorance of authority which would have been binding on the court; *and*
- that ignorance led to faulty reasoning.

The *and* is very important. To this the Court of Appeal has added that the rule can be applied only where, had the court reviewed these authorities, the court *would* (not just might) have reached a different decision. Thus, in *Williams* v *Fawcett* [1986] QB 604; [1985] 1 All ER 787 and *Duke* v *Reliance Systems* [1987] ICR 491; [1987] 2 All ER 858 the Court of Appeal has shown itself ready to use the *per incuriam* rule regarding its own decisions, but with reservations.

In the case of *Rakhit* v *Carty* [1990] 2 WLR 1107; [1990] 2 All ER 202, the Court of Appeal was faced with the situation where a Court of Appeal decision (*decision 1*) was plainly *per incuriam* as it had missed some vital statutory provisions. *Decision 1* had been followed without question in another Court of Appeal case (*decision 2*). Could the present Court of Appeal still declare *decision 1* to be *per incuriam* and therefore *decision 2* of no binding effect? Lord Donaldson MR said (at 208), 'If, that court [*in decision 2*], having all the relevant authorities before it, had concluded that [*decision 1*] was rightly decided, I would have felt bound to follow it, leaving it to the House of Lords to rectify the error.'

As this was not the case, the Court of Appeal in *Rakhit* v *Carty* declared *decision 1* to have been reached *per incuriam*, thereby invalidating both *decision 1* and *decision 2* as precedents.

The Court of Appeal confirmed all that has just been said above in *Peter Limb* v *Union Jack Removals Ltd and Honess* [1998] 1 WLR 1354; [1998] 2 All ER 513 (see section **6.8**).

In *Young* v *BAC* Lord Greene stated that a finding of *per incuriam* would only occur in the rarest of cases. This has been proved true: a search of the law reports reveals a great number of cases where a *per incuriam* argument has been tried but very few cases where it has proved successful. One case, however, interestingly combines two 'exception' heads: *Singh (India)* v *Secretary of State for the Home Department; R (on the application of Khalid)* v *Secretary of State for the Home Department* [2015] EWCA Civ 74. Here Underhill LJ found [at 41] that:

> If the outcome on issue (A) depended on making a choice between *Edgehill* and *Haleemudeen* I would follow *Edgehill*. Although formally the situation may fall within the first exception in *Young* v *Bristol Aeroplane Co Ltd* … in that we are confronted by two conflicting decisions of this court, the truth is that *Haleemudeen* was decided *per incuriam* because of the failure to draw the court's attention to the implementation provision; and in those circumstances I think that the better view is that we should treat ourselves as bound by *Edgehill*.

In *DN (Rwanda)* v *Secretary of State for the Home Department* [2018] EWCA Civ 273; [2018] 3 All ER 772 Arden LJ observed at [36]:

> In my judgment, it is not open to this court to refuse to follow an earlier decision simply because it overlooks (if it did) relevant authority. The doctrine of precedent forms part of law because it ensures consistency and certainty and enables the law to develop in a structured and disciplined way. As Lord Bingham of Cornhill reminded us in *Lambeth London BC* v *Kay, Leeds City Council* v *Price* [2006] UKHL 10, [2006] 4 All ER 128, [2006] 2 AC 465: [42], while adherence to precedent has been derided by some, at any rate since the time of Bentham, as a recipe for the perpetuation of error, it has been a cornerstone of our legal system.

Arden LJ then commented at [38], 'That leads me to the per incuriam rule … [It] is only available where there are conflicting decisions within the same tier. That must mean conflicting decisions on the same point, and there are none here.' This was the key point: though some earlier cases had not been taken into account, the court had followed a different line of cases. It therefore could not be said that the decision was 'demonstrably wrong'. Whether that was correct was a matter for appeal, not a ground on which the *per incuriam* exception could be invoked.

6.6 Are there any other exceptions to the application of *stare decisis* to the Court of Appeal that have emerged since 1944?

The short answer to this is: yes, but not many.

6.6.1 Criminal matters

The Criminal Division of the Court is traditionally more relaxed on *stare decisis*, especially where an individual's liberty is at stake. This seems a little strange, given that the House of Lords/Supreme Court has often espoused the view that, in order to promote certainty, it should rarely change its mind on criminal law matters (see, for instance, its reluctance to change its mind in *R v Shivpuri*). But then, in the hands of the Supreme Court rests the final appeal; which is the very issue that caused all the controversy discussed earlier.

The Court of Appeal addressed this issue again in *R v Parole Board, ex parte Wilson* [1992] 2 WLR 707; [1992] 2 All ER 576. The case concerned the right to see documents submitted to a parole board. The Court applied the principle that, where liberty is at stake and injustice might occur, *stare decisis* was not applicable. However, the Court of Appeal found the earlier precedents distinguishable in any case so that the comments on *stare decisis* were not strictly necessary. In *R v* [2003] EWCA Crim 1499; [2003] 3 All ER 531 the Court of Appeal affirmed this approach. There, Lord Woolf CJ stated that the power to depart from earlier decisions was not akin to the power of the House of Lords under the 1966 Practice Statement. He said:

> We appreciate that there may be a case for not interpreting the law contrary to a previous authority in a manner that would mean that an offender who otherwise would not have committed an offence would be held to have committed an offence. However, we do not understand why that should apply to a situation where a defendant, as here, wishes to rely upon a wrongly decided case to provide a technical defence. While justice for a defendant is extremely important, justice for the public at large is also important. So is the maintenance of confidence in the criminal justice system.

Thus, in dealing with criminal law matters the Court of Appeal generally adheres to *stare decisis* but also recognises that there have to be exceptions, given that a person's liberty is at stake. These exceptions arise, as *Halsbury's Laws* puts it: '(a) where the applicant is in prison and in the full court's opinion wrongly so; (b) where the court thinks that the law was misunderstood or misapplied; and (c) where the full court is carrying out its duty to lay down principles and guidelines in relation to sentencing . . .'.

This power is not exercised lightly, as illustrated in the conjoined cases of *R v Magro and others* [2010] EWCA Crim 1575; [2011] QB 398 (see also the article by Gillespie, 2010). A Court of Appeal decision the year before, *R v Clarke (Joseph)* (2009) *Times*,

1 July; [2009] 4 All ER 298; [2010] 1 WLR 223, had held that the Crown Court had no power to make a confiscation order against a defendant following conviction if he received an absolute or conditional discharge. This is what had happened to Magro and the others, so their appeal centred on this issue. The Crown argued that the decision in *Clarke* was made *per incuriam* and was not binding.

The Court of Appeal held that, even if the decision in *Clarke* was wrong and even though the Court here would indeed have reached a different conclusion had it not been for the authority of *Clarke*, it was still binding. The exercise of discretion set out in *Simpson* did not establish that a five-judge constitution was entitled to disregard or deprive the only previous decision of the three-judge court of its authority on a distinct and clearly identified point of law, reached after full argument and close analysis of the relevant legislative provisions. Interestingly, when the case went to the Supreme Court (under the name of *R v Varma* [2012] UKSC 42), it was held that *Clarke* had been wrongly decided—but not on the basis of its being decided *per incuriam*.

Nevertheless, instances can be found of the Court of Appeal not following its previous decisions in criminal law matters. One such case is *R v Ahmad and another* [2012] EWCA Crim 391; [2012] 1 WLR 2335, which received approval in *R v Hunter (Nigel) and others* [2015] EWCA Crim 631. A key reason for this departure from precedent in *Ahmad* was that the earlier authority had been the subject of academic and practitioner criticism. The Court of Appeal agreed with the criticisms (though not the rather patronising tone used by some critics). Further, Bettinson (2011) has argued that the Court of Appeal, in *R v C* [2011] EWCA Crim 1872; [2012] 1 Cr App R (S) 89, may have extended the notion of *per incuriam* (at least in criminal law) to include departing from an earlier decision: 'not on account of a lack of consideration of *legal* authorities, but due to the fact that . . .' certain material and significant arguments had not been before the Court in its earlier decision. It is respectfully submitted that this 'inadequate advocacy' argument is the gateway to a quagmire.

An interesting comment also emerged from Arden LJ's *per incuriam* comments in *DN (Rwanda) v Secretary of State for the Home Department* (above) that:

> [41] I am prepared to assume for the purposes of argument that there is an exception to the doctrine of precedent where the application of a prior decision of this court was unjust. However, if it exists, it must in my judgment be interpreted narrowly in the light of *Young* and be applicable only where the decision affects the liberty of the subject. Moreover, the liberty of the subject must be directly involved, and so the exception does not apply where the appellant is seeking a remedy after the event for a past deprivation of liberty.

6.6.2 Blocked appeals

If, in exceptional cases, the Supreme Court cannot review a decision of the Court of Appeal, then the Court of Appeal becomes the final point of appeal and can choose not to follow its own precedent: *Rickards v Rickards* [1989] 3 WLR 748; [1989] 3 All ER 193. The *Rickards* case involved very technical arguments concerning extensions of time in which to bring a case. Under those special rules the case could not go to the House of Lords: so, such occasions are not common.

6.6.3 Decisions of a two-judge Court of Appeal

The normal number for a panel in the Court of Appeal is three or five. In *Boys* v *Chaplin* [1968] 2 QB 1; [1968] 1 All ER 283 it was held that if the court consists of only two judges this will not bind a later full Court of Appeal. That is no longer the position. A two-judge Court of Appeal is now accorded the same powers of creating binding precedents as a full court: *Langley* v *North West Water Authority* [1991] 1 WLR 697; [1991] 3 All ER 610.

Historically, two-judge Court of Appeal panels dealt with what are called interim (previously called interlocutory) matters. An interim decision generally concerns pre-trial matters. For instance, if there is a dispute as to the procedure to be followed on, say, getting experts' reports, then this will be an interim matter. Injunctions are another example of interim orders. Here, one party is seeking to prevent the other doing something before the full case can be heard. Examples are domestic violence cases, where the injunction may exclude one party from the family home temporarily, defamation cases (used to prevent publication as, once published, it cannot be withdrawn even if it was defamatory), confidentiality, and restraint of trade claims.

However, over the years two-judge panels have taken on what are called more 'substantive' cases. 'Substantive' means cases that deal with the full issues. As two-judge panels have become more common, cases have therefore arisen which were not interim matters but proved to be important substantive decisions (e.g. *National Westminster Bank* v *Morgan* [1983] 3 All ER 85; *Harris* v *Wyre Forest District Council* [1988] QB 835; [1988] 1 All ER 691; and *Interfoto Picture Library* v *Stiletto Visual Programmes Ltd* [1988] 2 WLR 615; [1988] 1 All ER 348). The *Interfoto* case, as we shall see, had the added complication of the judges agreeing on the decision but disagreeing on the reasoning.

It is rare for a two-member Court of Appeal to disagree on the decision. However, this did happen in *Farley* v *Skinner* (Court of Appeal, unreported November 1999). One judge allowed the appeal and the other dismissed it. Therefore, there was no actual result. The parties sought a relisting of the appeal before a three-member panel, as is permitted under the Supreme Court Act 1981, s. 54(5), which states that: 'Where (a) an appeal has been heard by a court consisting of an even number of judges; and (b) the members of the court are equally divided, the case shall, on the application of any part to the appeal, be reargued before and determined by an uneven number of judges not less than three . . .'. The case was reheard accordingly (and expensively): see *Farley* v *Skinner* [2000] Lloyd's Rep. PN 516.

By way of contrast, in the Supreme Court, if you start with an odd number of judges, lose one on the way, and then find the voting divided equally, it seems that the old maxim *semper praesumitur pro negante* still applies. This means that the presumption is always in favour of the negative, which means that the appeal fails. A fascinating example of this arose in *Charter* v *Charter* (1874) LR 7 HL 364, where four of their Lordships were divided evenly as to the outcome and the remaining member died without leaving an opinion.

6.6.4 Decisions made by other courts

The Court of Appeal may find itself in the position where decisions on a topic have been made by the House of Lords/Supreme Court, the Judicial Committee of the Privy Council, the Court of Justice of the European Union, or the European Court of Human

Rights. If these decisions conflict with existing precedents of the Court of Appeal (or, indeed, with each other), what is the Court of Appeal to do?

Decisions of the House of Lords/Supreme Court and the Judicial Committee of the Privy Council

We saw earlier that where a Court of Appeal decision is followed by a House of Lords/ Supreme Court judgment, then any later Court of Appeal must follow the Lords/ Supreme Court (see section **6.4.3**). And, as we noted earlier at section **1.7.3**, whereas the Judicial Committee of the Privy Council (JCPC) was once the final court of appeal for the courts of the British Empire, it now acts as the final court of appeal for a diminishing number of countries in the Commonwealth. The JCPC is therefore not part of our system and cannot create **binding** precedent, but practically speaking, as the judges are made up from the Justices of the Supreme Court sitting in a different guise, any decision of the JCPC is treated as highly persuasive.

So, what should the Court of Appeal do in the light of a JCPC decision which conflicts with an earlier Court of Appeal authority? This issue arose in *Doughty v Turner Manufacturing Co. Ltd* [1964] 1 QB 518; [1964] 1 All ER 98 and the Court of Appeal chose to follow a JCPC decision (that of *The Wagon Mound (No. 2)* [1967] 1 AC 617; [1966] 2 All ER 709) rather than its own precedent, which had been set in *Re Polemis* [1921] 3 KB 560; [1921] All ER Rep 40.

In *HM Attorney General for Jersey v Holley* [2005] UKPC 23; [2005] 3 All ER 371 there was an appeal from the Court of Appeal of Jersey to the JCPC concerning the law on provocation as a (partial) defence to murder. Jersey law on this subject was the same as English law. This defence had been considered by the House of Lords as regards English law in *R v Smith (Morgan James)* [2000] 4 All ER 289; [2001] 1 AC 146. Unfortunately, the decision in *Smith* was in direct conflict with the decision of the JCPC in *Luc Thiet Thuan v R* [1996] 2 All ER 1033; [1997] AC 131. Further, *Smith* itself was not easy to reconcile with some other House of Lords' decisions. In *Jersey v Holley* the JCPC formed a specifically enlarged Board of nine to resolve this conflict and clarify both English and Jersey law. The majority disapproved the House of Lords' decision in *Smith* and approved the previous JCPC decision in *Luc Thiet Thuan*. So, what should be considered the precedent in English law: *Smith* or *Jersey v Holley*? The answer came fairly soon in the case of *R v Faqir Mohammed* [2005] EWCA Crim 1880: the Court of Appeal followed the JCPC without any hesitation as it represented the latest, considered, and authoritative statement on the law and this view was confirmed by the Court of Appeal in *R v James; R v Karimi* [2006] EWCA Crim 14.

'Normality' was restored, however, in *Sinclair Investments (UK) Ltd v Versailles Trade Finance Ltd (in administrative receivership)* [2011] 3 WLR 1153, where the Court of Appeal considered *R v James; R v Karimi* and held that the Court of Appeal should not follow a Privy Council decision in preference to a decision of its own, unless, as the practitioners' text *Archbold* (2019) puts it:

> there is domestic authority that shows that its own decision was *per incuriam* or at least of doubtful reliability ... the course taken in *R v James; R v Karimi* was, however, justified as it was a foregone conclusion that, if the case had gone to the House of Lords, they would have followed the Privy Council decision.

So, despite the fact that the JCPC is not part of our system and cannot create **binding** precedent, its decisions are still highly persuasive (sometimes to the point of overcoming the strict rules of *stare decisis*). Nevertheless, a court should not follow a decision of the JCPC if it is inconsistent with the decision of a court that is binding on it. In *Willers* v *Joyce (No. 2)* (see section **6.2**) the Supreme Court considered what it termed the 'difficult question' as to whether this rule is absolute, or whether it is subject to the qualification that it can be disapplied where a first instance judge or the Court of Appeal considers that it is a foregone conclusion that the view taken by the JCPC will be accepted by the Court of Appeal or Supreme Court (as the case may be). The Court concluded that it is safer if the rule is absolute—a judge should never follow a decision of the JCPC if it is inconsistent with the decision of a court which is otherwise binding on him.

Lord Neuberger did, however, add a rider to this, arising where an appeal to the JCPC might involve upsetting decisions of the Court of Appeal or Supreme Court. Here, his Lordship stated that the JCPC's existing Practice Direction of requiring the parties to notify the court of conflicting Supreme Court decisions should be extended to cover Court of Appeal decisions. Under the guidance of the President of the JCPC (who is the the same person as in the Supreme Court) the members of JCPC panel:

> can, if they think it appropriate, not only decide that the earlier decision of the House of Lords or Supreme Court, or of the Court of Appeal, was wrong, but also can expressly direct that domestic courts should treat the decision of the JCPC as representing the law of England and Wales.
>
> paras [19–21].

Decisions of the Court of Justice of the European Union

The Court of Justice (CJEU) is the only court that can make authoritative rulings on the meaning and interpretation of European legislation. Thus, all courts in the EU should follow the CJEU's decisions. It should be noted, however, that the CJEU only decides what the law means; it does not decide the cases themselves. In other words, once the CJEU has made an authoritative ruling on the *meaning* of the law, the *application* of that interpretation to the facts of the particular case is the province of the national court. So, if there is a decision of the CJEU on the meaning of European law which the Supreme Court then applies, the Court of Appeal should, strictly, follow the Supreme Court on the factual analysis and the CJEU on the pure legal analysis.

Once the UK leaves the EU, the CJEU will cease to play a continuing role in our legal system, though pre-Brexit rulings may still be relevant (for a full discussion on this see **Chapter 11**).

Decisions of the European Court of Human Rights

What should lower courts (such as the Court of Appeal) do when a House of Lords/ Supreme Court decision conflicts with one made by the European Court of Human Rights (ECtHR)? As you will see in **Chapter 10**, the ECtHR is not part of our system. Indeed, it is even less a part of our system than the CJEU. Decisions of the ECtHR must simply be 'taken into account' by our judges, but they do not create precedents (and the decisions are not enforceable in our courts).

The question of which decision to follow was considered in *Price* v *Leeds City Council* [2005] EWCA Civ 289; [2005] 1 WLR 1825. The case concerned the rights of gypsies to occupy land and whether attempts to remove them breached their rights under the European Convention on Human Rights, Art. 8 (Art. 8 concerns 'respect for private and family life'). The problem here was that a House of Lords' decision (*Harrow London Borough Council* v *Qazi* [2003] UKHL 43; [2004] AC 983) was incompatible with a subsequent decision of the ECtHR (*Connors* v *United Kingdom* (2005) 40 EHRR 9). Lord Phillips MR provided the solution on behalf of the Court at [33]:

> It seems to us that in these circumstances, the only permissible course is to follow the decision of the House of Lords but, to give permission, if sought and not successfully opposed, to appeal to the House of Lords, thereby and to that extent taking the decision in *Connors* into account. If in due course the House considers that we have not followed the appropriate course, it will no doubt make this plain.

That statement has been acknowledged as the rule in later cases.

6.6.5 International obligations

The court must have regard to the principle that Parliament is presumed to legislate in conformity with the United Kingdom's international obligations and, therefore, as an off-shoot of the *per incuriam* rule, a failure to take into account such obligations may mean that the previous case is not binding: *Crown Prosecution Service, Secretary of State for the Home Department* v *Varsha Bhadresh Gohil, Bhadresh Babulal Gohil* [2012] EWCA Civ 1550.

6.6.6 Patents

In *Actavis UK Ltd* v *Merck & Co Inc* [2008] EWCA Civ 444; [2009] 1 All ER 196 the Court of Appeal came to the conclusion that, as regards the very technical and specialist area of patents law, the international and commercial aspects of decisions in this area called for flexibility. They said [at 107] that:

> this court is free but not bound to depart from the *ratio decidendi* of its own earlier decision if it is satisfied that the [European Patents Office] Boards of Appeal have formed a settled view of European Patent law which is inconsistent with that earlier decision. Generally this court will follow such a settled view.

6.7 Does every case have to be heard by the Court of Appeal before it can proceed to the Supreme Court?

Fortunately, the answer is no. If the Court of Appeal is bound by the Supreme Court and itself, then a system which demanded it to hear every case anyway would be ludicrous. Thus, a civil case may be allowed to go on appeal from the High Court to the Supreme Court, bypassing the Court of Appeal. This is known as the 'leap-frogging' procedure. However, if the case began life in the county court, then an appeal from that court lies to the Court of Appeal, not the High Court; thus, the leap-frogging procedure would be irrelevant.

It is only fair to say that however much writers and judges try to explain the system on a rational basis there will always be some uncertainty and some cases that simply break the rules. For one thing, we have yet to consider in depth how one case can be distinguished from another so that the precedent in question (and therefore the application of *stare decisis*) is sidestepped. For another, judges occasionally surprise everyone with an admission that they were wrong in an earlier case (see Lord Denning in *Dixon v BBC* [1979] QB 546; [1979] 2 All ER 112, discussing his earlier judgment on the same issue in *BBC v Ioannou* [1975] ICR 267; [1975] 2 All ER 999, or even Lord Greene MR in *Young v BAC*, at 730:

> I should perhaps add, speaking for myself individually, with regard to the observations in *Unsworth's case* mentioned in this judgment, that I have carefully considered my own observations there mentioned in *Perkins' case* and I have come to the conclusion that the criticism of them in *Unsworth's case* is justified, and that what I said was wrong.

This is reassuring when considered in the context of human frailty, but likely to set a practising lawyer's teeth on edge and is little consolation to the party in the overruled case who originally lost (and probably paid costs which cannot be recovered). Even more surprising, perhaps, was Lord Denning's admission in one case that his own reasoning in an earlier case (which he now wished to avoid) was not legally correct, but that he had reached that earlier decision to do justice—'It was not really [a case which fell within the definition of dismissal] . . . but we had to stretch it a bit', he commented. The comment occurred in *Western Excavating v Sharp* [1978] ICR 221, 227; [1978] 1 All ER 713, 718 in relation to *Marriott v Oxford and District Co-operative Society Ltd (No. 2)* [1970] 1 QB 186; [1969] 3 All ER 1126.

It is also worth commenting at this stage (as we noted at section **6.4.2** on retrospective and prospective overruling), that when a decision of a higher court alters the law by overruling a line of established precedents, that decision does not merely affect the law from that moment on. The court setting the new precedent is stating the law as it *always has been*. Thus, commercial contracts concluded on the old law are in danger of being open to a different interpretation from that intended when they were formed; so too, property deals, licences, employment contracts, and so on. Therefore, one part of the work of lawyers is to review these earlier matters in the light of the new decision.

A question often posed by students is whether the aggrieved party in the case which has been overruled can now revive the case with the cry, 'There you are, I was right all along.' The answer is no. Parties to a case have to lodge an appeal within time limits. If these have expired it is unfortunately too late to do anything about it.

6.8 Precedent in the higher courts: summary

In discussing the *per incuriam* rule in section **6.5**, we noted the case of *Peter Limb*. That case also made some general comments on precedent and the Court of Appeal. Lord Justice Brooke stated that there were five main principles to be derived from the authorities:

(i) Where the court has considered a statute or a rule of law which has the force of a statute, the court's decision stands on the same footing as any other decision on a point of law (the reason for saying this is that there used to be a vague rule that precedents could not relate to decisions on statutory interpretation points).

(ii)   A decision of a two-judge Court of Appeal on a substantive appeal (as opposed to an application for leave) has the same authority as a decision of a three-judge or a five-judge Court of Appeal.

(iii) The doctrine of *per incuriam* applies only where another division of the Court has reached a decision in ignorance or forgetfulness of a decision binding upon it or of an inconsistent statutory provision, and in either case it must be shown that if the court had had this material in mind it must have reached a contrary decision. In *Cave* v *Robinson Jarvis & Rolf* [2001] EWCA Civ 245; [2002] 1 WLR 581 the Court of Appeal expressed the view that the decision in question had to be 'manifestly wrong' before it would be declared *per incuriam*.

(iv)   The doctrine does not extend to a case where, if different arguments had been placed before the court or if different material had been placed before it, it *might* have reached a different conclusion.

(v)   Any departure from a previous decision of the court is in principle undesirable. Even if the previous decision is manifestly wrong it will be necessary to take account of whether the decision purports to be one of general application and whether there is any other way of remedying the error, for example by encouraging an appeal to the Supreme Court.

Finally, it is worth noting a trend over recent years for the Court of Appeal to bunch together issues arising in a number of cases, set aside a specialist panel to look at all the cases, hear a selection, and issue general guidelines on the area. This has mainly happened in connexion with procedural matters (*Peter Limb* was such a case). The most famous occurrence was in *Bannister* v *SGB plc* [1998] 1 WLR 1123; [1997] 4 All ER 129 (which was also the first Court of Appeal decision to be published on the Internet immediately after the decision was given, so that all 200-plus affected parties could know the outcome as soon as possible). And, interestingly, in *Greig Middleton & Co. Ltd* v *Denderowicz* [1998] 1 WLR 1164; [1997] 4 All ER 181 (which was on the same issue as *Bannister*) the Court of Appeal took the opportunity to add as annexes to the *Greig* judgment some reserved judgments in other related cases and to produce a revised judgment of *Bannister*, directing that it would be the revised version which should appear in the law reports.

6.9 Other courts

6.9.1 Trial courts

All courts which are lower in status than the Court of Appeal (such as the High Court, Crown Court, magistrates' court, county court, and the various tribunals) are bound by *stare decisis* in the normal way. It should be noted, however, that the important tribunals also have their own appellate tribunals (e.g. the Employment Appeal Tribunal for employment tribunals) which often incorporate their own variations on the rules of right to appeal and the binding nature of precedent within that system (e.g. neither the Employment Appeal Tribunal nor the Competition Appeal Tribunal bind themselves). Courts like the Crown Court are trial courts, dealing for the most part with fact and evidence rather than questions of high legal analysis. They do not, therefore, create precedent. There is, however, some attempt to follow the reasoning employed in courts of the same level, for example as between divisions of the High Court when these courts are sitting as 'courts of first instance', i.e. trial courts. In *Colchester Estates (Cardiff)* v *Carlton Industries plc* [1984] 3 WLR 693; [1984] 2 All ER 601 it was stated that the latest decision should be preferred provided it was reached after full consideration of the earlier decisions. An example of this in operation arose from a decision of Butler-Sloss J (as she then was) in *Re Cherrington* [1984] 1 WLR 772; [1984] 2 All ER 285, which was not followed in a case on exactly the same point (*Re Sinclair* [1984] 3 All ER 362) because there had not been a full discussion of all the issues in *Re Cherrington*. However, one High Court decision cannot bind a later court: *R (Amin)* v *Secretary of State for the Home Department* [2009] EWHC 1085 (Admin).

In *Willers* v *Joyce (No. 2)* [2016] (discussed at section **6.2**) the Supreme Court discussed the rules of precedent and noted at para [9] that:

> So far as the High Court is concerned, puisne judges are not technically bound by decisions of their peers, but they should generally follow a decision of a court of co-ordinate jurisdiction unless there is a powerful reason for not doing so. And, where a first instance judge is faced with a point on which there are two previous inconsistent decisions from judges of co-ordinate jurisdiction, then the second of those decisions should be followed in the absence of cogent reasons to the contrary: see *Patel* v *Secretary of State for the Home Department* [2013] 1 WLR 63, para 59.

6.9.2 Divisional courts

For mainly historical reasons the High Court has a supervisory and limited appellate jurisdiction over the trial courts. Each division of the High Court—Queen's Bench, Family, and Chancery—has what is termed a 'Divisional Court'. Thus:

(i) the Divisional Court of the Chancery Division can hear appeals from a county court in bankruptcy cases;

(ii) the Family Division may hear appeals on guardianship matters from either the magistrates' courts or county courts.

(iii) the most common appellate function relates to the Queen's Bench Division. Say a party to a criminal case in a magistrates' court wishes to appeal on a question of law from the magistrates' decision; this can be done by asking the magistrates to **state their case**, i.e. to set out their legal reasoning. Strangely, for historical reasons, the issue goes before the Divisional Court of the Queen's Bench Division (which is a civil and not criminal court). This is known as an 'appeal by way of case stated'. A full rehearing (e.g. an appeal against the conviction relating to fact rather than law) of the case would go to the Crown Court. An appeal by way of case stated can also lie in limited circumstances, from the Crown Court to the High Court.

These Divisional Courts are bound by *stare decisis* in the usual way as regards decisions of higher courts. When it comes to Divisional Courts binding themselves, the rule is similar to that used in the Court of Appeal: on civil matters they are bound, but not necessarily so on criminal issues: *R* v *Governor of Brockhill Prison* [1997] 1 All ER 439,

451. In all cases, however, there is a reluctance to depart from earlier decisions, as noted by Sir Brian Leveson P in *R (on the application of JC and another)* v *Central Criminal Court* [2014] EWHC 1041 (Admin), where it was said, citing earlier judgments: 'it would only be in rare cases that a divisional court will think it fit to depart from a decision of another divisional court exercising this jurisdiction'.

6.10 Impact of human rights legislation

Under the Human Rights Act 1998 all common law rules and precedents that are incompatible with Convention rights are potentially open to challenge, especially if those precedents relate to the interpretation of statutory provisions. Further, the Act expressly requires the British courts to *take into account*, among other things, the judgments, decisions, and advisory opinions of the ECtHR, thereby adding another court to the list of things to be aware of in giving legal advice (though note the comments made at section **6.6.4** on the case of *Price* v *Leeds City Council* and the question of the precedent value of such decisions).

 CONCLUSION

Both the common law and the civil law traditions utilise the concept of precedent. No case has a meaning by itself; each case stands in a relationship to other cases. Like tracing one's ancestors, therefore, it is at least theoretically possible to go backwards in time, step by step, to see how a complicated principle emerged from perhaps a single case. It is not uncommon to find gross inconsistencies or jumps in logic, but for the most part the changes will be evolutionary rather than revolutionary. It is rare to make this journey in a practical or even academic setting, but it does beg the question: what came before the original case?

Sometimes the answer is that the seminal case derived its principle from a mixture of other cases on related (often barely related) principles: see, for instance *Rylands* v *Fletcher* (1868) LR 3 HL 330. On other occasions the principle may be derived from ancient Roman, Greek, or biblical laws. Occasionally the source may lie in a perception of fundamental rights and wrongs, such as laws prohibiting murder—crimes which are sometimes referred to as being *mala in se*, meaning 'bad in themselves' as opposed to specifically created laws on trading or parking, for instance, known as laws which are *mala prohibita* (bad because they are prohibited). Often the answer lies in works written by eminent scholars centuries ago—their views on the law being accepted by judges in later cases and then set as legal doctrine by the mechanisms of judicial precedent. The fact that these initial cases or scholarly writings were illogical, have exceeded their 'best before' date, or have been misinterpreted does not mean that they can be easily upset.

Much of this reification of (sometimes) archaic principles is due to the fact that there is a world of difference between merely recognising the source and value of precedent and the concept of *stare decisis*. Courts in nearly all major legal systems have a system of precedent (even in Islamic law, where the decisions are those of the judges acting as individuals under spiritual guidance). A notable historical exception was the Socialist bloc countries. Since the demise of the communist bloc most of the affected countries have adopted some form of civil law system.

However, the common law system (especially as practised in Britain) goes beyond the mere seeking of guidance by reference to a level of being constrained by deference: a previous decision may not only be helpful, it may be binding.

The great value of the doctrine of *stare decisis* is that it provides certainty. On the other hand, there are dangers: first, that in order to avoid the conclusions of *stare decisis* courts are sometimes forced to find hair-splitting distinctions between cases; secondly, the doctrine limits flexibility and can make unassailable some principles which should have been abandoned long ago. Equally, as Max Radin observed in 'The Trail of the Calf', noted in section **6.1.2**, '[T]he question has not really been whether precedent should be followed, but where and under what circumstances it was desirable to disregard it ...'. Thus, the research skills of a lawyer rest with finding the relevant authorities; the advocacy skills often rest with persuading a court not to follow a precedent.

A rare example of a long-established legal concept being overturned can be found in *R v R* [1991] 3 WLR 767; [1991] 4 All ER 481. In *R v R* public policy, together with historical and social considerations, came under review. This case concerned 'marital rape' and posed the question whether a husband could be criminally liable for raping his wife if he had sexual intercourse with her without her consent. The idea that a man would not be guilty in these circumstances could be traced back to Sir Matthew Hale in his *History of the Pleas of the Crown* written in 1736. Texts and cases since that time had taken this proposition as an accurate expression of the law (which it probably was in 1736). In *R v R*, however, the House of Lords took the opportunity to restate the law concerning marital rape and declared that the husband could be guilty of rape in these circumstances. As Lord Keith said: 'The common law is ... capable of evolving in the light of changing social, economic and cultural developments.'

You may, however, ask yourself one final simple question: why should we stand out from the rest of the legal world with our fixation that once a superior court has decided a matter an inferior court *must* follow it?

 CHAPTER REFERENCES

*ARCHBOLD, *Criminal Pleading Evidence & Practice* (2019) (London: Sweet & Maxwell).

BETTINSON, V. (2011), 'Has the Court of Appeal Extended the per incuriam Exception?', 75 *Journal of Criminal Law*, 448.

BROWN, L.N. and KENNEDY, T. (2000), *Brown and Jacobs: The Court of Justice of the European Communities* (5th edn, London: Sweet & Maxwell).

*BUXTON, R. (2009), 'How the Common Law Gets Made: *Hedley Byrne* and other Cautionary Tales', 125 *Law Quarterly Review*, 60.

*COOPER, T.M. (1950), 'The Common and the Civil Law: A Scots View' 63 *Harvard Law Review*, 468 at 471.

*CROSS, R. (1991), *Precedent in English Law* (4th edn, Oxford: Clarendon Press).

GILLESPIE, A.A. (2010), 'Precedent and the Limits of Simpson', 74 *Journal of Criminal Law*, 492.

HARRIS, B.V. (2002), 'Final Appellate Courts Overruling their Own "Wrong" Precedents: The Ongoing Search for a Principle', 118 *Law Quarterly Review*, 408.

HARRIS, J.W. (1990), 'Towards Principles of Overruling—When Should a Final Court of Appeal Second Guess?', 10(2) *Oxford Journal of Legal Studies*, 135.

LUNDMARK, T. (2003), '"Soft" Stare Decisis: The Common Law Doctrine Retooled for Europe', in R. Schulze and U. Seif (eds), *Richterrect und Rechtsfortbildung in der Europäischen Rechtsgemeinschaft*, 27, at 161–8.

MACCORMICK, N. (1987), 'Why Cases have *Rationes* and What These Are', in L. Goldstein (ed.), *Precedent in Law* (Oxford: Clarendon Press).

MACMILLAN, LORD (1937), *Law and Other Things* (Cambridge: Cambridge University Press).

PATTENDEN, R. (1984), 'The Power of the Criminal Division of the Court of Appeal to Depart from its Own Precedents', *Criminal Law Review*, 592.

*RADIN, M. (1946), 'The Trail of the Calf', 32 *Cornell Law Quarterly*, 137.

RODGER, A. (Lord) (2005), 'A Time for Everything under the Law: Some Reflections on Retrospectivity', *121 Law Quarterly Review*, 57.

SCANLON, G. (2004), '*Stare Decisis* and the Court of Appeal: Judicial Confusion and Judicial Reform', 23 (Jul) *Civil Justice Quarterly*, 212.

STEIN, P. (1984), *Legal Institutions: The Development of Dispute Settlement* (London: Butterworths).

*STEINER, J. and WOODS, L. (2017) in L. WOODS and P. WATSON (eds), *Steiner and Woods EU Law* (13th edn, Oxford: Oxford University Press). Editions 1–10 of this work were entitled *Textbook on EC Law*.

 ONLINE RESOURCES

Test your knowledge by trying the self-test questions that accompany **Chapters 1–6**.
Visit: www.oup.com/uk/holland-webb10e

7

How Precedent Operates: *Ratio Decidendi* and *Obiter Dictum*

7.1 Introduction

The concept of *stare decisis* as outlined in **Chapter 7** provides us with only the ground rules of precedent. It tells us that one court must follow the decision of a superior court when dealing with similar cases. It describes the environment in which our system of precedent operates. What it cannot tell us is *when* two cases are sufficiently similar that the doctrine should be applied.

If the facts of cases were identical, we would have no problem. But the facts change from case to case—sometimes in an obviously major way; other times in an apparently insignificant way. Clearly, we are not looking only for **identical cases**. What we must be trying to prove is that two (or more) cases are sufficiently similar to illustrate the same *principle* so that the doctrine of precedent can be applied. A comparison of facts will obviously help us achieve this. But we must also, and more importantly, try to see if the *reasoning* in the earlier case can be applied to the new set of facts in our case. It is worth remembering that lawyers cite cases in order to give authority to their argument. The question raised by the practitioner or academic is therefore: what is the principle of law for which that case is authority, and how does it relate to the case in hand? Or, to put it the other way: is there a case which is authority for the point I wish to make? This is the way that a busy practitioner is more likely to pose the question.

In **Chapter 7** we presented an exercise on fact comparison:

- In *case (1)* a man driving a Ford Mondeo runs over an old lady who was lawfully using a zebra crossing. The man is held to be liable in negligence.

- In *case (2)* a woman driving a BMW runs over an old man who was crossing the road. Should she be found liable too? Does the principle in *case (1)* apply to *case (2)*?

We asked whether you might examine the facts more closely, or ask more questions, before deciding on the answer. Students new to legal studies (and others who should know better) tend to say that the woman in *case 2* is liable. If asked why this is so, the poor student tends to say: 'It's obvious.' Such students may have a shorter or less successful career in law than they anticipated. Slightly better students say: 'The woman is liable because *case (2)* is the same as *case (1)*'—but with no explanation. Still better students say: 'The woman may not be liable because the old lady in *case (1)* was on a zebra crossing, but that is not so in *case (2) so the answer may be different.*' The best student will ask himself/herself: '**Why** was the man liable in *case (1)*? Before I know that I cannot really say whether *case (2)* will follow *case (1).*' For all we know, there may be a law against driving Ford Mondeos.

You might think this is a trite statement of the obvious. Don't! These examples of analysis (on a variety of facts) have all surfaced in seminars and tutorials, in different universities and colleges, in different countries, spoken by LLB undergraduates, undergraduates in other degrees who study law, and even by postgraduates. Karl Llewellyn offered these words of advice (or admonition) in 1930 to American Law students:

> Now the first thing you are to do with [a case] is to read it. Does this sound commonplace? Does this amuse you? There is no reason why it should amuse you. You have already read past seventeen [legal] expressions of whose meaning you have no conception . . . . The next thing is to get clear the actual decision, the judgment rendered . . . . You can now turn to what you want peculiarly to know . . . what has the case decided, and what can you derive from it as to what will be decided later?
>
> (1960: 41).

Any law lecturer will echo these words, but it is easy to forget as an academic or practitioner just how daunting reading cases for the first time can be. From the student perspective things look a little different, but the point we are making is still the same. To show you that you are not alone in the minefield of case law, consider the words in the highlighted box next, written by Scott Turow (1988: 28)—better known for his legal thrillers—detailing his experiences as a law postgraduate student at Harvard. Anyone who has ever studied law will have sympathy with these words.

> OK. It was nine o'clock when I started reading. The case is four pages long and at 10:35 I finally finished. It was something like stirring concrete with my eyelashes. I had no idea what the words meant. I must have opened *Black's Law Dictionary* twenty-five times and I still can't understand many of the definitions.

The aim of this chapter, therefore, is to emphasise that legal analysis is not just a question of comparing facts or using a set of balancing scales to see if the facts weigh about the same. The game is more complicated, more stimulating, and much more enjoyable than that.

7.2 Development of case law

Take a look at the following exercise. It sets out the facts of two well-known cases together with the result in each case. Ask yourself *why* the second case should be decided in the same way as the first.

EXERCISE 9 Dead snails and exploding underpants

 Case 1: *Donoghue* v *Stevenson* **[1932] AC 562**

Bare facts: Mrs May Donoghue and a friend went into a cafe in Paisley. The friend ordered ice cream and ginger beer for both of them. Francis Minchella, the shop-keeper, poured out some of the ginger beer over the ice cream. Mrs Donoghue con-sumed some of the mixture. Her friend poured out the remainder of the ginger beer for Mrs Donoghue and a decomposed snail fell out of the bottle. The bottle was of dark opaque glass so that the contents could not have been detected.

What was the claim? The claim was against the manufacturer of the ginger beer (Stevenson) for negligently causing Mrs Donoghue to suffer gastroenteritis and nerv-ous shock; the negligence arising from the manufacture of the product. So, we say that her cause of action (as explained at section **6.1.1**) was negligence and she was seeking damages (compensation) for her loss. As you will see in your contract law course, Mrs Donoghue could not claim against Mr Minchella because she had no contract with him (her friend had bought the ginger beer); and she had no claim in negligence against him either as there was no way he could have known the snail was in the bottle (made of opaque glass).

What was the decision? Mrs Donoghue succeeded in her claim; the House of Lords holding Stevenson liable by a majority of 3:2 (note how close such an important deci-sion was). Lord Atkin, in the majority, said that a manufacturer of products will be liable for want of reasonable care if he sells those products in a form which shows they are meant to reach the ultimate consumer in the same form as when they were manufactured (with no reasonable possibility of intermediate examination) and if he knows that the absence of reasonable care will cause injury.

 Case 2: *Grant* v *Australian Knitting Mills* **[1936] AC 85 (Privy Council**)

Bare facts: Grant purchased two pairs of underpants from a retailer in Australia. He contracted severe dermatitis (mainly around the ankles—they were 'long johns') owing to an excess of sulphites in the garments which should have been removed by the manufacturing process. He was ill for a year.

What was the claim? He sued the retailer for breach of contract; and brought a negligence action against the Australian Knitting Mills. This demonstrates that more than one claim can arise from one set of events. However, Grant would not be able to get damages twice: if Grant was successful, then one claim would be offset against the other.

What was the decision? Grant won the breach of contract action against the retailer, and the claim for negligence against the manufacturer was also successful, following the principles laid down in *Donoghue* v *Stevenson*.

continued

EXERCISE 9 *continued*

 QUESTIONS

(i)   Why do you think Grant was successful in his claim for negligence? Why should *Donoghue* v *Stevenson* apply to his case?

(ii) What arguments would you have used if you had been representing the Australian Knitting Mills?

A   ANSWERS

(i)   'Exploding underpants' and dead snails are not the same thing. If you have thought carefully about the cases you will have experienced some problems in assessing why *Donoghue* v *Stevenson* was applied in *Grant* v *Australian Knitting Mills*. But remember, both sides in *Grant* thought they had convincing reasons why they should win. Neither side could simply say 'dead snails equal (or do not equal) underpants'. The Privy Council assessed the principle of *Donoghue* v *Stevenson* by quoting Lord Atkin:

> A manufacturer of products, which he sells in such a form as to show that he intends them to reach the ultimate consumer in the form in which they left him with no reasonable possibility of intermediate examination, and with the knowledge that the absence of reasonable care in the preparation or putting up of the products will result in an injury to the consumer's life or property, owes a duty to the consumer to take that reasonable care.

The Privy Council stated that their understanding of *Donoghue* v *Stevenson* was that the principle in that case could be applied only where the defect is hidden and unknown to the consumer; in *Grant* the chemical in the underpants represented a latent (and therefore hidden) defect equivalent to the snail in the opaque bottle.

(ii) The lawyers acting for the Australian Knitting Mills raised a number of arguments. Among these were: (a) *Donoghue* v *Stevenson* only applied, at its widest, to cases of food and drink—that when Lord Atkin referred to 'products' he could only refer to the product in the case; (b) the decision was not unanimous, especially as regards the interpretation of earlier cases; (c) there had been no possibility of anyone tampering with the bottle, but the underpants were loosely packed (it was not alleged there had been any tampering, but the fact that this could have occurred was argued as being a distinctive difference between the cases); and (d) that Grant should have washed the underpants before wearing them (which would have removed the danger).

All these arguments failed. The principle behind a case concerning a dead snail in an opaque ginger-beer bottle had been applied to a very different set of facts.

So, however we try to compare the facts of two or more cases we cannot answer the question whether the woman in our example of *case (2)* should be liable for her negligent driving without first understanding *why* the man was liable in *case (1)*. What were the issues on which the first case turned? Was it important that the old lady was using a pedestrian crossing? Was it important that she was an old lady? The fact that you discover two cases which are similar on their facts is not enough. Two cases may look similar but produce different results because of a different perception of the apparently similar facts or because of a vital distinction in the reasoning employed by the judges. In other words, cases may be *distinguished* as well as *applied* on the material facts or the reasoning employed.

And if we are asking *why* the court decided one way, we must equally be aware that cases do not exist in isolation—there is a whole history behind the issues involved in a case. All these previous cases will have affected the language used by the judges and the decisions they reached. The way that a word was legally defined in, say, 1850 may have an enormous impact on the reasoning of a judge in 2019.

Thus, when we talk of a judge being bound by a precedent, we mean something more than matching the facts of cases—we say that a judge is bound to follow the *ratio decidendi* (the reason for deciding—usually referred to as the *ratio*) of the earlier higher authority. The judge only has to follow the *ratio*. It is not only the facts of the earlier case which are important, but also how the judge expressed the law in relation to those facts—how the judge justified the decision in law. For as long as you study law the *ratio* of any case will be vital to your investigations.

7.3 Trying to define *ratio decidendi*

Difficulties still lie ahead. Various judges and academics have tried to define what we mean by *ratio decidendi*. It is a surprisingly difficult problem. One complication is that a judgment may last for two, ten, or fifty pages. Somewhere in there is an account of the facts as found, a discussion of legal principles, a comparison with earlier cases, and a decision on the facts as to who won. A judge may apparently formulate a *ratio* only to continue with his judgment and formulate the *ratio* again; this time with slightly different words, with slightly different emphasis. For instance, a judge might say: 'A person cannot be excused from drinking and driving merely because they are called upon by friends to drive them when otherwise they would have been stranded', only later to say, 'As I have indicated, being surprised by a turn of events is no excuse for drinking and driving, unless arising from a genuine emergency.' The second statement confirms the first, but then goes wider by adding the proviso about 'genuine emergency': so which is the 'real' *ratio*? Well, as we shall see, one limiting factor is what actually happened in the case (was there an arguable emergency in the case or was the judge just speculating about what might be?).

Another example might be where the judge switches words around (which are not true synonyms). For instance, a judge might refer to a duty as arising unless it would be 'unreasonable' to impose it, but later say the duty arises unless it is 'impracticable' to impose it. These are not necessarily the same thing. This can prove galling. It happens. And nowhere will you find a sentence saying: 'Here comes the *ratio*.'

Yet another complication is that a judge in a later case may perceive the principle (the *ratio*) that is to be derived from the earlier case as something different from that which the original judge intended. If this strikes you as particularly odd, just consider the following everyday example: you always go to the local mall rather than the town centre because you think the shopping is better there. Your friend thinks you go there because the parking is easier. Maybe both are true, but there is a difference in perception and interpretation over a fairly simple decision. And even if you insist your reason is the quality of shopping, your friend may accept that but still think the parking point (although unsaid) can be inferred from your decision.

A question frequently posed by students at this stage is: 'So, how do I spot the *ratio*?' The question is a fair one. If there is an answer, it is the rather unsatisfactory one that, for both the practitioner and academic, this is a matter of skill and interpretation built on experience. After years of reading cases one instinctively formulates an opinion on what a case means (the basic theories of legal method having long been forgotten). The word we wish to stress here, though, is 'opinion'; and opinions can always be wrong, or at least open to argument. Further, saying that experience aids one's understanding does not provide any help to someone new to the study of law. Thus, in the following text we have attempted to take a practical line by trying to find the most understandable and useful starting point for analysing the *ratio* of a case.

There are a number of older, but excellent articles and books which take this academic debate to its limits: see, for example, MacCormick (1987); Montrose (1957); Goodhart (1959). However, our experience is that at the outset of legal studies such in-depth analysis tends to produce confusion rather than comfort. We are in some agreement with Twining and Miers (1991) that the intricacies of the debate can (at least with regard to students beginning their legal studies) be a 'long and rather sterile' one. Nevertheless, as you encounter a greater range of cases and gain in confidence you may then wish to explore the problem of defining *ratio* in more depth.

There is no set single test for defining what is meant by *ratio* or for establishing the *ratio* of a particular case. As Cross stated, 'It is impossible to devise formulae for determining the *ratio decidendi* of a case.' But before you lose heart altogether, Cross also stated that 'this does not mean it is impossible to give a tolerably accurate description of what lawyers mean when they use the expression' (1991: 72), and we shall see that that is true.

At its simplest, *ratio decidendi* is the 'because' factor. We can say things such as: the owner of a scrap metal yard was responsible for the injuries occasioned by trespassing children when metal fell on them *because* he had not taken sufficient care to fence the dangerous site and to keep them out. Or we can say that the owner of a scrap metal yard was not liable for the same injuries *because* he took sufficient care to protect potential trespassers (especially children), or *because* the trespassers were adults. We might even say: the owner was responsible *because* previous authority had determined that scrap metal dealers owe a duty of absolute liability to child trespassers. In all instances we are trying to get to the bed of reasoning employed in reaching the decision.

Like so many things in law this problem of identification is not unique to legal studies. Think of the plot to a book or a film. The facts are clear, the storyline can be described, but if some people were asked to say what the film, etc. was *about*, then opinions would vary. Some might see the film as nothing more than, say, an adventure film; others might see a social or political message in it; others might think the director was clearly paying tribute to an earlier famous director. Even if the writer or director was asked to spell out the meaning, the purpose, of the film (equivalent to reading the judgment of a case), the onlooker's reply could still be: 'You may have meant that, but you produced something different.'

Thus, to the student who asks, 'How do I spot the *ratio*?', Twining and Miers would respond:

> Talk of *finding* the *ratio decidendi* of a case obscures the fact that the process of interpreting cases is not like a hunt for buried treasure, but typically involves an element of choice from a range of possibilities.
>
> (2010: 306)

It is unwise, therefore, to presume that there is one and only one possible *ratio* to a case. As Jacob LJ said on behalf of the Court of Appeal in *Actavis UK Ltd* v *Merck & Co Inc* [2008] EWCA Civ 444; [2009] 1 All ER 196 (mentioned in **Chapter 6** at section **6.6.6** in relation to *stare decisis*):

> [78] . . . As every law student will know it is not always easy to find what the ratio of a decision is, and it can be harder the more there are different judgments.
>
> [79] Moreover there are cases where there is simply no *ratio*. It is wrong to assume that every decision must have a *ratio* if only it can be found. A clear example of a no-*ratio* decision would be where three judges in the Court of Appeal each reached the same ultimate conclusion for different reasons . . .
>
> [80] As for an individual judgment, although we suppose every judge who writes his or her own decision tries to articulate a ratio it would be an article of faith and contrary to reality to say that every judge has succeeded or that a ratio (or rationes) can readily be distilled from every judgment.

Be assured, however, that there are many cases—usually older cases dealing with fundamental principles in a particular area—where lawyers have accepted a general formulation of the ratio. For instance, textbooks will normally say more or less the same thing about the nineteenth-century 'offer-and-acceptance' cases in contract law, but reading a case is an exercise in interpretation; an exercise in exploring the range of possibilities. This is why we stressed the word 'opinion' earlier. Consequently, there is nothing wrong in reading a case and thinking: 'That case is not really authority for the proposition stated in the textbook; or even that stated by a judge.' All you have to do then is prove you are right; but it is surprising how many times the cases cited in footnotes as authority for a legal proposition turn out to be nothing of the sort (e.g. the famous Contract Law principle drawn from the 1602 case of *Pinnel* (1601) 77 ER 237—that part-payment of a debt is no payment at all—is based on an inadequate reading of the report so that it misses the fact that the case was actually decided on the basis of poor pleading of the defence and, had the case been presented better, the decision would have gone the other way).

Now, one of the classic ways of 'defining' what *ratio* means is to say that it is the material facts of the case, plus the decision made in relation to those facts. We will discuss what is meant by 'material facts' in section **7.7**. For the moment we will take the term as meaning those facts which were important in the judge's formulation of his decision; and so, the formulation of a rule which proceeds an inch beyond those material facts is suspect.

This approach was taken by Goodhart (1931: 25). It has been criticised mainly on the ground that Goodhart focused on the way in which the original judge formulated the *ratio* and that this fails to recognise sufficiently the role played by later judges in interpreting and applying the earlier case. We can agree with this criticism but it does not weaken the proposition that there is advantage to be gained in concentrating on what facts were material in a case, provided that one does not lose sight of the fact that a case does not stand in splendid isolation. How the case in question relates to other cases plays an important part in assessing its implications.

What the *ratio* of a case is *not* is a mere description of what happened. It is true that, at its simplest, finding the *ratio* of a case can be said to be like formulating a précis of the case—where one is trying to put into a few words or sentences an accurate summary of all that has been said (as you get when you read the headnote to a case). But in law we are looking for the *principle* that comes out of the case, not a mere description of the facts. We use the facts to illustrate that principle. If all one does is recount the facts, it is a bit like trying to say that the *ratio* of Shakespeare's *Macbeth* is: nobleman gets told by a bunch of witches that he will be king and cannot be slain by man born of woman; he and his wife set about murdering everyone in their way; there's a lot of blood that will not wash off for some reason; Macbeth becomes king but is in turn killed by Macduff—who conveniently happens to have been 'from his mother's womb untimely ripped' (i.e. through a Caesarean section), and so not 'born of woman' for the purposes of the story. This outlines the plot but it does not tell you what the play is really about, for example how one action can lead inexorably to another or the role of ambition. So, what we need to do is look for the principle in a case that is brought out by the material facts.

Think back to the case of *Whittall* v *Kirby* [1947] KB 194 to which we referred in **Chapter 6**. That was the case about the intoxicated lorry driver being disqualified from driving because what constituted a 'special reason' to avoid disqualification was said to have to be special to the offence, not to the offender. First, the decision as to what was meant by 'special reason' in the statute was a key part of the reasoning or the principle (and therefore the *ratio*) in this case. Secondly, merely being a lorry driver with a previously clean licence was not enough to constitute a 'special reason'; so this is part of the *ratio* too—and that reasoning was explained by Lord Goddard LCJ, stating that lorry drivers were not immune from disqualification merely because they were 'professional drivers'; that status did not amount to a special reason (so, this is also arguably part of the *ratio*). Thus, the principle to emerge from that case is that being a lorry driver (perhaps we might guess at extending this to being 'a professional driver') who is a first-time offender does not amount to a special reason under the Act so as to avoid disqualification.

7.4 Perception and *ratio*

The points raised in section **7.3** frequently cause students problems. It is not illogical when first studying law to believe that, if cases form the basis for legal propositions, you should be able to read a case and say what authority it stands for. After all, if you look at a maths equation you would expect to apply it time and time again in the same way. Why should the same not apply to legal cases?

First of all, maths equations are not always as certain and unchanging as we believe. For most of the time most mathematical equations will hold true; but in extreme circumstances they have to be modified. Thus, Newton's general laws of gravity stood the test of time until some modifications had to be made following Einstein's work on relativity. The same is true for law. Many basic principles are well established and safe; what you learn now will probably still be true in fifty years' time. But law, in particular, has two key problems to deal with. First, as new cases arise in a particular area they have to be set against the established principle; and it may be that the principle has to be modified to accommodate these new cases. Think of it this way. Begin with a simple rule, then start asking questions along the '*What if?*' line of reasoning. This is illustrated in **Table 7.1**.

Table 7.1 How rules are created and modified

Rule: A vehicle must never cross double white lines in the middle of the road (the rule may be derived from an early case or might be a section in a statute—it does not matter for our purposes here).		
What if. . .?	*Decision*	*Possible later alterations/additions to the original rule*
Case 1: The road is blocked by a parked car?	The general rule should not apply strictly in such cases.	*Case 1* has modified the original rule, so that the rule now reads: 'You must never cross double white lines in the middle of the road **unless your right of way is blocked by a car** (*or another vehicle*).'
Case 2: The left-hand side of the road is flooded?	The alteration to the general rule seen in *Case 1* should also apply here.	*Case 2* has modified the original rule (and added to the explanation in *Case 1*), so that the rule now reads: 'You must never cross double white lines in the middle of the road **unless your right of way is blocked by a car or passage is impossible because of an obstruction**.'
Case 3: You are turning right into a driveway and this means you must cross the white lines?	This is no different from *Cases 1* and *2*—an exception to the general rule.	*Case 3* has modified the original rule (and applied the reasoning in *Cases 1* and *2*), so that the rule now reads: 'You must never cross double white lines in the middle of the road **unless . . . or you are turning right into a driveway** (*and no other signs prevent you doing so*).'
Case 3 again:	**OR, if the decision was that you cannot cross the white line in such cases.**	Here, *Case 3* has limited the modifications seen in *Cases 1* and *2*, so that the rule now reads: 'You must never cross double white lines in the middle of the road **even when you wish to turn right (into a driveway)**.' **This case is distinguishable from *Cases 1* and *2*.**
Case 4: A police officer directs you to do so?	The instructions from the officer override the general rule.	*Case 4* has again modified the original rule, so that it now reads: 'You must never cross double white lines in the middle of the road **unless directed by a police officer** (*and no other danger is obvious*).'

Table 7.1 Continued

Case 5: The double white lines have been partially obliterated in some way?	Partial obliteration does not detract from the safety aspects of the general rule.	*Case 5* has applied the original rule but added a new role about knowledge being irrelevant, so that the new rule now reads: 'You must never cross double white lines in the middle of the road **even when they have been partially obliterated.**'
Case 5 again:	**OR, if the decision was that partial obliteration means that it would be unfair to enforce the general rule.**	This version of *Case 5* has modified the original rule, so that it now reads: '. . . **unless they have been partially obliterated** (*and no other signs warn you of the presence of restrictions*)'.

This is a very simple example and most of the answers are obvious, but the same principle applies here as with the comparison of previously decided cases.

Secondly, lawyers have to use words to express the principles and concepts, and particular words do not always mean the same thing to different people. It is at this point that problems of *perception* arise.

We are used to problems of perception when they concern the senses. Optical illusions are probably the best example of different perceptions, though hearing (e.g. music) and taste (e.g. of foods) also show the range of subjective responses to standard data. Somehow with *words* we expect our interpretation to be both universally accepted and certain. Any level of experience tells us this is not so; but the sanctity we impart to words (especially our own utterances) seems to overcome our experience.

7.5 *Ratio* and interpretation

Imagine that we have a case concerning the law on the protection of confidential information; we shall call it *Park Ltd* v *Moloney*. The issue is whether an employee, on leaving the company, can disclose his former employer's confidential information to another company. The case is heard in the Court of Appeal and the leading judgment is given by Tomlinson LJ. He rules that the employee is free to use the information. Tomlinson LJ states:

> During his employment an employee must not disclose any of his employer's confidential information to a third party. But once that employment has ended an employee should be free to use information which he has come by in the course of his employment unless that information amounts to a trade secret. The information in this particular case is confidential but not so confidential as to amount to a trade secret. Therefore the employee cannot be restrained from making use of it on termination of the contract of employment.

How might judges in later cases react to this ratio? Imagine we have a later case, *Harry George* v *Down Ltd*. Here are some examples of how judges in that case might express their different perceptions of Tomlinson LJ's *ratio* in *Park Ltd* v *Moloney*:

- **Judge 1**: 'In *Park* v *Moloney* Tomlinson LJ clearly established the principle that an ex-employee is bound to observe his former employer's secrets only in very limited circumstances. Unless Mr George's actions fit those exceptional circumstances, he will not be bound to keep his ex-employer's secrets once the contract of employment has come to an end.'

- **Judge 2**: 'In *Park* v *Moloney* Tomlinson LJ did not give ex-employees a free hand to disclose secrets on leaving employment. There are clear words of limitation in the phrase "trade secrets". All manner of things, in particular circumstances, may amount to a trade secret. We therefore need to explore what is meant by "trade secret".'

- **Judge 3**: 'When Tomlinson LJ stated that an employee "should be free to use information which he has come by in the course of his employment" he could not have meant this to apply where the employee has signed a contract specifically forbidding him from disclosing information once the contract has ended. The use of the word "should" clearly shows that there are limits to this freedom. In *Park Ltd* v *Moloney*, Mr Moloney had not signed such an agreement; here, Mr George had. The cases are distinguishable.'

- **Judge 4**: 'In *Park Ltd* v *Moloney* Tomlinson LJ clearly stated that an employee could use information which he has "come by in the course of his employment". The use of the words "come by" is interesting. I doubt whether his Lordship meant his judgment to include cases where the employee has not "come by" information by accident but has been specifically entrusted with the information by his employer, as is the case here.'

Although the *Park Ltd* v *Moloney* case and the comments are fictitious, they are based closely on real cases. They are simplified versions of how a judgment may be perceived by later judges, but they give you a taste of how a *ratio* is open to further interpretation.

7.6 Summary of the points covered

Before looking at a short exercise on this idea of 'interpreting the *ratio*', we can summarise the points made so far:

(i)   Many cases do not give rise to much argument as to what they mean, what the *ratio* was. Formulating a *ratio* can often be a simple and speedy exercise (especially if the textbooks give you a big clue). Indeed, sometimes you can use a sentence or paragraph from a judgment which sums up the case perfectly: it may not be labelled 'the *ratio*' but you can spot it quite easily. Or a later judge may have formulated a *ratio* for the earlier case which you can borrow (as with our fictitious example of *Park Ltd* v *Moloney*).

(ii) Every case is, however, open to some reinterpretation. As we noted in **Chapter 6** (and will return to in **Chapter 9**), this may prove to be a particularly significant point if the earlier case law is seen to be in conflict with principles of human rights as set out in the Human Rights Act 1998.

(iii) The earlier cases will have dealt with specific facts. Later cases will deal with different specific facts. Your job as a lawyer will be to show how these similarities or differences affect your case: what facts in each case are material?

(iv) The need to interpret the *ratio* of these earlier cases arises when you try to apply that case to the new set of facts in front of you. In a legal argument do not expect that your interpretation of the *ratio* will just be accepted.

(v) The judge's formulation of the *ratio* in any particular case is not always clear.

(vi) Whether it is clear or not, later judges have the right to interpret these words, to add an emphasis which the earlier judge may not have intended, or which the earlier judge would have intended had he or she been faced with the new set of facts in question.

(vii) Every time a case is decided in a particular area it may:

   (a) apply;

   (b) confirm;

   (c) extend;

   (d) reinterpret;

   (e) distinguish;

   (f) criticise;

   (g) narrow;

   (h) modify;

   (i) limit;

   (j) weaken;

   (k) obliterate; or

   (l) ignore

the principles established by the earlier cases.

Clearly, precedents do not simply develop in a 'straight line': they develop from encounters with different facts and different ways of viewing the facts.

EXERCISE 10 Things likely to do mischief

The case of *Rylands* v *Fletcher* (1868) LR 3 HL 330 is one of the more famous tort cases in English law. It was heavily criticised when it first appeared because many perceived the judges as having invented a legal principle not previously found in the case law (perhaps reflected in the fact that the form of liability derived from the case is simply known as the Tort of *Rylands* v *Fletcher*). Nevertheless, the case stood the test of time until fairly recently. It was criticised heavily in a 1994 case but is now considered to be a sub-species of another tort, namely 'nuisance'.

In *Rylands* v *Fletcher*, the House of Lords had to consider whether Fletcher could recover damages against Rylands when a reservoir constructed by Rylands burst through some disused mine shafts on his land and flooded the mines of Fletcher, who

continued

EXERCISE 10 *continued*

was Rylands' neighbour. On the facts, Rylands had not been negligent in constructing the reservoir. In holding that Rylands was nevertheless liable for the damage caused, Lord Cairns cited the judgment of Blackburn J. in the court below:

> We think that the true rule of law is, that the person who, for his own purposes, brings on his land and collects and keeps there anything likely to do mischief if it escapes, must keep it in at his peril; and if he does not do so, is prima facie answerable for all the damage which is the natural consequence of its escape.

Q QUESTIONS

(i) Do you think that this expresses a clear legal proposition which you could apply to other cases?

(ii) Earlier in Lord Cairns' speech he referred to the 'non-natural' use of land. Should this be read in to the statement given above?

(iii) Do you foresee difficulties with the words used? What do you think was meant by 'for his own purposes', 'brings on', 'escape', 'likely to do mischief'?

(iv) Do you think a later judge might say that the principle was expressed wider than was necessary to decide the actual case?

(v) Would later judges be justified in applying or not applying the words used to situations with very different facts? For instance, how would you use the principle where a visitor to a munitions factory is injured by the explosion of a shell which is being manufactured in the factory? (See *Read* v *J. Lyons & Co. Ltd* [1947] AC 156, [1946] 2 All ER 471.)

COMMENT

The first and second questions help to illustrate that the *ratio* is not set in stone but is subject to interpretation. The fact that textbooks give you the *rationes* of many cases only means that this is the conclusion the author reached after doing the same exercise. Textbooks are not legal authority. As was once said in criticism of an employment tribunal: 'The tribunal therefore took the bold step of not following a decision of [the Employment Appeal Tribunal] . . . and did so upon the basis of what had been written . . . in *Harvey*, which, albeit a leading text, is a textbook and is not legal authority . . . however correct it may later be held to be.'

However, if lawyers have been proposing *rationes* for centuries, then it is not an impossible art to master. For instance, quite often (as in *Rylands* v *Fletcher* itself) a fairly clear idea of the *ratio* can be found in one sentence or paragraph. It is also part of a lawyer's skill to gather the *ratio* from reading the whole judgment (or judgments). This may test one's ability to deal with concepts and linguistics, but it is not an insurmountable task. Although it is sacrilegious to say this, when starting out studying law a good idea of what most people will regard as being the *ratio* of a case is contained in the headnote to the case. This is written by an experienced barrister and

continued

EXERCISE 10 *continued*

most practitioners would admit that, on many occasions, this is all they have read in a case. Indeed, a US judge (Gleeson CJ) once said that there are some cases where those who write headnotes deserve a medal. But this is a dangerous practice when used long term. It gives only one interpretation, does not actually quote what the judges said, and, in some famous cases, may actually be wrong—even the most experienced barristers muck it up sometimes.

The third question illustrates the point that, even if the *ratio* is easy to spot, words do not always have a clear, single meaning. The word 'escape' was a major issue in the case of *Read v Lyons*, noted in question (v).

One question we did not pose, which can be dealt with only by reading the case itself is: what earlier authorities were cited by the court? We noted in the introduction to this exercise that Rylands v Fletcher was criticised for 'inventing law'. Nevertheless, the judges still referred to a number of cases; cases which they said were analogous to this situation. The judges drew together what they saw as a common idea occurring in different settings to create something distinct. Hence our previous comment that cases do not stand in splendid isolation.

Questions (iv) and (v) lead us into a discussion on another vital aspect of reading a case—the question of what constitutes a *material fact*. This question exemplifies the idea that the ratio of a case strictly relates only to the actual facts of that case, but is often expressed in wider terms. Question (v) asks you to decide whether changing a material fact (here, that Read was on the premises and not outside so how could the explosive material be said to have 'escaped'?) might make such a difference that the original ratio should not be applied. But before analysing what is meant by the term *material fact*, we will take the opportunity to note that not everything said by a judge when giving judgment can constitute a precedent. As Cross indicates (1991: 39), the ratio can only relate to pronouncements of law, not the facts of the case; and then only those pronouncements which the judge considers necessary for his decision are said to form part of the *ratio*.

7.7 Obiter dictum

Anything else said in the case that does not relate to the material facts is called an *obiter dictum* (this means 'a thing said by the way'—the plural, 'things said by the way', is *obiter dicta*). *Obiter dicta* statements are not binding on a later judge. MacCormick describes *obiter dicta* as 'statements of opinion upon the law and its values and principles in their bearing on the instant decision, statements which in some way go beyond the point or points necessary to be settled in deciding the case' (1987: 156).

Obiter comments can arise in many ways—here are a few examples:

(i)   where the judge makes a hypothetical pronouncement, for example, 'If the facts had been different (in some respect) then my decision would have been . . .'; or

(ii)   the judge might say what he would have decided had he not been bound by *stare decisis*; or

(iii)   the pronouncement by the judge might be entirely relevant to the material facts, but his or her judgment was in the minority. A minority judgment has its own *ratio*, but if a case is decided, say, 2:1, the judgment of the dissenting minority judge cannot form part of the *ratio* of the case, since that judge's view did not prevail;

(iv)   the judge may make a number of general comments on the topic of law under discussion. In *Donoghue* v *Stevenson*, for instance, Lord Atkin made a number of observations about liability for negligent acts. One observation was that one owed a duty of care not to injure one's 'neighbour'—a person so closely affected by one's acts that one must take reasonable care not to injure them. This is an *obiter* statement because it is not directly related to the facts; it proceeds far beyond that in its generality. To form part of the *ratio* the comment would have had to be narrower and closer to the actual facts: for example, relating to the duty owed by manufacturers to the ultimate customer.

As a broad summary: if the court is not being asked to decide the topic being discussed, or is bound by precedent to follow a particular line so that the judge's views cannot count anyway, the opinions are likely to be seen as *obiter*.

In our running example of *Whittall* v *Kirby* Lord Goddard CJ inserted into the judgment, towards the end, a comment that:

> It is certainly difficult to visualize what could amount to a special reason in the case of driving under the influence of drink or drugs, though perhaps one might be found if the court was satisfied that a drug had been administered to a driver without his knowledge, as for instance where a driver had taken a dose of medicine which he believed to be an ordinary tonic but which in fact contained a powerful drug.

These two thoughts would occupy the courts for many years to come, despite being said *obiter dicta*.

Most *obiter dicta* were never intended by the judge to be anything else. However, as you will see (especially in **Exercise 11**), a later court may always decide that what was said by a judge in the prior case was unnecessary to the decision and therefore not part of the *ratio*. This 'reassessment' is one of the devices used to overcome the binding element of precedent discussed in **Chapter 6**.

A judge can decline to follow anything that is not the *ratio*. This is why the classification is important. However, do not cast aside *obiter* comments. For one thing, if the *ratio* of a case is an arguable point you should not be too hasty in relegating a comment to the status of *obiter dictum*; one man's *obiter* may be the next man's *ratio* to a case. In *Whittall* v *Kirby* (section **6.1.2**) you may remember that Lord Goddard said: 'That a man is a professional driver cannot, as it seems to me, by any possibility be called a special reason.' The case concerned a lorry driver. Was the comment about 'professional drivers' part of the *ratio* or merely *obiter*?

Equally, *obiter* comments can turn out to be much more influential than the actual *ratio*. Lord Atkins's 'neighbour principle' was not an irrelevancy: far from it. Rather, it was used by later judges to form the basis upon which the law of negligence was to develop. From a case about dead snails the 'neighbour principle' has been extended to consumer items, industrial accidents, road accidents, misstatements, and many other areas.

The same is true of the *obiter* comment in *Whittall* v *Kirby*. In *Newnham* v *Trigg* [1970] RTR 107 the comment that a special reason might exist where a person took 'medicine which he believed to be an ordinary tonic' was tested when Mr Trigg's wife gave him some medicine containing whisky. He knew it contained whisky but not how much and, after taking it, drove a friend home; that is when he was stopped by the police. Lord Goddard CJ's *obiter* comment in *Whittall* on what may be a 'special reason' was held to be sound but not applicable here because of Mr Trigg's knowledge: he had not taken the whisky believing it to be ordinary medicine. But there was another *obiter* comment in *Newnham* v *Trigg*, this time from Lord Parker CJ:

> [This case] is quite different, it seems to me, from the case which may arise and may amount to a special reason though I am not saying that it does, where a man thinking he is drinking, we will say ginger ale, has, unknown to him, strong drink put into it behind his back. Ignorance of the quality of the drink may amount to a special reason, but ignorance of the exact quantity that he is drinking cannot in my judgment do so.

This led to a long line of cases as to when a person who had had their drink 'spiked' could avoid disqualification. So, one *obiter* had built influentially on another *obiter* comment.

Throughout the remainder of this chapter we concentrate on the two important aspects of analysing *ratio decidendi*: 'how precedents develop' and the 'material facts' of cases. These two topics are intertwined and, in our experience, it would be ideal to consider them both simultaneously. Unfortunately, there is no simple way of doing this. Therefore, by way of explanation and introduction we will summarise the points to begin with:

(i)   In section **7.8**, we will seek to show that, from the starting point of a single case, a line of cases can arise with similar facts that can apply or modify the *ratio* found in the first case. This exercise is something like analysing the history of computers. Forty years ago, it took a computer the size of a room a long time to produce fairly simple results. Working from the same principles as that early machine, computers became smaller and did the same job more quickly. The use of silicon chips changed the size again and brought about added refinements and advantages. The modern computer is the state of the art—but this will change yet again, so that each generation is, in many respects, quite unlike its ancestors—certainly its distant ancestors. However, the basic or underlying principles have generally remained the same. What we will stress is that in law it is the *reasoning* employed in a case that is passed on for examination to the next generation, even though the facts change with each case.

(ii) In section **7.11** 'Material Facts' we will attempt to explain which parts of the previous cases are considered vital to the decision. In other words, if the facts of each case are inevitably different to some degree, which facts do we consider material (vital) enough to say: 'That case was decided in a particular way and this case is sufficiently similar to it that it too should be decided in the same way'?

7.8 How precedents develop

7.8.1 Comparing the reasoning in cases

Once a case has been decided, it falls to judges in later cases sitting in an inferior court or one of equal status to apply the case, or find reasons not to apply it. This much is demanded by the doctrine of *stare decisis*. Even if there is no binding element attached to the earlier decision, it will not simply be ignored (the persuasive nature of precedent should not be underestimated) as we have seen with developments flowing from *Whittall* v *Kirby*. The reality is that the later judge will (to a greater or lesser extent) formulate his own opinion as to the *ratio* of the earlier case. This may not be exactly the same as the opinion held by the judge in that earlier case. There may be a difference of emphasis. It may be a wider *ratio* than the first judge intended; it may be narrower. It is rather like the writing and singing of a song: even when the same words are being sung the interpretation of different artists may be quite striking—consider the various versions of 'My Way' (e.g. that of Frank Sinatra and that of the Sex Pistols' Sid Vicious).

A common mistake made by law students, however, is to ignore all this and, as we indicated earlier, to discover a similarity and take the analysis no further. A lawyer cannot rest like this. Various arguments might be presented regarding the similarities of cases, such as:

- 'This present case is on all fours with the previous case'; or
- 'The facts are dissimilar at first sight, but both cases illustrate the same principle'; or
- 'The present case is clearly distinguishable from the earlier case because one of the material facts of the earlier case is missing here'; or
- 'The present case is clearly distinguishable from the earlier case because there are additional material facts in this case which were not present in the earlier case'; or even
- 'When Lord Justice Bloggs formulated the principle in the earlier case he paid insufficient attention to fact A which he should have treated as material.'

This last point is illustrated well by the discussion of 'materiality' in *Frozen Value Ltd v Heron Foods Ltd* [2012] EWCA Civ 473; [2012] 3 All ER 1328 where members of the Court of Appeal disagreed on the binding status of a previous decision which had dealt with the same area of law but had not covered what was now seen to be a material fact in the light of the facts before the 2012 court. Jackson LJ did not regard the earlier case as binding, arguing that it had failed to deal with the issue; Lloyd LJ regarded the earlier case as binding because the present issue had not been relevant to the facts in the earlier case (had not been material) so the lack of comment on it was understandable—if the issue had not been material to the earlier case (or even argued in the case) it was not surprising that the Court had not dealt with it.

There are therefore many ways in which one can try to use apparently dissimilar cases to argue your case; or argue that apparently similar cases are of little or no use at all. Remember, when you are arguing your client's case you are trying to persuade the judge to apply the *rationes* which are helpful to you and disapply the rest. It is a matter of legal ethics that you have a duty as an advocate to bring to the court's attention all relevant authorities. Advocates are required to cite the authorities they wish to rely upon (usually in what are termed 'skeleton arguments'), together with the proposition of law which the authority demonstrates, and the specific parts of the judgment which demonstrate this. This extends to informing the court of cases that are against you as well, but that does not stop you arguing that the ones against you are worthless or distinguishable.

By way of illustration, the simple time chart in **Figure 7.1** shows how a case might develop.

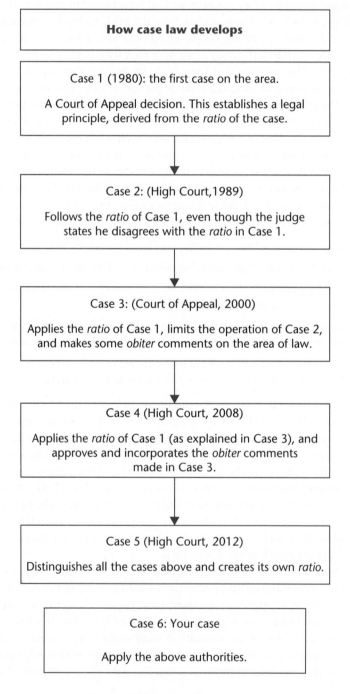

Figure 7.1 How case law develops

We can show this in action a little more specifically by returning to the example of the road accident first set out in **Chapter 6**. You may remember that the facts were: in *case (1)* a man driving a Ford Mondeo runs over an old lady who was lawfully using a zebra crossing. The man is held to be liable in negligence. In Brenda's case—*case (2)*—a woman driving a BMW runs over an old man who was crossing the road.

The question before the court is therefore: how does the decision in *case (1)* apply to the facts in *case (2)*? (We should state here that none of what follows is meant to be an accurate statement of the law—we have simplified many things to illustrate our general point.)

We shall start by assuming that *case (1)* took place in 2017 and the driver (we shall call him Alfred) argued that he was not liable because the old lady stepped onto the zebra crossing so late that he could not stop. The court did not accept that this was a legitimate excuse and Alfred was found liable in negligence to the old lady for the injury he caused her. Alfred's appeal to the Court of Appeal failed. By looking at the judgment of the trial judge and taking the comments of the Court of Appeal, we can put together the following **material facts**:

(i)   The weather conditions were excellent.

(ii)   The old lady was on a zebra crossing.

(iii) The fact that she stepped onto the crossing late did not, in law or on the facts, excuse Alfred from liability because:

(a) Alfred was speeding;

(b) Alfred's attention was distracted as he was using his mobile phone at the time.

We might say that the *ratio* of this case is: where a person is not paying adequate attention and is speeding, they will be liable for their negligence if they injure a pedestrian who is using a zebra crossing, even where the pedestrian steps onto the crossing late, provided a careful driver (taking account of the weather conditions) could have still avoided causing injury.

The fact that Alfred is male, that the injured person is female or old, that the car was a Ford Mondeo, have not been held to be relevant as **material facts**. Indeed, the court seems not to have concentrated on the use of the mobile phone (being a criminal offence in the United Kingdom), but taken a more general line about 'careful driving'. Now we have to apply this reasoning to *case (2)*—the woman (Brenda) driving a BMW, who hits an old man crossing a road. It is 2018. First, **Table 7.2** shows a simple comparison of (material) facts.

Table 7.2 Application of facts to *Brenda's case*

Material facts in Alfred's case	Facts in Brenda's case
Fact (i): use of a zebra crossing	Not present—this was a straight piece of open road
Fact (ii): speeding	Brenda was also speeding
Fact (iii): attention distracted by use of mobile phone	Similar—attention distracted by noisy child in the back seat
Fact (iv): the old lady stepped onto the crossing late	Not present—the man is not at a zebra crossing
Fact (v): weather conditions good	Same

We shall assume that the court in *Brenda's case* decides that the absence of facts (i) and (iv) does not affect the general principle to be found in *Alfred's case*. This means that the judge in Brenda's case believed that the fact the old lady in *Alfred's case* was injured *whilst using a zebra crossing* was not material to the *ratio* of *Alfred's case* when looked at in the light of the present case so that the same principle applies even where the injured person is crossing another part of the road. This is interesting: perhaps the textbooks written after *Alfred's case* thought that the protection given to the old lady only applied because she was using a zebra crossing—if so, the texts will have to be rewritten. The judge will have fixed on the presence of facts (ii), (iii), and (v) in *Brenda's case* as the determining factors (even though they are not identical to *Alfred's case*).

The *ratio* of *Brenda's case* **might then be: where a person is not paying adequate attention and is speeding, they will be liable for their negligence if they injure a pedestrian who is crossing the road, provided a careful driver (taking account of the weather conditions), could have still avoided causing injury.**

Our perception of the legal principles relating to driving negligently has been widened, even if only slightly. Gone is the requirement for the presence of the zebra crossing and the related fact of the person stepping onto it late. Also gone now is the basis for any argument which tried to limit the *ratio* of *Alfred's case* to inattention caused by the use of mobile phones. If we were being very precise, we only know that using a mobile phone or having a noisy child in the back of the car do not amount to sufficient excuses to overcome the 'inattention' point. Perhaps other distractions might be excused. However, we are at least beginning to get a clearer picture of what is required for liability and what does not matter.

We can now introduce a final example. *Carol's case* involves a woman driving a VW Golf, who runs over a student crossing the road (this time on a bend). It is 2019. **Table 7.3** sets out the material facts for this scenario.

Table 7.3 Application of facts to *Carol's case*

Material facts in Alfred's case	Material facts in Brenda's case	Material facts in Carol's case
Fact (i): use of a zebra crossing	Not present—this was a straight piece of open road	Not present—accident on the bend in a road
Fact (ii): speeding	Brenda was also speeding	Carol was *not* speeding
Fact (iii): attention distracted by use of mobile phone	Similar—Brenda was distracted by a noisy child in the back seat	Similar—Carol was distracted by seeing a dog, which was not on a lead and which was wandering around the roadside
Fact (iv): the old lady stepped onto the crossing late	Not present	Not present
Fact (v): weather conditions good	Same	Different—it was raining

You can see that the facts have moved on a little from each of the first two cases. It is possible that this shift will mean that Carol is not liable. It is also possible that the judge may find that the differences are immaterial to the general principle so that she is liable. This is what judges do: they make decisions. In any decision there is a point where a judgment has to be made and this is not a purely mechanical exercise (one reason why it is so difficult to invent a computer-based 'expert system' for deciding cases). As the great lateral thinker Edward de Bono once commented, 'In the end all decisions are emotional' and much of behavioural economics centres on this concept too. If it helps: we have described this moment of decision to our students as the 'Marmite moment'—a point where logic comes to an end and a judge either loves or hates your argument (to those readers who have not encountered the joys of Marmite, it is a yeast extract used as a spread on toast, etc.—even its own advertising campaign plays on the fact that people are divided on the taste).

We shall say that Carol is also found to be liable. This means that the judge has confirmed that the principles of liability as originally set out in *Alfred's case* are:

(i) not limited to cases involving zebra crossings (though this probably came out of *Brenda's case* anyway);

(ii) not limited to accidents occurring on straight roads (as had been the fact in *Brenda's case*);

(iii) not limited to cases where the driver is speeding (which was the position with both *Alfred* and *Brenda* but not Carol);

(iv) not limited to cases where the weather conditions were good (previously we would have been unsure, but in *Carol's case* it was raining and the same principles were still applied); and

(v) not limited by the fact that Carol's attention was distracted by a genuine and understandable concern that a loose dog might run into the road. On this, we can now speculate that any excuse regarding lack of attention will be very limited in its scope.

The *ratio* for *Carol's case* might be: where a person is not paying adequate attention, even where there is an understandable reason for that lack of attention, they will be liable for their negligence if they injure a pedestrian who is crossing on the bend of a road, provided a careful driver could have still avoided causing injury. The possible formulations of *ratio* in the three cases are compared in **Table 7.4**. How important are the minor differences?

This type of exercise is fine for examining decided cases—as you will do throughout your studies. But there is the practical 'prediction' aspect of law too. For instance, let us assume for a moment that you are a solicitor interviewing a client. The client, David, tells you that he injured a young man in a car accident. The man was crossing the road, at a junction, in a wheelchair. Can you say that the cases we have discussed will apply? Is the introduction of a new fact—that the injured person had been in a wheelchair—sufficiently different from the precedents that they may have no application?

One thing you would certainly have to do is to read the cases. We have simplified things. There are no statements here from judges as to *why* they reached these decisions. It might even be that there is an *obiter* comment in one of the cases where a judge said that had the injured person been in a wheelchair or similar device the decision would have been different. This *obiter* comment is not binding but it might be highly persuasive to a later judge; the judge in your case perhaps.

Table 7.4 *Rationes* of the three cases

Alfred's case	Brenda's case	Carol's case
Where a person is not paying adequate attention and is speeding, they will be liable for their negligence if they injure a pedestrian who is using a zebra crossing, even where the pedestrian steps onto the crossing late, provided the driver (taking account of the weather conditions) could have still avoided causing injury.	Where a person is not paying adequate attention and is speeding, they will be liable for their negligence if they injure a pedestrian who is crossing the road, provided a careful driver (taking account of the weather conditions) could have still avoided causing injury.	Where a person is not paying adequate attention, even where there is an understandable reason for the lack of attention, they will be liable for their negligence if they injure a pedestrian who is crossing on the bend of a road, provided a careful driver could have still avoided causing injury.

Distinguishing cases

When the material facts are found to be sufficiently similar, then the later court is bound to follow the decision of the earlier *superior* court (and possibly that of a court of equal status): it must apply the principle of law pronounced in the earlier case. The only other alternative is to **distinguish** the case. By this we mean that the lawyer or judge will seek to show a significant difference in the material facts or the reasoning employed in the two cases such that the court should not feel obliged to follow the earlier case. It is almost impossible to define coherently when courts will or will not feel inclined to distinguish a case. But do not be put off by this. The ability to argue differences in cases, to argue why a case should or should not apply, lies at the heart of the common law. This is what you are training to do. The fact that the judge finally disagrees with you may be annoying, but it's a fact of life. Sometimes your talents will be recognised even in the most hopeless of cases, as with Lord Donaldson's comment on David Pannick, QC in *Attorney-General* v *Barker* [1990] 3 All ER 257 at 261e: 'My abiding impression of this case is that I have confirmed my admiration for counsel . . . as an advocate in his ability to dress up the wholly unarguable as if it had a scintilla of a basis of reason.'

So, imagine you are David's lawyer in the driving case noted earlier. You wish to distinguish David's case from Alfred's, Brenda's, and Carol's. What arguments could you use? It will not be enough to show that the injured person was using a wheelchair. You will have to show that the injured person's use of the wheelchair in crossing the road at a dangerous point meant David was not at fault:

(i)   You will need David not to have been speeding because, even though that was irrelevant in *Carol's case*, if he was speeding, he will certainly be liable under the authority of *Alfred* and *Brenda*.

(ii) Even if he was not speeding you will need to show why *Carol's case* still does not apply. Maybe, when viewed more closely, you can show that Carol's speed was still close to the limit which, given that it was raining, affected the decision. Perhaps here the weather conditions were better and so the 'speeding' point is distinguishable. You would need to read the judgment in *Carol's case* carefully to see what was said by the judges and whether any comments were made *obiter* on this issue.

(iii) You will need David not to have been distracted (or, if he was, find a way of saying that the form of distraction was such that it went beyond what happened to Carol).

If you could show these things, you might be able to argue that the *principle* found in the earlier cases is not that a driver who injures a pedestrian is always liable, but that he is only liable where he is clearly at fault—and these facts show he was not at fault.

Because of our system of precedent, distinguishing cases is central to case law analysis. If, for instance, you feed the search term 'distinguish!' into Westlaw the system goes into overload and comes up with over 10,000 occurrences (the exclamation mark allows for different endings such as distinguish*ing*). Accepting that some are not directly relevant, this is still a huge number. Most distinctions are drawn in relation to a comparison of facts, though some relate to pure legal issues. An example of the first can be seen in *R v Pleydell (Michael Aaron)* [2005] EWCA Crim 1447, which distinguished another Court of Appeal judgment (*R v Woodward (Terence)* [1995] 1 WLR 375; [1995] 3 All ER 79). Both cases concerned causing death by dangerous driving. In *Woodward*, the fact that the driver had been seen with a glass of alcohol in his hands just before driving was held not to be admissible as proof that he had been over the limit while driving because there was no evidence of quantity consumed or effect (he had been injured in the crash and no samples had been taken). But this was **distinguished** in *Pleydell*, where there was evidence that the driver had consumed cocaine before driving. Here the court drew the distinction with these words:

> [30] In short, in our judgment, the mere fact that he had taken a drug, very shortly before the incident, if such could be established by the prosecution, was potentially relevant ... Quantification of the precise amount of cocaine consumed would not take matters any further.
>
> [31] In our judgment, therefore, the Crown were correct in asserting that the jury was entitled to view the consumption of the cocaine per se as relevant to the issue of driving dangerously, in contrast to perhaps modest consumption of alcohol.

There are, of course, many such examples. Sometimes the distinction is more technical and can cross different areas of law. In *Pacitti Jones (A Firm) v O'Brien* [2005] IRLR 888, for instance, the Employment Appeal Tribunal distinguished a House of Lords' decision (*Dodds v Walker* [1981] 1 WLR 1027; [1981] 2 All ER 609) when they held that the definition of a 'month' was different under an employment law statute than under a landlord and tenant statute.

This process is not unique to law. You distinguish things every day. At its simplest level, you distinguish physical objects—a television from a PVR for example. Their size, shape, and functions tell you that these objects are different. At a more complicated level, human beings share over 95 per cent of their DNA with chimpanzees and about 60 per cent with bananas, but, on the whole, we can tell the difference. More inexplicably we all distinguish the faces of billions of people, despite the fact that they are built of the same, limited number of component parts. We would submit that, saying *exactly* why

Deb and Jane are not the same person might, in the end, be more difficult than distinguishing between *Alfred's case* and *Carol's case* in our earlier examples.

What the 'negligent driving' exercise tells us is that the analysis of the *ratio* of a case involves a high degree of interpretation—of applying the *principle* in one case to the different facts in another. The principles that emerge from a case can thus often be seen only in retrospect. Looking back at *Alfred's case*, knowing that later cases have expanded upon such things as the position of the pedestrian on the road, we tend to generalise. Our account of the *ratio* of *Alfred's case* is much more general than it would have been immediately after *Alfred's case* was reported. When the decision in *Alfred's case* was given in 2017 you could not say with any certainty that the presence of the pedestrian crossing or the fact the driver was speeding would be irrelevant to liability. It might be that you now feel you could extract a wide principle from the three cases, for example that a driver who does not look where he or she is going, for any reason, is guilty of negligent driving. Perhaps this is accurate; but would you have been confident in saying this when *Alfred's case* was the only decided case?

It is like watching a game of chess where you have not been told all the rules. You might see a knight move and conclude that chess pieces move in an 'L' shape. Only in subsequent observations do you find that this principle applies to only one piece; and you may not have deduced yet that the knight has the ability to jump over other pieces. The real attributes of the knight—the first case—are seen only as things develop and by comparison with other events. This comparison was once used by the physicist Richard Feynman to describe the discovery of scientific principles; it applies equally here. And, as with Feynman's analogy, there is always the possibility that just when you think you understand everything about chess (or science, or legal principles) something totally unexpected happens, such as 'castling'.

For instance, assume that a new major case has just been reported. At this stage you cannot say with certainty how it will be used in the future. How will later judges apply it to different facts? Is the *ratio* going to be restricted to the particular facts of the case, or used in many other similar (but possibly only remotely similar) cases? In other words, how will judges in later cases use the precedent?

If we might borrow and adapt an example of this form of reasoning from Dworkin (1987: ch. 7), we can see that this twisting and turning of principles can apply outside the legal context too. Consider that Charles Dickens had never written *A Christmas Carol*. You have been commissioned to do so. In writing chapter 1, you have a completely free hand in deciding on the character of Scrooge and what will happen to him. Think of this as the first case in a line of precedents.

Now imagine that someone else is commissioned to write chapter 2. She takes your basic material, but places a different emphasis on it—maybe one you never intended. By the end of the novel (with even more authors having contributed) Scrooge, instead of seeing the error of his ways and being redeemed, is taught his lesson and still cast into hell. Your original idea has been changed out of all recognition, despite the fact that each chapter follows logically from the previous one.

7.8.2 Multiple and inconclusive *rationes*

It will not now come as a surprise that a case can be said to have different *rationes* in that there may be different interpretations of what is the proposition of law for which the case stands as authority. Equally, you need to be aware that: (a) even 'crystal-clear' judgments occasionally contain more than one *ratio*; and (b) that in some cases no one can find the *ratio*.

Different formulations of a *ratio*

At section **7.3** we noted that a judge may reformulate the *ratio* by using different words later in his judgment. That certainly adds confusion but, in many ways, it is part of a normal thought process. Here, we have in mind a slightly different position—where a judge says: 'I find for X for the following reasons . . . I would also say that there is another (unconnected) reason for which I find for X.' Which is the *ratio*? This occurred in the Court of Appeal case of *Turner* v *London Transport Executive* [1977] ICR 952. The traditional answer is that both statements are *ratio*. Later judges do not, however, follow a consistent line when dealing with such cases; they 'relegate' one of the statements to mere *obiter dictum*: see Lord Denning's comments on *Turner* in *Western Excavating* v *Sharp* [1978] ICR 221; [1978] 1 All ER 713 (also Court of Appeal).

This technique also even enables later judges in lower courts to reassess the *ratio* of an earlier case. Thus, in *Great Peace Shipping Ltd* v *Tsavliris Salvage (International) Ltd* [2002] EWCA Civ 1407; [2002] 4 All ER 689 Lord Phillips of Worth Matravers, MR in the Court of Appeal reassessed the words of Lord Atkin in the famous House of Lords contract law case of *Bell* v *Lever Bros* [1932] AC 161 and concluded that Lord Atkin had proposed two *rationes*, the first of which was based on very weak authority and so could be ignored in favour of the second *ratio*. Had he been alive at that time this would probably have been news to Lord Atkin.

No clear *ratio*

We also have in mind a number of confusing cases which the lawyer usually relates as being 'an authority for any proposition of law for which you care to use it'. This will arise where the judges are agreed as to the decision (X won) but present their reasons in quite different formulations. *Bell* v *Lever Bros* is one example.

Chaplin v *Boys* [1971] AC 356 has long been cited in this area as a case where their Lordships in the House of Lords agreed on the result but were faced with three possible grounds for reaching their decision; if one adds up the various opinions one discovers that each of the grounds was actually rejected by three of the five Law Lords. The High Court of Australia managed to do something similar in *Northern Sandblasting Pty Ltd* v *Harris* (1997) 188 CLR 313. Nicole Harris, a nine-year-old, had been electrocuted and reduced to a vegetative state when water pipes had become live owing to the negligence of an electrician. Because the case involved rented accommodation, the law on who was responsible had particular complications outside the scope of this text. In deciding to award substantial damages, two judges found for Nicole on what we shall call ground (a), but the other five judges rejected this reasoning; two found for Nicole on ground (b) but four of the remaining judges rejected this ground, the final judge not dealing with the issue.

Another case along the same lines is the contract law case of *Esso* v *Commissioners of Customs and Excise* [1976] 1 WLR 1; [1976] 1 All ER 117. The issue was quite simple. Esso had established a campaign whereby their garages were giving away free 'World Cup' coins (tokens bearing the faces of England's 1970 World Cup squad), with every four gallons of petrol. Customs and Excise claimed these coins were chargeable to purchase tax (the forerunner of VAT) because they were 'produced in quantity for general sale'. The customs officials placed a value on the coins and claimed £200,000.

The House of Lords held that Esso was not liable to purchase tax on the coins. But when one reads the judgments one finds that:

(i) two Law Lords held that there was no intent to create legal relations as regards the coins: they were gifts (see Viscount Dilhorne and Lord Russell);

(ii) two Law Lords held that the advertisement on the garage forecourts was an offer which the customers accepted when they bought the petrol. However, the coins themselves were ancillary to the main contract and were transferred only when the motorist bought the petrol. Therefore, the coins themselves were not produced for sale (Lord Simon and Lord Wilberforce).

(iii) Lord Fraser dissented, finding that there was intent to form a contract and the coins were part of that contract.

This summary ignores the many *obiter* statements which add greater confusion.

These cases do not occur that often, but they do exist. They help to illustrate our overriding point that cases are not merely objects that remain fixed and unaltered every time you look at them. Moreover, even if they could be considered as objects they would be more like audio systems than washing machines: the washing machine is a unit which does not change from purchase but the audio system can be altered substantially (new cables, speakers, etc.), and though it still performs its original purpose, it does so with very different results—and may even accommodate a completely new component such as the introduction of an HDMI interface.

Different elements to be drawn from the case

Leaving aside any question of confusion, a case may legitimately be authority for more than one principle. *Carlill* is usually cited, for instance, as a case on when an advertisement may amount to an offer. However, there is also much said in the judgments on when a person has effectively accepted an offer and, since this point was pertinent to the decision in *Carlill* it may also be cited as a distinct authority, but this time on the law relating to acceptance.

7.9 Summary of the position so far

- When we speak of the *ratio* of a case this relates to something more than the decision itself.

- Finding the *ratio* is not like discovering an object in a landscape (a 'Where's Wally?' exercise, if you will). It involves interpretation of the written material: combining what the judge said with the key or material facts which went to influence that judgment.

- The *ratio* must concern the necessary steps taken in reaching the final decision.

- There may be multiple, unclear, and inconclusive *rationes*.

- What the judge(s) in the key case believe is that the *ratio* is open to re-interpretation in later cases so that one can never be sure as to what is the 'accepted' *ratio* of the original case until it has been analysed in future cases.

- Later cases may avoid following the *ratio* of an earlier case by re-interpreting the *ratio* of that earlier case or by distinguishing it.

7.10 Answering legal questions on precedent

In **Exercise 11** we have drafted a problem on *ratio* and *stare decisis* based on both the information presented earlier and that in **Chapter 6**. Its aim is to reiterate some of the points made and to show you a general plan in answering legal questions. It also relates back to what we said in **Chapter 4** on writing essays and gives us an opportunity to note that in legal education, if not in practice, you will be asked to write essays relating to quotations as well as being asked to analyse problem situations.

EXERCISE 11 Precedent and the congenital idiot

 QUESTION

Lord Asquith once recounted a joke told to him regarding *ratio* and *obiter* that: 'The rule is quite simple, if you agree with the other bloke you say [the statement] is part of the *ratio*; if you don't you say it is *obiter dictum*, with the implication that he is a congenital idiot.'

Discuss.

 ANSWER

This question asks you to analyse how a judge uses or avoids precedent: what do the terms *ratio decidendi* and *obiter dictum* mean; and is a judge really bound by the doctrine of *stare decisis*? Thus, this is a specific question which demands a **specific** answer—not merely general comments. This style of question is one which is commonly found throughout all areas of law: a quotation questioning or denying the logic of a fundamental rule. For instance, the question might be: 'The formation of a contract is not based on assessing the parties' true intentions but on what the law defines as their intentions according to their conduct set against established case law. Discuss.' You are asked to perform four tasks, each of which is considered in turn in the following paragraphs:

(i) **Identify the area concerned**: in this case, this hardly presents a problem because of the introductory words. But a quotation on theft, or misrepresentation in contract, may have hidden points.

(ii) **Limit yourself to the topic in question**: in the context of this chapter, this again is not difficult; but when such a question appears at the end of a course the task becomes more difficult. It is vital to see at what limited area the question is aimed. Not all the topics that fall within 'legal method' are relevant to the question posed here. Thus, the **poor student** will tend to do one of two things:

(a) launch into a lengthy discussion of various or all aspects of precedent. This is known as the 'shotgun' approach: something has to hit the target. With a question on provocation in criminal law, for instance, nearly every defence under the sun will emerge at some time.

continued

EXERCISE 11 *continued*

(b) spend too much time on introductory matters, such as describing the court structure in detail. This would not be the crux of the question. This might be even more obvious when one glances down the examination paper to discover a question asking for just this type of information. With a question on contract law, for instance, there may be a page introduction setting out as many aspects of contract formation as possible when the question is only concerned with one aspect of offer and acceptance.

The **good student** will therefore focus on the key issue lying behind the quotation, namely, how a judge in one case deals with the ratio of an earlier case with which he or she disagrees. One method whereby the earlier inconvenient judgment can be avoided is to 'distinguish' the earlier authority by finding differences in the material facts of the two cases (see section **7.11** on 'material facts'). Another method (and the one alluded to here) is to 'reclassify' what the earlier judge said as not really being part of the ratio of the earlier case and so not binding. We saw this at section **7.5** in the fictitious case of *Harry George* v *Down Ltd*, where *Judges 3* and *4* redefined what had been said in the earlier case of *Park Ltd* v *Moloney*.

(iii) **Structure the answer**: do not leap into a discussion of the topic without planning the development of the essay. An examiner has difficulty following an answer that constantly repeats itself, restates points or arguments for no apparent reason, or makes sense from sentence to sentence but not from paragraph to paragraph. A safe bet is to begin with some (we stress some) introductory words.

For example:

The doctrine of precedent is central to the development of common law. The doctrine of *stare decisis* provides the mechanism for the operation of judicial precedent. *Stare decisis* demands that where a decision has been made on a particular point of law then later inferior courts (or courts of equal status in many cases) must not be merely persuaded by the earlier decision, but are bound to follow it. In its strictest form, therefore, this approach promotes certainty. However, the doctrine does not mean that all judges are simply machines, applying fixed rules already laid down. If that were so then the two sides would probably not be arguing the point. The difficulty is that the doctrine demands that *like cases should be decided in the same way*. This always leaves room for deciding when two cases are sufficiently similar that the doctrine of *stare decisis* should be applied: i.e. cases can very often be distinguished on their facts and the key point of *stare decisis* rests in the analysis of the *ratio* and *obiter dicta* of the earlier case. It is the principle in the earlier case that must be followed, not merely the decision.

You might then go on to explain the difference between ratio decidendi and obiter dicta.

(iv) **Refer to the question**: to obtain the best marks, you should try to relate your comments to the quotation. At various points in your answer review the relevance of parts of your answer to the quotation. Here is an example:

continued

EXERCISE 11 *continued*

We have said that the doctrine of *stare decisis* provides certainty. Thus, we can say that the 'law' on a topic can be discovered, and *stare decisis*, in particular, narrows down the enquiry. But such an approach assumes that the principle of a case (its authority) is not open to interpretation itself. If, however, **as the question implies or at least suggests**, the judge has at some early stage decided which way the case should go, then his task is one of showing how the authorities that he wishes to follow are very similar to the case before him; and how the other 'apparently' similar cases are based on entirely different facts. But even if one does not take such a cynical line, it is also true to say that the ratio of any case is not fixed and immutable. Different judges perceive cases as authority for differently stated principles.

(v) **Refer to some cases to illustrate your arguments**: here you could use cases which distinguished other cases on seemingly minor points, for instance—or cases where a judge felt compelled to follow earlier cases even when he believed them to be wrong. You could choose cases from areas you have studied, for example contract law or criminal law. Legal method, remember, is about how law is analysed; it is not a separate subject in itself.

Cases are cited in a number of ways. We shall take this opportunity to look at these methods of citation. Here are five general examples of alternative methods. The case is on employment law and the legal definition of 'dismissal'. Do not worry about understanding the legal issues. The key point is that if an employee resigns, he may still claim, in law, that he was dismissed. The aim of this provision is to prevent employers forcing an employee to resign without any remedy; it is referred to as 'constructive dismissal':

(a) In *Western Excavating* v *Sharp* an employee was short of money following disciplinary action by his employer. He asked for an advance of his pay but, in keeping with company regulations, this was refused. He resigned in order to obtain his holiday pay; and because he felt his employer was acting unreasonably. The question before the Court was: did a resignation because of 'unreasonable' conduct on the part of the employer fall within the legal definition of dismissal? The Court of Appeal held that a resignation could constitute a dismissal only where the employer had committed a serious breach of contract, not just because he may have been acting unreasonably. Hence there was no 'dismissal' here. **(NB: if you have time to do this for each case you cite in an examination you can write more quickly than any student we know!)**

(There is always a compromise to be drawn—even with coursework where there will be word limits—but the same is true in real cases where very often there are time limits to observe in making your submissions. So, the remaining examples make some form of compromise.)

(b) The principle was established in *Western Excavating* v *Sharp* that an employee can resign but still claim he was dismissed if the employer has seriously breached the

continued

EXERCISE 11 *continued*

contract. (NB: case names appear in italics in texts (underlined if handwritten). In essays it is always best to emphasise case names for clarity.)

(c) The Court of Appeal in *Western Excavating* v *Sharp* stressed that the employer must be in serious breach of contract, not just acting unreasonably, before an employee can resign and still claim he was dismissed.

(d) A resignation cannot be classed as a dismissal unless the employer has seriously breached the contract: *Western Excavating* v *Sharp*.

(e) In the 1970s there existed much judicial disagreement on when a resignation might constitute a dismissal. One camp argued that if the employer acted unreasonably this would constitute a constructive dismissal. Others pressed the point that what was required was a serious breach of contract on the employer's part. The issue was apparently settled in *Western Excavating* v *Sharp*, wherein the Court of Appeal pronounced in favour of the 'contract test'.

(vi) **Conclude**: the reality of the quotation is probably that some judges feel they must adhere to precedent at all cost because this promotes certainty; while others take a more creative standpoint. In the end it is probably true to say that judges do both things: they adhere to precedent and also use or adapt precedent to justify their decisions. The statement merely confirms that, despite our strict views of *stare decisis*, there exists the role of choice in our judicial process. Judges, after all, try to achieve 'fairness'. And if judges did not modify the law from one year to the next then, as Lord Goff commented in *Kleinwort Ltd* v *Lincoln Council* [1999] AC 349: 'the common law would be the same now as it was in the reign of Henry II ... [but it] is a living system of law, reacting to new events and new ideas ...'. The idea that judges merely 'declare' what existed in the common law all along and do not actively make law was also finally put to rest (if anyone ever believed it) by Lord Browne-Wilkinson in the same case.

The statement also recognises the interpretative element in describing the *ratio* of a case. The finer points of distinguishing cases, or showing how one case relates to others, can lead to a justifiable disagreement as to what is the *ratio* of a case.

7.11 Material facts

The facts of a case are revealed in the documents, statements, and evidence produced. All these are relevant to a case, but they are not all relevant to the *ratio* of the case. In our case of negligent driving, the legal reasoning is unlikely to hinge on whether the claimant was called Alfred, or what make of car he drove, or the colour of the car. Whether he was speeding is more *likely* to be material.

There is no set hierarchy of facts which will always be important or irrelevant. Change the issue before the court and different questions have to be posed. Alfred's name could be important where he is claiming that *he* is the 'Alfred' cited in a millionaire's will; so too his height, nickname, and age. The colour of the car might be the whole issue at stake in a breach of contract action where Alfred has ordered a red car and is presented with a yellow car which he refuses to accept, but most likely irrelevant in a road traffic accident.

7.11.1 Classifying material facts

Classifying which facts are 'material' and which are not is not an intuitive exercise; it is a skill developed through reading a lot of judgments. However, the first thing you always need to know is: what was the case about? What were the facts and what was the legal point being argued? In other words, what was the 'cause of action'? (see section **6.1.1** for the meaning of this term). Once you have established this, then certain facts cannot be material because they cannot relate to the issues involved. The same applies to the 'Charge' in a criminal case.

Here are some examples:

(i) *Cause of action: negligence.* The key parts of this to prove are:
- the claimant was owed a duty of care by the defendant;
- the defendant breached that duty;
- there was an unbroken chain of events between breach and loss; and
- the type of loss suffered (e.g. the particular injury) was foreseeable.

So, the facts that will be 'material' are those which go to show these elements of the cause of action—which facts show 'breach' and which show 'type of loss'?

(ii) *Cause of action: private nuisance.* The claimant must show that the defendant:
- committed an act or omission;
- which interfered with, disturbed, or annoyed the claimant;
- in the exercise or enjoyment of his ownership or occupation of land or some right used or enjoyed in connexion with land.

(iii) *Cause of action: breach of contract.* The claimant must show:

- that there was a properly formed contract (i.e. that there was an offer which was accepted, there was intent to create legal relations, and some consideration was exchanged);
- what the relevant terms were (express or implied) and that they were incorporated in the contract;
- breach by the defendant causing a type of loss which was within the contemplation of the parties when the contract was made.

Obviously not every case on each of these areas will be about all aspects of the cause of action. The cases will most likely focus on one legal issue. Strictly speaking, the only facts which can be 'material' are those relating to the parts of the case being argued about. So, any comments on other issues would not be 'material' and therefore not form part of the *ratio*. For instance, in a private nuisance action noted in (ii), the case might be about what is meant by 'the ownership or occupation of land or some right used or enjoyed in connexion with land'. Thus, the key feature of the case might be whether a person with a lease on a flat can bring an action for nuisance against a neighbour:

is a lease covered by the law? It may have been accepted by the parties that, *if* a lease-holder had the right to claim, there was evidence of disturbance, etc. So, even if the judge details the problems with noise—which generated the claim—these comments are not 'material' to the decision of the rights of a leaseholder. In a breach of contract action, the argument might be about whether a term can be implied in the contract, so it will be the findings of fact on this issue that will be material.

7.11.2 Abstraction of facts

The second thing you need to be aware of is that facts can be viewed as 'narrow' or 'general'. This depends upon the level of **abstraction** (or generalisation) with which one views the facts of a case; whether one takes only the literal facts as being relevant or one observes the facts as merely representing something wider. For instance: in **Figure 7.2**, how would you describe what you see?

Figure 7.2 Levels of abstraction

The different levels of 'abstraction' (ranging from the general to the more specific) include:

- a flower;
- a white flower;
- a Camellia;
- a white Camellia;
- a rose-form Camellia;
- a white, rose-form Camellia;
- a (white) rose-form Camellia, April 2006;
- a (white) rose-form Camellia in Bristol, April 2006.

So, to the question, 'How would you describe what you see?', all these answers are correct, but the level of detail is quite different. However, the relevance of this detail might not surface until you look back at the answer and try to apply it to a new question. That is when you face the problem whether the earlier case is authority for the law concerning (in our example) any flower or only Camellias, or even only white, rose-form Camellias.

In **Table 7.5** we show how this idea of abstraction of facts operates in a case law context. The three columns, each representing a wider abstraction of facts, are based on the analysis by Stone (1959) of the case of *Donoghue* v *Stevenson*. We considered *Donoghue* v *Stevenson* in **Exercise 9** in deciding why two cases should be decided the same way. To repeat the facts in brief: Mrs Donoghue and a friend went into a cafe in Paisley. The friend ordered ice cream and ginger beer for both of them. The shopkeeper poured out some of the ginger beer over the ice cream. Mrs Donoghue consumed some of the mixture. Her friend poured out the remainder of the ginger beer for Mrs Donoghue and a decomposed snail fell out of the bottle. The bottle was of dark opaque glass so that the contents could not have been detected. Mrs Donoghue sued Stevenson (the manufacturer of the ginger beer) for negligently causing her injury. She succeeded.

Table 7.5 Abstraction of facts—based on *Donoghue* v *Stevenson*

Narrow facts	Wider facts	Widest interpretation of facts
1. The case is only about dead snails	The case is about the presence of any animal	The case is concerned with liability for any foreign body
2. The material point is only about the sale of liquids	The material point is that the bottle was opaque; the liquid is irrelevant	The case is about articles in containers, not necessarily bottles
3. The defendant must be a manufacturer of ginger beer	The defendant simply has to be a manufacturer of foodstuffs	Anyone dealing with an item for consumption is potentially liable
4. It is material that the plaintiff was a Scottish widow	It is material that the plaintiff was a woman	Any person may claim
5. A key point is that the snail was not visible	The snail was not discoverable without damaging the container	The defect must not be discoverable by anyone who could reasonably be expected to inspect the item

Source: Stone 1959: 597.

In the first column is a material fact that relates very closely to what happened. The next two columns go wider in their interpretation. Picture yourself as a judge and ask which level of generalisation you would adopt in a later case to see whether the decision in *Donoghue* v *Stevenson* should be applied. Our experience is that students are attracted to the 'widest interpretation of the facts' on points 1, 2, and 4; the 'wider facts' column tends to be preferred on points 3 and 5. You may feel differently.

The point of this experiment is that the wider you set your *abstraction* of the facts, the easier it is to apply one decision concerning a particular set of facts to another case concerning different facts. Conversely, a narrower abstraction will provide a more accurate description of what actually happened (and therefore the less challengeable the conclusion will be). However, this also means that you have limited the usefulness of the precedent when dealing with new cases because it is unlikely that the same facts will arise again.

Assessing whether facts are 'material' or not can therefore be a difficult exercise. There is no set formula because it depends upon how narrowly or widely you view each fact. The case of *Donoghue* v *Stevenson* is about dead snails, ginger beer, and a Scottish widow, but if that was all it stood for as an authority, we would wait centuries before those facts resurfaced in a new case. Meanwhile, the slightest difference in facts would mean that when your client asked you for advice and she was an English widow, the drink was milk, and a dead mouse had emerged, you would be starting your argument afresh. Clearly you would abstract from *Donoghue* v *Stevenson* a slightly wider set of material facts than this, but how wide?

In this light you might look again at *Grant* v *Australian Knitting Mills* in **Exercise 9** and consider whether the Court took a narrow or wide view of the material facts in *Donoghue*. You can follow this up by looking at a textbook on torts to discover what has happened to the principles enunciated in a simple 1932 case about dead snails. You will discover, surprisingly perhaps, that the law went through many twists and turns before the modern, all-encompassing law of negligence appeared in about 1970 and that *Donoghue* v *Stevenson* did not receive immediate universal approval. For instance, in the leading textbook, *Salmond on Torts* (8th edn, Goodhart, 1934) it was said: 'We cannot do more than take Lord Atkin's general principle as a useful guide and it cannot be regarded as an authoritative proposition of law', and, in another leading text, as late as 1951, *Pollock on Tort* (Pollock, 1951): 'It is inconceivable that all these doctrines have been overruled by the *ipse dixit* [meaning 'an unsupported statement'] of a single Lord of Appeal.' This is not rapturous approval.

One method we have tried as an exercise in discovering material facts, and which has proved successful with students, is to analyse the importance of facts by removing them one by one from the description of the case in hand and asking whether this would have made a difference to the decision. If the reasoning would have been altered and the decision would consequently have been different, it seems highly likely that something hinged on the now-missing fact. Hence the removed fact would appear to be 'material' and crucial to the formulation of the *ratio*.

7.11.3 Material facts and the question of 'What if [x] happened?'

We can attempt to put this into practice with one of the most famous cases in law: *Carlill* v *Carbolic Smoke Ball Co.* [1893] 1 QB 256. The defendants placed an advertisement in various newspapers relating to their product, 'The Carbolic Smoke Ball'. The advertisement claimed that by using the smoke ball properly the purchaser could avoid influenza, colds, and a whole variety of other complaints ranging from neuralgia to whooping cough. The claim was made that many thousands of these smoke balls had been sold and in no ascertained case was influenza contracted by those using the smoke ball. It was stated that a £100 reward would be paid to anyone who used the smoke ball properly and who still contracted these illnesses. The advertisement went on to say: '£1,000 is deposited with the Alliance Bank, Regent Street, showing our sincerity in the matter.' Mrs Carlill read the advertisement, bought one of the smoke balls, used it as directed, and caught influenza. She claimed the £100 'reward'.

The issue was whether the advertisement constituted an offer which could be accepted, or whether it was only an 'advertising puff'. If it was an offer, and had been validly accepted by Mrs Carlill's correct use of the smoke ball, there was a contract and she was entitled to the £100. One of the main arguments propounded by the defendant was that the vagueness of the document showed that no contract was ever intended.

Following the outbreak of the 'Russian Flu' pandemic in 1889 there were many other advertisements like this: *Dr Drake's Universal Pill*, for instance, claimed to cure, amongst many things, bad blood, underdevelopment, flat feet, smarting loins, and weakness of knees. Dr Williams's superbly named *Pink Pills for Pale People* (a Canadian product) claimed to cure 'paralysis, aneamia and scrofula'. Medical science was not highly developed during this era and there were no key statutes dealing with quackery. Arguing a cause of action based on fraud would not have been seen as viable. Nor should one regard Mrs Carlill as some weak-minded, gullible individual. Many people bought these 'cures' and 'protections' in the hope of staving off illnesses, the causes of which were not understood.

When Mrs Carlill's claim came before the Court of Appeal she won her case. The question for us to address, then, is what should be the *ratio* of the case? For a true appreciation of this, of course, one would have to read the judgments. For the moment, however, we will take the case as described and ask: in formulating a *ratio* for *Carlill*, which facts would be material? Under the test proposed at the end of section **7.11.2** we will eliminate or alter some of the facts. If this alters the reasoning and result of the case, we can regard that affected fact as material:

- **If the advertisement had appeared in a shop window only, would that have made a difference to either the result or the *ratio*?** Unlikely. The case acknowledges that the offer was made to the 'world at large'. A smaller audience is hardly relevant. However, the use of a newspaper might carry with it more credibility than a shop window and so exhibit a greater degree of seriousness.

- **If Mrs Carlill had not used the smoke ball as directed, would that have made a difference?** This must be material because Mrs Carlill would otherwise not, in law, have accepted the terms of the offer. Hence, whatever the status of the advertisement, there could have been no contract and a key part of the 'cause of action' would be missing. It was also noted in the judgment that Mrs Carlill was under no duty to send any 'acceptance' to the company; merely using the smoke ball was enough as the company had waived their right to receive acceptance by the nature of the advertisement. Here, as noted above, is another principle hidden in the *ratio*—maybe even a separate *ratio* on the question of what constitutes acceptance.

- **If the sums of money had been £10 and £100, would that have made a difference?** The usual response to this is that the amount is generally immaterial. However, some would argue that the large amount (for 1893) indicated a serious intent on the part of the defendant, and so is material. For instance, one of our past students once argued persuasively that the converse was true: that the sums of £100 and £1,000 set against the cost of the smoke ball (ten shillings—now 50p) showed that the tenor of the company's claim was so extravagant that it was only on the outer limit of being taken seriously. A smaller 'reward' might indicate sincerity more easily. (£100 would now be worth about £10,000 using a 'purchasing power' comparison.)

- **If the defendants had not deposited the £1,000, would that have made a difference?** Our experience in conducting this exercise is that this question causes a split in the student vote. Many feel that it is this element which lent intention to the defendants' claim. Others feel that the *promise* to deposit was the key point.

- **If the defendant had not promised that it had deposited a sum of money, would that have made a difference?** Most students draw the line here. The presence of the promise is seen as a vital factor in the case. The Carbolic Smoke Ball Company clearly felt that this is why it lost: shortly after the decision a new advertisement appeared, this time offering £200 reward but now minus both the testimonials and the promise of having deposited £1,000.

- **If Mrs Carlill had not known about the advertisement, but had bought the smoke ball anyway, would that have made a difference?** Here we enter the realms of the relevance of other case law. Other cases had tackled the problem as to whether one needs to know of an offer before performing an act in order to accept it legally. We put this question to reiterate that, though the analysis of material facts aids our understanding of the authority of a precedent, we must be aware that one case stands in relation to others, for example here *Williams* v *Carwardine* (1833) 5 C & P 566.

- **Mrs Carlill contracted influenza whilst using the smoke ball. What if she had not done so until some weeks after using it: would that have made a difference?** If you read the case you will find that Lindley and Bowen LJJ agreed on the outcome and on most aspects of the reasoning for the decision but, on closer scrutiny, you will find that they disagreed as to whether the claim made by the company was that the product would be effective only during its consumption or for a reasonable time afterwards. This did not matter on the facts as Mrs Carlill contracted influenza whilst taking the medicine—so they were disagreeing on an *obiter* point. But if we take out the material fact of Mrs Carlill becoming ill whilst using the smoke ball and substitute that fact with one of her contracting the illness three weeks after finishing the course of medicine, this disagreement might matter. The third judge, AL Smith LJ, did not engage in the debate. He said as regards this 'time' factor: 'It is not necessary to say which is the correct construction of this contract, for no question arises thereon.'

One final question, to show that legal analysis need not be merely an abstract exercise but relates to the society in which it operates.

- **Influenza in the nineteenth century was a more serious illness than it is generally perceived to be now (though some recent influenza scares have given us an insight into the panic levels that can be generated) and many people died in the epidemics, including one of Queen Victoria's grandchildren. So, if the product claimed only to cure, say, bunions, do you think that that would have made a difference?** If you think there would have been a difference, is this because the question of seriousness and intent would have been affected? Or might it be that the judicial attitude would have been different for reasons really unconnected with legal technicalities, i.e. the social setting? Some years ago, one of our part-time degree students, a medical practitioner, once added a gloss to this: the smoke ball claimed to *prevent* an illness, whereas the 'bunion product' would be claiming to cure a condition. Thus, although concerned with a less serious topic, the bunion *cure* was less speculative and, as a *cure*, might be taken more seriously. Interestingly, while the advertisement in the *London Illustrated News* (the one we often see reprinted) claimed to 'positively cure' influenza, the advertisement in the *Pall Mall Gazette* (which Mrs Carlill read) did not make such a claim. It did not matter in the end, but had Mrs Carlill read the *London Illustrated News* her claim would have been even stronger.

We have been doing what many judges in later cases do when reviewing earlier authorities. Later judges must assess the extent to which the facts of the original case fit the case before them. In doing this, they interpret the *ratio* of the earlier case by evaluating the importance of the facts: placing them in a narrow or wide setting. What we have not the space to do, however, is to consider whether the order in which one removes the facts might matter, or the effect of removing groupings of facts. You might wish to consider this with *Carlill*.

One interesting feature of *Carlill* is how the Carbolic Smoke Ball Company's lawyers assessed what they perceived as the material facts of the case. Just after the case, a new limited liability company was formed. The new company started producing the smoke ball, accompanied by its infamous aggressive advertising campaign. A new advertisement appeared, stating that, '£100 reward was recently offered by the Carbolic Smoke Ball Company [and] many thousands of smoke balls were sold on these advertisements, but only three persons claimed the reward of £100, thus proving conclusively that this invaluable remedy will prevent and cure the above-mentioned diseases.' The company now offered a '£200 reward' should anyone use the smokeball and contract influenza, etc. This time, however, no promise was made of £1,000 having been deposited in a bank, use of the smoke ball had to be supervised by the company at their premises, and a three-month time period for bringing a claim appeared in the small print. So, it is clear that the company's lawyers regarded the 'promise' element as the key material factor—and also guarded against any 'time' or 'usage' arguments as raised by Bowen and Lindley LJJ by imposing these new specific terms.

Mrs Carlill lived until 1942. She died aged 96, principally from old age but also from the effects of contracting influenza. It is not often commented upon that her husband was in fact a solicitor and probably the driving force behind this claim. The Carbolic Smoke Ball Company only lasted until 1896.

7.12 What can happen to a case?

There are seven main possibilities:

(i) The case may be followed in its strictest form, or applied, in later cases. As we noted in **Chapter 6**, under the doctrine of *stare decisis* the earlier case may be followed even though the later judges disagree with it.

(ii) Sometimes the later court may be superior in status to the earlier court. If it follows the reasoning of the inferior court it is said to have *approved* the earlier case. Obviously, it may equally disapprove of or overrule the earlier case. Disapproval may diminish the status of the earlier case. In the case of overruling, the earlier case ceases to be an authority of any sort (unless an even more superior court reinstates it at a later date). Overruling is not that common, at least where the principle has been established for some time; but it does happen. In **Chapter 6**, for instance, we noted the case of *R v R* [1991] 3 WLR 767; [1991] 4 All ER 481 where the House of Lords overruled a long line of case law on marital rape; in *Pepper (Inspector of Taxes) v Hart* [1992] 3 WLR 1032; [1993] 1 All ER 42 the House of Lords did the same in connexion with the rules on statutory interpretation; in *Polkey v Dayton* [1987] AC 344; [1988] ICR 142 the House of Lords again overruled a decade's worth of Court of Appeal decisions on the question of determining fairness in an unfair dismissal; in *Patel v Mirza* [2016] UKSC 42; [2017] AC 467 (noted in section **6.4.1**) the Supreme Court reviewed the case law on the doctrine of illegality stretching back to the eighteenth century.

(iii) The term *overruling* tends to be applied when a court reviews previous precedents. However, if a court's decision is subject to an appeal the higher court obviously has to allow or dismiss the appeal. If the higher court reaches a different decision, it is said to *overturn* or *reverse* the decision of the lower court. The higher court might not overturn the actual result of the lower court (i.e. *x* still wins) but may reformulate the law or approve of only part of the decision in the lower court.

(iv) When the facts are found to be dissimilar the later court is said to distinguish the earlier case. The art of distinguishing cases is a major weapon used by advocates, especially when confronted with problems of *stare decisis*. The attack is usually concentrated on showing a difference in the material facts of the two cases (see section **7.8.1**).

(v) The later case may decide that the decision in the earlier case was reached *per incuriam*. As we noted in **Chapter 6**, this means that the earlier case missed some vital authority and that that omission would have made a difference to the decision.

(vi) An Act of Parliament may change the law. Ironically, the example we have used in (ii) since the first edition—the case of *Polkey v Dayton*—is a good illustration of this point too. In 2002, *Polkey* was limited in its effect by amendments made to the Employment Rights Act 1996 and the creation of a new section—s. 98A. The very case law *Polkey* had overturned was reinstated by this section. However, the Employment Act 2008 then removed s. 98A and thereby reinstated the analysis used in *Polkey*.

(vii) The later case may state that the earlier case has no clear *ratio* and is therefore not binding. See on this *Esso v Commissioners of Customs and Excise*, detailed in section **7.8.2**.

EXERCISE 12 Tales from the grave

This exercise centres on the law of succession, in particular the requirement for a testator to sign a will in order for it to be valid. The purpose of the exercise is to examine the possible ways you might attack an earlier precedent to show why it should not be applied in your case. Although we have used a particular case, this is by way of illustration only. The techniques and questions raised here can be used in any exercise on criminal law, torts, contract, etc. where you are comparing cases.

The earlier precedent: In *Wood v Smith* [1992] 3 All ER 556 the testator made a will two days before he died which started, 'My will by Percy Winterborne . . .'. He did not

continued

EXERCISE 12 *continued*

sign his name at the foot of the will and when the witnesses pointed this out to him, he replied that he had signed it at the top (referring to the opening statement) and that it could be signed anywhere. The will was contested on the ground that it was not validly executed. The Court of Appeal held that this was indeed a valid signature for the purposes of the Wills Act 1837, s. 9 (as amended), so that the will was valid.

The relevant statute: The Wills Act 1837, s. 9, states that no will shall be valid unless: '(a) it is in writing and signed by the testator . . . (b) it appears that the testator intended by his signature to give effect to the will; and (c) the signature is made or acknowledged by the testator in the presence of two or more witnesses present at the same time . . .'.

Your case: John Doe decided to make a will and purchased a 'will form' from a local shop. He started drafting it one day at work but was interrupted and did not complete the will until the following day. The first line of the will reads: 'John Doe—this is my last will and testament.' A witness pointed out to him that there was no signature on the will, but Doe said that this was all right since he had run out of space and provided wills were written on 'will forms' there was no need to sign them. The will was properly witnessed.

Q   QUESTION

What devices (e.g. distinguishing the cases) could you use to argue that *Wood* v *Smith* does not apply to this case?

A   ANSWER

The best way to approach this exercise is to read *Wood* v *Smith* and all the cases it cites. You should concentrate on four things in particular:

(i)   Which court are you in? This matters in relation to questions of *stare decisis*. Assume in this exercise that you are in the Court of Appeal.

(ii)   Exactly why did the Court of Appeal decide that the will was valid?

(iii)   What precise words did Scott LJ use to explain the decision?

(iv)   What differences in material facts can you find?

Whether or not you have had the opportunity to read the case, consider the following points in your argument.

Attack 1: Argue that the earlier case should not apply to the present one

(a)   Is the case of *Doe* distinguishable on its facts from *Wood* v *Smith*?

(b)   Is the case of Doe distinguishable as regards the issue of law raised in *Wood* v *Smith*?

Attack 2: If the case is not distinguishable, argue that *stare decisis* has no application

(c)   Was there a clear *ratio* in *Wood* v *Smith*?

(d)   Was the decision in *Wood* v *Smith* made *per incuriam*; or did it at least misinterpret the reasoning in earlier cases?

continued

EXERCISE 12 *continued*

(e)　When *Wood* v *Smith* had to decide matters that had not been raised in earlier cases, was the reasoning doubtful or unclear?

(f)　Has *Wood* v *Smith* been doubted in other cases?

(g)　Are there any decisions of the same level which conflict with *Wood* v *Smith*?

(h)　Are there substantive conflicts in the reports of the case found in the All England Law Reports and the Weekly Law Reports?

(i)　Were there any *obiter* statements which might help because they show that had the present facts arisen the Court would have decided differently?

Attack 3: Argue that the case should be bypassed on more general grounds

(j)　Has *Wood* v *Smith* been criticised by academic writers?

(k)　Were the words used by Scott LJ clear as to why the will was valid; and were those words limited to the special circumstances of *Wood* v *Smith*?

(l)　Have social conditions changed so radically that the earlier case should be doubted in a modern setting? (Not particularly useful in relation to *Wood* v *Smith* itself.)

One can see much of this at work in the cases flowing from *Donoghue* v *Stevenson*. However, by way of giving a different example we shall turn to the postal rules of acceptance in the law of contract to illustrate the development of a *ratio*.

7.13 The postal rule cases

In **Chapter 6** we took some of the 'postal rules' cases as examples of how judges use earlier authorities. We attempted to show that the doctrine of judicial precedent is not simply a mechanical process of matching similarities and differences; cases can appear to be similar at first glance, without necessarily proving to be so. As promised, we return to these cases to illustrate the development of a rule (see **Table 7.6**).

The format for this part of the chapter is to combine a description of the development of a simple rule with some exercise-type questions. You should be able to formulate opinions on the information provided; but, as always, you might devise better answers if you read the cases themselves.

As we explained in **Chapter 6**, a contract is formed when there is an offer which is accepted, without the addition of new terms, by the other party. The general rule is that acceptance has to be communicated. If the offeree communicates by post, when does the acceptance take place? When the letter of acceptance is posted, or only when it arrives with the offeror?

The first 'postal rule' case (some would argue, the first case on what we now term the rules of 'offer and acceptance') was *Adams* v *Lindsell* (1818) 1 B & A 681. Here an offer was made by post to sell some wool. The letter was sent on 2 September, reply to be by return of post. The letter was misaddressed and was not received until 5 September. It was accepted by post immediately. On 7 September the offeror had not received his reply by return of post and sold the wool elsewhere the day after. The letter of acceptance arrived on 9 September. Was there a contract established by these letters? If there was a contract, then the seller was in breach because he had sold the wool to another person.

Held: There was a contract at the moment the offeree posted the letter of acceptance. *Questions*:

- *How would you present the* ratio *of this case?*
- *Which facts should be seen as material; and how wide a description would you give to them?*
- *Should it be a material fact, for instance, that the offeror misaddressed the offer letter, but that the letter of acceptance did eventually arrive?*

Table 7.6   Development of a rule—based on the postal rule (1)

Possible narrow ratio	*Possible wider ratio*
Where an offer to form a contract is sent by post but is late reaching its destination because the letter was misaddressed by the offeror, the acceptance will be valid from the moment of posting, provided the offeree complies with the relevant conditions of the offer and the acceptance eventually arrives.	If the offeror chooses to use the post as a means of communicating an offer, he must take the consequences. Thus, he will be bound by a postal acceptance from the moment the acceptance is posted.

Dunlop v *Higgins* (1848) 1 HLC 381; 9 ER 805 was the next case to deal with this problem (see **Table 7.7**), as we noted in **Chapter 6**. Dunlop wrote to Higgins offering to sell some iron; reply to be by return of post. The offer was accepted by Higgins in a letter but bad weather delayed the post. In the meantime, there had been an increase in the price of iron. Dunlop maintained that because the reply had not been by return of post there was no contract—which would allow them to sell to other customers at the new price.

Held: The House of Lords decided that a contract existed when the letter of acceptance was posted.
Questions:

- *How would you present the* ratio *of this case?*
- *Which facts should be seen as material?*
- *Should it be a material fact that the parties were trading companies?*
- *How does this decision alter the original principle established in* Adams *v* Lindsell? *Is the 'postal rule' now (in 1848) wider or narrower? For instance, does it now matter that, in* Adams *v* Lindsell, *the offeror misaddressed the offer letter?*

Table 7.7   Development of a rule—based on the postal rule (2)

Possible narrow ratio	*Possible wider ratio*
Where an offer to form a contract is sent by post but the acceptance is late reaching its destination because of bad weather, the acceptance will be valid from the moment of posting, provided there is a trade usage to use the post and the letter of acceptance is properly addressed.	The use of the post is an exception to the rule that communication of acceptance must be effective. If the offeror chooses to use the post as the means of communicating an offer, he must take the consequences. Thus, he will be bound by a postal acceptance from the moment it is posted, provided the letter eventually arrives.

Effect on *Adams* v *Lindsell*: the narrow *ratio is* formulated differently and one would now (in 1848) need to ask whether the offeror's error in *Adams* v *Lindsell* is crucial to the point (see **Table 7.8**). The possible formulation of the wider *ratio* has not changed substantially. However, you will remember that in **Chapter 6** we saw that the judges in *Household Fire* v *Grant* (see immediately below) disagreed about the real meaning of *Dunlop* v *Higgins*.

In *Household Fire Insurance Co.* v *Grant* (1879) 4 Ex D 216 Grant made an application in writing to the company for shares. A deposit was paid, the remainder to be paid within twelve months. The company allotted shares to Grant and posted the allotment to him. The letter never arrived. The company later went into liquidation and the liquidator sought the balance of Grant's application, which was still outstanding. Grant maintained he had no contract with the company because his offer had not been accepted. No contract would mean no liability to pay. The company maintained that the offer had been accepted when their letter of acceptance had been posted, even though it never arrived.

Held: Grant was liable to pay the outstanding amount on the shares. The letter of acceptance was valid on posting, even though it never arrived.
Questions:

- *How would you present the* ratio *of this case?*
- *Which facts should be seen as material?*
- *Should it be a material fact that the letter of acceptance never arrived?*
- *How does this decision alter the original principle established in* Adams *v* Lindsell? *Is the 'postal rule' now (in 1879) wider or narrower?*

Table 7.8   Development of a rule—based on the postal rule (3)

Possible narrow ratio	*Possible wider ratio*
Where an offer to form a contract is sent by post the acceptance will be valid from the moment of posting even though it never arrives, provided the letter of acceptance is properly addressed and the parties expressly or impliedly agree to the use of the post as a means of communication.	If the offeror chooses to use the post as a means of communicating an offer, he must take the consequences. The non-arrival of the letter of acceptance does not alter the general rule.

Effect on *Adams* v *Lindsell:* the narrow *ratio* is formulated differently and one would now (in 1879) need to ask whether the late arrival of the letter of acceptance in *Adams* v *Lindsell* was crucial to the point.

In *Henthorn* v *Fraser* [1892] 2 Ch 27 (CA) Henthorn visited Fraser's offices. Henthorn was given an option to purchase a house (i.e. an offer). Fraser withdrew the offer by letter, but not before Henthorn had accepted by post. So, the letters crossed in the post. All letters arrived at their destinations on time (see **Table 7.9**).

Held: The acceptance was valid when posted. The rule was not limited to trade usage but, in the words of Lord Herschell, extended to: 'Where the circumstances are such that [the use of the post] must have been within the contemplation of the parties'.
Questions:

- *How would you present the* ratio *of this case?*
- *Which facts should be seen as material?*
- *Should it be a material fact that Fraser was attempting to withdraw the offer by use of the post?*
- *How does this decision alter the original principle established in* Adams v Lindsell? *Is the 'postal rule' now (in 1892) wider or narrower? For instance, has the fact that the offer was not made by post made a difference?*

Table 7.9 Development of a rule—based on the postal rule (4)

Possible *narrow* ratio	Possible *wider* ratio
An acceptance which arrives at its destination will be valid from the moment of posting, provided the letter of acceptance is properly addressed and the parties expressly or impliedly agree to the use of the post as a means of communication. This applies even where the offer was made in person and not by post.	Where the circumstances allow for the use of the post as a means of communicating an acceptance, the offeror must take the consequences. Where the parties live in different cities, there may be an indication that using the post is acceptable.

Effect on *Adams* v *Lindsell:* the narrow *ratio* is again formulated differently and one would now (in 1892) need to ask whether much of what actually happened in *Adams* v *Lindsell* is now regarded as crucial to the point.

Finally, for our purposes, we have the case of *Holwell Securities* v *Hughes* [1974] 1 WLR 155; [1974] 1 All ER 161. Here, an offer of an option to purchase property was sent by post. It stated: 'The option shall be exercisable by notice in writing to the vendor within six months.' Holwell accepted the offer, properly addressing the letter; but the letter never arrived (see **Table 7.10**).

Held: There was no contract. The acceptance was not valid on posting. The specific wording of the offer letter showed that the acceptance was only valid when delivered to the offeror. The postal rules were held not to apply in all cases where there is postal acceptance: '[They] probably do not operate if their application would produce manifest inconvenience and absurdity.' *Adams* v *Lindsell* was distinguished.

Questions:

- *How would you present the* ratio *of this case?*
- *Which facts should be seen as material?*
- *How does this decision alter the original principle established in* Adams v Lindsell? *Is the 'postal rule' now (in 1974) wider or narrower? For instance, can we now say that the postal rules can be excluded? If so, do we know which other forms of wording will be effective?*

Table 7.10 Development of a rule—based on the postal rule (5)

Possible narrow ratio	*Possible wider* ratio
Where an option (offer) is granted in writing and specifies that the acceptance must be 'by notice in writing to the vendor', an acceptance which is never delivered will not be valid from the moment of posting.	The language used in the offer may be such that the express terms override the postal rules. The postal rules are rules of convenience only.

We can now pose five questions to conclude this discussion:

(i) If you were writing a textbook on the law of contract, how would you present a general principle which would summarise these cases and describe the 'postal rules of acceptance'?

(ii) Do you think the development of this area of law was affected by socio-economic matters such as the fact that in 1818 there was no real postal service?

(iii) If the cases had occurred in a different sequence, do you think the rule might have been differently formulated?

(iv) Should these rules, by analogy, be applied to other forms of communication, for example telex, fax, email, text messages, or messenger rider?

(v) *Adams* v *Lindsell* was the seminal case from which all the other cases cited are directly descended. Do you think the judges in *Adams* v *Lindsell* could have forecast how their judgment would be applied in those later cases? After all, much of what seemed to matter in 1818 has probably disappeared. So, is the position analogous to Dr Jacob Bronowski's comment on the 'Ascent of Man': that the ancestors of humankind two million years ago would not recognise us today as their own descendants?

7.14 The 'uncertainty principle' of cases

Our final comment on the development of case law brings us to a theory in physics known as the 'Heisenberg Uncertainty Principle'. One of the themes we have tried to develop throughout this chapter is that later cases often change our perceptions of earlier cases. This often causes students problems, but, as we have said, discerning the *ratio* of a case is not like a hunt for buried treasure; it is one of interpretation and argument.

The problem is not unique to legal studies. The German physicist, Werner Heisenberg, argued in 1927 that as soon as you set about investigating an object you alter its state. If, for instance, you try to measure the temperature of a hot bath, then the introduction of the thermometer alters the temperature—however slightly (we accept the points made by physicists who have read this text and who have politely informed us that this is a bit of an oversimplification). The same is true with reading legal cases: the supposed *ratio* of an earlier case is open to reinterpretation by lawyers in later cases. Once the earlier case is looked at in the light of a new set of facts, the perception of the case may be altered. Further, the way you phrase your question as to the meaning of the earlier case has an impact—which facts you concentrate on; which judicial phrase you subject to scrutiny.

In *Adams* v *Lindsell*, for instance, there is a marked difference in asking: (a) is the case authority for the rule that acceptance does not always have to be communicated; and (b) is the case authority for the proposition that an offeror must always accept the risk for any mistakes he makes in *his* communication? The question posed as to the relevance of *Adams* v *Lindsell* will depend upon the facts of the case in front of you now and the issues thereby raised.

EXERCISE 13 Parking tickets and Jiffy bags

 QUESTIONS

1. **Please read the facts of *Thornton* v *Shoe Lane Parking*. What is your formulation of the ratio of the case?**

Question 2 follows the case description. It would be best if you could read the actual reports of the cases. Failing that, however, we provide a short summary of the issues raised.

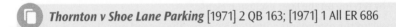 *Thornton v Shoe Lane Parking* [1971] 2 QB 163; [1971] 1 All ER 686

The plaintiff drove into the entrance to the defendant's automatic car park. A notice outside stated: 'All cars parked at owner's risk.' He took a ticket from the machine, the automatic barrier lifted, and he drove into the garage. He looked at the ticket to see the time printed on it. The plaintiff also noticed some printed words on the ticket, which he did not read. When he went to collect the car, an accident occurred in which he suffered personal injuries, partly through the negligence of the defendant garage.

The defendant admitted fault but relied on the ticket, which contained the clause: '. . . issued subject to the conditions of issue as displayed on the premises'. These conditions were displayed on the back of the ticket; they were lengthy, and excluded liability on the part of the garage for loss or damage to customers' property, or personal injury, howsoever caused. These, said the defendant, were contractual clauses which bound the plaintiff.

Mocatta J held the defendants liable. They appealed.

continued

EXERCISE 13 *continued*

Lord Denning reviewed the relevant cases, some of which are noted here:

- *Parker* v *South Eastern Railway* (1877) 2 CPD 416. The plaintiff deposited a bag in a railway cloakroom. He was handed a ticket on which were the words 'see back'; on the back there were printed conditions excluding liability for loss or damage. The bag was lost. The Court of Appeal held that the key questions were:

   (a) Did the plaintiff read the clause?

   (b) Did the railway company do what was reasonably sufficient to give the plaintiff notice of the clause?

- *Olley* v *Marlborough Court Ltd* [1949] 1 KB 532; [1949] 1 All ER 127. It was held that a notice in a hotel bedroom which excluded liability for damage to guests' luggage was not valid, as the contract had been made in the lobby of the hotel so that notice of the clause came too late.

Lord Denning dismissed the appeal. He indicated that the 'ticket cases' such as *Parker* were based on the theory that the customer, on being handed the ticket, could refuse it and decline to enter the contract on those terms. However real that theory was, it could not apply to a ticket which was issued by an automatic machine: 'The customer pays his money and gets his ticket. He cannot get his money back. He may protest to the machine, even swear at it; but it will remain unmoved.'

Lord Denning applied the reasoning given in *Olley* v *Marlborough Court*. In *Thornton* the offer was contained in the notice at the entrance giving the charges for garaging and saying. 'at owner's risk'. The acceptance took place when the customer put his money into the slot. The terms of the offer contained in the notice placed on or near the machine could be binding only if they were sufficiently brought to his notice before the contract was concluded. So, once the customer had accepted the offer, a contract was concluded on the terms known to exist, which could not then be altered.

Parker v *South Eastern Railway* meant that, unless the customer knows that the ticket is issued subject to a clause to be found on the back of the ticket, or the company did what was reasonably sufficient to give him notice of it, the company cannot avoid liability by relying on the later exclusion clause.

Counsel for the defendants admitted here that the defendants did not do what was reasonably sufficient to give the plaintiff notice of the exempting condition. Lord Denning held that the exclusion clause was:

> so wide and so destructive of rights that the court should not hold any man bound by it unless it is drawn to his attention in the most explicit way . . . In order to give sufficient notice, it would need to be printed in red ink with a red hand pointing to it, or something equally startling.

Lord Justice Megaw also dismissed the appeal. He declined to comment on when the contract was concluded. As regards the other points, His Lordship was in general agreement with Lord Denning MR. Under the three conditions noted in *Parker*, he concluded that the plaintiff in *Thornton* did not know of any printing on the ticket

continued

EXERCISE 13 *continued*

or, therefore, that there were any contractual conditions. As well as this, however, His Lordship laid stress on the fact that the conditions in this contract contained the sorts of restrictions that were unusual. Thus:

> at least where the particular condition relied on involves a sort of restriction that is not shown to be usual in that class of contract, a defendant must show that his intention to attach an unusual condition of that particular nature was fairly brought to the notice of the other party.

Lord Justice Megaw thus linked the type of clause in question (whether it was an unusual or usual clause in this type of contract) to the amount of effort needed on the defendant's part to bring the clause to the notice of the customer.

Sir Gordon Willmer agreed with both Lord Denning and Megaw LJ, saying, 'any attempt to introduce conditions after the irrevocable step has been taken of causing the machine to operate must be doomed to failure'.

 2. **Read this second case—***Interfoto Picture Library Ltd v Stiletto Visual Programmes Ltd* **[1988] 1 All ER 348; [1988] 2 WLR 615—and:**

(a)   decide whether the *ratio* of *Thornton* applies;

(b)   reach a decision on the *Interfoto* case;

(c)   formulate a *ratio* for your decision, either applying the *Thornton ratio* (in whole or part) or distinguishing *Thornton* on the facts.

> The defendant ordered certain photographic transparencies from the plaintiff. The photographs were consigned in a jiffy bag to the company messenger with the 'delivery note'. The defendant's manager ignored the note but, impressed by the contents of the bag, telephoned his acceptance.
>
> There were a number of conditions contained in the delivery note. Condition 2 set the daily charge for retaining the transparencies beyond the stipulated date of return. These charges were exorbitant, representing a figure ten times higher than that charged by other comparable agencies. The central issue was whether condition 2 was enforceable by the plaintiffs.

We provide no answer for this exercise except to indicate one or two salient points. The first is that the *Interfoto* case is interesting because it posed the question whether the logic used for a number of years and in a number of cases regarding one type of clause—one which excluded liability—could be applied to a 'similar' type of clause: one which sought to impose onerous terms on the other party. The second is that if you read the case in full you will see that there were only two judges in the Court of Appeal. It is as well that they agreed with each other as to the outcome of the case.

The final point is that the judges were not in full agreement as regards how the law should be expressed. The decision reached was the same—that condition 2 was not valid—but the reasoning employed by the judges differed greatly. Lord Justice Dillon took a conventional line of arguing from precedents. All the existing precedents concerned exclusion clauses and he drew a correlation between these 'exclusion' clauses

continued

EXERCISE 13 *continued*

and the 'onerous' clause contained in this contract. Lord Justice Bingham took a wider, more European, approach and looked to general notions of 'acting in good faith' to hold that the clause could not stand. This conceptual style of reasoning is very interesting; especially as there is no formula for defining 'good faith' in the English law of contract.

To see how academics reacted to this case at the time, we strongly recommend you to read the contrasting views seen in the following articles: Chandler and Holland (1988) 104 LQR, 359; McLean (1988) 47 CLJ, 172; MacDonald (1988) LMCLQ, 294.

To see how the case was employed in the next important case on this topic, see *Circle Freight International Ltd* v *Medeast Gulf Exports Ltd* [1988] 2 Lloyd's Rep 427. This case involved two businesses which had frequently dealt with each other on standard terms. These terms, which included an exclusion clause, had never been read by the party who suffered loss. Were these terms effectively incorporated into the contract?

CONCLUSION

Discovering the *ratio* of a case and predicting how that *ratio* will be interpreted and applied in the future are some of the skills with which a lawyer must come to grips. There is no magic formula for acquiring these skills; they develop from practice. In turn, that practice must have some thought behind it. Reading a coaching text on your favourite sport will not, in itself, make you an Olympic athlete; and practising without analysing your play will get you only marginally further.

The key point we wish to make with this chapter is that there is nothing resembling a template that can be placed over a decision to highlight and reveal the *ratio* of the case. Whether it is a student, a practitioner, or a judge reading the case, the exercise is still one of interpretation; and that form of exercise extends to persuasive precedents as well as binding ones.

The *ratio* of a case is not an object, it is more like an analytical process. Stone (1959) made the point that *ratio* comes in a 'descriptive' form (that which the judge in the case sets out or believes he or she has set out) and a 'prescriptive' form (how the *ratio* is actually applied in later cases). The 'descriptive' *ratio* therefore describes the effects of the judgment when first made; those effects may be different twenty years later after numerous applications and distinctions of the original judgment.

In court, each side presents their authorities to prove their legal point by relying on their portrayal of the *ratio* of those earlier cases, or their argument as to their application to or distinction from the case in hand. Each argument develops the story of the original precedent.

Perhaps the most helpful thing we can offer is to address some of the most commonly raised questions we have had from students over the years. In **Table 7.11** we have listed these student questions in the left-hand column and provided some short answers opposite.

Table 7.11 Students' FAQs relative to the *ratio* of a case

Does each case have one defined *ratio*?	No. There is no 'fixed' *ratio* to a case, though there may be a generally accepted one (e.g. to be found in textbooks or in later cases). When you first start to study law, you will have to accept these texts as accurate, but, later, with experience, you will develop your own ability to question the analysis of other lawyers.
Can a case stand for more than one legal principle?	Yes. A case may contain more than one *ratio*. This depends on what part of the case you are examining and why you are analysing it. The *Thornton* case in **Exercise 13** is a good example: there are statements about the incorporation of exclusion clauses and also statements as to when a contract is formed through the use of a ticket machine.
What does the *ratio* consist of?	In general terms the *ratio* of a case is made up of a legal principle based on: (a) existing case law prior to the case in hand; (b) the material facts of the case; (c) the decision in the case.
Materiality: do judges make this obvious?	No. Judges sometimes expressly state that they regard particular facts as 'material'. But, most often, you have to work this out by inference from the judgment.
Can later courts reassess the importance of the facts of the earlier case?	Yes. Facts may not appear to be 'material' until looked at later in comparison to a new case, i.e. even if a judge says that certain facts are material, that does not determine the status of those facts forever. The status of those facts can (*sometimes*) be reassessed in later cases *(see the* 'negligent driving' example earlier; and the development of 'non-natural use' *in Rylands v Fletcher).* This re-assessment also relates to Stone's point (1959) that there are 'descriptive' and 'prescriptive' *ratios* involved in a case.
Can later courts promote other facts (which the first judge seemed to rate as not a 'material' part of the decision) to the status of now being classed as 'material'?	Yes. Other facts which did not appear that important at first sight in the earlier case might be seen to be material when that case is later analysed. Again, we saw this with the driving example earlier. In fact, this reflects human nature—things that did not seem that important are viewed differently when new circumstances arise.
What is meant by 'abstraction of facts'?	Facts may be viewed as narrow or representative of something wider (see the 'Scottish widow' or 'dead snail' examples in *Donoghue v Stevenson* in **Exercise 9**). **This is the basis of arguing that an earlier case should be 'applied' or 'distinguished'.**
Can you have different 'levels' of *ratio*?	Yes. In the same way that one fact may be taken as a literal example (ginger beer) or representational (drink) or more abstract (consumable item, or even any product), so too can the *ratio* of a case exist at different levels. A case concerning a lorry driver, for instance, may just be about lorry drivers' liabilities, but it may also be about professional drivers, or even any drivers. This is one of the key points to observe in the 'abstraction of fact'.

Who creates the 'legal principles'?	Judges. Cases do not exist in a legal vacuum. It is very unlikely that the case you are examining was the first of its kind. There will be a whole history of similar cases before it. These have to be looked at, as the legal principle involved in those cases will have helped to determine the 'materiality' of the facts in the case being examined. You need to know why facts were regarded as material and the extent to which *stare decisis* has influenced the judge's analysis in order to formulate a *ratio*.
Is it important *how* the judge expresses the legal principle?	Vital: The exact words used by a judge are at the core of ascertaining the *ratio* of a case. The judge may have thought the words used were clear, but all words are open to interpretation. This is why reading a summary in a textbook or on a database (or even the headnote to the case) is inadequate legal research.
What happens when you have more than one judgment in a case?	Each judge in a case may give a judgment (formerly called an 'opinion' in the House of Lords, but this has changed to 'judgment' in the Supreme Court). Each judgment given will contain a *ratio*. The overall *ratio* of the case is derived from the *rationes* of the majority judgments. Thus, we have seen that there can be substantial argument as to what the *ratio* of a single judge's decision might be and this is made even more problematic when trying to formulate a 'general' *ratio* of the combined judgments. Differences in the individual *rationes* of judges (even those who agree on the overall result) often relate to different emphasis being placed on material facts or the use of particular words to describe the legal position (e.g. the *Interfoto* example in **Exercise 13**).

CHAPTER REFERENCES

BINGHAM, T. (2000), *The Business of Judging: Selected Essays and Speeches* (Oxford: Oxford University Press).

*CROSS, R. (1991), *Precedent in English Law* (4th edn, Oxford: Clarendon Press).

DWORKIN, R. (1987), *Law's Empire* (London: Fontana).

GOODHART, A. (1931), *Essays in Jurisprudence and the Common Law* (Cambridge: Cambridge University Press).

GOODHART, A. (1934), *Salmond on the Law of Torts* (8th edn, London: Wildy & Sons Ltd).

GOODHART, A. (1959), 'The *Ratio Decidendi* of a Case', 22 *Modern Law Review*, 117.

LANDON, P.A. (1951), *Pollock's Law of Torts* (London, Stevens & Sons).

LLEWELLYN, K. (1960), *The Bramble Bush* (Chicago, Ill.: University of Chicago Press).

MACCORMICK, N. (1987), 'Why Cases have *Rationes* and What these Are', in L. Goldstein (ed.), *Precedent in Law* (Oxford: Clarendon Press).

MONTROSE, J. (1957), 'The *Ratio Decidendi* of a Case', 20 *Modern Law Review*, 587.

STONE, J. (1959), 'Ratio of the *Ratio Decidendi*', 22 *Modern Law Review*, 597.

TUROW, S. (1988), *One L: What They Really Teach You at Harvard Law School* (London: Sceptre).

TWINING, W. and MIERS, D. (1991), (1999), and (2010), *How to Do Things with Rules* (3rd, 4th, and 5th edns, London: Weidenfeld & Nicolson and later Cambridge: Cambridge University Press).

ONLINE RESOURCES

Test your knowledge by trying the self-test questions that accompany **Chapters 7–9**. Visit: www.oup.com/uk/holland-webb10e

8

Making Sense of Statutes

8.1 Introduction

On the whole, statutes are not a fun read. Worse still, they are written in a style and format quite different from those of many other documents (though insurance documents and many credit card agreements are written in similarly dense styles). The language used is traditional (if not archaic) and often has a very flat-prose style and a dependence on complex phrasing and language (see Maughan and Webb, 2006). But, of course, an Act is not meant to be a piece of amusing literature; it is not designed to entertain, but to declare the law on a particular topic.

The aim of this chapter, therefore, is to introduce you to the techniques and problems of analysing the structure of statutes. Making sense of statutes (or, at least, some statutes) can be a real problem for students, practitioners, and judges alike. However, legal method tutors from around the world have told us that, for some reason, students are having more trouble reading statutes than used to be the case, and an interesting analysis of the debate in Australia on how to teach statutory interpretation can be found in Dharmananda and Lane's article (2018).

So, before we look at how to interpret statutes in **Chapter 9**, we need to begin by describing how statutes are set out, what tricks are employed, what particular catchphrases mean, and how to make sense of the opaque language often used. For an extremely good explanation of how we inherited the system we have today and also why, as one author puts it, 'The language of our legislation cannot be reduced to baby talk for consumption by the masses', see Hunt (2002: 24).

In **Chapter 3** we dealt with the basics of what statutes look like, for example how sections are organised and the use of subsections, schedules, long titles, etc. (recapped in **Table 8.1**) and in **Chapter 9** we will explore the techniques used to *interpret* words in a statute. In this chapter we are concerned with finding the best way to read, understand, and analyse the structure used—in other words, how to work your way through what is often a very complex layout. The problem arises because there are always many different ways of explaining even the simplest idea and what is an acceptable arrangement of the material to one person is confusion to another.

We have ignored the pattern by which legislation is grouped into 'Parts', 'Chapters', 'Headings', and 'Marginal notes' in this summary. Further, particularly with sections in an Act, there may be even more sub-divisions. Section 34 Theft Act 1968, for instance, breaks down to s. 34(2)(a)(i), while s. 2 Law of Property Act 1925 uses a slightly different layout, with the Roman numeral (v) coming before the lower case (a): s. 2(3)(v)(a). If further divisions are needed, draftsmen then conscript Greek letters.

Table 8.1 Recap on the basic structure of UK legislation

Title	Main division	Sub-division	Main sub-sub-division
Statute	Section, e.g. s. 1	Subsection, e.g. s. 1(1)	Paragraph, e.g. s. 1(1)(a)
Schedule to a statute	Paragraph, e.g. sch. 1, para. 1	Sub-paragraph, e.g. sch. 1, para. 1(a)	(None)
Statutory Instrument*	Regulations (or Rules), e.g. reg. 1 (or r. 1)	Paragraphs, e.g. reg. 1(1)	Sub-paragraphs, e.g. reg. 1(1)(a)

* Statutory Instruments often appear with the title 'Order', as with The Public Bodies (Abolition of the Commission for Rural Communities) Order 2012 or 'Regulation', as with The Transfer of Undertakings (Protection of Employment) Regulations 2006. Both forms have the same type of citation (year and number), as in SI 2006/246.

8.2 Drafting styles

Imagine you have been given the job of drafting a rule defining when a ball (in whatever sport) is 'in' play or 'out of' play. First, you need instructions from the rules committee as to what it wants: does it want a ball which is 'on the line' to be in play or out of play? (it varies with different sports; e.g. in football and tennis the line is in play but in golf the line itself is out of bounds). Let us assume here that the committee wants the line to be 'in play'. So, how could we put this into rule form?

The simplest method must be something like: 'A ball is always in play until it has completely crossed the line.' Rule 12 of the International Tennis Federation's Rules puts it like this: 'If a ball touches a line, it is regarded as touching the court bounded by that line' (so it is still in play). FIFA's rules for football (law 9) talk of a ball being in play until it 'leaves the field by entirely crossing a goal line or touch line'. But this still only provides us with a very simple formulation; it does not cover exceptions and does not add definitions. So, a draftsman has to consider how these extra elements will be woven into the document. Should he or she start with a general point and then add variations? Or maybe begin with definitions and then go on to the rule itself? Or deal with each individual aspect of the rule, bit by bit?

It is often quite easy to explain rules to someone orally because you can keep going back over points of confusion, or put things in slightly different ways. In a written document such devices are not available. So, a draftsman has to spell out the idea as fully as possible.

Table 8.2 provides an example of how two different draftsmen might use quite dissimilar methods of drafting to convey the same message using (very nearly) the same words but arranging them quite differently. We shall use the term 'playing field' here, though the rule could refer to a 'court' or 'pitch', etc.

Note that the first style uses phrases such as 'subject to . . .' in s. 1 and both styles use 'for the purposes of . . .', together with cross-references to later sections or schedules in the Act. This is not everyday speech. Both versions also attempt to state general points and then move onto the specific definitions, etc. The second version does this by avoiding using 'subject to . . .' and similar phrases, but it still has to include cross-references and has also had to include an additional section. In the end, both these methods of explanation say the same thing and each of them uses techniques common in drafting statutes. You will encounter various forms of drafting throughout your studies and in practice and we therefore aim in this chapter to give you some clues as to how to recognise and utilise them.

Table 8.2 Contrasting drafting styles

First drafting style	Second drafting style
Section 1: Subject to sections 2 and 3 of this Act a ball is always in play until the whole of the ball has crossed the relevant line forming the border of the playing field. ...	*Section 1*: A ball is always in play until the whole of the ball has crossed the relevant line forming the border of the playing field. ...
Section 2: For the purposes of section 1, and subject to section 3(1), the whole of the ball has crossed the relevant line only when it has cleared the outside boundary of the relevant line.	*Section 2*: For the purposes of section 1, 'whole of the ball' shall mean the full circumference of the ball, as would be evident if viewed directly from above.

Section 3: For the purposes of this Act:
(1) 'ball' shall mean only a ball which complies with the official measurements as authorised by [the governing body];
(2) 'line' shall mean only the official measurements of a line as authorised by [the governing body], these being set out in Schedule 1 to this Act.
(3) any reference to the term 'whole of the ball' shall be construed as relating to the full circumference of the ball as would be evident if viewed directly from above.
(4) a ball is:
  (a) in play unless and until it has been propelled by a player across any line of the playing area or it has been struck by a player and rebounds from the referee so as to cross the line; but
  (b) is out of play where the whole of the ball has crossed the line.
	Section 3: A ball will remain in play unless and until:
	(a) it has been propelled by a player across any line of the playing area; or
	(b) it has been struck by a player and rebounds from the referee so as to cross the line
	provided always that the whole of the ball, as defined in section 4, has not cleared the outside boundary of the relevant line.

	Section 4: For the purposes of this Act the words 'ball' and 'line' shall mean only balls and lines which comply with the official measurements as authorised by [the governing body], these being set out in Schedule 1 to this Act.

A good place to start with real drafting practices is with a fairly straightforward statute, namely the Theft Act 1968. Section 1 is headed 'Basic Definition of Theft' and it reads as follows:

> (1) A person is guilty of theft if he dishonestly appropriates property belonging to another with the intention of permanently depriving the other of it; and 'thief' and 'steal' shall be construed accordingly.
>
> (2) It is immaterial whether the appropriation is made with a view to gain, or is made for the thief's own benefit.
>
> (3) The five following sections of this Act shall have effect as regards the interpretation and operation of this section (and, except as otherwise provided by this Act, shall apply only for purposes of this section).

The language used is not particularly complicated, but there are a number of technicalities and hidden depths. For instance, what is meant by 'dishonestly'? What does 'appropriation' mean? Where would you find the answers to these questions? In one sense these are matters of interpretation and therefore fall within the province of **Chapter 9**, but, in structural terms, the Theft Act 1968 is set out in a very helpful way, so that all the words in s. 1 are expanded upon in subsequent sections. Therefore, to understand s. 1, you need to cross-refer to the definitions in ss 2–6.

For instance, s. 3 says that 'appropriation' means:

> (1) Any assumption by a person of the rights of an owner amounts to an appropriation, and this includes, where he has come by the property (innocently or not) without stealing it, any later assumption of a right to it by keeping or dealing with it as owner . . .

Thus, this meaning of 'appropriation' has to be 'read into' the definition of theft in s. 1(1). Equally, s. 4 tells you what the word 'property' means in this context; so, for instance, we can see the effect of ss 3 and 4 in *R* v *Greenberg* [1972] Crim LR 331. Here, a man was found not guilty of theft (under s. 1) when he drove into the petrol station, filled his car with petrol and, at that point, decided to drive off without paying. The reason for his acquittal was that he had appropriated the petrol (the property) honestly but become dishonest later in relation to what was then his own 'property' because in law property rights, but not ownership, passed when he mixed the new petrol with that in his tank.

Section 5 continues with another definition, this time dealing with what 'belonging to another' means, and s. 6 covers 'with the intention of permanently depriving the other of it'. This is a common method of drafting statutes. Other, similar, methods employ detailed explanations within the section itself, or make use of specific definition sections elsewhere in the Act, or provide more detail in the schedules. For example, in s. 8 of the Theft Act 1968, when the section uses the word 'steal', then, without anything else appearing in the statute to the contrary, that word takes on the meaning given to it in s. 1, even though there is no specific cross-reference. Section 8 states: 'A person is guilty of robbery if he steals, and immediately before or at the time of doing so, and in order to do so, he uses force on any person or puts or seeks to put any person in fear of being then and there subjected to force.'

We should also note that many draftsmen use words knowing that there is a body of case law which defines these words and upon which judges will rely, so no explanation is offered in the statute itself; for example where an Act uses the word 'offer' in a contractual setting the court will presume it bears the meaning derived from hundreds of years of case law (see the case of *Fisher* v *Bell* [1961] 1 QB 394; [1960] 3 All ER 731 as a good example—or the strange case of *R* v *Collins* [1973] QB 100; [1972] 2 All ER 1105, which centred on whether a man, naked except for his socks and perched on the sill of an open window was 'trespassing' for the purposes of committing burglary under the Theft Act 1968, s. 9 should any part of his anatomy cross the plane of the building).

One tends to be more sympathetic with the problems facing the draftsmen when one tries to draft a document oneself. It is worth spending a few minutes on the next exercise.

EXERCISE 14 The minimum speed limit

 QUESTION

In this exercise you are a parliamentary draftsman appointed to deal with the problems of slow-moving traffic. Assume that you have been instructed to draft legislation which will introduce a 'minimum speed limit' in country areas and on motorways. The purpose of this exercise is:

(i) to explore the style of wording you use—how many clauses you need; how concise the wording should be;

(ii) to see how difficult it can be to anticipate all the possible situations that may occur.

A ANSWER

There is of course no single right answer to this problem. Instead here are a few situations which we think your legislation should allow for. Glancing through them you may feel your drafting covers them, more or less. Our experience is that it is a sobering (or exasperating) exercise to get a friend to compare the situations with your piece of draftsmanship. The chances are that at one stage (at least) you will find yourself saying: 'Yes, but I meant it to cover that . . .' or 'Of course it covers that.' But does it?

Consider whether your legislation covers: stopping at junctions or traffic lights; stopping at hazards such as temporary roadworks; breakdowns; having to slow down because of moving hazards such as tractors; separate criteria for tractors and other agricultural vehicles (if so, how do you define an agricultural vehicle?). For that matter, how did you define 'vehicle'? Did you have the same speed limits for different roads, for example the B4106, the A4018, and the M5? Did weather conditions come into the definition, such as fog or bad visibility?

We will examine some of the problems of structure in more depth shortly. Before that, however, it is worth noting one or two points on why statutes are drafted this way.

8.3 The problems of drafting statutes in English law

Although for constitutional purposes primary legislation is created by Parliament, the actual drafting of statutes is the province of civil servants. Most of the work is done by the various government departments together with parliamentary draftsmen in the Office of Parliamentary Counsel (see www.gov.uk/government/organisations/office-of-the-parliamentary-counsel for further details and Regan (2013: 32) for an account of the problems of drafting from the perspective of a parliamentary draftsman). There are only about 50 of these specialist draftsmen (plus support staff). Their job is to translate the political objectives behind a proposed Bill into the appropriate legal form, to assess its impact upon the existing law, and to make sure that changes to the existing law are effected properly. This is a demanding task. So, how do the draftsmen approach that task? In a major article published some years ago Francis Bennion (1978), another former Parliamentary Counsel, identified nine targets of the draftsman's work; these he describes as:

(i)   **legal effectiveness**: the draftsman must take sometimes very generalised political policy and convert that into a legal form without losing sight of its intended aims. This is not always straightforward, particularly as one Bill may reflect a range of intentions, not all of which may be equally practicable;

(ii)   **procedural legitimacy**: the Bill must comply with the formal procedures for creating legislation laid down by both Houses of Parliament;

(iii) **timeliness**: the draftsmen are constrained by the fact that they must work within the time constraints created by the parliamentary timetable. A government wishing to push through large quantities of reforming legislation will inevitably impose considerable pressure on the draftsmen. Time pressures may mean, as one Member of Parliament has put it, Bills entering Parliament as 'ill-formed, ugly or premature progeny': Rhys Williams (1987: 138);

(iv)   **certainty**: (see section **8.3.1**);

(v)   **comprehensibility**: (see section **8.3.2**);

(vi)   **acceptability**: the language of legislation has to be 'acceptable'. By this Bennion means that it must obey the rules traditionally prescribed. Bennion himself once drew considerable criticism from within the House of Commons for using the phrase 'tried his best' rather than the more conventional 'used his best endeavours' and there is a long-running debate on whether the word 'shall' should be used in legislation;

(vii) **brevity**: one should not necessarily assume that brevity and clarity go hand in hand. One of the lessons we have already learned from attempts to develop 'plain English' styles of legal document drafting is that it may take *more* words, not fewer, to increase the clarity of legislation. Brevity itself is not always the answer: a classic example from the Law of Succession is the case of *Thorn v Dickens* [1906]

WN 54, where the will read 'All for Mother'. That appears reasonably clear but the will was contested successfully—'Mother' was the term used by the testator to refer to his wife, not his mother;

(viii) **debatability**: legislation should ideally be framed in such a way that the general principles are debatable in Parliament. This requires counsel to consider carefully both the complexity and even the order of clauses;

(ix) **legal compatibility**: the draftsman must finally work out how the proposals fit in with the existing law. This apparently simple statement disguises a number of difficulties. First, the draftsman needs to know what the existing law actually says. In that respect, the briefings from the instructing department are often an essential starting point, but any draftsman would then engage in research to determine not just what the law says but *how* it says it. As a general principle, a draftsman ought to attempt to use the same form of wording as appears in other legislation covering the same subject matter. Secondly, the draftsman should also indicate the manner in which and extent to which existing legislation is amended by the proposed Bill. This often requires further, sometimes difficult, research. Details of this will appear in the 'Repealing Schedule' to the Act.

Although we can describe points (i)–(ix) as targets, they are not all mutually compatible; as a result, drafting tends to be rather like negotiating a path through a maze of both political and technical legal constraints. All of these points are important but, for the purposes of this chapter, we will concentrate on 'certainty' and 'comprehensibility'. The ultimate aim of any draftsman is to produce as clear a version as possible of the law that Parliament wants. For sure, it is best to avoid clauses such as the one that appeared in a US statute: 'No one shall carry any dangerous weapon upon the public highway except for the purpose of killing a noxious animal or a policeman in the execution of his duty.' Chauvinistic smugness would be misplaced: there are English law equivalents. The most-cited example (said to relate to the ill-fated Tanganyika groundnuts scheme) is the supposed 1948 Statutory Instrument which read: 'In the Nuts (unground) (other than ground nuts) Order, the expression nuts shall have reference to such nuts, other than ground nuts, as would but for this amending Order not qualify as nuts (unground) (other than ground nuts) by reason of their being nuts (unground)'—we say 'supposed' because, sadly, this is probably an excellent and much-promulgated spoof; no such statutory instrument exists in the UK archives.

8.3.1 Certainty

Although it is desirable that a provision should normally only have one clear meaning, it is an ideal that is often difficult to achieve for a number of reasons:

(i) As we sought to show in **Chapter 5**, the English language itself is not always a very precise tool. In achieving certainty, the draftsman has to bear in mind the ordinary or, if necessary, technical meaning of the term he or she wishes to use. The draftsman must also be aware of the approach that the courts are likely to take when approaching questions of interpretation. Let us illustrate each of these points.

For instance, using a thesaurus, look up any word, for example *invention*. The range of synonyms is: contraption, design, device, discovery, gadget, fabrication, development, fantasy, fiction, illusion, creativity, ingenuity, innovation, inventiveness, originality.

But if you perform the same exercise with one of the words in the list, for example *fabrication*, then you get a further list: falsehood, fib, lie, prevarication, story, construction, manufacture, production.

A sentence in a statute that therefore reads:

> An employee must surrender to his employer any invention made in the course of his employment.

is unlikely to mean:

> An employee must surrender to his employer any fantasy made in the course of his employment.

but it could mean:

> An employee must surrender to his employer any fabrication made in the course of his employment.

or:

> An employee must surrender to his employer any design made in the course of his employment.

A design and a fabrication are not, however, the same thing, even accepting that 'fabrication' does not mean 'lie' or 'fib' in this context. 'Design' and 'fabrication', for instance, would have a different meaning in the fashion industry from that in the computer industry when applied to any definition of 'invention'. Clearly, the context of the word in the statute and the problem before the court must affect the meaning and accuracy of the application of the word.

Anticipating the reaction of the courts is not always easy. The word, or wording, does not even have to be complicated to cause problems. The statute can be about a very simple topic, and yet lead to many odd cases. Consider, as an example, the Wills Act 1837, s. 9. This section originally stated that the signature to a will must appear at 'the foot or end' of the will. But did this mean the physical positioning at the end of a document, or that the signature was the last thing written on the will, i.e. that the signature could appear anywhere as long as, in terms of time, it came at the end of making the will? Signatures appeared everywhere on wills because people always manage to do strange things. Some judges were lenient as to the physical positioning of the signatures; others were not (we will concentrate on how you can get variations in interpretation in **Chapter 9**). In 1852 the Act had to be amended to read that the signature should come:

> At or after, or following, or under, or beside, or opposite to the end of the will, that it shall be apparent on the face of the will that the Testator intended to give effect to the will.

This still produced problems and the wording to this section was changed again in 1982, by the Administration of Justice Act of that year. It became:

> No will shall be valid unless . . . it appears that the testator intended by his signature to give effect to the will . . .

This removed any reference to the position of the signature, so that should have resolved all the earlier problems. Nevertheless, the case of *Wood* v *Smith* [1993] Ch 90; [1992] 3 All ER 556, CA (which we touched on at section **7.11** in **Exercise 12**) shows that, even with the amended wording, the judges can still manage to disagree about the effect of the section. In this case the deceased had signed his will at the top, then written out the various bequests, and finally had it signed by his witnesses. At first instance, the High Court held that it was not a valid will. It was the natural construction of the words of the Act that the maker should sign the will *after* making the various dispositions, not before. There has to be something in the nature of a disposition before a will exists and can be signed. The Court of Appeal took a rather different view of the issue. It decided that a signature did *not* have to be appended after the dispositive provisions of the will had been written, provided that the writing of the will and its signing by the testator constituted 'one operation' (a concept which is barely defined by the courts). So, on this point the High Court was overruled, since there was no doubt on the facts that the testator had completed his will as a single operation. In its final version *Wood* v *Smith* thus appears to have done what the legislation intended, and, for the majority of cases, the decision shifts the court's focus away from the position of the signature, and on to the issue of testamentary intent. The logic of *Wood* v *Smith* did not, however, save a will in the case of *Marley* v *Rawlings* [2012] EWCA Civ 61; [2012] 4 All ER 630, where husband and wife had each managed (under the supervision of a solicitor, no less) to sign each other's will. As to the various interpretative techniques used by the Supreme Court in this case see Kelly (2017).

(ii) The desire for certainty frequently leads to undue verbosity, precisely because the draftsman is seeking to delineate meaning to such a high degree. That is why we find examples of such extremely dense prose as the Social Security Act 1975, s. 16(1):

> If a person is more than 5 years below pensionable age on the qualifying date in any period of inter-ruption of employment then, subject to the following provisions of this section, in respect of every day of that period in respect of which he is entitled to an invalidity pension, he shall also be entitled to an invalidity allowance at the appropriate weekly rate specified in relation thereto in Schedule 4, Part I, paragraph 3; and 'the qualifying date' means the first day in that period (whether before the coming into force of this section or later) which is a day of incapacity for work or such earlier day as may be prescribed.

It is not exactly light reading. If we look at what makes it so difficult, we can see a number of factors. One is the cross-referencing to other technical issues, both implicit in the use of terms such as 'pensionable age' or 'relevant amount', which are defined elsewhere in the Act, and explicitly in the reference to sch. 4. A second is the actual length of the sentence, and the number of dependent clauses it contains. By the time we reach the end, there is a real risk that we will have forgotten what the subsection first set out to do (i.e. define entitlement to invalidity allowance). The third factor is the use of terms that would be redundant in ordinary usage, but are used to emphasise the interrelationship between different parts of an Act. Here there are two such examples: 'subject to the following provisions of this section'; and 'specified in relation thereto'. Students find such phrases very difficult to deal with and we will shortly discuss how to handle these problematic terms.

(iii) Sometimes it may happen that a provision is left deliberately vague. As Bennion points out, this may well happen where the framers of the Act are themselves uncertain of how to handle it. Cynically, one might say that the courts are simply burdened with the responsibility. The most common 'signs' for this can be seen in phrases imposing duties on people such as factory owners to maintain health and safety standards 'where reasonably practicable' or where matters of judgment are deliberately left to 'the court's discretion' (e.g. s. 2 Health and Safety at Work Etc Act 1974 uses the (undefined) term 'reasonably practicable' to describe an employer's duty to his employees—and it does so on six occasions). Indeed, sometimes words are deliberately left vague as a political measure to get a clause through Parliament without inducing opposition from certain MPs (e.g. those opposing changes to family law). Then again, there are times when not defining a word was just the easiest thing to do, for example the Social Action, Responsibility and Heroism Act 2015, which creates a statutory duty for the courts to take into account a person's 'heroism' in deciding whether he has acted negligently (s. 4). Perhaps wisely, the Act does not define 'heroism' or tell the courts what to do once they have found it in terms of liability for the negligence in question. As the editor of *Statute Law* (Feb 2015) commented, 'So this is a direction to the courts to take an undefined and undefinable concept into account for an unspecified and incalculable purpose.'

8.3.2 Comprehensibility

Despite what we have just said, draftsmen do aim for legislation that is understandable. However, in so doing they tend to have a specialist audience in mind, in that legislation is designed to be read first and foremost by lawyers. Ideally it should also be comprehensible to Members of Parliament, who may not share the same degree of expertise as a legal audience. How effectively it reaches the latter audience is certainly debatable (e.g. Rhys Williams, 1987: 140). What is beyond doubt is that legislation is not drafted for lay people to read and understand with ease.

Comprehension also implies some degree of clarity and logical structure. We have already illustrated how linguistic problems affect clarity. However, clarity can also be influenced by the overall structure of an Act, particularly in the way it is broken down into composite parts and sections. In our system, it used to be considered good practice that draftsmen should start with matters of general principle, before getting buried in consequential detail, though this principle was frequently overlooked. Sir William Dale, one of the sterner critics of English drafting, has cited a number of examples of poor arrangement in an article published some years ago. One of those Acts, the Unfair Contract Terms Act 1977 (UCTA), was briefly introduced in **Chapter 3** (see Dale, 1981: 148–9). However, it has become more common practice to set out all the definitions used in the Act at the start of the document before laying out any principles (see, for instance, s. 2 of the Consumer Rights Act 2015, which has the heading 'Key definitions', or s. 3 of the Data Protection Act 2018, which is headed 'Terms relating to the processing of personal data' and cross-refers to an 'index of defined expressions' in s. 206). Lawyers are divided on the efficacy of this approach.

Another example of a confusing structure can be seen in the Public Interest Disclosure Act 1998, which this time starts (s. 1) by inserting a range of sections into another Act, numbering them as s. 43A, s. 43B and so on, and then states:

> • 43A. In this Act a 'protected disclosure' means a qualifying disclosure (as defined by section 43B) which is made by a worker in accordance with any of sections 43C to 43H.

It follows that up immediately with:

> • 43B(1)—In this Part a 'qualifying disclosure' means any disclosure of information which, in the reasonable belief of the worker making the disclosure, tends to show one or more of the following . . .

Five reasons follow in paras. (a)–(f). In s. 43B(2) the term 'relevant failures' appears. Only when we get to s. 43B(5) are we told:

> • In this Part 'the relevant failure', in relation to a qualifying disclosure, means the matter falling within paragraphs (a) to (f) of subsection (1).

So, only now do we know that a 'protected disclosure' is a 'qualifying disclosure', which consists of a worker showing a 'relevant failure' by the organisation.

This is not an isolated example. As we will explore in **Chapter 9** (notably section **9.4**), many words, phrases, and even grammatical structures are notorious 'death traps' in the area of interpretation. One such is the ambiguous word 'deemed' as in, 'For the purposes of this Act a house may be deemed a dwelling if . . .'. This is what Lord Radcliffe had to say about this word in *St Aubyn* v *Attorney General* [1952] AC, 15, 53:

> The word 'deemed' is used a great deal in modern legislation. Sometimes it is used to impose for the purposes of a statute an artificial construction of a word or phrase that would not otherwise prevail. Sometimes it is used to put beyond doubt a particular construction that might otherwise be uncertain. Sometimes it is used to give a comprehensive description which includes what is obvious, what is uncertain and what is, in the ordinary sense, impossible.

With all this in mind, therefore, it is worth looking at some examples of statutes to see how they are put together or, more importantly, what techniques you need to master in order to take them apart and apply them to factual situations (see also Stark (2002) on approaches to drafting statutes and Nowak (2016) on demystifying legislative drafting).

8.4 Examples of drafting practices and how to approach them

Students new to the study of law can sometimes be put off delving into statutes simply because the words or structure used are confusing. To show that, like all legal method techniques, this is not really a black art to be mastered by only the few, we have selected a few statutes which show some of the different drafting techniques you will encounter in your studies. These examples are drawn from statutes that have caused our own students problems in the past. Our aim is simply to reveal the tricks used and how very often the most complicated-looking provision is really nothing of the sort. The subject matter of each Act is irrelevant.

The most basic 'trick' of all sounds a little patronising, but it is still worth stating. *Each word counts: read the Act carefully, word by word, in the order it is set out.* One very common mistake students make when faced with an Act is to 'jump in' at the wrong point. For instance, a question asks you to determine whether there is a defence to a particular criminal charge; you see that section 8 is labelled 'exceptions', or even 'defences'. You cite section 8. This is not wrong in itself, but what has been missed perhaps is the definition of the offence in, say, s. 1, or some other exceptions in s. 2 (not so helpfully labelled). The offence (defined in s. 1) might have said that the defendant had to be 'negligent' or 'wilful' or 'malicious' or to 'have acted with knowledge', or even have other qualities such as being an adult or male, etc. These are constituent elements of the offence and therefore if the defendant has not been negligent, etc. there will have been no offence at all, so the exceptions will not even come into play.

This 'cascading' analysis is central to reading statutes. For instance, in s. 1 of the Criminal Damage Act 1971 we have an offence described thus:

> (2) A person who without lawful excuse destroys or damages any property, whether belonging to himself or another—
>
> (a) intending to destroy or damage any property or being reckless as to whether any property would be destroyed or damaged; and
> (b) intending by the destruction or damage to endanger the life of another or being reckless as to whether the life of another would be thereby endangered; shall be guilty of an offence.

There are key points here, not least what we mean by 'intending' or 'being reckless', but even before that we have the phrase 'without lawful excuse' and we do not know what that means. We can in fact discover what it means by turning to s. 5 of the Act, but that is not obvious on a first reading of s. 1.

All this is similar to reading a recipe. There is no point leaping in at instruction 7 (grill the steak) only to find that item 1 told you to marinade the steak for at least 24 hours.

We are still not yet concerned with how to *interpret* these (or any other) statutes; we are concerned only with how best to approach reading and understanding them. In particular, we are looking at how to deal with phrases such as 'subject to section 2 . . .', or 'notwithstanding the duties laid out in section 2 . . .', or 'Save as permitted by section 2 . . .'.

The best way to set about this is for you to read the wording of the Act given in the left-hand column in **Tables 8.3–8.7** in sections **8.4.1–8.4.5**, and see what sense you can make of it; then have a look in the right-hand column and you will see suggestions as to how to approach the statute.

8.4.1 The Knives Act 1997

We start with a reasonably simple section. This extract from the Knives Act 1997 illustrates the basic rules of structure noted earlier in section **8.4**—a general opening statement describing the offence followed by more specific 'definitional' matters (see **Table 8.3**).

Table 8.3 Understanding how to read rules (1)

Wording of section	Commentary
Unlawful Marketing of Knives 1. (1) A person is guilty of an offence if he markets a knife in a way which— (a) indicates, or suggests, that it is suitable for combat; or (b) is otherwise likely to stimulate or encourage violent behaviour involving the use of the knife as a weapon.	Section 1(1) sets up the offence, which has two disjunctive elements—(a) or (b). The use of the word 'or' creates two very different ways of committing the offence. Note, however, that it is the 'marketing' of the knife that is illegal, not the mere possession. At this stage in your reading of the statute you should also have been wondering what words such as 'markets', 'suitable for combat', or 'stimulate' mean. At first sight the Act appears unhelpful in that it does not tell you if these words are going to be defined (but they are, just a few subsections later). So, in reading the section, establish what you think is the basic offence; you can fill in details later.
(2) 'Suitable for combat' and 'violent behaviour' are defined in section 10.	Subsection (2) gives us a cross-reference to further explanations in s. 10, where you will find a long list of definitions. Thus, in s. 10 'suitable for combat' means 'suitable for use as a weapon for inflicting injury on a person, or causing a person to fear injury'. This definition is thus 'read into' s. 1.
(3) For the purposes of this Act, an indication or suggestion that a knife is suitable for combat may, in particular, be given or made by a name or description— (a) applied to the knife; (b) on the knife or on any packaging in which it is contained; or (c) included in any advertisement which, expressly or by implication, relates to the knife.	Another definition subsection (which applies to the whole Act—sometimes definitions only apply to particular sections or parts of Acts). Here, subsection (3) defines the rather vague terms we first saw in s. 1(1)(a). However, the wording of subsection (3) does not help much as you will notice that it has the term 'in particular' hidden halfway along. This must mean that although points (a)–(c) are clear examples, there may be others.

Table 8.3 Continued

Wording of section	Commentary
(4) For the purposes of this Act, a person markets a knife if— (a) he sells it or hires it; (b) he offers, or exposes, it for sale or hire; or (c) he has it in his possession for the purposes of sale or hire.	Finally, we get the meaning of the word 'markets', so, again, this has to be read back into the original description of the offence. Note that 'possession' still has to relate to the sale or hire of the knife. This subsection does not create a separate offence in this Act of 'possession'.

This statute was introduced following a public outcry when a headmaster was stabbed by a pupil outside his school. Legislation already existed prohibiting the carrying of offensive weapons: what society demanded was more legislation on the *sale* of knives. To outlaw the sale of all types of knife was obviously impracticable, so some other approach was needed—outlawing the marketing of knives which could be used as a weapon—the phrase eventually chosen being 'combat knives'.

8.4.2 The Wild Mammals (Protection) Act 1996

This next example looks like a mess on first reading (see **Table 8.4**). To start with it begins with the puzzling phrase 'If, save as permitted by this Act . . .' and then goes on to list a whole range of forbidden activities. But appearances can be deceptive: it is actually very straightforward. The phrase 'save as permitted . . .' appears quite often in statutes. It means that the actions listed in s. 1 might still be lawful if made so elsewhere in the Act. You are not told where this 'saving' provision might be, so it could appear anywhere in the Act and even arise from the context rather than specific wording.

Table 8.4 Understanding how to read rules (2)

Wording of section	Commentary
1. Offences If, save as permitted by this Act, any person mutilates, kicks, beats, nails, or otherwise impales, stabs, burns, stones, crushes, drowns, drags, or asphyxiates any wild mammal with intent to inflict unnecessary suffering he shall be guilty of an offence. [2. . . . *omitted here*] **3. Interpretation** In this Act 'wild mammal' means any mammal which is not a domestic or captive animal within the meaning of the Protection of Animals Act 1911 . . .	A formidable list, but not that confusing when dealt with one at a time. Any other act of cruelty you can think of might still fall within this section if it is *like* the action listed. Note also the key point at the end that 'intent to inflict unnecessary suffering' is required. So, if someone impales or burns a wild mammal accidentally or for some good reason, they will not have committed an offence under the Act. Section 3 gives definitions, but you need to refer to another Act to understand them. Such external source cross-referencing is very annoying but very common.

8.4.3 The Copyright, Etc. And Trade Marks (Offences and Enforcement) Act 2002

As with the Wild Mammals Act example, this section sets up a general rule but tells you, right at the start, that rule has to be read with exceptions. This time, instead of using the phrase 'save as permitted', it uses the more direct phrase 'subject to . . . [a particular subsection]',—so at least you know where to look this time. The trick here is to ignore the 'subject to . . .' part until you have worked out clearly what the general rule is. Students often make the mistake of trying to read the subsection referred to before establishing the general rule. That way lies madness.

This extract in **Table 8.5** deals with the situation where someone has breached another person's copyright and made illegal recordings of their material, for example pirated CDs. What should be done with those CDs?

Table 8.5 Understanding how to read rules (3)

Wording of section	*Commentary*
Section 4	*[Subsecs. (1)–(7)* omitted *here]*
(8) **Subject to subsection** (9), where any illicit recordings are forfeited under this section they shall be destroyed in accordance with such directions as the court may give.	A straightforward subsection which presents a *general* rule that illicit recordings which have been forfeited by the court will then be destroyed. But the opening words demonstrate that, whatever is said here, may be overridden by subsection (9).
(9) On making an order under this section the court may direct that the illicit recordings to which the order relates shall (instead of being destroyed) be forfeited to the person having the performers' rights or recording rights in question or dealt with in such other way as the court considers appropriate.	Subsection (9) sets out the exceptions referred to by the phrase in subsection (8), 'subject to subsection (9)'. In this case, illicit recordings will be destroyed unless the court decides: (a) to allow them to be forfeited for the benefit of certain people involved in their creation; or (b) to deal with them in another way. This latter point clearly allows the court a very wide discretion. So, subsection (8) is the normal procedure, but it can be varied according to subsection (9).

8.4.4 The Churchwardens Measure Act 2001

There is nothing particularly complicated about this next, rarely cited Act, but it is useful because it illustrates two things: (a) how a statute can set up an elaborate system and then provide exceptions; (b) the use of the word 'notwithstanding', which draftsmen love using (see **Table 8.6**).

Table 8.6 Understanding how to read rules (4)

Wording of section	*Commentary*
1 Number and qualifications of churchwardens *[Subsecs. (1) and (2) omitted here]* (3) The churchwardens of every parish shall be chosen from persons who have been baptised and— (a) whose names are on the church electoral roll of the parish; (b) who are actual communicants; (c) who are 21 years of age or upwards; and (d) who are not disqualified under section 2 or 3 below.	This subsection lists who may be churchwardens. Note the requirements are *cumulative* so if one condition is not met, the person cannot be a churchwarden. The 'and' which occurs between subsections (c) and (d) is meant to illustrate that the whole list is deemed to have 'ands' in it. Where an Act sets out alternatives (as in the Knives Act—see **Table 8.3**) it will usually have the word 'or' between each subsection but sometimes uses the device of just having the 'or' between the last two subsections.
(4) If it appears to the bishop, in the case of any particular person who is not qualified by virtue of paragraph (a), (b), or (c) of subsection (3), that there are exceptional circumstances which justify a departure from the requirements of those paragraphs the bishop may permit that person to hold the office of churchwarden notwithstanding that those requirements are not met. Any such permission shall apply only to the period of office next following.	Subsection (4) is an example where the word 'or' only appears once but applies to each paragraph. This subsection provides exceptions to subsection (3). There must be 'exceptional circumstances' (not defined) before this operates. The subsection allows a bishop to appoint a person as a churchwarden *even though* (in the Act the term used is 'notwithstanding the fact') that person does not meet the requirements of s. 3(a), (b), or (c). But what the bishop cannot do (and it is easy to miss this) is ignore the requirement set out in s. 1(3)(d) because only (a), (b), and (c) are mentioned here.

If you search for occurrences of the word 'notwithstanding' in LexisLibrary there are so many entries your search is automatically limited. The word 'notwithstanding' basically means 'despite', or 'in spite of', or 'even though' (the normal legal usages) as with a phrase such as: 'Notwithstanding the doctor's advice she went skiing anyway'. Less frequently it can mean 'although' or 'nevertheless'. It appears in sentences such as: 'Subsection (1) shall have effect **notwithstanding** any agreement to the contrary . . .' (meaning: subsection (1) will apply even if the agreement says otherwise); and 'The acts and proceedings of any person appointed to be a member . . . of a Service Authority and acting in that office shall, **notwithstanding** his disqualification or want of qualification, be as valid and effectual as if he had been qualified' (meaning: 'despite his disqualification'). It is quite common to see the phrase, in, say s. 5 of an Act: 'Notwithstanding the generality of s. 3 . . .'—meaning that however wide the rule in s. 3 appears to be s. 5 varies it, qualifies it, or expands upon it. An example appears in the Merchant Shipping (Fire Protection: Large Ships) Regulations 1998, where reg. 68 para. 1 sets out the 'means of escape' which must be provided on a ship, such as doors and stairways, and reg. 68 para. 2 states: 'Notwithstanding the generality of paragraph (1), in every ship the following shall be complied with . . .' and goes on to describe the size and shape of bulkheads that have to conform to the rules. With this in mind, note how the word is used in the following Act.

8.4.5 The Trustee Act 1925

We end this list of examples with this beauty—a section which always causes students problems. The law is not that complicated; it is the density of the prose that is the problem—s. 36(1) is actually all one sentence (see **Table 8.7**). However, though this looks daunting, it can be broken down into simpler elements (whether you use a flowchart approach or other device is a matter of preference). The key is to get the general picture of it first; later you can fill in the specific requirements and/or exceptions. If you can master this, you are well on your way to handling the structure of statutes.

Table 8.7 Understanding how to read rules (5)

Wording of section	Commentary
36 Power of appointing new or additional trustees (1) Where a trustee, either original or substituted, and whether appointed by a court or otherwise, is dead, or remains out of the United Kingdom for more than twelve months, or desires to be discharged from all or any of the trusts or powers reposed in or conferred on him, or refuses or is unfit to act therein, or is incapable of acting therein, or is an infant, then, subject to the restrictions imposed by this Act on the number of trustees— (a) the person or persons nominated for the purpose of appointing new trustees by the instrument, if any, creating the trust; or	**STEP 1:** The heading is usually a good indication of what the section is about (though, very occasionally, it can be misleading). So, we know this section concerns the appointment of trustees. **STEP 2:** First, take the opening words of s. 36(1) '**Where a trustee** . . .'. The next few clauses merely make clear *which trustees are covered,* so ignore them for the moment. **STEP 3:** The second key phrase is: '**is dead (or other things have happened)**'. We are merely trying to find out what the general position is here, so do not get concerned yet about these. **STEP 4:** The next key word is '**then** . . .,' i.e. what is going to happen or be allowed? So, the gist so far is: '**Where a trustee is dead (or something else has happened) then** . . .'.

Table 8.7 Continued

Wording of section	Commentary
(b) if there is no such person, or no such person able and willing to act, then the surviving or continuing trustees or trustee for the time being, or the personal representatives of the last surviving or continuing trustee; may, by writing, appoint one or more other persons (whether or not being the persons exercising the power) to be a trustee or trustees in the place of the trustee so deceased remaining out of the United Kingdom, desiring to be discharged, refusing, or being unfit or being incapable, or being an infant, as aforesaid.	**STEP 5:** The phrase '**Subject to the restrictions . . .** ' merely puts you on guard that the Act has other provisions covering the numbers of trustees which we will have to look at later. Ignore this for the moment. **STEP 6:** At first sight paras (a) and (b) look like the 'then' noted in STEP 4, but in fact they merely describe who has the power to act when the trustee is dead, etc. So, ignore this too for the moment. Annoying though this may be, this style of drafting is quite common (and, to be fair, it is difficult to set up such a rule without doing something like this). You need to look to the final para to see exactly what is going on. **The essence of the section so far is that when a trustee is dead (etc.) some people have the power to do certain things.** **STEP 7:** Finally, we get to what these persons may do. We find that they may appoint others to be trustees in place of the trustee who died (etc.). The only other point you have to note is that the appointment must be made 'by writing'. Amazingly straightforward in the end!

Statutes of course do not exist merely to provide exercises in analysis. They have to be applied in practice; so, having done your work on the wording of the Trustee Act 1925, you can now put that to use with a client's problem.

For example, say your client is a trustee of a charity and tells you that one of the other trustees has died and he wants to appoint a replacement.

- You know that s. 36(1) is generally about this sort of situation. You can now look at the detail to see that the first requirement of the section is met (i.e. that an existing trustee has died).

- You would next have to ask: does such an appointment fall foul of the number of trustees allowed under the Act? You would therefore need to look elsewhere in the Act. It is unlikely to be a problem, as the new appointment is merely a replacement. If there will be too many trustees, then there may have been too many all along but, of course, it is possible that when the trustees were appointed four were allowed but since then the law has changed and now only three are permitted—so you do need to check your law on this.

- If all is well, then you would need to see if your client falls within paras (a) or (b), i.e. does he/she have the right to make the appointment or do we need to get someone else to do it?

If all these requirements have been met, you would then advise that such an appointment has to be made in writing.

8.5 Amending earlier statutes

Another aspect of drafting practice you need to master arises when an Act (say, one passed in 2013) amends an earlier Act (say, one of 1990). The amendment may be wholesale: the earlier Act may be repealed and replaced by the later Act (or a whole string of Acts may be **consolidated** into the new Act). But, more commonly, the later Act will amend only parts of the earlier Act or Acts. It is quite common, therefore, for one Act to 'insert' new words or even new sections into an existing Act. There is nothing too puzzling about this and the new wording or section is simply referred to as if it had always been in the original Act; the real problem is that if you went and looked at the original Act you would not see the amendment (though you would in the electronic versions to be found on LexisLibrary and Westlaw). Laypersons representing themselves in court often make the mistake of relying on the original wording of the statute without realising there has been an amendment. Lawyers are presumed to know better.

8.5.1 Inserting and substituting words

Words or phrases in statutes may be amended by later Acts or Statutory Instruments. This is usually straightforward and databases such as Westlaw and LexisLibrary will contain the amended wording (usually with an accompanying note of where that amendment came from). To find the original wording (which is sometimes necessary when dealing with a claim which arose before the amendment) one needs to go to the relevant government website: www.legislation.gov.uk/ukpga

Figure 8.1 shows how Westlaw pages deal with this. The text reflects the law in practice and the footnotes demonstrate the changes made to the original statute.

8.5.2 Inserting new sections

The most usual method of inserting new sections is to put A or B, etc. after the old section number. We saw an example of this in section **8.3.2** with the Public Interest Disclosure Act 1998 in which s. 1 inserted a range of sections into a 1996 Act, numbering them as s. 43A, s. 43B, etc., so that the amended 1996 Act now reads: s. 43, s. 43A, s. 43B, s. 43C . . . s. 43M, then s. 44. The idea is that this saves having to renumber the whole Act. Here is an expanded example from the Theft Act 1968. Section 12 dealt with the taking of a vehicle without authority. Parliament later decided it needed to create a specific offence to cover the situation where a vehicle was taken without authority and then damage or injury resulted from that action—what is termed an 'aggravated' offence (here meaning 'intensified', 'heightened', or 'serious', not 'irritated' or 'provoked' as it is sometimes used). The Aggravated Vehicle-Taking Act 1992 came into being and, to more closely relate the basic offence with this 'add-on', s. 12A was placed in the Theft Act 1968 with appropriate cross-references to the original s. 12. The 1992 Act used these words to bring this about in s. 1:

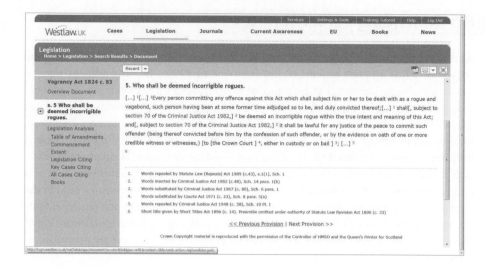

Figure 8.1 How databases deal with insertions and substitutions

New offence of aggravated vehicle-taking

(1) After section 12 of the [1968 c. 60.] Theft Act 1968 (taking conveyances without authority) there shall be inserted the following section—*[The new s. 12A was then set out, so the whole thing now reads:]*

12 Taking motor vehicle or other conveyance without authority

Subject to subsections (5) and (6) below, a person shall be guilty of an offence if, without having the consent of the owner or other lawful authority, he takes any conveyance for his own or another's use or, knowing that any conveyance has been taken without such authority, drives it or allows himself to be carried in or on it *[remainder omitted]*

12A Aggravated vehicle-taking

(1) Subject to subsection (3) below, a person is guilty of aggravated taking of a vehicle if—

(a) he commits an offence under section 12(1) above (in this section referred to as a 'basic offence') in relation to a mechanically propelled vehicle; and

(b) it is proved that, at any time after the vehicle was unlawfully taken (whether by him or another) and before it was recovered, the vehicle was driven, or injury or damage was caused, in one or more of the circumstances set out in paragraphs (a) to (d) of subsection (2) below . . .

Amendments do not make a great deal of sense when read in isolation and 'textual amendments' (such as the instruction, 'in s. 54 insert after the word "building" the words "or land thereon"') are usually wholly meaningless out of context. The points we made earlier on 'inserting words' regarding databases and the original text apply equally to 'inserting sections'.

CONCLUSION

Perfecting any legislation is a very difficult task. The balancing of clarity, generality, conciseness, precision, and the avoidance of excess verbiage to achieve a satisfactory statute requires a great deal of skill. Further, certain words are, as we saw in **Chapter 5**, probably beyond universally applicable definition—words such as 'reasonable' or 'practicable'. The 'common law' style adopted in the United Kingdom was summed up graphically in the description of it as 'fussy' (over-detailed) as opposed to the civil style in use in Europe, which might be termed 'fuzzy' (lacking in detail) (Campbell, 1996). Both styles have their strengths and weaknesses.

Approachability is also a matter of the form into which those words are put. The verbosity of British statutes is a throwback to the style of drafting which existed prior to the 1860s. Then sections were very densely written, with minimal punctuation (resulting in sentences that could run to many lines), and virtually no attempt to separate criteria within sections. Though that has changed, the hangovers are still present. Thus, to a lawyer trained in any other tradition, UK legislation comes as something of a shock; as a Bulgarian commentator has suggested:

> It is a challenging and arduous task to find one's way through the intricacies of English law when, as a translator, or professionally as a continental lawyer, one has to acquire a working knowledge of this uncommon law.
>
> (Dodova, 1989: 69)

In terms of structure, the way in which a British Act is put together can, at its best, aid interpretation by clarifying the relative degree of dependency that sections, subsections, and paragraphs have on each other. Sometimes, however, the structure imposed by the British draftsman can seemingly obscure that very same relationship. Thus the clarity that British statutes seek in the use of their highly technical structure does not always reap rewards. As Sir William Dale long argued, constant definition and re-definition does not make for certainty; his own position (which we support) was to agree with the Italian jurist Calamandrei that, 'The statutes cannot foresee all the cases that reality, much richer than the most fervid imagination, brings before the judge' (1981: 159). In other words, definition can often cause, as much as alleviate, uncertainty by creating doubt whether certain fact situations are covered.

In the UK, judges seek to implement the will of Parliament. But unlike the codified approach seen on the Continent, British judges have not (at least until recently) shown much inclination to claim extensive powers to look at the general purpose of the Act. For the most part, they will therefore adhere to the plain meaning of the words, so far as that proves possible. The way in which they go about these tasks forms the subject of **Chapter 9**.

CHAPTER REFERENCES

*BENNION, F. (1978), 'Statute Law Obscurity and the Drafting Parameters', 5 *British Journal of Law and Society*, 235.

CAMPBELL, L. (1996), 'Drafting Styles: Fuzzy or Fussy?', 3(2) *Murdoch University Electronic Journal of Law*.

DALE, W. (1977), *Legislative Drafting—A New Approach* (London: Butterworths).

DALE, W. (1981), 'Statutory Reform: The Draftsman and The Judge', *International and Comparative Law Quarterly*, 141.

DE BÚRCA, G. and GARDNER, S. (1990), 'The Codification of the Criminal Law', 10 *Oxford Journal of Legal Studies*, 559.

DHARMANANDA, J. and LANE, P. (2018), 'Teaching Statutory Interpretation in Australia: What's Next?', 39(1) *Statute Law Review*, 27.

*DODOVA, L. (1989), 'A Translator Looks at English Law', 10(1) *Statute Law Review*, 69.

DRIEDGER, E. (1976), *The Composition of Legislation* (2nd edn, Ottawa: Department of Justice).

EDITORIAL (2014), 'In Honour of the Moribund "Shall"', 35(2) *Statute Law Review, v*.

HANSARD SOCIETY (1992), *Making the Law* (London: Hansard Society).

HODGES, C. (1998), 'Development Risks: Unanswered Questions', 61 *Modern Law Review*, 560.

HUNT, B. (2002), 'Plain Language in Legislative Drafting: Is it Really the Answer?', 23(1) *Statute Law Review*, 24.

KELLY, M.D. (2017), 'Mixed-up Wills, Rectification and Interpretation: *Marley v. Rawlings*', 38(3) *Statute Law Review*, 265.

LAWS, S. (2011), 'Giving Effect to Policy in Legislation: How to Avoid Missing the Point', 32 *Statute Law Review*, 1.

LOBBAN, M. (1991), *The Common Law and English Jurisprudence*, 1760–1850 (Oxford: Clarendon Press).

MCEVOY, J. (1986), 'The Charter as a Bilingual Instrument', 64 *Canadian Bar Review*, 155.

MAUGHAN, C. and WEBB, J. (2006), *Lawyering Skills and the Legal Process* (London: Butterworths).

NOWAK, A. (2016), 'Demystifying Ambiguity in Legislative Writing', 37(2) *Statute Law Review*, 164.

REGAN, P. (2013), 'Enacting Legislation—a Civil Servant's Perspective', 34(1) *Statute Law Review*, 32–8.

*RENTON COMMITTEE (1975), *The Preparation of Legislation*, Cmnd 6053 (London: HMSO).

RHYS WILLIAMS, B. (1987), 'Legislation and Parliament', *Statute Law Review*, 38.

SALES, RT HON LORD JUSTICE (2017), 'Modern Statutory Interpretation' 38(2) *Statute Law Review*, 125.

SMITH, J. (1980), 'Legislative Drafting: English and Continental', 1 *Statute Law Review*, 14.

STARK, J. (2002), 'Learning from Samuel Johnson about Drafting Statutes', 23 *Statute Law Review*, 227.

 ## ONLINE RESOURCES

Test your knowledge by trying the self-test questions that accompany **Chapters 7–9**.
Visit: www.oup.com/uk/holland-webb10e

9

Interpreting Statutes

9.1 Introduction

Most people are willing to believe that case law can present problems because facts are never precisely repeated; at the same time most people also believe that statutes are precise and accurate so that anyone can 'look up' the law in a statute. For the most part the implementation of statutory provisions will indeed be a routine matter, but this is not universally true. Once words appear in a statute, they are open to all manner of argument and interpretation. Those arguments may be about the meaning of the language used in the statute (a sort of translation exercise), or about the application of the language to the facts (application exercise), or about both.

By a 'translation exercise' we mean instances where the court has to decide what a particular word or phrase means. These can be technical terms or plain, simple words. The court might be called upon to determine what specialised words like 'copyright', 'dismissal', or 'dishonesty' mean; equally the problem may centre on an apparently straightforward word such as 'vehicle' or 'animal'—or any other word you can think of. One thing you should bear in mind, though: the courts do not try to act like a dictionary editor; they are not trying to define a word for its own sake. Instead, they are trying to find the meaning of the word in the *context of the statute*. All that is said in this chapter concerns ascertaining meaning in context. So, you will see that we often have to investigate a wide range of sources in order to discover the meaning of a word or phrase. For instance, consider the meaning of the apparently simple word 'parent'. This may refer to a natural parent, a step-parent, to parents where the child was conceived through IVF or through a sperm donor, to adoptive parents, to foster parents, to people deemed to stand in the position of parents (the Latin phrase being *in loco parentis*, as might apply to teachers or child-carers) and so on—the meaning often turning on the context and the purpose of the statute.

We must also take account of punctuation and grammar. Words can change meaning with different punctuation. For example, note the significance of the hyphen in the term 'pickled-herring salesman'—with the hyphen, this is a salesman selling pickled herrings; without it we have a salesman of herrings who is pickled (taken from Lynne Truss's excellent book *Eats, Shoots & Leaves: The Zero Tolerance Approach to Punctuation*). Heathrow airport once had a sign which read: 'No passenger carrying vehicles beyond this point'. Good health advice—and avoids breaching the rules on hand luggage.

The same problems arise, of course, in ordinary life with insurance policies, contracts, and even the rules of games. We saw this in **Chapter 8** as regards the structure of statutes, and the same applies here when interpreting the words used. Take a look, for instance, at the rules of Monopoly. Under the heading *Landing on 'Chance'* or 'Community Chest' the rules state: 'A player takes the top card from the pack indicated and after following the instructions thereon, returns the card face down to the bottom of the pack.' Let's say you land on 'Chance'. You know (because you have been concentrating) that the only card still to come is a property repairs card; a fact which will cause you severe problems. Do you have to take the card? What arguments could you use not to? Do you have to show the card to anyone? Would the type of argument be the same as when you argued (but presumably lost) that you did not have to take the card at all?

When you look at any document the meaning attached to words is often influenced both by the fact that you wish your interpretation to be accepted and also by your general approach to life. What we mean by this last point is that some people are by nature apt to take words at their literal meaning—'it says X so it should mean X' (or, the Monopoly rules say 'take the card' so you must take the card)—while others naturally find themselves looking for the purpose behind the words—'what are these words trying to do?' (or what is the point in having cards marked 'Chance' if they leave you no choice whether to take them or not; surely there is a difference between 'Chance' and 'Community Chest'?).

Statutes are designed in the same way as the rules of a game or the rules of a committee. They seek to tell you what you can do, what you cannot do, and perhaps how you are meant to do it. Equally, as we have seen in **Chapter 8**, they need to be drafted very carefully. Written words are not like conversation: there is no inflexion, no stress, no sense of irony; no opportunity to ask, 'What do you mean?' The lifeblood of everyday speech is missing. The reader therefore has to give life to the words by interpreting what they mean and how they are meant to apply to particular situations. This is what is meant by statutory interpretation. The problem is: how do you do this? What rules do you use? When do you know you have found the *correct* meaning?

9.2 The so-called rules of interpretation

If you look in textbooks and cases written over the past five centuries, especially those on land law or the law of succession or the law of contract, you will see that lawyers have classified the basic means of reading documents under four headings:

- *the literal rule* (take only the plain, literal meaning of the words used because those are the words the draftsman chose to employ);
- *the golden rule* (take the whole of the statute together, placing the word or section in its context and giving the words their ordinary meaning unless this produces an absurdity or inconsistency—in which case the judge must try to give the words some other contextual meaning);
- *the purposive rule* (try to ascertain what the draftsman intended by the words by examining the general purpose of the section and the social, economic, or political context); and
- *the mischief rule* (which directs you to look to the previous common law and the history of the Act (or other document) to see what was wrong with the law, what was the mischief, that the draftsman sought to remedy).

These are rather crude labels for describing a complex mechanism, i.e. making sense of what someone else has written. The labels are still in common use, but they are dangerous. For a start, they use the word 'rule', and this gives the impression that if you follow a particular pattern you will not go wrong. They also have an aura of scientific authenticity about them when the reality is (as Lord Templeman said in the original Foreword to this book) that interpreting any document is more of an art than a science. Indeed, in the case of *Re M (A Minor) (Care Order: Threshold Conditions)* [1994] 2 FCR 871, Lord Templeman himself had to deal with an argument about a child's welfare under the Children Act 1989. The argument was about who should take care of the child and the complication was that the statute set out rules where the child 'is suffering . . . or . . . is likely to suffer significant harm'. The child had been in such danger but, at the time of the trial the circumstances had changed, so the case centred on the meaning of the phrase '*is* suffering'. Was this limited to one moment or did it have to have a continuing element? Lord Templeman had this to say about interpreting the statute: 'My Lords, this appeal is an illustration of the tyranny of language and the importance of ascertaining and giving effect to the intentions of Parliament by construing a statute in accordance with the spirit rather than the letter of the Act.' The Act was created to protect children and Lord Templeman regarded the arguments on the use of the present tense in the statute as a distraction from that aim. One might see this as a 'purposive' approach, but, in reality, this is an example of judicial practicality and a desire to see justice done. It is certainly more about art than science.

Generations of lawyers have had problems applying these 'rules'. It is almost impossible to resist believing that if you know what the 'rules' mean you can apply them universally in understanding a section, a statute, or any document. One of the great writers on statutory interpretation, Rupert Cross, experienced this problem as a student; and when he became a lecturer at Oxford, he found that his students shared his dilemma (Cross, 1995: Preface):

> Each and every pupil told me there were three rules—the literal rule, the golden rule and the mischief rule, and that the courts invoke whichever of them is believed to do justice in the particular case. I had, and still have, my doubts, but what was most disconcerting was the fact that whatever question I put to pupils or examinees elicited the same reply. Even if the question was, What is meant by 'the intention of parliament'? or What are the principal extrinsic aids to interpretation? back came the answer as of yore: 'There are three rules of interpretation—the literal rule . . .'.

The equivalent in legal practice (witnessed by one of the authors in the Court of Appeal) is:

> [Counsel] 'I urge the Court to adopt a literal interpretation.'
> [Judge's response] 'I have no idea what that means. Which one? I can see three possible literal meanings.'

In the text which follows we will explain these 'rules' in some more depth and will give some examples of their operation. The fact that we have chosen to do this seems almost hypocritical, given what we have just said. But we do so only because no matter what is written by commentators on statutory interpretation, lawyers and judges persist in using these terms because they are well-understood shorthand labels. But let us be blunt about this: they are, in fact, about as much use as the label on a product lambasted in *Which?* Magazine: the product was peanuts and the label contained the warning, 'This product may contain nuts.' In our own lectures we spend less than 15 minutes noting these 'rules'. In effect, they boil down to our common childhood experiences of trying to justify our actions to our mothers. So, when your mum says, 'Do not go to the shops on your own', how do you analyse her intention?

- The literal approach means you simply do not go to the shops on your own. You can go elsewhere on your own, or be accompanied by someone to the shops, but you take the words at their exact and limited meaning.
- The purposive approach means what your mum meant you should do or not do (i.e. 'Do not wander too far away from home—the shops being the limit and not a specific destination—unless I am with you'). This is therefore wider than the literal approach and limits you much more. Equally, you cannot be quite sure of those limits.
- The mischief rule means that the limitation relates to the behaviour or problem your mum was trying to correct (just beyond the shops lies a dangerous road on which a number of children have been injured). The action she is seeking to prevent you undertaking is about this danger element.

So, when, as a young child, you and a friend were discovered exploring beyond the shops and crossed the dangerous road you probably chose as your defence a literal approach ('I didn't actually go to the shops—and I wasn't alone'), but your mother will most likely have overruled you with a purposive approach or mischief rule interpretation to which your ill-judged childhood response was likely to be: 'If you meant that you should have said it.' Parents rely quite heavily on these approaches, even when using the interrogatory: 'What did I tell you not to do?'

9.2.1 Why do we still refer to the 'rules'?

In continuing to refer to these 'rules' we have, along with other writers, been accused of perpetuating an outdated approach to interpretation (Cross, 1995: 198). But, surprisingly, coming from such a distinguished text, this criticism misses the point we have made since the first edition of this book: no lawyer believes that by merely saying 'we should adopt a literal (or purposive) approach' one has *interpreted* the statute or constructed an argument. The terms are 'legal shorthand' for a complex analytical process—nothing more. However, as the terms appear in judgments and also in textbooks on contract, torts, etc. you need to be aware of their usage. Put another way: merely because a map or satnav has recognised or even recommended routes on it does not mean you have to follow them slavishly; but being ignorant of these routes is negligent, and trying to cut loose across country where there are no roads is unlikely to get you to your destination. The labels, the 'rules', are useful as map signs (especially when you are just starting your legal studies) but they do not tell you *how* to navigate, let alone how to drive.

The one *caveat* we would make at this point is that the 'purposive' approach is not a licence for invention or a substitute for that time-honoured phrase issued by students and unsuccessful litigants alike, 'But it's not fair'. Both your client and you (or any other combination) may well feel that the wording of a piece of legislation, or its interpretation, is 'unfair'. However, this is not an argument in itself, and no lawyer can afford to depart from the wording of a statute merely because it does not suit his or her client's case or his or her own sense of justice. Each interpretation offered has to have reasoning behind it and must actually bear some relevance to the words as they appear. And remember: what is fair or unfair is a question of opinion, not fact, and may be governed by other rules. This can apply even to things such as sports. In a tennis match, a player can win the match 0–6, 0–6, 6–4, 6–4, 6–4 because it is the number of sets which count; but if you tally the games, the winner only won eighteen games while the loser won twenty-four.

Perhaps the main difficulty with these 'rules' lies in the fact that, in order to see them in operation, one invariably looks at the reasoning given by the judge. Thus, you come across judicial utterances such as, 'If we apply the literal rule to these words we can see that . . .'. However, to analyse the 'rules' by looking at which one a particular judge chose to apply in any given case is a bit like looking at the results of a horse race and then pretending the outcome was clear all along, because it now seems so obvious. Looking at a judgment, or at a results sheet, means that you are looking at a **conclusion**; what you still need to know is why the conclusion was reached or why that particular horse won. The problem with reading statements like the one just mentioned is that an impression is gained that there was a *correct* analysis and that if only you had looked for it more carefully you could have found it. Instead, you need to think of these 'rules' as *approaches* to interpretation, as tools of argument.

Very often, one lawyer will try to argue a literal interpretation ('the words say this and nothing more'), while the other seeks to use a more purposive approach ('the words may say this but they cannot be taken so literally when you look at the purpose behind the section'). But there are many instances of a literal v literal argument or a purposive v purposive one. The essence of statutory interpretation is the construction of arguments which favour your client's case. The judgment reflects whether you were successful; and this depends on a whole host of things, such as how well you and your opponent presented your arguments, whether the judge was by nature more inclined to accept one approach, the context in which the words appear, and whether there were any precedents that helped or hindered you.

9.2.2 How do we use these 'rules' in legal argument?

General textbooks cannot spend much time on approaches to statutory interpretation and so present these 'rules' as though they are fixed and adhered to in an unchanging logical form. Such generalisatons are attractive because they look simple, but they are misleading. Here, we certainly agree with Cross. The reality is much less certain because these 'rules' are really nothing more than techniques of reading a document, and may be used singularly or in any combination. There is nothing wrong, for instance, in an argument which runs:

(i) 'The plain meaning of these words show that my client's actions conformed with the requirements of the section [*a literal approach to the wording*].

(ii) Further, if we look at the purpose behind this section we find that it was designed to remedy the very problem for which my client seeks redress [*a purposive argument*].

(iii) And indeed, if we look at why this Act came about, the history of this area shows that the Act was necessary to overcome the problems with previous cases in this field [*use of the mischief rule*].'

In *Oliver Ashworth (Holdings) Ltd* v *Ballard (Kent) Ltd* [1999] 2 All ER 791, Laws LJ explained the reality of these 'rules' (at 805):

> [I]t is now misleading—and perhaps it always was—to seek to draw a rigid distinction between literal and purposive approaches . . . frequently there will be no opposition between the two, and then no difficulty arises. Where there is a potential clash, the conventional English approach has been to give at least very great and often decisive weight to the literal meaning of the enacting words. This is a tradition which I think is weakening. . . .

So do not get too worried about these rules for now. You must know what they are seeking to do, but only as a tool for the way you argue your case; and so that you can make some guess at how the judge might decide the issue. Instead of thinking about statutory interpretation as just another legal topic—like homicide, theft, or offer and acceptance—you should think about the ideas outlined shortly and try to make use of them, either in academic discussion or in practice, across the whole range of legal subjects.

But we must emphasise again that these are not fixed rules of law; for the most part they are examples of the use of language generally. Cross, for instance, refers to cases which decided such awe-inspiring questions as 'Is a bicycle a "carriage"? Is a goldfish an "article"?' and concludes:

> Conundrums of this sort are part of the daily bread of judges and practitioners. In solving them the courts usually pay due regard to the context, but, in many instances, the answer must . . . be treated as a matter of common sense.
>
> (1995: 75)

Being aware of the 'rules' of statutory interpretation is important, therefore, because:

(i)   Judges are not robots; their personality affects the way they will approach a problem of interpretation. Judges do not follow a 'critical path' analysis, progressing from one rule of interpretation to another in a logical fashion. If they did, we would have far more 'expert systems' available where people could just answer a series of questions generated by a computer and obtain an answer at the end. At some point a judge reaches what we called (in **Chapter 7** when looking at case law) the 'Marmite Moment'—the stage at which all argument has been made and he or she has to favour one or the other. You need to be aware, therefore, what range of analytical options are open to a judge in reaching that point.

(ii)   When arguing your case, or analysing the advantages and disadvantages of pursuing that case, you need to know the framework in which you are operating. It is often said that a bad workman always blames his tools; a workman who does not even know which tools exist deserves all he gets.

(iii) It helps if you can combine (i) and (ii), but that means you need to know how the judge is likely to react to the approach you have chosen. An argument based on the grand purpose of a statute delivered to a judge who believes firmly in a literal interpretation of words will fall on stony ground. You will discover from reading cases which senior judge favours which approach. This may not help on your first appearance in court before an unknown junior judge—which is why point (ii) is important.

Lundmark and Waller (2017) have argued cogently that not only are the same statutory interpretation problems (with effectively the same analytical solutions) encountered and dealt with in other jurisdictions such as Germany and California, but the method employed in analysing statutes is also not different, if at all, from the method used in analysing cases. The authors draw comparisons, for instance, in the desire of judges to delve into the history of precedents and critically examine their rationale, on the one hand, with, on the other, the so-called 'mischief rule'—which is one of the methods which enquires into the history of legislation to discover the purpose behind a statute.

9.3 Examples of the 'rules' in action

These traditional 'rules' may be explained as follows.

9.3.1 The literal rule

The 'literal rule' is founded on the assumption that the words chosen by Parliament in the Act clearly show its intentions in passing that Act. The rule demands that one looks at what was said, not at what it *might* mean; that one is concerned with linguistics rather than considerations of the purpose of the Act or the wider context in which the statute was enacted. To do otherwise, as was said in *Duport Steel* v *Sirs* [1980] 1 WLR 142; [1980] 1 All ER 529, 541, might mean that the court is not interpreting the Act but really making law. There, Lord Diplock said:

> Where the meaning of the statutory words is plain and unambiguous it is not for the judges to invent fancied ambiguities as an excuse for failing to give effect to its plain meaning because they consider the consequences of doing so would be inexpedient, or even unjust or immoral.

Presented in this way the rule is seen as a safe bet—judges simply apply what is there. Safe bet or not, it is not a true reflection of reality. If the words were that clear, nobody would have brought the case in the first place. The literalist is prepared for this challenge. What the literalist would be looking for is the *primary* or most *obvious* meaning of the word, not any *general* or *secondary* meaning. And he will usually do this by looking at the way the word or sentence fits into the rest of the section or even the Act as a whole (see Summers and Marshall, 1992: 213). But, as Slocum comments, 'Courts generally do not, however, have good answers to the question of what makes a given meaning the ordinary one, as opposed to an inappropriately broad or narrow or technical meaning' (2012: 39).

The literal rule at its most extreme echoes the approach of a fundamentalist: consideration of the word or phrase as written is sacrosanct. The rule does not demand that the word be viewed in isolation from the rest of the sentence or section, but demands steadfastly that the investigation as to meaning does not stray beyond this point.

Thus, the literal rule does not call upon a judge to consider the consequences of the interpretation. Sometimes this can still lead to what appear to be pretty odd results. The literal rule does not always generate a feeling that justice has been done, even though it may be linguistically precise. Nor does it bear mathematical precision. As Willis stated:

> it is quite possible for all the members of the court to agree that the meaning of a section is so plain that it cannot be controlled by the context and yet to disagree as to what the plain meaning is.
>
> (1938: 2)

Many examples can be given of judges relying upon the literal rule. But if we listed 100 cases all we would see is 100 different examples of the rule being used. The examples would not necessarily tell us how to interpret the next case. However, here are three examples that might help to give a flavour of literal interpretation in action.

In *R* v *Harris* (1836) 7 C & P 446 a statute made it an offence to 'stab, cut or wound' another person. Harris bit off her friend's nose in a fight—and then the policeman's finger. Was she guilty under the statute? The answer was no. The words in the statute pointed towards the use of a *weapon*. Teeth (even false?) are not a weapon. This conclusion was given further force by the fact that elsewhere in the section were references to the use of weapons, such as the word 'shooting'. You may think she should be guilty of something, but she was not guilty **as charged**.

It is also well worth reading the strange case of *R* v *Munks* [1964] 1 QB 304; [1963] 3 All ER 757 on the meaning of the word 'engine' in the Offences Against the Person Act 1861, s. 31. Here, the question was whether the action of Munks in wiring up a metal-framed doorway so as to electrocute his wife amounted to constructing an 'engine'. The judgment deals with literal interpretations and also a rule of grammar we shall return to (*eiusdem generis*). The judgment in *Munks* essentially limited the meaning of 'engine' to a 'mechanical contrivance' but this has been re-examined in *R* v *Cockburn* [2008] EWCA Crim 316; [2008] QB 882. It is also worth noting that *Cockburn* is an interesting example of the courts using all three of these so-called 'rules' in reaching their judgment as the discussion also deals with the purpose behind the 1861 Act and the 'legal mischief' which brought it into being. This is a good example of how 'applying the rules' is not some form of box-ticking exercise.

In *Fisher* v *Bell* [1961] 1 QB 394; [1960] 3 All ER 731, an Act of 1959 made it an offence to 'sell or hire or offer for sale or hire' certain offensive weapons such as flick knives. Bell placed a flick knife in his Bristol shop window with a price tag on it. Was he guilty of the offence? Again, the answer was no. As you will see in the law of contract, placing an item on display is not the same thing as 'offering it for sale'. If the statute had used the phrase 'expose for sale', the answer would, on this analysis, have been different.

EXERCISE 15 Are we still on strike?

Take a look at the following case summary. We pose a few questions at the end of the account.

 Stock v Frank Jones (Tipton) Ltd [1978] 1 WLR 231; [1978] 1All ER 948

This concerned the dismissal of employees who were on strike. Under the Trade Union and Labour Relations Act 1974 an employee who was dismissed for striking could not claim unfair

continued

EXERCISE 15 *continued*

dismissal unless 'one or more of the employees, who also took part in that [strike], were not dismissed for taking part'. So, all employees taking part in the strike had to be treated the same way. If one employee, for example the shop steward, was victimised by being the only person dismissed, he could claim that the dismissal was unfair (which would be decided on the facts). In this case the employees were on strike and, following fairly normal industrial relations tactics, the employer threatened them with dismissal if they did not return to work. Some did return. The employer dismissed those who did not return and they claimed unfair dismissal.

Q **QUESTIONS**

Using the literal rule, what do you think the words 'employees who took part in that [strike]' mean? Do they mean:

(i)   all the employees who originally took part in the [strike]; or

(ii) those employees who were still taking part in the [strike] when some of the others had returned to work following the threat?

What are the consequences of choosing each option?

A **ANSWERS**

Under the law which applied at the time of the case the House of Lords decided that 'employees who took part in the [strike]' could only refer to those employees who were participating in the strike when the strike began. Thus, when some employees returned and were not dismissed, they still counted in the number of those who 'took part in the [strike]'. The employees who had been dismissed had therefore been 'victimised' and could claim unfair dismissal.

If the House of Lords had taken the second and less literal option, then, provided all those who stayed out on strike had been dismissed (which had happened), the employer would have been protected against any claim for unfair dismissal. After this case employers argued that this made nonsense of industrial relations, for if the employer threatened to dismiss anyone not returning to work and one person out of a thousand did return, the employer would either have to dismiss no one or dismiss everyone, including the one who returned! As a consequence, the legislation was changed soon afterwards and it has changed considerably on many occasions since.

It is often said that the literal rule will not be used when it would lead to inconsistency or absurdity. This must not be taken too widely. Merely disliking the provision in the Act does not mean it produces an absurd result. If judges are seen to 'second-guess' Parliament by failing to treat the words used with respect the accusation that they are usurping the power of Parliament becomes an easy one to make. Thus, judges are looking for something that is illogical or indefensible within the ambit and spirit of the Act. This journey of discovery to find that spirit, ambit, or intention of the Act starts with the wording in the Act itself (e.g. definition sections and schedules). If a solution can be found within the confines of the Act, that is likely to be determinative, but the investigation can go wider at times, and we shall explore what may be taken into consideration below.

9.3.2 The golden (and purposive) rules

The first two methods of exploration that take us beyond the immediate text of the section are the golden and purposive rules. The golden rule can be best described as an *adaptation* of the literal rule. It tells you to read the word in the context of the statute as a whole. We use this form of interpretation every day when reading signs such as 'Stop Children'; hardly an instruction to act like Herod! The context aids the interpretation. The classic exposition of the rule is to be found in *River Wear Commissioners v Adamson* (1876–77) 2 App Cas 743, at 764–5, *per* Lord Blackburn:

> I believe that it is not disputed that what Lord Wensleydale used to call the golden rule is right, viz, that we are to take the whole statute together and construe it all together, giving the words their ordinary signification unless when so applied they produce an inconsistency, or an absurdity or inconvenience so great as to convince the court that the intention could not have been to use them in their ordinary signification and to justify the court in putting on them some other signification which, though less proper, is one which the court thinks the words will bear.

Sadly, his Lordship did not offer us much assistance on *how* the interpretation is to proceed once we have discovered the absurdity. We can overcome this by arguing that the only logical way to deal with an absurd interpretation is to correct it by assessing what Parliament was trying to do. But how is this to be ascertained? In its strictest form the golden rule still required the judge to focus only on the text of the Act and therefore the internal context of the word or phrase in question. Slowly but surely other (external) aids were brought to bear in trying to give meanings to words. This led to a more purposive approach.

The golden rule is a bridge between literalism and purposiveness. Whereas literalism focuses only on the words themselves, the golden rule developed this by making more use of context: the widest context is the setting which brought the Act into being (its purpose). One word of warning here: the term 'purposive' is not used consistently by the judges, as we shall at section **9.3.2**.

In *Stock v Frank Jones (Tipton) Ltd* [1978] ICR 347; [1978] 1 All ER 948 Lord Simon advocated departure from the literal rule only when:

(i)   there is a clear and gross anomaly;

(ii)   Parliament could not have envisaged the anomaly and would not have accepted its presence;

(iii) the anomaly can be obviated without detriment to the legislative intent; and

(iv)   the language of the statute allows for such modification.

This is in keeping with the tenor of statements made by judges in the nineteenth century, particularly Lord Wensleydale in *Grey v Pearson* (1857) 6 HL Cas 61, which linked the idea of absurdity with the situation where a literal meaning would prove repugnant or inconsistent with the rest of the section or Act (the *internal* context). The emphasis is laid on establishing that the literal meaning is nonsense when the rest of the statute is considered; it clearly does not mean that an absurdity can be said to arise merely because a literal meaning might offend one's sense of justice.

Viewed this way the golden rule can be seen as an accessory to, or shadow of, the literal rule. It does not exist independently of the literal rule but comes into play only as a back-up when the literal rule has failed; usually focusing on the range of secondary meanings of the word or phrase in question. The literal rule will be departed from mainly where there is confusion *within* the Act—that a clear interpretation is not possible because of surrounding words and sections. It is interesting to note, however, that many of the cases which developed the golden rule were in fact cases on the interpretation of another type of document: testators' wills. And even a cursory study of the interpretation of wills in the law of succession reveals that there has always been a major conflict of judicial attitude here: do you follow only what the testator wrote, or do you look for other evidence of his intentions? The law of succession has had the same problems, as seen in statutory interpretation. It has not produced a satisfactory answer. Even Lord Wensleydale, the sometime father of the golden rule, was known to adopt a strong literal approach when interpreting wills (see, for instance, *Abbott* v *Middleton* (1858) 7 HLC 68).

It is respectfully submitted that Lord Simon's guidelines are still useful, although they leave us with the one major problem with the golden rule: how do we know when something is an anomaly, an ambiguity, or absurd? This is a question most frequently avoided by commentators and even recourse to dictionaries does not solve the problem. The *Oxford English Dictionary*, for instance, says of 'absurdity' that it is: 'the quality or state of being extremely unreasonable, illogical, or inappropriate . . .'; and on the meaning of 'absurd': 'against or without reason or propriety; incongruous, unreasonable, illogical'. This does not in reality help too much. Cross, however, does make a number of helpful points on this problem (1995: 81–92).

First, says Cross, the primary meaning cannot be abandoned, 'simply because it produces a result which [the judge] believes is contrary to the purpose of the Act. No judge can decline to apply a statutory provision because it seems to him to lead to absurd results.' That is always worth remembering. As noted above, it is not the function of a judge to create law; judges are creative in the law's interpretation and application, but they cannot just make things up or disregard a law they do not like.

Equally, however, judicial treatment of the topic does not lend itself to simply saying judges are concerned only with the *internal* context of the words. Cross is forced to conclude that judicial applications of the rule tend to show that 'absurdity' 'does mean something wider than irreconcilability with the rest of the instrument' (1995: 89). In other words, some judges at least will go beyond merely examining the words of the section, etc. and probe into the purpose of the Act. Discovering whether something is absurd when matched against the purpose of the Act may involve examining the wider legal, and even social, setting of the Act. That is to say, judges, to a greater or lesser extent, will look to the *external context* of the statute.

Indeed, it is fair to say that the *purposive approach* has become the dominant judicial interpretation technique. Judges may not ignore the words written in statutes, but they are now more inclined to adopt a purposive interpretation whenever possible. This is partly due to the effects and influence of EU legislation over the past forty years. It may also be related to the questionable standard of drafting seen in modern statutes.

Again, there are many cases which illustrate the rule, but that is all they do—*illustrate*. As a lawyer you are concerned with using the rule to argue—it is of little value citing a case which simply proves that the courts do occasionally use the rule if the case cited has nothing to do with your argument. So, an essay which involves interpreting a statute on tax law, say, which tells the reader that the court could use a purposive approach and then simply cites *River Wear Commissioners* as an example of when the courts used this approach has taken the argument nowhere.

Here, however, are two famous examples of the golden rule in operation.

R v Allen (1872) LR 1 CCR 367: Allen, who was already married, married a woman called Harriet Crouch. The statute in question said: 'whosoever being married shall marry any other person during the lifetime of his spouse' shall commit bigamy. Now, Harriet was in fact closely related to Allen so this apparently bigamous marriage was actually void. Thus, Allen argued that he had not married Harriet (because at law this was impossible) and so had not committed bigamy. He argued that the second marriage had to be a legal marriage before bigamy could be committed. But this would of course produce an absurdity because logically no bigamous marriage is lawful by its own definition; so, if Allen's argument was accepted, the judges would have had to pretend that the section was meaningless. Therefore, they took a more purposive approach and read the words in the section 'shall marry' as meaning 'going through the ceremony'.

Re Sigsworth [1935] Ch 89; [1934] All ER Rep 113: Mrs Sigsworth was found dead. An inquest found that she had been murdered by her son, who was also found dead.

Mrs Sigsworth's will left everything to her son. However, old rules of public policy dictated that the son (and therefore his estate) could not inherit in these circumstances. Therefore, Mrs Sigsworth died intestate. But, under the Administration of Estates Act 1925, s. 46, the person entitled on intestacy was her son and, through him, his estate. The money had gone around in a circle; and the statute dealing with intestacy said nothing about murderers being barred from inheriting.

The Court held that the statute could not have been intended to allow murderers to inherit, despite being silent on the point. The old rule which applied to inheriting under a will was applied to intestacy on the grounds that cases such as *Sigsworth* would be 'obnoxious' to that old principle and must be read as being subject to it.

A more recent example arose in *R v Lehair* [2015] EWCA Crim 1324; [2015] 1 WLR 4811. The case centred on the Proceeds of Crime Act 2002. This allows for courts to recover money (which is termed 'tainted') from criminals in certain circumstances. For instance, how does the law regard money given away by the criminal? Section 77(5) deals with the position: 'A gift is tainted if it was made by the defendant at any time after—(a) the date on which the offence was committed.' Lehair had been convicted of a bank robbery and had disposed of the money in question on the day of the robbery. A literal interpretation therefore meant the money was not recoverable as it had been transferred on the day itself rather than after the date of the crime: the argument would be that the section does not cover the transfer of any gift at any time on the day during which the offence concerned was committed, only those on days subsequent.

In response, the Crown argued that Parliamentary intent is clear and that the date referred to in s. 77(5)(a) must refer to the actual **time** of the offence from which the benefit was obtained. Any disposal after the offence itself was covered. Macur LJ gave the decision of the court. Her Ladyship reviewed many leading authorities on the use of the literal rule and concluded.

[19] We are satisfied that a literal interpretation of section 77(5)(a) is anomalous to the explicit purpose of the Act. It could not have been intended that criminals have a day's grace to dispose of their assets or to require either the prosecution, the enforcement agencies or the court to devise a scheme, outside the Act, to catch relevant assets. A literal interpretation of section 77(5) would require this.

[22]. We have no hesitation in endorsing the argument that there must be a purposive construction of the provision and in doing so, the subsection must read as though the **date** upon which an offence is committed must refer to the actual **time** of commission and after which any tainted gift will fall for the consideration in the court's powers of confiscation.

EXERCISE 16 Not all there; or, present and correct?

Please read the following case summary. We pose only one question at the end of the account.

Under the Statute of Frauds 1677 it was a requirement that a will had to be signed by the testator 'in the presence' of witnesses.

In *Casson* v *Dade* (1781) 28 ER 1010 Miss Honora Jenkins went to her attorney's office to execute her will. She signed the will but then felt faint and was taken outside to sit in her carriage with her maid. The witnesses to the will remained in the office and gave their signatures to the will. The maid gave evidence that at the moment the witnesses were signing the carriage horses reared up, causing the carriage to move into a line of sight with the office window. The maid stated that, had Miss Jenkins looked through the window she would have seen the witnesses sign.

 QUESTION

Was the will validly witnessed?

 ANSWER

The Court held that the will had been properly witnessed. Miss Jenkins was 'in the presence' of the witnesses even though she was not physically present in the same room. The fact that she was in the line of sight of the witnesses and could have seen them sign had she looked was enough. For, as had been said in the 1687 case of *Shires* v *Glascock* 21 ER 1134, to demand otherwise would mean that 'if a man should but turn his back, or look off, it would vitiate the will'. In modern parlance, it would be absurd to hold otherwise!

9.3.3 The mischief rule

Akin to the purposive rule is a much older aid to interpretation called the mischief rule, or the rule in *Heydon's Case* (1584) 3 Co Rep 7a, 7b.

Like both the golden rule and the purposive rule, the mischief rule stresses the need to interpret an enactment in such a way as to give effect to its objectives: in this case, what problem was the Act meant to overcome? However, the mischief rule is, formally, of narrower application, in that the approach is located purely in the context of an identifiable common law status quo which existed prior to the Act. Thus, the courts are required to consider four things:

(i)   What was the common law before the Act?

(ii)   What was the 'defect or mischief' for which the common law did not provide?

(iii) What remedy did Parliament intend to provide?

(iv)   What was the true reason for that remedy?

Great care must be taken when relying upon this rule in argument: first, when *Heydon's Case* was determined the mischief could in fact be discovered within the Act itself because the reason for the Act's existence was always stated in the **preamble**. Thus, a judge did not have to go beyond the bounds of the Act to discover the mischief it sought to remedy. The *internal* context was sufficient. A classic example of the use of preambles comes in the **Charitable Uses Act 1601**, which states:

> WHEREAS Lands, Tenements, Rents, Annuities . . . have been heretofore given, limited, appointed and assigned, as well by the Queen's most excellent Majesty, and her most noble Progenitors, as by sundry other well disposed Persons; some for Relief of aged, impotent and poor People, some for Maintenance of sick and maimed Soldiers . . . which Lands, Tenements, Rents, Annuities . . . nevertheless have not been employed according to the charitable Intent of the givers and Founders thereof by reasons of Frauds, Breaches of Trust, and Negligence in those that should pay, deliver and employ the same: For Redress and Remedy whereof Be it enacted . . .

Lord Diplock recognised this in *Black-Clawson International Ltd* v *Papierwerke Waldhof-Aschaffenburg Aktiengesellschaft* [1975] AC 591; [1975] 1 All ER 810 when he said:

> So, when it was laid down, the 'mischief rule' did not require the court to travel beyond the actual words of the statute itself to identify the 'mischief and defect for which the Common Law did not provide' . . . the mischief rule must be used with caution to justify any reference to extraneous documents for this purpose.

The point concerning 'extraneous documents' is significant. As we will see shortly, judges have not, traditionally, been allowed to look at any and every source in order to discover the mischief. Recently this approach has altered.

Secondly, 'mischief' itself can be difficult to define. All Acts came about for *some* reason, be it social, economic, political, or because of some technical legal defect. This last reason is a reasonably safe basis upon which to attach the tag 'mischief'. One can easily find out what the law was before the Act came into effect and thereby see the apparent changes the Act sought to make in the law. The other means of identifying the mischief are fraught with danger because they clearly involve making value judgements.

Thirdly, as was noted by Lord Bingham in *R* v *Secretary of State, ex parte Spath Holme* [2001] 1 All ER 195 (HL), an Act may have more than one mischief and the interrelationship between these may affect the question of interpretation. Two good examples of the mischief rule in operation are the cases of *Gorris* v *Scott* (1874) LR 9 Ex 125 and

Smith v *Hughes* [1960] 1 WLR 830; [1960] 2 All ER 859. In *Gorris* v *Scott*, Scott contracted to transport some sheep by sea. The sheep were swept overboard because they had not been fenced in. Orders in Council made under the Contagious Diseases (Animals) Act 1869 required that the sheep should have been put in pens. Gorris thus claimed that Scott was in breach of the Act. The Court of Exchequer held that the purpose of the Act (which was clear from the preamble) was to prevent the spread of diseases among sheep or cattle en route to Britain; not to give a right to claimants like Gorris.

In *Smith* v *Hughes*, the Street Offences Act 1959, s. 1 stated: 'It shall be an offence for a common prostitute to loiter or solicit in a street or public place for the purposes of prostitution.' Prostitutes began trying to attract customers by signalling to the men from balconies or from windows. The report notes that the prostitutes would indicate the price by raising three fingers—and that on one occasion they received a counter-offer of two raised fingers! The Divisional Court of the Queen's Bench Division (on an appeal by way of case stated) decided that the mischief of the Act was to 'clean up the streets'. The words of s. 1 did not indicate *who* had to be in the street, and so an offence had been committed under the section.

It is probably fair to say that, today, the distinction between the mischief and golden rules is, in the minds of some judges, so fine as to be virtually non-existent. It could even be argued that both rules have become subsumed within a general purposive approach. An example of such thinking can be seen in Lord Diplock's approach to the Abortion Act 1967 in *Royal College of Nursing* v *DHSS* [1981] AC 800; [1981] 1 All ER 545. His Lordship began by defining his method for discovering the purpose of the Act:

> one starts by considering what was the state of the law relating to abortion before the passing of the Act, what was the mischief that required amendment, and in what respect was the existing law unclear.

He continued his analysis by looking at the whole context of the abortion problem—its social and economic aspects, as well as its legal history. He then concluded that:

> the wording and structure of the section are far from elegant, but the policy of the Act, it seems to me, is clear. There are two aspects to it: the first is to broaden the grounds upon which abortions may be lawfully obtained; the second is to ensure that the abortion is carried out with all proper skill and in hygienic conditions.

Be careful, however, not to assume that, in discovering the 'purpose' of an Act the judges are dealing with some sort of absolute, clearly definable, objective. Be prepared for contrary argument. Discovering the purpose of a rule is often an act of creative interpretation by the judge. Purposes and reasons for legislating are at least as indeterminate as the rules themselves.

9.4 Secondary aids to construction

The three 'canons of construction' so far considered are sometimes called **primary** aids to interpretation. It is now necessary to consider a set of **secondary rules** that can be employed within the framework of the primary aids to facilitate interpretation. These relate either to the use that can be made of parts of the statute itself, or to external (*extrinsic*) materials. Many of the rules noted later in the chapter are simply rules of grammar which are not unique to legal terminology. For instance, to borrow part of the exercise we have set at the end of this chapter, consider the following list: *cats, dogs, horses, cattle, sheep, pigs, and snakes or insects common to the British Isles.* Is it only snakes and insects that have to be common to the British Isles?

9.4.1 The title of the Act

It is very tempting to point to the long or short title in order to show the purpose of the Act. It should be stressed that the long title is rarely used for this purpose and the short title is practically irrelevant. A classic example of this is the case of *R* v *Galvin* [1987] QB 862; [1987] 2 All ER 851. Galvin acquired 'restricted' Ministry of Defence documents. When Galvin was charged under the Official Secrets Act 1911, he argued that the documents had ceased to be secret and had never actually been 'official'—which, he said, is what the title of the Act demanded. Nevertheless, he was found guilty because the section referred only to 'documents' and the title, being merely a label, had to give way to the words actually used in the section. The conviction, however, was quashed on other grounds.

On the use of the long title, see *Vacher* v *London Society of Compositors* [1913] AC 107. Here, the House of Lords referred to the long title of the Act but only to supplement and explain the meaning of the words in the section, not to contradict them. Note also that special rules will apply to the use of the Schedules that often appear at the end of an Act: see *Buchanan & Co. Ltd* v *Babco Forwarding & Shipping Ltd* [1978] AC 141; [1977] 3 All ER 1048.

9.4.2 Inclusory words and lists

A word which often arises in a statute is 'include': thus, you find a section which might read:

> For the purposes of this Act references to sending include delivering, causing to be sent or delivered, transferring and posting.

The question would then be whether the word 'include' meant all the subsequent terms were included **and everything else was excluded** or that the subsequent terms were examples only, so that other terms might also be included. For instance, should 'distributing' or 'handing out' be included? In *R* v *Sheppard and another* [2010] EWCA Crim 65; [2010] 1 WLR 2779 the Court of Appeal had to consider whether racially inflammatory material published on the web fell within the ambit of s. 29 of the Public Order Act 1986 in the phrase: '"written material" includes any sign or other visible representation', or whether the term was limited to things such as 'signs'. It held that the phrase extended to the web, i.e. that 'includes' here did not close off the list.

Again, think of an everyday example: if you say that the Football Association Premiership includes Manchester United, Liverpool, and Arsenal, does this mean that there is no other team in the league? On the other hand, if you say that the Grand Slam tournaments in golf include the US Masters, the (British) Open, the US Open, and the US PGA, there are in fact no others, so this list has 'included' everything.

This problem was considered in *Coltman v Bibby Tankers* [1988] AC 276; [1987] 3 All ER 1068. In this case a ship sank off the coast of Japan with the loss of all hands. The administrators of the estate of one of the engineers sued the ship's owners under the Employer's Liability (Defective Equipment) Act 1969, alleging that the owners had provided defective equipment inasmuch as the ship was unseaworthy. The House of Lords therefore had to decide whether the words in s. 1(1) of the Act—'equipment provided by his employer for the purposes of the employer's business'—as explained in s. 1(3)—'equipment *includes* any plant and machinery, vehicle, aircraft, and clothing'—covered a ship. What was the effect of the italicised word 'includes'? The House of Lords solved the problem by looking at other sections in the Act which listed things. These other lists were very specific when not introduced by the word 'include'. This tended to indicate that when the word 'include' did occur it was merely stating examples, so that items not stated in the list might still fall within the definition of 'equipment' in the Act. So, although a ship was not mentioned in the Act specifically it was nevertheless 'included' in the definition of equipment. Lord Oliver stated:

> [I]t is quite clear . . . that the word 'includes' in subsection (3) cannot be construed as 'means and includes' so as to confine that which is embraced in the word 'equipment' to the exemplars there specified. Granted that there may be circumstances in which an inclusive definition of this sort can have a restrictive effect, that cannot, in my judgment, possibly apply in the case of this statute. Here, where the draftsman intends a restricted meaning, he makes it quite clear. One has only to contrast the definitions of 'business,' 'equipment' and 'personal injury,' all of which are by reference to what is included, with those of 'employee' and 'fault,' where the Act makes it clear that there is to be a single exclusive meaning for the purposes of the Act. Subsection (3) cannot, therefore, be used to cut down the meaning of the word 'equipment' as it is used in subsection (1). It must have been inserted in the statute either for the purpose of enlarging the word by including in it articles which would not otherwise fall within it in its ordinary signification or it must have been inserted for clarification and the avoidance of doubt.

Thus, the mere fact that a list is introduced by the word 'includes' does not automatically mean that the list is open ended. Much more needs to be considered. Indeed, we strongly recommend that you read this case, as it encompasses many of the techniques of statutory interpretation discussed in this chapter—including a reference to the long title of the Act which is introduced without excuse or explanation (showing how judges—if not students—can bend the rules when they so wish).

Lists in statutes are problematic (as we shall see below with maxims such as the *eiusdem generis* rule). Introductory words to lists cause their own headaches. In addition to 'includes', for instance, we have the term 'in particular'. In *R (on the application of (Zimbabwe)) v Secretary of State for the Home Department* [2017] EWCA 1669; [2018] 2 All ER 1015 the section began with the term 'in particular' and then listed eight very specific requirements. Did this mean that these eight points were examples of what needed to be done or was this a closed list? The Court of Appeal decided that the words had a natural meaning of 'by way of example' or 'especially' rather than, as was being argued, a meaning of exclusivity (similar to the arguments on the meaning of 'includes').

Legal maxims (there are more to come and many we do not cover) used to be the lifeblood of any lawyer; today they are looked on with some disdain, especially as they are often contained in Latin phrases. But this loses sight of the history by which they came about (we are not the first generation of lawyers to struggle making sense of a document) and the fact that they are still useful grammatical tools. As long as we do not regard ourselves as slaves to these maxims, they can still help a great deal (see also Graham, 2001). Nevertheless, we know from bitter experience that students do not like dealing with these maxims (not least because of the problems of pronunciation).

9.4.3 *Expressio unius est exclusio alterius*

Closely connected to the problem of what is meant by 'include' is the position where a simple list of words appears. Can other words be added to the list? As always there is a Latin maxim to cover this: *expressio unius est exclusio alterius* ('the expression of one thing is the exclusion of another'). Using this maxim one can argue that if the legislature produces a list of items, then it is logical that all other items were specifically excluded. Why else would the legislators have provided a list? Thus, one might use this rule to decide whether a faith healer fell within 'clairvoyant, fortune teller, or diviner'. This maxim might have applied in *Coltman* had it not been for the presence of the word 'include'. Similarly, where words like 'such as' or 'etc.' appears in the list the maxim does not work. One should take care with this maxim, however. It is not seen as a particularly strong presumption and is frequently overridden by examining the context of the words. Hence, Lord Bingham's statement in *R (on the application of Smith) R (on the application of West) v Parole Board* [2005] UKHL 1; [2005] 1 WLR 350 [29] that 'the maxim *expressio unius exclusio alterius* can seldom, if ever, be enough to exclude the common law rules of natural justice'. A similar negative view appeared in *Government of the Republic of France v Royal Borough of Kensington and Chelsea* [2017] EWCA Civ 429; [2017] All ER (D) 185, where Hickinbottom LJ said at [64]:

> Nor do I consider that the expressio unius maxim is of any substantial assistance. I agree with the learned authors of Cross on Statutory Interpretation (3rd edition (1995), Butterworths) at page 140 . . . '. . . it is doubtful whether the maxim does more than draw attention to a fairly obvious linguistic point, viz that in many contexts the mention of some matters warrants an inference that other cognate matters were intentionally excluded'.

9.4.4 *Eiusdem generis*

What should happen when an Act employs a generic but non-exhaustive list? For example, an Act may state that a licence is required to keep 'dogs, cats, budgerigars and **other animals**'. Would you consider that a cow could be included on that basis? Obviously, it is difficult to say without more information about the context in which those words appear. We can, however, identify a specific legal method of dealing with such a problem by saying that where general words follow a list of specific words, then the general words must be read according to the *genus* (i.e. type or group) of the preceding specific words. It is the legal equivalent of explaining what one means by 'et cetera'. Thus, we must discover the *genus* which our named categories have in common and then interpret the general words ('other animals') so that they do not conflict with the specific words ('dogs', etc.). This is called the *eiusdem generis* rule.

    Although this is a very useful rule of grammar (and one which the Court of Appeal in *Tillmanns & Co. v SS Knutsford Ltd* [1908] 2 KB 395 said should apply before others), that is all it is; one still has to persuade the court that the *genus* of the preceding words is what you say it is. A good example of the arguments that may surround this rule arose in *Massey* v *Boulden* [2002] EWCA Civ 1634; [2003] 1 WLR 1792, where the Court of Appeal had to decide whether a person had the right to drive a vehicle along a track which ran across a village green, owned by another person, in order to gain access to his home. The owner of the village green submitted that the use of the track contravened the Road Traffic Act 1988, s. 34(1)(a), which states that a person commits an offence if 'without lawful authority [they drive] a mechanically propelled vehicle—(a) on to or upon any common land, moorland or land of any other description, not being land forming part of a road . . . '. The Court held that it was quite difficult to identify what the *genus* might be here but a village green would certainly fall within its scope (other types of land might be more difficult to decide upon). The use of the track therefore contravened s. 34.

In our example concerning the phrase 'or other animals' we could therefore argue, depending upon context, that 'other animals' could refer to any commonly domesticated animal, or to *any* commonly domesticated animal normally **kept as a pet**. Either interpretation might be feasible, which is why it is important to remember that such rules are secondary aids—and therefore used only within the context of our understanding of the provision as a whole.

See, for examples of this rule in operation:

(i)   *Powell* v *Kempton Park Racecourse* [1899] AC 143 on whether Tattersall's Ring (a place where horses are sold at a racecourse) fell within 'other place' in the phrase 'house, office, room or other place'—it did not (but only on a majority decision and involving detailed interpretational arguments on both the 'literal meaning' and the 'purpose' behind the legislation); and

(ii)   *R* v *Staniforth, R* v *Jordan* [1976] 3 WLR 887; [1976] 3 All ER 775 on whether pornographic material could fall outside the definition of obscene material under the Obscene Publications Act 1959 as being 'in the interests of science, literature, art or learning, or of other objects of general concern'. The argument was that the obscene material had psychotherapeutic value, so falling within the definition. That argument failed in the House of Lords.

9.4.5 *Noscitur a sociis*

Linked with the *eiusdem generis* approach is the maxim *noscitur a sociis*—a word is known by its associates. The meaning of a word is affected by the surrounding words and should be interpreted accordingly. This rule is similar to the *eiusdem generis* rule and students often confuse the two (so do practitioners). The *noscitur* rule is in fact of wider application than *eiusdem generis.* Indeed, Bennion (2017) classes the *eiusdem generis* rule as a sub-set or branch of this rule.

The *eiusdem generis* rule is more limited because it comes into effect only when dealing with *general words at the end of a list*, usually introduced with the words 'or other'. Thus, if we take the Wills Act 1837, s. 20 as an example, one of the ways of revoking a will is by 'burning, tearing, or otherwise destroying'. The *eiusdem generis* rule tells us that 'or otherwise destroying' is to be read in the light of burning and tearing; the cases showing us that this requires an act of physical violence rather than, say, amending the text or crossing things out.

The *noscitur a sociis* rule would not be used in this example merely because the *eiusdem generis* rule performs the same sort of task as regards general words at the end of lists. However, one would turn to the *noscitur a sociis* rule if the section read: 'burning, tearing, mutilating, or defacing' as there are no general words at the end of the list. In reality, though, you perform nearly the same analysis by asking, 'What type of burning or defacing is included in this section?' So, one could ask: what if the will had been partially destroyed by fire? How should you read the word 'burning'? Does the burning have to be complete before the will is revoked, or is partial burning enough? From the surrounding words, especially 'mutilating' and 'defacing', it seems that this action does not have to be complete—that burning could be read as including partial burning.

Another good illustration comes from *Tektrol Ltd v International Insurance Co. of Hanover Ltd and another* [2005] EWCA Civ 845. Tektrol carried on business in the provision of computer-related energy-saving devices. A 'source code' played a crucial part in the business. By a very unusual series of unrelated incidents involving both a computer virus and a burglary, Tektrol lost all of its copies of that code and sought to recover money through its insurance policy. The case hinged on what was meant by 'loss' in the insurance policy. Sir Martin Nourse concluded:

[27] 'Loss' is a word whose meaning varies widely with the context in which it is used. If a man said to you: 'I have lost my wife', you would understand him to mean one thing outside the maze at Hampton Court and another outside an undertakers in the high street.

[28] Here we have to decide what . . . is meant by 'other . . . loss . . . of information on computer systems or other records programmes or software.' Judging those words as they stand, I would find it difficult to say that they comprehended a loss of information caused by the loss of a computer in which the information was stored. That would not seem to be a loss of information on computer systems, etc. The computer could be lost but the information retained.

[29] If, however, 'loss' is read in its context, its meaning becomes plain. The expression [in the policy] 'other erasure loss distortion or corruption of information' demonstrates that the loss contemplated is loss by means of electronic interference; **noscitur a sociis**. It is not just the effect of the other three words, but the order in which the four appear. 'Loss' follows 'erasure'. While erasure can be expected to result in loss, a careful draftsman would not necessarily assume that it was the only way in which information might be lost. Then follow 'distortion or corruption', which seem to refer to interference causing something less than erasure or loss and between which, as Buxton LJ has observed, it is difficult to suggest a clear distinction. I agree with him that all four are overlapping words used by the draftsman to ensure that he had not omitted any case in which the information on the computer systems, etc. was interfered with by electronic means.

In *McDonald (deceased) (Represented by Mrs Edna McDonald) v National Grid Electricity Transmission plc* [2014] UKSC 53, [2015] AC 1128 the Supreme Court had to decide whether regulations on the use of asbestos covered the death of a former worker. One part of the case hinged on whether his work, which involved mixing asbestos with water, amounted to 'mixing' within the statute because the surrounding words seemed to limit the word 'mixing' to a more technical meaning used in the industry. Two Supreme Court Justices held that the *noscitur a sociis* rule applied: the word was in the company of other technical words and so limited by them. However, three went the other way to say that the term 'mixing' in the Regulations should be read in a wider context and so should not be given a restricted, technical meaning, but should include the work in question—mixing asbestos powder.

Such a divergence of opinion by the most senior judges in this case demonstrates quite vividly that all these are merely rules of grammar. A judge does not have to apply these rules if he or she believes the wording of the Act does not justify their use. Thus, a detailed examination of the enactment may show a list that is clearly meant to be closed or a list that cannot accommodate the disputed fact or action within it (i.e. the words in the list are not closely related). Such an instance was *R (on the application* of *(Zimbabwe))* v *Secretary of State for the Home Department*, noted above at section **9.4.2** (concerning the use of the words 'in particular'). This was a case concerning deportation under s. 35 Asylum and Immigration (Treatment of Claimants, etc.) Act 2004. Section 35(2) placed demands on the potential deportee, those being:

> In particular, the Secretary of State may require a person to—(a) provide information or documents to the Secretary of State or to any other person; (b) obtain information or documents; (c) provide biometric information (within the meaning of section 15 of the UK Borders Act 2007), or submit to a process by means of which such information is obtained or recorded; (d) make, or consent to or co-operate with the making of, an application to a person acting for the government of a state other than the United Kingdom; (e) co-operate with a process designed to enable determination of an application; (f) complete a form accurately and completely; (g) attend an interview and answer questions accurately and completely; (h) make an appointment.

It was held that s. 35(2) provided a clear exhaustive list and, further, that it did not contain sufficiently common items to form a class to which the *noscitur a sociis* maxim could attach.

9.4.6 *Ignorantia legis non excusat*

Perhaps the most famous maxim of all: ignorance of the law is no defence (though this is in fact derived from Roman law and was a maxim created when laws were fewer and more widely published, though not necessarily simpler). A 'Charlie Brown' cartoon once included this maxim. In the cartoon, Charlie Brown states the maxim and a puzzled Snoopy responds with: 'But what if you never know what's going on?'

9.4.7 Other statutes

Provided statutes are *in pari materia* a word in one Act can be given the same meaning it had in an earlier Act. *In pari materia* means concerning the same matter. This interpretive technique should be used cautiously: as has been noted on a number of occasions, *par* or *pari* means 'equal' not just 'similar'. Thus, the way the word 'horse' was interpreted in an Act concerning breeding rights could not be used readily to interpret the same word in an Act pertaining to the definition of a dangerous animal.

As a good example of the use of *in pari materia*, see *R* v *Wheatley* [1979] 1 WLR 144; [1979] 1 All ER 954 on whether 'explosive substance' in the Explosive Substances Act 1883, s. 4, included a pyrotechnic device. The 1883 Act gave no definition, but the Explosives Act 1875 dealt with the same subject matter and encompassed pyrotechnic devices in the term 'explosive'. Note also *British Amusement Catering Trades Association v Westminster City Council* [1988] 2 WLR 485; [1988] 1 All ER 740, in which, in order to decide whether video games in an amusement arcade fell within the meaning of 'exhibition of moving pictures' in the Cinematograph Act 1982, the Court considered every occurrence of this phrase within the long line of Cinematograph Acts dating from 1909 and the Cinemas Act 1985. The device can even be seen in operation across common law geographical boundaries; for example in *Wing Joo Long Ginseng Hong (Singapore) Co Pte Ltd* v *Qinghai Xinyuan Foreign Trade Co Ltd* [2009] SGCA 9; [2009] FSR 13 the Court of Appeal of Singapore found that the Trade Marks Act 1992, s. 39(1) (Singapore) was *in pari materia* with ss 46 and 47 of the UK Trade Marks Act 1994.

The principle does not involve a hindsight factor—the meaning of words used in later Acts cannot be used as authority for establishing the meaning of the same words or phrases in earlier Acts: see *R (On the application of George)* v *Secretary of State for the Home Department* [2014] UKSC 28, [2014] 1 WLR 1831.

Linked with the idea of *in pari materia* interpretation is what is sometimes referred to as the 'Barras principle'. It is taken from the speech of Viscount Buckmaster in *Barras* v *Aberdeen Steam Trawling and Fishing Co. Ltd* [1933] All ER Rep 402, 411:

> It has long been a well established principle to be applied in the consideration of Acts of Parliament that where a word of doubtful meaning has received a clear judicial interpretation, the subsequent statute which incorporates the same word or the same phrase in a similar context, must be construed so that the word or phrase is interpreted according to the meaning that has previously been assigned to it.

One would have to say, however, that this is not really a principle of interpretation, more a useful starting point or presumption. It should be used with great caution (as was stated by the other Law Lords in *Barras* itself and again *per* Lords Scarman, Roskill, and Templeman in *R* v *Chard* [1984] AC 279; [1983] 3 All ER 637), but was applied most recently by the Supreme Court in *R (on the application of CN)* v *Lewisham London Borough Council; R (on the application of ZH)* v *Newham London Borough Council (Secretary of State for Communities and Local Government, interested party)* [2014] UKSC 62; [2014] 3 WLR 1548, the court finding that the word 'dwelling' should have the same meaning in the Housing Act 1996 as had been given by the court in relation to the same word in the Protection from Eviction Act 1977.

9.4.8 The Interpretation Act 1978

You should be aware of the existence of this Act, but it is not as helpful as it first sounds. The Act simply states that certain words will have a standard meaning unless specifically changed.

Thus 'month' means a calendar month and not 30 days; 'he' is read as including 'she'; singular words include the plural, 'oath' and 'affidavit' include affirmation and declaration, and 'swear' includes affirm and declare; 'distance' is measured in a straight line on a horizontal plane; 'British Islands' means the United Kingdom, the Channel Islands, and the Isle of Man; 'Land' includes buildings and other structures, land covered with water, and any estate, interest, easement, servitude, or right in or over land, and so on.

The Act itself may be amended to include new definitions, such as the term 'exit day' in relation to Brexit (taking its definition from the European Union (Withdrawal) Act 2018 and allowing for the application of that term to other legislation).

9.4.9 Punctuation and marginal notes

The modern view is that punctuation can be used as an aid to interpretation. Traditionally, however, this was not true of headings and marginal notes in a statute. That approach changed following *R* v *Montilla* [2004] UKHL 50; [2004] 1 WLR 3141.

Marginal (or side) notes are just what they sound like. Prior to 2001, when a Bill was going through Parliament each clause of the Bill had a note (drafted by Parliamentary Counsel) in the margin explaining the function of the clause for ease of reference. In 2001 these notes were moved so that they now appear in bold type as headings to each clause (later to become section) in the version of the statute which is published by the Stationery Office. Parliamentary Counsel very occasionally, on the advice of the Bill's drafter, alter marginal notes and headings which, because of amendments or for some other reason, have become inaccurate, but for the most part they stay the same even if the clause/section is redrafted. The question then is whether headings and marginal/ sidenotes, although generally unamendable, can be considered in construing a provision in an Act of Parliament.

The resistance to making use of these notes has always been justified on the grounds that they can sometimes be misleading. An example of this can be seen in the Animals Act 1971, where s. 3 reads: '*Where a dog causes damage by killing or injuring livestock, any person who is a keeper of the dog is liable for the damage . . .*' and s. 11 adds, '*In this Act "damage" includes the death of or injury to any person*' but the marginal note to s. 3 states: '*Liability for injury done by dogs to livestock*'—which is not quite the same thing.

Nevertheless, in *R* v *Montilla* the House of Lords decided that they could be used: 'the headings and sidenotes are as much part of the contextual scene as these materials, and there is no logical reason why they should be treated differently' (at [36]). Interestingly, the Irish Supreme Court has held to the traditional approach (see *Fitzgibbon* v *Law Society of Ireland* [2014] IESC 48).

Montilla does not mean that all such sidenotes, etc. are determinant of the meaning of the section. They are aids only. As Arden LJ put it this way in *Murphy* v *Wyatt* [2011] EWCA Civ 408 at [75]: '[W]hile **marginal notes** to a statute do not have great weight in the interpretation of a statute they have some weight' (see also Horn (2011) on the use of headings and drafting techniques). Further, where statutes have been amended by later Acts it may well be the case that the accompanying notes (unamended) become misleading. Such was noted in *R (on the application of Smith)* v *Parole Board; R (on the application of West)* v *Parole Board* [2005] UKHL 1; [2005] 1 All ER 755. Here, the side-note to the Criminal Justice Act 1991, s. 39 referred to both long-term and life prisoners. This was an accurate description of the contents of the 1991 Act when it was enacted. However, as a result of a complex series of repeals, s. 39 no longer dealt with life prisoners. The sidenote therefore had to be ignored and their Lordships suggested that similar misunderstandings could be avoided by draftsmen and Parliament in the future if a section whose substance has been so changed as to make the sidenote an unreliable guide to its contents were to be repealed and replaced by an entirely new section, with its own appropriate sidenote.

9.4.10 Explanatory notes

Explanatory notes have been appended to statutory instruments for some time and began to accompany Acts in 1999. As with marginal notes these explanatory notes are attached to Bills and draft statutory instruments as they go through Parliament. They seek to offer a simplified guide to the legislation. As well as appearing in printed form you can also find them on the internet (at www.legislation.gov.uk). The opening part contains a 'health warning', such as appears in the Child Benefit Act 2005:

> These explanatory notes relate to the Child Benefit Act, which received Royal Assent on 24th March 2005. They have been prepared by the Inland Revenue in order to assist the reader in understanding the Act. They do not form part of the Act and have not been endorsed by Parliament.

One would presume from this that they cannot be used to interpret the Act itself. Not so. That these notes could be used as a means of identifying the mischief behind a *statutory instrument* was established in *Pickstone v Freemans plc* [1989] AC 66; [1988] 2 All ER 803, at least in a European setting. More recently they have been applied to statutes.

This is how it came about. In *Coventry and Solihull Waste Disposal Co. Ltd v Russell (Valuation Officer)* [1999] 1 WLR 2093; [2000] 1 All ER 97 it was said that an explanatory note may be referred to as an aid to construction where the statutory instrument to which it is attached is ambiguous. And in *R (on the application of Westminster City Council) v National Asylum Support Service* [2002] UKHL 38, [2002] 1 WLR 2956 Lord Steyn commented specifically on explanatory notes—this time in relation to a statute (the Immigration and Asylum Act 1999). He did not rely on the notes to the Act but sought to clarify their status (his comments were therefore *obiter*). He observed that:

> [5] The question is whether in aid of the interpretation of a statute the court may take into account the explanatory notes and, if so, to what extent. The starting point is that language in all legal texts conveys meaning according to the circumstances in which it was used. It follows that the context must always be identified and considered before the process of construction or during it. It is therefore wrong to say that the court may only resort to evidence of the contextual scene when an ambiguity has arisen . . . Insofar as the explanatory notes cast light on the objective setting or contextual scene of the statute, and the mischief at which it is aimed, such materials are therefore always admissible aids to construction. They may be admitted for what logical value they have. . . .
>
> [6] If exceptionally there is found in explanatory notes a clear assurance by the executive to Parliament about the meaning of a clause, or the circumstances in which a power will or will not be used, that assurance may in principle be admitted against the executive in proceedings in which the executive places a contrary contention before a court . . . What is impermissible is to treat the wishes and desires of the government about the scope of the statutory language as reflecting the will of Parliament. The aims of the government in respect of the meaning of clauses as revealed in explanatory notes cannot be attributed to Parliament. The object is to see what is the intention expressed by the words enacted.

A short time later came *Regina (Confederation of Passenger Transport UK) v Humber Bridge Board and another* [2003] EWCA Civ 842; [2004] QB 310. This case also concerned a statutory instrument, but, here, one in which there was no ambiguity *per se*: instead there was a clear drafting error. The error was that, in setting the level of tolls to be paid for crossing the Humber Bridge no provision had been made for tolls on buses carrying sixteen passengers or more ('large buses'). Previous statutory instruments on the tolls had included large buses. The history of these previous relevant statutory instruments and the explanatory notes to the statutory instrument made it obvious that large buses should have been included.

The Court of Appeal therefore had to consider whether, when construing a statutory instrument, it was permissible to add, omit, or substitute words in order to correct an obvious drafting error. It was held that, having regard to the historical context of the Orders, it was inconceivable that the bridge company or the Secretary of State had intended to exclude large buses from the classes of vehicle expected to pay tolls. The Court of Appeal held that, provided that the court was sure:

(i)   of the intended purpose of the provision in question;

(ii) that the draftsman had failed to give effect to that purpose by inadvertence; and

(iii) of the substance of the provision that would otherwise have been made,

then reference to material extraneous to the statutory instrument could be made as an aid to its construction where the instrument was ambiguous, obscure, or led to absurdity and the material made the intention of the instrument clear.

Again, in *R v Montilla* it was noted that it had become common practice for their Lordships to ask to be shown the explanatory notes when issues were raised about the meaning of words used in an enactment. Their Lordships cited themselves with approval (which is handy if somewhat circular) in *R (on the application of S) v Chief Constable of South Yorkshire* [2004] UKHL 39; [2004] 4 All ER 193 (*per* Lord Steyn at [4]: 'they may potentially contain much more immediate and valuable material than other aids regularly used by the courts, such as Law Commission reports, government committee reports, Green Papers, and so forth'). So, whatever the 'health warning' in the notes themselves, it seems that they can be used to interpret provisions in an Act: see, for instance *R (on the application of the Public and Commercial Services Union) v Minister for the Civil Service* [2010] EWHC 1027 (Admin); [2011] 3 All ER 54, which distinguished 'notes on clauses' distributed to MPs privately to explain the nature of a Bill from 'explanatory notes'. The privately distributed notes were excluded as an aid to interpretation in direct contrast to the explanatory notes which were simply accepted as a normal part of statutory interpretation techniques.

Despite this, some judges are still wary of relying on explanatory notes or other such material and the full extent to which they can be used is tied up with the debate on another House of Lords' decision (*Pepper v Hart*) which we will discuss at section **9.5**, so we shall leave this for the moment. One interesting aside here comes from Underhill LJ in *Jessemey v Rowstock Ltd and another* [2014] EWCA Civ 185; [2014] 3 All ER 409 with the line [at 36]: 'this explanation cannot be reconciled with para 353 of the explanatory notes (*at least if these were produced by the draftsman of the section, rather than by someone else trying to reconstruct his thinking*)'. The highlighted section rather begs the question as to the strength of a note depending on proof of authorship.

9.4.11 Dictionaries

Dictionaries can be used by judges where a word has no specific legal meaning. One must be careful here, however, as words can change meaning by dint of time, usage, and context.

One example of a court using dictionaries to interpret sections arose in *Flack* v *Baldry* [1988] 1 WLR 393; [1988] 1 All ER 412. The case concerned the legality of possessing a 'stun gun' which could administer an electric shock of 46,000 volts. Did this offend against the Firearms Act 1968 as a 'weapon designed for the **discharge** of any noxious liquid, gas, or other thing'? The Court found that 'discharge' had a dictionary meaning of 'emit' rather than 'physical ejection', so that the stun gun was caught by the Act. Dictionaries also came to hand in *R (on the application of Robinson)* v *Torridge DC* [2006] EWHC 877 (Admin); [2007] 1 WLR 871 in deciding that a bridge could 'choke' a river under the Public Health Act 1936, s. 259 (see Munday (2008) for a discussion on this slightly weird problem of interpretation).

One has to tread carefully here, though. Different dictionaries often give different slants to the meaning of words. For instance, in one exercise we have given to our students a key question arises whether a person has committed an act of 'violence' when he has been found guilty of causing criminal damage to a snack bar. Depending upon which dictionary is used, you tend to get definitions which will stress either that 'violence' relates only to causing injury to people, or that it includes damage to property as well as injury to people. Finding the one dictionary that most favours your interpretation is sometimes referred to as 'dictionary shopping'.

9.4.12 *Travaux préparatoires*

This translates literally as 'preparatory works'. In the English context it refers to the consideration of public materials by the courts in order to discern the purpose of the legislation. A common example is the reports or working papers (though not the recommendations) of law reform bodies such as the Law Commission or Criminal Law Revision Committee. The question as to whether White Papers may be referred to in aid of interpretation has been inconclusively mooted by the Court of Appeal in *Thomas* v *Chief Adjudication Officer and Secretary of State for Social Security* [1990] IRLR 436; [1990] 3 CMLR 611; but for earlier contrary authority see *Katikiro of Buganda* v *Attorney-General* [1961] 1 WLR 119.

In the European context, the willingness to consider *travaux préparatoires* has traditionally been greater. European Union case law, for instance, thus includes references to the use of legislative proposals as published in the *Official Journal* and parliamentary debates in Member States. Similarly, in the Commonwealth, the (English) exclusionary rules have gradually been relaxed across most jurisdictions since the early 1980s: see Zander (2004) for examples.

9.5 The use of Hansard

In contrast to what we have just said about the use of *travaux préparatoires* in European courts, the English courts used to take a restrictive view of the range of documents which may be so used. For instance, all parliamentary debates in the House of Commons and House of Lords are recorded in a text called Hansard, which seeks to provide an account of proceedings (it is not a transcript but an edited record). Traditionally, Hansard could not be referred to explicitly by a court in order to gauge Parliament's intention (although some judges have admitted over the years to looking at the debates anyway). In the international context, such as dealing with the interpretation of international treaties, the English courts had already taken a more relaxed attitude: see *Fothergill* v *Monarch Airlines* [1981] AC 251; [1980] 2 All ER 696. Further, in the European context, as more and more legislation has owed its origins to the European Union, the House of Lords began to use Hansard on several occasions and moved more towards harmonisation with European methods of interpretation in the use of *travaux préparatoires*: see *Pickstone* v *Freemans* [1988] 3 WLR 265; [1988] 2 All ER 803; *Litster* v *Forth Dry Dock* [1990] AC 546; [1989] 1 All ER 1134; and *R* v *Secretary of State for Transport, ex parte Factortame Ltd* [1990] 2 AC 85; [1989] 2 All ER 692.

9.5.1 *Pepper* v *Hart*

In 1992 the House of Lords delivered a blockbuster in the case of *Pepper (Inspector of Taxes)* v *Hart* [1992] 3 WLR 1032; [1993] 1 All ER 42. By a 6:1 majority (Lord Mackay LC dissenting) the House of Lords decided to allow reference to be made to Hansard in limited circumstances. Reference to parliamentary materials would be allowed where:

(i)   legislation is ambiguous or obscure, or leads to an absurdity;

(ii)   the material relied upon consists of one or more statements by a minister or other promoter of the Bill, together if necessary with such other parliamentary material as is necessary to understand such statements and their effect;

(iii)   the statements relied upon are clear.

In this case, the effect of permitting reference to Hansard was that the literal meaning of the statute in question was not followed (and it is probably fair to say that justice was therefore done).

Some comments by their Lordships are worth noting here. Lord Bridge stated (at 1039H, WLR) that:

> It should, in my opinion, only be in rare cases where the very issue of interpretation which the courts are called on to resolve has been addressed in Parliamentary debate and where the promoter of the legislation has made a clear statement directed to that very issue, that reference to Hansard should be permitted.

Lord Oliver commented (1042H, WLR):

> It can apply only where the expression of the legislative intention is genuinely ambiguous or obscure or where a literal or prima facie construction leads to a manifest absurdity . . .

Lord Mackay (dissenting) observed:

> I believe that practically every question of statutory construction that comes before the courts will involve an argument . . . [on (a) to confirm the meaning of a provision as conveyed by the text, its object and purpose; (b) to determine a meaning where the provision is ambiguous or obscure; or (c) to determine the meaning where the ordinary meaning is manifestly absurd or unreasonable] . . . It

> follows that the parties' legal advisors will require to study Hansard in practically every such case to see whether or not there is any help to be gained from it. I believe this is an objection of real substance. It is a practical objection not one of principle . . .
>
> (1037G, WLR)

> Such an approach appears to me to involve the possibility at least of an immense increase in the cost of litigation in which statutory construction is involved.
>
> (1038B, WLR)

Lord Bridge further commented on the issue of additional costs:

> Provided the relaxation of the previous exclusionary rule is so limited, I find it difficult to suppose that the additional cost of litigation or any other ground of objection can justify the court continuing to wear blinkers which, in such a case as this, conceal the vital clue to the intended meaning of an enactment . . . [W]here Hansard does provide the answer, it should be so clear to both parties that they will avoid the cost of litigation.
>
> (1039H, WLR)

9.5.2 The rise and 'fall' of *Pepper* v *Hart*

Despite Lord Bridge's reassurances, *Pepper* v *Hart* initially cut major inroads into the traditional methods of statutory interpretation. In the six months immediately following the decision the House of Lords itself had made express use of Hansard in no fewer than three important cases: *Chief Adjudication Officer* v *Foster* [1992] 2 WLR 292; [1993] 1 All ER 705, *Stubbings* v *Webb* [1993] 2 WLR 120; [1993] 1 All ER 322, and *R* v *Warwickshire County Council, ex parte Johnson* [1993] 2 WLR 1; [1993] 1 All ER 1022.

In contrast to this, however, reservations or scepticism concerning this new-found research source began to emerge. Thus, in *Sheppard* v *Commissioners of Inland Revenue* [1993] STC 240, Aldous J expressed concern regarding the problem of determining what is an 'ambiguity' for the purposes of reference to Hansard (on which, see section **9.5.4**) and on the level of clarity required in a Minister's statement specifically on the issue in question. Indeed, in *Melluish (Inspector of Taxes)* v *BMI (No. 3)* [1996] AC 454 the House of Lords itself expressed reservations on the over-use of *Pepper* v *Hart* (e.g. *per* Lord Browne-Wilkinson, who had been one of the Law Lords in *Pepper* v *Hart* itself, that the statement by the appropriate minister must be 'directed to the very point in question in the litigation', effectively creating a fourth condition).

However, before that, the full potential of *Pepper* v *Hart* was realised in *Thomas Witter Ltd* v *TBP Industries Ltd* [1996] 2 All ER 573. This case neatly illustrates the true width of the problem: the potential ambiguity of *any* statutory provision and the fragility of our existing understanding of established areas of the law. This case involved examining the Misrepresentation Act 1967, s. 2(2). Jacob J considered this subsection to be ambiguously drafted and, relying on the support of *Pepper* v *Hart*, decided to examine the relevant extracts from Hansard. His Lordship concluded that these extracts were sufficient to establish that the accepted meaning of the subsection was incorrect. This of course meant that the previous understanding of the great majority of academic writers (endorsed by judicial *obiter* comments) and practitioners since the inception of the

Act was erroneous. Given the quality of the actual debate cited, taking place at 3.30 am in a near-empty chamber, this case does not provide the best example of when to make these references. For contemporary comment on this case, see Chandler and Holland (1995: 503).

More recently, however, case law has shown that the practice of referring to debates which, at the date when they took place, would not have been admissible as evidence in court of Parliament's intention (i.e. debates prior to 1992), may no longer be permissible: see *McDonnell* v *Congregation of Christian Brothers Trustees* [2003] UKHL 63; [2004] 1 AC 1101.

After all this initial confusion and enthusiasm things began to calm down. A trawl through the cases shows an increasing reluctance to rely on extracts from Hansard unless the guidelines noted earlier have been shown to justify the search. It is not surprising, therefore, to find more and more decisions where the courts are reluctant to allow references to Hansard without a fair bit of persuasion.

A good example of this can be seen in the comments of Silber J in *Zafar* v *Director of Public Prosecutions* [2004] EWHC 2468 (Admin); [2004] All ER (D) 06 (Nov.). The case involved the law relating to drink-driving and the accuracy of intoximeters when the driver being tested was suffering from heartburn and stomach reflux. The argument centred on the meaning of the word 'breath' in the Road Traffic Act 1988, s. 5 and the Road Traffic Offenders Act 1988, s. 15(2). When invited to refer to statements made by Baroness Blatch, as recorded in Hansard, Silber J concluded:

> [20] In my view, the appellant cannot rely on the statements of Baroness Blatch as an aid to construing the sections with which the Case Stated is concerned because first the word 'breath' in section 5 of the RTA is not ambiguous, second the statement of Baroness Blatch was not made in relation to section 5, which is the section under review and third, her statement was made not by the promoter of section 5 but as the promoter of an amendment, which was made eight years later.

The case clearly demonstrated that, merely because a particular interpretation is arguable or may lead to a perceived injustice against your client, it does not mean that the word or section is ambiguous or absurd so as to trigger a reference to Hansard. The court must be persuaded that such a reference is justified. One way to do this is to show internal inconsistencies within the Act, or to demonstrate the logical consequences of following only one line of interpretation, or to show that case law on this area has already been divided on the topic, as was the case in *Mirvahedy* v *Henley* [2001] EWCA 1749; [2002] QB 769.

Equally, it should be stressed that the mere discovery of a ministerial statement does not mean anything in itself. Not only must that statement be clear but one must also have regard to the context in which the statement was made: sometimes, for instance, it is apparent that, looking at the full text of the speech, the minister had not been purporting to construe the relevant legislation at all. One might regard this cautionary note as effectively imposing an additional requirement for the citation of Hansard. Indeed, to many, it would not even be a fourth requirement but a fifth for, as we noted earlier in this section, even in 1996 Lord Browne-Wilkinson (who set out the original 'rules') had confined references to parliamentary statements directed *to the specific statutory provision under consideration* or to the problem raised by the litigation (see *Melluish (Inspector of Taxes)* v *BMI (No. 3)* [1996] AC 454; [1995] 4 ALL ER 453).

The Irish approach, given that they use the same methods of interpretation, to this question is again interesting. There, s. 5(1) of the Interpretation Act 2005, entitled 'Construing ambiguous or obscure provisions, etc', provides similar rules to *Pepper* v *Hart* for referencing other material where there is ambiguity. It states that, 'the provision shall be given a construction that reflects the plain intention of the Oireachtas [the National Parliament] . . . where that intention can be ascertained from the Act as a whole'. Thus, investigation as to Parliament's intention is restricted to the Act itself. There are real obstacles to making use of Hansard reports. However, one method used to persuade a court to look at Hansard is to ask the judge to take the point *de bene esse*.

9.5.3 The *de bene esse* approach

This means 'For what it's worth'. A judge may take a point *de bene esse*, which means he or she will allow it to be argued for the present (i.e. conditionally or provisionally) but to make no ruling on whether, once things have been more fully argued, it will be accepted. In other words, to overcome the rather circular arguments that can arise over whether there is an absurdity and what Parliament really meant to do, judges sometimes allow the lawyer to refer them to Hansard—'without prejudice', one might say. It is a bit of a cheat—rather like looking at the answers to a crossword 'just to check' you are on the right lines. For instance, the most common application of this approach is where the court acknowledges having looked at Hansard as a confirmation of what the court has already decided, as in this example from *R* v *MK (also known as D); R* v *Gega (also known as Maione)* [2018] EWCA Crim 667; [2018] 3 All ER 566 per Lord Burnett CJ:

> [46] We have found it unnecessary to consider the Parliamentary debates in order to reach this conclusion, and we doubt whether the rule in Pepper v Hart would have permitted that course. However, having considered the material de bene esse we do not consider that it sheds any further light on Parliament's intentions.

Another example of the *de bene esse* approach in operation (though not specifically referred to) is *R* v *Hinks* [2000] 4 All ER 833 (a case dealing with the meaning of 'appropriates' in the Theft Act 1968, s. 1). Lord Steyn quoted a famous statement by Lord Reid in the *Black-Clawson* case (see section **9.3.3**) that: 'We often say that we are looking for the intention of Parliament, but that is not quite accurate. We are seeking the meaning of the words which Parliament used. We are seeking not what Parliament meant but the true meaning of what they said.' Lord Steyn used this as the basis for his refusal to allow counsel to submit (supposedly under the rule in *Pepper* v *Hart*) a memorandum written by the drafter of the Theft Act to the Larceny Sub-Committee of the Criminal Law Revision Committee, explaining what he had thought he had meant by the term 'appropriates'. At the time this was perhaps not too surprising, as it really was pushing the boundaries to argue that such a memorandum fell within the *Pepper* v *Hart* guidelines. However (illustrating the divergence of approaches in this area) within three years of *Hinks* the Court of Appeal, in *R* v *Humber Bridge Board* (noted earlier), had admitted both explanatory notes and even a 'decision letter' from the relevant Secretary of State in the interpretation of a statutory instrument (a 'decision letter' is a ministerial response to a matter arising from a formal inquiry; these letters are not statements made in Parliament and have no connexion with legislation). That documents such as 'decision letters' might be referred to therefore cast doubt on the exclusion of the memo-randum in *Hinks*.

9.5.4 What is meant by 'ambiguity'?

The triggers set out by Lord Browne-Wilkinson in *Pepper* v *Hart* for the use of Hansard require there to be an ambiguity, obscurity, or absurdity evident in the legislation. In *R* v *Secretary of State, ex parte Spath Holme* [2001] 2 AC 349; [2001] 1 All ER 195 the House of Lords confirmed the importance of these 'trigger events'.

On the facts, their Lordships held that, as the words in question were not ambiguous, reference to Hansard was not permissible. However, the key area of disagreement in this case ironically concerned what was meant by 'an ambiguity'. Their Lordships were clear that if the words in the statute were ambiguous, then Hansard could obviously now be referred to. This does not mean that just because a word may be difficult to define precisely it is ambiguous. In *Cooke* v *MGN Limited* [2014] EWHC 2831; [2015] 2 All ER 622, for instance, the High Court refused a *Pepper* v *Hart* reference on the term 'serious harm' in a defamation case on the basis that 'serious' was an ordinary word in common usage.

However, what if the words themselves were clear but there was some 'ambiguity' as to what the words were *meant to do*: what was the policy or purpose behind the statute? Could this type of ambiguity justify a reference to Hansard?

The issue in *Spath Holme* was whether a minister could issue an order capping rent increases for certain types of tenants. The words were clear as to the minister's powers; the argument was as to when he could exercise those powers. The history of the relevant statutes showed that such a power was first introduced because of massive problems of inflation in the 1970s, but updating and consolidating legislation had since been added, when no such inflation existed. All the Acts were silent as to whether the policy or pur-pose was limited to introducing capping only where there were problems of inflation or on wider grounds, but there were some statements to be found in Hansard. So, the ministerial power was clear, but was it limited to interfering only when there was high inflation, or could it be invoked for other reasons?

Lords Bingham, Hope, and Hutton felt that *Pepper* v *Hart* was never designed to allow reference to Hansard in order to ascertain what the Executive (the Government) had in mind as their policy. Their Lordships felt that this was extending the decision in *Pepper* v *Hart* well beyond its limits, which usurped the power of Parliament and the courts. However, Lords Bingham and Hope thought there might be rare instances where this would be permissible. As Lord Bingham stated (at 212a):

> Only if a minister were, improbably, to give a categorical assurance to Parliament that a power would not be used in a given situation, such that Parliament could be taken to have legislated on that basis, does it seem to me that a Parliamentary statement on the scope of a power would be properly admissible.

However, Lords Nicholls and Cooke took the opposite line and felt that *Pepper* v *Hart* 'ambiguities' *could* extend to matters of policy: 'The purpose for which a statutory power is conferred is just as much a question of interpretation of the statutory provision as is the meaning of a particular word or phrase' (*per* Lord Nicholls at 218b). Though Lord

Cooke also noted that 'Government statements, however they are made and however explicit they may be, cannot control the meaning of an Act of Parliament . . . it is for the court . . . to decide how much importance, or weight, if any, should be attached to a government statement' (at 218h).

An interesting application of *Pepper* v *Hart* and also the use of explanatory notes can be found in *The Queen (on the application of Minton Morrill Solicitors)* v *The Lord Chancellor* [2017] EWHC 612 (Admin). Here Kerr J analysed the various sources and concluded:

> [40] The explanatory notes are admissible only to help elucidate the purpose of the enactment, not to determine its meaning. . . . [The explanatory notes were found not to help here.]
>
> [42] . . .That brings me to the next question: whether recourse to Hansard is permissible and provides the answer. I have to ask myself first whether the provision is ambiguous or whether, literally construed, it leads to an absurdity. There is no question of absurdity here . . . [but] . . .
>
> [47] [T]he first of the *Pepper v. Hart* tests is satisfied: the provision is sufficiently ambiguous that recourse to Hansard is permissible for the purpose of resolving the ambiguity, subject to considering the second and third of the *Pepper v. Hart* requirements, to which I turn next.
>
> [48] The second requirement is straightforward. The Access to Justice Bill was introduced in the House of Lords. The responsible Minister was the Lord Chancellor. It is accepted that the statements relied upon come from the Lord Chancellor, who was responsible for promoting the Bill. The second requirement is satisfied. The question is then whether the third requirement is also satisfied.
>
> [49] Mr Offer says that the statements of the then Lord Chancellor in the House of Lords do not resolve the ambiguity, if there is one. He argues that the statements are silent on the critical issue, , , ,
>
> [50] In my judgment, the utterances of the Lord Chancellor make it clear that the words added to the end of what was then clause 18 of the Bill, following the query raised by Lord Ackner, were intended to ensure that legal help would be available. . . .
>
> [52] I take the view that these statements are clear and that they exclude the interpretation for which the claimant contends.

9.5.5 The practice direction

To help deal with the real and practical difficulties of referring to Hansard material, there is a practice statement relating to the use of Hansard: *Supreme Court Practice Direction* (Hansard: *Citation*) [1995] 1 WLR 192 (repeated in later consolidating Practice Directions covering the Court of Appeal (Civil Division at [1999] 1 WLR 1059, and Criminal Proceedings at [2002] 1 WLR 2870). This demands, for instance, that anyone wishing to rely on Hansard must serve copies of the extract on the court and other parties, together with a brief summary of argument, not less than five working days before the hearing.

9.5.6 Views on *Pepper* v *Hart*

There is extensive division in the legal world as to the efficacy of *Pepper* v *Hart*. Indeed, there is some division between the authors of this book. There are certainly undoubted advantages in making use of all relevant materials to interpret a statute, and the cases to date have often allowed perceived justice to win over technicalities. The rule was being eroded prior to 1992 anyway, in practice if not in law. Equally, Lord Mackay's words as to the extra level of research and costs involved in litigation should not be disposed of lightly. Possibly more pertinent to this book is the fact that practitioners, academics, and law students have to include such references in their research. On a wider scale, however, one of the objections to *Pepper* v *Hart* might be that it encourages (perhaps even obliges) the courts to adopt an assumption of ministerial infallibility when describing the meaning or purpose of statutory language.

9.5.7 Current trends regarding *Pepper* v *Hart*

After the initial 'settling-in' period it became obvious that all was not well within the judiciary as regards the operation of *Pepper* v *Hart*. Some judges took a very strict approach to the use of Hansard; some made use of the *de bene esse* approach (though usually concluded that the reference had either been of no help or simply confirmed the decision they would have come to anyway). Others were minded to allow reference, even where the rules for reference laid out in *Pepper* v *Hart* were not adhered to (but then neither did their Lordships do so in *Pepper* v *Hart* itself).

By the late 1990s and the early part of the twenty-first century the divisions of opinion on *Pepper* v *Hart* (even within the House of Lords) were becoming very obvious. In 1997 Lord Hoffmann and Lightman J expressed their views, extrajudicially (meaning, not in a case but in a lecture or article), that there were problems with *Pepper* v *Hart*. Lord Millett, in another lecture, referred to the case as 'a regrettable decision'. Then, in 2000, a powerful attack on the use of Hansard was launched by Lord Steyn in his Oxford Hart Lecture and published shortly afterwards in the *Oxford Journal of Legal Studies* (see Steyn, 2001)— the reference to 'Hart' is coincidental and relates to one of our great jurists. Although another extrajudicial statement, this lecture was viewed as sounding warning bells that *Pepper* v *Hart* should only be used in limited cases; or even as sounding its death knell.

From that moment on the cases show what has been called a 'retreat from *Pepper* v *Hart*'. Even one of the early uses of *Pepper* v *Hart* by the House of Lords (in *Stubbings* v *Webb*) has been overturned by another House of Lords' case for placing too much weight on non-statutory material (see *A* v *Hoare* [2008] UKHL 6; [2008] 1 AC 844).

Yet, in the midst of this 'retreat', as we have seen, there were cases such as *R* v *Humber Bridge Board*, permitting references to explanatory notes (the reference to which does not require an ambiguity in the Act) and *R (on the application of Amicus-MSF Section)* v *Secretary of State for Trade and Industry* [2004] EWHC (Admin) 860, admitting a letter from the General of the General Synod and the Archbishops' Council to the Parliamentary Joint Committee on statutory instruments. So, while references to Hansard were falling into disuse, other non-statutory material was being admitted. Lord Steyn defended such to-ing and fro-ing in *R (Westminster City Council)* v *National Asylum Support Service* [2002] UKHL 38; [2002] 1 WLR 2956 on the basis that references to explanatory notes did not evoke the same sort of constitutional arguments witnessed in Hansard references. However, that dodges the unequal resources argument and the possible deliberate influencing of statutory interpretation by ministers and their civil servants, using extra-legislative material to aid their cause.

Equally, as noted in a fascinating article by Professor Vogenauer (designed as a reply to Lord Steyn's lecture) the Court of Appeal throughout this time has not shown the same level of antagonism to *Pepper* v *Hart* as had been witnessed in the House of Lords— which is ironic given that they started the whole thing. On a key point, for instance, the

House of Lords have demonstrated time and again that references to Hansard are generally inadmissible except to bind Parliament to ministerial assurances given on the limitations of the legislation (what is sometimes called the 'estoppel' argument, meaning that the government should be stopped or prevented from relying on statements which support their own later preferred interpretation).

At the same time the Court of Appeal has tended to disregard this view and perceive *Pepper* v *Hart* references in a much more welcoming light on a much wider range of issues (see Vogenauer, 2005). However, even here the Court of Appeal (*obiter*) has at times shown antagonism to *Pepper* v *Hart* as regards its use in interpreting penal statutes (see *Massey* v *Boulden* [2002] EWCA Civ 1634; [2003] 1 WLR 1792). The doubts on using Hansard references in criminal cases were expressed forcefully by Lord Phillips of Worth Matravers CJ again in *Thet* v *Director of Public Prosecutions* [2007] 1 WLR 2002 but *obiter* observations from the same learned judge in *R* v *Tabnak* [2007] EWCA Crim 380; [2007] 1 WLR 1317 indicated that *Pepper* v *Hart* could be invoked by a *defendant* in a criminal case. Interestingly, in *R* v *JTB* [2009] UKHL 20; [2009] 2 WLR 1088 the same judge made use of Hansard (and the other Law Lords agreed) but this time in favour of the prosecution. The case was a criminal case where the defendant was tried on counts of causing or inciting a child under 13 to engage in sexual activity. He had been 12 years old at the time of the alleged offences. At one time there was a rebuttable presumption that a child aged 10–14 was *doli incapax* (incapable of committing an offence). However, the Crime and Disorder Act 1998, s. 34 stated: 'The rebuttable presumption of criminal law that a child aged 10 or over is incapable of committing an offence is hereby abolished.' The technical argument was whether only the presumption had been abolished or the whole defence. To decide this, Lord Phillips used a number of aids described earlier but also turned to entries in Hansard, stating at [35]:

> I further consider that this is one of the rare cases where it is both legitimate and helpful to consider ministerial statements in Parliament under the principle in *Pepper* v *Hart* [1993] AC 593. Furthermore, the proposed amendment was moved on the premise that the clause, as drafted, would abolish not merely the presumption but the defence of doli incapax.

On this analysis, the boy was not able to make use of the defence—so here is a case where a *Pepper* v *Hart* reference was used in a criminal case as against the defendant. All their Lordships referred to this as a 'rare event' but it demonstrates that there is no hard-and-fast rule here.

It is worth noting the words of the editor of *Statute Law Review* here as regards both *Pepper* v *Hart* and the use of other materials in a 2014 setting:

> [L]aw students have always been taught to identify the range of materials to which the courts will have regard in determining the mischief or context of legislation. Nowadays it would be more tempting to give students a list of materials to which the courts will not have regard; except that since Pepper v. Hart it is not at all clear that there would be any items on the list.
>
> Year on year the courts appear to expand both the range of materials to which they are happy to have regard in making decisions about interpretation and application and also the extent of the reliance that they are prepared to place on those materials.
>
> (2014: v)

We conclude this account with a fascinating comment from Lord Hope DP made back in 2010, in *Bocardo SA* v *Star Energy UK Onshore Ltd and another* [2010] UKSC 35; [2010] 3 All ER 975 at [106]:

> I have come to this conclusion in the light of the legislation and general principles of law applicable to compulsory acquisition. It is true that what was said on the second reading of what became the 1934 Act (quoted by Lord Brown at [76]) supports the view that what was envisaged was loss of amenity value. But I prefer not to take that into account in the light of the continuing controversy over Pepper (Inspector of Taxes) v Hart [1993] 1 All ER 42, [1993] AC 593 and its limits.

Certainly, nearly all modern references to *Pepper* v *Hart* in the case law concern rejection of the use of Hansard rather than acceptance. To many, *Pepper* v *Hart* is like the visitor who has overstayed his welcome.

9.5.8 *Pepper* v *Hart* and human rights cases

The Human Rights Act 1998 (see section **9.7** and the full discussion in **Chapter 10**), has also arguably added to the pressure on courts to look to Hansard in the process of assessing whether legislation is compatible with the United Kingdom's obligations under the European Convention on Human Rights. It has become increasingly common for evidence from government departments in such cases to contain lengthy memoranda detailing the legislative history and debate about the statutory provision under examination. This practice has, however, also attracted a certain amount of criticism from the judiciary, most notably in *Wilson* v *First County Trust* [2003] UKHL 40, where Lord Nicholls observed:

> 66. I expect that occasions when resort to Hansard is necessary as part of the statutory 'compatibility' exercise will seldom arise. The present case is not such an occasion. Should such an occasion arise the courts must be careful not to treat the ministerial or other statement as indicative of the objective intention of Parliament. Nor should the courts give a ministerial statement, whether made inside or outside Parliament, determinative weight. It should not be supposed that members necessarily agreed with the minister's reasoning or his conclusions.
>
> 67. Beyond this use of Hansard as a source of background information, the content of parliamentary debates has no direct relevance to the issues the court is called upon to decide in compatibility cases and, hence, these debates are not a proper matter for investigation or consideration by the courts . . .

So, even in the context of human rights legislation, *Wilson* did not really change the pattern of the 'retreat' from *Pepper* v *Hart*. At the moment, therefore, we can only say that any reliance on references to Hansard, in the context of human rights or wider, is fraught with difficulties.

9.5.9 Summary of *Pepper* v *Hart*

Pepper v *Hart* represented a major shift in interpretive techniques (as well as stirring up a whole range of constitutional issues). After initially being received by many with enthusiasm, it now looks a bit like last year's Christmas toy. The current rules appear to be:

- The starting point now seems to be to regard Hansard as generally inadmissible. Consequently, even the sleight-of-hand *de bene esse* arguments have generally fallen from favour.

- If it is admissible, the three triggers originally identified in *Pepper v Hart* itself must be present. On the meaning of 'ambiguity' see *R v Secretary of State, ex parte Spath Holme* and *Mirvahedy v Henley*.

- If it is admissible it seems that it is confined to cases which turn on the meaning of words in the legislation, not on questions of the policy behind the Act.

- An exception to this is seen in *Spath Holme*, where references can be used as *against the Government* to show how a minister gave a categorical assurance on the use of discretionary powers—what is sometimes termed the 'estoppel' argument (*estoppel* being a Norman-French word meaning that where a person acts on your words or conduct there are limitations on how much you can then change your position if this adversely affects the other person).

- The High Court and Court of Appeal have adopted a more liberal attitude to references to Hansard. There is therefore some conflict between the Supreme Court and the lower courts.

- Even the Court of Appeal has intimated that Hansard cannot be used in certain situations (see the *obiter* comments in *Massey v Boulden* as regards use in penal statutes).

- The use of material such as explanatory notes and headings does not fall under the same set of limitations (*R v Montilla*). Such materials—once thought irrelevant to interpretation—now regularly make an appearance in counsels' arguments and judges' decisions.

- If there is authority on a point which was reached at a time when Hansard was not admissible, this should not be departed from (*McDonnell*). Contrast this to the case of Thomas Witter (dealt with at section **9.5.2**).

9.6 From rules to reality

The question posed by all students at some stage is: in what order will the rules be applied? The analysis of statutory interpretation found in many textbooks begs the same question. Most of them fail to answer it. The reality is that not only is there no answer; it is the wrong question to ask.

The right question is: how do judges choose to explain the construction they have placed on the statute? Posed this way the question recognises, as Willis put it, that there is not 'one great sun of a *principle*, "the plain meaning rule", around which revolves in planetary order a series of minor rules of construction. . . . Any one of these approaches may be selected by your court' (1938: 1). There is no rule that says a judge must look at the literal meaning of words first. The fact that many judges do this is simply the recognition that most English judges do not want to be seen to be *creating* law, and a logical starting point in reading any document is to see what has actually been written. By examining the literal meaning of the words, judges appear to take a logical and safe line. However, if they wish then to rely on a more purposive argument, they will do so by finding absurdity or inconsistency; they have at least guarded against some criticism.

9.6.1 Styles of interpretation

We would suggest that interpretation is a question of *style*, not rules. By emphasising the *style* of judging we would draw a parallel with Llewellyn's analysis of how judges use case law (a view now supported by Lundmark and Waller: 2017). In 1960 Llewellyn drew attention to two different approaches used by judges; he termed these 'grand' and 'formal'. The 'grand' style reflects a judicial willingness to base a decision on public policy and to take a creative or flexible approach to precedent. Conversely, the 'formal' style demands rigid adherence to traditional doctrine and the denial of a creative judicial function.

So too, we submit, is this the case with statutory interpretation. Judges who employ the 'grand' style place substantial emphasis on the external context of the statute. They place less weight on the dictionary meaning of words, preferring to seek out the sense of the provision in question. One who adopts the 'formal' style, however, is more concerned with the form the statute takes, the internal context, and the perceived hierarchy of the rules.

The formalist will, therefore, frequently seek to find a safe embarkation point in a literal approach. This does not prevent the formalist then making use of the golden and mischief rules; but this method of 'follow the pathways' analysis provides appropriate justification for departing from a strictly literal interpretation. Such 'formalism' can be seen extensively in the House of Lords' decision in *Duport Steel* v *Sirs* (cited in section **9.3.1**).

On the other hand, the 'grand' style will encompass those judges who will tend to move much more easily to reliance on the external context for interpretation. Such can be seen in *Royal College of Nursing* v *DHSS*; but equally its ranks will also be filled by judges prepared to go beyond this point to using a 'teleological' approach. A teleological approach is a rather grandiose name for an interpretation which is based on the purpose or object of the text confronting the judge. It goes beyond the inquiry as to the external context of the Act; examining instead the broader social, economic, perhaps political reasons behind the Act. It thereby attempts to give the fullest effect to the grand design of the law. It is, in the end, not really different from a purposive approach; it is more an extreme method of discovering that purpose and surfaces more in the analytical styles of European judges than in English law.

The hallmark of the 'grand' style is often that the approach is extremely credible from a common-sense viewpoint: the authority for such (often) sweeping statements is less clear.

9.6.2 Example of the use of different styles

In support of the foregoing analysis any examples are inevitably somewhat selective. However, we suggest that a good illustration of these styles in action is a case we first mentioned in **Chapter 6** concerning *stare decisis*: *Davis* v *Johnson* [1979] AC 264; [1978] 1 All ER 841 (CA) and 1132 (HL).

Jennifer Davis and Nehemiah Johnson were joint tenants of a council flat. Davis was subjected to extreme violence by Johnson and eventually fled the flat with her infant child. She applied to the county court, under the Domestic Violence and Matrimonial Proceedings Act 1976 (DVA), s. 1, for an injunction restraining Johnson from assaulting or molesting her or the child and ordering him to vacate the flat and not return. At first the injunction was granted and then withdrawn. We are concerned with the case in the Court of Appeal and the House of Lords. The case illustrates the points we have been making because, even when the various judges were agreed as to the outcome, their approaches to the question of interpretation differed extensively.

The case is dealt with in texts mainly as regards the issue of *stare decisis* raised by the Court of Appeal's judgment. We will not dwell on that aspect of the case in this analysis. However, the case is a fine example of the areas of judicial precedent and statutory interpretation overlapping; and this is an aspect of statutory interpretation that is worth noting. As with judicial precedent, cases concerning statutory interpretation do not exist in isolation. When a court is considering the meaning of a statute it will frequently have to interpret it in the light of previously decided cases.

Returning to *Davis v Johnson*: in the Court of Appeal Lord Denning MR, Sir George Baker P., and Shaw LJ found in favour of Ms Davis and the injunction was granted. Lords Justices Goff and Cumming-Bruce dissented. The House of Lords unanimously dismissed Johnson's further appeal. These are three points we need to examine here:

(i)   What was the question of interpretation?

(ii)   How did the judges in the Court of Appeal set about the question of interpreting the statute?; and

(iii) How did the House of Lords interpret the statute?

We shall now consider each of these.

What was the question of interpretation?

The DVA, s. 1 stated:

> (1) Without prejudice to the jurisdiction of the High Court, on an application by a party to a marriage a county court shall have jurisdiction to grant an injunction containing . . . [(a) and (b) are irrelevant here] . . . (c) a provision excluding the other party from the matrimonial home . . .
>
> (2) Subsection (1) above shall apply to a man and a woman who are living with each other in the same household as husband and wife as it applies to the parties to a marriage and any reference to the matrimonial home shall be construed accordingly.

So, did this section apply to the case in hand? It was argued that s. 1 was procedural in its effect; it had not changed the existing law on property rights and could not have been meant to do away with these rights. In other words, if the man had property rights in the home (e.g. as a joint tenant, as was the case here), he could not be excluded from the property.

The *stare decisis* point (see **Chapter 6**) was that there were two binding Court of Appeal decisions where similar applicants to Davis had failed: *B v B* [1978] Fam 26; [1978] 1 All ER 821 and *Cantliff* v *Jenkins* [1978] 2 WLR 177n; [1978] 1 All ER 836.

How did the judges in the Court of Appeal set about the question of interpreting the statute?

Lord Denning began by recounting the history of the Act—an Act designed to protect 'battered wives'. He then commented that 'No one, I would have thought, could possibly dispute that those plain words [s. 1 above] by themselves cover this very case.' One sees here a reliance on the literal reading of the section (though without full explanation) and hence the 'formal' style in operation.

In reviewing the two earlier Court of Appeal decisions, Lord Denning set about proving they had inadequately interpreted the section. If *B* v *B* was right, he argued, the only woman who could obtain an injunction would be one who owned the property solely. Thus, he said, 'In order to give s. 1 any effect at all, the court must be allowed to override the property rights of the man' (849b). Even when faced with House of Lords authority which appeared to give preference to the protection of property rights, Lord Denning reacted: 'Social justice requires that personal rights should, in a proper case, be given priority over rights of property . . . I prefer to go by the principles underlying the legislative enactments rather than the out-dated notions of the past' (849e–f). This is a purposive approach in the 'grand' style. The term 'social justice' looks like a logical and analytical argument, but in fact it has appeared from nowhere. Try to look up 'social justice' as a legal term of art: you will have difficulty.

Lord Denning then returned to the history of the Act and investigated Reports of Select Committees and statements made in Parliament. This was more than simple reliance on the 'mischief rule' and again demonstrates a 'grand' style purposive approach.

Sir George Baker P. began by discerning the 'mischief' on which the DVA centred by reference to legal history and the long title of the Act. There is nothing apparently unconventional in this. On the whole this is still a 'formal' approach; though it moves away from the strict canons of interpretation by its premature use of the long title. That mischief was the protection of family partners (married or unmarried) from violence. His analysis continued on a 'formal' basis: he rejected the idea that only a woman who was a sole owner could bring such an action. This interpretation he justified on the grounds that any other interpretation would deprive the Act of any practical meaning or purpose. Although Sir George Baker P. talks of 'purpose', the style of the judgment is still 'formal'. He had to make the point as to 'purpose' in order to overcome the decision in *B* v *B*. What he is actually saying is that:

(i) a literal reading of s. 1 produces this solution; it gives the woman a right to have the violent male excluded; it does not even mention a limit to be placed on this; and

(ii) it was the earlier cases which had gone beyond this literal reading by importing into the wording the sanctity of property rights and, in doing so, had not implemented the purpose of the Act. He is therefore arguing that it is the use of a 'formal' style which produces the real purpose and not the 'grand' style.

Lord Justice Shaw first considered that the meaning of the section was plain: nothing in the wording took account of the 'other party's' property rights so it could not have intended this to be relevant. He reviewed the arguments to the contrary, and, though attracted by them, concluded that the 'section would be utterly stultified' if nobody but a sole owner could gain the injunction. The general theme of the section was to subordinate property rights to the need to protect the victim of violence. Lord Justice Shaw's decision thus has a strong 'formalist' feel about it, though there are odd hints of a wider approach such as: 'The construction of a statute dealing with a morbid aspect of society must, it seems to me, be pursued in the practical context of the evil sought to be remedied rather than with analytical detachment' (876a).

Lord Justice Goff (dissenting) dwelled on the *stare decisis* aspect and felt bound by the earlier decisions, although he expressly did not agree with them. However, he made some comment on the interpretation of the section. He reiterated the point that a woman should not have to be sole owner of the home in order to make the application, for this would deprive the section of all effect. Lord Justice Goff continued in a classic 'formalist' vein by analysing the relationship of s. 1 to other parts of the Act. He concluded that, if he were free of binding precedent, he would adopt a 'liberal approach' and grant the injunction because:

> the strict construction . . . virtually strikes the power of eviction in s. 1(1)(c) . . . since where the (woman) is sole owner of the property she does not need it . . . yet where she is not sole owner and so the Act is needed to protect her from just the same evil, it is held inapplicable.
>
> (874: d)

His Lordship was prepared to make reference to the mischief of the Act, but only by discovering that mischief on the accepted (limited) grounds. The meaning of Parliament, he said, must still be found in the words used in the Act.

Lord Justice Cumming-Bruce (also dissenting) agreed with the decision in *B v B* and, for the most part, with Goff LJ; but concentrated his reasoning on points of precedent. The tenor of his judgment is in the 'formal' style. This is particularly noticeable in his references to the mischief rule and his consequent disapproval of using debates in Parliament to assess the purpose behind the Act on which he says (at 885):

> The task of this court is to decide what the words of the Act mean. The subject should be able, as in the past, to read the words of an Act and decide its meaning without hunting through Hansard to see whether the Act has a different meaning from that which is to be collected by application of the subtle principles of construction that this court has worked out over the last three centuries.

How did the House of Lords interpret the statute?

The House of Lords unanimously dismissed Johnson's appeal but the Law Lords were not of one mind in their reasoning.

Lord Diplock stated a preference for a narrow 'formal' approach to the interpretation of s. 1, to which he added adverse comment on the practice of looking at reports on parliamentary debate to discern the meaning of a statute. This latter point was treated in the same way by the other Law Lords.

Viscount Dilhorne stated (at 1145) that the 'language is clear and unambiguous and Parliament's intention apparent'. To differentiate between married and non-married women would 'frustrate the intention of Parliament'. At first sight this appears to be a 'formal' style; but it is difficult to see from where Viscount Dilhorne derives his conclusions apart from the line (at 1145): 'Subsection (1) is not concerned with property rights.'

Lord Kilbrandon took a literal approach to the section; expressly agreeing with Lord Salmon and Lord Scarman.

Lord Salmon adopted a 'formal' style, moving from a literal reading ('It has been said that its [s. 1] meaning is as plain as a pikestaff. I agree') to a more purposive stance based on an examination of the legal history of the Act and the mischief it sought to remedy. This also illustrates our point that judges can use any of the so-called 'rules of interpretation' as they feel it necessary to do so in order to explain their conclusions.

Finally, Lord Scarman also looked to the mischief the Act was designed to remedy. Out of this Lord Scarman identified the purpose of the Act and had no difficulty extending this purpose to allow an unmarried woman with no property rights to be, nevertheless, granted the injunction. His Lordship's speech lies between the 'formal' and 'grand' styles. Lord Scarman concentrates on the mischief. There are wide statements of purpose (at 1156): 'I would expect Parliament, when dealing with the mischief of domestic violence, to legislate in such a way that property rights would not be allowed to undermine or diminish the protection being afforded.'

All this illustrates the point that the logic of decision-making (and the method of reaching those decisions) does not follow one particular, predictable, line. For instance, if one just adds up the decisions of all the judges (merely who won and who lost) in this case as well as *B v B* and *Cantliff v Jenkins*, one finds seven Lords Justices on one side and the Master of the Rolls, the President of the Family Division, and two Lords Justices, together with five Law Lords on the other. And, as we have shown, this simple arithmetic does not reveal the diversity of approach. Even where the judges are in agreement as to the outcome, the route they followed in getting there is not always shared by others. And one judge does not always maintain a consistent style. You may recall that Lord Denning, in *Davis v Johnson*, relies on a literal reading of the section at one stage, only to turn to the purpose of the Act later. He was not alone in doing this and you, as an advocate, should be prepared, in the same way, to advance arguments along different fronts.

9.6.3 Criticisms of the styles of interpretation

Two final points need to be made here. First, it is very tempting to criticise those who adopt the 'grand' or purposive style as inventing reasons to fit decisions they have already reached. But on closer examination, when a judge adopts a more 'formal' style it is still often difficult to understand exactly where *the purpose* to which he refers came from, as we can see with the treatment of the phrase 'living with each other'. The 'formal' style, ranging from literalism through to a more purposive approach, is not automatically entitled to be termed logical.

Secondly, if you approach the problems of interpretation by only asking 'Which rule will be used?', you will miss the point. To adapt the chess analogy we used in **Chapter 7**: knowing that your opponent *can* 'castle' does not tell you that he *will* 'castle'. There is no set moment when your opponent will 'castle'—if at all. And if you are playing chess and do not know what 'castling' is, and when it may be used, you are at a serious disadvantage. Thus, the rules describe the limits of what *may* happen; and they tell you what will *not* happen. Your opponent cannot move his pawn as if it were a knight, for instance. Equally there are limitations placed, by convention and common sense, on even the most purposive of judges. The rules may tell you *what* will happen in terms of basic structure; they cannot tell you *how* the game will progress. Each player has his own style.

We agree, therefore, with Twining and Miers that 'We do not believe that there is one right answer in hard cases or that problems of interpretation can be solved primarily by rules' (1991: 376) and with Zander that 'The rules and principles of interpretation therefore do nothing to solve problems. They suggest arguments that can be advanced and then justify conclusions often reached on other grounds' (2004: 184). It is not unfair for a student new to legal studies to ask which rule will be used; it is unfair, however, for us to pretend there is a 'right' answer.

However, most of your academic life will be spent presenting an argument for one side (the same will be true if you go on to practise law). Your problem does not therefore lie in which approach you should use to *determine* a case: that will not be your function. Instead, your problem lies in determining which approach to adopt so that your argument is at its most convincing. Consequently, if you can master the types of reasoning available to you described in this chapter and learn to judge when one style is more applicable than another, then you will have done all you can in presenting your argument professionally. The fact then that there is no single correct way to read a statute becomes a less daunting prospect.

9.7 Interpretation and the Human Rights Act 1998

In **Chapter 10** we will deal with the topic of human rights at some length. For the moment we can note the following:

- The Human Rights Act (HRA) 1998 selectively incorporates elements of the European Convention on Human Rights by giving them a special legal status as 'Convention rights' under s. 1 of the Act.
- The HRA 1998 requires judges to interpret legislation, so far as possible, consistently with Convention rights, and where consistency cannot be achieved, to declare such laws incompatible with Convention rights.

Thus, there is the potential that courts may be presented with arguments which require the judges to embark upon a radical rethink of all legislation that comes before them, whenever that legislation was enacted. However, it should also be noted that the case of *Price* v *Leeds City Council* [2005] EWCA Civ 289; [2005] 1 WLR 1825 determined that where there is a conflict between (what are now) Supreme Court decisions and those of the European Court of Human Rights, precedent demands that the Supreme Court be followed.

9.8 Interpreting secondary legislation

When looking at the rules of statutory interpretation, it is easy to forget that much legislation is not created by statute but by statutory instrument or by-law. You will recall that we considered the growth, and importance, of this whole area of 'secondary legislation' in **Chapter 1**. We now need to consider the principles of interpretation that apply to secondary, or delegated, legislation.

As a starting point, we can say that generally the same rules do apply, which is a relief. The courts will look at the words used in a regulation, and interpret them according to their immediate linguistic context, only straying beyond this point in cases where the judge finds some absurdity or ambiguity demanding a more purposive approach. However, within this framework there are a number of substantive differences which reflect the fact that delegated legislation is, ultimately, a different creature from primary legislation.

This is because delegated legislation does not stand alone, in the way that an Act of Parliament does; it forms part of a legislative 'package' which includes the parent Act, and possibly other sets of regulations, which may affect our assessment of meaning. It is also because the courts are less constrained by problems of sovereignty when dealing with secondary as opposed to primary legislation.

These various differences can be explored in relation to two issues: the way in which we define the context of secondary legislation; and the way in which the courts handle questions of validity.

9.8.1 Defining the context

As we have said, delegated legislation is to be read within a potentially wider context than statute law. The meaning of a particular provision is to be ascertained from the whole body of regulations of which it forms part, the parent Act and the common law. Exceptionally, the environment within which the regulations operate may also be considered as part of the context. The part played by each of these will be considered.

The regulations

The principle here is the same as that applied to statute. Just as you would not take one section of an Act out of context, so you should not consider a regulation outside its instrument. This may be particularly important if a reading of the parent Act offers alternative interpretations.

The parent Act

This is of central importance in defining meaning. This is emphasised by the fact that the Interpretation Act 1978, s. 11 requires words used in secondary legislation to be read as having the same meaning as in the parent Act, unless a contrary intention appears. That is fine, of course, so long as the meaning in the empowering legislation is clear! If it is not, the court has to work it out for itself, from possibly a variety of competing explanations. Where there are doubts about the meaning of a word used within the parent Act, then it seems permissible for the court to look at both the parent Act and the regulations in assessing meaning: see *Nurse* v *Morganite Crucible Ltd* [1989] AC 692; [1989] 1 All ER 113.

The common law

This can also be of significance. The courts will be reluctant to interpret any delegated legislation in such a way that it conflicts with an established and fundamental principle of common law. For example, in *R* v *Secretary of State for the Home Department ex parte Anderson* [1984] QB 778; [1984] 1 All ER 920, the Court had to assess the validity of order 5A(34) made by the Secretary of State under powers contained within the Prison Rules 1964, which were themselves made under the authority of the Prison Act 1952, s. 47(1). The order sought to prevent prisoners from obtaining visits from their legal advisers regarding complaints about their treatment in prison. Section 47(1) was silent in respect of such rights of access, so the Court resorted to the common law. As a result, it held that the fundamental right of access to the courts was wide enough to include a prisoner's right of access to legal advice. Parliament could not be deemed to have legislated against that right purely by implication, so order 5A(34) was held invalid. The courts' powers to declare secondary legislation invalid is a point we now also need to address.

9.8.2 The principle of validity

We noted in **Chapter 1** that the courts have the power to declare secondary legislation invalid where it involves an exercise of power exceeding that granted by Parliament. The decision to invalidate is thus dependent upon a question of interpreting, first, the scope of the powers contained within the delegated legislation and, secondly, the scope of the grant within the parent Act. In dealing with these situations, the courts have developed a number of principles.

First, in some specific instances, they have ruled that delegated legislation may only do certain things if there is express authorisation within the parent statute. There are two particularly significant situations where this applies:

(i) The courts apply a presumption against retrospectivity to prevent instruments affecting events which precede their introduction. The presumption may be used to require not only that the possibility of retrospective effect is specifically alluded to within the instrument, but that it was also within the ambit of the original grant of power by Parliament—see, for example, *Marshall's Township Syndicate Ltd* v *Johannesburg Consolidated Investment Co. Ltd* [1920] AC 420, *Webb* v *Ipswich Borough Council* (1989) 21 HLR 325.

(ii) Parliament will not be presumed to have authorised the amendment of primary legislation by secondary legislation without clear authority within the parent Act. Thus, in the case of *McKiernan* v *Secretary of State, Guardian*, 28 October 1989, the Court of Appeal refused to imply that social security regulations modified an otherwise mandatory condition laid down under the parent Act in the absence of express authority. Even where such powers have been granted, the courts have tended to construe them narrowly.

Secondly, the courts have, as we suggested at the beginning of this section, shown a marked reluctance to allow secondary legislation to be invalidated purely because of problems of ambiguity or uncertainty—*Percy* v *Hall* [1996] 4 All ER 523. The courts have used the maxim *ut res magis valeat quam pereat* ('it is better for a thing to have effect than to be void') to justify whichever of competing interpretations would be a valid exercise of power. This principle has become widely used in common law jurisdictions to avoid treating delegated legislation as *ultra vires*. Strictly speaking, it should not be adopted in cases where the meaning of the regulation is clear from the face of the document, or where its application would require a virtual rewriting of the legislation. In that respect it is no more than a manifestation of the rules against ambiguity.

Thirdly, in cases where delegated legislation is only partially invalid, the courts recognise that they have a power of 'severance'. Severance is a process whereby invalid portions of a document may be separated from those which are valid, leaving those valid parts still standing. As such, it can be seen as a derivative of the principle of validity. The mechanics of 'severance' are extremely complex and we do not recommend that you consider them in any greater detail at this stage in your studies.

9.9 Illustration of how to analyse a case on statutory interpretation

The following case illustrates a number of these points on statutory interpretation. After the headnote, etc., the judgment is noted in the left-hand column, with notes on legal method aspects appearing in the right-hand column. The case contains many of the aspects discussed throughout this book and highlighted earlier in the chapter—the notable exceptions, because of the specific issues and the date the case was heard, being that of any EU law or human rights references.

Director of Public Prosecutions v Bull [1994] 3 WLR 1196
[QUEEN'S BENCH DIVISION]
1994 March 28: Mann LJ and Laws J
May 5

CATCHWORDS

Crime—Sexual offences—Soliciting—Man charged as common prostitute—Whether 'common prostitute' applying exclusively to women—Street Offences Act 1959 (c. 57), ss. 1(1), 2(1)

HEADNOTE

The term 'common prostitute' in s. 1(1) of the Street Offences Act 1959 applies exclusively to female prostitutes. Where, therefore, a stipendiary magistrate accepted a submission of no case to answer to a charge that a male respondent, being a common prostitute, loitered in a street or public place for the purpose of prostitution, contrary to s. 1(1) of the Act of 1959, and the prosecution appealed:
Held, dismissing the appeal, that the submission of no case to answer had been rightly accepted (post, p. 1201C–D, G).

CITATIONS

The following cases are referred to in the judgment of Mann LJ:
Fothergill v *Monarch Airlines Ltd* [1981] AC 251; [1980] 3 WLR 209; [1980] 2 All ER 696, HL(E)
Pepper v *Hart* [1993] AC 593; [1992] 3 WLR 1032; [1993] 1 All ER 42, HL(E)
R v *De Munck* [1918] 1 KB 635, CCA
R v *McFarlane* [1994] QB 419; [1994] 2 WLR 494; [1994] 2 All ER 283, CA
Wicks v *Firth* [1983] 2 AC 214; [1983] 2 WLR 34; [1983] 1 All ER 151, HL(E)

The following additional cases were cited in argument:
Dale v *Smith* [1967] 1 WLR 700; [1967] 2 All ER 1133, DC
R v *Ford (Graham)* [1977] 1 WLR 1083; [1978] 1 All ER 1129, CA
R v *Gray* (1981) 74 Cr App R 324, CA
R v *Kirkup* [1993] 1 WLR 774; [1993] 2 All ER 802, CA
R v *Webb* [1964] 1 QB 357; 3 WLR 638; [1963] 3 All ER 177, CCA

FACTS

Case Stated by the Wells Street Metropolitan Stipendiary Magistrate.
(Statement of facts as appears in the report omitted. Facts are stated in the judgment below.)

COUNSEL

Jeremy Carter-Manning QC and John McGuinness for the applicant.
Adrian Fulford for the respondent.
Cur. adv. vult.

JUDGMENT	COMMENTS ON THE TEXT

5th May

Mann LJ read the following judgment: There is before the court an appeal by way of case stated. The appellant is the Director of Public Prosecutions and the respondent is Andrew John Bull. The case has been stated by Mr Ian Michael Baker, metropolitan stipendiary magistrate for the Inner London commission area, in respect of his adjudication as a magistrates' court sitting at Wells Street Magistrates' Court, London, W1, on 27 April 1993.

§ *History of the case*

§ *A stipendiary magistrate is now called a District Judge (Criminal) or District Judge (Magistrates' Court)*

On that day Mr Baker had before him a charge against the respondent to the effect that on 4 December 1992 he, being a common prostitute, did loiter in a street or public place for the purpose of prostitution contrary to section 1(1) of the Street Offences Act 1959. At the conclusion of the prosecution case counsel for the respondent submitted that there was no case to answer on the basis that section 1(1) applies only to female prostitutes. This submission was upheld by the magistrate, who has now posed this question for the opinion of the court:

§ *Outline of facts and arguments*

Whether I was correct in construing section 1(1) of the Street Offences Act 1959 so as to limit it to the activities of female prostitutes and to exclude from its scope the activities of male prostitutes.

§ *Phrasing of the Case Stated by the magistrate for consideration in the High Court*

The magistrate made certain findings of fact to which I think it unnecessary to refer. Suffice to say that he remarks in paragraph 7 of the case stated that had the submission not been accepted he would have held that there was a case to answer. So far as is material, the long title to the Act of 1959 is:

An Act to make, as respects England and Wales, further provision against loitering or soliciting in public places for the purpose of prostitution . . .

§ *Indeterminate reference made to long title*

The further provision is to be found in sections 1 and 2. The material subsections of section 1 are subsections (1) (2) (as substituted by the Criminal Justice Act 1982, section 71) and (3):

§ *Key aspects of section 1 highlighted*

1. It shall be an offence for a common prostitute to loiter or solicit in a street or public place for the purpose of prostitution.

§ *Wording of the Act (as later amended)*

2. A person guilty of an offence under this section shall be liable on summary conviction to a fine of an amount not exceeding level 2 on the standard scale . . . or, for an offence committed after a previous conviction, to a fine of an amount not exceeding level 3 on that scale.

3. A constable may arrest without warrant anyone he finds in a street or public place and suspects, with reasonable cause, to be committing an offence under this section.

The material subsection of section 2 is subsection (1), which provides:

§ *Reference to a related section in the Act*

Where a woman is cautioned by a constable, in respect of her conduct in a street or public place, that if she persists in such conduct it may result in her being charged with an offence under section 1 of this Act, she may not later than 14 clear days afterwards apply to a magistrates' court for an order directing that there is to be no entry made in respect of that caution in any record maintained by the police of those so cautioned and that any such entry already made is to be expunged; and the court shall make the order unless satisfied that on the occasion when she was cautioned she was loitering or soliciting in a street or public place for the purpose of prostitution.

The other legislative provision which is material is the earlier section 32 of the Sexual Offences Act 1956, which provides: 'It is an offence for a man persistently to solicit or importune in a public place for immoral purposes.'

§ *Reference to a related Statute (of three years earlier)*

As Mr Jeremy Carter-Manning for the appellant pointed out, there are differences between the components of an offence under section 32 of the Act of 1956 and those of an offence under section 1(1) of the Act of 1959. Thus (i) section 32 requires actual soliciting *or importuning*; section 1(1) requires either actual soliciting *or loitering* (ii) section 32 requires *persistence*;

Section 1(1) does not, and (iii) section 32 requires *an immoral purpose*; section 1(1) requires a *prostitutional purpose*.

§ *Key differences in the working of the two Acts observed*

The submission for the appellant was that section 1(1) of the Act of 1959 is unambiguous and is not gender specific. Our attention was drawn to the following factors which were relied upon:

§ *Reference to the arguments put to the court*

(i) The phrase in section 1(1) 'a common prostitute' was linguistically capable of including a male person.

§ *Linguistic argument*

The *Oxford English Dictionary*, 2nd edn (1989), includes within the possibilities for 'prostitute,' 'a man who undertakes male homosexual acts for payment'.

§ *Use of dictionary*

(ii) Lord Taylor of Gosforth CJ has recently said in *R* v *McFarlane* [1994] QB 419 424D that 'both the dictionary definitions and the cases show that crucial feature in defining prostitution is the making of an offer of sexual service for reward'. I do not regard this factor as of significance. Lord Taylor CJ was speaking in a case which concerned a woman who had been clipping.

§ *Case quoted but distinguished ('clipping' means offering sexual services for reward, being paid in advance, but never intending to provide the service)*

(iii) Section 1(2) and 1(3) of the Act of 1959 refer respectively to 'a person' and 'anyone'.

(iv) In contrast section 2(1) refers specifically to 'a woman'. The reason for this is conjectured by Mr Carter-Manning to be that until the Sexual Offences Act 1967 homosexual acts between men were criminal offences and thus cautioning was inappropriate.

§ Wording of related section and sub-sections analysed

§ Historical analysis

(v) Since 1967 male prostitution has been in certain circumstances not unlawful and accordingly in the new environment it is open to the court to interpret section 1(1) of the Act of 1959 as being applicable to prostitutes who are male 'even if this was not the original intent of the provision'. This in my opinion is a bold submission.

§ Response to Counsel's invitation to read present law and social attitudes into the Act

It was based upon observations by Lord Bridge of Harwich in *Wicks* v *Firth* [1983] 2 AC 214, 230C–E, but Lord Bridge was dealing with a situation where an enactment has been re-enacted in a new context.

§ Use of earlier case rejected on the ground it is distinguishable

(vi) Where Parliament intends to deal with gender specific prostitution it uses specifically the word 'woman', 'girl', or 'her' as in sections 22, 28, 29, 30 and 31 of the Sexual Offences Act 1956. See also section 5 of the Sexual Offences Act 1967 as regards a 'woman' living on male prostitution.

§ Analysis of terms in other Acts in pari materia

It is to be observed, for completeness, that Mr Carter-Manning recognised he could obtain no assistance from the gender provisions of section 6 of the Interpretation Act 1978 because the provision that words importing the feminine gender, as does ordinarily the phrase 'common prostitute', include the masculine is inapplicable to enactments such as the Act of 1959 (see Part I of Schedule 2 to the Act of 1978). Mr Adrian Fulford, who appeared for the respondent, submitted that the phrase 'common prostitute' was for many years before 1959, and is now, regarded as a term of art which had the meaning formulated by Darling J when delivering the judgment of the Court of Criminal Appeal in *R* v *De Munck* [1918] 1 KB 635. He said, at pp. 637–638: 'The court is of opinion that the term "common prostitute" in the statute is not limited so as to mean only one who permits acts of lewdness with all and sundry, or with such as hire her, when such acts are in the nature of ordinary sexual connection. We are of opinion that prostitution is proved if it be shown that a woman offers her body commonly for lewdness for payment in return.'

§ Application of section 6 Interpretation Act 1978—which states that, 'In any Act, unless the contrary intention appears,—(b) words importing the feminine gender include the masculine'—rejected because later parts of the 1978 Act state that these words do not apply here

§ Reference to case law to show what might have been the draftsman's presumptions in using the terms and comment on an earlier related Act

The statute referred to was section 2(2) of the Criminal Law Amendment Act 1885 (48 & 49 Vict. c. 69) which however was gender specific for it spoke of 'women or girls'. Although the decision was in that context, I believe there to be great force in Mr Fulford's submission that 'common authority prostitute' is ordinarily regarded as signifying a woman. The statute was

§ Statutory history of the area

referring to a common law concept. Mr Fulford drew our attention to the only text-book which appears to deal with the problem, Rook and Ward, *Sexual Offences* (1990), where at para. 8.12 the authors state: 'The better view is that the offence under section 1(1) may be committed as principal only by a woman.'

§ *Reference to an academic text*

However, Mr Fulford's main submission was that the court should avail itself of the report which led to the Act of 1959 and of the parliamentary debate upon the Bill for the Act *Pepper* v *Hart* [1993] AC 593.

The availability of a report which led to an Act as an aid to interpretation is discussed in Bennion, Statutory Interpretation, 2nd edn (1992), p. 450. He cites *Fothergill* v *Monarch Airlines Ltd* [1981] AC 251, 281, where Lord Diplock said:

§ *Reference to* Pepper v Hart

§ *Reference to a practitioners' text*

Where the Act has been preceded by a report of some official commission or committee that has been laid before Parliament and the legislation is introduced in consequence of that report, the report itself may be looked at by the court for the limited purpose of identifying the 'mischief' that the Act was intended to remedy, and for such assistance as is derivable from this knowledge in giving the right purposive construction to the Act.

§ *Discussion of the method of identifying the mischief*

Section 1(1) of the Act was a result of a recommendation in paragraph 256 of the Report of the Departmental Committee on Homosexual Offences and Prostitution (1957) (Cmnd. 247) ('the Wolfenden committee'). The relevant chapters of the report are Chapters VIII and IX and a perusal of them leaves me in no doubt that the committee was concerned only with the female prostitute. Thus, and for example:

§ *Analysis of mischief as recounted by the report of the investigating committee*

223. It would have taken us beyond our terms of reference to investigate in detail the prevalence of prostitution or the reasons which lead women to adopt this manner of life

261. .... The problem of the prostitute is, in terms of numbers, far greater than that of the male importuner and, for that matter, far more of a public nuisance. In any event, we think it would be too easy to evade the formula by a game of 'general post' in which an individual prostitute would not loiter in a particular place though the number of prostitutes in that place at a given time might be constant.

262. Our second difficulty related to the criteria which would enable the police to infer that a person was loitering 'for the purposes of prostitution'. We have in mind the possibility that any woman might, from ignorance or in discretion, put herself in a position in which she might be said to be loitering, and by conduct which was quite innocent give rise to a suspicion in the mind of an observant policeman that she was loitering for the purposes of prostitution.

It is plain that the 'mischief' that the Act was intended to remedy was a mischief created by women. The assistance which I derive from the report confirms my strong impression that, notwithstanding the use of 'a person' and 'anyone' in subsections (2) and (3), section 1(1) of the Act of 1959 is confined to women. The term 'common prostitute' is ordinarily regarded as applying to a woman and, importantly, it seems improbable that Parliament intended to create a new male offence which was but subtly different from the extant section 32 of the Sexual Offences Act 1956.

§ *Conclusion on the mischief and a return to the analysis of the wording in the Act*

Accordingly I would dismiss this appeal and answer the magistrate's question in the affirmative. I add this. I have not sought to avail myself of the doctrine in the parliamentary debates it would become plain that section 1(1) of the Act of 1959 was intended to be applicable only to women. Had I concluded as a matter of interpretation that section 1(1) applied to male prostitutes, then a curious situation would have arisen. The judicially ascertained expressed intention of Parliament would have been at variance with what the court had been told was the actual intention of the promoters. The ensuing problems may have to be addressed if concessions of the type made here are repeated on another occasion.

§ *Decision*

§ *Further comments on the rejection of use of* Pepper v Hart

§ Obiter *comment on the use of* Pepper v Hart
§ *Recognition of the duty of counsel to cite all matters for and against him*

Laws J: I agree.

§ *Other judgment in the case*

ORDER Costs out of central funds.

§ *Appeal dismissed*
§ *Someone has to pay the costs and an order always has to be made (though not always reported)*

CONCLUSION

By way of conclusion we would like to suggest a rough guide on how you might approach the problem of interpreting a statute and then end with a short exercise on answering problems in this area.

Checklist for reading a statute

Table 9.1 contains a checklist of research points you need to consider when reading a statute. The left-hand column sets out the general headings you should bear in mind, and the right-hand column explains these in more detail.

Table 9.1 Checklist for reading a statute

1.	Read the section(s) carefully.	This may include:
		(1) noting any technical legal terms. For example, words such as 'property'; 'possession'; 'dismissal'; 'recklessness' all have technical legal meanings. In particular, check whether the word is covered by the Interpretation Act 1978 or case law;
		(2) noting any other technical terms relating to specialist areas, or trades or industry. The Act (e.g. a Finance Act) may well have been drafted with these in mind;
		(3) checking dictionaries;
		(4) referring to any related sections in the Act;
		(5) checking the schedules to the Act;
		(6) checking for interpretations in the section and/or later interpretation sections;
		(7) checking related statutes which are *in pari materia* with this Act.
2.	Research academic texts which will provide general guidance on the meaning of the section and point you to other authorities.	(1) textbooks;
		(2) articles and case notes in legal journals;
		(3) monographs (generally shorter books, often borne from Ph.D. theses, written on a very specific topic such as misrepresentation in contract, defamation, etc.);
		(4) practitioners' texts;
		(5) the internet (with great care). General Google searches and Wikipedia are not authorities in legal argument.
3.	Understand the mischief of the Act.	(1) refer to any annotations, e.g. in 'Current Statutes Annotated';
		(2) check for any Law Commission Reports;
		(3) look at social, economic, or political background;
		(4) check whether you have found the mischief or whether there are multiple mischiefs;
		(5) check Hansard under the rules in *Pepper* v *Hart*;
		(6) check the long title of the act: *Vacher* v *London Society of Compositors*.
4.	Check for any European derivation.	Does the Act in question derive from a Treaty, Regulation, or Directive? If so, even after Brexit, the European case law may still be relevant.
5.	Research existing or related case law.	(1) Are you sure your legal research has unearthed all the authorities?
		• English case law?
		• Possibly decisions of the Judicial Committee of the Privy Council?
		• Relevant cases in foreign jurisdictions?
		• European case law at the Court of Justice or as applied in the UK?
		(2) How will you present the *ratio* of each case?
		(3) How will you deal with *obiter dicta*?
		(4) You must decide how you are going to argue the relevance of helpful cases and distinguish unhelpful authority.

6.	Are there any Human Rights Act 1998 implications?	(1) Direct reference to human rights on the basis that any case will be taken against a public authority? (2) Possible 'horizontal' use of Human Rights Act 1998?
7.	Be aware of any technical rules of grammar.	For example, the *eiusdem generis* rule.
8.	Be aware of judicial trends in methods of interpretation.	Are judges now more purposive in their approach? How will this affect your argument?
9.	Be aware from which perspective you are viewing the problem and adopt the appropriate style of argument.	Are you acting as an advocate? Are you arguing the general possibilities? Answering an examination problem is quite different from acting as an advocate in a moot, for example. Even in real-life advocacy or the provision of legal advice, you must decide how to pitch your case in terms of emphasis on literal or purposive approaches.
10.	Decide how to marshal your authorities to substantiate your approach.	For example, what degree of emphasis will you put on each case or other relevant material? Good arguments emphasise the key points, not every single point.

EXERCISE 17 Perilous poodles and rabid fish

This very short exercise explores the basic methods of interpreting statutes.

PROBLEM

It is to be assumed that, as a result of a recent outbreak of rabies (and following a consequent Law Commission recommendation) the **Rabies and Dangerous Animals Act 2015** has been passed. It states:

Section 1: It is an offence to leave animals unattended in any hotel, public house, restaurant, or other public place.

Section 2: The keeping of any animal, other than a domesticated one, without an appropriate licence, is an offence. The form and cost of such a licence will be determined by orders issued from time to time by the Minister. A domesticated animal is one so defined by sch. 9 of this Act.

Section 3: Private dwelling houses are exempted from the provisions of this Act.

Schedule 9: For the purposes of this Act a 'domesticated animal' includes cats, dogs, horses, cattle, sheep, pigs, and snakes or insects common to the British Isles.

continued

EXERCISE 17 *continued*

Using the rules of statutory interpretation that have been developed, present arguments **as if you were counsel for the defence** in the following cases.

(1) *R v Alfred*

Alfred left his poodle in the changing rooms at his local tennis club while he played tennis. He is charged with contravening s. 1 of the Act.

(2) *R v Bert*

Bert keeps piranha fish in a pond in his front garden. The garden is unfenced. He is charged with not having the appropriate licence under s. 2.

Points to note in this exercise:

1. *Alfred*

Start any problem of this nature by breaking down the constituent elements of the section(s) involved. What is required for conviction here?

- There must be an animal (not a problem here).

- That animal must be left unattended;

- in any hotel, public house, restaurant, or other public place.

However simplistic this may seem, it really is not (especially if the section is more complicated). As we noted earlier, you will find in seminars that many of your colleagues, when asked to analyse a problem like this, 'jump in' all over the place commenting on different aspects of the offence (or saying 'this is nonsense'). Structure matters and wins hands down over a disorganised argument. Here, remember, if the Crown fails to prove any one of the constituent elements of the offence, there can be no conviction.

Next, make sure there are no other parts of the Act which have to be taken into account, for example a definitions section. Here, the only one that could be of relevance to *Alfred* is s. 3.

Next, marshal your authorities (case law, statutes in pari materia, explanatory notes to this Act, any possible *Pepper* v *Hart* references, etc.). Let us say, for instance, that you find a reference in Hansard to a speech made by the Home Secretary which might help your case. When can you use this? If you can use it, is it precise enough to help your argument?

From this we can say that the defence may rest on three grounds:

(i) The Act refers to 'hotel, public house, restaurant, or other public place'. Does a tennis club, therefore, come within that last, general, category? The phrase 'or other public place' could be read *eiusdem generis* to restrict the general words to the genus of the preceding specific words. What is the genus of the preceding words? The prosecution will argue that these words show that the tenor of the section is to prevent animals being left in a place to which the public have general access. The defence could argue that the words indicate a place restricted to food and drink establishments. Further, if the tennis club is private (or has a limited membership) there might be a defence here. The express exclusion of private

continued

EXERCISE 17 *continued*

dwellings under s. 3 could also be cited in support of this interpretation (since we are entitled to look at the effect of the *whole* Act).

This is a weak point but could be used by ignoring the problematic word 'dwelling' and concentrating on the privacy element.

(ii) In the alternative, the defence could argue that this phrase is not sufficiently specific to create a genus, and that therefore, since a literal interpretation of such general words is virtually meaningless, the court should inquire into the purpose of the Act. A formal style of discovering 'purpose' would be to analyse the Act mainly by referring to the internal context. The short title of the Act is the Rabies and Dangerous Animals Act. This cannot itself be used, unlike the long title, as an aid to construction: *R* v *Galvin*. However, it does suggest that the Act is particularly concerned with the threat of dangerous animals (note the exclusion of domesticated animals by s. 2 and sch. 9). This argument could be used to deny the application of the section to pet dogs, and the long title of the Act (if it has one) could be cited in support (if it offers that support—the question is silent on this). See *Vacher* v *London Society of Compositors*, where it was stressed that the long title could be used as a minor aid to construction, provided it did not contradict the express language of the Act.

Seeking the purpose in the 'grand' style one can move away from the Act itself to matters such as social conditions. Similarly, the Law Commission's report could also be used in support, if that was the case (*Black-Clawson*), and even Hansard might prove useful on this point if the court will admit it. Perhaps the Home Secretary answered a question on the scope of the Act by saying: 'The Act is designed to ensure people's safety, but we cannot seriously banish dogs from all public places. We have sought to balance personal freedoms and public safety by prohibiting dogs from being left unattended in public areas where people are being entertained.' Is this useful or not?

(iii) Finally, one could argue that 'unattended' does not mean the animal always has to be in the owner's presence (or that 'presence' simply means 'in the line of sight' as in *Casson* v *Dade*).

2. Bert

Use the same structure as with *Alfred*. Here, the relevant section is s. 2. What is required for conviction here?

- An animal must be involved (will a fish be included?).

- The Act does not apply to domesticated ones.

- There must be no appropriate licence.

Again, make sure there are no other parts of the Act which have to be taken into account, for example a definitions section. Here, there are two: s. 3 (exempting private dwelling houses) and sch. 9 (defining domesticated animals).

continued

EXERCISE 17 *continued*

The first point to note is that you may have to do some research on what is an 'animal' (see various dictionaries, biology books, etc.). It comes as a surprise to many that fish are animals and so will require a licence unless sch. 9 exempts them.

The defence is threefold:

(i) The most obvious line of attack is the purposive argument that, although fish may be animals, they are incapable (to the best of the authors' knowledge) of carrying rabies. The prosecution may well point out that the Act is concerned with both rabid *and* dangerous animals; a dangerous fish falls within the provisions of the Act. However, the purpose of the Act, as exemplified perhaps in the long title (not provided here) and gained through an examination of the social setting for the Act, would probably demonstrate that the two ideas were connected.

(ii) The offence created by s. 2 is absolute, save for the exclusion of domesticated animals in sch. 9. Though a literal approach apparently catches Bert, he might be able to utilise s. 3. One must argue an extended meaning to 'private dwelling houses'. Land is usually included in such terms.

Bert could try to argue that as the fish are kept in his garden, they should be excluded under s. 3. This could be argued on the basis that the purpose of the Act is only to protect the public in places to which they normally have resort. As such, there is an argument that an individual's garden is as much his private property as his house, and that any wider meaning could create absurd results. One might try to find other statutes which have defined the term in an acceptable way for the defence. Finding one *in pari materia* might be more difficult. One such possible example might be the Dangerous Dogs Act 1991. And, indeed, the very question whether a garden path constituted a 'public place' under s. 10 of the Act arose in *Fellowes* v *DPP, The Times* 1 February 1993. Fellowes was convicted of having a dog which was dangerously out of control in a public place contrary to the Dangerous Dogs Act 1991 s. 3(1), after his dog bit a paper boy who was delivering a newspaper to the house. The Queen's Bench Division Divisional Court held that this was not a public place because of the purpose of the Act and that people entered the private premises only as visitors, not as general members of the public. Again, the same court has decided that a dangerous dog in a private car in a public car park had to be muzzled because, although a car is not in and of itself a public place, when the car is in a public place everything inside the car is deemed to be in a public place for the purposes of the Act (*Bates* v *DPP, The Times*, 8 March 1993; (1993) 157 JP 1004). So, if the mischief in our fictitious Act is perceived as relating to 'danger', the unfenced pond is still a problem in our argument.

However, a different slant was put on this in *R* v *Roberts (Leroy Lloyd)* [2003] EWCA Crim 2753; [2004] 1 WLR 181, where the accused had a 'lock knife' in his own (very narrow) front garden. This was held not to have occurred in a 'public place' for the purposes of the Criminal Justice Act 1988, s. 139(7). The Court decided it was inappropriate to construe the phrase 'public place' in s. 139(7) as embracing land adjacent to areas where the public had access, so long as the harm against which the Act was designed to provide protection could not be inflicted from that place.

continued

EXERCISE 17 *continued*

(iii) The categories of animals referred to in sch. 9 are wide; wider, perhaps, than a literal reading of the word 'domesticated' would lead us to expect; although it is presented as an inclusive definition. The case of *Coltman* v *Bibby Tankers* [1988] AC 276 considered the dual meaning that can be given to 'inclusive' definitions. The list might be either exemplary or exhaustive. It is notable that fish are excluded, and so if the definition is exhaustive, the prosecution might seek to argue the principle *expressio unius est exclusio alterius*. This would be difficult to counter, and the defence's only response, it is submitted, might be to argue that the definition is exemplary; that 'domesticated' here is sufficiently wide to include all animals that are in fact kept as 'pets'. Whether piranhas are on that basis common to the British Isles might nonetheless be a difficult point to argue!

CHAPTER REFERENCES

ARDEN, M. (2008), 'The Changing Judicial Role: Human Rights, Community Law and the Intention of Parliament', 67 *Cambridge Law Journal*, 487.

BAILEY, D. and NORBURY, L. (eds) (2017), *Bennion on Statutory Interpretation* (7th edn, London: LexisNexis).

*CHANDLER, A. and HOLLAND, J. (1995), '*Pepper* v *Hart*: Unearthing the Meaning of Rescission', *Journal of Business Law*, 503.

*CROSS, R. (1995), *Cross: Statutory Interpretation* (3rd edn, by Bell, J. and Engle, G., London: Butterworths).

FELDMAN, D. (1992), 'Commencement, Transition and Retrospective Legislation', 108 *Law Quarterly Review*, 212.

GRAHAM, R.N. (2001), 'In Defence of Maxims', 22 *Statute Law Review*, 45.

GRAHAM, R.N. (2009), 'What Judges Want: Judicial Self-interest and Statutory Interpretation', 30(1) *Statute Law Review*, 38.

*HORN, N. (2011), 'Legislative Section Headings: Drafting Techniques, Plain Language, and Redundancy', 32 *Statute Law Review*, 186.

KRISHNAPRASAD, K.V. (2011), 'Pepper v. Hart: Its Continuing Implications in the United Kingdom and in India', 32(3) *Statute Law Review*, 227.

LLEWELLYN, K. (1960), *The Common Law Tradition* (Boston, Mass.: Little Brown).

LUNDMARK, T. and WALLER, H. (2017), 'Using Statutes and Cases in Common and Civil Law' (Routledge, Transnational Legal Theory, DOI: 10.1080/20414005.2016.1275590).

MANCHESTER, C. and SALTER, D. (2011), *The Dynamics of Precedent and Statutory Interpretation* (4th edn, London: Sweet & Maxwell).

*MUNDAY, R. (2008), 'The Bridge that Choked a Watercourse or Repetitive Dictionary Disorder', 29(1) *Statute Law Review*, 26.

*SLOCUM, B.G. (2012), 'Linguistics and 'Ordinary Meaning' Determinations', 33 *Statute Law Review*, 39.

SMITH, J.C. (1995), 'The Criminal Appeals Act 1995: (1) Appeals against Conviction', *Criminal Law Review*, 920.

STEYN, J. (2001), '*Pepper* v *Hart*: A Re-examination', 21 *Oxford Journal of Legal Studies*, 59.

SULLIVAN, R. (2001), 'Some Implications of Plain Language Drafting', 22 *Statute Law Review*, 175.

*SUMMERS, R. and MARSHALL, G. (1992), 'The Argument from Ordinary Meaning in Statutory Interpretation', 43 *Northern Ireland Legal Quarterly*, 213.

*TWINING, W. and MIERS, D. (1991), *How to Do Things with Rules* (3rd edn, London: Weidenfeld & Nicolson; 5th edn, Cambridge: Cambridge University Press).

VOGENAUER, S. (2005), 'A Retreat from *Pepper* v *Hart*? A Reply to Lord Steyn', 25 *Oxford Journal of Legal Studies*, 629.

*WILLIS, J. (1938), 'Statute Interpretation in a Nutshell', XVI *Canadian Bar Review*, 1.

YIHAN, G. (2008), 'A Comparative Account of Statutory Interpretation in Singapore', 29 *Statute Law Review*, 195.

*ZANDER, M. (2004), *The Law-Making Process* (6th edn, Cambridge: Cambridge University Press).

 ONLINE RESOURCES

Test your knowledge by trying the self-test questions that accompany **Chapters 7–9**.
Visit: www.oup.com/uk/holland-webb10e

10

'Bringing Rights Home': Legal Method and the Convention Rights

10.1 Introduction

In **Chapter 1** we introduced the idea that English law has become subject to two powerful pan-European legal forces: with (a) EU law, and, (b) since 2000, the impact of the limited incorporation of the European Convention on Human Rights (ECHR) by the Human Rights Act (HRA) 1998. As we shall see in this chapter the HRA has had a significant substantive impact on English law, extending the scope of protection of what are often called the 'fundamental' human rights and freedoms of those living within this jurisdiction. At this point you may, however, be wondering why the Act merits a whole chapter in a book on legal methods. It is a fair question; the answer lies in the fact that the HRA has set specific constraints on how the courts must interpret and apply English law, and has given the courts unusual powers to deal with legislation that is inconsistent with so-called 'Convention rights' incorporated by the HRA. In summary form what this means is, that when coming to a decision where there is a human rights issue under the HRA:

(i)   all courts must apply common law precedent so as to comply with the scope and principles of the Convention;

(ii) all courts and tribunals must interpret *all* relevant legislation, so far as is possible, to comply with Convention rights;

(iii) in interpreting the scope of the Convention rights, all courts and tribunals must take into account the decisions of the European Court of Human Rights (abbreviated to ECtHR);

(iv) the higher courts may declare primary legislation incompatible with Convention rights, but they cannot disapply it.

Whilst in **Chapter 1** we also noted that Brexit will, over time, greatly reduce the influence of EU law on UK legal systems, it is important to remember that the ECHR is independent of the EU. Consequently, the role of the HRA, and through it the influence of the ECHR, will not be directly affected by Brexit.

In the remainder of this chapter we set out to do three things:

(i)   to outline what the ECHR is and why it is important;

(ii) to explain how the HRA has incorporated 'Convention Rights' into English law, and explore how those rights can be enforced;

(iii) to enable you to understand more fully the impact that the HRA has had on legal method—both precedent and statutory interpretation.

10.2 The European Convention on Human Rights

10.2.1 What is the ECHR?

The ECHR is an international treaty which was signed in Rome on 4 November 1950, and came into force on 3 September 1953. It sets out basic civil and political rights. The ECHR was the first major convention to be created under the auspices of a body called the Council of Europe. Although a number of other treaties have followed, the ECHR remains probably the most significant.

The Council itself was established by treaty in 1949, largely as a reaction to the failures of democracy and ethics that accompanied the rise of fascism in inter-war Europe. It exists as a political association of European states committed to advancing European unity, social and economic progress, and human rights. Although, historically speaking, it shares certain common roots with the EU, it is institutionally and politically quite separate. There has, of course, been significant overlap in membership of the Council of Europe and the European Economic Community (EEC)/EU, though the Council has always tended to be the larger body. There were ten original members of the Council (as compared with the EEC's six), namely the Benelux states (Belgium, the Netherlands, and Luxembourg) together with Denmark, France, Italy, Ireland, Norway, Sweden, and the United Kingdom; the Council today has forty-seven members, with most of the former Eastern bloc states having joined since 1989.

States signing up to the Convention have been allowed to enter reservations to or derogations from particular provisions of the ECHR. A *reservation* is a statement made by a signatory, at the time of signing, that it recognises and reserves a position in which its laws are (to some specified extent) inconsistent with the Convention. A *derogation*, on the other hand, is a statement whereby a state notifies the Council that it is suspending certain rights under the Convention 'in time of war or other public emergency threatening the life of the nation' (ECHR, Art. 15). This is a fairly elastic concept, though there are certain Convention rights from which it is not possible to derogate (under Arts 2, 3, 4, and 7). The power of derogation was carried over into the HRA 1998 by s. 14 of that Act.

10.2.2 The Scope of the ECHR

The ECHR is concerned with the identification and protection of only certain specific 'fundamental' human rights and freedoms. These are prescribed in quite broad terms in the various substantive sections or 'Articles' of the Convention. The main substantive rights are set out in **Figure 10.1**.

Rights under the ECHR are expressed either as 'absolute' or 'qualified' rights. Where rights, such as the right to life or freedom from torture, are absolute, this means that they cannot be restricted or derogated by signatory states. Where rights are qualified, there is scope to balance different rights and interests, and some restrictions can be justified. The basis for legitimate constraint is expressed in terms within the relevant articles of the Convention. Thus, for example, freedom of expression may be curtailed provided it is in a manner 'prescribed by law' and 'necessary in a democratic society' in the interests of national security, or for the protection of health or morals, or to prevent disclosure of confidential information. However, the extent of constraint in specific cases must

Art. 2	Right to life
Art. 3	Prohibition of torture, inhuman or degrading treatment or punishment
Art. 4	Prohibition of slavery or forced labour
Art. 5	Right to liberty and security of person
Art. 6	Right to a fair trial
Art. 7	Prohibition of punishment without law
Art. 8	Right to respect for privacy and family life
Art. 9	Right to freedom of thought, conscience and religion
Art. 10	Right to freedom of expression
Art. 11	Right to freedom of assembly and association
Art. 12	Right to marry and establish a family
Art. 14	Prohibition of discrimination with respect to rights under the ECHR

Figure 10.1 Rights and freedoms under the ECHR

then be determined by reference to the principle of *proportionality*. Proportionality is an extremely important general principle of human rights law. It provides what has been described as:

> a common analytical framework . . . [which] influences (some would say controls) how courts reason to conclusions in many of the great moral and political controversies confronting political communities.
>
> (Hustcroft *et al.*, 2014: 2)

Different formulations of the proportionality test are used in different contexts (the precise detail goes beyond the concerns of this chapter), but, broadly, it can be said that proportionality always requires that the body seeking to limit a right must demonstrate that a reasonable relationship or 'balance' exists between the (legitimate) policy objective to be achieved and the means used to achieve it. If the means used are disproportionate, then the restriction or interference will be struck down. Thus, for example, in *Campbell* v *United Kingdom* (1992) 15 EHRR 137, the Court determined that opening and reading all correspondence between prisoners and their solicitors was a disproportionate interference in the prisoners' rights. By contrast, it would be reasonable for the prison service to open letters without reading them, to see if they contained illicit enclosures. As we shall see, proportionality is also used as the balancing test in England, where cases are brought under the HRA.

10.2.3 Enforcement

The Convention created its own enforcement procedures, separate from any measures taken by individual contracting states. Under Convention procedures, complaints about breaches of the ECHR may be brought by a signatory state or, in some circumstances, by an individual petitioner. An action can only be brought against the *state* allegedly in breach. There is generally no possibility of one individual suing another before the ECtHR. A state, moreover, can only be sued if it is a signatory to the Convention.

A party must have exhausted all domestic remedies before petitioning the ECtHR. Admissibility is determined in a preliminary hearing, with court data suggesting that about 85 per cent of cases fall at this hurdle.

10.3 The Human Rights Act 1998

The HRA came into force in England and Wales on 2 October 2000. It has thus been instrumental in creating a more substantial human rights dimension to UK (not just English) law for nearly two decades. Examples of its impact include cases where the HRA:

- is playing an important, but gradualist role in marking out the boundaries of a modern privacy law in the United Kingdom (see, e.g., *Douglas* v *Hello! Ltd (No 1)* [2001] QB 967; [2001] 2 All ER 289; *Wainwright* v *Home Office* [2003] UKHL 53; *Campbell* v *MGN* [2004] UKHL 22);

- has played a substantial part in clarifying rights relating to personal identity, same-sex relationships, and, more generally, the scope of the right to enjoyment of family life (e.g. *R (Mellor)* v *Secretary of State for the Home Department* [2001] EWCA Civ 472; *Bellinger* v *Bellinger* [2003] UKHL 21; *Ghaidan* v *Godin-Mendoza* [2004] UKHL 30); *R (Baiai)* v *Secretary of State for the Home Department* [2008] UKHL 53);

- has influenced modern legal debate about fundamental moral and medico-legal issues such as the right to life (*In re A (Children) (Conjoined Twins: Surgical Separation)* [2000] EWCA Civ 254; [2001] Fam 147) and assisted dying (*R* v *DPP ex parte Pretty* [2001] UKHL 61; *R (Nicklinson)* v *Ministry of Justice* [2014] UKSC 38);

- has been instrumental in defining the scope of executive and legislative powers over individual liberty and freedom from wrongful detention, for example in respect of powers to detain suspected terrorists (*A* v *Secretary of State for the Home Department* [2004] UKHL 56); as regards prisoner's rights during their incarceration (e.g. *Black* v *Secretary of State for Justice* [2009] UKHL 1), or the rights of those detained under the Mental Health Act 1983 (*R (H)* v *North and East London Regional Mental Health Review Tribunal* [2001] EWCA Civ 415; and

- has also enabled the courts to rule unequivocally against the admissibility before a British court of evidence obtained by torture (*A* v *Secretary of State for the Home Department* [2005] UKHL 71).

It has achieved these things by a fairly typical piece of British pragmatism. Unlike the European Communities Act 1972, which simply incorporated by reference all current and future EEC and subsequently EU law wholesale into English law, the HRA expressly gives the selected Convention rights a statutory basis *in* English law by a process of direct incorporation in the Act itself (see HRA 1998, sch. 1).

One of the great arguments against incorporation of the ECHR had been the damage that it could cause to parliamentary sovereignty by increasing the powers of unelected judges—both by ceding authority directly to the ECtHR, and by giving greater constitutional power to the British judiciary. The HRA 1998, its supporters claim, has maintained a balance between enabling judicial protection of human rights and protecting the sovereignty of Parliament (though this continues to be contested by the Act's opponents). As Dwyer (2005: 362) points out, the HRA:

> maintains the dualist distinction between the United Kingdom's obligations in international law and the provisions of domestic law. The United Kingdom's international obligations are not directly applicable in domestic law.

The HRA further seeks to preserve sovereignty by requiring that any action to deal with incompatibility of primary legislation rests with Parliament, not the courts. Breach of Convention rights cannot, unlike fundamental breaches of EU Law, post-*Factortame*, empower the courts to disapply an Act of Parliament. We come back to this in section **10.3.2**.

10.3.1 Constructing a claim: how does the HRA work in practice?

The HRA 1998 is designed to work in one of two ways. First, it gives claimants a 'direct' cause of action against any 'public authority' that has allegedly acted in a way that is incompatible with the complainant's Convention rights. Secondly, in any substantive legal action, it requires the courts to interpret domestic law consistently with Convention rights. This may give litigants an 'indirect' route to enforcement, including against other individuals, not just public bodies. Let's now look at each of these in turn.

Sections 6 and 7 HRA 1998 can be said to create a distinction akin to that in EU law between horizontal and vertical effect. By virtue of these provisions, the HRA creates a cause of action that only has vertical effect, so that an individual can sue the state or a 'state-like' body; it does not have the direct horizontal effect that allows enforcement of Convention rights between individuals. Section 6 achieves this vertical effect by imposing a duty on all public authorities to act compatibly with the Convention rights. This is important because it places a proactive duty on public bodies to take human rights issues into consideration in all their activities. Where, contrary to s. 6, a public authority has acted in breach of Convention rights, HRA, s. 7(1)(a) then enables a person harmed by that breach (the 'victim' in the language of the Act) to bring proceedings against that authority. Section 7 is thus the key provision that makes the breach of Convention rights actionable under English law. This is a broad power, but three particular requirements set some limits to it and, in the latter two points that follow, also manage to create some uncertainty around the courts' exercise of their responsibility under these sections.

First, as noted, the Act limits the ability to bring proceedings to those who are 'victims'. In many instances this does not cause problems, but it does act as a barrier to cases being brought to clarify purely hypothetical legal questions, or as public interest litigation by bodies that are not themselves victims, or acting on behalf of a specific victim—see *In the matter of an application by the Northern Ireland Human Rights Commission for Judicial Review (Northern Ireland)* [2018] UKSC 27. We return to this point in **10.3.2** below.

Secondly, the notion of 'public authority' is crucial. A cause of action can only be sustained where a Convention right has been infringed by such an authority. However, the concept is only broadly defined in s. 6(3) HRA. Bodies such as central government departments, the courts, and local councils are clearly included, but there are also many bodies whose status as public or private is debatable. Section 6 tries to deal with this by recognising that the public–private distinction is not so much about status or ownership of the organisation, but rather about its *function*. If it exercises a 'public function', then under s. 6(3) it is a public body. But that is where the statutory definition ends, as Parliament deemed it better to leave the actual boundary determination to the courts on a case-by-case basis. If a body is publicly funded, exercises statutory powers, taking on a function otherwise performed by or for central or local government, or otherwise providing a public service, then it is more likely to be regarded as a public authority under the HRA. However, difficulties arise with hybrid entities that are essentially private bodies carrying out only limited public functions. Some, such as privatised utility companies or professional regulatory bodies have been found to come within the reach of the Act for all or some of their activities, but others have not—for example private care homes that receive local authority funding in respect of (some of) their residents (*YL v Birmingham City Council* [2007] UKHL 27). This approach creates some obvious uncertainty. It requires courts to undertake what Rix LJ has called a 'multi-factorial assessment' (*R (Weaver)* v *London & Quadrant Housing Trust* [2009] EWCA 587 at [119]), in circumstances where a myriad of factors might be relevant. It also raises concerns that governments may seek to use powers to delegate public functions to private bodies in an attempt to circumvent their obligations under the HRA, contrary to the principles of the ECHR (see *Wos* v *Poland*, App. No. 22860/02, 1 March 2005, para. 60).

Thirdly, the court will only restrict the activities of a public authority if they are a disproportionate interference with the rights of citizens. This is, of course, a sensitive exercise, and how far the courts *should* go in substantively scrutinising governmental or administrative action is a question of real practical and constitutional importance. Human rights cases are, in theory, still distinctive in this regard; they are the only domestic context in which English courts use a pure proportionality test as a justification to interfere with governmental decision-making (Boughey, 2017: 138). This contrasts with the conventional approach in England, which has been to focus on the reasonableness of the decision-maker's actions. This is widely regarded as a less 'intense' standard of review than proportionality under the ECHR. Proportionality, moreover, is often seen as both more objective and structured (*Keyu* v *Secretary of State for Foreign and Commonwealth Affairs* [2015] 3 WLR 1665); and less inclined to give undue weight, or even 'deference' to the reasoning of the original decision-maker (cf. *R(SB)* v *Governors of Denbigh School* [2006] 2 WLR 719; *R (Carlile)* v *Secretary of State for the Home Department* [2014] UKSC 60). Some uncertainty arises because there continues to be a divergence of opinion, even among the Supreme Court, as to whether the difference between proportionality and reasonableness review is essentially one of degree, or something more fundamental (compare, e.g., Lords Mance and Carnworth in *Kennedy* v *Charity Commission (Secretary of State for Justice intervening)* [2015] AC 455, at [54], [267]). What is also striking, however, is the extent to which more recent cases like *Pham* v *Secretary of State for the Home Department* [2015] UKSC 19 and *Youssef* v *Secretary of State for Foreign and Commonwealth Affairs* [2016] UKSC 3 point to an increasing and pervasive acceptance of the value of the European proportionality approach, even in non-human rights cases. As we see elsewhere where English and European approaches have come into substantial contact, there is a marked blurring of old systemic distinctions.

Turning to our second basis of making a claim under the HRA, a person may *indirectly* rely on the rights contained in the HRA in actions against people who are not public authorities. This is permissible on two bases, first, in respect of common law rights and responsibilities, because the courts themselves fall within the definition of a 'public authority' under s. 6 HRA. Consequently, any decision they reach must itself comply with Convention principles. Secondly, there is what is commonly referred to as 'statutory horizontality', which is a way of describing the express duty imposed on the courts to interpret legislation consistently with convention rights under s. 3 HRA—discussed further in section **10.3.2**.

The way these provisions work is that the claimant brings a claim, for example under contract or tort, or in terms of a specific statutory duty, (not under the HRA as such) and asks the court to (re)interpret the scope and effect of these existing legal rights in the light of the Convention. To illustrate, consider the following two example of the process,

In *Campbell* v *MGN Ltd* [2004] UKHL 22, the model Naomi Campbell was photographed coming out of a Narcotics Anonymous ('NA') meeting having previously denied she was addicted to drugs. The *Mirror* newspaper published the photographs with the faces of other attendees at the meeting pixelated to protect their identities. The article contained in general terms information relating to Ms Campbell's treatment for drug addiction, including the number of NA meetings she had attended. The Claimant admitted that there was a public interest justifying publication of the fact that she was a drug addict and was having therapy, but claimed damages for breach of confidentiality in respect of the publication of information about the location contained in the photographs, and the specific details of her treatment. The House of Lords agreed. Although the HRA does not create any new cause of action between private persons, where there is already a relevant cause of action, the court as a public authority under s. 6 must act compatibly with both parties' Convention rights. In this case the tort of breach of confidence had already shaken off the requirement for an initial confidential relationship, and should, consistent with Art. 8 ECHR, be better construed as a tort governing the misuse of private information more broadly.

In contrast, the process of claiming under conditions of statutory horizontality can be seen in the recent case of *Lee* v *Ashers Baking Company Ltd* [2018] UKSC 49, which has garnered a lot of public attention. Here the appellant, a gay man, had sought to obtain a cake from the respondents. The cake, which the appellant wished to take to a private party organised to mark the end of Northern Ireland anti-homophobia week in 2017, was to be decorated with the *Sesame Street* characters Bert and Ernie, and the slogan 'Support Gay Marriage'. The respondents initially accepted the order but later advised that they could not complete it on conscience grounds, based on their religious beliefs, and offered Mr Lee a refund. The appellant subsequently sued, not under the HRA itself (as Ashers was clearly a private company, no 'vertical effect' could be claimed), but under Northern Irish equality law, and regulations prohibiting discrimination in the supply of goods and services. Questions then arose in the litigation as to how those regulations should, by virtue of the requirement of consistent statutory interpretation, be interpreted in the context of the parties' Convention rights. One of the interesting facets of this case was that human rights arguments were actually engaged on both sides of the case: in terms of Mr Lee's rights to 'political speech', and not to be discriminated against, and the respondents' entitlement to exercise their own freedom of religion and freedom of expression.

As these examples show, these are *indirect* effects because, they do not constitute a cause of action in themselves—they do not create a distinct right to sue a particular *person*. There is some theoretical debate about whether s. 6 might properly ground a strong version of horizontal effect in common law cases such as to create new common law rights, but, as cases like *Campbell* v *MGN* show, there is no great support for this in case law so far. (The issues go beyond the scope of this book, but see, e.g., Young (2011) for a fuller account.) However, what these horizontal provisions do clearly provide is some entitlement to have the existing *law* interpreted in a particular way, or at least act as some constraint on the courts in narrowing the range of interpretations that are permissible.

One final point of note regarding the operation of the HRA is that the Act does not entirely exclude the jurisdiction of the ECtHR. A person may still take a case to the court at Strasbourg, but only after having exhausted all domestic remedies. If the Court rules in their favour, the government is required, by Art. 46 of the ECHR, to give effect to the Court's ruling. As a matter of international law this is, as Lord Sumption has observed, an absolute obligation: *R (Chester)* v *Secretary of State for Justice; McGeoch* v *Lord President of the Council* [2013] UKSC 63; it does not, however, impose any equivalent obligation on the UK courts to follow that ECtHR decision—see further section **10.6**.

10.3.2 The declaration of incompatibility

The powers under HRA, ss 3 and 4 to declare legislation incompatible with a Convention right were based by the draftsman on similar powers contained in the New Zealand Bill of Rights Act 1990, s. 6, requiring the New Zealand courts to interpret legislation consistently with the rights and obligations of the International Covenant on Civil and Political Rights. The UK approach, however, goes further. It imposes a stronger duty to achieve a consistent interpretation under s. 3, *and*, unlike the New Zealand legislation, where no consistent interpretation is possible, it gives the domestic courts a clear *statutory* power to declare the legislation incompatible (s. 4).

A 'declaration of incompatibility' under s. 4 is simply a statement that the legislation is not 'Convention compliant', and it serves to put the government on notice of that fact. The only courts with the power to make a declaration of incompatibility are, in England and Wales, the High Court, the Court of Appeal, the Supreme Court, the Judicial Committee of the Privy Council, and the Courts Martial Appeal Court. In Scotland, the power can be exercised by the Court of Session and the High Court of Justiciary, in addition, of course, to the Supreme Court.

An important procedural question here is whether proceedings can be brought 'in the abstract' to establish incompatibility, or only in the context of a specified allegation of an unlawful act. The requirement for there to be a 'victim' would seem to exclude that possibility. Nonetheless, in *In the matter of an application by the Northern Ireland Human Rights Commission for Judicial Review (Northern Ireland)* [2018] UKSC 27 the Northern Ireland Human Rights Commission (NIHRC) had argued, under ss 69 and 71 of the Northern Ireland Act, that it could challenge the compatibility of legislation under (the equivalent of) ss 3 and 4 HRA, irrespective of whether there has been any specific unlawful act by a public authority. The essence of this argument is that the human rights legislation creates separate rules of standing (a) in respect of substantive complaints by victims to bring proceedings in respect of an unlawful act of a public authority, or to rely on such an unlawful act in other proceedings, pursuant to s. 7(1); and (b) as a broader power to challenge the compatibility of legislation under ss 3 and 4, irrespective of whether there had been any unlawful act by a public authority. This would have meant that NIHRC had standing to bring the latter proceedings. However, the majority of the Supreme Court (by 4:3) held that the power to bring an incompatibility claim was constrained by the need to identify an actual or potential victim of an unlawful act to which the proceedings related. On the facts of the case, it was thus not sufficient for the NIHRC to assert generally that the failure to abrogate or amend the relevant (abortion) laws was likely to give rise to victims. This decision thus seems to put beyond doubt that the bringing of incompatibility claims is only feasible where victims are also bringing substantive claims for breaches of their Convention rights.

A declaration does not in any way affect the validity of the Act in question. It remains law unless and until Parliament deals with the incompatibility. Thus, the court must still apply the legislation as it stands and the positions of the parties to the actual case are unchanged by the declaration.

It is important to note that the courts have the *power* to make a declaration; it is not a *duty*, or certainly not in all cases. In particular, where the question of consistency falls within the UK's margin of appreciation (discussed in section **10.3.2**), the courts may determine not to issue a declaration, on the basis either that Parliament is better placed to assess where the line falls, or that Parliament should at least be given an opportunity to consider the issue first: see *R (Nicklinson)* v *Ministry of Justice* [2014] UKSC 38, though such arguments for not issuing a declation are considered by the courts on their merits. If the court is not satisfied that delay is merited, it can (and will) issue a declaration—*R (Steinfeld and Keidan)* v *Secretary of State for International Development* [2018] UKSC 32. Relatively few declarations have in fact been made: a total of 37 between October 2000 and July 2017, i.e. an average of only just over two per year; moreover only 25 of these had become final (Ministry of Justice, 2017: 32).

There is no legal duty on the government to repeal or amend incompatible legislation, nor upon Parliament to accept the remedial measures the minister may propose, though the political or moral pressure to do so could be considerable. As a consequence, the ECtHR has been reluctant to regard the declaration procedure as an 'effective remedy' under the ECHR: see *Hobbs* v *UK* (2002) (App. No. 63684/00, 18 June 2002). However, in the context of evidence that the UK government had acted to change the law in 15 of the 18 declarations that had become final since the passing of the HRA, the Grand Chamber of the Court in *Burden* v *UK* [2008] 2 FLR 787 expressed the view that future evidence of an established ministerial practice of giving effect to declarations could be sufficient to persuade the Court that the procedure is effective.

As Greer (1999: 15–16) points out, practically speaking, the declaration process is, nonetheless, somewhat unsatisfactory as it must create uncertainty about how public authorities will deal with incompatible but not (yet) amended legislation. To try and minimise these practical problems, there is a 'fast-track' procedure under HRA 1998, s. 10 whereby ministers can amend non-compliant legislation by 'remedial order'— provided the minister concerned finds 'compelling reasons' (undefined by the Act) for doing so. Moreover, 'fast track' is itself a relative term, and it is perfectly legitimate for the minister to await the exhaustion of the normal appeals process before taking any action. This can add significant delays to the process and, possibly in some cases, hardship to litigants. The Parliamentary Joint Committee on Human Rights recommended in 2008 that a clear timetable for implementation should be established, with a normal expectation that action to address an incompatibility should be completed within six months of the declaration. This recommendation was, however, rejected by the then government (Ministry of Justice, 2009).

10.3.3 Incompatibility of delegated legislation

The powers under s. 4 do not extend to secondary legislation. So, how do we deal with potentially incompatible secondary legislation?

The first issue is always whether the delegated legislation can be interpreted compatibly with Convention rights—the duty to achieve a consistent interpretation under HRA, s. 3 expressly extends to delegated or subordinate legislation. If consistency can be achieved, then that is the end of the problem—see **Figure 10.2**.

If a compatible reading cannot be achieved, we need to identify clearly where the potential incompatibility lies. If the real cause of incompatibility is the parent Act, then it is the Act that should be challenged, not the subordinate legislation. In this situation the subordinate legislation must remain in force unless and until the parent Act is repealed or amended, since, even if the parent Act is incompatible, it is still the law until that time. Both the courts and the minister or council (etc.) who made the rules can, in these circumstances, rely on the 'defence' that they are giving effect to laws necessarily made under primary legislation. If, on the other hand, the incompatibility lies within

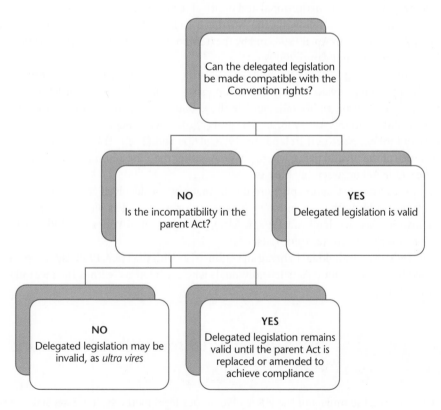

Figure 10.2 Addressing the compatibility of secondary legislation

the secondary legislation itself, then, in the unlikely case that it cannot be reinterpreted to be Convention compliant, it may be struck down by the normal process of judicial review. In effect, the secondary legislation would be declared *ultra vires* its parent Act, because the Act did not require its powers to be used in a way that is incompatible with the Convention.

10.4 Incorporation under the Devolution Acts

The HRA applies across all UK jurisdictions, but in the devolved nations of the United Kingdom, the Convention rights were also built into the legislation which created the Welsh Assembly, the Scottish Parliament, and the Northern Ireland Assembly. This means that actions in respect of the compatibility of devolved legislation are dealt with under the devolution Acts, whereas other matters in these juridictions are pursued under the HRA.

Devolution of legislative powers to the National Assembly for Wales and Scottish Parliament was achieved through Acts of the UK Parliament: the Government of Wales Acts 1998 and 2006, and the Scotland Act 1998. An important feature of this legislation is that both bodies are statutorily obliged to legislate in accordance with Convention rights as defined by the HRA 1998. The position in Northern Ireland is theoretically similar by virtue of the Northern Ireland Act 1998, but also in practice more complicated by virtue of the constitutional and political technicalities of governance arrangements in the Province following the Northern Ireland Peace Agreement (the 'Good Friday Agreement') in April 1998, and by the (temporary) suspension of the assembly in Northern Ireland in the mid-2000s.

The requirement for compatibility has distinct legal consequence in respect of devolved primary and secondary legislation First, primary devolved legislation which breaches Convention rights falls outside those bodies' legislative competence, and is thus invalid (Scotland Act 1988, s. 29(1) and (2)(d); Government of Wales Act 2006, s. 94(3) and (6)(c)); Northern Ireland Act 1998, s. 6(1) and (2)(c)). This seems to envisage severance of the invalid parts, where possible, rather than the automatic striking down of the whole Act or Assembly Measure.

Any secondary legislation purported to be made by the devolved governments which is not compatible with Convention rights is statutorily defined as *ultra vires* and therefore invalid—see Scotland Act 1998, s. 54(2), Government of Wales Act 2006, s. 81(1), and Northern Ireland Act 1998, s. 24(1)(a).

The right of an individual to bring an action, is, as with the HRA 1998 itself, explicitly limited by the devolution Acts to individuals who are 'victims' within the meaning of ECHR, Art. 34.

10.5 The consequences for legal method (1): statutory interpretation

To understand the impact of the HRA 1998 on our legal methods, it is essential first to remember the distinctive basis on which incorporation is to be achieved. The 1998 Act, you will recall, has *not* made the ECHR, with the attendant jurisprudence of the Court, 'lock, stock and barrel' part of English law. This leaves British judges relatively free to arrive at their own version of Convention rights, guided, but not bound, by the *principles,* the approach and meanings adopted by the ECtHR, not necessarily the 'precedent' as such. We will now consider the implications of this, first, for methods of interpretation and second, for precedent.

10.5.1 Interpreting UK legislation

The primary role of the national courts under the HRA 1998 is an interpretative one; they must interpret UK legislation in the light of the Convention rights, and this in turn means that they must interpret the scope and meaning of the Convention rights themselves. How will they go about these processes?

The key provision in the HRA 1998, for our purposes, is s. 3(1). As we have already noted, this imposes a statutory duty on all courts and tribunals to interpret primary and subordinate legislation in a manner consistent with the Convention rights. This duty extends to all legislation, including Acts and regulations passed before the HRA came into force. It follows also that, where there is an issue of compliance, the courts are no longer bound by pre-HRA precedent on the meaning of any particular statutory language—see *per* Lord Hope in *R* v *Lambert* [2001] UKHL 37; [2001] 3 All ER 577 at [81].

The duty under the HRA is concise: it expressly requires the courts to achieve compatibility only *in so far as it is possible to do so*. Not surprisingly, the choice of this form of words has been crucial to the way the courts have approached their interpretative task, and has been the subject of substantial academic and judicial debate. We now need to look at the arguments that have framed that debate.

Section 3 and the art of the possible

The core argument about s. 3 turns on the fact that there are essentially two ways of determining the effect of the phrase 'in so far as it is possible': one is to read it restrictively; the other is to read it expansively. These options were being debated in the academic literature even as the HRA came into force. The case for a restrictive approach was advanced by Marshall (1998), who suggested that s. 3(1) does not really change the task of the courts. It obliges the courts to find consistency only where that is achievable within the bounds of the recognised principles of statutory interpretation. In other words, the courts should not artificially strain the meaning of statutory language to make it fit the Convention. This is also, arguably, consistent with the strong emphasis on parliamentary sovereignty implicit in the whole structuring of the Act, and particularly the procedures for a declaration of incompatibility.

Alternatively, it is possible to argue that the intention of s. 3 is to impose a stronger duty on the courts, akin, as Hunt (1999: 97–8) suggests, to the *Marleasing* obligation in EC law, which, by virtue of similar language to that of HRA 1998, s. 3(1), has been taken to oblige courts to achieve consistency except where that is manifestly *impossible* on the language of the legislation (see further, Case C–106/89 *Marleasing SA* v *La Comercial Internacional de Alimentación SA* [1990] ECR I-4135, explored in **Chapter 11**). This position too had its supporters in the early days of the Act (see, e.g., Ewing, 1999: 87; Bennion, 2000), who saw it is a logical consequence of incorporating human rights standards into UK law. Moreover, it was consistent with the view of the Lord Chancellor in debate on the Human Rights Bill that the courts should apply the declaration of incompatibility only where it is *impossible* to construe legislation consistently with Convention rights (Hansard HL Debates, vol. 583, col. 535, 18 November 1997). The difficulty, then, is that the courts have very little assistance from the Act in defining the boundaries of interpretation. As Lord Nicholls admitted in *Ghaidan* v *Godin-Mendoza* [2004] UKHL 30, at [27]:

> What is not clear is the test to be applied in separating the sheep from the goats. What is the standard, or the criterion, by which 'possibility' is to be judged? A comprehensive answer to this question is proving elusive. The courts, including [the House of Lords], are still cautiously feeling their way forward as experience in the application of section 3 gradually accumulates.

The high watermark of expansive interpretation so far has been the case of *R* v *A* [2001] UKHL 25; [2001] 2 AC 45; it also highlights the tensions that have existed between different judicial styles. The accused in this case had been charged with rape and wished at his trial to bring evidence of previous consensual sexual relations with the complainant as part of his defence. This, he argued, he was precluded from doing by the Youth Justice and Criminal Evidence Act 1999, s. 41(1) and (3), which had introduced a new 'rape shield defence' into English law, prohibiting a defendant from bringing evidence or asking questions about any prior sexual behaviour of the complainant without the leave of the court. This change in the law reflected longstanding concerns that questions about sexual history were too often used by defendants unfairly to undermine the evidence of alleged rape victims in court. On the other hand, there were also concerns that s. 41 had in fact gone too far in protecting the victim, to the extent that it now undermined the rights of the accused (see, e.g., Birch, 2000).

The House of Lords accepted that s. 41 had gone too far, and had denied the defendant his due process rights under ECHR, Art. 6. In what is clearly the leading judgment Lord Steyn takes us through a number of steps. These are instructive in terms of approach.

First, his Lordship undertakes an extensive review of the content and legislative history leading up to the passing of s. 41. He then explores the scope of s. 41 itself, drawing extensively on both academic commentary and the Canadian 'rape shield' laws that were influential in shaping s. 41, while also considering proposals from the New South Wales and New Zealand Law Commissions. On this basis, he concludes that s. 41 is too widely drafted and makes an 'excessive inroad into the right to a fair trial' (para. 36). His third step is to explore the interpretive options open to the complainant in the light of HRA, s. 3(1), *if* 'ordinary methods of purposive and contextual interpretation' (para. 39) fail. Using these options, his Lordship rejects a number of ways of restricting the breadth of s. 41 as impossible under both ordinary rules and HRA, s. 3(1). Finally, his Lordship focuses on two of the statutory exceptions built into s. 41. These give a judge discretion to admit evidence of a complainant's sexual history where:

- behaviour is relevant to the issue of consent and the relevant behaviour either took place at or about the same time as the event out of which the complaint came: s. 41(3)(b); or
- it was so strikingly similar to the behaviour of the complainant at or about the time complained of, that it ought to be admitted: s. 41(3)(c).

Having ruled out any possibility of using subsection (3)(b) in this case (because too much time had elapsed between any previous sexual activity and the event complained of), the Court focused on s. 41(3)(c). Lord Steyn argued that, although the subsection was not sufficient under ordinary methods of statutory interpretation to cure the problem, it was possible, by using HRA, s. 3(1) 'to subordinate the niceties of language' (para. 45) to interpret the provision to take account of 'modern considerations of relevance judged by logical and commonsense criteria of time and circumstances' (ibid.). Consequently, the House of Lords decided by a majority that the test of admissibility under s. 41(3)(c) in such cases becomes whether, 'due regard always being paid to the importance of seeking to protect the complainant from indignity and humiliating questions . . . the evidence . . . is nevertheless so relevant to the issues of consent that to exclude it would endanger the fairness of the trial under Article 6 of the convention' (para. 46).

Now, whatever the House of Lords may call it, this involves a quite breathtaking disregard of statutory language—to the extent that one of their Lordships, Lord Hope, was clearly uncomfortable with what was being done. A narrow statutory exception, concerned only to admit what in the jargon we call 'similar fact' evidence, has consequently been rewritten as a much more generalised test of relevance.

Lord Steyn's approach to s. 3 in this case thus takes the 'strong consistency' approach to something of an extreme. Compatibility is to be achieved, even if the resulting interpretation is 'linguistically strained'—as it was (to say the least) in *R* v *A*. Only if there is an express restriction on Convention rights 'stated in terms' (i.e. made explicit on the face of the Act) should a declaration of compatibility be considered under s. 4.

By contrast, Lord Hope's position, taken in both *R* v *A* and in *R* v *Lambert* [2001] UKHL 37, is much closer to what we have called the 'Marshall interpretation'. Legislation cannot be made compatible with the ECHR if it contains provisions which, either expressly *or by necessary implication*, contradict Convention rights. The phrase in italics thus seems to run counter to Lord Steyn's expansive view. Case law since *R* v *A* can perhaps be read as indicating some attempt to consolidate practice and clarify common principles and approaches. Both Lords Steyn and Hope subsequently made statements which suggested that their positions were in fact closer than this initial juxtaposition would indicate (see Lord Hope's later opinion in *Lambert* and Lord Steyn in *R (Anderson)* v *Secretary of State for the Home Department* [2002] UKHL 46 [2003] 1 AC 837). Some commentators have taken this as indicative of a general retrenchment by the House of Lords. Danny Nicol (2004) thus argues that their Lordships' approach in *Re S, ex parte Anderson*, and *Bellinger* v *Bellinger* [2003] UKHL 21; [2003] 2 WLR 1174 indicates a move towards a more restricted use of s. 3 and a correspondingly greater willingness to issue a declaration of incompatibility under s. 4. However, others are less certain. Aileen Kavanagh (2004a), by contrast, sees evidence of judicial sensitivity to the context of each case rather than a clear trend. She points to the fact that the s. 4 declaration was a relatively 'easy' option for the courts in those cases. In *Anderson* and *Bellinger* in particular, there was already a strong indication that Parliament would change the law. This was not the case in *R* v *A*, which involved legislation that was already supposed to be HRA compliant.

Certainly, it is our view that judicial practice today is still geared very much to treating the declaration of incompatibility as a remedy of last resort. This view is consistent with the House of Lords' approach in the leading case of *Ghaidan* v *Godin-Mendoza* [2004] UKHL 30, which concerned rights of succession to a statutory tenancy under the Rent Act 1977. The respondent had lived in a stable homosexual relationship with the deceased tenant. But the Rent Act only gave a right of succession to a person living with the original tenant 'as his or her wife or husband'—and, in any strict or proper sense of the terms, this could not therefore encompass same-sex partnerships. The respondent alleged that this violated his right under ECHR, Art. 14. The House of Lords agreed (Lord Millet dissenting) and construed the 1977 Act to allow succession, regardless of gender, provided the parties had been living together in a stable relationship.

The majority in *Ghaidan* agreed that any non-compliant literal meaning of a provision must readily give way, except where, in Lord Nicholls' words, such an interpretation would conflict with a 'fundamental feature' of the legislation. Moreover, Lord Steyn (at [45]), strongly supported by Lord Rodger, once again explicitly rejected a narrow construction of s. 3(1):

> First, it applies even if there is no ambiguity in the language in the sense of it being capable of bearing two *possible* meanings. The word 'possible' in section 3(1) is used in a different and much stronger sense. Secondly, section 3(1) imposes a stronger and more radical obligation than to adopt a purposive interpretation in the light of the ECHR. Thirdly the draftsman of the Act had before him the model of the New Zealand Bill of Rights Act which imposes a requirement that the interpretation to be adopted must be reasonable. Parliament specifically rejected the legislative model of requiring a reasonable interpretation.

Subsequently, the superior courts have delivered a range of statements stressing the extent to which s. 3 itself imposes a 'strong interpretative duty on the courts, so that a declaration of incompatibility should be treated as exceptional': see, for example, *Sheldrake* v *DPP* [2004] UKHL 43; [2005] 1 AC 264, para 28; *R v Waya* [2012] UKSC 51; [2012] 3 WLR 1188, para. 14. A number of cases have explicitly drawn, or at least accepted in argument, a comparison with the *Marleasing* approach in the way that Hunt (1999) has suggested—see, for example, *Johnson v Medical Defence Union* [2007] EWCA Civ 262; *Vodafone 2 v Revenue and Customs Commissioners* [2009] EWCA Civ 446.

None of these cases, however, entirely resolve the uncertainties we have been discussing. Despite the direction of travel, we are not necessarily much closer to Lord Nicholl's elusive 'test'. And perhaps that is because the search for such a test is ultimately unrealistic. Aileen Kavanagh (2007: 132) thus makes the point that:

> Such an answer is elusive . . . because of the necessarily evaluative nature of the task which judges have to undertake when applying s. 3 by balancing two sets of values which pull in different directions.

In other words, we are back to the old truism that it really does depend on the circumstances of the case.

That in turn still leaves us with some uncertainty about just how far, practically, a court should be prepared to go to achieve consistency. What emerges from the case law is a range of techniques that the courts are prepared to use, and a few that they are not.

First, a court may *read down* the words of the Act to give them a narrower than usual scope and thereby make the offending provision Convention compliant.

Secondly, a court can *read in* Convention rights by implying words into a statute that are not there on a literal reading—*Ghaidan* is a good example of this; *R v A* perhaps the most extreme example so far.

Thirdly, there is some suggestion that, as Lord Hope expressed it in *Lambert* (at [81]), the courts can engage in a process of *translation*, that is, a process in which incompatible words are to be changed and read as if they were compatible. Both 'reading in' and 'translation' represent potentially radical departures from the tradition of literal interpretation.

There are also some things that the courts are reluctant to do. As we have noted already, the courts will not use s. 3 to interpret legislation compatibly if such a construction:

- clearly conflicts with the express words—see *Anderson*, earlier in this section;
- conflicts with a foundational aim or function of the statute—see *Re S*, earlier in this section;
- requires reading in a substantially new provision (e.g. a whole new section) or the substantial redesign of a statutory scheme: *R (MH)* v *Secretary of State for the Health Department* [2004] EWCA Civ 1609; *R (Wright)* v *Secretary of State for Health* [2009] UKHL 3.

You need to be aware that, on the whole, the problem cannot be quantified in simple terms, such as 'it is OK to read in a few words, but not a whole subsection'. Section 3 cases are difficult precisely because it is hard to say *in general* where the dividing line between interpreting and legislating *should* be drawn. The courts, in their pragmatic fashion tend to treat s. 3 problems as largely contextual decisions which may be influenced by a number of general interpretive principles (see Kavanagh, 2004b), but which ultimately have to be decided on a case-by-case basis. While it would certainly be inconsistent with the spirit of the ECHR and the purpose of HRA, s. 3 to focus narrowly on literalist, linguistic approaches to interpretation, the current rather pragmatic emphasis on teleological interpretation does also carry with it some risks. In particular, we suggest, there must be a point where the proper, parliamentary redrafting of fundamentally non-compatible legislation is desirable. This would at least maintain some relative transparency and certainty in the meaning of statute law, and help sustain the distinction between legislative and judicial functions. It would also allow Parliament rather than the judges to determine the merits of what may be important changes to social policy.

The process of interpretation under section 3

Whatever uncertainties we may face in determining when s. 3 will be used, there is an increasingly clear reasoning process by which the question of construction is decided. We summarise these various steps in **Figure 10.3**.

The critical first step is that we must identify precisely which statutory provision contravenes the Convention (see *per* Lord Nicholls in *Re S*, at [41]). It is not enough simply to raise a general allegation of incompatibility against the statute as a whole.

If the court then decides there is a breach of Convention rights, it is not necessary to go straight to s. 3. If the problem can be resolved by reference to normal principles of construction, then the court should do so. If—and only if—this is not possible, then the court must consider s. 3. In so doing, you should be aware that the court's approach will differ somewhat, depending on whether the Act in question was passed before or after the HRA. Where it was passed before the HRA, legislative intent is unlikely to be a decisive factor in any question of construction (unless, unusually, Convention compliance was identified as an issue at the time). Moreover, any pre-HRA authorities on statutory

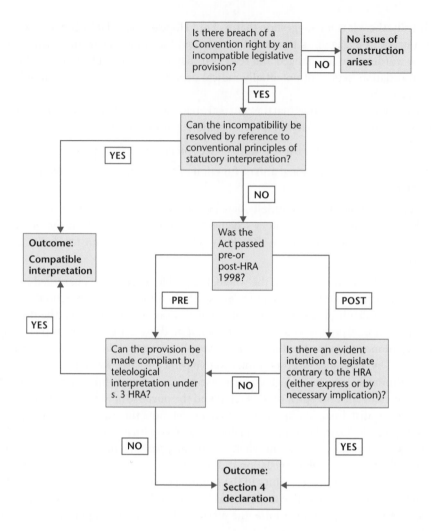

Figure 10.3 Steps to construction under HRA, s. 3

meaning will not be binding on the court—*per* Lord Hope in *Lambert*, at [81]. In the case of post-HRA legislation, both legislative intent—as in *R* v *A*, discussed earlier in the section, and relevant precedents do need to be taken into account, though any assertion that Parliament intended to legislate contrary to the HRA is likely to require very clear supporting evidence.

Legislative intent, Hansard, and the HRA

One final point, before we leave the discussion of s. 3, concerns the role of Hansard and other documentary sources that may provide evidence of legislative intent or legislative scope to the courts. As we saw in **Chapter 9**, following *Pepper* v *Hart*, under certain strict conditions it has become acceptable for the courts to refer to Hansard, the record of proceedings in Parliament. There was a concern that the HRA might add to the pressure on courts to look to Hansard, particularly in assessing whether legislation is compatible with the Convention. In fact, as with *Pepper* v *Hart*, more generally the courts have tended to discourage extensive reliance on legislative history. As Lord Nicholls observed in *Wilson* v *First County Trust* [2003] UKHL 40:

> 66. I expect that occasions when resort to Hansard is necessary as part of the statutory 'compatibility' exercise will seldom arise. The present case is not such an occasion. Should such an occasion arise the courts must be careful not to treat the ministerial or other statement as indicative of the objective intention of Parliament. Nor should the courts give a ministerial statement, whether made inside or outside Parliament, determinative weight. It should not be supposed that members necessarily agreed with the minister's reasoning or his conclusions.
>
> 67. Beyond this use of Hansard as a source of background information, the content of parliamentary debates has no direct relevance to the issues the court is called upon to decide in compatibility cases and, hence, these debates are not a proper matter for investigation or consideration by the courts . . .

Similarly, the courts have also been reluctant to permit Hansard to be used in interpreting the HRA itself. Thus, the House of Lords in both *Aston Cantlow Parochial Church Council* v *Wallbank* [2003] UKHL 37; [2004] 1 AC 546 and *YL* v *Birmingham City Council* [2007] UKHL 27 declined to use Hansard to assist in understanding the scope of 'public authority' under HRA s. 6.

10.5.2 Interpreting the Convention rights

The second point we need to explore is the courts' approach to interpreting the Convention rights themselves. There is, of course, already a substantial 'bank' of interpretive material in the jurisprudence of the ECtHR. However, one consequence of the 'free-standing' model of incorporation is that the English courts are not obliged to follow the interpretations laid down by the Court, though they are expected to have some regard to the decisions of that body (see section **10.6** for more detail on this). Accordingly, it is conceivable that the English courts could develop a distinctive human rights jurisprudence which deviates significantly from the approach of the Court, provided that it does not fall below the threshold standards set by the ECtHR. This is because the HRA 1998 does not oust the jurisdiction of the ECtHR (though it does make the journey to Strasbourg rather longer). Claimants who fail to establish a breach of Convention rights before the UK courts are still entitled to appeal to Strasbourg for redress. If they win, under the ECHR, Art. 46 the UK government is obliged to apply the decision of the ECtHR (unless it has entered a derogation), thereby overriding the inconsistent approach of the domestic courts. A controversial example of this was the *Abu Qatada* case: see *Othman* v *United Kingdom* App. No. 8139/09, 17 January 2012. The Law Lords had considered that it would not be a violation of the Convention to deport the radical Islamic cleric Abu Qatada (Omar Othman) to Jordan, where he had been convicted in his absence of serious terrorist offences. However, the Strasbourg court held that Abu Qatada's deportation would be a 'flagrant' breach of Art. 6 on account of what was seen as a real risk that the Jordanian court would use evidence at the applicant's retrial that had been obtained by the torture of third persons. The ECtHR had never before found that deporting or extraditing a person would be a violation in those circumstances, and its decision 'sent political shockwaves through the UK establishment' (Dickson, 2012: 373). As a result, the United Kingdom and Jordan had to enter into a treaty agreeing that evidence of torture would not be used before Qatada could be deported. (He was subsequently acquitted in Jordan from involvement in two bomb plots, and released from prison in September 2014.)

Cases like this indicate that too much independence on the part of the British courts could be counter-productive if it simply generated more appeals to Strasbourg than the present system. At the same time, this does not mean that the English and European courts should necessarily proceed in absolute tandem. The ECtHR itself recognises that scope may exist for local variation in the application of the Convention and, regardless of whether a state has incorporated the Convention or not, allows a 'margin of appreciation'. This rather technical doctrine means that, in assessing compliance, the Court will in some respects defer to the appreciation of a problem by the national authorities, including the courts, thereby giving them some element of discretion. The extent of the margin of appreciation will depend on the nature of the rights involved. Where 'a particularly important facet of an individual's existence or identity is at stake' (*Dickson v United Kingdom* [2007] 41 EHRR 21; [2007] ECHR 44362/04 at 78), that margin will be reduced accordingly.

The operation of a margin of appreciation also helps explain why there is an obligation on national courts only to take the ECtHR's jurisprudence into account. The limit to this obligation means that domestic courts are permitted to take local conditions and local needs into consideration in applying the Convention. However, this framing of the obligation also means that the margin of appreciation is actually a 'two-way street'. While it prevents the ECtHR from applying the Convention too strictly across different national legal systems, it also prevents national courts from ignoring the Court's jurisprudence entirely. That would not be to take it into account.

Related to this is the question of what interpretative principles the domestic courts will bring to their analysis of Convention rights. We have already pointed out that the Convention rights are not necessarily capable of the kind of precise and detailed exposition that characterises a lot of domestic legislation. While the Convention may specify that we have a right to life and a right to privacy, the potential boundaries of these rights are difficult to define in the abstract, or in the detail often expected of legislation; similarly, problems will arise in defining the boundaries between competing rights. For example, is the practice of abortion to be protected because it constitutes an integral part of the woman's right to a private life, or challenged as a violation of the foetus's right to life itself? At what point may one right supersede the other? Resolving such problems requires not just analysis of the text, but a sensitivity to the 'spirit' of the Convention and to the social and ethical issues that such problems raise. Arguments about human rights often do not lend themselves to the narrower brands of legal literalism. In theory this should not be an insurmountable problem. British judges today are, given the EU context, far more familiar with broader, principles-based drafting and purposive styles of interpretation than they were 30 years ago, and generally more prepared for the kind of judicial activism that the ECHR demands. But the EU law analogy gives rise to a further question: should British judges consciously adopt the style of analysis used by the ECtHR? This is in some respects distinctive, reflecting both the special character of the ECHR and the general principles of interpretation developed under the Vienna Convention on the Law of Treaties (1969). The interpretive style of the Court is thereby characterised by three key elements: the 'textuality principle'; a 'teleological' approach to interpretation; and a capacity to supplement the express terms of the Convention by the recognition of 'implied terms'.

The **textuality principle** describes the Court's starting point, which, in common with all widely accepted traditions of interpretation, demands respect for the text of the Convention. As the Vienna Convention, Art. 31(1) puts it: 'A treaty shall be interpreted in good faith in accordance with the ordinary meaning to be given to the terms of the treaty in their context and in the light of its object and purpose.' It is an approach, therefore, which avoids the extremes of literalism by accepting that the ordinary meaning is in large part determined by the context—both textual and social. This is reinforced by an expectation that the Court will look at the meaning of words or provisions within the context of the Convention as a whole. This has created some interesting problems, because the Court has sometimes found areas of overlap between different provisions of the ECHR, rather than, say, assuming that the express inclusion of one right in one part of the Convention precludes its implicit inclusion in another article. For example, in *Rasmussen*, Series A, No. 87, a question arose as to Danish paternity law. Denmark had ratified the Convention but not the Seventh Protocol, which, in Art. 5, expressly defined the rights of parents with regard to their children, and the Danish government therefore sought to argue that the case was not justiciable. The Court rejected this argument by finding that, despite the omission of the Seventh Protocol, the case could also be considered under ECHR, Art. 8. In theory at least this could raise interesting questions in the British context, given that the Protocols not ratified by Britain are excluded from the Convention rights within the HRA 1998.

The idea of a **teleological approach** is primarily a very European way of describing purposiveness; it operates in the EU courts as well. The ECtHR has adopted a fairly cautious approach in this regard, seeking to tread a fine line between possibly excessive interference with the domestic jurisdiction and powers of individual states, and the need to give full effect to the aims and objectives of the Convention in securing individual rights and freedoms. Consequently, the Court has established a number of basic guidelines. For example:

(i)   Where an article limits or qualifies an individual right, such limits are normally to be interpreted narrowly.

(ii) The Convention should be read as a 'living instrument', that is, by reference to current values and conditions, not those that existed when the Convention was adopted in the 1950s.

(iii) Closely related to this, following the Vienna Convention, Art. 31(3)(b) the interpreter is entitled to take account of the subsequent practice of the state in the application of the treaty. The precise scope and meaning of subsequent practice, however, is a contested and somewhat thorny issue, beyond the scope of our present concerns.

(iv) In addition, the Court has recourse to a number of *general principles*, notably, the 'margin of appreciation' and the principles of proportionality (see section **10.3.2**) and legal certainty (self-explanatory!), which it will use to determine the limits of state liability and individual rights. This approach is again one with which British judges have become more familiar through EU law, and, as we have seen, increasingly have had to engage with under the HRA. This may be particularly difficult when it forces judges further into the political arena than they might wish when interpreting the Act.

The signs are, for the most part, that the English judiciary has adapted effectively, though some might say rather conservatively, to both the Strasbourg jurisprudence and approach. Signs are too that it is starting to find its way towards a more distinctive UK jurisprudence, though there has been little evidence so far of the HRA free-standing model being used as a justification to depart dramatically from the ECtHR line.

10.6 The consequences for legal method (2): precedent

In looking at the impact of Convention rights and the HRA 1998 on precedent there are essentially two questions: what is the likely impact of the 1998 Act on the doctrine of precedent, and what is the status of decisions of the ECtHR under the HRA 1998?

As regards the first of these points, all common law rules and precedents that are incompatible with Convention rights are potentially open to challenge. This principle extends *expressly* to those precedents which are interpretations of statutory provisions, since, if inconsistent with Convention rights, they will be caught explicitly by HRA 1998, s. 3, and *implicitly* to all common law rules *per se*. This argument is based on the fact that all courts and tribunals are, as we have seen in section **10.3.1**, themselves 'public authorities' under the Act. As such they are obliged to achieve consistency with the Convention in respect of the substantive and procedural rules they have made. The interesting technical question is how the courts face that particular challenge.

There is clearly an expectation with regard to previous (inconsistent) interpretations of legislation caught by s. 3 that all courts/tribunals will be required to disregard such precedents, even though this is implicit in s. 3 rather than expressly spelled out in the Act (but see Home Office (1997), para. 2.8, where the point is made explicit). The extent to which common law precedents are necessarily open to review and potential rejection is more difficult. In practice, the sanctity of precedent is often related, but perhaps secondary in common law matters to larger policy questions regarding the Court's preparedness to use the HRA to extend or create new causes of action.

We noted above, in our discussion of indirect effects under s. 6, that the courts (on the whole) have tended to operate with caution in extending common law causes of action. Thus, in cases like *Wainwright* and *Campbell* v *MGN,* the courts have moved relatively slowly in developing privacy principles out of existing causes of action, rather than use the HRA to create, wholesale, a new common law of privacy. We suggest this cautious approach is not unique to privacy matters. It is, for example, also apparent in recent cases where the courts have been invited to align, via the HRA and Arts 2 and 3 of the Convention, the public law and private law (negligence) accountability of the police for failing to safeguard victims or potential victims of serious crime. It is established in ECtHR and UK jurisprudence that the police may be liable as a public authority for harms caused to the victims of crime by serious and substantial failures in its response to or investigation of those crimes—see particularly now *Commissioner of Police for the Metropolis* v *DSD* [2018] UKSC 11 (affirming decisions of both the High Court and Court of Appeal). However, in *Smith* v *Chief Constable of Sussex Police; Van Colle* v *Chief Constable of the Hertfordshire Police* [2008] UKHL 50 and *Michael* v *Chief Constable of South Wales Police* [2015] UKSC 2, the courts saw strong policy grounds for *not* using the HRA to extend police liability in negligence. These policy grounds were not outweighed by the issue of matching private and public law obligations under the HRA. Put simply, the tort and HRA regimes were not functionally analogous, and did not need to march in step just by virtue of the HRA.

A related question is whether the HRA actually disrupts the normal practice of *stare decisis* to the extent of requiring courts to disregard otherwise binding authority. Since all courts and tribunals are caught by the duties contained in HRA 1998 s. 6, there is clearly some basis for saying that the duty to override inconsistent precedents *in general* lies with all courts and tribunals, regardless of the status or authority of the precedent involved. The Court of Appeal's decision in *D v East Berkshire NHS Trust* [2004] QB 558 offers some limited authority consistent with this view. Here the Court of Appeal held, contrary to normal principles of *stare decisis* that the House of Lords' decision in *X (Minors) v Bedfordshire County Council* [1995] 2 AC 633 could not survive the introduction of the HRA 1998, because the HRA undermined the policy considerations that had shaped the House of Lords' reasoning in that case. This decision was affirmed subsequently in *Kay v London Borough of Lambeth; Leeds City Council v Price* [2006] UKHL 10. However, in *Kay*, their Lordships also affirmed the priority of the common law principles of precedent, and stressed that the circumstances in *D v East Berkshire* should be regarded as wholly exceptional. Since then, in various twists and turns, the Court of Appeal decision in *D* has itself been treated as impliedly overruled on substantive grounds (see *CN v Poole Borough Council* [2017] EWCA Civ 2185), but without further comment on the issue of precedent. Consequently, we must assume for the present that courts should follow established precedent, even if there is a conflict with Convention rights, except in the most extreme circumstances. In effect, it means that the Supreme Court becomes virtually the sole arbiter of whether or not domestic precedents are compliant, or should be overruled as non-compliant with Convention rights.

As regards the status of decisions of the ECtHR, HRA 1998, s. 2(1) expressly requires the British courts to *take into account*, among other things, the judgments, decisions, and advisory opinions of the Court and opinions and decisions of the (now defunct) European Commission. This was interpreted by the Court of Appeal in *Barclays Bank plc v Ellis* [2000] All ER (D) 1164 to mean that lawyers had to bring to the court's attention to *all* the relevant case law of the ECtHR. Mere reference to the Convention, it was said, did not help the court and was not sufficient.

However, this is also an obligation only to consider; there is no express statutory duty to *follow* the established European case law on the ECHR. This is consistent with the free-standing model adopted by the United Kingdom, and different from the United Kingdom's obligations as regards decisions of the CJEU under the European Communities Act, s. 2. That said, certainly for the first decade of the HRA, the courts tended to treat themselves as ordinarily obliged to adopt a consistent interpretation. In *R (Alconbury) v Environment Secretary* [2011] UKHL 23, for example, the majority of the Law Lords undoubtedly treated the Strasbourg jurisprudence as *prima facie* binding, even if only for pragmatic reasons. In Lord Slynn's words (para. 20):

[i]n the absence of some special circumstances it seems to me that the [UK] court should follow any clear and constant jurisprudence of the European Court of Human Rights. If it does not do so there is at least a possibility that the case will go to that court, which is likely in the ordinary case to follow its own constant jurisprudence.

This approach came to be reflected (no pun intended) even more strongly by the superior courts following the leading case of *R (Ullah)* v *Special Adjudicator* [2004] UKHL 26. This decision came to epitomise the development of the so-called 'mirror principle', by which the UK courts sought not just to apply the established Strasbourg jurisprudence, but to anticipate the way in which ECtHR would apply it to the case in hand. This was, as commentators have observed, a narrow, common law-influenced, approach to adopt. It only began to be disrupted at the end of the last decade as senior judges began to take a more circumspect—if not actually critical—look at ECtHR decision-making (see, e.g., Bates, 2015: 60).

Lord Neuberger's decision in *Manchester City Council* v *Pinnock* [2010] UKSC 45; [2011] 2 AC 104, is considered a marker for this sea change in approach. Lord Neuberger thus reminded the UK courts that their duty was to 'take account' of Strasbourg jurisprudence, which might mean following a clear and constant line of decisions, but only provided their:

> 48 . . . effect is not inconsistent with some fundamental substantive or procedural aspect of our law, and whose reasoning does not appear to overlook or misunderstand some argument or point of principle.

As Bates (2015: 61–2) has observed, no court has yet had to cross this 'constitutional redline' constructed by *Pinnock*, but the decision can nonetheless be seen as part of a 'new equilibrium' between the UK courts and Strasbourg, the other side of which is the ECtHR's openness to a more dialogical approach with national courts, a move that was strongly signalled in the wording of the Council of Europe's 2012 Brighton Declaration on the future working of the Court.

Latterly, this move away from the mirror principle can also be observed in a willingness in the UK courts to apply Convention principles in the absence of ECtHR authority. Thus, in *Rabone* v *Pennine Care NHS Foundation Trust* [2012] UKSC 2 it was held that, notwithstanding the absence of authority from ECtHR, a hospital was under a positive obligation to protect the life of a mentally ill young woman who had been admitted informally because of serious attempts to take her own life. Similarly, in *Moohan* v *Lord Advocate* [2014] UKSC 67, Lord Wilson observed (at [105]):

> . . . where there is no directly relevant decision of the ECtHR with which it would be possible (even if appropriate) to keep pace, we can and must do more. We must determine for ourselves the existence or otherwise of an alleged Convention right . . .

Our discussion of s. 2(1) so far leaves unresolved one other issue: what should an English court do when confronted by the post-HRA precedent of a superior English court, which is inconsistent with a *later* decision of the ECtHR? This rather mind-bending question arose for the Court of Appeal in *Leeds City Council* v *Price* [2005] EWCA Civ 289. Here the Court was faced with the House of Lords' decision in *Harrow LBC* v *Qazi* [2004] 1 AC 983. This was a decision that was made, obviously, after the passing of the HRA, and was one in which the Lords had taken into account the relevant ECtHR jurisprudence. Unfortunately, it was also obvious that *Qazi* was 'unquestionably' incompatible with the later decision of the ECtHR in *Connors v United Kingdom* (2004) 40 EHRR 189. What do you think the Court of Appeal should have done? Well, what the Court actually did was to follow *Qazi* and distinguish its own earlier decision in *D v East Berkshire NHS Trust* (discussed earlier in the section), despite the conflict with the *Connors* decision. This was a decision made with some reluctance. Clearly, the judges felt caught between the proverbial rock and hard place. The *Price* case was appealed to the House of Lords—see *Kay v London Borough of Lambeth*; *Leeds City Council v Price* [2006] UKHL 10, where, as we have seen, the Court of Appeal's decision was affirmed. Thus, it seems that a court faced by a conflict between a binding domestic precedent, and a contrary ECtHR decision must *normally* follow the domestic precedent. This was justified (*per* Lord Bingham at paras [43]–[44]) on the need to preserve legal certainty, even in the Convention context, and by reference to the margin of appreciation granted by the Convention to national authorities, including the courts. However, the House of Lords did leave a loophole by allowing that in very exceptional circumstances departure from an otherwise binding precedent could be justified.

By an interesting twist, the consistency of the substantive decision in *Kay* with the ECHR was subsequently brought into question by the decision of the Strasbourg Court in *McCann v United Kingdom* (2008) 47 EHRR 40 [2008] ECHR 19009/04. As a result, the standing of the *Kay* decision itself fell to be considered again by the House of Lords in *Doherty v Birmingham City Council* [2008] UKHL 57. In *Doherty*, their Lordships declined to overturn the majority view in *Kay*, arguing that *Kay*, as a recent precedent, could only be overturned by a hearing before a panel of nine Law Lords (which it was not, as the problem of inconsistency was not foreseen at the time the case was listed), and that, in any event, inconsistencies with *McCann* could be dealt with by 'modifying' the majority view to take account of *McCann*.

Taken together, these decisions indicate (a) the strong reluctance of the courts to set aside notions of *stare decisis*; and (b) their willingness to use their obligations under s. 6 to justify creatively reinterpreting their own precedents (as *Qazi* was in *Kay*, and then *Kay* itself was in *Doherty*), rather than overruling them. While some may see this as a complicated way of making UK law Convention-compliant, it nevertheless fits with an idea that we discussed earlier in the section; that is, as Lord Bingham asserted in *Kay*, that the principle of a margin of appreciation allows national courts some freedom of action, not just as regards the extent of substantive compliance with ECtHR jurisprudence, but particularly in the choice of methods whereby compliance is achieved.

The search for consistency, as we have seen, may also arguably leave the UK law on human rights in a rather unsatisfactory position. It both limits the opportunity to develop a more distinctive UK jurisprudence, and also leaves the superior UK courts, and particularly the Supreme Court, in the position of playing 'catch-up' with Strasbourg. To some extent this may be inevitable. Our courts should not necessarily be expected successfully to anticipate the Strasbourg jurisprudence, particularly when, as in response to cases like *Al-Skeini* [2008] 1 AC 153 (see *Al-Skeini v United Kingdom* (2011) 53 EHRR 18) and *Abu Qatada*, the ECtHR decides to extend its own jurisprudence. Nonetheless, an approach that seems predominantly focused on hitting the required minimum standard will almost certainly see a continuing, if relatively small number of applicants beating a path to Strasbourg (see Dickson, 2012).

10.7 Legal research and argumentation

The HRA 1998 raises a number of important practical and conceptual issues around legal research and argumentation.

First, it has created an obligation on all British lawyers (rather than just the human rights specialists) to become familiar with new sources of law. This is not a small task. There is not just the matter of developing a familiarity with the Convention itself (one probably needs to understand the Convention as a whole, not just the Convention rights enacted in the HRA 1998, for the reasons of interpretation already considered), there is also the slight matter of over 50 years of case law. Reading decisions of the ECtHR is also a somewhat distinctive process. The judgments are drafted as something of a compromise between the common law and civil law styles we saw in **Chapter 3**. Until 1968, decisions of the Court adopted very much the continental style still used in modified form by the CJEU, with numbered paragraphs giving the Court's reasoning, followed by a short judgment. This has been abandoned for a more flowing, narrative, style of analysis, with reference to its own earlier authorities as required (as we have briefly seen, the Court does abide by its own system of precedent, albeit not with the full rigour of the English model of *stare decisis*). Like the British courts, the Court requires decisions to be made by at least a majority, rather than expecting unanimity. Judges may also, therefore, in common law fashion, offer separate opinions. This is clearly different from the collegial approach of the CJEU. In practice, it is relatively rare for judges of the Court to deliver separate opinions (though for a recent example, see *Sher* v *United Kingdom* [2015] ECHR 5201/11 (20 October 2015). Judges appear to have been very cautious in their use, and aware of the risk of undermining the authority of the Court by extensive divisions of opinion. Consequently, when the power has been used it is generally to deliver a dissent from the majority view, rather than a concurring judgment giving some distinctive reasoning. Joint dissenting opinions may also be delivered.

At a deeper level, as Hunt (1999) points out, the HRA 1998 more than ever forces lawyers to confront matters of morality and fundamental values, and this itself has implications for the form and content of legal argumentation. The traditional 'positivistic' conception of law has tended to keep law and morality separate. This is not to say that law is routinely assumed to have no moral content or foundation, but it does mean that legal and moral principles and reasoning have generally been treated as distinct species, with the courts being primarily concerned with the enforcement of law, not morals. By blurring that distinction, the 1998 Act sometimes obliges lawyers, including the judges, to take account of a wider range of resources and forms of argument. This may involve both a wider academic literature, including the ethical and philosophical, not just the legal. As Lord Steyn acknowledged, instead of trawling through endless *dicta* on *Wednesbury* unreasonableness, 'it may be more helpful to dip into Isaiah Berlin' (cited in Hunt, 1999: 99). Comparative material, particularly from other common law jurisdictions that have adopted a culture of positive rights, such as Canada, South Africa, New Zealand, and the United States, is also relevant, and sometimes cited at length. Indeed, much of the HRA case law cited in this chapter illustrates the extent to which such materials are considered.

10.8 The future of the Human Rights Act

'Bringing rights home' has been given a new twist by debates over whether the HRA should be repealed and replaced by a 'British Bill of Rights'. Up until British political life was dominated by Brexit, the future of the Act had become a political hot potato. A Commission on a Bill of Rights (2012) was established by government to 'investigate the creation of a UK Bill of Rights that incorporates and builds on all our obligations under the European Convention' (Commission on a Bill of Rights, 2012). Though the Commission was split in its conclusions, the majority favoured a move, in principle, to a British Bill of Rights, and the Conservative Party subsequently went into the 2015 General Election with a manifesto commitment to scrap the Act.

Whether the future of the HRA becomes a critical issue for government post-Brexit remains to be seen. Repeal of the HRA can be seen as consistent with a growing maturity and sense of the United Kingdom as a rights-based rather than liberties-based democracy. Proponents of the move see it as more consistent with British traditions of parliamentary sovereignty, though this is often coupled with concerns that the HRA is open to abuse by certain undesirable or undeserving litigants. Amongst the most politically contentious issues have been voting rights for prisoners, the Art. 6 rights of suspected terrorists, and the rights or otherwise of the state to deport foreign national prisoners at the end of their sentence (see, e.g., Horne and Miller, 2015).

A new Bill of Rights could thus be seen as an opportunity to break the link with the ECtHR so as to allow a more distinctively 'British' culture of rights to develop (see, e.g., Commission on a Bill of Rights, 2012). It would also be an opportunity to address some of the technical problems we, and others, have identified with the HRA in its current form.

On the other side, many supporters of the HRA see the attacks on the Act as largely politically motivated and based on a mistaken conception of Strasbourg 'interference' in the domestic legal process, fuelled in part by media antagonisms and inaccuracies.

Aside from the political arguments, whilst not in the same league as Brexit, the technical legal difficulties of constructing a British Bill of Rights would be substantial. The HRA is deeply embedded in UK law, and particularly in the new 'constitutional DNA' of the devolved nations. How far the UK could disentangle itself from Strasbourg and the ECHR is also highly debatable. This was reflected in the terms of reference of the Independent Commission, which precluded any question of the United Kingdom withdrawing from the ECHR as such.

 CONCLUSION

There is no doubt that the HRA has had a significant impact in moving the United Kingdom from a system historically built around a loosely defined set of civil liberties to a far more pro-active, rights-based model. The move to a Bill of Rights might set new limits, but it is unlikely to reverse that underlying seismic shift in legal culture.

In the fourth edition of this book we suggested that the HRA 1998 was likely to have some impact on what we have previously called 'judicial style'. At the very least, we suggested that it would curb some of the more pragmatic and unprincipled (in the sense of being without an underlying 'deep' rationale) decision-making that has frequently substituted for a more sophisticated discourse of rights in the English courts. As our discussion of proportionality in *Carlile*, and of the impact of HRA, s. 3 shows, such effects are now quite deeply embedded in English legal method and reasoning, though perhaps still not as deeply as we suspected in 1999. In short, with some exceptions, we take the view that the courts, and particularly the House of Lords and Supreme Court, have approached this revolution in a relatively conservative and careful fashion. Indeed, some might say in too conservative a fashion, though that is not the perception that one would tend to get from the pages of the *Daily Mail*.

One of the problems of legislation like the HRA is that it does seem to bring the courts much more obviously into the political arena. As Lord Irvine, the Lord Chancellor who introduced the HRA, made clear at the time, the intention of the HRA was 'to provide as much protection as possible for the rights of individuals against the misuse of power by the state' (Hansard HL Debates vol. 583, col. 808, 24 November 1997). In seeking to achieve that somewhat controversial objective, it is not surprising that the Act and the courts have attracted political criticism from both left and right.

Fifteen years after it came into force, the big questions for the future are how much longer the HRA will survive in its present form, and, if it does not, what implications that will have, both for human rights and legal method. Whatever happens, it is unlikely that the courts will simply be able to forget the accumulated experience and precedents built up over the past decades.

EXERCISE 18 Concept check

This is simply a short comprehension exercise designed to assist you to become more comfortable with concepts used in this chapter. After reading the chapter, try to complete the following without referring back; then check your answers. Repeat the process of reading, answering, and checking until you are satisfied that you *understand* the material. Alternatively, you can do this as a group task by swapping answers and checking each other's. If you find you have different answers, consider why. Sometimes this may bring out important differences in understanding.

 QUESTION

What do the following concepts mean? Try to define them in your own words:

free-standing model of incorporation	margin of appreciation
declaration of incompatibility	textuality
right of individual petition	victim
principle of proportionality	Convention rights
legislative competence	indirect horizontal effect

CHAPTER REFERENCES

BATES, E. (2015), 'The UK and Strasbourg: A Strained Relationship—The Long View', in K.S. Ziegler, E. Wicks, and L. Hodson (eds), *The UK and European Human Rights—A Strained Relationship?* (Oxford: Hart).

BENNION, F. (2000), 'What Interpretation is "Possible" under Section 3(1) of the Human Rights Act 1989?', *Public Law*, 77.

BIRCH, D. (2000), 'A Better Deal for Vulnerable Witnesses?', *Criminal Law Review*, 223.

BOUGHEY, J. (2017), 'Proportionality and Legitimate Expectations' in M. Groves and G. Weeks (eds), *Legitimate Expectations in the Common Law World* (Oxford: Hart Publishing).

COMMISSION ON A BILL OF RIGHTS (2012), *A UK Bill of Rights?—The Choice Before Us*, www.justice. gov.uk/about/cbr.

DICKSON, B. (2012), 'The Record of the House of Lords in Strasbourg' 128 *Law Quarterly Review*, 354.

DWYER, D. (2005), 'Rights Brought Home', 121 *Law Quarterly Review*, 359.

EWING, K.D. (1999), 'The Human Rights Act and Parliamentary Democracy', 62 *Modern Law Review*, 79.

*GREER, S. (1999), 'A Guide to the Human Rights Act 1998', 24 *European Law Review*, 2.

HOME OFFICE (1997), *Rights Brought Home: The Human Rights Bill*, Cm. 3782 (London: The Stationery Office).

*HORNE, A. and MILLER, V. (2015), *A British Bill of Rights?* House of Commons Library, Briefing Paper No. 7193 (19 May 2015), https://researchbriefings.parliament.uk/ResearchBriefing/ Summary/CBP-7193.

HUNT, M. (1999), 'The Human Rights Act and Legal Culture: The Judiciary and the Legal Profession', 26 *Journal of Law & Society*, 86.

HUSCROFT, G., MILLER, B.W., and WEBBER, G. (eds) (2014), *Proportionality and the Rule of Law: Rights, Justification, Reasoning* (Cambridge: Cambridge University Press).

KAVANAGH, A. (2004a), 'Statutory Interpretation and Human Rights after *Anderson*: A More Contextual Approach', *Public Law*, 537.

*KAVANAGH, A. (2004b), 'The Elusive Divide between Interpretation and Legislation under the Human Rights Act 1998', 24 *Oxford Journal of Legal Studies*, 259.

KAVANAGH, A. (2007), 'Choosing between Sections 3 and 4 of the Human Rights Act 1998: Judicial Reasoning after *Ghaidan v Mendoza*', in H. Fenwick, G. Phillipson, and R. Masterman (eds), *Judicial Reasoning under the UK Human Rights Act* (Cambridge: Cambridge University Press).

*MARSHALL, G. (1998), 'Interpreting Interpretation in the Human Rights Bill', 3 *Public Law*, 167.

MINISTRY OF JUSTICE (2009), *Responding to Human Rights Judgments: Government Response to the Joint Committee on Human Rights' Thirty-first Report of Session 2007–08*, Cmd 7524 (London: The Stationery Office).

MINISTRY OF JUSTICE (2017), *Responding to Human Rights Judgments: Report to the Joint Committee on Human Rights on the Government's Response to Human Rights Judgments 2016–17*, Cmd 9535 (London: The Stationery Office), www.gov.uk/government/publications/ responding-to-human-rights-judgments-2016-to-2017.

Nicol, D. (2004), 'Statutory Interpretation and Human Rights after *Anderson*', *Public Law*, 273.

Poole, T. (2008), 'Courts and Conditions of Uncertainty in "Times of Crisis"', *Public Law*, 234.

Young, A. (2011), 'Mapping Horizontal Effect' in D. Hoffman (ed.), *The Impact of the UK Human Rights Act on Private Law* (Cambridge: Cambridge University Press).

 ONLINE RESOURCES

Test your knowledge by trying the self-test questions that accompany **Chapters 10–11**. Visit: www.oup.com/uk/holland-webb10e

11

European Legal Method

The United Kingdom (UK) joined what is now called the European Union in 1973. Following the Brexit referendum of 2016, the UK triggered Article 50 of the Treaty on European Union—often called the Lisbon Treaty (and containing the 'notice to leave' clause)—and is now set to leave the EU on 29 March 2019 ('Exit Day'). The publication timetable means the reader will have a better view of the outcome of the Brexit negotiations than we can offer here but, for the authors, writing in the autumn of 2018, the position is far from clear and there are several possible outcomes which will affect the role of EU law in the UK after Exit Day. To help overcome this uncertainty, we would refer readers to OUP's Brexit-related online resources covering developments in this field, at www.oxfordtextbooks.co.uk/orc/eulaw. The possibilities, roughly speaking, are set out here:

1. The United Kingdom could leave the EU without any agreement in place (a 'No-deal Brexit'). Leaving aside the political and trade ramifications (such as access to the Single Market and free movement of persons) this would mean that EU law would cease to have effect in the United Kingdom. The European Union (Withdrawal) Act 2018 would operate and we will explore the consequences of that in this chapter.
2. The United Kingdom could formally leave the EU but transitional arrangements may be in place (at one time set to last until 31 December 2020, but perhaps lasting for longer). Some (or all) parts of EU law might continue to operate for that period and the CJEU might continue to have a role in how the agreement operates or, as proposed at one stage, a 'joint institutional framework' would interpret any agreement and deal with compliance by each side.
3. The United Kingdom could join another organisation (such as the European Free Trade Association) to gain access to the EU market, but would be subject to EU law indirectly.
4. There might be a compromise agreement, which could combine some of the points above together with other ideas (especially as regards the Northern Ireland/Republic of Ireland border).
5. The United Kingdom might, for various political reasons, revoke Article 50 of the Lisbon Treaty and remain in the EU for an indeterminate time.

Commentators on EU law stress that law students will still need to study EU law for some time, even in the case of a 'No-deal Brexit', in order to understand the 'hangovers' of EU law as laid out in the European Union (Withdrawal) Act 2018, and especially in the case of any transitional arrangements operating. The commentators also stress that, because trade with the EU states will continue in some form, lawyers advising clients on export and import matters, food regulations, or wider commercial law topics will need to be aware of EU laws come what may. That is certainly true, though the same could be said of dealings with the United States, or Japan, or other countries. What it does mean, though, from a legal perspective, is that EU law will not just go away instantly in 2019: it will either continue to have direct (maybe limited direct) effect or will have to be taken into account by our courts in some indirect form. It will at least have a legacy in the UK.

However, it would be unrealistic to give the same weight to this area as we have done in previous editions. Consequently, this streamlined chapter now covers the absolute essentials; it will describe how the European Union (Withdrawal) Act 2018 will operate post-Brexit and how our courts will deal with laws which were originally the creatures of the EU, before looking very briefly at the sources and general operation of EU law. These latter points are relevant for the reasons noted above: namely, any continuing effect of EU law in our system after Exit Day and as regards commercial enterprises dealing with EU companies, etc. in the future.

This chapter is therefore organised as follows:

- section **11.1**: the European Union (Withdrawal) Act 2018 and how the different outcomes to the Brexit negotiations may play out in terms of the Act's application;
- section **11.2**: the **sources** of EU law and the EU institutions;
- section **11.3**: how EU law is enforced.

11.1 The European Union (Withdrawal) Act 2018

The purpose of the 2018 Act is to set out what happens to laws which originated in the EU and which have become part of our legal framework but will cease to have effect after Brexit (e.g. many areas of employment law and consumer law). To avoid having to create an Act that repealed or amended every single relevant measure, the Act preserves the laws that were in force at the time of withdrawal ('exit day' as it is termed).

11.1.1 How were EU laws incorporated into UK law?

To allow for the United Kingdom to become a member of the (then) EEC and for the integration of EEC law to take effect, the UK Parliament passed the European Communities Act in 1972. It had to do this because merely signing the Treaty of Rome 1957 did not incorporate European Economic Community (EEC) laws into our system. International treaties are not automatically part of our law: they require an Act to be passed before they are incorporated. Thus, the 1972 Act incorporated the Treaty provisions (including future ones) into our law as from 1 January 1973. Section 2(1) of the Act stated:

> All such rights, powers, liabilities, obligations and restrictions from time to time created or arising by or under the Treaties, and all such remedies and procedures from time to time provided for by or under the Treaties, as in accordance with the Treaties are without further enactment to be given legal effect…

By these means EU law took supremacy over UK law in selected areas. As noted in *R (on the application of Miller and another)* v *Secretary of State for Exiting the European Union (Appellant)* [2017] UKSC 5, the 1972 Act was a conduit for EU laws to flow into the United Kingdom. The European Union (Withdrawal) Act 2018—the EU (W) Act 2018—now has to unpick 40 years of incorporated EU legislation.

EU laws are generally contained in four types of legislation: Teaties, Regulations, Directives, and Decisions. The Treaties are the big policy documents, laying out the principles of the EU. Regulations are like 'mini treaties' dealing with more specific topics. Treaties and Regulations apply to all Member States. They are published in all the official languages of the EU and are binding without further action on the part of the Member States. This means that once a Treaty or Regulation has been signed by all Member States (and any operational date has passed) the articles become law across all Member States—no Act of Parliament is needed to introduce the new law. This is called 'direct application'. Though political in nature, Treaties and Regulations can sometimes create rights affecting individuals. If so, they are also said to be 'directly effective' as well as having direct application.

A **Directive** addresses very specific topics such as how many hours an employee may work, what type of ingredient may be used in a food product, or how toys need to comply with health-and-safety measures. They do not have 'direct application', so each Member State must bring in its own legislation to implement the Directive. A Directive is binding on Member States only as to the *result* to be achieved. The Treaty on the Functioning of the European Union (TFEU), Art. 288 puts it this way: 'A Directive shall be binding, as to the result to be achieved, upon each Member State to which it is addressed, but shall leave to the national authorities the choice of form and methods.' Thus, the implementation of a directive in, say, Finland and Ireland may be quite different in detail, even though the overall result must be the same. The general principle is that a Directive has no effect in law until it is implemented by the state, and Member States are invariably given a time limit for implementation—usually three years from enactment. Thus, Directives become part of our law through Acts of Parliament or Statutory Instruments. Most EU-derived laws come from Directives and Directives have 'direct effect', which means they can be enforced by individuals against other individuals or companies. We will expand upon 'direct effect' at **11.3** below.

A **Decision** is not something of judicial origin, though it sounds as if it should be. Instead it is a binding 'order' issued by an institution of the EU and addressed to an individual or state. These frequently arise in competition law cases. They will not be preserved after exit day unless they were directed at the United Kingdom.

Thus, the laws set out in EU Directives can be found in our statutes and secondary legislation; the wording is ours, though it must express the principle contained in the directive. These pieces of legislation can therefore be incorporated into UK laws quite easily as they are effectively already there. The laws contained in EU Treaties and Regulations, however, do not appear on our statute books and, as we have noted, sometimes these laws may have 'direct effect' and so be enforceable by individuals. These are more difficult to incorporate and we shall see how this is done in section **11.1.2**.

11.1.2 How will these laws be treated?

The EU (W) Act 2018 has five basic stages.

- First s. 1 repeals the 1972 Act on 'exit day' so that any EU laws cease to have effect in the United Kingdom from that point.
- Second, s. 2 maintains those EU-derived laws already in force in the United Kingdom through incorporation into our domestic legislation by using the fiction that they

had been UK-derived legislation all along (termed 'EU-derived domestic legislation' or 'preserved legislation'). As we have noted, in the case of Directives this fiction is easy to implement because they have already been converted into Acts or Statutory Instruments (S.I.s). In other cases (notably to do with the Health and Safety Act 1974), legislation was not derived from EU law originally but complies with later EU legislation. Different though this may be, it does not present a great problem and is also covered as part of 'EU retained law'.

- Third, following exit day the United Kingdom will not be bound by EU Treaties and, where the EU-derived material comes from Regulations and Treaties, it has never been incorporated into our domestic law via an Act or secondary legislation, so here the solution in s. 3 is to treat the full English translation text of the EU legislation as being converted into domestic law and counting as EU retained law 'so far as operative immediately before exit day'. Section 4 goes further and acknowledges that where a Treaty or Regulation creates directly effective rights for individuals, then those principles (but not the text of the EU document) are incorporated into UK law. Examples would include non-discrimination on the grounds of nationality, equal pay, free movement of capital, state aid, and many more.

- Fourth, as the Explanatory Notes to the Act state: '[the Act] creates temporary powers to make secondary legislation to enable corrections to be made to the laws that would otherwise no longer operate appropriately once the UK has left, so that the domestic legal system continues to function correctly outside the EU.'

- Fifth, it allows for Parliament (and, within devolved competence, the devolved legislatures of the United Kingdom) to decide which elements of that law to keep, amend, or repeal once the United Kingdom has left the EU.

Additionally, the Notes add that: '[the] Act also enables domestic law to reflect the content of a withdrawal agreement under Article 50 of the Treaty on European Union once the UK leaves the EU, subject to the prior enactment of a statute by Parliament approving the final terms of withdrawal'. Thus, another Act—the EU (Withdrawal Agreement) Act—will be necessary to implement the outcome of the negotiations and Parliament's approval of that outcome. This will legislate for the specific terms of the agreement reached, time periods involved, and the rights of EU citizens within the United Kingdom.

Consequently, we have a two-stage process: the EU(W) Act 2018 deals with what happens to existing laws (retained EU Law) and how these may be changed in the future; the Withdrawal Agreement Act will cover the specifics of the outcomes of the negotiations. Each will reflect the other.

As we noted above, various outcomes are possible. One such outcome is that there are transitional arrangements lasting for a specific time. This might mean that some or all of the EU-derived legislation continues to operate after Exit Day under the auspices of the EU and not as part of the fiction of its being domestic law. Say, for instance, that it is agreed that for two years the CJEU will still have authority to interpret EU-derived laws in the United Kingdom in one or more areas of life, then the 2018 Act will have to reflect this. Another outcome is that the United Kingdom leaves the EU but, in gaining access to the Single Market, for instance, agrees to the CJEU's continuing authority.

Equally, the United Kingdom might join an organisation such as the European Free Trade Association (presently consisting of Iceland, Lichtenstein, Norway, and Switzerland—an organisation which, ironically the United Kingdom helped create). In very simple terms, members of that organisation do not belong to the EU but, aside from Switzerland, join with the EU to form the European Economic Area (EEA). The EEA allows for things such as the free movement of people, goods, and services across EEA states (Switzerland, though part of EFTA, has its own series of bilateral agreements with the EU). The EFTA/EEA members pay for access to the Single Market, etc. and have to accept EU legislation in a number of commercial activities (notable exceptions being agriculture and fisheries).

EFTA has its own court, based, rather peculiarly, in Luxembourg. That court, as a rule, but not always, follows the CJEU in all its decisions on the meaning of EU-derived legislation that affects the EFTA countries. Equally, the CJEU can follow EFTA Court case law and the EFTA Court is proud to point out that it is the only court of general jurisdiction whose jurisprudence is regularly taken into account by the CJEU when interpreting EU law. Nevertheless, in joining EFTA the United Kingdom would be subject to indirect control by the CJEU in these circumstances. One key difference is that EFTA does not apply the principle of supremacy of EU laws, which is a hallmark of the EU and the CJEU's role within the EU.

Obviously, other arrangements involving or not involving EU institutions may also arise and the Withdrawal Acts will need to create appropriate operational rules.

Section 13 EU(W) Act 2018 deals with the specific arrangements for Parliamentary approval of the outcome of the Brexit negotiations and the procedures that must be followed and s. 19 states that:

> Nothing in this Act shall prevent the United Kingdom from—
>> (a) replicating in domestic law any EU law made on or after exit day, or
>> (b) continuing to participate in, or have a formal relationship with, the agencies of the EU after exit day.

11.1.3 Decisions of the CJEU and interpretation of retained EU law

Section 6(3) EU(W) Act 2018 provides that:

> Any question as to the validity, meaning or effect of any retained EU law is to be decided, so far as that law is unmodified on or after exit day and so far as they are relevant to it—
>> (a) in accordance with any retained case law and any retained general principles of EU law.

Thus pre-exit case law of the CJEU, or UK case law applying CJEU interpretations of EU law, is still relevant and the general laws of precedent operate in relation to those cases. Section 6(4), however, makes it clear that the Supreme Court or the High Court of Justiciary in Scotland (on relevant matters) are not bound by any retained EU case law. Although s. 6(3) refers to 'unmodified' law, s. 6(6) states that 'modified' law may still draw on pre-exit day cases if doing so is consistent with the intention of the modifications. However, any principles laid down or decisions made by the CJEU after exit day are not binding and no UK court can refer a matter to the CJEU. One presumes that UK courts will treat future decisions of the CJEU on pre-exit legislation as persuasive, provided that legislation has not been changed substantially in the meantime.

11.1.4 Powers to change legislation

Some 'retained EU law' will not make sense after exit day, as it will include terms that are no longer relevant (such as the need to refer matters to some EU body) or will include wording (such as 'other EU states') which, again make no sense. Power is therefore granted to Ministers under ss 8 and 9, including those exercising devolved legislative powers, to make suitable alterations in legislative wording to deal with what are termed 'deficiencies' arising from withdrawal. Specific limitations exist, such as the inability to create criminal offences or amend the Human Rights Act 1998. These are laid out in ss 8(7) and 9(3).

Equally, some EU bodies exercising control over, say, environmental issues will no longer be relevant and suitable UK replacements will need to be appointed, and fees established. International agreements and tariffs will also need modifications. Such Ministerial powers are often referred to as 'Henry VIII clauses' (a derogatory term used to describe absolute monarchy, or, here, ministers having the power to override legislation without having to go through Parliament). The inclusion of such powers has given rise to some debate as to their use.

11.2 The sources of European Union law

EU law is made up from the originating and amending Treaties of the EU (what might be seen as the EU's foundations), the 'Acts' of the various EU institutions (sometimes referred to as secondary sources, e.g. 'Directives'), and the judgments of the CJEU.

11.2.1 Origins and Treaties

Various Treaties have been signed over the years dealing with specific developments. The Lisbon Treaty (2007) is the latest in a long line of Treaties, and it was this Treaty that simplified legislative matters with the introduction of two main consolidating Treaties: the Treaty on the Functioning of the European Union (TFEU) and the Treaty on European Union (TEU). The Lisbon Treaty also activated Article 50 TEU—the mechanism for a Member State to leave the EU. The TFEU and TEU form the backbone of the EU legislative framework and the text of the consolidated versions of TFEU and TEU can be found in the EU's major publication, the Official Journal, at http://eur-lex.europa.eu/legal-content/EN/ALL/?uri=OJ:C:2010:083:TOC.

Treaties are mainly political or quasi-constitutional documents but they do contain laws which are of general application across the EU relating to matters such as equality, trade, and free movement. Each Treaty is subdivided into *Articles*, which are the equivalent of our *sections* in UK legislation. The EU website contains details of the history, membership, laws, and Treaties: see http://europa.eu.

11.2.2 The Acts of the institutions

Treaties do not appear that often and so clearly someone has to have the power to make law within the EU on a year-by-year basis. That power falls to two bodies, termed the *Council of the European Union* and the *Commission* (see section **11.2.4**). The pieces of legislation produced by these bodies are published in the *Official Journal* of the EU. We noted these above at **11.1.1** as being:

(i)   Regulations;

(ii)   Directives; and

(iii) Decisions.

To these three binding legal provisions we can also add **recommendations** and **opinions**, which will be of persuasive authority and which do not concern us here.

11.2.3 The Court of Justice of the European Union

The Court is the supreme authority on the law relating to the EU. Many publications refer to this court as some form of court of appeal, and its perceived over-arching and interfering authority was one reason people voted for Brexit. **However, it deals only with the interpretation and validity of EU-generated law and does not decide cases as such.** The court is usually referred to as the CJEU but until 2009 it was referred to in the UK as the European Court of Justice (ECJ). We will generally refer to the CJEU but, when we are speaking historically, we will use the abbreviations 'ECJ'.

The CJEU is modelled on European systems, and most of its procedure and legal method bears little relationship to the common law world. TFEU Section 5 deals with the jurisdiction of the Court. It states: 'The Court of Justice shall ensure that in the interpretation and application of (the Treaties) the law is observed.' The EU's own website says this:

> The Court of Justice interprets EU law to make sure it is applied in the same way in all EU countries. It also settles legal disputes between EU governments and EU institutions. Individuals, companies, or organisations can also bring cases before the Court if they feel their rights have been infringed by an EU institution.

Thus, the job of the Court is to make sure that EU law is interpreted and applied in the same way in all EU countries, thereby ensuring that the law is equal for everyone. It ensures, for example, that national courts do not give different rulings on the same issue. This does not affect the fact that a Directive might be implemented differently in Member States: the CJEU is concerned with whether the Directive has been implemented properly and the fact that, say, Italy has 'added' to a Directive by giving consumers in Italy even better rights than found elsewhere in the EU, for instance (but still complying with the requirements of that Directive), is not the concern of the CJEU.

The Court is located in Luxembourg and has one judge drawn from each Member State. The various Treaties give it a wide jurisdiction. From a legal method viewpoint, the key element is that it receives *preliminary references* and provides *preliminary rulings* under Art. 267 TFEU concerning the interpretation of EU legislation, when asked to do so by a court of a Member State. We will concentrate most of our attention in this chapter on these '*preliminary references*' and will explain shortly what these are and how they work. For the moment we can say that a preliminary reference is a question of law sent by a domestic court (e.g. the Court of Appeal) to the CJEU asking for an authoritative interpretation of the meaning of EU legislation. We should also note that the CJEU actually consists of a number of courts: the Court of Justice itself, 'The General Court', which generally deals with companies or individuals seeking annulments of decisions made by EU bodies, notably in competition law and trade, and the 'EU Civil Service Tribunal' (which, as the name implies, covers disputes between the EU and its officials and other servants). We are concerned only with the main court here.

11.2.4 The institutions

There are six major institutions of the European Union. The first four listed next are the law-making bodies:

- The European Council;
- The European Commission (which is the driving force and executive body);
- The Court of Justice (the court which ensures compliance with EU law);
- The European Parliament (the body elected by the peoples of the Member States);
- The European Central Bank; and
- The Court of Auditors (not actually a court but a body which oversees the sound and lawful management of the EU budget).

All institutions are equal, at least on a formal basis. In this book we shall not deal with the Court of Auditors, the EU Civil Service Tribunal, the European Central Bank, or some of the other institutions such as the Economic and Social Committee.

The European Council

Article 15 TEU and Arts 235–6 TFEU state that the Council will ensure that the objectives set out in the Treaties are attained. The Council is based in Brussels and is a political body that has the final say on nearly all legislative matters. It is a key point of the EU that the parliaments of the Member States do not create EU legislation; nor is EU legislation subject to the approval/rejection of the national parliaments. The responsibility of the national parliaments is merely to implement the Regulations, Directives, and Decisions of the EU.

The Council is effectively the sovereign body of the EU. However, national power is not given up so easily: the Council is not an autonomous organisation of the EU, distinct from the national governments. It is made up of one ministerial representative appointed by each Member State. The representative sent by each state varies according to the issue at hand; economic matters will draw the Chancellors, other matters will require the appropriate minister, for example for agriculture or education. At the highest level the heads of national governments will meet up to four times a year. When this occurs, the Council is referred to as the European Council, or more informally as a 'summit'.

The Council is a policy or strategy body: it does not generate the legislation itself. That function rests with the Commission. The importance of the Council, however, is that it decides whether proposals from the Commission shall take effect. The Council itself is not a fixed body, it is not in permanent session, and the ministerial representatives change frequently in 'reshuffles'.

The Commission

The Commission is based in Brussels and is the driving force in the legislative process. It meets at least once a week. Like the Council, the Commission consists of nationals drawn from each Member State—one member per state. This time, however, although nominated by their respective government, they are not representatives, and are supposed to act independently of their national governments. Each Commissioner is allocated a special task, such as trade or international cooperation. The Commission plays a vital role in the legislative process of the EU. It initiates legislation, safeguards the objectives of the Treaty by acting as its 'watchdog', and acts as the EU's executive.

The Parliament

This body sits in Strasbourg, though many of its activities are carried out in Luxembourg (its administration) and Brussels (its committees). It was originally called the Assembly and its members were drawn from national parliaments. It was not a directly elected democratic body until 1979. Consequently, it never was a legislative body in the way we would understand the term 'Parliament'. Rather it had the function of supervising and advising. This has changed in recent years, with the Lisbon Treaty increasing both its supervisory and law-making powers.

The Parliament can accept, amend, or reject legislation proposed by the Council. It describes itself as a 'co-legislator, sharing with the Council the power to adopt and amend legislative proposals and to decide on the EU budget. It also supervises the work of the Commission and other EU bodies . . .' (see www.europarl.europa.eu/about-parliament/en).

The Court of Justice of the European Union

The CJEU sits in Luxembourg and actually pre-dates the creation of the EEC (now the EU). Unhelpfully, the UK's European Communities Act 1972 refers to it as the 'European Court' (and consequently some media coverage confuses this court with the European Court of Human Rights, which is also often referred to as the 'European Court').

The CJEU presently consists of one judge from each Member State, together with two sets of characters which have no equivalent in our system: the Advocates General and the Judge-Rapporteur. The role of an Advocate General is to act as filtering system in a case, assisting the Court by delivering independent opinions on cases for the judges to consider. They hear the cases alongside the judges and then present their legal views on the matter to those judges. There are eleven Advocates General. A Judge-Rapporteur (drawn from the panel of judges hearing the case) is responsible for the general management of the proceedings and the writing up of the decision.

The Court may sit in courts of 3, 5, or 15 judges, depending on the issues. As we have noted, the Court deals with EU law only; it is not some supreme European court of appeal. Instead, it is a 'court of reference'. By this we mean that, although it can hear cases brought by Member States or EU institutions against other Member States regarding violations of the Treaties, or even by individuals in cases of annulment of legal acts or to sue for damages arising from EU actions (and in this sense it can be a 'trial court'), its main function lies in relation to *preliminary references*. This jurisdiction is defined in Art. 267 TFEU and appears a strange beast to the English law practitioner or law student.

What is a preliminary reference?

It is a basic premise of EU law that it is the duty of each court in Member States, not just the CJEU, to apply EU law and that EU law takes precedence over national law. However, where an authoritative interpretation of EU law is needed, that can be supplied only by the CJEU. Whatever the CJEU says is the *meaning* of an EU Directive, for instance, is binding on all courts in all Member States. Even after Brexit, UK courts will still follow these pre-exit day decisions (though the Supreme Court will not be bound to do so).

In most instances the national courts can interpret EU legislation quite happily themselves, but where that is not possible, then any country's domestic courts or tribunals can ask the CJEU for a ruling—for clarification on the meaning of a piece of EU legislation. The domestic court will do this under Art. 267 TFEU. The question posed is called a *preliminary reference*; the answer given is called a *preliminary ruling*, and that judgment by the CJEU is definitive; no domestic court (in any country, not just the one which made the reference) can ignore it. So, a preliminary ruling in response to a preliminary reference posed by a Belgian court will apply to courts in Spain, Sweden, etc.

How does a preliminary reference come before the CJEU?

Only the domestic court hearing the case can decide whether to make a reference or not—the parties to the case will be consulted but have no rights in the matter. Thus, once a court or tribunal is faced with a problem involving the application of EU law it may ask the CJEU for an authoritative interpretation of a Treaty Article or, for instance, an EU Directive. Equally, it may not. However, if it does refer a case, it does so by posing legal questions in the abstract; it does not ask for the solution to the particular case.

The CJEU has issued Practice Directions on the conduct of cases in preliminary hearings (see Protocol (No. 3) to the Statute of the Court of Justice of the European Union, and OJ L31, 31 January 2014 for the latest version), which allow for expedited procedures in simpler cases or ones which raise no new issues, and in the United Kingdom there is a specific direction on how cases should be referred to the CJEU: see Part 68 of the Civil Procedure Rules and Practice Direction 68, and Rule 75.3 of the Criminal Procedure Rules. It is the responsibility of the Court, not the parties, to settle the terms of the reference. That reference will identify the parties, summarise the nature of the proceedings, give the relevant facts, make reference to the rules of domestic law, and summarise the contentions of the parties. The reference will then identify the EU provisions at issue and formulate the question(s) to which an answer is requested—we give an example of this shortly—with an eye on the fact that these will have to be translated into the various EU languages.

A key point to emphasise is that the CJEU does not decide the result of the cases itself, i.e. it makes no findings of fact, nor does it apply the law to the facts: it makes rulings on interpretation, not decisions on who wins or loses the case. **On most issues, therefore, the CJEU is a court of reference, not a court of appeal**. It assists the domestic court in making its decision by giving authoritative rulings on the interpretation of the EU-derived legislation.

This role of the (then) ECJ drew specific comment from Laddie J in *Arsenal Football Club plc v Reed (No. 2)* [2002] EWHC 2695 (Ch); [2003] 1 All ER 137. The case concerned the alleged misuse of Arsenal FC's trade marks by Reed and was referred to the ECJ regarding the meaning of a Trade Marks Directive. In giving its judgment, the ECJ drew specific conclusions of fact. When the trial resumed back in the United Kingdom, Laddie J pointed out in no uncertain terms that the ECJ had exceeded its jurisdiction and the domestic court was not bound by its conclusion (although later again, the Court of Appeal disagreed with Laddie J's interpretation on whether the ECJ had actually overstepped the mark).

How does the case proceed at the CJEU?

The question has been formulated and the case is now lodged with the Court of Justice—and joins the backlog! A reference to the Court of Justice is, in this procedure, just a step in the action being heard by the domestic court; it is not an appeal because the case in the domestic court has simply been adjourned pending the opinion of the Court of Justice. Thus, although we call it a 'preliminary ruling' this is a little misleading: the reference to the Court of Justice is made *during* the case before the domestic court, not before the case has started. It is preliminary to a decision being made by the domestic court, not preliminary to the proceedings themselves.

Assuming the matter is not expedited as being simple or not being novel, the basic pattern for a case involving a preliminary reference can be outlined as follows:

1. The domestic court decides to make the reference. This constitutes the start of the 'written stage'.
2. The court, with the aid of the parties, sets about formulating the relevant question(s) and establishing a statement of facts and law which will accompany the reference, as noted earlier in the section. We note below some examples of the form these questions take.
3. The reference is translated by the CJEU into the working languages of the EU and published. Written submissions may be made within two months by interested parties, including Member States' governments.
4. The case is assigned to a specific Judge-Rapporteur and an Advocate General, if thought necessary.
5. The Judge-Rapporteur produces an initial report and advises on the forum (e.g. to be heard in a chamber or in plenary) and whether further inquiries of fact or law are necessary. He or she summarises the legal background to the case and the observations of the parties submitted in the first, written phase of the procedure. In the light of the conclusions of the Advocate General appointed to the case, the Judge-Rapporteur draws up a draft ruling, which is submitted to the other members of the Court.
6. The parties prepare for the hearing, provided the court thinks this is necessary. This begins the 'oral stage'—a public hearing.
7. The oral hearing takes place. Any interested party may make a submission.
8. If the court so requests, the Advocate General prepares and delivers an opinion on the case (the Judge-Rapporteur may also provide an opinion, especially if disagreeing with the Advocate General).
9. The Court discusses the case and goes into deliberation.

10. The Court produces a judgment in whichever of the official languages the case was heard. This is then translated. No dissenting opinion is delivered.

This procedure can take well over a year to complete, before the case is then taken up again at the domestic court. However, there is an accelerated procedure for cases of 'exceptional urgency'. The normal procedure is illustrated in **Figure 11.1**.

Once the case comes before the CJEU we see a difference in approach from the common law system. As we noted earlier in the book, English law still bears some relation to its roots in 'trial by battle'. The champion is now replaced by the solicitor or barrister, the swords replaced by words; but the basic plot is the same. Our system concentrates on the

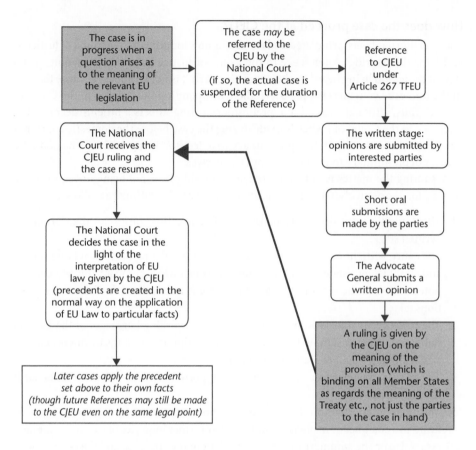

Figure 11.1 Preliminary rulings in the CJEU

adversarial approach and depends greatly on oral argument. The continental approach depends far more on an inquisitorial procedure and written argument (though note that our own courts are increasingly demanding written submissions in advance of oral argument—called 'skeleton arguments'). Indeed, if the case is concerned with a *preliminary reference* there are, strictly speaking, no parties involved—the domestic court has sought an opinion, not a fight.

All documents are sent by the Court of Justice's Registry to the parties in the domestic court, the Member States, the Commission, and (possibly) the Council. All these parties have a right to make submissions on the case. For instance, in a case concerning part-time workers in Germany (Case 171/88 *Rinner-Kühn v FWW Spezial-Gebäudereinigung GmbH and Co. KG* [1989] ECR 2743; [1989] IRLR 493) a number of Member States (recognising that the case was of great importance) made submissions to the Court even though they were not directly involved. The next major difference lies in the presence of the Advocate General. The Advocate General, as already noted, acts as an adviser to the Court, sifting through the law on behalf of the Court and producing a reasoned opinion in each case. The Court is then free to follow that opinion or derogate from it in any way it thinks fit. Sometimes the Court will simply adopt the Advocate General's opinion wholesale.

Remember, the Court of Justice is concerned only with ruling on the abstract question of law, not with deciding the case. There is thus no appeal from a judgment of the Court of Justice on a preliminary reference (though there are various mechanisms whereby the Court can review its own decision). Further, as we shall note again in relation to legal method in section **11.2.5**, there is only one judgment given by the Court; no dissenting voices are heard. That judgment is relatively short and sometimes without detailed reasons. One can find the presentation of reasoning which resembles that of the English judge in the opinion delivered by (accepted or not by the Court) the Advocate General.

When will a case go to the Court of Justice?

We said earlier that it is for the domestic court to decide whether it wishes to refer a matter to the Court of Justice. Article 267 TFEU states that where a question of interpretation of the Treaties:

> is raised before any court or tribunal of the Member State, that court or tribunal may, if it considers that a decision on the question is necessary to enable it to give judgment, request the Court of Justice to give a ruling thereon.
>
> Where any such question is raised in a case pending before a court or tribunal of a Member State, against whose decisions there is no judicial remedy under domestic law, that court or tribunal shall bring the matter before the Court of Justice.

It has to be said that any perusal of the Reports (CMLR or ECR) reveals some of the most boring questions and issues ever encountered in legal texts (usually concerned with import duties, VAT, and regulations concerning agricultural matters). The range of topics that can be covered is nevertheless very extensive and getting wider by the day. There are glimmers, therefore, of real-life questions. Many of these centre on employment issues such as discrimination and equal pay. Some take on more expansive parameters, such as the case of Case C–415/93 *Union Royale Belge des Sociétés de Football Association* (*ASBL*) v *Bosman* [1995] ECR I-4921; [1996] 1 CMLR 645, for instance, which set the soccer world alight when it declared that certain transfer fees were in breach of Community Law, *viz* the Treaty of Rome, Art. 48.

On most EU law matters, any court or tribunal may refer a case to the CJEU; the court does not require permission from any higher court (though Part 68 Civil Procedure Rules, for instance, states that lower courts such as the County Court will not *normally* make a reference). It is clear, however, that national rules of precedent have no effect on a court's power to refer a matter to the CJEU, except that only the final appeal court (usually that has meant the Supreme Court in the United Kingdom) may make a reference to the CJEU as regards certain matters relating to the maintenance of law and order or internal security. Linked with this is the idea (which has always been present in EU law) that, if a court is dealing with any question of EU law and that court is the final appeal court, it *must* refer the point to the CJEU. However, this does not always happen. The Supreme Court and other final appeal courts do not refer all relevant cases to the CJEU because the key part of Art. 267 TFEU requires them to do that only when it is 'necessary' to give judgment.

What does 'necessary' mean?

The decision to refer a case to the CJEU lies with the domestic court alone. This was decided early in the CJEU's life in Case 6/64 *Costa* v *ENEL* [1964] ECR 585. The decision to refer or not to refer cannot be restricted by any domestic system of precedent, nor does it matter whether the parties request such a reference to be made.

In Case 283/81 *CILFIT Srl* v *Ministero della Sanità* [1982] ECR 3415; [1983] 1 CMLR 472 the ECJ ruled that a reference is *not necessary* if:

(i)   the question of EU law is irrelevant; or

(ii)   the provision has already been interpreted by the Court of Justice; or

(iii) the correct application is obvious (an idea borrowed from the French system, called *acte clair*).

Steiner and Woods (2017) point out that this latter point is a deceptively simple idea, because what is clear and obvious to one person is not necessarily clear to another, as we saw in **Chapters 8** and **9** on statutory interpretation. Indeed, this was illustrated in *R v Henn (No. 1)* [1978] 1 WLR 1031; [1978] 3 All ER 1190, where the Court of Appeal did not ask for a preliminary ruling on the ground of *acte clair*; the House of Lords did not find the matter so obvious and pursued a reference (*DPP v Henn and Darby* [1980] 2 CMLR 229). Equally, as we noted before, the CJEU is not bound by *stare decisis* and so is free to change its mind on a matter. This means that you are never entirely sure whether the key ruling by the CJEU on a point might be overturned by the CJEU on another day if the matter was referred to the court.

Taken to an extreme, the notion of *acte clair* could spell disaster for the Court of Justice because there is no mechanism to force a domestic court to make a reference. But with one or two exceptional bursts of chauvinism from national courts (usually French), the spirit of cooperation and collaboration has prevailed.

A reference is made in the form of a question. The CJEU is keen to convert any question which seeks an answer on how to *apply* the law into a more abstract question on what the Treaty or other provision *means* or whether the provision is valid. As we have said, it is not there to decide the case itself. There is no set formula for putting these questions. The following is an extract taken from a House of Lords' Reference to the ECJ in *R v Secretary of State for Employment, ex parte Seymour-Smith and Perez* [1997] ICR 371 (it reads remarkably like a set of examination questions):

1. Does an award of compensation for breach of the right not to be unfairly dismissed under national legislation such as the Employment Protection (Consolidation) Act 1978 constitute 'pay' within the meaning of Art. 119 of the EC Treaty?

2. If the answer to question 1 is 'yes', do the conditions determining whether a worker has the right not to be unfairly dismissed fall within the scope of Art. 119 or that of Directive 76/207?

3. What is the legal test for establishing whether a measure adopted by a Member State has such a degree of disparate effect as between men and women as to amount to indirect discrimination for the purposes of Art. 119 of the EC Treaty unless shown to be based upon objectively justified factors other than sex?

Here is another example, this time from the Court of Appeal in *Société des produits Nestlé SA* v *Mars UK Ltd* (Case C–353/03):

May the distinctive character of a mark referred to in Article 3(3) of Directive 89/104 and Article 7(3) of Regulation No 40/94 be acquired following or in consequence of the use of that mark as part of or in conjunction with another mark?

What this referred to is a little more approachable. Nestlé wanted to register the term, 'Have a break' as a trade mark. They argued that the term had acquired a distinctive character as a result of its use in advertisements in the slogan, 'Have a break ... Have a KIT KAT'—the term being therefore linked to the chocolate bar 'KIT KAT' which was already a registered trade mark. The rival confectioner, Mars Ltd, opposed this. The argument centred on the meaning of the Directives noted earlier which sought to approximate the laws of the Member States relating to trade marks.

11.2.5 The effect of preliminary rulings on common law legal method

Once the United Kingdom leaves the EU, there can be no further preliminary references from our courts, as the CJEU will cease to have any authority here. However, s. 6(3) EU(W) Act 2018 preserves the pre-exit day rulings of the CJEU on EU law as 'Retained EU Law' and where the CJEU rules in the future on such topics their views will undoubtedly be persuasive for our courts in dealing with the same issues.

11.3 How is EU legislation enforced?

As we have seen, the main classification of EU legislation into Treaties, Regulations, and Directives carries with it important concepts which determine how these various rules are actually implemented within the EU by the Member States. Those concepts are:

- direct applicability;
- direct effect; and
- indirect effect.

11.3.1 Direct applicability

Because Treaty obligations and Regulations of the EU are designed to have over-riding and universal application across Member States, we have noted previously that they are given special status, termed *direct applicability*. This means that these rules *automatically* become part of the law of each domestic legal system without the need (in most cases) for confirmation of their legitimacy by formal enactment in the legislatures of the Member States. Thus, you will not find these rules in any UK statute book; you must research the treaty or regulation itself. Section 3 EU(W) Act 2018 will incorporate the text of these documents into our law after Exit Day. The idea of *direct applicability* is really aimed at the Member States; it tells them that they are not required to do anything more to implement the relevant rule.

The importance of this concept of *direct applicability* is that each Member State is bound by the rules contained in these Treaties and Regulations. *Direct applicability* is therefore reserved for rules which need to have immediate and EU-wide-binding enforceability. Matters such as equal pay and the free movement of workers, for instance, appear in Treaty articles. On the other hand, Common Agricultural Policy matters will generally surface in the form of Regulations. These laws are all directly applicable.

Directives, on the other hand, do not have direct applicability because they lay down a **result** to be achieved, rather than fixed and universal rules. A Directive is like an instruction which reads, 'When driving from home to work you may not use the motorway system': you (or the Member State if this were a legal direction) are then left to determine which roads (other than motorways) you may use. So, each driver/Member State can then dictate (within the given confines) what are the permissible routes, such as, 'You can only use A-roads', or 'You cannot use roads with a speed limit of 60 mph or more', etc. Each country might produce different systems, but they would all be legitimate within the Directive if they followed the general 'non-motorway' rule. It would not be legitimate, for, say, Ireland to allow motorway driving to go to work if the journey was more than a certain distance. What might still happen, however, is that at some point a reference might be made to the CJEU as to the exact meaning of 'motorway' (with all its translations) in this Directive.

We noted earlier that Directives have no effect at all on the laws of a Member State until that state's legislature incorporates the goals set out in the Directive into its own law. In the United Kingdom this means that Parliament must have legislated on the matter. Each Member State is given a time limit to achieve this (often two or three years from the date of the Directive). Thus, the process for implementation is as set out in **Figure 11.2**.

Directives therefore seek only to harmonise the laws of Member States, to make them approximately the same while still taking into account the economic, political, social, and legal differences that exist in each state. Directives *cannot* have direct applicability because they are too general and vague in what it is they are trying to achieve. Let us draw an analogy with the laws of Association Football: the rules on the size of playing

Figure 11.2 The procedure for implementing Directives

area set out maximum and minimum measurements only (the length must be between 100 and 130 yards, for instance). This allows for the varying size of stadia, and can be likened to the way Directives are often framed. Thus, as long as the football club does not infringe the maximum or minimum size, its ground measurements do not have to be identical to those of any other club.

In the end, though, the fact that Member States are bound to obey directly applicable rules only really tells us about their obligations as between themselves and as between them and the EU. We are still left with the problem of how EU legislation can be enforced by individuals and companies within the EU. After all, the domestic courts of Member States are under a duty to interpret and apply EU law (Treaties, Regulations, and Directives alike) to any relevant matters arising in the domestic courts. They are also bound to interpret domestic laws to maintain consistency with EU law. Thus, there has to be a system whereby EU legislation can be relied upon by citizens of the EU in suing the state or, possibly, companies and individuals. This is achieved by courts across the EU using two devices—giving *direct effect* and *indirect effect* to EU legislation.

It is unfortunate that the terms 'direct applicability', 'direct effect', 'indirect effect', and even 'Directive' all sound so similar. They are often used, erroneously, as interchangeable terms—even by the courts occasionally. However, these are terms of major significance and one needs to be clear about the distinction and the interrelationship. We need, therefore, to examine what is meant by *direct* and *indirect* effect. We shall consider *direct effect* first.

11.3.2 Direct effect

The basic idea underlying direct effect is straightforward. *Direct effect* means that someone may cite a Directive as law without having to cite any domestic legislation that was meant to implement that Directive. It may seem strange that this is not done all the time. But remember that a Directive is designed to be implemented by the Member States rather than stand as domestic law in its own right. So, what we are dealing with here is the situation where a Directive is used as the governing source of law, thus bypassing the domestic legislation. The principle of *direct effect* was not established by the Treaty of Rome. Instead, in a famous and controversial judgment (Case 26/62 *NV Algemene Transport-en Expeditie Orderneming Van Gend en Loos* v *Inspecteur der Invoerrechten en Accijnzen, Veulo (10852T) (Tariefcommissie (NL))* [1963] ECR 1; [1963] CMLR 224) the ECJ said that where EU legislation creates '**clear and unconditional**' obligations on Member States, these were capable of creating individual rights enforceable in domestic courts. All forms of EU legislation are *capable* of having direct effect, provided they meet certain conditions. There are normally four overlapping conditions for a Directive to have direct effect, and these are set out in **Table 11.1**.

The operation of the principle of direct effect has spawned an extensive body of case law, before both the CJEU and domestic courts. This has added greatly to the complexity of the principle, but the central idea is quite simple: a person in any Member State can refer to the *wording* of the Directive *as law*, no matter what the domestic statute says, *provided* the Directive is clear enough in its aims to be so enforceable. At this stage in your studies, judging exactly when a Directive meets these conditions is not something you should worry about.

Table 11.1 Conditions for direct effect

(a) *The provision of EU law must be clear and unambiguous.*	The approach of the CJEU to this issue is highly flexible; e.g. in the joined cases of Cases C–6/90, C–9/90 *Francovich and Bonifaci* v *Italy* [1992] IRLR 84 the Court recognised that the provisions of Directive 80/987/EEC, guaranteeing compensation to individuals for loss of employment through the insolvency of their employer, gave Member States a wide element of discretion (and so were not unambiguous). Nevertheless, the ECJ felt that it could discern a sufficient 'minimum guarantee' to make the provision precise enough to be capable of direct effect. In Case C–91/92 *Faccini Dori* v *Recreb srl* [1995] ECR I-3325; [1995] All ER (EC) 1, the ECJ returned to this concept and indicated that the provisions of a Directive can be sufficiently precise if they enable a domestic court to determine upon whom, and for whose benefit, the obligations are imposed, i.e. is it possible to determine minimum rights from the provision in question?
(b) *The provision must be unconditional.*	For example, it must not be subject to conditions requiring implementation by Member States, or giving Member States substantive discretion in respect of the period for implementation. However, as was noted in the case of *Maribel Dominguez* v *Centre informatique du Centre Ouest Atlantique* C–282/2010, [2012] IRLR 321: 'Even though [a Directive Article] leaves the Member States a degree of latitude when they adopt the conditions … [of the Directive] … that does not alter the precise and unconditional nature of the obligation laid down in that article.'
(c) *The provision must be capable of taking effect without further action by the EU or a Member State.*	For example, the EU legislation should not be dependent upon further clarifying regulations being passed in each Member State. Again, this test is of crucial significance in respect of both treaty obligations and Directives which are initially expressed to be conditional but become unconditional with the passing of time and thereby become directly effective.
(d) *The provision must be capable of creating rights for individuals.*	The provision in question must go beyond merely imposing obligations on Member States, e.g. in their relationship with other Member States or the EU as an entity. The provision must be drafted in such a way that an individual gains some enforceable right to sue the state or another individual.

The next thing you do have to worry about, however, is the question: can all Directives which have direct effect be relied upon by anyone suing another person or being prosecuted by the state?

The answer to this question is, 'No', because there is a further complication. A distinction is made between Directives having *vertical direct effect* and *horizontal direct effect*:

'Vertical effect'

The word 'vertical' refers to the relationship between the parties. Something is a vertical action where an individual (including a 'legal person' such as a company) is suing or being sued by the state (or, in criminal law, the individual is being prosecuted by the state).

If a Directive has vertical direct effect it means that an individual may rely on the specific words set out in a treaty, Directive (etc.) in any action against an organ of the state (see *Van Gend en Loos*) or against some other body having special powers to provide public services under the control of the state. Such bodies include, for example, a privatised industry under a statutory duty to provide a public utility—see Case C–188/89 *Foster* v *British Gas* [1990] ECR I-3313; [1991] 1 QB 405; [1990] 3 All ER 897 (ECJ); [1991] 2 AC 306; [1991] 2 All ER 705 (HL). The Court of Appeal has indicated that the definition of a 'public body' for these purposes should be a broad one: *National Union of Teachers* v *Governing Body of St Mary's Church of England (Aided) Junior School* [1997] 3 CMLR 630.

'Horizontal effect'

The word 'horizontal' again refers to the relationship between the parties. This time, a case can be described as a horizontal action where an individual is suing someone of equivalent legal standing—another person or a company, for instance—unlike vertical actions where the state exists in a superior (and therefore vertical) relationship with the individual.

What distinctions are drawn between these two types of action in terms of relying on directly effective Directives? Table 11.2 maps these out.

Table 11.2 Key points on vertical and horizontal direct effect

Vertical direct effect	Horizontal direct effect
It is now well accepted by the CJEU that Directives may have a vertical direct effect, for to deny a vertical direct effect (i.e. an individual against an organ of the state) would thus enable a Member State to rely upon its own non-implementation of EU law to avoid liability.	Whether Directives can have a horizontal effect has been hotly debated for many years. For the moment, we should say that Directives do not have horizontal direct effect.

All that we have already said regarding vertical and horizontal direct effect has been concentrated on Directives. We should note here that Treaty provisions are directly applicable and may also have direct effect (provided they are certain, unconditional, etc.).

Note: where treaty provisions have direct effect, they will have *both* vertical and horizontal direct effect. For instance, you will find Directives which deal with discrimination and equal pay matters. However, the basic idea of 'equal pay' actually appears in Art. 157 of the Treaty on the Functioning of the European Union. So, when an air stewardess brought an equal pay claim against her employer (using the wording of the forerunner of TFEU) in Case 43/75 *Defrenne* v *SA Belge de Navigation Aérienne (SABENA) (No. 2)* [1976] ECR 455, the ECJ held that, because the article in question was part of a Treaty and because it was clear and unconditional, it could be relied upon in this 'horizontal' action between employee and employer.

11.3.3 Indirect effect

Case 14/83 *Von Colson* v *Land Nordrhein-Westfalen* [1984] ECR 1891 is credited with creating a further principle, termed *indirect effect*. Indirect effect sidesteps some of the problems created by the vertical/horizontal direct effect distinction and allows for some very creative judicial reasoning.

If a Directive does not have horizontal direct effect, it may be effective *indirectly* by means of domestic courts adopting an appropriately purposive form of interpretation for related domestic legislation. In other words, courts can read into the wording of the domestic legislation the *purpose* declared in the Directive. A court may thus give the citizen a right under domestic law where there would otherwise be none because the EU Directive lacks direct effect. The relationship between direct and indirect effect is a problematic feature of European jurisprudence. In many ways, the idea of *indirect effect* is more important than direct effect as it means that, irrespective of who is suing whom, the courts can try to implement the spirit of the Directive in a wider range of cases.

It does not matter, for the purposes of *indirect effect* whether there is a vertical or horizontal relationship between the parties as the court will try to do whatever lies within its powers to ensure that the Directive in question is fully effective and will have regard to the whole body of national law in doing so.

Indirect effect enables a court to 'read in' to the statute the wording and even the aims of the original Directive. It is called indirect effect for this reason, since it gives an individual a right of action through national law, but based *indirectly* on the Directive. This takes us full circle because we are now back in the field of *how* the courts interpret statutes, as seen earlier.

We have to say that the position has become more and more convoluted. The guidelines issued by the ECJ in *Von Colson* were less than clear and at one time it was argued that the concept of indirect effect did nothing more than create a rule for dealing with ambiguities in domestic implementing legislation. In Case C–106/89 *Marleasing SA* v *La Commercial Internacional de Alimentación SA* [1990] ECR I-4135; [1992] 1 CMLR 305 the ECJ clarified this position to some extent by reaffirming the views expressed in *Marshall* and by noting that it is **domestic law** (not just legislation) which must comply with EU legislation, whether the Directive has been implemented, implemented improperly, or not implemented at all, once the time limit for implementation has passed.

An easily understandable example can be seen in *Webb* v *EMO Air Cargo (UK) Ltd* [1990] ICR 442 (EAT); [1992] ICR 445; [1992] 2 All ER 43 (CA); [1993] 1 CMLR 259 (HL), which posed the question whether the dismissal of an employee on grounds of pregnancy constituted sex discrimination when the dismissed employee had been engaged specifically to cover for another employee's absence. The Employment Appeal Tribunal and the Court of Appeal thought not. They said that a claim fell under the Sex Discrimination Act 1975 only where a pregnant woman was treated less favourably by her employer than a hypothetical man would be in 'comparable' circumstances; for example, where he is suffering from an illness of similar severity and duration. Ms Webb had argued that the dismissal was discriminatory, based on the fact that a man can never be in the same position as a pregnant woman.

There was authority supporting Ms Webb's argument, derived from the Equal Treatment Directive EC/76/207, to be found in Case 177/88 *Dekker* v *Stichting Vormingscentrum voor Jong Volwassen Plus* [1990] ECR I-3941; [1991] IRLR 27. Ms Webb's counsel argued that the Directive as interpreted in *Dekker* (although not having direct horizontal effect) should be applied, using the *Marleasing* principles of indirect effect. The House of Lords in *Webb* indicated that, in its view, there was no discrimination here on a 'proper construction' of the 1975 Act. But their Lordships also stated that (*per* Lord Keith [1993] 1 CMLR 259, at 270):

> [I]t is for a United Kingdom court to construe domestic legislation so as to accord with the interpretation of the Directive as laid down by the European Court, if that can be done without distorting the meaning of the domestic legislation... This is so whether the domestic legislation came after or, as in this case, preceded the Directive...

Their Lordships found that the *Dekker* case was not direct authority on the facts in *Webb* (and so implicitly not 'binding' upon them), and sought a preliminary ruling from the ECJ on the meaning of the Directive.

The ECJ in Case C–32/93 *Webb* v *EMO Air Cargo (UK) Ltd* [1994] ECR I-3567; [1994] ICR 770 ruled that under Council Directive 76/207/EEC, Arts 2(1) and 5(1), 'dismissal of an employee who is recruited for an unlimited term with a view, initially, to replacing another employee during the latter's maternity leave and who cannot do so because, shortly after her recruitment, she is herself found to be pregnant' is precluded. In other words, there does not have to be a 'male comparator'; dismissal of a pregnant employee for that reason is discrimination. In turn the case came back to the House of Lords (*Webb* v *EMO Air Cargo (UK) Ltd (No. 2)* [1995] ICR 1021), where their Lordships held that the Sex Discrimination Act 1975 must be interpreted in a manner consistent with the ruling by the ECJ.

Thus, the specific wording of the Sex Discrimination Act 1975 was subsumed within the broad principles enunciated by the ECJ so that this decision certainly complies with the idea of indirect effect.

Another down-to-earth example may help. In the Irish case of *Smith* v *Meade* [2009] IEHC 99 a passenger was injured while being driven in the back of a van. He was not in a seat and the insurance policy did not cover passengers who were not seated. The relevant Directive had not been implemented by Ireland; had it been, the passenger would have been covered by the insurance. The insurance company was not an emanation of the state, so direct effect was inapplicable. Nevertheless, the Irish High Court ruled that, using the principles of indirect effect, the clause in the insurance contract excluding the passenger from compensation was to be regarded as void.

The concept of *indirect effect* still continues to be the subject of much argument, especially as regards the extent to which domestic courts may disapply national legislation in order to seek compliance with EU law. As regards civil liability the ECJ/CJEU has demonstrated that it is prepared to see EU law dominant, and use the principle of indirect effect to achieve this, even when this means exposing individuals to liabilities which were not there under national law (see *Pfeiffer*, joined Cases C–397/01 to C–403/01, [2004] ECR I-8835).

In C–144/04 *Mangold* v *Helm* [2006] IRLR 143 the ECJ extended the concept of EU law dominating domestic legislation by determining that the prevention of age discrimination was a 'general principle' of EU law so that domestic legislation could be overridden and horizontal direct effect could apply in such instances. However, these 'general principles' and 'fundamental rights' have no single accepted definition, so exactly which principles and rights are so sacrosanct as to be 'general' is not entirely clear (some attempts have been made, such as with the case of *Kadi* v *European Union Council* (Joined Cases C–402/05, C–415/05), [2008] ECR I-6351). In their chapter on the judicial method of English courts utilised in EU law cases, contained in Neergaard *et al.* (2011), Hervey and Sheldon note that this emerging doctrine of the primacy of 'general principles' of EU law is the latest challenge for English courts on legal method. It is an approach, illustrated by another case, *Kücükdeveci* v *Swedex Gmbh & Co* (C-555/07) [2010] 2 CMLR which, say the authors, 'blurs the boundaries between direct and indirect effect' (Neergaard *et al.*, 2011: 372) by taking a Directive which did not have direct effect and stating that domestic legislation should nevertheless be dis-applied (this was another case on age discrimination being held to be a 'general principle' of EU law).

The CJEU is much more reluctant to do anything which may impose on an individual criminal liability which was not present under national legislation (see Case C–168/95 *Arcaro* [1996] ECR I-4705; [1997] 1 CMLR 179).

11.3.4 Summary of enforcement methods

- The idea of *direct applicability* is that the EU can instigate major and overriding legislation without having to rely on each Member State to implement it through its own parliamentary systems. Apart from matters such as Treaty obligations, this is not a common method of legislating. Member States, of course, have the right to vote on and sometimes even to veto such Treaties and Regulations. Some states allow for referenda on new Treaties and, in such cases, the voting population may get to have a say on adoption or rejection and in some cases these matters may be regarded as constitutional issues.

- The idea of *direct effect* is to provide a mechanism whereby individuals can rely on the wording of EU legislation, even when the Member State has implemented EU legislation (usually a Directive) incorrectly, or not at all. For any EU legislation to have *direct effect* it must satisfy additional conditions of certainty, and the time limit for implementation must have passed.

- Treaty obligations generally have *direct applicability*. In some cases, this will mean that they also have *direct effect*, provided that they are certain and create rights for individuals (though even specific Treaty obligations may be couched in terms of desirability rather than detailed rules).

- Regulations also generally have *direct applicability*. In most cases this will mean that they also have *direct effect*, again provided that they are certain and create rights for individuals.

- Directives are not *directly applicable* and will have direct effect only in limited situations: 'They do not impose obligations as between private individuals' (Hervey and Sheldon in Neergaard *et al.*, 2011: 371). The present position is that, even in these limited cases, they may have only vertical *direct effect*.

- The exact status of *indirect effect* cannot be stated with any clarity; it should be seen more as a tool of interpretation available to judges than as a fixed method of analysis. It can be used whether the Directive has direct effect or not.

- The key element in the relationship between national and EU law is that EU law trumps any national laws where there is conflict. Usually, the courts will try to interpret the national law so as to make it comply with EU law. Sometimes this will involve 'reading in' to the statute some key words derived from the Directive (as happened in *Litster* v *Forth Dry Dock & Engineering Co. Ltd* [1990] 1 AC 546; [1989] 2 CMLR 194). Occasionally even this will not be possible, in which case the national law must be disapplied. This (complicated) position was summed up nicely by Lord Walker in *Fleming (t/a Bodycraft)* v *HM Revenue & Customs; Condé Nast* v *HMRC* [2008] UKHL 2 [24]; [2008] 1 CMLR 48, where he says:

It is a fundamental principle of the law of the European Union (EU), recognised in s. 2(1) of the European Communities Act 1972, that if national legislation infringes directly enforceable Community rights, the national court is obliged to disapply the offending provision. The provision is not made void but it must be treated as being…without prejudice to the directly enforceable EU rights of nationals of any member state of the EEC….

Disapplication is called for only if there is an inconsistency between national law and EU law in the way we have already described. In an attempt to avoid an inconsistency the national court will, if at all possible, interpret the national legislation so as to make it conform to the superior order of EU law and will make extensive use of the concept of *indirect effect* to do so: *Pickstone v Freemans Plc* [1989] AC 66; [1988] 3 CMLR 221; *Litster v Forth Dry Dock & Engineering Co Ltd* [1990] 1 AC 546; [1989] 2 CMLR 194. Sometimes, however, a conforming construction is not possible, and disapplication cannot be avoided.

In *Robertson* v *Swift* [2014] UKSC 50; [2014] 4 All ER 869 the Supreme Court cited the Court of Appeal decision in *Vodafone 2* v *Commissioners for Her Majesty's Revenue and Customs* [2009] EWCA Civ 446, [2010] Ch 77 to summarise the obligations on the English courts to construe domestic legislation consistently with Community law obligations as being:

(i) that the court is not constrained by conventional rules of construction;

(ii) ambiguity in the legislative language is not a requirement;

(iii) this is not simply an exercise in semantics or linguistics;

(iv) courts are permitted to depart from the strict and literal application of the words which the legislature has elected to use;

(v) the implication of words necessary to comply with Community law obligations is permitted; and

(vi) the precise form of the words to be implied does not matter.

Their Lordships added that: 'It is important to note that, in order to observe the imperative that this guidance contains, the court must not only keep faith with the wording of the Directive but must have closely in mind its purpose.'

Practical problem areas

In reality, the case law reveals that there are three main areas where the problem of *direct* and *indirect effect* will arise, and they all relate to Directives:

(i) where the Member State implements the Directive but there is a conflict between the relevant statute and the wording of the Directive;

(ii) where the Member State fails to implement the Directive at all;

(iii) where the general laws of the Member State (e.g. precedents not based on statutes) seem to be in conflict with the Directive.

If a Directive is not implemented or is not implemented properly, there is the question of whether a UK citizen can nevertheless enforce the rights given under the Directive. We saw in section **11.3.2** that if the Directive satisfies the conditions of certainty and has vertical direct effect, then the answer is generally 'Yes'; but if an individual wishes to rely on the Directive in suing another individual he/she must argue that the Directive has horizontal effect. This is more problematic. To give Directives horizontal direct effect, it is argued, equates them with Regulations—so what would be the distinction?

In one of the leading equal treatment cases, Case 152/84 *Marshall* v *Southampton and South West Hampshire AHA (Teaching)* [1986] ECR 723; [1986] 1 CMLR 688;

[1986] 2 All ER 584, the ECJ denied the possibility of giving horizontal effect to Directives. Both the ECJ and the Advocate General agreed that the relevant Directive could be relied upon only in actions against the state (i.e. having vertical effect). On the facts, Ms Marshall succeeded in her claim, as it was conceded that her employer (the health authority) was an emanation of the state. If, on the other hand, she had been employed by, say, BUPA, the Directive would not have had direct effect because the relationship would have been 'horizontal'. This analysis was affirmed by the ECJ in *Faccini Dori* v *Recreb* [1995] ECR I-3325; [1995] All ER (EC) 1. Here, the ECJ decided that there could be no such thing as *horizontal direct effect* as regards Directives—and again in Case C–192/94 *El Corte Inglés SA* v *Blázquez Rivero* [1996] ECR I-1281; [1996] 2 CMLR 507.

Like most things involving EU law, that was not to be the final word. A series of cases in 1996 cast some doubt on this, for example Case C–194/94 *CIA Security International SA* v *Signalson SA* [1996] ECR I-2201; [1996] 2 CMLR 372, Case C–441/93 *Pafitis and others* v *TKE and others* [1996] ECR I-1347; [1996] 2 CMLR 551, Case C–129/94 *Ruiz Bernáldez* [1996] ECR I-1829; [1996] 2 CMLR 889, and Case C–168/95 *Arcaro* [1996] ECR I-4705; [1997] 1 CMLR 179. However, we are in some agreement with the editor of the *European Law Review* that these cases do not destroy the principle of the ineffectiveness of horizontal direct effect; indeed, *Arcaro* illustrates and confirms the point that a Member State which fails to comply with EU law cannot use that failure against an individual. *Arcaro* concerned criminal proceedings relating to pollution. Had the state been allowed to pursue an action against the individual based on Directives (i.e. a vertical action, but 'top down') when there was doubt whether the Italian criminal legislation conflicted with EU Directives, this would have allowed Italy to benefit from its own failure to implement the Directive.

Indeed, more recent cases, focusing on both EU law and human rights law, have affirmed the *Faccini Dori* view of the inapplicability of horizontal direct effect.

11.3.5 State liability: the *Francovich* principle

The final stage in this saga is to note the joined Cases C–6/90 and C–9/90 *Francovich and Bonifaci* v *Italy* [1991] ECR I-5357; [1992] IRLR 84, where the ECJ held that, under certain conditions, a Member State is liable to make good damage to individuals if loss is suffered because the state failed to implement an EU Directive.

In Case C–46/93 *Brasserie du Pêcheur SA* v *Federal Republic of Germany* and Case C–48/93 *R* v *Secretary of State for Transport, ex parte Factortame Ltd and others* (both reported at [1996] ECR I-1029; [1996] 1 CMLR 889) the ECJ considered this area again. These two cases concerned, respectively, damages suffered by a French company based in Alsace, which had lost a substantial sum of money owing to German import laws regarding beer (held to be in breach of EU legislation), and our old friends, the Spanish fishermen.

The ECJ identified three main conditions governing state liability:

(i)   The EU legislation must have been intended to confer rights on individuals. The interpretation of this in the United Kingdom is that there must be an intention to create rights, not just a harmonisation of the law that incidentally creates such a right: *Three Rivers District Council* v *Bank of England* [1996] 3 All ER 558.

(ii)   The breach by the Member State must be 'sufficiently serious'. 'Sufficiently serious' breaches occur, according to the ECJ in Case C–127/95 *Norbrook Laboratories* v

Ministry of Agriculture [1998] ECR I-1531, 'where a Member State, in the exercise of its legislative powers, has manifestly and gravely disregarded the limits on its powers'.

(iii) There must be established a causal link between the breach and the damage suffered.

11.3.6 Direct and indirect effect: a working example

Imagine that a new Council Directive has appeared—the Fairness in Life Assurance Contracts Directive. This seeks to impose a duty on insurance companies to identify and explain clearly all 'surrender value' clauses in their policies. You wish to stop payments on your life assurance and receive the surrender value of the policy. You are told by the company that the wording of their surrender value clause means that they do not have to pay anything. You claim that the company's clause does not comply with the Directive. Can you make use of the Directive?

To answer this, you will need to take account of the information set out in **Table 11.3**.

Table 11.3 Direct and indirect effect: a worked-through example

(a) Has the time passed when the Directive was meant to be implemented?	If not, the Directive is, strictly, irrelevant.
(b) Assuming that the time period for implementation has passed, has the UK implemented the Directive?	(i) *If it has done so,* then the primary source for establishing your rights will be the UK legislation and the Directive will be relevant only as an aid to interpretation (indirect effect).
	(ii) *If it has done so but there is a conflict* between the relevant UK legislation and the wording of the Directive (e.g. difference in wording or gaps in the UK Act), the wording of the Directive itself can be used if the Directive is certain enough to have direct effect (but this will only apply to cases of *vertical effect*, i.e. actions against the state).
	(iii) *If the UK has failed to implement the Directive* at all, the position is the same as in (ii) above. But since our fictional case is a claim against a company the claim is a horizontal one: effectively individual v individual.
	(iv) As vertical direct effect is not relevant, and horizontal direct effect is not possible, the courts may invoke the principle of *indirect effect*.
(c) In any case, if the government is at fault for not having implemented the Directive at all (or, more arguably, having implemented it incorrectly), the government may be liable to individuals, companies, etc. under the *Francovich* principle.	*This applies whether the Directive does or does not have direct effect.* The Commission may also take action, but this is irrelevant to your particular claim.

We have sought to sum up this position in diagrammatic form (see **Figures 11.3** and **11.4**). We do not pretend that this level of uncertainty and complexity is justified.

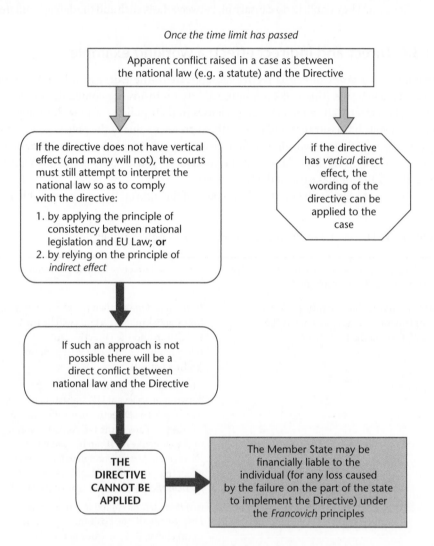

Figure 11.3 Directive improperly implemented

Once the time limit has passed

Figure 11.4 Directive not implemented at all

CONCLUSION

In previous editions we have drawn comparisons as to how the European and English and Welsh lawyers analyse problems: the similarities and differences and, despite this, most commonly how they often reach the same conclusions. That is no longer the focus of this chapter. Instead, we have had to look at how the United Kingdom disengages from the EU in legal terms and what lawyers still need to know about how EU law operates for the future. For the present, we have kept the explanations of the workings of Directives, etc. because this provides the groundwork for the 'Retained EU Law' we will be dealing with over many years to come, and also because EU law will continue to be relevant to the United Kingdom for reasons stated at the start of this chapter.

Some of our speculation will look quite weak from the perspective of hindsight in late 2019 and beyond but, in the autumn of 2018, these are our best guesses. As we noted at the start of the chapter, OUP's online resources as regards the status of the law post-Brexit is highly recommended, see www.oxfordtextbooks.co.uk/orc/eulaw.

One final comment in this area has survived all editions of this text since 1990—the (perhaps apocryphal) early twentieth-century headline in *The Times*: 'Fog in the Channel—Europe Isolated'.

 CHAPTER REFERENCES

BROWN, L. and KENNEDY, T. (2000), *Brown and Jacobs: The Court of Justice of the European Communities* (5th edn, London: Sweet & Maxwell).

DAVID, R. and BRIERLEY, J. (1985), *Major Legal Systems in the World Today* (3rd edn, London: Stevens).

FOSTER, N. (2017), *Foster on EU Law* (6th edn, Oxford: Oxford University Press).

MARKESINIS, B.S. (1994), 'A Matter of Style', 110 *Law Quarterly Review*, 607.

NEERGAARD, U. and NIELSEN, R (eds) (2013), *European Legal Method: Towards a New Legal Realism* (Copenhagen: DJØF Publishing).

*NEERGAARD, U., NIELSEN, R., and ROSEBERRY, L. (eds) (2011), *European Legal Method—Paradoxes and Revitalisation* (Copenhagen: DJØF Publishing).

STEINER, J. (1993), 'From Direct Effect to *Francovich*: Shifting Means of Enforcement of Community Law', 18 *European Law Review*, 3.

STEINER, J. (1995), *Enforcing EC Law* (London: Blackstone Press).

*STEINER, J. and WOODS, L. (2017) in L .WOODS and P. WATSON (eds), *Steiner and Woods EU Law* (13th edn, Oxford: Oxford University Press). Editions 1–10 of this work were entitled *Textbook on EC Law*.

 ONLINE RESOURCES

Index